D1540749

INTERNAL AUDITING:
Assurance & Consulting Services

Second Edition

Kurt F. Reding, PhD, CIA, CPA, CMA
Paul J. Sobel, CIA, CPA
Urton L. Anderson, PhD, CIA, CCSA, CGAP, CCEP
Michael J. Head, CIA, CPA, CMA, CBA, CISA
Sridhar Ramamoorti, PhD, CIA, CPA, CITP, FCPA, CFE, CFSA, CGAP
Mark Salamasick, CIA, CISA, CSP
Cris Riddle, MA

The IIA Research Foundation

Book design by Rule and Renco, www.ruleandrenco.com
Illustration by Linda Frichtel

Copyright © 2009 by The Institute of Internal Auditors Research Foundation (IIARF), 247 Maitland Avenue, Altamonte Springs, Florida 32701-4201. All rights reserved. Printed in the United States of America. No part of this publication may be reproduced, stored in a retrieval system, or transmitted in any form by any means — electronic, mechanical, photocopying, recording, or otherwise — without prior written permission of the publisher.

The IIARF publishes this document for informational and educational purposes. This document is intended to provide information, but is not a substitute for legal or accounting advice. The IIARF does not provide such advice and makes no warranty as to any legal or accounting results through its publication of this document. When legal or accounting issues arise, professional assistance should be sought and retained.

The Institute of Internal Auditors' (IIA's) International Professional Practices Framework (IPPF) comprises the full range of existing and developing practice guidance for the profession. The IPPF provides guidance to internal auditors globally and paves the way to world-class internal auditing.

The mission of The IIARF is to expand knowledge and understanding of internal auditing by providing relevant research and educational products to advance the profession globally.

The IIA and The IIARF work in partnership with researchers from around the globe who conduct valuable studies on critical issues affecting today's business world. Much of the content presented in their final reports is a result of IIARF-funded research and prepared as a service to The Foundation and the internal audit profession. Expressed opinions, interpretations, or points of view represent a consensus of the researchers and do not necessarily reflect or represent the official position or policies of The IIA or The IIARF.

ISBN 978-0-89413-643-6

09/09 First Printing
04/11 Second Printing

TABLE OF CONTENTS

Chapter 10 Audit Evidence and Working Papers 10-1

Chapter 11 Audit Sampling 11-1

CONDUCTING INTERNAL AUDIT ENGAGEMENTS

CONTENTS OF CD-ROM

PREFACE

Welcome to the second edition of *Internal Auditing: Assurance & Consulting Services*. The primary impetus for updating the textbook after only two years is The Institute of Internal Auditors' (IIA's) International Professional Practices Framework (IPPF), which was published in January 2009. There are, however, additional important changes, some of which are based on other professional guidance that has emerged since the publication of the first edition. Other changes were made in response to recommendations for improvement from independent reviewers who used the first edition. Yet other changes reflect new ideas of the authors.

The authors' continuing goal, carried forward from the first edition of the textbook, is to provide students with the fundamental knowledge and a sense of the skills they will need to succeed as entry-level internal audit professionals. Accordingly, our primary target audience is undergraduate and graduate college students enrolled in introductory internal audit courses. We believe, however, that internal audit practitioners also will find the second edition of the textbook useful as a training and reference tool.

Significant Changes in the Second Edition

As indicated above, the second edition of the textbook includes several important changes:

- Chapter 2, "The International Professional Practices Framework: Authoritative Guidance for the Internal Audit Profession," has been completely rewritten to reflect the new IPPF. Emphasis is placed on enabling students to clearly understand the mandatory guidance and strongly recommended guidance contained in the IPPF.
- Chapter 3, "Governance and Risk Management," of the first edition has been divided into two chapters: Chapter 3, "Governance," and Chapter 4, "Risk Management." This division will make it easier for students to separately focus on these two related, but independently important, topics.
- Chapter 5, "Business Processes and Risks," has been substantially reorganized to make it easier for students to read and understand the relationship between business processes and the risks they are designed to manage.
- Chapter 6, "Internal Control," has been updated to include a discussion of the Committee of Sponsoring Organizations of the Treadway Commission's (COSO's) Guidance on Monitoring Internal Control Systems, which was published in January 2009.
- Chapter 7, "Information Technology Risks and Controls," has been revised substantially to better convey fundamental IT-related concepts that all internal auditors need to understand. This chapter also introduces students to the two IT audit guidance series included in the IPPF as Practice Guides: the Global Technology Audit Guides (GTAG) and the Guide to the Assessment of IT Risk (GAIT).
- Chapter 8, "Fraud Risks and Controls," has been updated to encompass the guidance provided in Managing the Business Risk of Fraud: A Practical Guide, which was cosponsored by The IIA, the AICPA, and the ACFE and published in 2008. New, more recent incidents of fraud also are covered.

- Chapter 9, "Gathering and Documenting Audit Evidence," of the first edition has been divided into three chapters: Chapter 10, "Audit Evidence and Working Papers," Chapter 11, "Audit Sampling," and Chapter 12, "Introduction to the Engagement Process." This separates three very important topics into smaller chapters that will better enable both teaching and learning.
- Chapter 15, "The Consulting Engagement," has been updated to better reflect the IPPF guidance regarding consulting engagements.
- Three case studies were developed during 2008:
  - Case Study 1, "Auditing Entity-level Controls."
  - Case Study 2, "Auditing the Compliance and Ethics Program."
  - Case Study 3, "Performing a Blended Consulting Engagement."

  These three case studies are included on the CD-ROM that accompanies the textbook. Two new case studies, "Conducting an Integrated IT Audit" and "Conducting an Operational Audit" are under development.
- The end-of-chapter questions and cases have been refined and expanded.
- Specific steps have been taken to make the textbook more global in nature.

Content and Organization of the Textbook

The textbook continues to include the following key components:

- Extensive coverage of governance, risk management, and internal control, the core components of the Definition of Internal Auditing.
- A risk-based, process and controls-focused internal audit approach.
- Integration of IT and fraud risks and controls.
- Alignment with the IPPF and CIA examination content specifications.
- Callouts of key terms in the margins of each chapter to reinforce key concepts.

Chapters 1 through 11, which are collectively referred to as Fundamental Internal Audit Concepts, cover topics that all internal auditors need to know and understand. Chapters 12 through 15, which are collectively referred to as Conducting Internal Audit Engagements, focus on the planning, performing, and communicating phases of internal audit assurance and consulting engagements.

The end-of-chapter materials include review questions, multiple-choice questions, discussion questions, and application-oriented cases. Unless otherwise indicated, all end-of-chapter questions and cases are the original work of the authors or have been adapted from the Certified Internal Auditor Model Exams, published by The IIA in 1998 and 2004, or from CIA exams prior to The IIA's closure of the exam in 1997.

The Glossary contains the authors' definitions of key terms used throughout the textbook. The IIA's Code of Ethics and the *International Standards for the Professional Practice of Internal Auditing* (*Standards*) are reproduced in Appendix A and Appendix B, respectively.

Textbook Supplements

The following supplemental materials are included on the CD-ROM that accompanies the textbook:

- **ACL and IDEA Software.** Both ACL and IDEA, the two most widely used commercially available audit analytics software programs, are included on the CD-ROM. Instructors can decide individually the extent to which they want to give their students practical, hands-on experience with generalized audit software using ACL and/or IDEA.
- **Case Studies.** The CD-ROM contains three supplemental case studies, which are intended to provide students with more in-depth, application-oriented coverage:
  - Case Study 1, "Auditing Entity-level Controls."
  - Case Study 2, "Auditing the Compliance and Ethics Program."
  - Case Study 3, "Performing a Blended Consulting Engagement."

  Other case studies will be distributed separately, as they are developed, to instructors who want to use them.
- **The IIA's Code of Ethics and *Standards*.** In addition to being reproduced in the textbook appendices, The IIA's Code of Ethics and *Standards* are included on the CD-ROM as a convenience to students who want to access them electronically.

The following supplemental materials are available separately for instructors upon request via e-mail (iiatextbook@theiia.org):

- **Solutions Manual.** The Solutions Manual contains answers prepared by the textbook authors for the end-of-chapter questions and cases.
- **Textbook Exhibits.** Each of the textbook exhibits has been reproduced individually for instructors who want to use them separately as visual aids and/or handouts.
- **Slide Templates.** Slide templates have been prepared for each chapter. Instructors can use these templates as a starting point for preparing their personal sets of slides.
- **Illustrative Exams.** The illustrative exams prepared by the authors are intended to give instructors a head start on constructing exams best suited for their classes.
- **Internal Audit Project.** Urton Anderson and Mark Salamasick describe how they have successfully integrated real-world internal audit projects into their IAEP Program curricula.

ACKNOWLEDGMENTS

The authors would like to thank the organizations and individuals, including college instructors and students, who used the first edition of the textbook. We especially want to thank the following professors who graciously reviewed portions of the first edition and provided constructive improvement recommendations for the second edition:

- David M. Cannon, PhD, CIA, CPA, CISA, CCP, Assistant Professor of Accounting, Grand Valley State University.
- Richard R. Clune, EDM, CIA, CPA, Assistant Professor of Accounting, Kennesaw State University.
- Penelope Sue Greenberg, PhD, CPA, CMA, Director of Graduate Programs and Associate Professor, School of Business Administration, Widener University.
- Simon Petravick, PhD, CIA, Professor of Accounting, Bradley University.
- Deborah W. Tanju, PhD, CIA, CPA, CMA, Professor of Accounting, University of Alabama at Birmingham.
- Douglas E. Ziegenfuss, PhD, CIA, CPA, CMA, Chair and Professor of Accounting, Old Dominion University.

In addition, the authors would like to thank the following organizations and individuals for their contributions to the second edition of the textbook:

- The Institute of Internal Auditors Research Foundation for sponsoring the writing of the textbook.
- The Institute of Internal Auditors for permission to incorporate the International Professional Practices Framework and other materials, including questions from the Certified Internal Auditor Model Exams and from past CIA examinations.
- ACL Services Ltd for contributing the education edition of ACL audit software that is on the CD-ROM that accompanies the textbook.
- Audimation Services Inc. for contributing the IDEA audit software that is on the CD-ROM that accompanies the textbook.
- The Institute of Internal Auditors – United Kingdom and Ireland, the IT Governance Institute, The Committee of Sponsoring Organizations of the Treadway Commission (COSO), the American Institute of Certified Public Accountants (AICPA), and The University of Texas at Austin, for granting us permission to copy and/or adapt proprietary information.
- Bonnie Ulmer, Vice President, The Institute of Internal Auditors Research Foundation, for again coordinating and directing the project.
- Lee Ann Campbell, Senior Publications Editor, Educational Materials, The Institute of Internal Auditors, for editing the entire textbook, including the supplemental Case Studies contained on the accompanying CD-ROM.
- Joe Sorrentino, Director, Retail Operations, The Institute of Internal Auditors Research Foundation, for managing the production process.
- Nicki Creatore, Operations Manager, The Institute of Internal Auditors Research Foundation, for editing the three Case Studies included on the CD-ROM that accompanies the textbook.
- Rule & Renco for handling all aspects of textbook design and composition.

ABOUT THE AUTHORS

Kurt F. Reding, PhD, CIA, CPA, CMA

Grant Thornton Faculty Fellow
Assistant Professor of Accounting
W. Frank Barton School of Business
Wichita State University

Kurt currently serves on The Institute of Internal Auditors' (IIA's) Academic Relations Committee and The IIA's Wichita chapter's Board of Governors. He has previously served on The IIA's Board of Directors, North American Board, Board of Research and Education Advisors, and Board of Research Advisors and as an ex officio member of The IIA's Kansas City chapter's Board of Governors.

He received The IIA's 2003 Leon R. Radde Educator of the Year Award. He also has received both The IIA's John B. Thurston Award and the Institute of Management Accountants' Lybrand Gold Medal, the highest annual writing awards bestowed by these organizations. He coauthored *Introduction to Auditing: Logic, Principles, and Techniques*, a textbook published by The IIA in 2002, and has published articles in *Internal Auditor, Internal Auditing, Managerial Auditing Journal, Management Accounting Quarterly*, and other journals.

Kurt has more than 25 years of experience as an audit educator and practitioner and holds a PhD in Accounting from The University of Tennessee. He is a member of The Institute of Internal Auditors, the American Institute of Certified Public Accountants, the Institute of Management Accountants, and the American Accounting Association.

Paul J. Sobel, CIA, CPA

Vice President, Internal Audit
Mirant Corporation

Paul is responsible for directing Mirant's worldwide internal audit activities, and developing and implementing risk assessment and ERM methodologies. In addition to reporting to Mirant's Audit Committee and Nominating & Governance Committee, he sits on the company's Risk Oversight Committee, IT Steering Committee, and Disclosure Committee. Before joining Mirant, Paul was Vice President, Risk Assessment at Aquila, Inc. where he had responsibilities similar to those at Mirant. He was a Senior Manager in Arthur Andersen's Business Risk Consulting practice, with focus on risk assessments and internal audit co-sourcing arrangements. His career has also included the positions of Audit Director with Harcourt General and International Audit Manager for PepsiCo. He began his career with Arthur Andersen, focusing on financial and information systems audits.

He is a frequent speaker on ERM, governance, and internal audit topics at IIA and other conferences, and achieved Distinguished Faculty honors as an instructor of IIA seminars. He has published a book titled *Auditor's Risk Management Guide: Integrating Auditing and ERM*. He has also authored or co-authored articles for *Internal Auditor* magazine and *Management Accounting Quarterly*. One of his articles was honored with an Outstanding Contributor Award by The IIA, and he was also awarded the Institute of Management Accountants' Lybrand Gold Medal in 2004.

Paul has been an active volunteer with The IIA. He has served as a Director on The IIA's Board of Directors, Vice Chair of Research on The IIA's Executive Committee, Senior Vice Chair on the North American Board, President of The IIA Research Foundation, and as the Midwest Region Representative and Midwest District #1 Representative. He has also served on the Board of Governors of The IIA's Atlanta, Kansas City, and Central Florida chapters, and was President of the Kansas City chapter. Paul is also currently serving an appointment to the Standing Advisory Group of the Public Company Accounting Oversight Board (PCAOB).

Urton L. Anderson, PhD, CIA, CCSA, CGAP, CCEP

Clark W. Thompson, Jr., Professor in Accounting Education
Chair, Department of Accounting
McCombs School of Business
The University of Texas at Austin

Urton joined the Department of Accounting at the University of Texas at Austin in 1984, teaching auditing and managerial accounting. He received his PhD from The University of Minnesota in 1985. His research has addressed various issues in internal and external auditing — particularly corporate governance, compliance, enterprise risk management, and internal control. He has written several books, his most recent being *Implementing the International Professional Practices Framework, 3rd Edition* (with Andrew Dahle), as well as papers published in a variety of scholarly and professional journals.

Urton is active in The IIA. He has been a member and Chair of The IIA's Board of Regents and served on the CCSA Steering Committee, which developed the professional examination for Control Self-Assessment and the CGAP Steering Committee for the new professional examination in governmental auditing. He has also been a member and Chair of the International Internal Auditing Standards Board. In 1997 he was named Leon R. Radde Educator of the Year by The IIA. In June 2006, The IIA recognized his outstanding contributions to the field of internal auditing by awarding him The Bradford Cadmus Memorial Award. Urton also has served on the Board of Directors for the Health Care Compliance Association and the Advisory Board of the Society of Corporate Compliance and Ethics.

Michael J. Head, CIA, CPA, CMA, CBA, CISA

Managing Director of Corporate Audit
TD AMERITRADE

Mike is responsible for the coordination and delivery of risk-based and process-driven review, assurance, and advisory services specific to internal controls and risk management throughout TD AMERITRADE. During his 29-year career he has served in various capacities, including director of internal audit, audit manager, and controller, with companies including PricewaterhouseCoopers, KPMG, The Guarantee Life Companies Inc., Bank of America (formerly NationsBank), FirsTier Financial, Inc., and Standard Havens, Inc. His experience includes the development and implementation of comprehensive, risk-based internal audit functions, and strategic, financial, operational, and compliance control consultant to the financial services industry.

In addition to earning numerous professional designations — the Certified Internal Auditor, Certified Public Accountant, Certified Management Accountant, Chartered Bank Auditor, and Certified Information Systems Auditor — Mike is a FINRA Registered General Securities Representative (Series 7), General Securities Principal (Series 24), and a Financial and Operations Principal (Series 27). He is also an active member and director of The IIA, serving on the International Board's Audit Committee. In the past, he served on The IIA's North American Board and also as The IIA's Midwestern Region District Advisor. Mike, who earned a BSBA degree at the University of Missouri – Columbia, is also a member of the American Institute of CPAs, the Nebraska Society of CPAs, Missouri Society of CPAs, Information Systems Audit & Control Association, and Institute of Management Accountants.

Sridhar Ramamoorti, PhD, CIA, ACA, CPA, CITP, FCPA, CFE, CFSA, CRP, CGAP, CGFM, CICA

Partner, National Corporate Governance Group
Grant Thornton LLP
Chicago, Illinois

Sri contributes to the firm's thought leadership efforts in the areas of corporate governance and accountability, and consults on Sarbanes-Oxley, technical matters in financial reporting and auditing, and anti-fraud programs and controls. He assists with global client pursuits across Grant Thornton's practices, helps design in-house professional development programs, and mentors younger professionals. He was part of the Grant Thornton authoring team for the recently issued COSO Guidance on Monitoring Internal Control Systems (2009).

Previously, Sri was the Sarbanes-Oxley Advisor for the National Advisory Practices of Ernst & Young in North America. As an Ernst & Young Fraud Investigation & Dispute Services faculty member, he conducted training on fraud awareness for more than 1,000 U.S. audit partners and principals. Earlier in his career, Sri was a principal with Arthur Andersen's Professional Standards Group. He was the Andersen representative on the AICPA's financial instruments task force that produced SAS 92: Auditing Derivatives, Hedging Activities, and Investments in Securities, and served as a key liaison for the Andersen-MIT research collaboration.

He earned a Bachelor of Commerce (BCom) degree from Bombay University, India, and the MAcc. and PhD degrees from The Ohio State University. After finishing his PhD, Sri served on the accountancy faculty of the University of Illinois at Urbana-Champaign. He has published extensively in journals such as *Management Science*, *European Management Journal*, *International Journal of Accounting*, *Journal of Information Systems*, *Research in Accounting Ethics*, *Journal of Government Financial Management*, *Internal Auditor*, *The White Paper*, and *Internal Auditing*. Among his IIA-funded research monographs are: *Research Opportunities in Internal Auditing* and *Using Neural Networks for Risk Assessment in Internal Auditing*. He has won several research and teaching excellence awards.

Sri has been an active volunteer as the Chairman of the Academy for Government Accountability, a member of The IIA Research Foundation's Board of Trustees, Chairman of The IIA's Academic Relations Committee, and a member of the Board of Governors of The IIA's Chicago chapter. He is currently co-chair of The IIARF's Global Common Body of Knowledge

2010 study. Over the last 10 years, he has made professional presentations in the United States, Brazil, Canada, France, India, Japan, Qatar, South Africa, Spain, the Netherlands, Turkey, and the United Arab Emirates.

Mark Salamasick, CIA, CISA, CSP

Director of the Center for Internal Auditing Excellence
University of Texas at Dallas

Mark is currently Director of the Center for Internal Auditing Excellence at the University of Texas at Dallas, which is one of the five largest internal audit programs worldwide. He started the program six years ago with an extensive curriculum in internal auditing, technology, audit software, information security, and forensic accounting. He teaches Internal Audit, Information Technology Audit, and Risk Management and Advanced Auditing.

He was the principal researcher on a project with The IIA Research Foundation and Intel on PC Management Best Practices along with another publication, *Auditing Vendor Relationships*, both published in 2003. He was previously with Bank of America for more than 20 years. He worked within the Internal Audit Group for 18 years, serving as Senior Vice President and Director of Information Technology Audit with responsibility for various technology, financial, and operational audits. He was responsible for partnering and auditing technology, information security, and business continuity. Before joining Bank of America, Mark was a senior consultant with Accenture (Andersen Consulting).

Mark currently serves on the Board of Trustees of The IIA Research Foundation and has served on The IIA's Board of Research and Education Advisors and its predecessor, the Board of Research Advisors, since 1997. He received the 1994 IIA International Audit and Technology Award. In 2005 he was named Leon R. Radde Educator of the Year by The IIA.

He is a frequent conference speaker on emerging technology issues and internal audit practices. He is on The IIA's Dallas chapter's Board of Governors. Mark holds a BS in Business Administration and an MBA from Central Michigan University, where he taught accounting and information systems as a graduate student and as a full-time faculty member.

Cris Riddle, MA

Audit Administration Analyst
TD AMERITRADE

Cris is the Audit Administration Analyst for TD AMERITRADE. She is responsible for managing the processes, systems, and databases for the administration of the Internal Audit department. Additionally, she reviews and edits audit materials, including audit reports, meeting presentations, and the Audit Manual. Cris also teaches English Composition and World Literature at Creighton University and Nebraska Methodist College.

She is a member of The IIA as well as a FINRA Registered General Securities Representative (Series 7). She received both her B.A. and M.A. degrees in English/Creative Writing from Creighton University in Omaha, Nebraska, where she held a Presidential Fellowship as a graduate student. Cris writes and presents on numerous topics and is currently working on a novel.

CHAPTER 1
INTRODUCTION TO INTERNAL AUDITING

Learning Objectives

- Obtain a basic understanding of internal auditing and the internal audit process.
- Understand the relationship between auditing and accounting.
- Distinguish between financial reporting assurance services provided by internal auditors and those provided by independent outside auditors.
- Become familiar with the internal audit profession and The Institute of Internal Auditors (IIA).
- Understand the competencies needed to excel as an internal auditor.
- Be aware of the various internal audit career opportunities it is possible to pursue.

Think about the term "internal auditing" for a moment. What pops into your mind? What does the term mean to you? For many people, the term has no particular significance, and for some, it may invoke negative thoughts. Now consider the following statements.

> Time *names Cynthia Cooper, WorldCom Vice President of Internal Audit, one of three Persons of the Year.*[1]

> *"Each listed company must have an internal audit function."*
>
> — New York Stock Exchange[2]

> *"[Internal] auditors are rock stars now. This is their day in the sun."*
>
> — Bruce Nolop
> Chief Financial Officer, Pitney Bowes Inc.[3]

> *"Today more than ever, audit committees need to work closely with internal auditors to ensure strong internal controls, accurate financial reporting, and adequate risk management in every company they serve . . . By understanding internal audit standards, audit committees can strengthen their own work of oversight."*
>
> — Roger Raber
> Former CEO, National Association of Corporate Directors[4]

Internal Auditing

An independent, objective assurance and consulting activity designed to add value and improve an organization's operations.

Add Value

Value is provided by improving opportunities to achieve organizational objectives, identifying operational improvement, and/ or reducing risk exposure through both assurance and consulting services.

Did your initial thoughts about internal auditing coincide with these statements? Probably not. Internal auditing has not, until recently, been widely viewed as a prestigious, high profile profession. Many people have long held the view that auditing is merely a boring branch of accounting — only a nerd would want to sit behind a desk working with numbers day after day. To others, internal auditing conveys an even more negative connotation — after all, the only thing auditors do is check other peoples' work and report the mistakes they make, sort of like a police function. These are just two of the misperceptions about internal auditing.

As the authors of this textbook, we hope to dispel these misperceptions. The fact is that the stature of the internal audit profession has never been higher. The demand for talented individuals at all levels of internal auditing far exceeds the supply. Chief audit executives (CAEs) of most public companies report directly to the audit committee of the board of directors and are viewed as peers among senior management executives. Membership in The IIA exceeded 160,000 at the beginning of 2009.

We also hope to convey our shared passion for internal auditing — we really like it. We even enjoy getting together and talking about it. We want to share our collective expertise about internal auditing with you in a way that enables you to make informed decisions as to whether it is a career option you should consider.

We begin this introductory chapter by walking through the definition of internal auditing and introducing you to the internal audit process. We next clarify the relationship between auditing and accounting and distinguish the financial reporting assurance services provided by internal auditors from those provided by independent outside auditors. We then introduce you to the internal audit profession and The IIA. We conclude the chapter by discussing the competencies needed to excel as an internal auditor and the various internal audit opportunities interested, competent individuals can pursue.

DEFINITION OF INTERNAL AUDITING

The IIA's Board of Directors adopted the current definition of internal auditing in 1999:

> *Internal auditing is an independent, objective assurance and consulting activity designed to add value and improve an organization's operations. It helps an organization accomplish its objectives by bringing a systematic, disciplined approach to evaluate and improve the effectiveness of risk management, control, and governance processes.*[5]

The key components of this definition are listed here and discussed in turn below:

- Helping the organization accomplish its objectives.
- Evaluating and improving the effectiveness of risk management, control, and governance processes.
- Assurance and consulting activity designed to add value and improve operations.
- Independence and objectivity.
- A systematic and disciplined approach (specifically, the engagement process).

Helping the Organization Accomplish Its Objectives

An organization's objectives define what the organization wants to achieve, and its ongoing success depends on the accomplishment of its objectives. At the highest level, these objectives are reflected in the organization's mission and vision statements. The mission statement expresses, in broad terms, what the organization wants to achieve today. The vision statement conveys what the organization aspires to achieve in the future.

There is no single right way to categorize business objectives. This textbook uses the following categorization promulgated by the Committee of Sponsoring Organizations of the Treadway Commission (COSO) in 2004.

- **Strategic objectives** pertain to the value creation choices management makes on behalf of the organization's stakeholders. Hereafter the term *objectives* is used when referring to what an organization wants to achieve and the term *strategy* when referring to how management plans to achieve the organization's objectives. For example, an organization may specify "increase market share" as an objective and implement a strategy of "acquire other companies" to achieve this objective.
- **Operations objectives** pertain to the effectiveness and efficiency of the organization's operations, including performance and profitability goals and safeguarding resources against loss.
- **Reporting objectives** pertain to the reliability of internal and external reporting of financial and nonfinancial information.
- **Compliance objectives** pertain to adherence to applicable laws and regulations.[6]

Understandable and measurable business objectives represent achievement targets and, accordingly, establish parameters for evaluating actual achievements over time. From an internal auditor's perspective, business objectives provide a foundation for defining engagement objectives (in other words, what the internal auditor wants to achieve). The direct link between business objectives and internal audit engagement objectives sets the stage for internal auditors to help the organization achieve its objectives. This is an important concept that will be emphasized throughout the text. Exhibit 1-1 illustrates a set of business objectives and corresponding internal audit engagement objectives.

Internal Auditing

It helps an organization accomplish its objectives by bringing a systematic, disciplined approach to evaluate and improve the effectiveness of risk management, control, and governance processes.

Evaluating and Improving the Effectiveness of Risk Management, Control, and Governance Processes

An organization cannot achieve its objectives and sustain success without effective risk management, control, and governance processes. These processes are complex and interrelated; an in-depth discussion of them at this point would be premature. They are covered extensively in later chapters.

Simple definitions are provided here to facilitate thinking about the various roles internal auditors might play in evaluating and improving these processes. Governance provides a good starting point because it is generally viewed as the broadest of the three. *Governance* is the *process conducted by the board of directors to authorize, direct, and oversee management toward the achievement of the organization's objectives.*

EXHIBIT 1-1

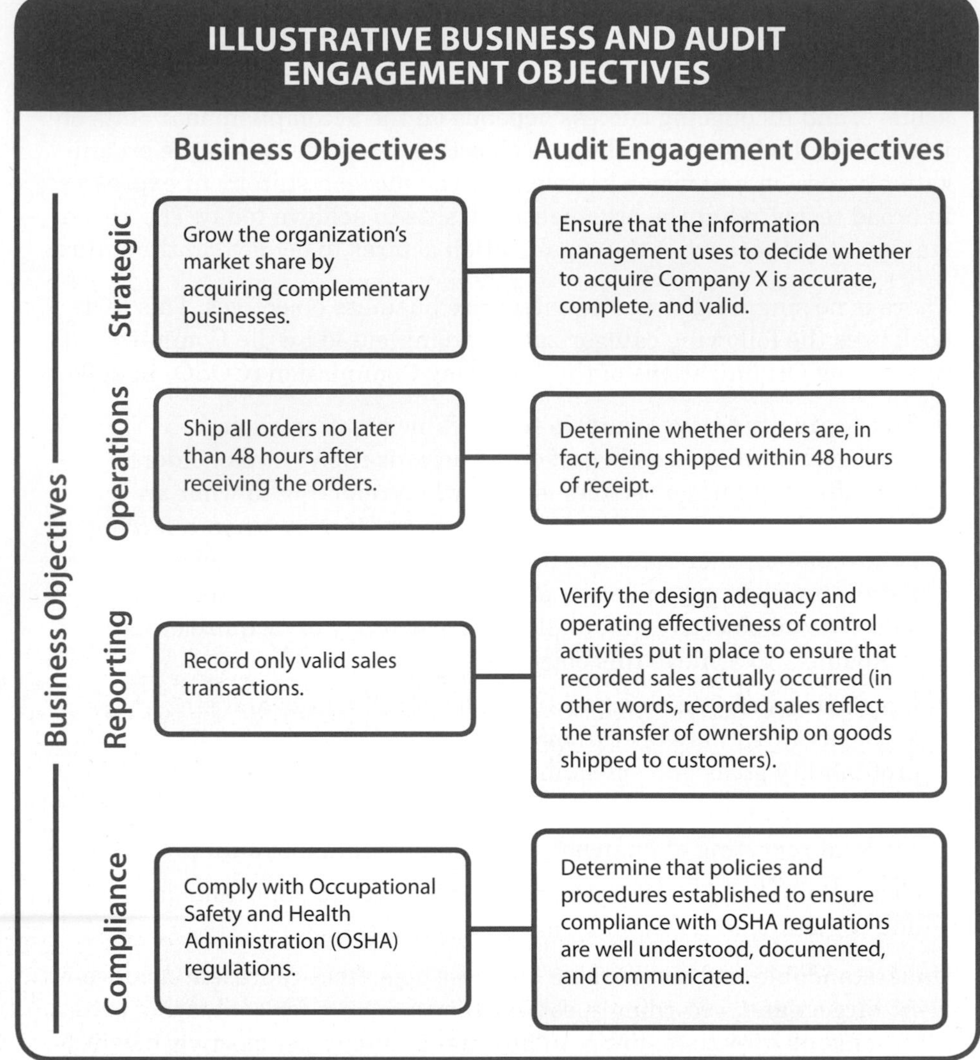

ILLUSTRATIVE BUSINESS AND AUDIT ENGAGEMENT OBJECTIVES
Business Objectives
Audit Engagement Objectives
Business Objectives
Strategic
Grow the organization's market share by acquiring complementary businesses.
Ensure that the information management uses to decide whether to acquire Company X is accurate, complete, and valid.
Operations
Ship all orders no later than 48 hours after receiving the orders.
Determine whether orders are, in fact, being shipped within 48 hours of receipt.
Reporting
Record only valid sales transactions.
Verify the design adequacy and operating effectiveness of control activities put in place to ensure that recorded sales actually occurred (in other words, recorded sales reflect the transfer of ownership on goods shipped to customers).
Compliance
Comply with Occupational Safety and Health Administration (OSHA) regulations.
Determine that policies and procedures established to ensure compliance with OSHA regulations are well understood, documented, and communicated.

Risk management, which is closely interlinked with governance, is the *process conducted by management to understand and deal with uncertainties (risks and opportunities) that could affect the organization's ability to achieve its objectives*. Hereafter, *risk* is used when referring to the possibility that an event will occur and negatively affect the achievement of objectives (for example, employee fraud) and *opportunity* is used when referring to the possibility that an event will occur and positively affect the achievement of objectives (for example, introducing a new product).

Control, which is imbedded in risk management, is the *process conducted by management to mitigate risks to acceptable levels*.

Objectives

What an organization wants to achieve.

All three processes focus on the achievement of the organization's objectives. Whereas the board of directors is responsible for conducting the governance process, management is responsible for conducting the risk management and control processes. The term *conducting* here means guiding or leading the process as opposed to unilaterally performing or completing the steps in the process. The board and management need each other to effectively implement governance, risk management, and control. They also need the internal audit function, which plays a prominent role in evaluating and improving these processes. However, the internal audit function's responsibility stops well short of actually guiding or leading governance, risk management, and control. Chapter 3, "Governance," Chapter 4, "Risk Management," and Chapter 6, "Internal Control," discuss in detail the internal audit function's responsibilities in these areas.

Assurance and Consulting Activity Designed to Add Value and Improve Operations

The title of this textbook, *Internal Auditing: Assurance & Consulting Services*, was chosen because it clearly identifies the two types of services — assurance and consulting — that internal auditors provide to add value and improve operations. Assurance and consulting engagements differ in three respects: the primary purpose of the engagement, who determines the nature and scope of the engagement, and the parties involved. The terms used to refer to these parties vary widely. Hereafter, *auditee* is used to denote the people subject to assessment in an assurance engagement and *customer* is used to denote the people seeking services in a consulting engagement.

The primary purpose of internal assurance services is to assess evidence relevant to subject matter of interest to someone and provide conclusions regarding the subject matter. The internal audit function determines the nature and scope of assurance engagements, which generally involve three parties: the *auditee* directly involved with the subject matter of interest, the *internal auditor* making the assessment and providing the conclusion, and the *user* relying on the internal auditor's assessment of evidence and conclusion.

The primary purpose of internal consulting services is to provide advice and other assistance, generally at the specific request of engagement customers. The customer and the internal audit function mutually agree on the nature and scope of consulting engagements, which generally involve only two parties: the *customer* seeking and receiving the advice, and the *internal auditor* offering and providing the advice.

Independence

The freedom from conditions that threaten objectivity or the appearance of objectivity. Such threats to objectivity must be managed at the individual auditor, engagement, functional, and organizational levels.

Independence and Objectivity

Both The IIA's Code of Ethics and The IIA's *International Standards for the Professional Practice of Internal Auditing* (*Standards*) emphasize the criticality of independence and objectivity to the practice of internal auditing. *Independence* refers to the organizational status of the internal audit function. *Objectivity* refers to the mental attitude of individual internal auditors.

Objectivity

An unbiased mental attitude that allows internal auditors to perform engagements in such a manner that they have an honest belief in their work product and that no significant quality compromises are made. Objectivity requires internal auditors not to subordinate their judgment on audit matters to that of others.

For the internal audit function to be independent, the CAE must report to a level within the organization that has sufficient authority to ensure broad engagement coverage, due consideration of engagement outcomes, and appropriate responses to those outcomes. The IIA recommends that ideally the CAE report functionally to the organization's board of directors and administratively to the organization's CEO (Practice Advisory 1110-1: Organizational Independence).

Objectivity means that an auditor is able to make impartial, unbiased judgments. To ensure objectivity, internal auditors should not involve themselves in day-to-day operations, make management decisions, or otherwise put themselves in situations that result in actual or potential conflicts of interest. For example, if an individual moves into the internal audit function from another area of the organization, the internal auditor may not provide assurance services to that area for one year (Standard 1130.A1-1). The reasoning behind this policy is that the internal auditor would be put in a position of auditing his or her own work. Chapter 2, "The International Professional Practices Framework: Authoritative Guidance for the Internal Audit Profession," goes into greater depth on the subjects of independence and objectivity.

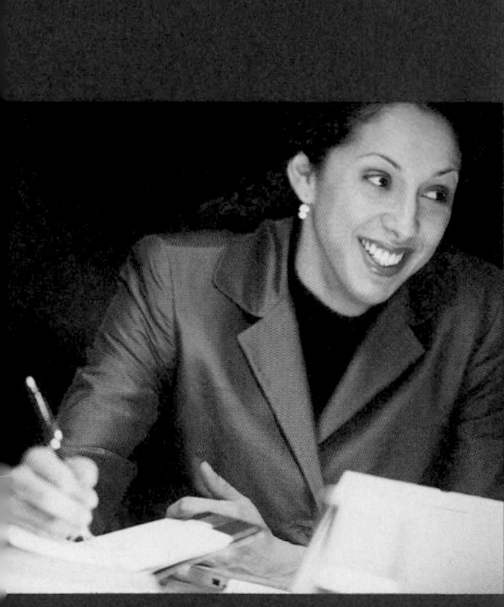

A Systematic and Disciplined Approach: The Engagement Process

To truly add value and improve operations, internal assurance and consulting engagements must be performed in a systematic and disciplined manner. The three fundamental phases in the internal audit engagement process are planning the engagement, performing the engagement, and communicating engagement outcomes. These three phases are introduced in Chapter 12, "Introduction to the Engagement Process," and covered in depth in Chapter 13, "Conducting the Assurance Engagement," Chapter 14, "Communicating Assurance Engagement Outcomes and Performing Follow-up Procedures," and Chapter 15, "The Consulting Engagement." However, a brief overview is provided here.

Engagement

A specific internal audit assignment or project that includes multiple tasks or activities designed to accomplish a specific set of objectives. See also Assurance Services and Consulting Services.

Planning the engagement involves, among other activities:

- Obtaining an understanding of the auditee or customer. An internal auditor cannot provide value-adding assurance or consulting services to an auditee or customer that is not well understood. The internal auditor needs to understand the auditee's or customer's business objectives and the risks that threaten the achievement of those objectives. Other aspects of the auditee or customer that the internal auditor must understand include, for example, the auditee's or customer's personnel, resources, and operations.
- Setting the engagement objectives. Because the overall purpose of internal assurance and consulting services is to help the organization achieve its objectives, the internal auditor will use the auditee's or customer's business objectives as a foundation for defining the desired outcomes of a specific engagement.
- Determining the required evidence. The internal auditor must design the engagement to obtain sufficient appropriate evidence to achieve the engagement objectives.
- Deciding the nature, timing, and extent of the audit tests. These decisions will influence the internal auditor's testing approach that is necessary to gather the required evidence.

Performing the engagement involves the application of specific audit procedures. Procedures include, for example, making inquiries, observing operations, inspecting documents, and analyzing the reasonableness of information. A second important aspect of gathering evidence is documenting the procedures performed and the results of performing the procedures.

Evaluating the evidence gathered during an assurance engagement involves reaching logical conclusions based on the evidence. For example, an internal auditor might reach the conclusion that controls over sales transactions are effective. Evaluating the evidence gathered during a consulting engagement involves formulating practical advice based on the evidence. For example, an internal auditor might advise the customer that specific application controls need to be built into a new computerized information system.

Communicating outcomes is a critical component of all internal assurance and consulting engagements. Regardless of the content or form of the communications, which may vary, communications of engagement outcomes "must be accurate, objective, clear, concise, constructive, complete, and timely" (Standard 2420: Quality of Communications).

THE RELATIONSHIP BETWEEN AUDITING AND ACCOUNTING

Students beginning their first auditing course have a tendency to assume that auditing is a subset of accounting. Although such an assumption is understandable, it is not correct. Exhibit 1-2 contains a quote from *The Philosophy of Auditing* that explains the difference between auditing and accounting.

Although the context of this quote is the audit of financial statements conducted by an independent outside auditor, the ideas expressed are just as relevant to internal assurance and consulting services. Internal assurance and consulting services are analytical and investigative; they are based on logic, which involves reasoning and drawing inferences. Internal auditors use logic when they reach conclusions or formulate advice based on evidence they gather and evaluate. The quality of internal auditors' conclusions or advice depends on their ability to gather and evaluate sufficient appropriate evidence.

FINANCIAL REPORTING ASSURANCE SERVICES: EXTERNAL VERSUS INTERNAL

Publicly traded companies in many countries are required by law or the requirements of the stock exchange on which they trade to have their

EXHIBIT 1-2

RELATIONSHIP BETWEEN AUDITING AND ACCOUNTING

"The relationship of auditing to accounting is close, yet their natures are very different; they are business associates, not parent and child. Accounting includes the collection, classification, summarization, and communication of financial data; it involves the measurement and communication of business events and conditions as they affect and represent a given enterprise or other entity. The task of accounting is to reduce a tremendous mass of detailed information to manageable and understandable proportions. Auditing does none of these things. Auditing must consider business events and conditions too, but it does not have the task of measuring or communicating them. Its task is to review the measurements and communications of accounting for propriety. Auditing is analytical, not constructive; it is critical, investigative, concerned with the basis for accounting measurements and assertions. Auditing emphasizes proof, the support for financial statements and data. Thus, auditing has its principal roots, not in accounting, which it reviews, but in logic on which it leans heavily for ideas and methods."

Mautz, R. K., and Hussein A. Sharaf, *The Philosophy of Auditing* (Sarasota, FL.: American Accounting Association, 1961), p. 14.

annual financial statements audited by an independent outside auditor, for example, a chartered accounting (CA) or certified public accounting (CPA) firm. A financial statement audit is a form of assurance service in which the firm issues a written attestation report that expresses an opinion about whether the financial statements are fairly stated in accordance with Generally Accepted Accounting Principles (GAAP). Many privately held companies, government organizations, and not-for-profit organizations also have annual financial statement audits.

COSO

The Committee of Sponsoring Organizations of the Treadway Commission.

The U.S. Sarbanes-Oxley Act of 2002 requires a U.S. public company's independent outside auditor (frequently referred to as the external auditor) to also attest to the effectiveness of the company's internal control over financial reporting as of the balance sheet date. The CPA firm's opinion on internal control over financial reporting must be based on a recognized framework such as *Internal Control – Integrated Framework* issued by COSO. The COSO framework, as it is often called, and other internal control frameworks are discussed in detail in Chapter 6, "Internal Control." Both the CPA firm's financial statement audit report and the firm's report on the effectiveness of internal control over financial reporting are public documents — they are included in the company's annual report and submitted to the U.S. Securities and Exchange Commission (SEC). This requirement is not restricted to the United States. Many other countries have similar financial reporting laws with similar requirements.

Independent outside audit firms provide their financial reporting assurance services primarily for the benefit of third parties. Third parties rely on a firm's independent attestations when making financial decisions about the organization. The independent attestations provide credibility to the information being used by the third-party decision makers and, accordingly, increase the users' confidence regarding the accuracy, completeness, and validity of the information upon which they base their decisions.

Internal auditors also provide financial reporting assurance services. The primary difference between internal and external financial reporting assurance services is the audience. Internal auditors provide their financial reporting assurance services primarily for the benefit of management and the board of directors. For example, the Sarbanes-Oxley Act requires the CEO and chief financial officer (CFO) of U.S. public companies to certify the company's financial statements as part of their quarterly and annual filings. It also requires management to assess and report on the effectiveness of internal control over financial reporting. Management relies on the financial reporting assurance services provided by the company's internal audit function to provide them with confidence regarding the truthfulness of their financial reporting assertions.

THE INTERNAL AUDIT PROFESSION

Modern Internal Auditing: A Dynamic Profession in High Demand

> *"The profession of auditing in general, and internal auditing in particular, is ancient."* [7]

Although historians have traced the history of internal auditing to centuries B.C., many people associate the genesis of modern internal auditing

TIMELINE OF SELECTED IIA MILESTONES	
1941	The Institute of Internal Auditors is established. IIA membership totals 24.
1947	The *Statement of Responsibilities of the Internal Auditor* is issued.
1948	The first chapters outside North America are formed in London and Manila.
1953	"Progress Through Sharing" is adopted as The IIA's official motto.
1957	The *Statement of Responsibilities of the Internal Auditor* is revised to include more responsibility for operational areas.
1968	The IIA Code of Ethics is approved.
1973	The first Board of Regents is appointed. The Certified Internal Auditor (CIA®) program is established.
1976	The Foundation of Auditability, Research, and Education (FARE) is founded; the name is later changed to The IIA Research Foundation.
1978	The *Standards for the Professional Practice of Internal Auditing* is approved.
1979	The National Institute Agreement is approved; five national institutes are established.
1980	IIA membership totals 21,549.
1984	*The Quality Assurance Review Manual* is published. A pilot school is established at Louisiana State University. The first *Statement on Internal Auditing Standards* (SIAS) is published.
1986	The target school program is started.
1988	An IIA National Institute is established in The People's Republic of China.
1989	The United Nations grants consultative status to The IIA.
1990	The IIA elects A.J. Hans Spoel as the first chairman from outside North America.
1995	The IIA becomes an official member body of the American National Standards Institute (ANSI) and the sole U.S. representative to the International Standards Organization (ISO).
1996	*Accounting Today* names IIA President, William G. Bishop III, CIA, as one of the "top 100 most influential people in accounting." The IIA begins to aggressively promote the CIA® program in Europe, Asia, the Middle East, and South America.
1998	The first all-objective CIA® exam is offered with a record-breaking 5,165 candidates sitting for one or more parts.
1999	The new definition of internal auditing is introduced. The 25th anniversary of the CIA® designation is celebrated.
2000	The new *International Standards for the Professional Practice of Internal Auditing* is introduced. IIA membership totals 68,985.
2002	The *Standards* becomes mandatory guidance for all IIA members and CIAs.
2003	The new IIA Professional Practices Framework is issued.
2006	IIA membership exceeds 120,000.
2007	To continue to use the statement "conducted in accordance with the *Standards*," internal audit functions that existed as of January 1, 2002, must have an external quality assessment completed by January 1, 2007.
2008	Computer-based testing is introduced for all professional examinations administered by The IIA.
2009	The International Professional Practices Framework is issued, which specifies mandatory guidance (Definition of Internal Auditing, Code of Ethics, and the *International Standards for the Professional Practice of Internal Auditing*) and strongly recommended guidance (Practice Advisories, Position Papers, and Practice Guides).

Source: www.theiia.org

EXHIBIT 1-3

with the establishment of The IIA in 1941. At its inception, The IIA was a national organization with 24 charter members.[8]

Both The IIA and the internal audit profession have evolved dramatically since then. A timeline of selected IIA milestones is presented in Exhibit 1-3. Two items that stand out in the timeline are the phenomenal growth of The IIA, especially during the last 30 years, and its globalization. IIA members now reside in 165 countries and territories, with more than 50 percent of the membership residing outside North America.[9] Internal auditing is now a truly global profession and the demand for internal audit services continues to grow.

A number of interrelated circumstances and events have fueled the dramatic increase in demand for internal audit services over the past 30 years. The business world during this time has changed dramatically. Examples of these changes include globalization, increasingly complex corporate structures, e-commerce and other technological advances, and a global economic downturn. Simultaneously, the business world has experienced a rash of devastating corporate scandals, which have precipitated a groundswell of new laws and regulations and professional guidance. These forces, in combination, continue to generate an ever-widening array of risks that corporate executives must understand and address. As a result, internal auditors are increasingly being called upon to help organizations strengthen their corporate governance, risk management, and control processes.

The Nature and Scope of Modern Internal Audit Services

The overarching objective of the internal audit function is to help an organization achieve its business objectives. Consequently, the targets of internal audit attention may include:

- Operational effectiveness and efficiency of business processes.
- Reliability of information systems and the quality of the decision-making information produced by those systems.
- Safeguarding assets against loss, including losses resulting from management and employee fraud.
- Compliance with organization policies, contracts, laws, and regulations.

Compliance

Conformity and adherence to applicable laws and regulations as well as policies, plans, procedures, contracts, or other requirements.

The internal audit function helps the organization achieve its business objectives by evaluating and improving the effectiveness of governance, risk management, and control processes. Evaluating and improving these processes propels the internal audit function into virtually all areas of the organization, including, for example, production of goods and services, financial management, human resources, research and development, logistics, and information technology. The stakeholders served by the internal audit function include the board of directors, management, employees, and interested parties outside the organization.

Internal auditors use a wide variety of procedures to test the design adequacy and operating effectiveness of the organization's governance, risk management, and control processes. These procedures include:

- Inquiring of managers and employees.
- Observing activities.
- Inspecting resources and documents.
- Reperforming control activities.
- Performing trend and ratio analysis.
- Performing data analysis using computer-assisted audit techniques.
- Gathering corroborating information from independent third parties.
- Performing direct tests of events and transactions.

THE IIA'S VISION, MISSION, AND MOTTO

Vision:

The IIA will be the global voice of the internal audit profession: Advocating its value, promoting best practice, and providing exceptional service to its members.

Mission:

The Mission of The Institute of Internal Auditors is to provide dynamic leadership for the global profession of internal auditing. Activities in support of this mission will include, but not be limited to:

- Advocating and promoting the value that internal audit professionals add to their organizations;
- Providing comprehensive professional education and development opportunities; standards and other professional practice guidance; and certification programs;
- Researching, disseminating, and promoting to practitioners and stakeholders knowledge concerning internal auditing and its appropriate role in control, risk management, and governance;
- Educating practitioners and other relevant audiences on best practices in internal auditing; and
- Bringing together internal auditors from all countries to share information and experiences.

Motto:

Progress Through Sharing

EXHIBIT 1-4

The Professionals Who Perform Internal Audit Services

Providers of internal audit services are employed by all types of organizations: public and private companies; local, state, and federal government agencies; and nonprofit entities. Until recently, these services were provided exclusively "in-house," in other words, by employees of the organizations employing them. This is no longer the case. Some organizations are choosing to outsource their internal audit functions, either fully or partially, to external service providers. External providers of internal audit services include public accounting firms and other third-party vendors. The most common form of outsourcing is referred to as "co-sourcing." Co-sourcing means that an organization is supplementing its in-house internal audit function to some extent via the services of third-party vendors. Common situations in which an organization will co-source its internal audit function with a third-party service provider include circumstances in which the third-party vendor has specialized internal audit knowledge and skills that the organization does not have in-house and circumstances in which the organization has insufficient in-house internal audit resources to fully complete its planned engagements. Chapter 9, "Managing the Internal Audit Function," goes into more detail regarding co-sourcing.

THE INSTITUTE OF INTERNAL AUDITORS

The IIA, headquartered in Altamonte Springs, Florida, is recognized around the world as "the internal audit profession's global voice, standard-setter, and resource for professional development and certification."[10] The IIA headquarters, with a staff of approximately 125 professionals, serves the internal audit profession at the international level, with members in 165 countries.[11]

The IIA's vision, mission, and motto are presented in Exhibit 1-4.

The IIA Motto

Progress Through Sharing

The IIA Leadership Structure

The IIA headquarters' executive leadership team includes the president and CEO, the executive vice president and chief financial officer, and the vice presidents. Hundreds of volunteers also provide IIA leadership. These leaders include The IIA's Board of Directors, international committees, district representatives, and officers and board members of the various institutes.

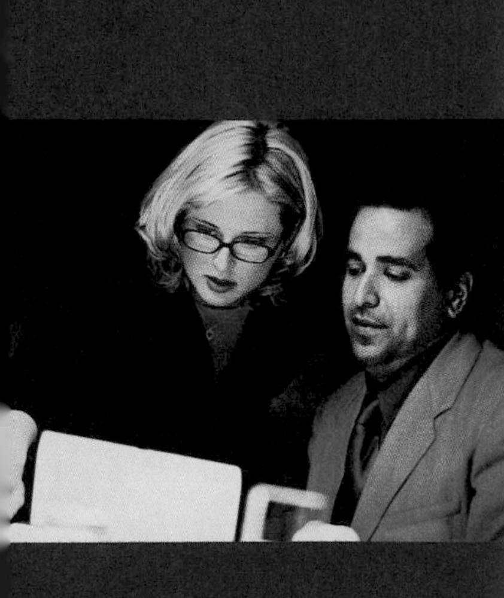

The 38-member Board of Directors oversees the affairs of The IIA. The Board's Executive Committee comprises the chairman of the board, the senior vice chairman, four vice chairmen, the treasurer, the secretary, and the two most recent former chairmen of the board. The board also includes the North American Board, which holds specific authority and oversight of North American activities, certain institute directors, directors-at-large, and The IIA president as an ex-officio director.[12] Exhibit 1-5 depicts an abridged version of The IIA's volunteer structure. Additional details on this structure can be found at www.theiia.org.

Numerous international committees undertake specific tasks directed at meeting the ever-changing needs of the IIA membership. Twenty-nine district representatives oversee the activities of approximately 153 North American chapters in Canada, the United States, Bermuda, and the Caribbean.[13] Each of the nearly 93 institutes worldwide elects its own officers and board members.

Professional Guidance

Professional guidance provided by The IIA is embodied in the International Professional Practices Framework (IPPF). The following is a brief introduction to the IPPF. It is described in detail in Chapter 2, "The International Professional Practices Framework: Authoritative Guidance for the Internal Audit Profession."

IPPF

International Professional Practices Framework, which consists of both *mandatory* and *strongly recommended* guidance.

The IPPF comprises two categories of guidance:

Category 1: Mandatory Guidance. Conformance with the principles set forth in the mandatory guidance is required and essential for the professional practice of internal auditing. The mandatory guidance is developed following an established due diligence process, which includes a period of public exposure for stakeholder input. The three mandatory elements of the IPPF are the Definition of Internal Auditing, the Code of Ethics, and the *Standards*.[14]

Category 2: Strongly Recommended Guidance. The strongly recommended guidance is endorsed by The IIA through a formal approval process. It describes practices for effective implementation of The IIA's Definition of Internal Auditing, Code of Ethics, and *Standards*. The three strongly recommended elements of the IPPF are Practice Advisories, Position Papers, and Practice Guides.[15] More detailed information about the IPPF and the other guidance resources provided by The IIA can be found on its website (www.theiia.org).

Professional Certifications

The premier certification sponsored by The IIA is the Certified Internal Auditor (CIA), the only globally accepted certification for internal auditors. The CIA examination tests a candidate's expertise in four parts: The

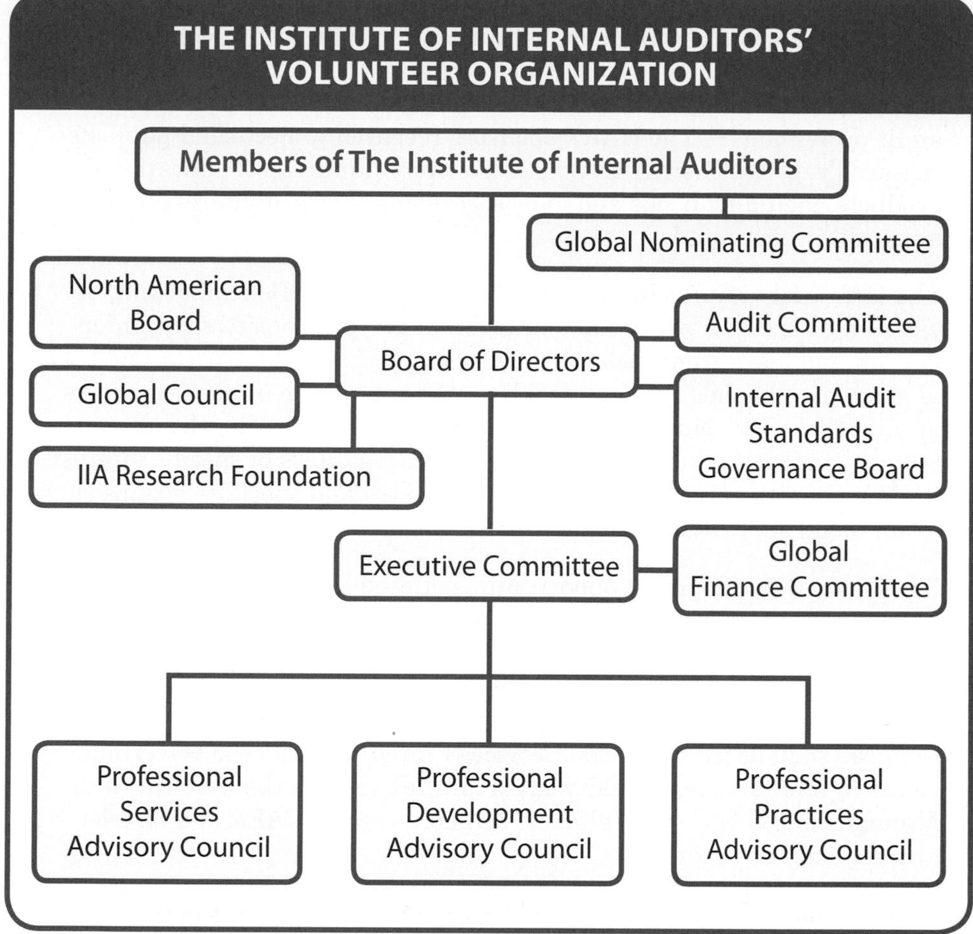

EXHIBIT 1-5

Internal Audit Activity's Role in Governance, Risk, and Control; Conducting the Internal Audit Engagement; Business Analysis and Information Technology; and Business Management Skills. In addition to passing the CIA examination, candidates must have a minimum of two years of internal audit experience or its equivalent to become a CIA.

Certified Internal Auditor (CIA)

The premier certification sponsored by The IIA; the only globally accepted certification for internal auditors.

The IIA also sponsors three specialty certification programs: Certification in Control Self-Assessment; Certified Government Auditing Professional; and Certified Financial Services Auditor. Detailed information about each of the certification programs can be found on The IIA's website.

Other professional organizations also sponsor certification programs relevant to internal auditors. For example, the ISACA (formerly known as the Information Systems Audit and Control Association) sponsors the Certified Information Systems Auditor program and the Association of Certified Fraud Examiners sponsors the Certified Fraud Examiner program.

Research and Educational Products and Services

The IIA is widely known as the chief educator and global leader in professional development for the profession of internal auditing. The wide variety of research and education products and services offered by The IIA are briefly described below. More detailed information can be found on The IIA's website.

The IIA Research Foundation (IIARF) was established in 1976. Its mission is "to expand knowledge and understanding of internal auditing by providing relevant research and educational products to advance the profession globally." Its major objective is "to support research and education in internal auditing, thereby enhancing the development of the internal audit profession."[16] The IIARF sponsors research projects and publishes research reports. The IIARF Bookstore offers hundreds of educational products, including books and videos, covering topics of interest to internal audit professionals.

IIA Research Foundation

Established in 1976, its mission is "to expand knowledge and understanding of internal auditing by providing relevant research and educational products to advance the profession globally."

The IIA's Global Audit Information Network (GAIN) Benchmarking Services and Flash Surveys enable internal audit functions to share information and learn from each other. *Internal Auditor*, The IIA's bi-monthly magazine, publishes articles of widespread interest to internal auditors around the world. Numerous newsletters published by The IIA also cover topics of interest to internal auditors, including topics of specific interest to CAEs and to various internal audit industry and specialty groups such as financial services, gaming, and information technology (IT) auditing.

Professional development opportunities offered by The IIA include meetings, seminars, and conferences as well as technology-based training, books, and webcasts. The premier IIA conference is the annual International Conference, which attracts thousands of internal auditors from around the world. Other IIA opportunities include industry-specific conferences such as the Financial Services Conference and the Government Auditing Conference, specialty opportunities such as the General Audit Management Conference, which is targeted toward CAEs, and district and regional conferences.

Internal Auditing Education Partnership (IAEP)

Sponsored by The IIA, the IAEP program provides an internal audit curriculum in approved colleges and universities.

The IIA, through its Academic Relations Committee, also promotes and supports internal audit education around the world. The Internal Auditing Education Partnership (IAEP) program is designed to support universities and colleges that have made formal commitments to offer internal audit education. The level of support provided by The IIA to a particular school is directly related to the level of development of the internal audit program at that school.

COMPETENCIES NEEDED TO EXCEL AS AN INTERNAL AUDITOR

> *"I keep six honest serving men*
> *(They taught me all I knew);*
> *Their names are What and Why and When*
> *And How and Where and Who."*[17]

The above is the beginning of the poem "I Keep Six Honest Serving Men ..." by Rudyard Kipling from his story "The Elephant's Child." It conveys two important points relevant to internal auditors: they must continue to learn and always ask questions.

Reflecting back on the definition and description of internal auditing presented earlier in this chapter, what else must individuals know to achieve success as internal auditors? What must they be able to do? Are there certain personal characteristics that are indicative of success? The good news is that there is no single right answer to these questions; different people with different competency profiles can achieve success as internal auditors. Moreover, the competencies needed to succeed are not unique to internal auditing.

There are, however, certain competencies that tend to be common among successful internal auditors. Some of these competencies are inherent personal qualities. Others are knowledge and skills that can be learned and developed. An understanding of these competencies provides information with which an informed decision can be made about internal auditing as a desirable vocation.

Inherent Personal Qualities

Different people have different inherent personal qualities or characteristics. For example, some people are by nature more introverted (shy and reserved), while others are more extroverted (outgoing and sociable). Personal qualities that are common among successful internal auditors at all levels include:

Integrity. Integrity is not an option for internal auditors; they must have it. People with integrity build trust, which in turn establishes the foundation for reliance on what they say and do. Users of internal audit work products rely on internal auditors' professional judgments to make important business decisions. These stakeholders must have confidence that internal auditors are trustworthy.

Passion. It is virtually impossible to be very good at something you do not really like to do. Successful internal auditors have a deep interest in, and intense enthusiasm for, their work. Some show this passion more than others, but long-term success cannot be achieved or sustained without this passion.

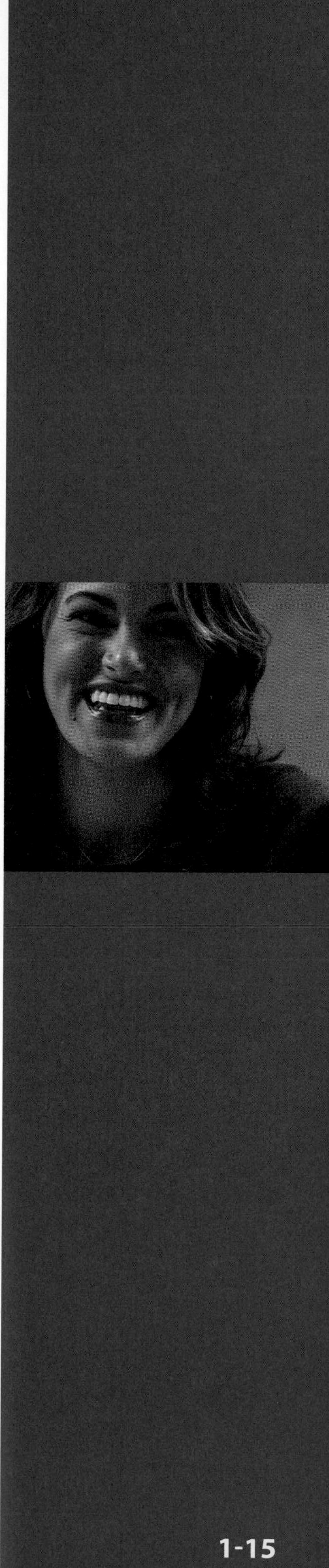

Work ethic. Success in business requires the ability to consistently meet the quality, cost, and timing expectations of "customers." But this success does not come without hard work. The same applies to successful internal auditors, who must not only work hard, but also work smart. They get the right things done, the right way, at the right time.

Curiosity. The information needed to make judgments during internal audit engagements may not always be obvious. Thus, successful internal auditors must be inquisitive and go beyond asking "checklist" type questions. They may need to ask more probing questions to gain the necessary understanding of how things work and why they work the way they do.

Creativity. Most internal auditors like to solve problems. However, the solutions to many problems are not always obvious. Therefore, successful internal auditors must be creative and "think outside the box" to generate the types of ideas valued by management and other stakeholders.

Initiative. Successful internal auditors are self-starters. They voluntarily seek out and pursue opportunities to add value and want to play the role of change agent within their organizations.

Flexibility. Change is the only constant in today's business world. Successful organizations continuously adapt to change, and change brings new risks that must be managed. Successful internal auditors embrace change; they adapt quickly to new situations and challenges.

The characteristics described above are illustrative of the inherent personal qualities that are required to succeed as an internal auditor. Does this mean that someone lacking one or more of these traits is destined to fail as an internal auditor? Not necessarily. Integrity is imperative and it would be foolish for anyone to pursue a vocation they really do not believe in or to which they are not fully committed. The other qualities can be exercised — they can be strengthened, if desired. However, it is important to recognize and understand how each of these qualities enables internal auditors to be successful. For those seeking long-term success, most of these qualities will be necessary.

Knowledge, Skills, and Credentials

Proficiency

Internal auditors must possess the knowledge, skills, and other competencies needed to perform their individual responsibilities. The internal audit activity collectively must possess or obtain the knowledge, skills, and other competencies needed to perform its responsibilities. (Standard 1210)

The IIA's *Standards* require internal auditors to perform their assurance and consulting engagements with proficiency, which means they must possess the knowledge and skills needed to fulfill their responsibilities (Standard 1210). What knowledge and skills are needed to succeed as an internal auditor? The answer to this question will depend, to a certain extent, on the current stage in a person's career and the responsibilities they are undertaking. Those planning to pursue a long-term career in internal auditing will need to continuously advance their knowledge and skills. For example, an internal auditor will be expected to know and do things as an in-charge auditor with four years of experience that would not be expected of someone directly out of school. Accordingly, one of the most important skills to begin developing while in school is learning how to learn — internal auditors continue to learn throughout their careers.

Nobody is an expert internal auditor when they graduate from college. Internal auditing, like any other profession, is learned primarily by doing, in other words, through on-the-job experience. It is like learning how to drive a car. It is impossible to learn how to drive merely by reading about it, listening to someone talk about it, or watching someone else drive. It must be experienced — it is necessary to get in a car and practice, preferably under the supervision of a well-qualified instructor. Such is the case with internal auditing — it is learned by doing it under the watchful eyes of experienced supervisors and mentors.

Recognizing that internal auditors need a wide variety of competencies, The IIA developed an Internal Auditor Competency Framework. This framework can help individual internal auditors and internal audit functions assess their current competency levels and identify areas for improvement. The framework outlines the minimum level of knowledge and skills needed in four areas to effectively operate and maintain a successful internal audit function. Exhibit 1-6 provides an outline of these four areas and the specific attributes recommended for each.

At first glance, this framework may look imposing and overwhelming. However, these competencies are not necessary for an entry position and can be developed over time. There are many things a student can do to prepare for an entry-level internal audit position. Certain levels of knowledge and skills can be obtained through:

- Education in auditing, accounting, information systems and technology, business risks and controls, management, finance and economics, commercial law, or quantitative methods. Knowledge in more than one area is especially beneficial. For example, knowledge in both internal auditing and information systems is in very high demand.
- Hands-on experience with audit-related software such as flowcharting, spreadsheet, database, and generalized audit software.

INTERNAL AUDITOR COMPETENCY FRAMEWORK

EXHIBIT 1-6

1. Interpersonal Skills

a. Influence: Wielding effective tactics for persuasion
b. Communication: Sending clear and convincing messages, listening
c. Management
  i. Policies and procedures
  ii. Staffing
  iii. Priority setting, planning, performance management, and customer focus
  iv. Time management, achieving goals and tasks, and organizational skills
d. Leadership: Inspiring and guiding groups and people, building organizational commitment, and entrepreneurial orientation
e. Change catalyst: Initiating, managing, and coping with change
f. Conflict management: Negotiating and resolving disagreements
g. Collaboration and cooperation: Working with others toward shared goals
h. Team capabilities: Creating group synergy in pursuing collective goals

2. Tools and Techniques

a. Operational and management research tools
b. Forecasting
c. Project management
d. Business process analysis
e. Balanced scorecard
f. Risk and control assessment techniques (including self-assessment)
g. Governance, risk, and control tools and techniques
h. Data collection and analysis tools and techniques
i. Problem-solving tools and techniques
j. Computer assisted auditing techniques (CAATs)

3. Internal Audit Standards, Theory, and Methodology

a. Definition of Internal Auditing
b. Code of Ethics
c. *International Standards for the Professional Practice of Internal Auditing*
  i. Attribute standards
  ii. Performance standards

4. Knowledge Areas

a. Financial accounting and finance
b. Managerial accounting
c. Regulatory, legal, and economics
d. Quality: understanding of the quality framework in your organization
e. Ethics and fraud
f. Information technology
g. Governance, risk, and control
h. Organizational theory and behavior
i. Industry knowledge

Source: www.theiia.org

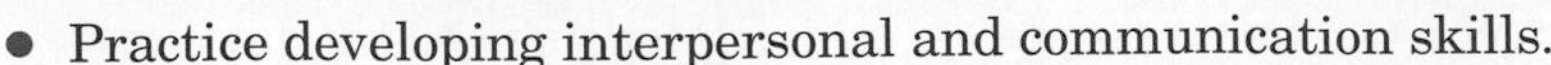

- Practice developing interpersonal and communication skills.
- Projects that allow students to think analytically, assimilate new information quickly, cope with ambiguity, handle unstructured multidimensional tasks, and effectively manage several projects simultaneously.

The credentials students attain and report on their resumes will reflect the knowledge and skills they have obtained. The completion of a degree with a good grade point average displays mastery of a field of study. Working while in school or actively participating in extracurricular activities shows the ability to multitask successfully. Scholarships and other awards signify respect for a student's achievements. Completion of an internship demonstrates the ability to apply what has been learned. Serving as an officer in a student organization signifies motivation and the ability to lead. Completing the CIA examination before graduation demonstrates not only competency in internal auditing and related subjects, but also motivation to succeed.

Progression from a staff internal auditor to an experienced in-charge internal auditor indicates a readiness to coach and share expertise with subordinates, make presentations and facilitate meetings, communicate persuasively with all levels of people, build rapport and lasting relationships with auditees and customers, and proactively stimulate change. Credentials to accrue during this stage of an internal audit career may include, for example, a track record of engagement successes, testimonials from auditees and customers (being recognized as a "go to" person), a Master of Business Administration degree, multiple professional certifications, and a volunteer leadership position in a professional organization such as a local IIA chapter.

Internal audit professionals who continue to develop their management and leadership skills can progress into internal audit management. These individuals must be able to coach and mentor subordinates, adeptly address strategic management issues, and command respect among senior executives and professional colleagues. As an individual gains a reputation as an internal audit thought leader, he or she will likely be called upon to share his or her expertise by doing such things as serving as an IIA volunteer at the international level, delivering presentations at professional meetings or conferences, and writing articles for professional journals.

INTERNAL AUDIT CAREER PATHS

Pathways into Internal Auditing

Until very recently, most internal auditors began their careers in public accounting. Accounting graduates would start out as financial statement auditors in public accounting and, after gaining experience, move into internal audit positions, oftentimes with former clients. While this is still a recognized pathway into internal auditing, it is by no means the only one.

Hiring of internal auditors directly out of school has become much more common in recent years. Public and private companies, governmental entities, not-for-profit organizations, and firms providing internal audit services are increasingly recruiting internal auditors directly out of colleges and universities. Colleges and universities that have established internal audit programs endorsed by The IIA are growing in number and popularity among recruiters. Top-tier students with degrees in accounting, information systems, and other business and nonbusiness fields from these and other schools are in high demand. Those students who have completed one or more internal audit-related internships are in especially high demand because of the real-world experience they have gained.

Some organizations consider internal auditing to be an important component of their management trainee programs because it offers management candidates a unique opportunity to gain relevant governance, risk management, and control expertise across many areas of the organization. In these organizations, prospective managers from different areas of the organization are required to spend a certain amount of time in the internal audit function as a prerequisite to moving upward into management.

Pathways Out of Internal Auditing

The majority of people who work in internal auditing do not spend their entire careers there. As indicated above, experience in an internal audit function serves as an excellent training ground for aspiring business executives. Many internal auditors use the expertise they gain in internal auditing as a stepping stone into financial or nonfinancial management positions, either in the organization they have been working for or another organization.

Moving from internal auditing into a position with a professional services firm that provides internal assurance and consulting services was virtually unheard of a few years ago. This is now a viable opportunity, especially for individuals with specialized, highly valued expertise in a particular industry (for example, energy or banking) or subject matter (for example, information systems or fraud prevention, deterrence, and detection).

Careers in Internal Auditing

Some people, however, do choose to make internal auditing their career and even they have options. One option is to progress upward through the ranks of a single organization's internal audit function into internal audit management. Another option is to stay in internal auditing but advance up the ladder toward internal audit management, moving from one organization to another. A third option is to move upward through the various levels in a professional services firm that provides internal assurance and consulting services.

CAE

The chief audit executive is a senior position within the organization responsible for internal audit activities.

The ultimate destination of a career internal auditor in an organization is CAE. CAEs are highly respected within their organizations, often holding senior executive positions. They interact with the highest levels of senior management and the board of directors. They commonly report functionally to the audit committee of the board of directors and administratively to a senior executive such as the CEO or CFO. Chapter 9, "Managing the Internal Audit Function," comprehensively addresses the roles and responsibilities of the CAE.

In a firm that provides internal audit services to many organizations, an internal auditor can rise to the level of a partner or comparably prestigious position. Unlike CAEs in an organization, they interact with and report to senior executives and boards of directors of several organizations.

Regardless of the career path chosen, present day internal auditors have many more career opportunities than they did just a few years ago. Internal auditors who develop a wide range of skills and gain experience in different areas will be in a good position to pursue a wide variety of career options.

SUMMARY

This chapter provided a basic understanding of internal auditing and introduced the internal audit process. The difference between auditing and accounting and the difference between the financial reporting assurance services internal auditors provide and those that public accountants provide was covered. An introduction to the internal audit profession and The IIA also was provided. Finally, the competencies needed to excel as an internal auditor and the various internal audit career paths that are available were outlined.

This textbook covers both the concepts that are necessary to understand internal auditing as well as the steps to conduct internal audit engagements. The first 11 chapters are part of the *Fundamental Internal Audit Concepts* section of the textbook. These chapters cover just that — fundamental internal audit concepts that internal auditors need to know and understand. A firm grasp of these concepts is necessary, but not sufficient, to understand internal auditing. The last four chapters are part of the *Conducting Internal Audit Engagements* section of the textbook. These chapters focus on the steps necessary to plan, perform, and communicate results of assurance and consulting engagements. Finally, the case studies that accompany the textbook can be used to practice and reinforce the concepts and steps provided throughout the textbook.

Review Questions

1. How does The IIA define internal auditing?
2. What is the primary difference between an organization's objectives and its strategy?
3. According to COSO, what are the four categories of business objectives?
4. What are the definitions of governance, risk management, and control provided in this chapter?
5. What is the difference between internal assurance services and internal consulting services?
6. What is the difference between independence and objectivity as they pertain to internal auditors?
7. What are the three fundamental phases in the internal audit engagement process?
8. What is the relationship between auditing and accounting?
9. What is the primary difference between internal and external financial reporting assurance services?
10. What are some of the factors that have fueled the dramatic increase in demand for internal audit services over the past 30 years?
11. What types of procedures might an internal auditor use to test the design adequacy and operating effectiveness of governance, risk management, and control processes?
12. What is co-sourcing? Why might an organization choose to cosource its internal audit function?
13. What is The IIA's official motto?
14. How is The IIA's leadership organization structured?
15. What are the two categories of guidance included in the IPPF?
16. What are the four areas of expertise tested on the CIA exam?
17. What is the major objective of The IIARF?
18. What are the seven inherent personal qualities listed in the chapter that are common among successful internal auditors?
19. Why is it imperative that internal auditors have integrity?
20. What are the four areas outlined in The IIA's Internal Auditor Competency Framework?
21. What are the three common ways individuals enter the internal audit profession?
22. Do most people who work in internal auditing spend their entire careers there? Explain.
23. What options does an individual have if he or she chooses to be a career internal auditor?

Multiple-choice Questions

Select the best answer for each of the following questions.

1. AVF Company's new CFO has asked the company's CAE to meet with him to discuss the role of the internal audit function. The CAE should inform the CFO that the overall responsibility of internal auditing is to:
   a. Serve as an independent assurance and consulting activity designed to add value and improve the company's operations.
   b. Assess the company's methods for safeguarding its assets and, as appropriate, verify the existence of the assets.
   c. Review the integrity of financial and operating information and the methods used to accumulate and report information.
   d. Determine whether the company's system of internal controls provides reasonable assurance that information is effectively and efficiently communicated to management.

2. Which of the following statements is not true about business objectives?
   a. Business objectives represent targets of performance.
   b. Establishing meaningful business objectives is a prerequisite to effective internal control.
   c. Establishing meaningful business objectives is a key component of the management process.
   d. Business objectives are management's means of employing resources and assigning responsibilities.

3. Within the context of internal auditing, assurance services are best defined as:
   a. Objective examinations of evidence for the purpose of providing independent assessments.
   b. Advisory services intended to add value and improve an organization's operations.
   c. Professional activities that measure and communicate financial and business data.
   d. Objective evaluations of compliance with policies, plans, procedures, laws, and regulations.

4. Internal auditors must have competent interpersonal skills. Which of the following does not represent an attribute of interpersonal skills?
   a. Communication.
   b. Leadership.
   c. Project management.
   d. Team capabilities.

5. While planning an internal audit, the internal auditor obtains knowledge about the auditee to, among other things:
   a. Develop an attitude of professional skepticism about management's assertions.
   b. Develop an understanding of the auditee's objectives and risks.
   c. Make constructive suggestions to management concerning internal control improvements.
   d. Evaluate whether misstatements in the auditee's performance reports should be communicated to senior management and the audit committee.

Discussion Questions

1. Describe the relationship between objectives and strategies. What is your foremost objective as a student in this course? Explain your strategy for achieving this objective.

2. Ina Icandoit has an 8:00 a.m. class each day. The professor has instilled in the students the importance of getting to class on time, so Ina has made this one of her objectives for the semester. What risks threaten the achievement of Ina's objective? What controls can Ina implement to mitigate these risks?

3. Prim Rose owns five flower shops in the suburbs of a large Midwestern city. Each shop is managed by a different person. One of the tests Prim performs to monitor the performance of his shops is a simple trend analysis of month-to-month sales for each shop. Assume that Prim's analysis of the reported sales performance for his flower shop on Iris Street shows that monthly sales remained relatively consistent from January through June. Should Prim be pleased or concerned about the sales performance report for the shop on Iris Street over this six-month period? Explain.

4. Discuss:
   a. The inherent personal qualities common among successful internal auditors.
   b. The knowledge, skills, and credentials entry-level internal auditors are expected to possess.
   c. Additional knowledge, skills, and credentials in-charge internal auditors might be expected to possess.
   d. Additional knowledge, skills, and credentials CAEs might be expected to possess.

CASE

Visit The Institute of Internal Auditors' website (www.theiia.org). Locate, print, read, and prepare to discuss the following items:

A. Frequently asked questions about internal auditing.

1. What is internal auditing?
2. Why should an organization have internal auditing?
3. What should be the reporting lines for the CAE?
4. How does internal auditing maintain its independence and objectivity?
5. How do internal and external auditors differ and how should they relate?
6. What is enterprise risk management (ERM) and what role in it does internal auditing play?
7. Is it mandatory to have an internal audit activity?
8. What standards guide the work of internal audit professionals?

B. The CIA exam content outlines for "Part I: The Internal Audit Activity's Role in Governance, Risk, and Control" and "Part II: Conducting the Internal Audit Engagement."

REFERENCES

[1]Lacayo, Richard, and Amanda Ripley, "Persons of the Year," *Time*, Dec. 30, 2002 - Jan. 6, 2003, 30.

[2]NYSE Listed Company Manual, Section 303A.07(d), http://www.nyse.com/pdfs/finalcorpgovrules.pdf.

[3]Lieb, Scott, "New Terrain," *CFO Magazine*, Feb. 1, 2004, p. 40.

[4]Audit Committee Briefing, *Internal Auditing Standards – Why They Matter* (Altamonte Springs, FL: The Institute of Internal Auditors, 2005).

[5]International Professional Practices Framework (Altamonte Springs, FL: The Institute of Internal Auditors, 2009), p. 2.

[6]Committee of Sponsoring Organizations of the Treadway Commission (COSO), *Enterprise Risk Management – Integrated Framework* (Jersey City, NJ: AICPA, 2004), pp. 35-36.

[7]Calloway, David, *Internal Auditing: A Guide for the New Auditor* (Altamonte Springs, FL: The Institute of Internal Auditors, 1995), p. 1.

[8]www.theiia.org.

[9]Ibid.

[10]Ibid.

[11]Ibid.

[12]Ibid.

[13]Ibid.

[14]International Professional Practices Framework (Altamonte Springs, FL: The Institute of Internal Auditors, 2009), p. iii.

[15]Ibid.

[16]www.theiia.org.

[17]Kipling, Rudyard, "The Elephant's Child." *Just So Stories. Everyman's Library Children's Classic Series* (New York: Knopf Doubleday Publishing Group, 1992).

Ethics

CHAPTER 2
THE INTERNATIONAL PROFESSIONAL PRACTICES FRAMEWORK: AUTHORITATIVE GUIDANCE FOR THE INTERNAL AUDIT PROFESSION

Learning Objectives

- Know the history behind the current professional guidance for the practice of internal auditing.
- Describe the structure of the new International Professional Practices Framework (IPPF) and the categories of authoritative guidance it provides.
- Understand the mandatory IPPF guidance: the Definition of Internal Auditing, the Code of Ethics, and the *International Standards for the Professional Practice of Internal Auditing* (*Standards*).
- Understand the strongly recommended IPPF guidance: Practice Advisories, Position Papers, and Practice Guides.
- Describe how the IPPF is kept current.
- Understand how the authoritative guidance promulgated by other professional organizations affects the practice of internal auditing.

The stature and reputation of any profession can be measured to a large extent by the rigor of its ethics and practice standards. This is true for the medical, engineering, law, public accounting, and other professions. It also is true for the internal audit profession.

This chapter explains how authoritative guidance from The Institute of Internal Auditors (IIA) answers questions such as:

- What should the stakeholders of internal audit services expect from internal audit professionals?
- What makes an internal audit function successful?
- What does it take to be a good internal auditor?
- What are the responsibilities of the chief audit executive (CAE)?
- How do the board and senior management evaluate internal audit services?
- In sum, how does internal auditing add value?

The Definition of Internal Auditing introduced in Chapter 1, "Introduction to Internal Auditing," describes internal auditing as " . . . an independent, objective assurance and consulting activity designed to add value and improve an organization's operations." Internal auditors provide these professional services to a diverse set of organizations ranging from publicly traded and private companies to government and not-for-profit entities. Within these organizations, internal auditors serve a number of stakeholders, each with their own needs and demands. These stakeholders include internal parties such as the organization's board of directors (particularly the audit committee), senior management, financial and operating managers, and external parties such as investors, creditors, regulators, suppliers, and customers. This chapter explains how the internal audit profession's authoritative guidance enables internal audit professionals to deliver value-adding services that meet the needs of this wide array of stakeholders.

The Institute of Internal Auditors

Headquartered in Altamonte Springs, FL, it is recognized around the world as the internal audit profession's leader in certification, education, research, and technological guidance.

The chapter begins with an historical overview of how the guidance for the professional practice of internal auditing has evolved since the inception of The IIA in 1941. The IIA's new IPPF, which reflects the global nature of the internal audit profession, is then introduced. The mandatory guidance and the strongly recommended guidance contained in the IPPF are then discussed in detail. This is followed by a description of how authoritative guidance for the profession of internal auditing is developed and issued. The chapter concludes with an explanation of how the authoritative guidance promulgated by other professional organizations affects the practice of internal auditing.

THE HISTORY OF GUIDANCE SETTING FOR THE INTERNAL AUDIT PROFESSION

The practice of internal auditing has been developing over a long period of time. As organizations grew in size and complexity and developed geographically dispersed operations, senior management could no longer personally observe operations for which they were responsible nor have sufficient direct contact with people reporting to them. This distancing of senior management from the operations for which they were responsible created a need for other people in the organization to assist them by examining the operations and providing reports based on those examinations. These people began performing internal audit-type activities to provide this assistance. Over time these activities became more formalized and, with the founding of The IIA, the practice of internal auditing began evolving into a profession. Consensus among practitioners about the role of the internal audit function and the basic concepts and practices of internal auditing began to emerge.

The development of guidance for the profession of internal auditing began shortly after the formation of The IIA. The first formal guidance, the *Statement of the Responsibilities of the Internal Auditor* (*Statement of Responsibilities*), was issued in 1947. This short document defined the objectives and scope of internal auditing. As the profession evolved, the broadening of its scope was reflected in subsequent revisions. For instance, the scope of internal audit activities covered in the original 1947 *Statement of Responsibilities* was restricted primarily to financial matters, but by 1957 the scope had been broadened to include operations as well.[1] The scope of internal audit activities continued to expand as the profession evolved over the years and the *Statement of Responsibilities* was revised accordingly in 1971, 1976, 1981, and 1990.

In 1968, The IIA provided ethical guidance for its members with the issuance of a Code of Ethics. The code consisted of eight articles, the basic principles of which are still found in the current code. With the publication of the Common Body of Knowledge (CBOK) in 1972 and implementation of the Certified Internal Auditor (CIA) certification program in 1973, The IIA provided additional professional guidance on the necessary competencies (that is, knowledge and skills) for internal audit practitioners. In 1978, The IIA issued the *Standards for the Professional Practice of Internal Auditing* (the 1978 *Standards*). These standards consisted of five general and 25 specific guidelines for how the internal audit function should be managed and how audit engagements should be performed. The standards were widely adopted and translated into a number of different languages. They also were incorporated into the laws and regulations of various government entities.

The 1978 *Standards* proved to be sufficiently robust to accommodate the evolving profession, remaining relatively unchanged for the next 20 years. However, The IIA provided a large amount of additional guidance to facilitate the interpretation of these standards. This additional guidance included:

- Guidelines that accompanied the 1978 *Standards*,
- Professional Standards Practice Releases providing responses to frequently asked questions,
- Position papers, and
- Research studies.

By the end of the 1990s, the levels of authority among the various forms of guidance were no longer clear and instances of conflicting guidance began to occur.

Moreover, the landscape of the internal audit profession began changing in the 1980s. The use of risk assessment as a method of allocating internal audit resources (that is, risk-based auditing) rapidly gained popularity. In the 1990s, many organizations began outsourcing internal audit activities to external service providers. The time allocated to traditional internal audit services decreased, while the time allocated to the effectiveness and efficiency of operations increased. Nontraditional internal audit services such as control self-assessment programs, proactive training on internal control, participation as advisors in system implementation projects, and other consulting activities consumed a growing proportion of the internal audit resources. The 1978 *Standards* did not adequately address these emerging issues.

Recognizing the important role that the *Statement of Responsibilities*, the Code of Ethics, and particularly, the 1978 *Standards* had played in advancing the now global internal audit profession, The IIA established a Guidance Task Force in 1997 to consider the needs and mechanisms for providing guidance to the profession in the future. After more than a year of study, the Guidance Task Force issued its report — *A Vision for the Future: Professional Practices Framework for Internal Auditing*. This report proposed a new definition of internal auditing to replace the one found in the *Statement of Responsibilities* and a new structure for providing relevant and timely guidance to the profession. The proposed definition and structure were approved in 1999. Implementation began with the revision of the Code of Ethics in 2000 and the completion of the *International Standards for the Professional Practice of Internal Auditing* (*Standards*) in 2002.

By 2006, the *Standards* had become recognized globally, with authorized translations in 32 languages. Moreover, the number of countries and jurisdictions around the world incorporating the *Standards* into laws and regulations continues to increase. With the increased recognition and status of The IIA's professional guidance, IIA leadership saw the need to ensure that its authoritative guidance was clear, current, relevant, and internationally consistent. The guidance-setting process also needed to be sufficiently responsive to the needs of the profession and suitably transparent to the profession's stakeholders. A task force and steering committee were established to review the existing guidance structure and the process for developing, reviewing, and issuing guidance. The review resulted in a new International Professional Practices Framework (IPPF) and a reengineering of the guidance-setting process. A new Guidance Oversight Board, composed predominately of outside stakeholders, was created to oversee establishment of the mandatory guidance.

THE INTERNATIONAL PROFESSIONAL PRACTICES FRAMEWORK

International Professional Practices Framework (IPPF)

The only globally recognized guidance for the internal audit profession.

The IIA's depiction of the IPPF components is presented in Exhibit 2-1. The IPPF is the only globally recognized guidance for the internal audit profession and contains what are considered the essential elements for the delivery of internal audit services that add value. These elements include the attributes of the individual internal auditor, the characteristics of the function providing these services, the nature of internal audit activities, and associated performance criteria. Thus, the IPPF provides guidance to the profession and sets expectations for its stakeholders regarding the performance of internal audit services.

The components of the IPPF include both mandatory guidance (Definition of Internal Auditing, the Code of Ethics, and the *Standards*) and strongly recommended guidance (Practice Advisories, Position Papers, and Practice Guides). Conformance with the mandatory guidance is considered essential. This guidance is developed following a rigorous due process, including a period of public exposure. Strongly recommended guidance describes practices supporting effective implementation of the principles found in the Definition, Code of Ethics, and *Standards*. The IIA endorses and strongly encourages conformance with this guidance, but recognizes that there may be other, equally effective practices. The process for developing strongly recommended guidance is less rigorous.

The IPPF encompasses the full range of internal audit guidance promulgated by The IIA and makes it easily accessible to internal audit professionals globally. It provides the foundation for internal audit functions to fulfill their role and effectively meet their responsibilities. The IPPF reflects the global nature of the internal audit profession and has achieved worldwide acceptance with approved translations of the Definition of Internal Auditing, the Code of Ethics, and the *Standards* into more than 20 languages.

THE INTERNATIONAL PROFESSIONAL PRACTICES FRAMEWORK

EXHIBIT 2-1

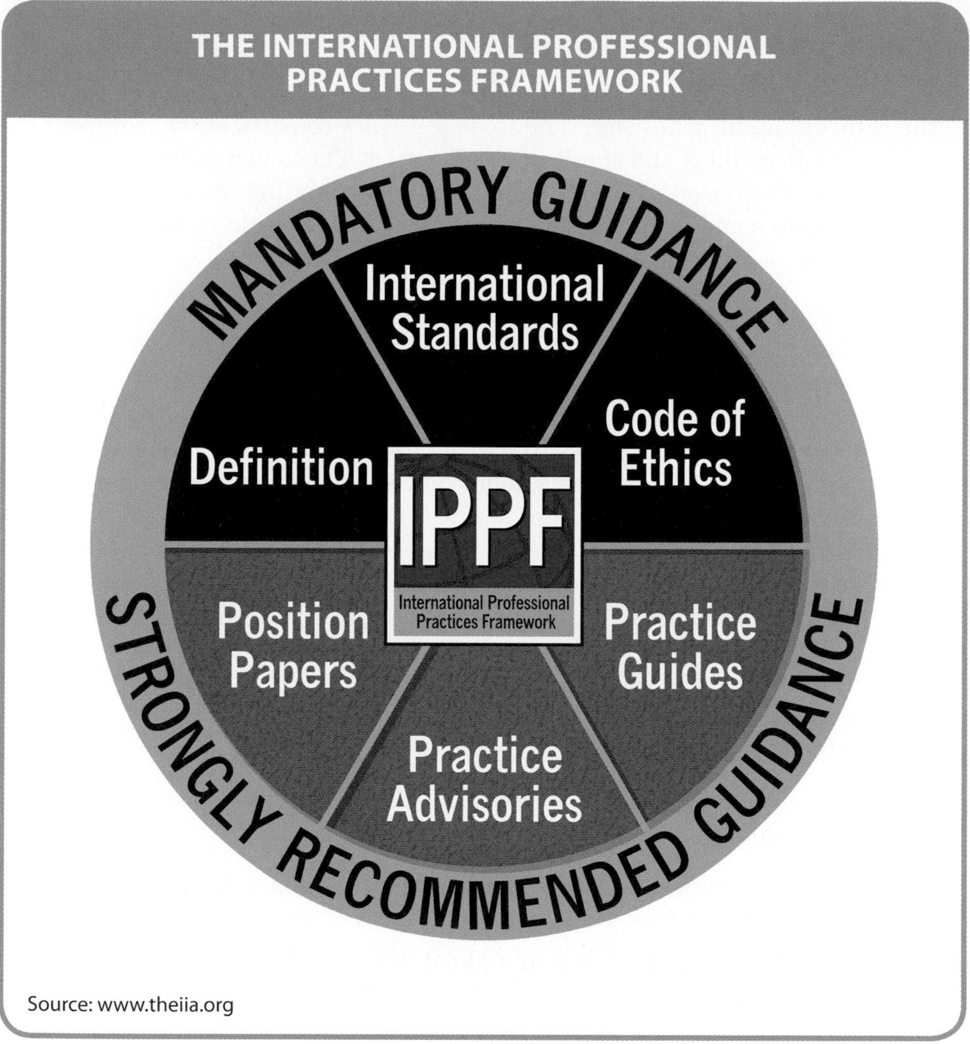

Source: www.theiia.org

MANDATORY GUIDANCE

The Definition

The IPPF provides the following Definition of Internal Auditing:

> *Internal auditing is an independent, objective assurance and consulting activity designed to add value and improve an organization's operations. It helps an organization accomplish its objectives by bringing a systematic, disciplined approach to evaluate and improve the effectiveness of risk management, control, and governance processes.*

This definition recognizes that the ultimate goal of the internal audit profession as a whole, and individual internal audit functions in particular, is to add value to the organization by providing assurance and consulting services. It focuses internal auditors' attention on the evaluation and improvement of the effectiveness of the organization's risk management, control, and governance processes. The definition's reference to independence and objectivity, and the systematic, disciplined approach provides the foundation for performing internal audit services. These elements are discussed further in the remaining components of the IPPF.

The Code of Ethics

The purpose of the Code of Ethics is to promote an ethical culture in the internal audit profession. The Code of Ethics consists of two components: the Principles and the Rules of Conduct. These two components go beyond the Definition of Internal Auditing by expanding upon the necessary attributes and behaviors of the individuals providing internal audit services.

The Principles express the four ideals internal audit professionals should aspire to maintain in conducting their work and represent the core values that internal auditors must uphold to earn the trust of those who rely on their services. The Rules of Conduct describe 12 behavioral norms that internal auditors should follow to put the Principles into practice. While some might have differing views about how specific engagements are carried out or whether internal audit services are better provided by external providers or an internal function, it is hard to imagine there is anyone who would not want internal audit professionals to follow these four Principles and 12 Rules of Conduct, as presented and discussed below.

Integrity — According to the Code of Ethics, "The integrity of internal auditors establishes trust and thus provides the basis for reliance on their judgment."

Integrity

Establishes trust and provides the basis for reliance on internal auditors' judgment.

The Rules of Conduct associated with the integrity principle state that "Internal auditors:

1.1. Shall perform their work with honesty, diligence, and responsibility.

1.2. Shall observe the law and make disclosures expected by the law and the profession.

1.3. Shall not knowingly be a party to any illegal activity, or engage in acts that are discreditable to the profession of internal auditing or to the organization.

1.4. Shall respect and contribute to the legitimate and ethical objectives of the organization."

Integrity is the "price of admission" for internal auditors. It is so fundamental that, without it, an individual cannot serve as an internal audit professional. For example, how could a stakeholder rely on an internal audit report that contains intentionally false or deceptive statements? Or, would stakeholders be comfortable if an internal auditor was fired from a previous job for committing fraud? Internal auditors must model the ethical values of the organization to gain the trust and respect needed to fulfill their professional responsibilities.

Objectivity

Internal auditors are not unduly influenced by their own interests or by others in forming judgments.

Objectivity — The Code of Ethics requires that, "Internal auditors exhibit the highest level of professional objectivity in gathering, evaluating, and communicating information about the activity or process being examined. Internal auditors make a balanced assessment of all the relevant circumstances and are not unduly influenced by their own interests or by others in forming judgments."

The Rules of Conduct associated with the objectivity principle state that "Internal auditors:

2.1. Shall not participate in any activity or relationship that may impair or be presumed to impair their unbiased assessment.

This participation includes those activities or relationships that may be in conflict with the interests of the organization.

2.2. Shall not accept anything that may impair or be presumed to impair their professional judgment.

2.3. Shall disclose all material facts known to them that, if not disclosed, may distort the reporting of activities under review."

Objectivity is a fundamental attribute of internal auditing. In performing their work, internal auditors must be aware of potential threats to their objectivity such as personal relationships or conflicts of interest. For example, accepting gifts from auditees, auditing an operation in which their spouse works, or agreeing with the divisional manager to transfer to the division at the end of the audit would be perceived as impairing an internal auditor's objectivity. Moreover, internal auditors must be objective in their communications and avoid misleading language. For example, it is inappropriate to state that inventory controls were at the same level of effectiveness as in the last audit but neglect to point out that such controls were assessed as unsatisfactory at that time.

Confidentiality — The Code of Ethics also requires that "Internal auditors respect the value and ownership of information they receive and do not disclose information without appropriate authority unless there is a legal or professional obligation to do so."

Confidentiality

Internal auditors do not disclose information they receive without proper authority unless there is a legal or professional obligation to do so.

The Rules of Conduct associated with the confidentiality principle state that "Internal auditors:

3.1. Shall be prudent in the use and protection of information acquired in the course of their duties.

3.2. Shall not use information for any personal gain or in any manner that would be contrary to the law or detrimental to the legitimate and ethical objectives of the organization."

In providing internal audit services, the internal auditor needs unrestricted access to all relevant data. To grant such access, management must have confidence that the internal auditor will not inappropriately disclose or use data in such a manner that harms the organization, violates laws or regulations, or results in personal gain. Similarly, internal auditors must protect data within their possession to ensure confidential information is not inadvertently disclosed to inappropriate parties. For instance, passwords, encryption, and other security measures should be used when carrying personally identifiable information on a laptop. Likewise, an internal auditor who is aware of material nonpublic information cannot disclose it to outsiders or use it for personal gain (such as insider trading).

Competency — Finally, the Code of Ethics requires that "Internal auditors apply the knowledge, skills, and experience needed in the performance of internal audit services."

Competency

Internal auditors apply the knowledge, skills, and experience needed in the performance of internal audit services.

The Rules of Conduct associated with the competency principle state that "Internal auditors:

4.1. Shall engage only in those services for which they have the necessary knowledge, skills, and experience.

4.2. Shall perform internal audit services in accordance with the *International Standards for the Professional Practice of Internal Auditing*.

4.3. Shall continually improve their proficiency and the effectiveness and quality of their services."

Internal audit services can be performed by people who have integrity, are objective, and maintain confidentiality, but those services are of little value if such persons do not have the necessary knowledge and skills to perform the work and reach valid conclusions. That is why there are specific standards requiring internal auditors to be competent and continuously strive for improvement.

The Code of Ethics applies to all individuals and entities that provide internal audit services, not just those who are IIA members or hold IIA certifications. However, The IIA is only able to exercise enforcement over IIA members and recipients of, or candidates for, IIA professional certifications. Breaches of the Code of Ethics by those in the purview of The IIA can result in censure, suspension of membership and/or certifications, and expulsion and/or revocation of certification as determined by The IIA's Ethics Committee. It should also be noted that conduct need not be explicitly mentioned in the Rules of Conduct for it to be considered unacceptable or discreditable and thus subject to disciplinary action.

The *International Standards for the Professional Practice of Internal Auditing*

The basic principles of internal auditing are outlined in The IIA's *Standards*. The introduction to the *Standards* recognizes that "Internal auditing is conducted in diverse legal and cultural environments; within organizations that vary in purpose, size, complexity, and structure; and by persons within or outside the organization." While the differences that exist among organizations may affect the practice of internal auditing, "conformance with [the *Standards*] is essential in meeting the responsibilities of internal auditors and the internal audit activity."

***The* Standards**

Principles-focused, mandatory requirements consisting of Statements and Interpretations.

"The purpose of the *Standards* is to:

1. Delineate basic principles that represent the practice of internal auditing.
2. Provide a framework for performing and promoting a broad range of value-added internal auditing.
3. Establish the basis for the evaluation of internal audit performance.
4. Foster improved organizational processes and operations." (Introduction to the *Standards*)

"The *Standards* are principles-focused, mandatory requirements consisting of:

- *Statements* of basic requirements for the professional practice of internal auditing and for evaluating the effectiveness of performance, which are internationally applicable at organizational and individual levels [italics added].
- *Interpretations*, which clarify terms or concepts with the Statements [italics added]." (Introduction to the *Standards*)

For example, in Standard 2040: Policies and Procedures the *Statement* is: "The chief audit executive must establish policies and procedures to guide the internal audit activity." The *Interpretation* is: "The form and content of policies and procedures are dependent upon the size and structure of the internal audit activity and the complexity of its work." In this case, the interpretation explains that the appropriate form and content of policies and procedures will vary across internal audit functions because of size, organizational structure, and types of services provided.

The *Standards* include a Glossary of terms that have been given specific meanings. The Statements, their Interpretations, and terms defined in the Glossary must be considered together to understand and apply the *Standards* correctly. The *Standards* are reproduced in their entirety in Appendix A of this textbook.

Three types of **Standards**

- **Attribute Standards**
- **Performance Standards**
- **Implementation Standards**

There are three types of *Standards*:

- **Attribute Standards** "address the attributes of organizations and individuals performing internal auditing."
- **Performance Standards** "describe the nature of internal auditing and provide quality criteria against which the performance of these services can be measured."
- **Implementation Standards** " . . . expand upon the Attribute and Performance Standards, by providing the requirements applicable to assurance . . . or consulting . . . activities." (Introduction to the *Standards*)

The *Standards* are organized using a system of numbers and letters. Attribute Standards make up the 1000 series and Performance Standards the 2000 series. The Attribute Standards and Performance Standards apply equally to both assurance and consulting activities. The Implementation Standards are presented directly under the related Attribute and Performance Standards and are indicated by an "A" if they pertain to assurance services or by a "C" if they pertain to consulting services. This system is illustrated in Exhibit 2-2.

Assurance and Consulting Services

The two types of internal audit services — assurance and consulting — were introduced in Chapter 1, "Introduction to Internal Auditing." These two types of services are defined in the Glossary to the *Standards* as follows:

> **Assurance Services —** An objective examination of evidence for the purpose of providing an independent assessment on governance, risk management, and control processes for the organization. Examples may include financial, performance, compliance, system security, and due diligence engagements.
>
> **Consulting Services —** Advisory and related [customer] service activities, the nature and scope of which are agreed with the [customer], are intended to add value and improve an organization's governance, risk management, and control processes without the internal auditor assuming management responsibility. Examples include counsel, advice, facilitation, and training.

The difference in purpose between these two types of services is clear. Assurance engagements are performed to provide independent assessments.

EXHIBIT 2-2

ILLUSTRATION OF THE NUMBERING SYSTEM USED IN THE *STANDARDS*

1220 – Due Professional Care
Internal auditors must apply the care and skill expected of a reasonably prudent and competent internal auditor. Due professional care does not imply infallibility.

1220.A3 – Internal auditors must be alert to the significant risks that might affect objectives, operations, or resources. However, assurance procedures alone, even when performed with due professional care, do not guarantee that all significant risks will be identified.

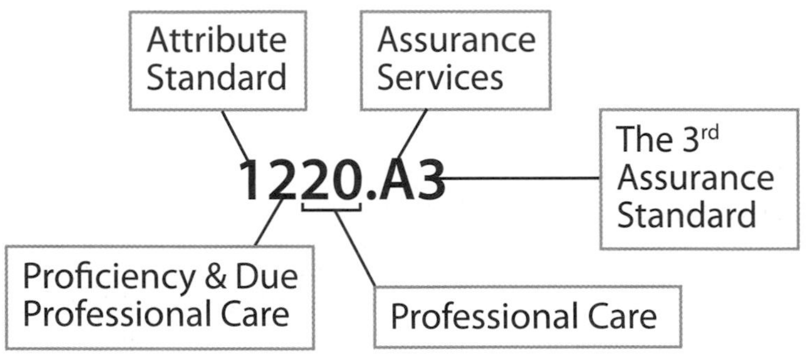

Consulting engagements are performed to provide advisory, training, and facilitation services.

The structural difference between assurance and consulting engagements is not as obvious and is illustrated in Exhibit 2-3. The structure of consulting engagements is relatively simple. They typically involve two parties: (1) the party requesting and receiving the advice — the customer and (2) the party providing the advice — the internal audit function. The internal audit function works directly with the customer to tailor the engagement to meet the customer's needs. The structure of assurance engagements is more complex. They typically involve three parties: (1) the party directly responsible for the process, system, or other subject matter being assessed — the auditee, (2) the party making the assessment — the internal audit function, and (3) the party/parties using the assessment — the user(s). The users of the internal audit function's assessment are not involved directly in the engagement and in some cases are not identified explicitly.

The relative complexity of assurance engagements is reflected in the *Standards*. The internal audit function must plan and perform an assurance engagement and report the engagement results in a manner that meets the needs of the third-party users who are not involved directly in the engagement. Moreover, the internal audit function must take care to avoid any potential conflicts of interest with these users. Many of the attributes and practices required by the *Standards* and Code of Ethics are particularly concerned with keeping the interests of assurance service providers and the third-party users aligned. Accordingly, the Implementation Standards for assurance services are more stringent and numerous than the Implementation Standards for consulting services.

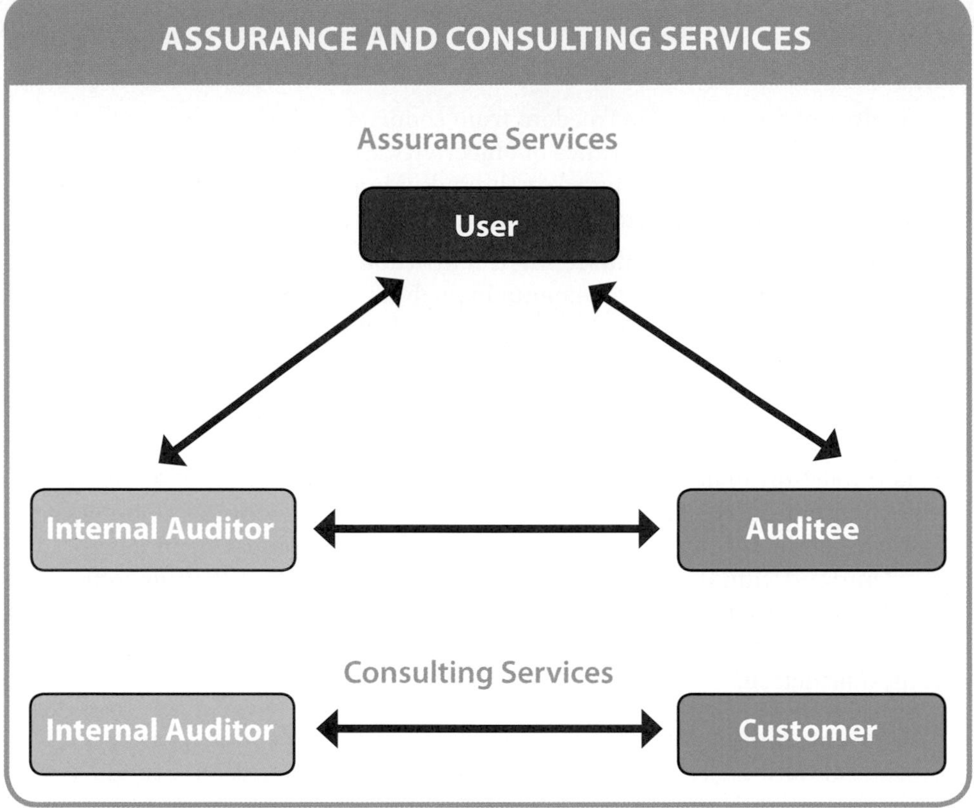

EXHIBIT 2-3

Coverage of the Implementation Standards is integrated in the following discussion of Attribute Standards and Performance Standards.

The Attribute Standards

The Attribute Standards, which address the characteristics that the internal audit function and individual internal auditors must possess to perform effective assurance and consulting services, are divided into four main sections:

1000 – Purpose, Authority, and Responsibility

1100 – Independence and Objectivity

1200 – Proficiency and Due Professional Care

1300 – Quality Assurance and Improvement Program

Purpose, Authority, and Responsibility. The internal audit function must have a charter that clearly states the function's purpose, authority, and responsibilities and specifies the nature of the assurance and consulting services the function provides. The charter also must acknowledge the internal audit function's responsibility to adhere to the Definition of Internal Auditing, the Code of Ethics, and the *Standards*. Such information may be documented in the form of a service contract when internal audit services are outsourced to a third-party service provider. The CAE "must periodically review the internal audit charter and present it to senior management and the board for approval" (Standard 1000: Purpose, Authority, and Responsibility). Final approval of the charter is the responsibility of the board. More information about the internal audit charter is presented in Chapter 9, "Managing the Internal Audit Function."

Independence and Objectivity. "The internal audit [function] must be independent, and internal auditors must be objective in performing their work" (Standard 1100: Independence and Objectivity). The Glossary to the *Standards* defines independence and objectivity as follows:

> **Independence —** The freedom from conditions that threaten objectivity or the appearance of objectivity. Such threats to objectivity must be managed at the individual auditor, engagement, functional, and organizational levels.
>
> **Objectivity —** An unbiased mental attitude that allows internal auditors to perform engagements in such a manner that they have an honest belief in their work product and that no significant quality compromises are made. Objectivity requires internal auditors not to subordinate their judgment on audit matters to others.

Independence

The freedom from conditions that threaten objectivity or the appearance of objectivity.

Objectivity

An unbiased mental attitude.

It is important to note that independence and objectivity are two distinct, yet interrelated, concepts that are fundamental to providing value-adding internal audit services — the internal audit function must be independent and individual internal auditors must be objective. Whereas independence is an attribute of the internal audit function, objectivity is an attribute of the individual auditor. This is a subtle, yet extremely important, distinction.

The extent to which an internal function can be independent depends on the relative status of the function within the organization. Standard 1110: Organizational Independence states that "The chief audit executive must report to a level within the organization that allows the internal audit [function] to fulfill its responsibilities . . . and confirm to the board, at least annually, the organizational independence of the internal audit [function]." Standard 1111: Direct Interaction With the Board requires the CAE to "communicate and interact directly with the board." Positioning the internal audit function at a high level within the organization facilitates broad audit coverage and promotes due consideration of engagement outcomes. Conversely, positioning the internal audit function lower within the organization greatly increases the risk of conflicts of interest that impair the function's ability to provide objective assessments and advice. For example, it would be difficult for an internal audit function to assess objectively the controls over financial reporting if the CAE reports to the controller who is responsible for the design adequacy and operating effectiveness of those controls.

As shown in Exhibit 2-4, independence and objectivity is one of three pillars supporting effective internal audit services. Organizational independence of the internal audit function facilitates the objectivity of individual auditors. Objectivity is a state of mind and is defined as freedom from bias. It involves the use of facts without distortions by personal feelings or prejudices.[2] In an applied sense, it would mean that two people with the same level of expertise and facing the same facts and circumstances will come to similar conclusions.

Conflicts of interest impair independence and objectivity. A conflict of interest is "a situation in which an internal auditor, who is in a position of trust, has a competing professional or personal interest" (Interpretation of Standard 1120: Individual Objectivity). Potential conflicts of interest often arise as a result of naturally occurring events, such as:

- A senior manager from another area of the organization is asked to be the CAE.

EXHIBIT 2-4

THE THREE PILLARS OF EFFECTIVE INTERNAL AUDIT SERVICES

Effective Internal Audit Services

Independence & Objectivity

Proficiency

Due Professional Care

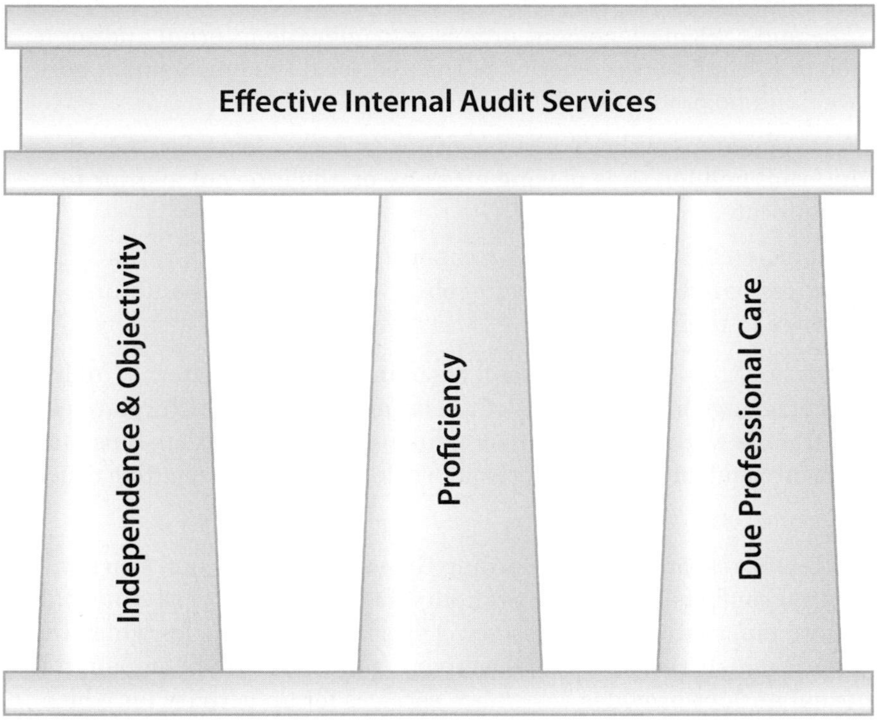

- An employee moves into the internal audit function from another area of the organization or rotates through the internal audit function as part of his or her training regimen.
- An internal auditor with specialized accounting expertise is asked to assume a temporary accounting position.
- An internal auditor with management experience is asked to fill a vacated management position while the organization searches for a suitable replacement.
- An internal auditor is asked to design control policies and procedures in an area of the organization that does not have the requisite expertise to address existing control deficiencies.
- The CAE manages functions in addition to internal audit, such as risk management, security, or compliance.

Task-related threats to independence and objectivity arise from the nature of the work itself. For example, an individual who recently joined the internal audit function might be asked to audit the area for which they were previously responsible. This individual would, in effect, be auditing his or her own work. Objectivity is threatened in such situations because people sometimes have trouble recognizing or acknowledging personal deficiencies or errors in their own work. Human beings exhibit an unconscious "self-serving bias" that is a cognitive weakness. Research has shown, for example, that people are not as good at identifying weaknesses in systems they design as they are in identifying weaknesses in systems designed by others.[3]

Independence and objectivity also can be undermined by incentives and personal relationships. *Incentives* involve conditions in which internal auditors have economic stakes in the outcomes of their work that could impair their judgment. Examples of such conditions include:

- The auditee's management promises to offer the internal auditor a job or to support a promotion of the auditor if the engagement goes well and no problems are found.
- A manager or employee gives a gift to, or does a favor for, the internal auditor, thus placing pressure on the internal auditor to reciprocate.
- The internal audit function's compensation structure awards bonuses based on the number of observations internal auditors include in their reports.

Conflict of Interest

Any relationship that is, or appears to be, not in the best interest of the organization.

Personal relationships cause conflicts of interest when internal auditors perform engagements in areas of the organization in which relatives or close friends work as managers or employees. Such relationships may tempt internal auditors to overlook problems or soften negative conclusions.

The CAE is responsible for guarding the internal audit function against potential conflicts of interest. Standard 1130.A1 states that "Internal auditors must refrain from assessing specific operations for which they were previously responsible. Objectivity is presumed to be impaired if an internal auditor provides assurance services for an activity for which the internal auditor had responsibility within the previous year." Standard 1130.A2 states that "Assurance engagements for functions over which the chief audit executive has responsibility must be overseen by a party outside the internal audit [function]."

The standards pertaining to consulting services are not as stringent. Standard 1130.C1 states that "Internal auditors may provide consulting services relating to operations for which they had previous responsibilities." Per Standard 1130.C2, they must, however, disclose potential impairments to independence or objectivity to the prospective customer before accepting a consulting engagement.

Impairment of independence or objectivity, in fact or appearance, may be unavoidable in certain circumstances. Standard 1130: Impairment to Independence or Objectivity indicates that in such instances the CAE must disclose the details of the impairment to appropriate parties. To whom the details of the impairment should be reported depends on the nature of the impairment and the CAE's responsibilities to senior management and the board as covered in the internal audit charter. This prevents the users of internal audit services from unknowingly placing unwarranted confidence in the internal audit function's work products and allows the users to determine for themselves the extent to which they want to rely on the work of the internal audit function.

Proficiency and Due Professional Care. As illustrated in Exhibit 2-4, proficiency and due professional care are the second and third pillars supporting effective internal audit services. Assurance and consulting services provided by internal auditors lacking the requisite knowledge, skills, and other competencies (that is, proficiencies) to perform the work or failing to apply the care and skills required will be of little, if any, value. Thus the *Standards* require that internal audit functions and individual auditors possess the knowledge, skills, and other competencies needed to fulfill their responsibilities and apply due professional care.

The *Standards* do not mandate a specific set of knowledge, skills, and other competencies. Strongly recommended guidance regarding proficiency is provided in Practice Advisory 1210-1: Proficiency. Further guidance can be found in The IIA's Competency Framework (discussed in Chapter 1, "Introduction to Internal Auditing") and in the syllabus for the Certified Internal Auditor (CIA) examination.[4]

One specific competency that is required by the *Standards* is knowledge of fraud risks. Standard 1210.A2 states that "Internal auditors must have sufficient knowledge to evaluate the risk of fraud and the manner in which it is managed by the organization . . . " They are not expected, however, "to have the expertise of a person whose primary responsibility is detecting and investigating fraud." Chapter 8, "Fraud Risks and Controls," covers in detail the nature of fraud risks and the controls that organizations can put in place to mitigate these risks.

Likewise, Standard 1210.A3 states that "Internal auditors must have sufficient knowledge of key information technology risks and controls and available technology-based audit techniques to perform their assigned work." However, every internal auditor need not possess "the expertise of an internal auditor whose primary responsibility is information technology auditing." Chapter 7, "Information Technology Risks and Controls," covers in detail the nature of IT risks and the controls that organizations can implement to mitigate these risks. Chapter 10, "Audit Evidence and Working Papers," provides an overview of computer-assisted audit techniques. The CD-ROM that accompanies this textbook contains both ACL and IDEA, the two most widely used commercially available audit software programs.

Proficiency applies to the internal audit function as a whole as well as to the individual internal auditor. The CAE is responsible for ensuring that the internal audit function possesses the knowledge, skills, and other competencies required to fulfill the function's responsibilities as specified in its charter. In cases in which the function lacks competencies required to perform all or part of an assurance engagement, the CAE "must obtain competent advice and assistance" from other sources (Standard 1210.A1). Chapter 9, "Managing the Internal Audit Function," discusses how such advice and assistance may be obtained from outside service providers. When the internal audit function is asked to perform a consulting engagement for which the internal audit function does not possess the necessary competencies, the CAE must either decline the engagement or obtain competent advice and assistance (Standard 1210.C1).

Standard 1220: Due Professional Care requires internal auditors to "apply the care and skill expected of a reasonably prudent and competent internal auditor." This does not mean that internal auditors can never make mistakes or imperfect judgments, but rather that they will demonstrate the level of concern and competence expected of a professional. Due care also does not mean that internal auditors will examine every transaction, visit every location, or speak with every employee of the engagement auditee or customer. It does, however, mean that they will put forth the same level of effort as other internal audit professionals would in similar situations.

Proficiency

The knowledge, skills, and other competencies needed to fulfill internal audit responsibilities.

Due Professional Care

The care and skill expected of a reasonably prudent and competent internal auditor.

The *Standards* prescribe what needs to be considered in determining the appropriate level of care for assurance and consulting engagements. Standard 1220.A1 indicates that internal auditors must consider the following for assurance engagements: "the

- Extent of work needed to achieve the engagement's objectives;
- Relative complexity, materiality, or significance of matters to which assurance procedures are applied;
- Adequacy and effectiveness of governance, risk management, and control processes;
- Probability of significant errors, fraud, or noncompliance; and
- Cost of assurance in relation to potential benefits."

Internal auditors also must consider "the use of technology-based audit and other data analysis techniques" (Standard 1220.A2) and "be alert to the significant risks that might affect objectives, operations, or resources" (Standard 1220.A3).

Standard 1220.C1 indicates that internal auditors must consider the following for consulting engagements: "the

- Needs and expectations of [customers], including the nature, timing, and communication of engagement results;
- Relative complexity and extent of work needed to achieve the engagement's objectives; and
- Cost of the consulting engagement in relation to potential benefits."

Certifications Sponsored by The IIA:

- **Certified Internal Auditor (CIA)**
- **Certified Government Auditing Professional (CGAP)**
- **Certified Financial Services Auditor (CFSA)**
- **Certification in Control Self-Assessment (CCSA)**

Standard 1230: Continuing Professional Development states that "Internal auditors must enhance their knowledge, skills, and other competencies through continuing professional development." Individuals aspiring to become internal auditors and internal auditors who have not yet achieved professional certification should pursue education, training, and experience programs that qualify them to obtain one or more certifications relevant to their professional responsibilities. Certifications sponsored by The IIA include the Certified Internal Auditor (CIA), Certified Government Auditing Professional (CGAP), Certified Financial Services Auditor (CFSA), and the Certification in Control Self-Assessment (CCSA). Other professional organizations also sponsor certifications that internal audit professionals may find worthwhile to pursue. Examples include the Certified Information Systems Auditor (CISA) certification sponsored by ISACA (previously known as the Information Systems Audit and Control Association) and the Certified Fraud Examiner (CFE) certification sponsored by the Association of Certified Fraud Examiners (ACFE). Internal auditors possessing professional certifications need to meet specified continuing professional education requirements to retain their certifications. This standard complements rule 4.3 of The IIA's Code of Ethics, which requires internal auditors to continually improve their proficiency and the effectiveness and the quality of their services.

Quality Assurance and Improvement Programs. The basic concept of quality assurance for internal audit services is the same as it is for the manufacturing of products or the delivery of other types of services. Quality assurance instills confidence that the product or service possesses the essential features and characteristics it is intended to have. For example, quality assurance associated with manufacturing a particular metal bolt would focus on ensuring that the bolt is made in accordance with the prescribed engineering specifications. In a similar vein, an internal audit function's quality assurance and improvement program "is designed to enable an evaluation of the internal audit [function's] conformance with the Definition of Internal Auditing and the *Standards* and an evaluation of whether internal auditors comply with the Code of Ethics. The program also assesses the efficiency and effectiveness of the internal audit [function] and identifies opportunities for improvement" (Interpretation to Standard 1300: Quality Assurance and Improvement Program).

Quality Assurance

Instills confidence that the product or service possesses the essential features and characteristics it is intended to have.

"The chief audit executive must develop and maintain a quality assurance and improvement program that covers all aspects of the internal audit [function]" (Standard 1300: Quality Assurance and Improvement Program). The CAE also "must communicate the results of the quality assurance and improvement program to senior management and the board" (Standard 1320: Reporting on the Quality Assurance and Improvement Program) and "state that the internal audit [function] conforms with the *International Standards for the Professional Practice of Internal Auditing* . . . if the results of the quality assurance and improvement program support this statement" (Standard 1321: Use of "Conforms with the *International Standards for the Professional Practice of Internal Auditing*"). "When nonconformance with the Definition of Internal Auditing, the Code of Ethics, or the *Standards* impacts the overall scope or operation of the internal audit [function], the chief audit executive must disclose the nonconformance and the impact to senior management and the board" (Standard 1322: Disclosure of Nonconformance).

Standard 1310: Requirements of the Quality Assurance and Improvement Program states that "The quality assurance and improvement program must include both internal and external assessments." "Internal assessments must include:

- Ongoing monitoring of the performance of the internal audit [function]; and
- Periodic reviews performed through self-assessment or by other persons within the organization with sufficient knowledge of internal audit practices" (Standard 1311: Internal Assessments).

"External assessments must be conducted at least once every five years by a qualified, independent reviewer or review team from outside the organization. The chief audit executive must discuss with the board:

- The need for more frequent external assessments; and
- The qualifications and independence of the external reviewer or review team, including any potential conflicts of interest" (Standard 1312: External Assessments).

Exhibit 2-5 provides a framework for designing a quality assurance program, which includes an underlying principle of substitutability. Quality assurance elements can be substituted for those higher in the hierarchy if specific independence conditions are met. For example, an internal review may be conducted in lieu of an external review if the reviewers are independent (that is, outside the line of authority and responsibility of the work they are reviewing). Large internal audit functions with several decentralized internal audit units (for example, an Asian office, a North and South American office, and a European office) may internally review

EXHIBIT 2-5

FRAMEWORK FOR QUALITY ASSURANCE PROGRAM DESIGN
Hierarchy of Quality Assurance Elements

Control Element	Control Objective	Source	Assurance Level
Professionalism (Due Care)	Individual Auditor's Work	Individual	Individual Internal Auditor
Supervisory Review	Engagement	Supervisor *Within* Line of Responsibility	Internal Audit Function Management
Internal Review	Aggregate of Engagements or Divisional Offices or Autonomous Internal Audit Units	Supervisor/Peer *Outside* Line of Responsibility	Chief Audit Executive
External Review	Internal Audit Function as a Whole	Qualified Persons From Outside the Organization	Audit Committee and Senior Management

the work performed by internal auditors on individual assurance and consulting engagements. In such situations, external reviewers may focus on the internal audit function's quality assurance process, organizational independence, risk assessment process, and relationships with the audit committee and senior management. Conversely, reviews of individual assurance and consulting engagements conducted by small, centralized internal audit functions must be performed by qualified external reviewers.

Chapter 9, "Managing the Internal Audit Function," provides more details regarding the implementation of quality assurance and improvement programs. Further guidance for conducting internal and external reviews can be found in The IIA's *Quality Assessment Manual*.

The Performance Standards

The Performance Standards, which describe the nature of internal audit services and the criteria against which the performance of these services can be assessed, are divided into seven main sections:

2000 – Managing the Internal Audit Activity

2100 – Nature of Work

2200 – Engagement Planning

2300 – Performing the Engagement

2400 – Communicating Results

2500 – Monitoring Progress

2600 – Resolution of Senior Management's Acceptance of Risks

Managing the Internal Audit Activity. Standard 2000: Managing the Internal Audit Activity indicates that the CAE is responsible for managing the internal audit function (referred to throughout the *Standards* as the internal audit activity) and ensuring that the function adds value to the organization. Even when an organization outsources the internal audit function to an outside service provider, the organization must have an in-house CAE. In such cases, the CAE is responsible for approving the service contract, overseeing the quality of the service provider's work, reporting assurance and consulting engagement outcomes to senior management and the board, and following up on engagement results and observations. "The internal audit activity is effectively managed when:

- The results of the internal audit activity's work achieve the purpose and responsibility included in the internal audit charter;
- The internal audit activity conforms with the Definition of Internal Auditing and the *Standards*; and
- The individuals who are part of the internal audit activity demonstrate conformance with the Code of Ethics and the *Standards*" (Interpretation to Standard 2000: Managing the Internal Audit Activity).

Subsequent standards go on to indicate that, to meet his or her management responsibilities, The CAE must:

- ". . . establish risk-based plans to determine the priorities of the internal audit activity, consistent with the organization's goals" (Standard 2010: Planning).
- ". . . communicate the internal audit activity's plans and resource requirements, including significant interim changes, to senior management and the board for review and approval." The CAE "must also communicate the impact of resource limitations" (Standard 2020: Communication and Approval).
- ". . . ensure that internal audit resources are appropriate, sufficient, and effectively deployed to achieve the approved plan" (Standard 2030: Resource Management).
- ". . . establish policies and procedure to guide the internal audit activity" (Standard 2040, Policies and Procedures).
- ". . . share information and coordinate activities with other internal and external providers of assurance and consulting services to ensure proper coverage and minimize duplication of efforts" (Standard 2050: Coordination).
- ". . . report periodically to senior management and the board on the internal audit activity's purpose, authority, responsibility, and performance relative to its plan." The CAE also must report "significant risk exposures and control issues, including fraud risks, governance issues, and other matters needed or requested by senior management and the board" (Standard 2060: Reporting to Senior Management and the Board).

These responsibilities of the CAE are discussed further in Chapter 9, "Managing the Internal Audit Function."

Nature of Work. Standard 2100: Nature of Work is consistent with the Definition of Internal Auditing discussed earlier in this chapter. It states that "The internal audit activity must evaluate and contribute to the improvement of governance, risk management, and control processes using a systematic and disciplined approach."

The internal audit function assesses and makes appropriate recommendations for improving the organization's "governance process in its accomplishment of the following objectives:

- Promoting appropriate ethics and values within the organization;
- Ensuring effective organizational performance management and accountability;
- Communicating risk and control information to appropriate areas of the organization; and
- Coordinating the activities of and communicating information among the board, external and internal auditors, and management" (Standard 2110: Governance).

Likewise, the internal audit function evaluates the effectiveness and contributes to the improvement of the organization's risk management process (Standard 2120: Risk Management). Determining whether the organization's risk management processes are effective is based on the internal audit function's "assessment that:

- Organizational objectives support and align with the organization's mission;
- Significant risks are identified and assessed;
- Appropriate risk responses are selected that align risks with the organization's risk appetite; and
- Relevant risk information is captured and communicated in a timely manner across the organization, enabling staff, management, and the board to carry out their responsibilities" (Interpretation to Standard 2120: Risk Management).

Thirdly, the internal audit function assists "the organization in maintaining effective controls by evaluating their effectiveness and efficiency and by promoting continuous improvement" (Standard 2130: Control).

The internal audit function evaluates risk exposures and evaluates the design adequacy and operating effectiveness of controls "regarding the:

- Reliability and integrity of financial and operational information;
- Effectiveness and efficiency of operations;
- Safeguarding of assets; and
- Compliance with laws, regulations, and contracts" (Standards 2120.A1 and 2130.A1).

Chapter 3, "Governance," Chapter 4, "Risk Management," and Chapter 6, "Internal Control," discuss governance, risk management, and control processes in detail and discuss the internal audit function's responsibilities for evaluating and contributing to the improvement of these processes.

The Engagement Process. The performance of internal audit engagements, whether assurance or consulting, can be divided into three phases. These engagement phases are illustrated in Exhibit 2-6. The following Performance Standard sections pertain directly to the engagement process:

2200 – Engagement Planning

2300 – Performing the Engagement

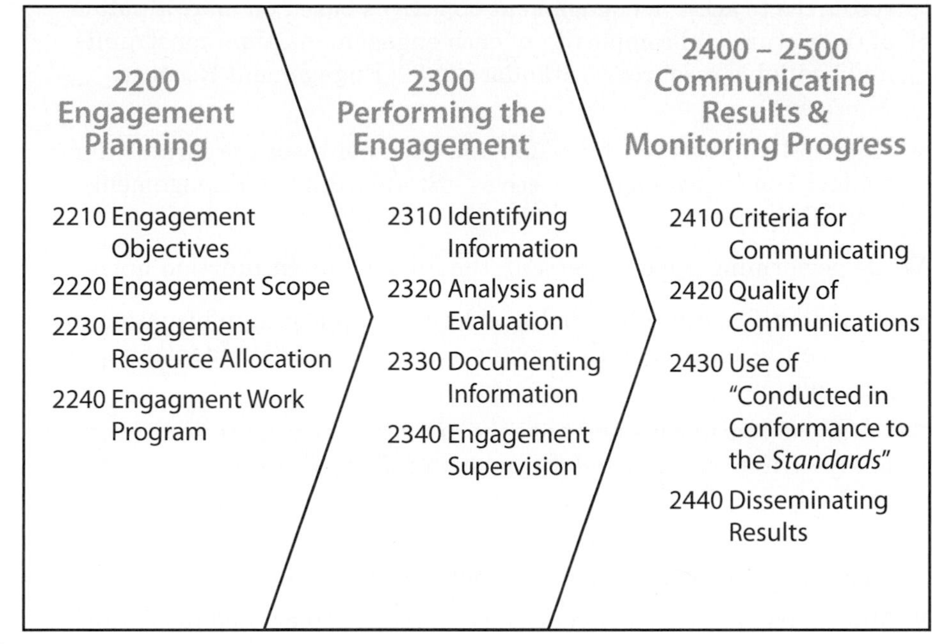

EXHIBIT 2-6

2400 – Communicating Results

2500 – Monitoring Progress

The last two sections have been combined in the "Communicate" phase of the engagement process illustrated in Exhibit 2-6. The standards pertaining specifically to the engagement process are intentionally general in nature to accommodate the varying nature of internal audit engagements.

Standard 2200: Engagement Planning states that "Internal auditors must develop and document a plan for each engagement, including the engagement's objectives, scope, timing, and resource allocations." In planning the engagement, the internal audit function "must consider:

- The objectives of the activity being reviewed and the means by which the activity controls its performance;
- The significant risks to the activity, its objectives, resources, and operations and the means by which the potential impact of risk is kept to an acceptable level;
- The adequacy and effectiveness of the activity's risk management and control processes compared to a relevant control framework or model; and
- The opportunities for making significant improvements to the activity's risk management and control processes" (Standard 2201: Planning Considerations).

The following standards apply when planning the internal audit engagement:

- "Objectives must be established for each engagement" (Standard 2210: Engagement Objectives).

- "The established scope must be sufficient to satisfy the objectives of the engagement" (Standard 2220: Engagement Scope).
- "Internal auditors must determine appropriate and sufficient resources to achieve engagement objectives based on an evaluation of the nature and complexity of each engagement, time constraints, and available resources" (Standard 2230: Engagement Resource Allocation).
- "Internal auditors must develop and document work programs that achieve the engagement objectives" (Standard 2240: Engagement Work Program).

While performing the engagement, the internal audit function must:

- " . . . identify sufficient, reliable, relevant, and useful information to achieve the engagement's objectives" (Standard 2310: Identifying Information).
- " . . . base conclusions and engagement results on appropriate analyses and evaluations" (Standard 2320: Analysis and Evaluation).
- " . . . document relevant information to support the conclusions and engagement results" (Standard 2330: Documenting Information).
- Make sure that the engagement is "properly supervised to ensure objectives are achieved, quality is assured, and staff is developed" (Standard 2340: Engagement Supervision).

Criteria for Communicating

Communications must include the engagement's objectives and scope as well as applicable conclusions, recommendations, and action plans.

For internal audit engagements to have value, their outcomes must be communicated timely to the appropriate users. It is not enough, however, for the users to receive a report. The communication must be in a form that minimizes the risk of misinterpretation. Standard 2410: Criteria for Communicating states that "Communications must include the engagement's objectives and scope as well as applicable conclusions, recommendations, and action plans." Standard 2420: Quality of Communications further states that "Communications must be accurate, objective, clear, concise, constructive, complete, and timely." Moreover, Standard 2421: Errors and Omissions states, "If a final communication contains a significant error or omission, the chief audit executive must communicate corrected information to all parties who received the original communication."

Quality of Communications

Communications must be accurate, objective, clear, concise, constructive, complete, and timely.

Internal audit functions "may report that their engagements are 'conducted in conformance with the *International Standards for the Professional Practice of Internal Auditing*,' only if the results of the quality assurance and improvement program support the statement" (Standard 2430: Use of "Conducted in Conformance with the *International Standards for the Professional Practice of Internal Auditing*). "When nonconformance with the Definition of Internal Auditing, the Code of Ethics, or the *Standards* impacts a specific engagement, communication of the results must disclose the:

- Principle or rule of conduct of the Code of Ethics or Standard(s) with which full conformance was not achieved;
- Reason(s) for the nonconformance; and
- Impact of nonconformance on the engagement and the communicated engagement results" (Standard 2431: Engagement Disclosure of Nonconformance).

The CAE is responsible for communicating internal audit engagement results to the appropriate parties (Standard 2440: Disseminating Results) and for establishing and maintaining a system to monitor the disposition of engagement results communicated (Standard 2500: Monitoring Progress). For assurance engagements, this means that the CAE must ascertain that "management actions have been effectively implemented or that senior management has accepted the risk of not taking action" (Standard 2500.A1). For consulting engagements, the internal audit function "must monitor the disposition of results . . . to the extent agreed upon with the [customer]" (Standard 2500.C1).

The engagement process is covered extensively in Chapter 12, "Introduction to the Engagement Process," Chapter 13, "Conducting the Assurance Engagement," Chapter 14, "Communicating Assurance Engagement Outcomes and Performing Follow-up Procedures," and Chapter 15, "The Consulting Engagement."

Resolution of Senior Management's Acceptance of Risks. Standard 2600: Resolution of Senior Management's Acceptance of Risks addresses the issue of accepting "a level of residual risk that may be unacceptable to the organization . . . " The Glossary to the *Standards* defines residual risk as "The risk remaining after management takes action to reduce the impact and likelihood of an adverse event, including control activities in responding to a risk." The textbook Glossary contains a slightly different, but consistent definition of residual risk: the portion of inherent risk that remains after management executes its risk responses (sometimes referred to as net risk). When a potentially unacceptable level of residual risk is believed to exist, "the chief audit executive must discuss the matter with senior management. If the decision regarding residual risk is not resolved, the chief audit executive must report the matter to the board for resolution."

Residual Risk

The portion of inherent risk that remains after management executes its risk responses (sometimes referred to as net risk).

STRONGLY RECOMMENDED GUIDANCE

The IIA's mandatory guidance (Definition of Internal Auditing, Code of Ethics, and *Standards*) is relatively general in nature because it is applicable to all internal audit activities. Internal audit assurance and consulting engagements are conducted in a wide variety of organizations, by in-house internal audit functions or outside service providers, in a centralized or decentralized organizational structure, and in diverse cultures and legal environments.

Strongly recommended guidance (Practice Advisories, Position Papers, and Practice Guides) provide more specific, nonmandatory guidance. In some cases, strongly recommended guidance may not be applicable to all internal audit functions. In other cases, it may represent only one of many acceptable alternatives. However, this guidance is authoritative in the sense that The IIA has endorsed it through a formal endorsement process, which includes review by the Ethics Committee and the Internal Audit Standards Board for consistency with the mandatory guidance.

Practice Advisories

Provide concise and timely guidance as to how the *Standards* might be implemented.

Practice Advisories. The Practice Advisories provide concise and timely guidance as to how the *Standards* might be implemented. They address approaches, methodologies, and factors for an internal audit function to consider, but are not intended to provide detailed processes and procedures for internal audit functions to follow. They may pertain to specific types of engagements or clarify geographical or industry internal audit practices. Each practice advisory is correlated by number to the standard to which it pertains and also refers to the Code of Ethics where applicable.

The IIA's Professional Issues Committee is responsible for developing Practice Advisories. The Professional Issues Committee may, however, work with other IIA committees such as the Ethics Committee or the Advanced Technology Committee to develop advisories for which specialized expertise is needed. As of 2009, more than 50 Practice Advisories have been issued. The Practice Advisories are available in the published edition of the IPPF, which is usually updated every three years, and the accompanying CD, which is updated annually. All issued Practice Advisories are available to IIA members on The IIA's website.

Exhibit 2-7 presents an example of a practice advisory. Practice Advisory 1000-1: Internal Audit Charter provides advice pertinent to Standard 1000: Purpose, Authority, and Responsibility. In addition to the advisory text, the practice advisory contains the related standard and, if applicable, the interpretation. In this case, the practice advisory augments the standard by providing supplemental guidance regarding the internal audit charter.

Position Papers. Position Papers provide guidance on issues that extend beyond the specifics of how the CAE, internal audit function, and individual internal auditors should conduct their work. They are written

EXHIBIT 2-7

EXAMPLE OF PRACTICE ADVISORY

Practice Advisory 1000-1

Internal Audit Charter

1. Providing a formal, written internal audit charter is critical in managing the internal audit activity. The internal audit charter provides a recognized statement for review and acceptance by management and for approval, as documented in the minutes, by the board. It also facilitates a periodic assessment of the adequacy of the internal audit activity's purpose, authority, and responsibility, which establishes the role of the internal audit activity. If a question should arise, the internal audit charter provides a formal, written agreement with management and the board about the organization's internal audit activity.
2. The chief audit executive (CAE) is responsible for periodically assessing whether the internal audit activity's purpose, authority, and responsibility, as defined in the internal audit charter, continue to be adequate to enable the activity to accomplish its objectives. The CAE is also responsible for communicating the result of this assessment to senior management and the board.

***

Issue: January 2009

Primary Related Standard

1000 – Purpose, Authority, and Responsibility
The purpose, authority, and responsibility of the internal audit activity must be formally defined in an internal audit charter, consistent with the Definition of Internal Auditing, the Code of Ethics, and the *Standards*. The chief audit executive must periodically review the internal audit charter and present it to senior management and the board for approval.

Interpretation
The internal audit charter is a formal document that defines the internal audit activity's purpose, authority, and responsibility. The internal audit charter establishes the internal audit activity's position within the organization; authorizes access to records, personnel, and physical properties relevant to the performance of engagements; and defines the scope of internal audit activities. Final approval of the internal audit charter resides with the board.

Origination date: January 1, 2009

not only for internal auditors but for other interested parties outside the profession. Such parties include management, board and audit committee members, and external stakeholders such as legislators, regulators, and other professionals with whom internal auditors work (for example, independent outside auditors or other service providers involved in organizations' ethics and compliance programs or risk management initiatives). Position Papers currently address the role of internal auditing in the organization's enterprise risk management system and how the organization sources the internal audit function. Future Position Papers may address significant governance, risk management, and control issues with the intent of clarifying the issues and enhancing internal auditors' and stakeholders' understanding of the issues.

Position Papers

Provide guidance on issues that extend beyond the specifics of how the CAE, internal audit function, and individual internal auditors should conduct their work.

The IIA's Professional Issues Committee usually initiates Position Papers, but any international committee or local IIA institute may do so. Position Papers drafted by local IIA institutes must be submitted for review by, and feedback from, The IIA's international technical committees to ensure that the guidance is consistent with the IPPF. Position Papers also may be developed and issued in partnership with other professional organizations. Managing the development and writing of the Position Papers rests with the Professional Issues Committee. Unlike other types of strongly recommended guidance, Position Papers require a one-month exposure period to local IIA institutes and other international technical committees before they are issued.

Practice Guides. Practice Guides provide detailed guidance on internal audit tools and techniques. Practice Guides are currently composed of the Global Technology Audit Guides (GTAG) and the Guide to the Assessment of IT Risk (GAIT) series, both of which were developed by The IIA's Advanced Technology Committee. Both the GTAG series and GAIT series are available to IIA members on The IIA's website. Chapter 7, "Information Technology Risks and Controls," provides more information about this IT-related guidance.

Practice Guides

Provide detailed guidance on internal audit tools and techniques.

Any of The IIA's technical committees may propose the concept for a Practice Guide, but the Professional Practices Advisory Council (composed of the chairs of The IIA's international technical committees) oversees their development and issuance. The Professional Practices Advisory Council approves the concept and assigns it to one of the committees to develop. The committees most likely to be asked to develop Practice Guides are the Professional Issues Committee, the Advanced Technology Committee, and the Committee on Quality.

HOW THE INTERNATIONAL PROFESSIONAL PRACTICES FRAMEWORK IS KEPT CURRENT

The IPPF is not intended to be a static body of guidance. It will continue to evolve as the profession responds to a continuously changing environment.

The Professional Practices Advisory Council is responsible for coordinating the initiation, development, issuance, and maintenance of the authoritative guidance that makes up the IPPF. The Council comprises The IIA's vice president of professional practices and the chairs of The IIA's six international technical committees. These committees are the Ethics Committee, the Internal Audit Standards Board, the Professional

Issues Committee, the Advanced Technology Committee, the Committee on Quality, and the Board of Regents. The first three committees have direct responsibility for maintaining specific portions of the IPPF.

Each year, the Professional Practices Advisory Council develops a work plan for the next year as well as a tentative plan for the following two years that lays out the work for the Ethics Committee, the Internal Audit Standards Board, and the Professional Issues Committee. The Council also coordinates the review of all existing guidance on a three-year cycle.

The Ethics Committee. The Ethics Committee's mission is to serve the global profession of internal auditing by maintaining The IIA's Code of Ethics; promoting an understanding of and compliance with The IIA's Code of Ethics; assessing, investigating, and sanctioning complaints concerning noncompliance with The IIA's Code of Ethics; and advocating ethics as part of the governance process. The committee is required to complete a formal review of the existing Code of Ethics every three years. Any changes in the Code of Ethics, such as adding additional rules, must be initiated by this committee. Adoption of new rules requires a 90-day exposure period for public comment. Final approval of changes to the Code of Ethics rests with The IIA's Board of Directors. The Ethics Committee also evaluates the conduct of IIA members and candidates for, or holders of, IIA professional certifications, when necessary.

The Internal Audit Standards Board. The Internal Audit Standards Board's mission is to promulgate, monitor, and promote the *Standards* on a worldwide basis. The board is required to complete a review of the existing *Standards* every three years. New standards or modifications to existing standards are initiated with this committee and require a 90-day exposure period for public comment. Exposure includes translation into Spanish and French, and often into other major member languages (for example, Chinese, Italian, German, Japanese, and potentially others). After due consideration of responses to the exposure draft, a majority vote of the committee is required for final issuance.

Professional Issues Committee. The Professional Issues Committee's mission is to provide thought leadership and timely professional guidance to the members and stakeholders of the internal audit profession on methodologies, techniques, and authoritative positions included in the IPPF and to comment on or support other matters that impact the internal audit profession. This committee initiates, develops, and maintains the Practice Advisories and reviews existing Practice Advisories on a three-year cycle. The Professional Issues Committee also is a primary initiator and developer of Position Papers and Practice Guides. Drafts of proposed Practice Advisories, Position Papers, and Practice Guides are circulated to the Ethics Committee and the Internal Audit Standards Board for a review of consistency with existing mandatory guidance before they are issued. Position Papers also require a 30-day exposure period to local IIA institutes.

The process for developing the mandatory and strongly recommended guidance included in the IPPF is summarized in Exhibit 2-8.

To improve transparency and enhance the trust that legislators, regulators, and other users of internal audit services have in the profession's authoritative guidance, The IIA's 2006 Vision for the Future Task Force recommended the establishment of an independent Guidance Oversight

THE IPPF GUIDANCE DEVELOPMENT PROCESS

EXHIBIT 2-8

IPPF Element/ Responsibility	Process	Final Approval
The Definition		
——	Board of Directors establishes special task force: • 90-day public exposure period.	IIA Board of Directors
Code of Ethics		
Ethics Committee	Developed and maintained by Ethics Committee: • 90-day public exposure period.	IIA Board of Directors
International Standards for the Professional Practice of Internal Auditing		
Internal Audit Standards Board	Developed and maintained by the Internal Audit Standards Board: • 90-day public exposure period.	Internal Audit Standards Board
Practice Advisories		
Professional Issues Committee	Developed and maintained by the Professional Issues Committee: • Drafts reviewed by Ethics Committee and Standards Board for consistency. • No additional exposure.	Professional Issues Committee
Position Papers		
Professional Issues Committee	Professional Issues Committee primary developer but can be initiated by local IIA institutes or other IIA committees: • Drafts reviewed by Ethics Committee and Standards Board for consistency. • 30-day exposure period to local IIA institutes.	IIA Executive Committee
Practice Guides		
Professional Practices Council	Professional Practices Council responsible for development, approval, and maintenance: • Council assigns development of guide to an international technical committee. • Drafts reviewed by Ethics Committee and Standards Board for consistency. • No additional exposure.	Professional Practices Council

Committee. The Guidance Oversight Committee represents the interests of stakeholders outside the internal audit profession and provides assurance that The IIA follows its stated protocol in developing, issuing, and maintaining the IPPF.[5] The majority of the members of this committee are prominent individuals from the global business community. Committee representatives observe the guidance-setting process and certify that appropriate procedures are followed before mandatory guidance is issued.

As the internal audit profession continues to grow in size and stature, the IPPF, especially the *Standards*, are increasingly being recognized as the global criteria for the practice of internal auditing. For example:

- The National Treasury of South Africa requires that all public sector entities implement internal auditing following The IIA's Definition of Internal Auditing and *Standards*.[6]
- The King II Report endorses The IIA's Definition of Internal Auditing and *Standards* for publicly listed companies in South Africa.[7]
- A 2007 report by the Council of Europe recommends for member states that internal audit functions be established at the local and regional level of government pursuant to generally accepted international standards, such as those promulgated by The IIA.[8]
- The Finnish Financial Supervision Authority, which regulates financial markets and banks, investment firms, and the Stock Exchange in Finland, requires that the entities it supervises have internal audit functions and recommends that these internal audit functions follow The IIA's *Standards*.[9]
- The Government of Canada and its departments have adopted the [International] Professional Practices Framework and the *Standards* for their internal audit work.[10]

STANDARDS PROMULGATED BY OTHER ORGANIZATIONS

The IIA recognizes that guidance promulgated by other organizations is pertinent to the profession of internal auditing. In fact, some internal audit functions need to follow other professional guidance in addition to the IPPF. Such guidance includes, for instance, the U.S. Government Accountability Office's (GAO's) Governmental Auditing Standards, Standards for the Professional Practice of Environmental, Health, and Safety Auditing, and standards issued by the International Standards Organization (ISO). For example, it is common for the internal audit functions in many state and local government agencies in the United States to incorporate both The IIA's *Standards* and the *Government Auditing Standards* (*Yellow Book*) issued by the GAO in their internal audit charters.

The introduction to The IIA's *Standards* provides the following directive as to how to handle situations in which multiple standards apply:

> If the *Standards* are used in conjunction with standards issued by other authoritative bodies, audit communications may also cite the use of other standards, as appropriate. In such a case, if inconsistencies exist between the *Standards* and other standards, internal auditors and the internal audit activity must conform with the *Standards*, and may conform with the other standards if they are more restrictive.

The IIA's *Standards* are principles-focused and intended for use by internal audit functions in a wide range of organizations in a variety of legal and cultural environments. For this reason, there is little, if any, direct conflict between The IIA's *Standards* and the standards promulgated by other professional organizations. The differences that do exist typically involve a situation in which one set of standards is more stringent than another regarding a particular requirement. For example, ISACA's Standard S9.10 requires information systems auditors to obtain written representation from management at least annually that acknowledges management's responsibility for the design and implementation of internal controls to prevent and detect illegal acts.[11] The IIA's *Standards* contain no specific requirements for obtaining written representations from management, but obtaining such representations does not in any way conflict with the *Standards*.

Standards for Internal Auditing in Government. The GAO has issued standards for governmental audits in the United States. These standards are commonly referred to as the *Yellow Book* standards because of the yellow cover used when publishing the standards. The *Yellow Book* standards apply to U.S. federal financial audits, performance (or operational) audits, and other audit-related activities. Federal legislation requires that both federal and nonfederal auditors comply with the *Yellow Book* standards for audits of federal organizations, programs, and functions. The standards are generally relevant to, and are recommended for use by, state and local government auditors and public accountants who conduct state and local government audits. The *Yellow Book* explicitly recognizes The IIA's *Standards* as relevant for internal audit work in governmental entities. However, it does require that in cases of conflict, or when the *Yellow Book* standards are more restrictive, that the *Yellow Book* be followed. For example, The IIA's *Standards* require internal audit functions to have an external quality review every five years, but the *Yellow Book* requires such a review every three years.

The U.S. GAO

Issues standards for governmental audits known as Government Auditing Standards (Yellow Book).

Like the United States, most countries have established standards for audit of governmental entities and contracts. Many have modeled their standards after the principles established by the International Organization of Supreme Audit Institutions (INTOSAI). Like the *Yellow Book*, these standards tend to focus on financial statement and performance audits for external users.

Standards for Information Technology Audits. Auditing computerized information systems is integral to internal auditing. While The IIA's *Standards* provide a sufficient framework for auditing computerized systems, ISACA (previously know as the Information Systems Audit and Control Association) provides more detailed and specialized guidance. The ISACA Standards are very similar in nature to The IIA's *Standards* except for the fact that they are directed to a much more specific practice. ISACA issues "Standards," "Guidelines," and "Procedures" for conducting information systems audits. ISACA's "Guidelines" provide more specific information about how to apply their "Standards" and require justification for departure from them when appropriate. "Procedures" provide examples of what an information systems auditor might do in performing an internal audit engagement, but these procedures are not required. There is not, at present, any incompatibility between The IIA's *Standards* and ISACA's Standards. However, internal audit functions whose work

ISACA

Issues standards, guidelines, and procedures for conducting information systems audits.

involves a significant portion of information systems audits should be aware of the ISACA guidance and consider adopting this guidance for their information systems audit work.

The BEAC

Issues standards to address the needs of environmental, health, and safety audit professionals.

Standards for the Professional Practice of Environmental, Health, and Safety Auditing. The Board of Environmental, Health, and Safety Auditor Certifications (BEAC) has developed *Standards for the Professional Practice of Environmental, Health, and Safety Auditing* to address the needs of environmental, health, and safety audit professionals. Some organizations have functions other than the internal audit function that provide assurance that the organization is complying with environmental protection, health, and safety laws and regulations. Other organizations consider such assurances to be within the scope of their internal audit functions' responsibilities. When internal audit functions perform environmental, health, and safety audit engagements, they can use the BEAC Standards to direct their work. The BEAC Standards are consistent with The IIA's *Standards*.

The PCAOB and AICPA

Issue standards for audits of companies' financial statements in the United States.

IFAC

Issues international audit standards adopted by a number of countries.

Standards for Financial Audits. The U.S. Public Company Accounting Oversight Board (PCAOB) and the American Institute of Certified Public Accountants (AICPA) currently set the standards for audits of companies' financial statements in the United States. Standards for audits of companies' financial statements are set separately in other countries as well. However, as is the case with accounting standards, there are initiatives under way to unify the financial audit standards among certain countries. For example, the International Auditing and Assurance Standards Board (ISAB), which is a part of the International Federation of Accountants (IFAC), has issued international audit standards which are being adopted by a number of countries. Although these standards pertain directly to independent audits of companies' financial statements, they can have a bearing on internal audit work, particularly those standards pertaining to the coordination of work between internal audit functions and outside independent auditors.

Other Relevant Guidance. Guidance promulgated by other professional organizations also is relevant to internal auditors. For example:

- The International Standards Organization (ISO) sets standards for quality and environmental audits.
- Standards Australia promulgates standards for risk management and governance processes.
- The Committee of Sponsoring Organizations of the Treadway Commission (COSO) has issued four frameworks pertaining specifically to internal control and risk management.
- The Society of Corporate Compliance and Ethics (SCCE) provides guidance for ethics and compliance practitioners.
- The Health Care Compliance Association (HCCA) provides guidance for compliance professionals specifically operating in the healthcare industry.
- The Basel Committee on Banking Supervision has specific requirements (referred to as *Basel 1* and *Basel 2*) for internal audits of banking and financial institutions' risk management and rating systems.

These are just a few of the many organizations that promulgate guidance of relevance to internal auditors. Internal auditors must be cognizant of these organizations and the nature of the guidance they issue. Internal auditors practicing in specific countries or in certain industries must be knowledgeable of existing guidance, other than The IIA's IPPF, that is relevant to their work.

SUMMARY

This chapter covered in detail The IIA's IPPF. This framework contains two categories of authoritative guidance — mandatory and strongly recommended — that enable internal audit functions to provide value-adding assurance and consulting services. Mandatory guidance includes the Definition of Internal Auditing, the Code of Ethics, and the *Standards*. Strongly recommended guidance includes Practice Advisories, Position Papers, and Practice Guides. The process through which The IIA maintains and develops the IPPF also was discussed, as was guidance of relevance to internal auditors that is promulgated by professional organizations other than The IIA.

The Code of Ethics articulates the ethical principles and behavioral norms relevant to the practice of internal auditing. The Attribute Standards prescribe the attributes that internal audit functions and individual internal auditors must have to deliver assurance and consulting services effectively. The Performance Standards provide authoritative guidance on managing the internal audit function and conducting assurance and consulting engagements. The Implementation Standards expand upon the Attribute and Performance Standards by providing guidance that is specifically applicable to either assurance services or consulting services. Practice Advisories, Position Papers, and Practice Guides provide guidance that is helpful to internal auditors in implementing the Definition of Internal Auditing, Code of Ethics, and *Standards*. Finally, standards promulgated by other organizations that are relevant to internal auditors were discussed.

The IPPF, especially the *Standards* and Practice Advisories, will be referred to extensively throughout the remainder of this book.

Review Questions

1. What are the circumstances that precipitated the need for internal audit-type activities?
2. What are the six components of the IPPF? Which components constitute mandatory guidance? Which components constitute strongly recommended guidance?
3. What is the purpose of The IIA's Code of Ethics?
4. Identify the four principles of the Code of Ethics. Why should internal auditors strive to comply with these principles?
5. What is the purpose of The IIA's *Standards*? Explain the difference between Attribute and Performance Standards.
6. Explain the difference between assurance and consulting services. Why does each type of service have its own Implementation Standards?
7. What is the definition of independence as it pertains to an internal audit function? What is the definition of objectivity as it pertains to individual internal auditors?
8. What are the seven main sections of the Performance Standards?
9. What is the relationship between *Standards* and Practice Advisories?
10. What are the responsibilities of The IIA's Professional Practices Advisory Council?
11. What organizations, other than The IIA, promulgate guidance that is pertinent to internal auditors?

Multiple-choice Questions

Select the best answer for each of the following questions.

1. A primary purpose of the *Standards* is to:
   - a. Promote coordination of internal and external audit efforts.
   - b. Establish a basis for evaluating internal audit performance.
   - c. Develop consistency in internal audit practices.
   - d. Provide a codification of existing practices.
2. Which of the following are "mandatory guidance" in The IIA's IPPF?

   I. Practice Advisories.
   II. The Code of Ethics.
   III. The Definition of Internal Auditing.
   IV. The *Standards*.

   - a. I, II, and IV.
   - b. II and IV.
   - c. II, III, and IV.
   - d. I, II, III, and IV.

3. An internal auditor provides income tax services during the tax season. For which of the following activities would the auditor most likely be considered in violation of The IIA's Code of Ethics?
   a. Preparing, for a fee, a division manager's personal tax returns.
   b. Appearing on a local radio show to discuss retirement planning and tax issues.
   c. Receiving a stipend for teaching an evening tax class at the local junior college.
   d. Working on weekends for a friend who has a small CPA firm.

4. An internal auditor is auditing a division in which the division's CFO is a close personal friend. The auditor learns that the friend is to be replaced after a series of critical contract negotiations with the Department of Defense. The auditor relays this information to the friend. Which principle of The IIA's Code of Ethics has been violated?
   a. Integrity.
   b. Objectivity.
   c. Confidentiality.
   d. Privacy.

5. The IIA's *Standards* require internal auditors to exercise due professional care while conducting assurance engagements. Which of the following is not something an internal auditor is required to consider in determining what constitutes the exercise of due care in an assurance engagement of treasury operations?
   a. The audit committee has requested assurance on the treasury function's compliance with a new policy on use of financial instruments.
   b. Treasury management has not instituted any risk management policies.
   c. The independent outside auditors have requested to see the engagement report and working papers.
   d. The treasury function just completed implementation of a new real-time investment tracking system.

6. In which of the following situations does the internal auditor potentially lack objectivity?
   a. A payroll accounting employee assists an internal auditor in verifying the physical inventory of small motors.
   b. An internal auditor discusses a significant issue with the vice president to whom the auditee reports prior to drafting the audit report.
   c. An internal auditor recommends standards of control and performance measures for a contract with a service organization for the processing of payroll and employee benefits.
   d. A former purchasing assistant performs a review of internal controls over purchasing four months after being transferred to the internal audit department.

7. Which of the following is/are components of the *Standards*?
    I. Statements.
    II. Interpretations.
    III. The glossary.
    a. I only.
    b. I and II.
    c. I and III.
    d. I, II, and III.

8. According to the *Standards*, which of the following must the internal audit manager think about when considering appropriate due care while planning an assurance engagement?
    a. The opportunity to cross train internal audit staff.
    b. The cost of assurance in relationship to potential benefits.
    c. Job openings in the area that may be of interest to internal auditors assigned to the engagement.
    d. The potential to deliver consulting services to the auditee.

9. Which of the following types of IPPF guidance require(s) an exposure to the various IIA national institutes prior to its issuance?
    I. A new Practice Advisory.
    II. A new Standard.
    III. A new Position Paper.
    IV. A new definition in the *Standards* glossary.
    a. III only.
    b. II and IV.
    c. II, III, and IV.
    d. I, II, III, and IV.

10. Which of the following are required of the internal audit function per the *Standards*?
    a. Evaluate annually the effectiveness of the audit committee.
    b. Issue annually an overall opinion on the adequacy of the organization's system of internal controls.
    c. Obtain an annual representation from management acknowledging management's responsibility for the design and implementation of internal controls to prevent illegal acts.
    d. Assess whether the information technology governance of the organization sustains and supports the organization's strategies and objectives.

Discussion Questions

1. Why is it important for a profession, such as internal auditing, to promulgate standards?
2. Refer to Appendix A, "The IIA's Code of Ethics," and answer the following questions:
   a. Why is it important for the internal audit profession to have a code of ethics?
   b. How do Principles differ from Rules of Conduct?
   c. Who must abide by the Code of Ethics?
   d. What are the ramifications of breaching the Code of Ethics?
3. How does The IIA's Code of Ethics differ from the *Standards* in governing the behavior and activities of internal auditors?
4. Does including the CAE in a company's stock option program violate either The IIA's Code of Ethics or the *Standards*? Explain your answer.
5. The CAE for Sargon Products reports administratively to the CFO and functionally to the audit committee. The scope of the internal audit function assurance services includes financial, operational, and compliance engagements.

   Is the internal auditors' objectivity regarding accounting-related matters impaired in each of the situations described below? Briefly explain your answer.
   a. The internal auditors are frequently asked to make accounting entries for complex transactions that the company's accountants do not have the expertise to handle.
   b. A staff accountant reconciles the company's monthly bank statements. An internal auditor reviews the bank reconciliations to make sure they are completed properly.
6. Review Exhibit 2-7 and answer the following questions.
   a. Why is it important for an internal audit function to have a charter?
   b. What information should an internal audit charter contain?
7. You are part of a three-person internal audit function that was asked by your company's CEO to conduct an audit of the internal controls over the company's commodities trading and hedging activities. No member of the internal audit function has any training or experience in auditing trading and hedging activities.
   a. Refer to Appendix B, "The *International Standards for the Professional Practice of Auditing*." Which standard(s) would you consult for guidance regarding the situation described above? Explain.
   b. Refer to the list of Practice Advisories on The IIA's website (www.theiia.org). Which Practice Advisories would you consult for guidance? Explain.

CASES

CASE 1 A 1999 *Wall Street Journal* article (April 7, 1999, page c1) described a now settled U.S. Securities Exchange Commission (SEC) case against W. R. Grace & Co., claiming that the company engaged in "profit management" in its National Medical Care unit.

> In the early 1990s, executives at W.R. Grace & Co became troubled about the performance of the company's National Medical Care Inc. unit. The Problem: earnings were growing too fast. Profit was increasing more than 30% a year, exceeding the unit's growth target. While most companies would be ecstatic, Grace executives worried that the unit couldn't keep it up. So they quietly stashed the excess profit in an all-purpose reserve, which they later would tap in a way that masked real problems — including slowing earnings.
>
> The profit stockpile soon was discovered by _______* auditors, who repeatedly told Grace that this was wrong, internal ________* memos show. But instead of standing firm, the accountants gave the financial statements a clean bill of health . . .
>
> Internal company and audit-firm memos, as well as deposition excerpts, show a breakdown in controls at Grace and far larger distortions to earnings than previously disclosed. At least six _________* auditors and Norman Eatough, Grace's former in-house audit chief, questioned the propriety of Grace's accounting maneuvers . . .
>
> Some business people insist the SEC's initiative is much ado about very little, noting that companies have leeway to use accounting techniques to deliver consistent earnings, as long as any adjustments aren't "material." That's the fuzzy disclosure standard under securities laws, often defined by accountants as events that have more than a 5% or 10% impact on earnings.
>
> "Any CFO anywhere has managed earnings in a way the SEC is now jumping up and down and calling fraud," maintains Wallace Timmeny, a lawyer . . .
>
> Mr. Eatough, Grace's in-house audit chief, meanwhile was growing concerned . . . . (in a report to the CFO he laid out what he called "deliberate deferral of reported income.") But, fearing his job was in jeopardy, he stopped short of calling it fraud . . . [12]

What would you advise Mr. Eatough to do in this situation? Justify your advice with the guidance provided in The IIA's IPPF, referencing specific sections of the *Standards* and the Code of Ethics and taking practical considerations into account.

*A current Big Four public accounting firm.

CASE 2[13] Mark Hobson is an internal auditor employed by Comstock Industries. He is nearing completion of an audit of the Avil Division conducted during the first five weeks of the year. The Avil Division is one of three manufacturing divisions in Comstock and manufactures inventories to supply about 50 percent of Comstock's sales. In addition to the manufacturing divisions, Comstock has two marketing divisions (domestic and international) and a technical service division that offers worldwide technical support. Each customer is assigned to the most suitable manufacturing division, which functions as the supplier for that customer. The manufacturing division then approves the customer's credit, ships against orders obtained by the sales representatives, and collects the customer receivables when due. This allows order-to-order monitoring of customer credit limits against customer orders received.

Two Potential Observations

Two items concern Mark. First, there was a material dollar amount of inventory of part number A2 still carried on the Avil books at year-end, despite the fact that the Fast-tac machining component in which part A2 was used is now considered first generation and is no longer manufactured. Company policy requires an immediate write-off of all obsolete inventory items. Second, some accounts receivable still carried as collectible at year-end were over 180 days old. All receivables are due in 30 days, which is standard for the industry. Mark believes many of these old accounts are uncollectible.

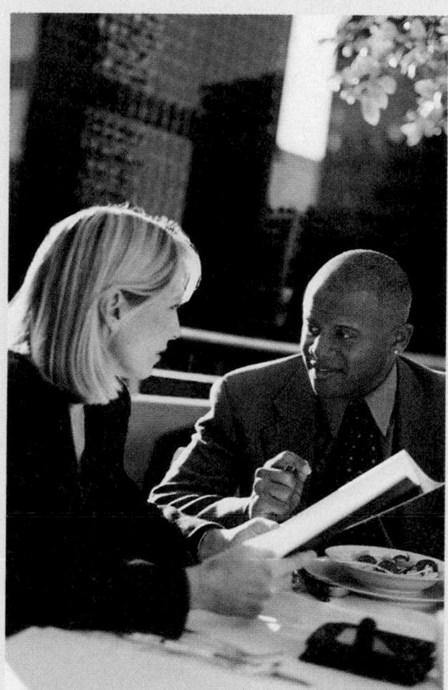

The division manager's administrative assistant, Brenda Wilson, performed the aging of accounts receivable rather than the division accountant, as is standard practice. The division accountant refused to discuss the circumstances of Brenda's actions.

The Auditee's Comments

Mark scheduled a meeting with Brenda to discuss his concerns.

"Well, Mark," Brenda responded, "I know that policy requires that obsolete inventories be written off, but part A2 is just not being used at present. We might start to make those Fast-tac components again. Who knows? Wide ties are coming back again, aren't they? Fast-tac could, too. There are plenty of customers, especially in the third world, that are finding those second- and third-generation machines pretty expensive to maintain. I mean, there is a policy that states obsolete inventories should be written off, but there is no policy defining an obsolete part.

"And as for those receivables," Brenda continued, "that is certainly a judgment call, too. Who knows if those accounts will be collected?

We're in a slight recession now. When things pick up, we'll probably collect a few. There isn't even a policy in this division on writing off receivables. I checked. Nothing says I have to write them off. So who are you to say I have to?"

"Brenda, be straight. You know those parts will never be used. And you know those receivables are bad."

"Look, Mark," Brenda finally bargained, "it's only two weeks from the close of the year. Let's let these items ride till after the close so that everyone gets their bonuses. Then, I promise I'll take a fresh look at both inventories and receivables. I'll write them down after year-end, after the financial reports are issued. No one will know. And, after all, who's to be hurt?"

The Division Manager

Mark continued his audit, drafted his report containing observations related to the inventory and receivables, and reviewed the report with the division manager, Hal Wright. Hal was visibly disturbed.

"Gee, Mark, this couldn't have come at a more awkward time. Our figures just passed muster by the independent outside auditors. There was a guy out here for our inventory count in November and Brenda already sent her spreadsheet on year-end receivables to corporate headquarters. No one up there, in our group or on the CPA audit team, was the least bit critical. If you go raising a big stink, particularly now, the independent outside auditors will catch us writing off inventory and receivables, they'll adjust profit, and there will be hell to pay for all of us. And, Mark, this is no clear-cut issue either. I mean, I can see how you can write a report calling for clearer policy, but not one calling for specific write-downs. That's way out of your jurisdiction. But still, I promise, we'll look at all this after our statements go to bed. Right now, I feel the managers of this division have worked their hearts out and I intend to fight to protect what little bonuses they have coming. If we write down as you suggest, those bonuses will go and the stockholders will lose too. Earnings per share (EPS) will drop like a rock. They might even close this division. Now you don't want that, do you, boy?"

"Well, Hal, I could word my observations as they are in the draft but include your response." Hal was suddenly angry. "What? And let the audit committee decide the issue? They have nothing to do with this. They accepted the CPA's report. If you want to make the audit committee happy, you'll accept it, too, and leave this adjustment stuff alone."

The Internal Audit Director

Concerned, Mark delayed finalizing his report and discussed the draft with Gail Wu, director of Internal Audit. Gail is not trained as an auditor and was promoted to director of Internal Audit from Corporate Finance so that she might develop a better understanding of operating relationships. Still, Gail is very smart and Mark has always respected her opinion. The discussion was by telephone, with Mark still at the Avil Division headquarters and Gail at the corporate office.

"Mark, Hal is right. If you, in essence, blow the whistle on management bonuses this year, we can kiss goodbye all the goodwill I've been struggling to build for this department. It will all go out the window."

"I know you've been trying to put us on a better footing, Gail, but Hal is intractable. As far as he is concerned, the only observation he will accept in the report is that of deficient policy, with nothing mentioned about the inventory or receivables needing adjustment."

"Well, do what you have to," Gail ended the discussion. "But I insist that you submit a report that Hal agrees to and has signed. I don't want to stir up hornets and then have to try to explain my loose cannon to the board when everyone is howling about the bonus problem."

- **A.** Refer to The IIA's Code of Ethics. Identify *three* specific Rules of Conduct relevant to this case. Using the Rules of Conduct you identify as the context, discuss the ethical issues raised in the case.
- **B.** Discuss how the ethical dilemma Mark faces might have been avoided. In other words, discuss specific things Comstock's management and/or the internal audit function might have done to reduce the risk of such a situation arising.
- **C.** Clearly indicate what you would do if you found yourself in Mark's position. Briefly explain why.

REFERENCES

[1]Ramamoorti, Sridhar, "Internal Auditing: History, Evolution, and Prospects," in Bailey et al. *Research Opportunities in Internal Auditing* (Altamonte Springs, FL: The Institute of Internal Auditors, 2003), p. 5.

[2]*Independence and Objectivity: A Framework for Internal Auditors* (Altamonte Springs, FL: The Institute of Internal Auditors, 2001), p. 15.

[3]Plumlee, R. David, "The Standard of Objectivity for Internal Auditors: Memory and Bias Effects." *Journal of Accounting Research*, (Autumn, 1985), pp. 683-699.

[4]The "Exam Content" (the syllabus) for the CIA examination is available from the IIA's website under "Certification."

[5]*A Vision for the Future: Guiding the Internal Audit Profession to Excellence – Report from The IIA's Vision for the Future Task Force* (Altamonte Springs, FL: The Institute of Internal Auditors, 2007), p. 11.

[6]*Treasury Regulations for Departments, Trading Entities, Constitutional Institutions and Public Entities*. (Cape Town and Pretoria: National Treasury, Republic of South Africa, March 2005, Section 3.2).

[7]Institute of Directors in Southern Africa, *King Report of Corporate Governance For South Africa – 2002 (King II Report)*, (Johannesburg: IOD, 2002, Section 4.1).

[8]*Internal Audit at Local and Regional Level*, European Practice Reports: Local and Regional Democracy (Paris: Council of Europe, 2007), p. 40.

[9]*Standard 1.3 Internal Governance Organisation of Activities* (Helsinki: Finnish Financial Supervisory Authority, 2008, section 5.6, para 100).

[10] *Internal Auditing Standards for the Government of Canada* (Ottawa, ON: The Treasury Board of Canada Secretariat, October 21, 2005).

[11]ISACA, All ISACA IS Standards, Guidelines and Procedures for Auditing and Control Professionals, www.isaca.org/Template.cfm?Section=Standards&Template=/TaggedPage/TaggedPageDisplay.cfm&TPLID=29&ContentID=42792, 17.

[12]Davis, A., "SEC Case Claims Profit 'Management' by Grace," *The Wall Street Journal*, April 7, 1997, C1.

[13]Adapted from Case 37, "Comstock Industries," by G. Thomas Friedlob and E. Lewis Bryan included in *Case Studies in Internal Auditing: Volume 2*, compiled by M. Dittenhofer and R. A. Roy, and issued by The Institute of Internal Auditors' Academic Relations Committee, March 1994.

CHAPTER 3
Governance

Learning Objectives

Define governance and contrast the different roles and responsibilities within governance.

- Articulate the different enterprise-wide governance principles.
- Describe the changes in regulations and how governance has evolved into its present state.
- Describe the role of the internal audit function in the governance process.
- Know where to find information about governance codes and regulations from countries around the world.

Any successful organization must establish a basic framework through which both long-term and day-to-day decisions will be made. Think about how a university is structured, or the business through which you gained your first part-time job. Reflect on any clubs or athletic teams in which you participated. All had some form of structure that helped them be successful. In most organizations, internal auditing can be a key enabler to that success. Before you can fully understand how an internal audit function can serve such a role, it is important first to understand how organizations are structured and operate to achieve success. Although the actual organizational structure will vary from one organization to the next, each must establish an overall governance structure to ensure key stakeholder needs are met. This governance structure provides direction to those executing the day-to-day activities of managing the risks inherent in an organization's business model. These day-to-day activities represent internal control. These elements are depicted in Exhibit 3-2.

This figure shows that governance surrounds all activities in an organization. The governance structure may be established to comply with laws and regulations in the jurisdictions in which an organization operates. These laws and regulations are typically promulgated to protect the public's interest. Additionally, the board and management of an organization may establish governance structures to ensure the needs of key stakeholders are met and that the organization operates within the boundaries and values established by the board and senior management.

EXHIBIT 3-1

PROFESSIONAL STANDARDS RELEVANT TO CHAPTER 3

2010 – Planning

2100 – Nature of Work

2110 – Governance

Risk management is the next layer in the governance structure. Risk management is intended to (1) identify and mitigate the risks that may adversely affect the organization's success, and (2) exploit the opportunities that enable that success. Management develops strategies regarding how to best manage the key risks and opportunities. Risk management activities should operate within the overall direction of the governance structure. Risk Management is discussed in greater detail in Chapter 4, "Risk Management."

Internal control is shown in the center since the system of internal controls represents a subset, but integral part, of the broader risk management activities. Risk responses, which include controls, are designed to execute the risk management strategies. Refer to Chapter 6, "Internal Control," for additional discussion about controls and the overall system of internal controls.

Finally, there are arrows that represent the flow of information throughout the governance structure. The board provides direction to senior management to guide them in carrying out the risk management activities. Senior management in turn provides direction to lower levels of management who are responsible for the specific controls. However, lower level managers are accountable to senior management with regard to the success of those controls. And senior management is accountable to provide the board assurances regarding the effectiveness of risk management activities. The arrows in the figure depict that flow of direction and accountability from one layer to the next.

Governance

The combination of processes and structures implemented by the board to inform, direct, manage, and monitor the activities of the organization toward the achievement of its objectives.

This chapter describes governance in detail, discussing key elements and principles of governance, as well as the roles and responsibilities. Other illustrations are provided to depict, in greater detail, how one might envision the key elements of governance. The chapter also includes a discussion about the internal audit function's assurance role in governance, as well as the role other assurance activities can play.

GOVERNANCE CONCEPTS

To perform effective internal assurance and consulting services, it is imperative to have an understanding of an organization's business. As part of gaining that understanding, it is necessary to determine how an organization operates from a top-down perspective. The overall means by which organizations operate is commonly referred to as corporate governance (referred to more generally as "governance" throughout this chapter).

EXHIBIT 3-2

DEPICTION OF KEY GOVERNANCE ELEMENTS

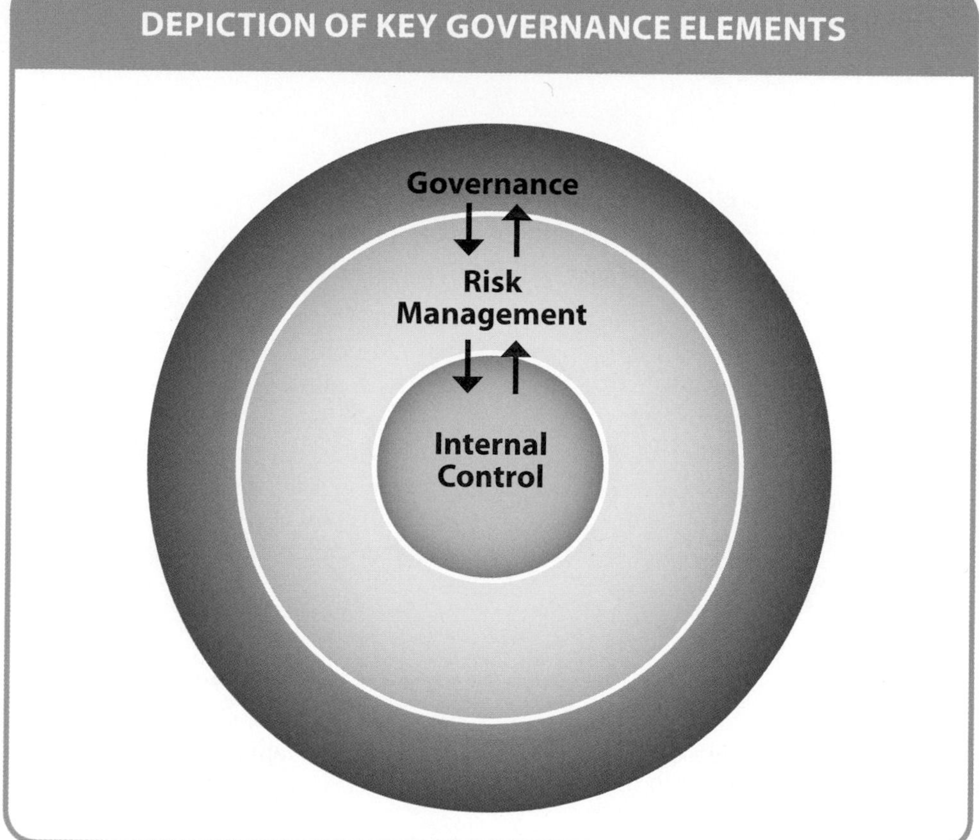

Definition of Governance

As discussed in Chapter 1, "Introduction to Internal Auditing," governance is the process conducted by the board of directors to authorize, direct, and oversee management toward the achievement of the organization's objectives. An often-used definition of governance comes from the Paris-based forum of democratic markets, the Organisation for Economic Co-operation and Development (OECD):

> Corporate governance involves a set of relationships between a company's management, its board, its shareholders, and other stakeholders. Corporate governance also provides the structure through which the objectives of the company are set, and the means of attaining those objectives and monitoring performance are determined.[1]

Although there are many other definitions of governance, there are certain common elements present in most of them. [Readers should refer to http://www.ecgi.org/codes/all_codes.php for a comprehensive list of codes from around the world, many of which relate to governance.] The glossary to The IIA's *International Standards for the Professional Practice of Internal Auditing* (*Standards*) captures these elements in its definition, which describes governance as "The combination of processes and structures implemented by the board to inform, direct, manage, and monitor the activities of the organization toward the achievement of its objectives."[2]

In addition to the elements described by the OECD and The IIA, the discussion of governance that follows will include the elements of organizations determining their objectives and values, and establishing boundaries for conduct. Taking into consideration the different governance defi-

EXHIBIT 3-3

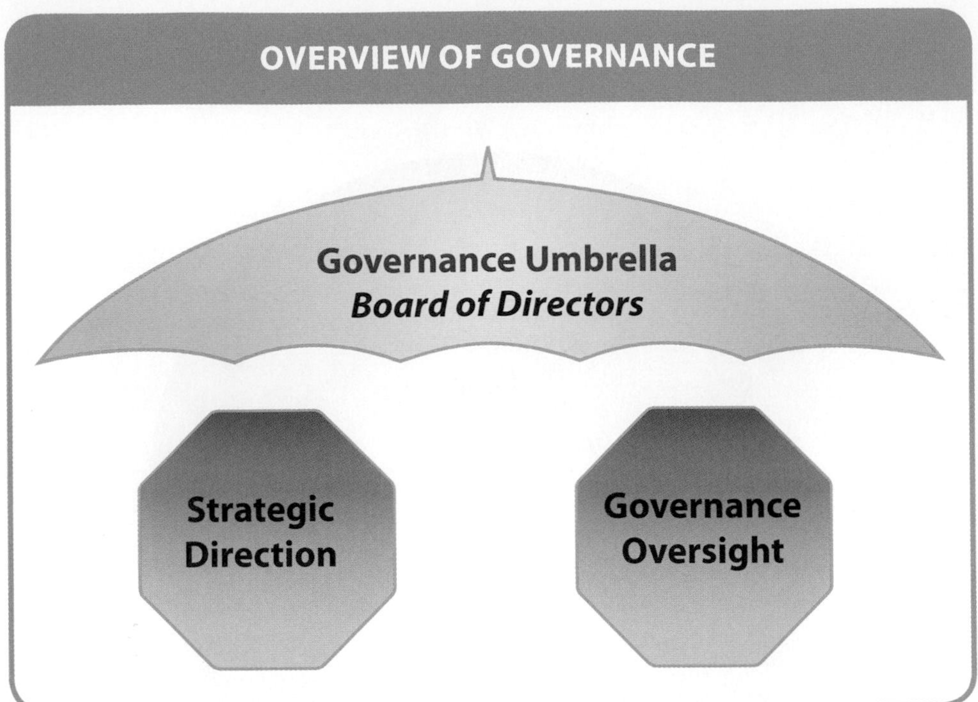

Board

An organization's governing body, such as a board of directors, supervisory board, head of an agency or legislative body, board of governors or trustees of a nonprofit organization, or any other designated body of the organization.

Strategy

Refers to how management plans to achieve the organization's objectives.

nitions and associated elements, governance can be depicted in a diagram as shown in Exhibit 3-3.

The first broad area of governance is depicted in the exhibit as strategic direction. The board is responsible for providing strategic direction and guidance relative to the establishment of key business objectives, consistent with the organization's business model and aligned with stakeholder priorities. Directors bring varied and diverse business experience to the board and, thus, are in a position to provide the strategic direction and guidance that will help ensure the organization is successful. The board also can influence the organization's risk-taking philosophy and establish broad boundaries of conduct based on the organization's overall risk appetite and cultural values. Monitoring progress toward meeting the goals and objectives of the organization is another key reason for the board's existence.

The second broad area of governance is depicted in the exhibit as governance oversight. Expanding on the view in Exhibit 3-3, the key components of governance oversight are shown in Exhibit 3-4. Because this oversight responsibility is where the risk management and internal audit activities are most relevant, governance oversight is discussed in much greater detail following this exhibit.

The key points that should be taken from this depiction of governance are:

- Governance begins with the board of directors and its committees. The board serves as the "umbrella" of governance oversight for the entire organization. It provides direction to management, empowers them with the authority to take the necessary actions to achieve that direction, and oversees the overall results of operations.
- The board must understand and focus on the needs of key stakeholders. Ultimately, the board has a fiduciary responsibility to stakeholders.

EXHIBIT 3-4

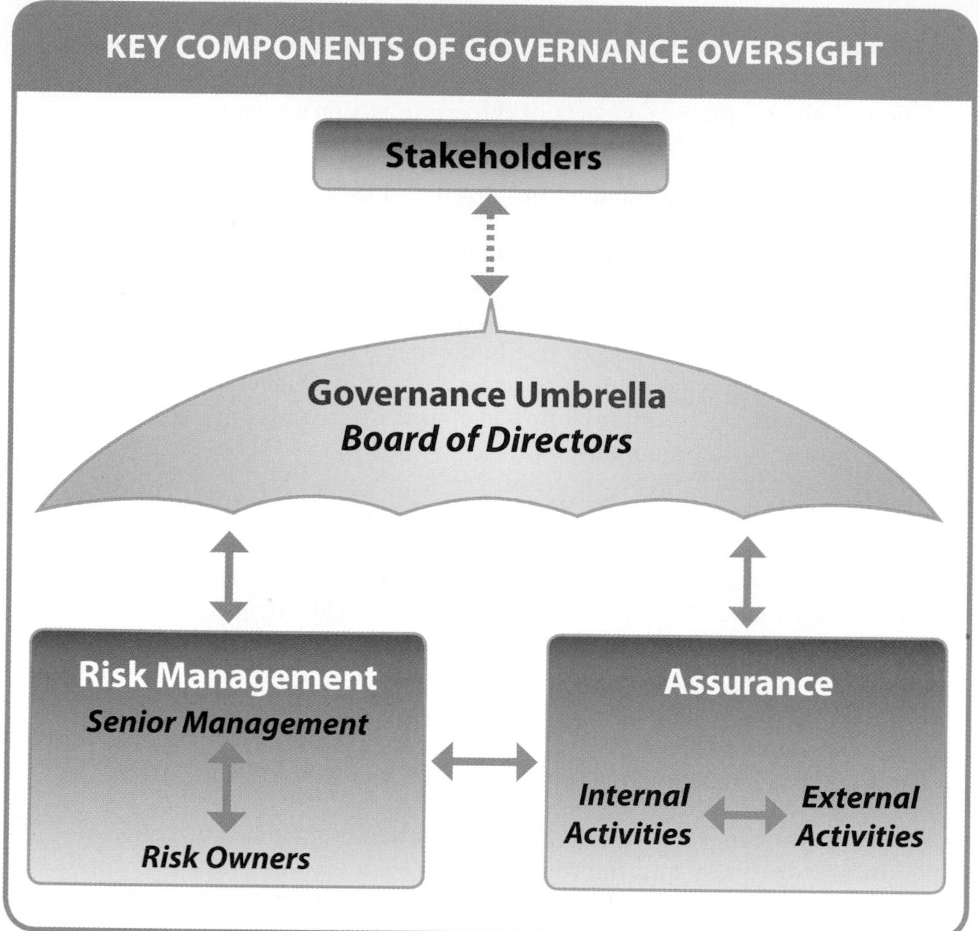

- Day-to-day, governance is executed by management of the organization. Both senior executives and line managers have important, although somewhat different, roles in governance. These roles are carried out through risk management activities.
- Internal and external activities provide management and the board with assurances regarding the effectiveness of governance activities. These parties include, but are not limited to, internal auditors and the independent outside auditors.

Roles and Responsibilities within Governance

Governance Umbrella
Board of Directors

The Board and Its Committees

Governance is ultimately the responsibility of the board, although this responsibility is frequently carried out by its various committees (for example, the audit committee). The first of the board's responsibilities is to identify the key stakeholders of an organization. A stakeholder is any party with a direct or indirect interest in an organization's activities and outcomes. Stakeholders can be viewed as having one or more of the following characteristics:

Stakeholders

- Some stakeholders are *directly involved* in the operation of the organization's business.
- Other stakeholders are not directly involved, but are *interested* in the organization's business; that is, they are affected by the success or other outcomes of the business.

- Some stakeholders are neither involved nor interested in the success of an organization's business, but these stakeholders may nonetheless *influence* aspects of the organization's business and, as a result, the organization's success.

The most common stakeholders are discussed below:

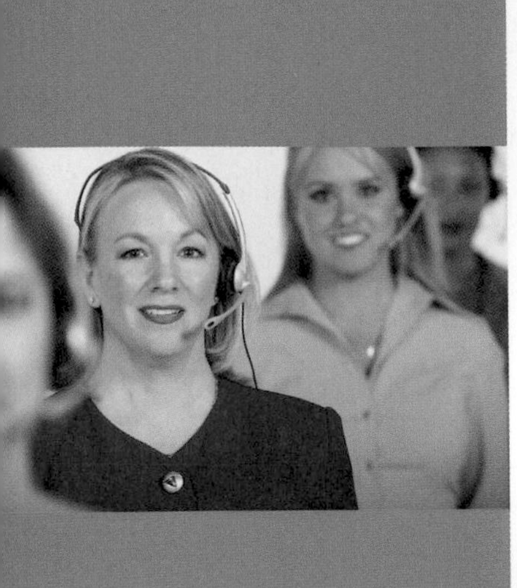

Employees work for an organization and, therefore, are *directly involved* in the conduct of the organization's business. Employees also have a vested *interest* in the organization's ongoing viability and success. If the organization ceases to exist, or has to downsize due to the lack of success in a market, employees may lose their source of livelihood. Therefore, a board must ensure an organization is operating in a manner that serves the best interest of its employees.

Customers are typically the lifeblood of an organization's success, and, as such, are *directly involved* in that success. Customers also are *interested* in an organization's success because failure of the organization may reduce the number of viable options from which the customer can obtain a needed good or service. In exchange for some form of payment, customers rely on an organization to build safe and reliable products, deliver agreed-upon services, and comply with other aspects of sales contracts and arrangements. Because the organization has obligations to customers, the board has a responsibility to ensure these obligations are met.

Vendors provide the goods and services needed for an organization to conduct its business and, therefore, are *directly involved* in the business. Similar to customers, vendors will have an *interest* in the ongoing viability of the organization as a key customer of the vendor. An organization has certain obligations to vendors, the most obvious of which is the obligation to pay for the goods and services received from those vendors. Therefore, a board has oversight responsibilities to ensure that the organization meets its obligations under vendor contracts and arrangements.

Stakeholder Types
- **Directly involved**
- **Interested**
- **Influence**

Shareholders/Investors are not directly involved in the business but have a strong *interest* in the organization's success. These stakeholders own an investment in the company, either through shares of stock, ownership units, or some other legal instrument that vests them in the future success of the company. Shareholders may be individual investors, institutions, or funds that invest on behalf of a group of investors. Typically, shareholders have the right to elect individuals to serve as directors on the board who they believe will best serve and protect their interests. Therefore, because they can *influence* the board, shareholders are frequently considered the most important and powerful stakeholders from the board's perspective.

Regulatory Agencies represent governmental agencies that may have either an *interest* in the organization's success or may be able to *influence* that success. The rules and regulations promulgated by these agencies may dictate certain operational and reporting requirements of an organization, or influence the decisions made by management of the organization. For example, the U.S. Securities and Exchange Commission (SEC) influences all publicly held companies in the United States. Examples of regulatory agencies affecting most U.S. companies include the Department of Labor, the Environmental Protection Agency, and the Occupational Safety and Health Administration. Additionally, some industries are subject to specific regulators such as banking (the Federal Deposit

Insurance Corporation and others) and utilities (for example, the Federal Energy Regulatory Commission and state regulatory commissions that are responsible for approving the rates that can be charged to customers). These regulators are responsible for ensuring organizations comply with regulations that meet a public good and, as such, have a strong interest in the operations of the organizations. Virtually every country or legal jurisdiction will have agencies or similar bodies that promulgate regulations. A board must understand the requirements of these agencies to exercise their oversight responsibilities.

Financial Institutions impact the capital structure of an organization. Capital structures typically are composed of debt and/or equity. The equity component was covered under the discussion of shareholders above. Debt stakeholders are typically financial institutions, such as banks or other institutions, that provide financing to an organization. Financial institutions are willing to provide financing in exchange for a return, most commonly in the form of an interest rate on the outstanding balance. However, such institutions frequently have other stipulations, or covenants, with which an organization must comply. These covenants typically relate to the overall financial health and liquidity of an organization, and provide ongoing assurances to the financial institutions regarding the organization's ability to repay its obligations. This creates both an *interest* in the success of an organization and *influence* on how the organization will operate to comply with covenants. Therefore, a board must provide oversight to ensure management is mindful of, and complying with, all relevant covenants of financing arrangements with these influencing stakeholders.

Although the above are the most common types of stakeholders, there may be other parties who have an *interest* in or can *influence* an organization. Examples include rating agencies, industry associations, financial analysts, and competitors of the organization. The key point is that a board must make the effort and spend the time to ensure it has identified all of the key stakeholders in an organization.

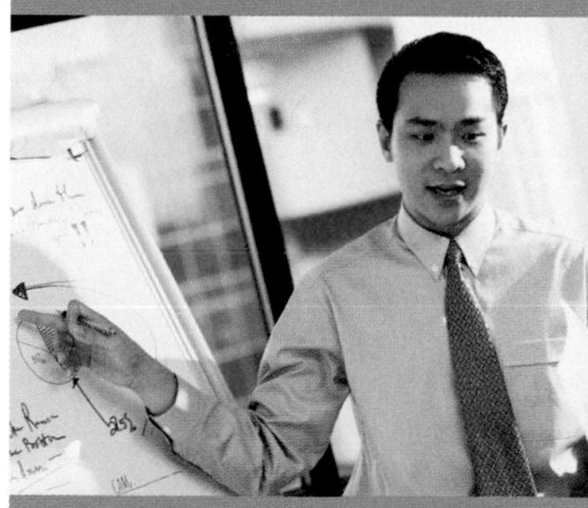

Once the key stakeholders are identified, the next step the board must undertake is to understand the needs and expectations of these stakeholders. Some of those needs and expectations are self-evident. For example, customers expect that products are generally free of defects and vendors expect obligations to be paid on time. However, other expectations, such as shareholders' desire for dividends versus share price growth, may require some research and analysis to fully understand. Boards may be able to determine these expectations through internal discussions, but they also may need to discuss expectations directly with key stakeholders.

Finally, the board should identify the potential outcomes that would be unacceptable to key stakeholders. For example, certain investors may be disappointed if the organization misses its earnings estimate by one cent per share in a given quarter, but may not find that unacceptable, as some components of earnings are more volatile than others. However, if the organization misses its earnings estimates for several consecutive quarters, investors may find that unacceptable and question whether the board should consider a change in senior management. Note that when considering unacceptable outcomes, it is important to think both in terms of outcomes that cause harm to the organization as well as outcomes that represent failure to effectively exploit opportunities.

Because the various stakeholders will likely have different expectations, the outcomes each type of stakeholder deems unacceptable will vary as well. The board may need to consider the following types of outcomes:

- **Financial** — for example, earnings per share, cash liquidity, credit rating, return on investments, capital availability, tax exposures, material weaknesses, and disclosure transparency.
- **Compliance** — for example, litigation, code of conduct violations, safety and environmental violations, restraining orders, governmental investigations, indictments, and arrests.
- **Operations** — for example, achievement of objectives, efficient use of assets, protection of assets (insurance coverage, asset impairments, asset destruction), protection of people (health and safety, work stoppages), protection of information (data integrity, data confidentiality), and protection of community (environmental spills, plant shutdowns).
- **Strategic** — for example, reputation, corporate sustainability, employee morale, and customer satisfaction.

Once the board determines the outcomes that key stakeholders deem unacceptable, it can establish tolerance levels based on those outcomes. The tolerance levels, which are consistent with the organization's overall risk appetite, can be communicated to management as boundaries within which the board would like the organization to operate. While the concepts of risk appetite and tolerance are discussed in greater depth in Chapter 4, "Risk Management," a broad understanding of these concepts will be helpful to appreciate the board's role.

Risk Appetite

The amount of risk, on a broad level, an organization is willing to accept in pursuit of its business objectives.

Risk appetite can be thought of in terms of an eating metaphor, thinking quite literally about an individual's appetite for food. This appetite represents the total amount of food that can be consumed to achieve certain objectives, such as maintaining good health and a desired weight. It is possible to satiate an appetite by consuming all of one type of food (for example, chocolate). However, while it is possible to feel "full" at that point, eating only chocolate will not likely support the longer term objectives of maintaining good health and a desired weight. Thus, the brain of a human being (which is analogous to the board of an organization) determines how much of certain types of foods, including minimum and maximum amounts, should be consumed. These amounts are analogous to tolerance levels that support the achievement of business objectives.

Risk Tolerance

The acceptable levels of risk size and variation relative to the achievement of objectives, which must align with the organization's risk appetite.

Using the concepts discussed above, the board can best execute its governance responsibilities by:

- Establishing a governance committee.
  - This committee could be a new committee or an expansion of responsibilities for an existing committee (for example, many public companies have expanded the responsibilities of the nominating committee to become a nominating and governance committee).
  - It should be made up of independent directors.
  - The committee should have the responsibilities outlined above.
- Articulating requirements for reporting to the board.

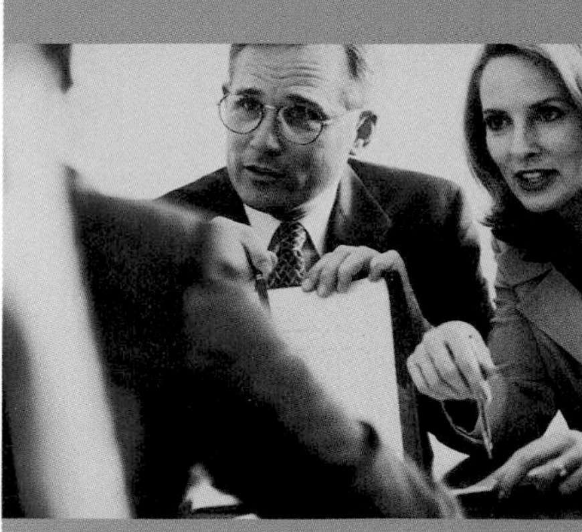

- The board should delegate to management the authority to operate the business within the board's tolerable limits relative to unacceptable outcomes. Management must have the authority to make day-to-day business decisions, but also must have a clear understanding of the board's tolerance limits within which to manage the business.
- As part of its oversight role, the board also must establish reporting thresholds for management — that is, which outcomes must be approved by the board, reported directly to the board, or summarized for the board as part of quarterly meetings.

- Reevaluating governance expectations periodically (probably annually).
  - Key stakeholder expectations may evolve and change. Therefore, the board must identify those changes and reevaluate its governance direction.
  - As a result of those changes, the board's tolerance levels also should be reevaluated.

In summary, the board of directors plays a very key and comprehensive role in corporate governance. Without that umbrella of authority, direction, and oversight, governance will not be sufficiently effective over the long term.

Risk Management
Senior Management

Senior Management

Although the board provides the umbrella of governance oversight, management executes the day-to-day activities that help ensure effective governance is achieved. Once the board determines its tolerance levels relative to the boundaries of operations, it must next delegate authority to members of senior management so they can manage the operations within those tolerance levels. Senior management then has the responsibility to execute the board's direction in a manner that achieves corporate objectives, but within the tolerance limits outlined by the board.

To execute its governance responsibilities, senior management is responsible for:

- Ensuring that the full scope of direction and authority delegated is understood appropriately. Senior management must understand the board's governance expectations, the amount of authority the board has delegated to management, its tolerance levels relative to unacceptable outcomes, and requirements for reporting to the board.
- Identifying the processes and activities within the organization that are integral to executing the governance direction provided by the board. That is, senior management must determine:
  - Where in the organization to manage the specific risks that could result in unacceptable outcomes.
  - Who will be responsible for managing those risks (that is, risk owners).
  - How those risks will be managed.
- Evaluating what other business considerations or factors might create a justification for delegating a lower tolerance level to risk owners than that delegated by the board. For example, the board may specify that management must maintain controls to ensure

there are no control weaknesses beyond a certain level of severity. However, senior management, desiring to avoid the situation in which multiple significant control deficiencies aggregate to an unacceptable level, may specify to risk owners that controls be maintained to ensure there are no control deficiencies exceeding a lower level of severity.

- Ensuring that sufficient information is gathered from the risk owners to support its reporting requirements to the board.

Senior management can best execute its governance responsibilities by:

- Establishing a risk committee.
  - This committee is typically led by a senior executive: a chief risk officer (CRO), if one exists, or some other executive who has broad risk oversight responsibility.
  - It is responsible for determining that all key risks are identified, linked to risk management activities, and assigned to risk owners. As part of this responsibility, the committee must ensure that it comprehensively considers all possible outcomes for key risks, not just the financial outcomes.
  - It evaluates the organization's ongoing risk appetite and ensures that tolerance levels delegated to the risk owners are consistent with this risk appetite.
- Articulating reporting requirements.
  - Risk owners must understand the nature, format, and timing of communications regarding the effectiveness of the risk management activities. These communications typically should be consistent with the tolerance levels delegated to the risk owners.
  - This reporting may occur through regularly scheduled risk committee meetings or as part of the process of compiling information for reporting to the board.
- Reevaluating governance expectations periodically (probably annually).
  - As an organization evolves and changes, senior management must reevaluate its governance direction and the corresponding tolerance levels that have been delegated to risk owners. These changes may come from the board or from other external and internal factors. Such changes may result in the need for new risk management activities or modifications to existing risk management activities.
  - As a result of those changes, senior management's tolerance levels also should be reevaluated.
  - This also gives senior management the opportunity to evaluate the overall effectiveness of the organization's risk management program.

Risk

Possibility that an event will occur and adversely affect the achievement of objectives.

Senior management plays an integral role in risk management, which is a key component of governance. Refer to Chapter 4, "Risk Management," for a more in-depth discussion of these risk management concepts.

Risk Owners

Individuals who have day-to-day responsibility for ensuring that risk management activities effectively manage risks within the organization's risk appetite are called risk owners. Many would argue that the chief executive officer and the other chief officers are ultimately the owners of risk within an organization. However, the term is used here in reference to the individuals who conduct day-to-day activities to manage specific risks. These individuals are responsible for identifying, measuring, managing, monitoring, and reporting on risks to the members of senior management to whom they report, typically the chief officers. In some instances, risk owners may be individuals who are lower in the organizational hierarchy. However, risk owners certainly work with senior management to carry out the risk management activities of an organization. The responsibilities of risk owners include:

- Evaluating whether the risk management activities are designed adequately to manage the related risks within the tolerance levels specified by senior management. Although senior management may provide direction relative to the risk management activities, the risk owners typically will determine the specific tasks that are necessary to carry out those activities.
- Assessing the ongoing capabilities of the organization to execute those risk management activities. This assessment should evaluate the maturity of the procedures in place, the competence and experience of the people performing those procedures, the sufficiency of any enabling technologies (for example, computer systems), and the availability of external and internal information to support decision-making.
- Determining whether the risk management activities are currently operating as designed — that is, whether the people and systems are executing the processes consistently with the desired objectives.
- Conducting day-to-day monitoring activities to identify, in a timely manner, whether anomalies or divergences from expected outcomes have occurred.
- Ensuring that the information needed by senior management and the board is accurate and readily available, and is provided to senior management on a timely basis.

Risk owners can best execute their governance responsibilities by:

- Presenting governance recommendations to the risk committee.
  - If an individual becomes a new risk owner, or is responsible for a risk that was not previously subject to formal risk management and reporting, the risk owner should prepare a recommendation for the risk committee. This recommendation should cover the inherent nature and source of the risk, its potential impact, proposed tolerance levels, and expected risk management activities. This information is presented to, discussed with, and approved by the risk committee.
- Reevaluating risk management activities periodically (at least annually, but potentially more frequently).
  - The design of risk management activities should continue to align with organization-wide risk strategies and ensure the risks are managed within the delegated tolerance levels.

- The risk management capabilities should be reassessed in light of personnel turnover, systems changes, and other events that could impact the maturity and effectiveness of those capabilities.
- Risk management monitoring activities should provide the risk owners with timely information on the effectiveness of the risk management activities.
- The reporting of risk management results to senior management should be reassessed periodically to ensure the reporting continues to meet senior management's expectations.

Assurance Services

An objective examination of evidence for the purpose of providing an independent assessment on governance, risk management, and control processes for the organization.

Risk owners are on the front lines of managing risks and, as such, are key contributors to good governance. Their role in executing and monitoring risk management activities, along with reporting on the effectiveness of those activities, will greatly influence the success an organization will have in avoiding or mitigating unacceptable outcomes. Refer to Chapter 4, "Risk Management," for a more in-depth discussion of these risk management concepts.

Assurance
Internal Activities ↔ *External Activities*

Assurance Activities

The final component of governance is independent assurance activities, which help provide the board and senior management with an objective assessment regarding the effectiveness of the governance and risk management activities. These independent assurance activities can be performed by a variety of parties, either internal or external to the organization. The most common internal group to provide such assurances is the internal audit function.

IIA Standard 2110: Governance states the following regarding the internal audit function's role in governance activities:

> "The internal audit activity must assess and make appropriate recommendations for improving the governance process in its accomplishment of the following objectives:
>
> - Promoting appropriate ethics and values within the organization;
> - Ensuring effective organizational performance management and accountability;
> - Communicating risk and control information to appropriate areas of the organization; and
> - Coordinating the activities of and communicating information among the board, external and internal auditors, and management."

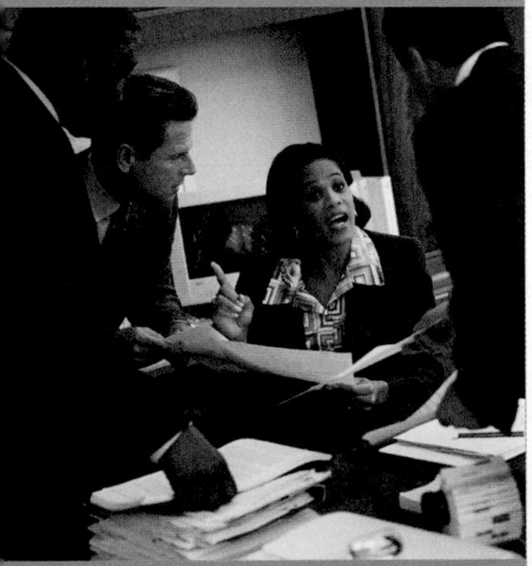

IIA Standard 2120: Risk Management states "The internal audit activity must evaluate the effectiveness and contribute to the improvement of risk management processes." Embedded in both of these standards is the notion that an internal audit function may provide both assurance and consulting services to an organization. The extent of assurance activities performed by the internal audit function will depend on (1) the internal audit charter, which specifies the internal audit function's role in governance assurance, and (2) specific direction from the board regarding current or ongoing expectations to perform such activities. Depending on these two factors, the internal audit function's governance responsibilities may include any or all of the following:

- Evaluating whether the various risk management activities are designed adequately to manage the risks associated with unacceptable outcomes.
- Testing and evaluating whether the various risk management activities are operating as designed.
- Determining whether the assertions made by the risk owners to senior management regarding the effectiveness of the risk management activities accurately reflect the current state of risk management effectiveness.
- Determining whether the assertions made by senior management to the board regarding the effectiveness of the risk management activities provide the board with the information it desires about the current state of risk management effectiveness.
- Evaluating whether risk tolerance information is communicated timely and effectively from both the board to senior management and from senior management to the risk owners.
- Assessing whether there are any other risk areas that are currently not included in the governance process, but should be (for example, a risk for which risk tolerance and reporting expectations have not been delegated to a specific risk owner).

The internal audit function can be an effective part of the governance process by:

- Ensuring it fully understands the board's governance direction and expectations.
  - The internal audit function should understand the direction provided to senior management, including the tolerance levels and reporting expectations.
  - Additionally, it is important to understand the board's expectations of the role the internal audit function should play with regard to governance assurance.
- Supporting management's risk management program.
  - The internal audit function can help bring structure and discipline to the risk management program, which may be managed in a manner similar to managing internal audit activities.
  - The internal audit function can help educate management and other employees on risk and control topics.
  - Organizational and divisional risk assessments can be facilitated or monitored by the internal audit function.
  - Ongoing oversight and input can be provided formally (for example, sitting on a risk steering committee) or informally (for example, periodic discussions with management).
- Developing an internal audit plan that appropriately encompasses the governance assurance activities and allows for periodic communications to senior management and the board on the effectiveness of risk management activities.

Some organizations have other groups that may provide independent assurance (for example, environmental and safety departments, quality

Consulting Services

Advisory and related services, the nature and scope of which are agreed to with the customer, and which are intended to improve an organization's governance, risk management, and control processes without the internal auditor assuming management responsibility.

assurance groups, or trading control activities). These groups may provide assurance directly to the board, or they may communicate to members of management who provide the assurance to the board.

Assurances from external parties are less common but still can be important to the board. For example, although the attestation opinions provided by independent outside auditors are primarily for the purpose of meeting regulatory or contractual requirements, such opinions also may provide the board and management with assurance regarding the effectiveness of activities designed to mitigate financial reporting risks. Similarly, third-party consultants may be hired to provide management or the board with assurance regarding specific risk management activities. Finally, regulatory auditors, who assess regulatory compliance for the benefit of the sponsoring agency, also can provide forms of assurance to management.

Independent Outside Auditor

Registered public accounting firm, hired by the organization's board or executive management, to perform a financial statement audit providing assurance for which the firm issues a written attestation report that expresses an opinion about whether the financial statements are fairly presented in accordance with applicable Generally Accepted Accounting Principles.

The independent assurance activities performed by internal auditors as well as other parties provide valuable information to senior management and the board to help them monitor the ongoing effectiveness of governance and risk management activities.

THE EVOLUTION OF GOVERNANCE

Despite the publicity that corporate governance has received in recent years, effective governance is not a new concept. An underlying premise of the public equity markets is that investors will provide capital to organizations in exchange for a potential return on that investment. To instill confidence in the capital markets, investors need sufficient appropriate information to evaluate the potential risks and rewards of their investments. They also need assurance that it is a level playing field — that is, all investors will be able to transact consistently and fairly. Various regulations and standards have been written to achieve this objective and provide greater transparency in publicly available information. Frequently, new regulations and standards have been promulgated in response to events in the business world. These regulations and standards were designed to eliminate or minimize the undesirable outcomes of those events. Exhibit 3-5 summarizes some of those key business events in the United States and the legislation that resulted. Appendix 3-A, "Summary of Key U.S. Regulations," at the end of this chapter presents a summary of key U.S. regulations and a description of each piece of legislation shown in Exhibit 3-5.

Regulations in Other Parts of the World

Similar business events have occurred in other countries around the world, resulting in the promulgation of legislation by their legislative bodies. Each piece of legislation was designed to improve overall governance, as well as the controls surrounding the preparation of financial statements, and enhance the fairness and transparency of financial reporting.

A description of key guidance/regulations from other countries can be found in Appendix 3-B, "Summary of Governance and Risk Management Codes From Other Countries." Additionally, Appendix 3-C, "Other Governance References," provides links to sources of governance information promulgated by other countries.

KEY U.S. BUSINESS EVENTS AND RESULTING LEGISLATION

EXHIBIT 3-5

Key Business Events	Legislation/Guidance
The U.S. stock market crash in 1929, combined with the subsequent failures of several major corporations because of fraud, precipitated the need for investor faith to be restored. The intent of the resulting regulations was to provide a level playing field for investors through consistent, timely, complete, and relevant public reporting of financial information.	Securities Act of 1933 Securities Exchange Act of 1934
In the aftermath of the Watergate investigation at the beginning of the 1970s, more than 450 American companies were reported to have paid bribes or made questionable payments to foreign government officials or political parties.	Foreign Corrupt Practices Act (FCPA) of 1977
In the 1980s, there were multiple incidents of financial reporting that were inaccurate, incomplete, or misleading.	Report of the National Commission on Fraudulent Financial Reporting (Treadway Commission Report) 1987
In the 1980s, several savings and loan institutions required bailout by the federal government, bringing into question, among other things, the strength of their system of internal controls.	Federal Deposit Insurance Corporation Improvement Act (FDICIA) of 1991
After the turn of the new century, several U.S. corporations were beset by fraud and bankruptcy (for example, Enron Corp. and WorldCom).	U.S. Sarbanes-Oxley Act of 2002, which amends the 1933 and 1934 Securities Acts U.S. Stock Exchange Listing Standards (NYSE and NASDAQ)

Commonly Identified Governance Principles

As is probably evident from the previous discussions, governance is a broad concept. Organizations around the world have posted their governance principles on their websites. Visits to these websites make it clear that approaches to governance vary. However, as described in a widely distributed IIA paper on governance, principles often included in defining effective governance processes are:

1. Ensure a properly organized and functioning board that has the correct number of members; an appropriate board committee structure; established meeting protocols; sound, independent judgment about affairs of the organization; and periodically reaffirmed membership.
2. Ensure board members possess appropriate qualifications and experience, with a clear understanding of their role in the governance activities, a sound knowledge of the organization's operations, and an independent/objective mindset.
3. Ensure that the board has sufficient authority, funding, and resources to conduct independent inquiries.

4. Maintain an understanding by executive management and the board of the organization's operating structure, including structures that impede transparency.
5. Articulate an organizational strategy against which the success of the overall enterprise and the contributions of individuals are measured.
6. Create an organizational structure that supports the enterprise in achieving its strategy.
7. Establish a governing policy for the operation of key activities of the organization.
8. Set and enforce clear lines of responsibility and accountability throughout the organization.
9. Ensure effective interaction among the board, management, [independent outside] and internal auditors, and any other assurance providers.
10. Secure appropriate oversight by management, including establishment and maintenance of a strong set of internal controls.
11. Make sure that compensation policies and practices — especially related to senior management — are consistent with the organization's ethical values, objectives, strategy, and control environment, and encourage appropriate behavior.
12. Communicate and reinforce throughout the organization an ethical culture, organizational values, and appropriate tone at the top, which includes an environment that allows employees to raise concerns without fear of retaliation, as well as monitors and investigates potential conflicts of interest.
13. Effectively use internal auditors, ensuring the adequacy of their independence, resources, scope of activities, and effectiveness of operations.
14. Clearly define and implement risk management policies, processes, and accountabilities at the board level and throughout the organization.
15. Effectively use [independent outside] auditors, ensuring their independence, adequate resources, and scope of activities.
16. Provide appropriate disclosure of key information, in a transparent manner, to stakeholders.
17. Provide disclosure of the organization's governance processes, comparing those processes with recognized national codes or best practices.
18. Ensure appropriate oversight of related-party transactions and conflict of interest situations.

Although there may be additional principles cited in other resources, this list comprehensively supports the discussion of governance provided earlier in this chapter.

EXHIBIT 3-6

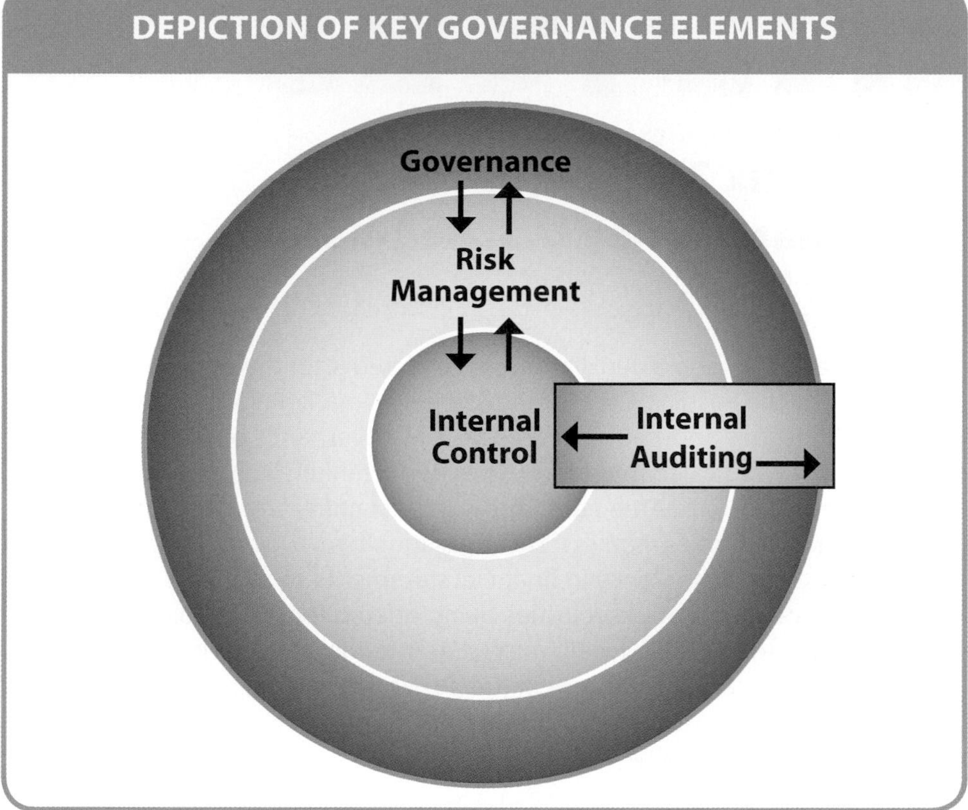

SUMMARY

Organizations must take great care to implement effective governance structures and risk management approaches. The governance structure provides direction to those executing the day-to-day activities of managing the risks inherent in an organization's business model. These activities must be monitored to ensure consistent operation. The three elements of governance can be depicted as shown in Exhibit 3-6.

Governance involves a set of relationships between an organization's management, its board, and its stakeholders. The board typically provides the "umbrella" of governance direction, authority, and oversight. The board must understand and strive to meet the needs and expectations of the organization's various stakeholders. Thus, the board must articulate its direction, advise on the creation of business objectives, establish boundaries of business conduct, and empower management to carry out its direction. Management executes its risk management activities to fulfill the direction of the board. These activities may be carried out by lower-level risk owners in the organization, but senior management is ultimately accountable for the effectiveness of risk management activities. Finally, internal and external parties, in particular the respective auditors, carry out activities that can provide levels of assurance to management and the board regarding the effectiveness of risk management activities.

Finally, it should be clear that the internal audit function fulfills an important role in governance. This will become even more evident in Chapter 4, "Risk Management," and Chapter 6, "Internal Control." As a result, Exhibit 3-6 adds a box depicting the fact that internal auditing is a key element in governance.

APPENDICES

Appendix 3-A
Summary of Key U.S. Regulations

Securities Act of 1933

This piece of U.S. federal legislation was enacted after the market crash of 1929 and the ensuing Great Depression. The market crash raised some serious questions about the effectiveness of governance over the sale of securities. It was signed into law by President Franklin D. Roosevelt as part of his "New Deal" with America to bring back stability and investor confidence in the securities markets. The legislation had two main goals: (1) to ensure greater transparency in financial statements so investors can make informed decisions about securities being offered for public sale, and (2) to establish laws against deceit, misrepresentation, and other fraudulent activities in the sale of securities in the public markets.

Securities Exchange Act of 1934

The Securities Exchange Act of 1934 was created to provide governance of securities transactions on the secondary market (after issue) and regulate the different exchanges and broker-dealers to protect the investing public. From this act, the U.S. Securities and Exchange Commission (SEC) was created. The SEC's responsibility is to enforce securities laws. Primary requirements include registration of any securities listed on U.S. stock exchanges, disclosure, proxy solicitations, and margin and audit requirements. Contrasted with the Securities Act of 1933, which regulates these original issues, the Securities Exchange Act of 1934 regulates the secondary trading of those securities between persons often unrelated to the issuer. Trillions of dollars are made and lost through trading in the secondary market.

Foreign Corrupt Practices Act

Due to questionable corporate political campaign finance practices and foreign corrupt practices in the mid-1970s, the SEC and the U.S. Congress enacted campaign finance law reforms and the 1977 Foreign Corrupt Practices Act (FCPA), which criminalizes transnational bribery and requires companies to implement internal control programs. Specifically, the FCPA requires publicly traded companies to "make and keep books, records, and accounts, which, in reasonable detail, accurately and fairly reflect the transactions and dispositions of the assets of the issuer . . . "[3] The act, in effect, broadens the focus on internal control to provide reasonable assurance that transactions are appropriately authorized and accurately recorded, assets are physically safeguarded, and there is periodic substantiation of recorded assets.

Report of the National Commission on Fraudulent Financial Reporting (Treadway Commission Report)

This private-sector initiative, called the National Commission on Fraudulent Financial Reporting (commonly known as the Treadway Commission), was formed in October 1985. Its mission was to identify causal factors that could lead to fraudulent financial reporting and determine the steps necessary to reduce the incidence of those factors. The Treadway Commission studied cases that had been brought before the SEC during the years leading up to its initial report in 1987. This report recommended that the organizations sponsoring the Treadway Commission work together to develop integrated guidance on internal control. Additionally, it had recommendations for public companies, independent public accounting firms, the SEC and others with regulatory power, and educators.

As a result of this report, the Committee of Sponsoring Organizations of the Treadway Commission (COSO) was created. COSO was composed of the American Institute of Certified Public Accountants (AICPA), American Accounting Association (AAA), Financial Executives International (FEI), The Institute of Internal Auditors (IIA), and the Institute of Management Accountants (IMA). COSO commissioned the creation of an internal control framework, which was issued in 1992, titled *Internal Control – Integrated Framework*. This framework became the only widely accepted internal control framework in the United States.

FDICIA

The U.S. Federal Deposit Insurance Corporation Improvement Act of 1991 requires FDIC insured depository institutions with assets in excess of US $500 million to certify that their system of internal controls is functioning effectively. It also requires the institution's independent outside auditors to attest to management's assertions regarding the effectiveness of its system of internal controls. Many aspects of this act were later included in the U.S. Sarbanes-Oxley Act of 2002.

U.S. Sarbanes-Oxley Act of 2002

After a series of significant bankruptcies and incidents of fraudulent financial reporting at major U.S. corporations (for example, Enron Corp., Tyco, WorldCom), legislation was passed in the United States with the overall objectives of creating more accountability over the integrity of financial reporting by chief executive and chief financial officers, and restoring investor confidence in the capital markets. This legislation, the Sarbanes-Oxley Act, contained numerous sections promulgating rules and regulations on many aspects of governance for public companies. The two sections that received the most public awareness and scrutiny were Sections 302 and 404.

- Section 302 requires the chief executive and chief financial officers of public companies to certify each quarter, in connection with the company's quarterly filing of its financial results on Form 10-Q, as to the effectiveness of the disclosure controls and procedures that were in place in connection with preparing that filing.
- Section 404 requires the company to provide assertions, in connection with the annual filing of its financial results on Form 10-K, as to the effectiveness of internal control over financial reporting. This section, in particular, requires most companies to improve the documentation and testing surrounding those internal controls to support the required assertions.

U.S. Stock Exchange Listing Standards

The major stock exchanges in the United States (New York Stock Exchange [NYSE] and NASDAQ [National Association of Securities Dealers Automated Quotations]) have promulgated certain standards that must be met by any public company that desires to be listed on those exchanges. These listing standards cover such items as the organization and responsibilities of the board and audit committee, code of business conduct, personal loans to executives, the need for an internal audit function, and stock options.

Appendix 3-B Summary of Governance and Risk Management Codes From Other Countries[4, 5]

Many nations have promulgated regulations or issued codes pertaining to governance principles. Following is a summary of those from certain countries.

Australia — The Corporate Governance Council of the Australian Stock Exchange (ASX) issued Principles of Good Corporate Governance and Best Practice Recommendations in 2003, which was revised in 2007. This document outlines eight essential corporate governance principles and includes recommendations regarding the composition and role of the audit committee. The ASX recommends that audit committees be composed of nonexecutive directors, a majority of whom are independent, and that the audit committee's role include, among other things, assessing the performance and objectivity of the internal audit function, reviewing results of risk management and internal compliance and control systems, and assessing whether external reporting is consistent with audit committee members' information and knowledge and is adequate for shareholder needs. The 2007 update requires management to report to the board on how effectively the company is managing material business risks, and for internal auditing to give independent assurance on the risk management framework.

Canada — Canadian Securities Administrators issued rules to improve investor confidence in early 2004. The rules mandate an independent audit committee, require written committee charters, authorize audit committees to communicate directly with internal audit functions, and cover a variety of other issues.

China — The China Securities Regulatory Commission, Code of Corporate Governance for Listed Companies in China (2001), requires at least one-third of board members to be independent directors, and its rules provide for the optional appointment of an audit committee. If an audit committee is established, a majority of its members must be independent, and at least one independent director must be an accounting expert. The committee's principal responsibilities should include supervision of the internal audit function.

France — The Financial Security Act (LSF) of August 1, 2003, as modified to transpose the 4th and 7th European directives, requires the chairman of the board to describe in an annual report the company's internal control and risk management procedures. Moreover, this report must be approved by the board of directors. The chairman must indicate if the company voluntarily complies with a corporate governance code (such as the corporate governance of listed companies established in 2003 and modified in 2008 by AFEP-MEDEF — Association of major French corporations and Association of French private sector companies) or explain the reason for noncompliance. More recently, the law transposed the 8th European directive on the statutory audit, indicating that the audit committee must monitor the effectiveness of the company's internal control and risk management systems.

Germany— A government commission appointed by the Ministry of Justice adopted the German Corporate Governance Code (Kodex) in February 2002. In July 2002, the Transparency and Disclosure Act was passed, requiring publicly listed companies to publish an annual declaration of conformity with the code's recommendations. The recommendations of the code are marked in the text by use of the word "shall." Companies can deviate from them, but are then obliged to disclose this annually. This enables companies to reflect sector and enterprise-specific requirements. Thus, the code contributes to more flexibility and more self-regulation in the German corporate constitution. Furthermore, the code contains suggestions which can be deviated from without disclosure; for this, the code uses terms such as "should" or "can." The remaining passages of the code not marked by these terms contain provisions that enterprises are compelled to observe under applicable law. The code, which has been amended since it was originally published, recommends — among other things — the establishment of audit committees to deal with issues of accounting, auditing, and risk management.

Hong Kong — The Rules Governing the Listing of Securities on the Stock Exchange of Hong Kong Limited and The Rules Governing the Listing of Securities on the Growth Enterprise Market of the Stock Exchange of Hong Kong Limited require listed companies to establish an audit committee composed of nonexecutive directors, a majority of whom are independent. The audit committee should have clear terms of reference, including oversight of the financial reporting system and internal control procedures. For issuers with an internal audit function, the audit committee should review and monitor its effectiveness and ensure it has adequate resources and appropriate standing. The rules also require directors to report to shareholders annually on whether they have conducted a review of the effectiveness of the system of internal controls and, if not, the reasons why.

Italy — The Corporate Governance Code issued by Borsa Italiana in 2006 significantly changed the 2002 version of the code. In particular, it requires the establishment of an internal control committee made up of nonexecutive directors (the majority of whom need to meet additional independence requirements), and the appointment of an executive director position (one of the managing directors) specifically responsible for internal control. The internal controls committee is a distinct committee from the Board of Auditors, which oversees the auditing of financial statements. An internal audit function is also required.

Japan — The Standards and Implementation Standards for Evaluation and Auditing of Internal Control Over Financial Reporting were issued in early 2007. These standards, which support the Japanese Financial Instruments and Exchange Law, require all listed companies to submit internal control reports on a consolidated basis. Management must evaluate and report on the sufficiency of internal control over financial reporting. Under the Company Law enforced from May 2006, companies are required to resolve to develop a system to ensure appropriate company management and to describe the content of the resolution in the business reports. A Cabinet Office Ordinance requires listed companies to disclose information relating to corporate governance in financial reports (or annual reports) since fiscal year starting after April 2003. Finally, the Tokyo Stock Exchange formulated "Principles of Corporate Governance for Listed Companies" in March 2004, and since June 2006, requires listed companies to prepare a report on corporate governance.

Mexico — The Securities Market Law, Ley del Mercado de Valores, was last updated in 2004. It requires listed companies to establish an audit committee with a majority of independent directors. The Mexican Securities and Banking Commission recommends that all public companies adopt its Code of Best Practices, which recommends the size, role, and responsibilities of the audit committee. Among those responsibilities are assisting the board in reviewing financial information for external reporting and helping to oversee internal control systems and evaluate their effectiveness.

The Netherlands — The Dutch Corporate Governance Code, issued in 2003, recommends practices for the supervisory board and the audit committee. The supervisory board should supervise the operation of the internal risk management and control systems. To give the code more corporate governance structure, the committee proposes that listed companies that fail to adhere to certain aspects of the code must state the reasons for this noncompliance in their annual report (the "comply or explain" principle).

Russia — A Corporate Behavior Code was developed through the efforts of regulators and professional advisers and recommended by the government in November 2001. The Federal Commission for Financial Markets in April 2002 recommended the code for adoption by all regulated exchanges and listed companies. Compliance is voluntary. The code recommends the establishment of an audit committee for purposes of implementing and monitoring controls over an organization's financial and business activities. The code also recommends that the audit committee consist solely of independent directors.

South Africa — The King Report on Corporate Governance (King II Report), issued in 2002, focuses on board and audit committee practices and their conduct to improve governance. The role, function, and reporting requirements of internal auditing are specifically covered. Audit committees are required to concur in the appointment and dismissal of the chief audit executive (CAE). The report also recommends that internal audit plans be based on risk assessment as well as on issues highlighted by the audit committee and senior management.

A draft version of King III was made available in February 2009 (www.iodsa.co.za) for public comment with a planned final effective date in March 2010, until which King II will apply. King is endorsed by the Johannesburg Securities Exchange. The report considers, among other issues:

- The link between governance and law,
- Key principles pertaining to leadership, sustainability, and corporate citizenship,
- Emerging governance trends such as alternative dispute resolution, IT governance and risk-based internal audit, shareholders and remuneration, and
- Business rescue.

United Kingdom — The Combined Code on Corporate Governance, updated in 2008, has appended guidance on internal control from the Turnbull Committee, guidance on audit committees from the Smith Group, and suggestions for good practice from the report authored by Sir Derek Higgs. Regarding internal auditing, audit committees are advised to monitor and review the effectiveness of the internal audit function — including reviewing the internal audit function's remit, appointing or terminating the CAE, and meeting privately with the CAE at least annually. The Turnbull guidance recommends that directors acknowledge, in annual reports, their responsibility for the company's system of internal controls and for reviewing its effectiveness. It also recommends that boards disclose whether there is an ongoing process for identifying, evaluating, and managing significant risks faced by the company.

Appendix 3-C
Other Governance References

Many different references are available on the Internet with relevant information regarding governance and ERM principles. The authors have found the following sample to be of interest in terms of their comprehensiveness and relevance relative to the topics in this textbook.

- Links to various countries' governance codes or guidelines as assembled by the European Corporate Governance Institute. http://www.ecgi.org/codes/all_codes.php.
- The Basel Committee on Banking Supervision is an institution created by the central bank governors of the Group of Ten Nations. The Basel Committee formulates broad supervisory standards and guidelines and recommends statements of best

practice in banking supervision. The purpose of the committee is to encourage convergence toward common approaches and standards. http://www.bis.org.

- The Open Compliance and Ethics Group focuses on compliance matters. http://www.oceg.org.
- National Association of Corporate Directors. http://www.nacdonline.org.
- Committee of Sponsoring Organizations of the Treadway Commission (COSO). http://www.coso.org.
- The Business Roundtable. http://www.businessroundtable.org/.
- RiskMetrics Group (Owner of Institutional Shareholder Services Inc.). http://www.riskmetrics.com.
- The International Corporate Governance Network. http://www.icgn.org.
- Standard & Poor's Article, Standard & Poor's To Apply Enterprise Risk Analysis To Corporate Ratings, http://www2.standardandpoors.com/portal/site/sp/en/us/page.article/3,2,2,0,1204836988994.html (Users must register, at no charge, with Standard & Poor's to access this site.)

Review Questions

1. Why are there arrows flowing in both directions between the different elements of governance depicted in Exhibit 3-2?
2. What is the OECD's definition of corporate governance?
3. What is the difference between the two areas of governance depicted in Exhibit 3-3?
4. What are the three different types of stakeholders that the board must understand? Give examples of each type.
5. What types of outcomes might a board need to consider to understand stakeholders' expectations?
6. In governance, what are the key responsibilities of:
   a. The board of directors?
   b. Senior management?
   c. Risk owners?
7. What role does the internal audit function play in governance?
8. In addition to the internal audit function, what other internal functions may provide independent assurance to the board or senior management?

Multiple-choice Questions

Select the best answer for each of the following questions.

1. Which of the following is not an appropriate governance role for an organization's board of directors?
   a. Evaluating and approving strategic objectives.
   b. Influencing the organization's risk-taking philosophy.
   c. Providing assurance directly to third parties that the organization's governance processes are effective.
   d. Establishing broad boundaries of conduct, outside of which the organization should not operate.
2. Which of the following are typically governance responsibilities of senior management?
   I. Delegating risk tolerance levels to risk managers.
   II. Monitoring day-to-day performance of specific risk management activities.
   III. Establishing a governance committee of the board.
   IV. Ensuring that sufficient information is gathered to support reporting to the board.
   a. I and IV.
   b. II and III.
   c. I, II, and IV.
   d. I, II, III, and IV.

3. ABC utility company sells electricity to residential customers and is a member of an industry association that provides guidance to electric utilities, lobbies on behalf of the industry, and facilitates sharing among its members. From ABC's perspective, what type of stakeholder is this industry association?
   a. Directly *involved* in the operation of the company.
   b. *Interested* in the success of the company.
   c. *Influences* the company.
   d. Not a stakeholder.

4. Who is responsible for establishing the *strategic* objectives of an organization?
   a. The board of directors.
   b. Senior management.
   c. Consensus among all levels of management.
   d. The board and senior management jointly.

5. Who is ultimately responsible for identifying new or emerging key risk areas that should be covered by the organization's governance process?
   a. The board of directors.
   b. Senior management.
   c. Risk owners.
   d. The internal audit function.

Discussion Questions

1. Describe ways in which an organization's business model may affect its approach to governance oversight. Provide examples that contrast publicly held companies from privately held companies.

2. Discuss why it is important, from a governance perspective, to have independent outside directors on a board of directors?

3. Given that directors typically do not interface directly with key stakeholders, how might a board of directors obtain an understanding of key stakeholder expectations? How might that process vary among the various stakeholder groups identified in the chapter?

4. In Exhibit 3-4 the internal audit function is included in the Assurance box. In light of this assurance role, discuss the pros and cons of the CAE reporting to the board of directors (or one of its committees) versus the CFO. Relate your answer to the concepts described in Standard 1100: Independence and Objectivity.

5. Information technology (IT) governance has become a "hot topic" in recent years. Using the governance framework shown in Exhibit 3-4, customize each of the components to describe how they might specifically relate to governing IT objectives and risks of an organization.

6. The General Auditor's Office (GAO) of ABC jurisdiction issued a report on the XYZ Electric Cooperative, a large member-owned utility. This report reviewed the work of MNO Consulting. MNO found numerous internal control weaknesses. The GAO concurred with MNO's conclusion and recommendations regarding the overall lack of effective internal controls. In particular, the GAO went on to recommend that the ABC jurisdiction's legislature should require by law that each cooperative:
   - Create a board of directors (board) and maintain a separate audit committee.
   - Employ an internal auditor who reports to the board.

   A reporter for the local newspaper has a couple of questions for you.

   a. Typically, what is a governing board's responsibility for internal controls?

   b. Why would the GAO want each cooperative board to employ an internal auditor?

CASES

CASE 1 Review the governance regulations for Australia, South Africa, and the United Kingdom. Conduct additional research on the Internet to answer the following questions:

A. What events may have been the impetus for each of these countries promulgating these regulations?

B. Describe ways in which these regulations are similar.

C. Describe at least one notable difference between each of these regulations.

D. Which of these regulations do you believe has the most comprehensive governance requirements? Why?

CASE 2 The IIA has different blogs on its website. One of these is a governance blog (www.theiia.org/blogs/marks). Find this site on The IIA's website and review the last three postings, as well as the comments related to each. Be prepared to discuss in class your thoughts on each of the three original postings and the related comments.

REFERENCES

[1]Organization for Economic Co-operation and Development, Preamble to the OECD Principles of Corporate Governance, Revised May 2004.

[2]International Professional Practices Framework (Altamonte Springs, FL: The Institute of Internal Auditors, 2009), p. 18.

[3]U.S. Foreign Corrupt Practices Act, Section 78m.(b) (2)(a). Available at http://www.usdoj.gov/criminal/fraud/fcpa/.

[4]*Factors Affecting Corporate Governance and Audit Committees in Selected Countries* (Altamonte Springs, FL: The Institute of Internal Auditors Research Foundation, 2005).

[5]Bromilow, Catherine L., Barbara L. Berlin, and Richard J. Anderson, "Stepping Up," *Internal Auditor*, December 2005.

CHAPTER 4
RISK MANAGEMENT

Learning Objectives

- Define risk and enterprise risk management.
- Discuss the different dimensions of the Committee of Sponsoring Organizations of the Treadway Commission's *Enterprise Risk Management - Integrated Framework.*
- Articulate the relationship between governance and enterprise risk management.
- Describe the different roles the internal audit function can play in enterprise risk management.
- Evaluate the impact of enterprise risk management on internal audit activities.

Life is full of uncertainty. If you stop to think about it, there are many day-to-day activities about which you simply do not know what the outcome will be in advance. How you deal with those uncertainties determines what kind of success you will have in life.

Operating a business is no different. Organizations face uncertainties in all aspects of conducting business, and their success is dependent on how well they manage those uncertainties. Internal auditing can be a key enabler to that success.

Refer back to Exhibit 3-2 in Chapter 3, "Governance." Risk management is depicted as the middle layer in the governance structure. Risk management is intended to (1) identify and mitigate the risks that may adversely affect the organization's success, and (2) exploit the opportunities that enable that success. Management develops strategies regarding how to best manage the key risks and opportunities. Risk management activities should operate within the overall direction of the governance structure.

Similar to the discussion of governance in Chapter 3, this chapter describes risk management in detail, discussing key risk management elements and principles, as well as the various roles and responsibilities. Other illustrations will be provided to depict, in greater detail, how one might envision the key elements of risk management.

The chapter ends with discussions about how the internal audit function can play an integral role in risk management. The specific roles of the internal audit function are discussed, as is the impact risk management may have on the annual internal audit plan.

EXHIBIT 4-1

PROFESSIONAL STANDARDS, PRACTICE ADVISORIES, AND POSITION PAPERS RELEVANT TO CHAPTER 4

2010 – Planning

2100 – Nature of Work

2120 – Risk Management

Practice Advisory 2010-1: Linking the Audit Plan to Risk and Exposures

Practice Advisory 2120-1: Assessing the Adequacy of Risk Management Processes

Practice Advisory 2210.A1-1: Risk Assessment in Engagement Planning

Position Paper: The Role of Internal Auditing in Enterprise-wide Risk Management

Practice Advisory 2010-2: Using the Risk Management Process in Internal Audit Planning

Before beginning the discussion about risk management, it is important to understand why this area is a frequent topic of discussion in the business world. Many organizations have found that implementing effective risk management programs is more difficult than first thought. However, there are an increasing number of reasons for organizations to establish strong capabilities in these areas. For example, ratings agencies in the Unites States are now focusing more heavily on risk management in their ratings evaluations. Moody's Investors Services incorporates governance into their ratings and considers risk management as well. Beginning in 2008, Standard & Poor's began evaluating risk management with the intention of formally incorporating it into their ratings in the future. These are examples of why it is so important for organizations to implement an appropriate risk management structure.

OVERVIEW OF RISK MANAGEMENT

A Brief History of Risk

The concept of risk is not a recent phenomenon or new way of approaching the management of a business. Peter L. Bernstein provides an extensive history of risk in *Against the Gods: The Remarkable Story of Risk*. His book outlines the evolving acceptance and understanding of risk over the centuries. For example:

- Gambling has been documented back several centuries to early Greek and Egyptian civilizations as well as in the Bible (for example, Pontius Pilate's soldiers cast lots for Christ's robe as he suffered on the cross). While games of chance have been common throughout history, the theory of probability was not discovered until the Renaissance period in the mid-17th century. After that discovery, probability theory advanced from the mathematical exercise of explaining outcomes in games of chance to a key tool used in the business world to support decision-making.
- Chinese and Babylonian traders displayed risk transfer and distribution practices as early as the third and second century B.C., respectively. The Greeks and Romans introduced early forms of

health and life insurance around A.D. 600. Toward the end of the 17th century, the growing importance of London as a center for trade led to rising demand for marine insurance. In the late 1680s, Edward Lloyd opened a coffeehouse that became a popular haunt of ship owners, merchants, and ships' captains, and thereby a reliable source of the latest shipping news. It became the meeting place for parties wishing to insure cargoes and ships, and those willing to underwrite such ventures. Today, Lloyd's of London remains one of the world's leading specialty insurance companies.

- Similar to insurance businesses, banks and other financial institutions have been dealing with risks in all aspects of their businesses throughout the years. The first banks were probably the religious temples of the ancient world. There are records of loans from the 18th century B.C. in Babylon that were made by temple priests to merchants. The Greek and Roman empires helped evolve banking practices surrounding loans, deposits, and currency exchange. Banks use concepts of risk to determine the rates they can charge for loans based on their own cost of funds and the probabilities of default. Financial institutions also have developed financial instruments, such as options, swaps, and derivative instruments, that create value based on the probabilities of uncertain future events.[1]

Risk

The possibility that an event will occur and adversely affect the achievement of objectives.

Definitions of Risk

The English language word risk comes from the Italian word "risicare," which means "to dare: a choice under uncertain conditions (rather than fate)."[2] The key to this definition is the notion of uncertainty. Expanding on that definition, The Committee of Sponsoring Organizations of the Treadway Commission (COSO) defines risk as " . . . the possibility that an event will occur and adversely affect the achievement of an objective."[3]

Embedded in COSO's definition of risk are certain key, fundamental points that must be understood before proceeding to the concepts of risk management:

- Risk begins with strategy formulation and objective setting. An organization is in business to achieve particular strategies and objectives, and risks represent the barriers to successfully achieving those objectives. Therefore, because each organization has somewhat different strategies and objectives, they also will face different types of risks.
- Risk does not represent a single point estimate (for example, the most likely outcome). Rather, it represents a range of possible outcomes. Because many different outcomes are possible, the concept of a range is what creates uncertainty when understanding and evaluating risks.
- Risks may relate to preventing bad things from happening (risk mitigation), or failing to ensure good things happen (that is, exploiting or pursuing opportunities). Most people focus on preventing bad outcomes — for example, a hazard that needs to be mitigated or eliminated. While many risks do, in fact, present a threat to an organization, failure to achieve positive outcomes also may create a barrier to the achievement of an objective and is also a risk.

Opportunity

The possibility that an event will occur and positively affect the achievement of objectives.

Business Risk

Risks that are specifically associated with organizations conducting a form of business: uncertainties regarding threats to the achievement of business objectives.

- Risks are inherent in all aspects of life — that is, wherever uncertainty exists, one or more risks exist. The examples provided in the previous section on the history of risk illustrate how the understanding of risk has evolved. Those risks specifically associated with organizations conducting a form of business are commonly referred to as business risks. This can be thought of in quite simple terms: uncertainties regarding threats to the achievement of business objectives are considered business risks.

Using this definition of risk, it becomes apparent that there are an extensive number of risks that organizations face as they try to execute their strategies and achieve their objectives. This extensiveness can be somewhat overwhelming, which brings greater appreciation for the need to have a process to effectively understand and manage risks across an organization. This need can be addressed through enterprise risk management (ERM).

COSO ERM Framework

In the United States, COSO published its *Enterprise Risk Management – Integrated Framework* (COSO ERM, or ERM framework) in 2004. COSO identified a need for a robust framework to help companies effectively identify, assess, and manage risk. The resulting framework expanded on the previously issued *Internal Control – Integrated Framework*, incorporating all key aspects of that framework in the broader ERM framework.

COSO defines ERM as:

> A process, effected by an entity's board of directors, management and other personnel, applied in strategy setting and across the enterprise, designed to identify potential events that may affect the entity, and manage risk to be within its risk appetite, to provide reasonable assurance regarding the achievement of entity objectives.[4]

Enterprise Risk Management

The process conducted by management to understand and deal with uncertainties (that is, risks and opportunities) that could affect the organization's ability to achieve its objectives.

COSO explains that this definition reflects certain fundamental concepts. ERM is:

- A process that is ongoing and flows throughout an organization.
- Effected by people (that is, employees) at every level of an organization.
- Applied when setting an organization's strategy.
- Applied across the organization, at every level and unit.
- Focused on taking an entity-level portfolio view of risk.
- Designed to identify potential events that, if they occur, will affect the organization.
- A means to enable the management of risks within an organization's risk appetite.
- Able to provide reasonable assurance to an organization's management and board of directors.
- Geared toward achievement of objectives in one or more separate but overlapping categories.

The ERM framework was graphically depicted as a three-dimensional matrix, in the form of a cube, recreated in Exhibit 4-2. This depiction shows the interrelationship between the types of objectives (vertical

COSO ENTERPRISE RISK MANAGEMENT CUBE

EXHIBIT 4-2

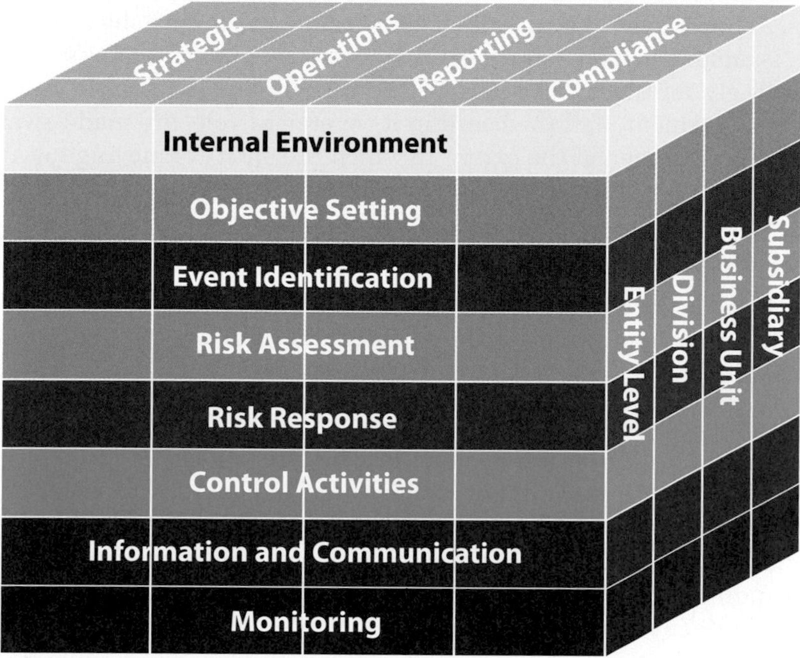

Copyright 2004 by The Committee of Sponsoring Organizations of the Treadway Commission. Reproduced with permission from the American Institute of Certified Public Accountants acting as authorized copyright administrator for COSO.

columns across the top of the cube), the components of ERM (horizontal rows), and an organization's business structure (side of the cube). It portrays the ability to focus on the entirety of an organization's ERM, or by objective type, component, organizational unit, or any subset thereof.

Types of Objectives

When an organization establishes its mission and vision, management also establishes a variety of objectives that support the mission and are aligned and cascade throughout the organization. As discussed in Chapter 1, "Introduction to Internal Auditing," the ERM framework is geared to achieving an organization's objectives in the following four categories:

- **Strategic Objectives.** High-level goals that are aligned with and support the organization's mission.
- **Operations Objectives.** Broad goals promoting the effective and efficient use of resources.
- **Reporting Objectives.** Goals focusing on the reliability of reporting (both external and internal).
- **Compliance Objectives.** Goals enforcing compliance with applicable laws and regulations.

This categorization of an organization's objectives supports a focus on separate but equally important aspects of ERM. These distinct but overlapping categories of objectives — a particular objective can fall into more than one category — address different organizational needs and may be under the direct responsibility of different members of senior management.

Objectives

What an entity desires to achieve. When referring to what an organization wants to achieve, these are called business objectives, and may be classified as strategic, operations, reporting, and compliance.

COSO states the following about achievement of objectives: "Because objectives relating to reliability of reporting and compliance with laws and regulations are within the entity's control, enterprise risk management can be expected to provide reasonable assurance of achieving those objectives. Achievement of strategic objectives and operations objectives, however, is subject to external events not always within the entity's control; accordingly, for these objectives, [ERM] can provide reasonable assurance that management, and the board in its oversight role, are made aware, in a timely manner, of the extent to which the entity is moving toward achievement of the objectives."[5]

Components of ERM

COSO ERM consists of eight interrelated components. These are derived from the way management runs an enterprise and are integrated with the management process. These components are:

- **Internal Environment.** "Management sets a philosophy regarding risk and establishes a risk appetite. The internal environment encompasses the tone of an organization, and sets the basis for how risk and control are viewed and addressed by an entity's people. The core of any business is its people — their individual attributes, including integrity, ethical values, and competence — and the environment in which they operate."[6]

  COSO goes on to state that "The internal environment is the basis for all other components of ERM, providing discipline and structure. It influences how strategies and objectives are established, business activities are structured, and risks are identified, assessed, and acted upon. It also influences the design and functioning of control activities, information and communication systems, and monitoring activities."[7]

  The internal environment is influenced by an organization's history and culture. It comprises many elements, including the following, which COSO discusses in greater detail:

  - **Risk management philosophy,** which represents a set of shared beliefs and attitudes characterizing how the organization considers risk in everything it does.
  - **Risk appetite,** which represents the amount of risk, on a broad level, an organization is willing to accept.
  - **Board of directors,** which provides the structure, experience, independence, and oversight role played by the organization's primary governing body.
  - **Integrity and ethical values,** which reflect the preferences, standards of behavior, and style.
  - **Commitment to competence,** including the knowledge and skills needed to perform assigned tasks.
  - **Organizational structure,** as characterized by the framework to plan, execute, control, and monitor activities.
  - **Assignment of authority and responsibility**, reflecting the degree to which individuals and teams are authorized and encouraged to use initiative to address issues and solve problems, as well as limits to their authority.

Risk Management Philosophy

Set of shared beliefs and attitudes characterizing how the organization considers risk in everything it does.

Risk Appetite

The amount of risk, on a broad level, an organization is willing to accept in pursuit of its business objectives.

- **Human resource standards,** composed of the practices pertaining to hiring, orienting, training, evaluating, counseling, promoting, compensating, and taking remedial actions.

- **Objective Setting.** "Objectives are set at the strategic level, establishing a basis for operations, reporting, and compliance objectives. Every entity faces a variety of risks from external and internal sources, and a precondition to effective event identification, risk assessment, and risk response is establishment of objectives."[8]

  Objectives must be aligned with the organization's risk appetite, which drives risk tolerance levels for the organization. Risk tolerances are the acceptable levels of size and variation relative to the achievement of objectives, and must align with the organization's risk appetite.

Risk Tolerance

The acceptable levels of risk size and variation relative to the achievement of objectives, which must align with the organization's risk appetite.

- **Event Identification.** "Management identifies potential events that, if they occur, will affect the entity, and determines whether these events represent opportunities or whether they might adversely affect the entity's ability to successfully implement strategy and achieve objectives. Events with negative impact represent risks, which require management's assessment and response. Events with positive impact represent opportunities, which management channels back into the strategy and objective-setting processes. When identifying events, management considers a variety of internal and external factors that may give rise to risks and opportunities, in the context of the full risk scope of the organization."[9]

  COSO cites external factors, along with examples of related events, including:

  - **Economic events,** such as price movements, capital availability, or lower barriers to competitive entry.
  - **Natural environment events,** such as flood, fire, earthquake, or weather-related events.
  - **Political events,** such as election of government officials with new political agendas, or enactment of new laws and regulations.
  - **Social events,** such as changing demographics, social mores, family structures, or work/life priorities.
  - **Technological events,** such as new means of electronic commerce, storage, or processing.[10]

  COSO also cites internal factors, along with examples of related events, including:

  - **Infrastructure factors,** such as increasing capital allocation to preventive maintenance or call center support.
  - **Personnel factors,** such as workplace accidents, fraudulent activities, or labor agreement expiration.
  - **Process factors,** such as process modifications, process execution errors, or outsourcing decisions.
  - **Technology factors,** such as increasing resources to handle volume volatility, security breaches, or systems downtime.[11]

Inherent Risk

The combination of internal and external risk factors in their pure, uncontrolled state, or, the gross risk that exists, assuming there are no internal controls in place.

Residual Risk

The portion of inherent risk that remains after management executes its risk responses (sometimes referred to as net risk).

- **Risk Assessment.** "Risk assessment allows an entity to consider the extent to which potential events have an impact on achievement of objectives. Management assesses events from two perspectives — likelihood and impact — and normally uses a combination of qualitative and quantitative methods. The positive and negative impacts of potential events should be examined, individually or by category, across the entity. Risks are assessed on both an inherent and residual basis."[12]

  In simplest terms, inherent risk represents the "gross" risk while residual risk is the "net" risk. Inherent risk is the risk to an organization in the absence of any actions management might take to alter either the risk's likelihood or impact. These risks may be inherent in the organization's business model or relate to decisions management has made regarding how to operate and execute that business model. Residual risk is the risk that remains after management's response to the risk (for example, to reduce or transfer the risk). Risk assessment should be applied first to inherent risks. Once the risk responses have been developed, management then considers residual risk.

  There are many different ways to assess the impact and likelihood of risks, ranging from obtaining the overall judgments and perspectives of individuals, to benchmarking against other companies, to running sophisticated probabilistic models. Regardless of which option, or combination of options, is used, it is important that the assessment consider the relationships between risks. That is, the realistic worst-case impact and likelihood of risk events may be dependent on how combinations of risks interrelate. Assessing each risk on its own may overlook realistic worst-case scenarios that the organization needs to consider.

- **Risk Response.** "Having assessed relevant risks, management determines how it will respond. Responses include risk avoidance, reduction, sharing, and acceptance. In considering its response, management assesses the effect on risk likelihood and impact, as well as costs and benefits, selecting a response that brings residual risk within desired risk tolerances. Management identifies any opportunities that might be available, and takes an entity-wide, or portfolio, view of risk, determining whether overall residual risk is within the entity's risk appetite."[13]

  As indicated, risk responses fall within four categories, which COSO defines as:

  - **Avoidance.** Exiting or divesting of the activities giving rise to the risk. Risk avoidance may involve exiting a product line, declining expansion to a new geographical market, or selling a division.
  - **Reduction.** Action is taken to reduce risk likelihood or impact, or both. This typically involves any of a myriad of everyday business decisions [such as implementing controls].
  - **Sharing.** Reducing risk likelihood or impact by transferring or otherwise sharing a portion of the risk. Common techniques include purchasing insurance products, engaging in hedging transactions, or outsourcing an activity.

- **Acceptance.** No action is taken to affect risk likelihood or impact. [In effect, the organization is willing to accept the risk at the current level rather than spend valuable resources deploying one of the other risk response options.][14]

It is important to consider the portfolio, or aggregated, effect of risk responses. In some cases, a certain risk response may not appear to be the best or most cost-effective response for a given risk. However, if that risk response helps manage other risks, the benefit to the organization may justify the selection of that particular option. By looking at risks from a portfolio perspective, management can best ensure that risks are optimally managed within the organization's established risk appetite.

- **Control Activities.** "Control activities are the policies and procedures that help ensure that management's risk responses are carried out. Control activities occur throughout the organization, at all levels and in all functions."[15]

While control activities are most commonly associated with risk reduction strategies, certain control activities also may be necessary when executing one of the other risk responses. They are classified in a variety of ways and include a range of activities that may be preventive or detective, manual or automated, and at the process level or the management level. Refer to Chapter 6, "Internal Control," for a further discussion of the different types of controls. Examples of commonly used control activities provided by COSO include:

  - **Top-level reviews** are controls that are typically executed at the entity level, such as performance against budget reviews, updated forecasts, monitoring of competitor actions, or cost containment initiatives.
  - **Direct functional or activity management** are controls executed by managers running specific functions or activities, such as reviewing performance reports for the area or overseeing the execution of detailed level controls (for example, reconciliations).
  - **Information processing controls** are designed to check the accuracy, completeness, and authorization of transactions. Additionally, this area includes general infrastructure controls, such as physical and logical security; controls over systems implementation, upgrades, or modifications; disaster recovery; and systems operations controls.
  - **Physical controls** include (1) physical counts of cash, securities, inventories, equipment, or other fixed assets, and comparing those counts with amounts recorded in the books and records, and (2) physical barriers or restrictions such as fences and locks.
  - **Performance indicators** involve analyzing and following up on deviations from expected or targeted performance norms.
  - **Segregation of duties** involves separating the duties of different people to reduce the risk of error or fraud. For example, individuals who establish a new vendor in the system should not be able to authorize a transaction to pay that vendor.[16]

- **Information and Communication.** "Pertinent information is identified, captured, and communicated in a form and time frame

Control

Any action taken by management, the board, and other parties to manage risk and increase the likelihood that established objectives and goals will be achieved.

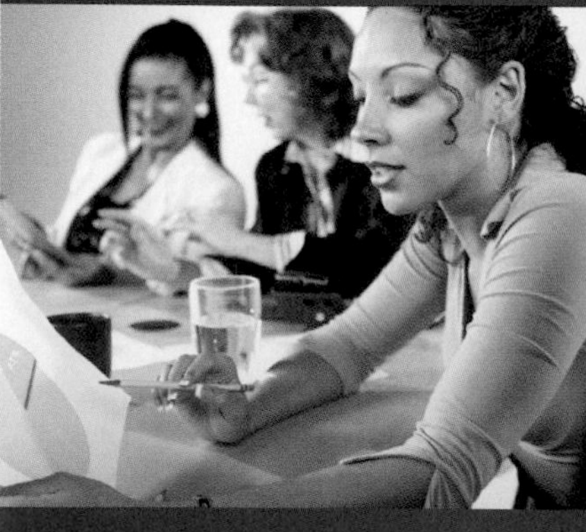

Monitoring

A process that assesses the presence and functioning of governance, risk management, and control over time. There are three types of monitoring:

- **Ongoing**
- **Separate evaluation**
- **Combination**

that enable people to carry out their responsibilities."[17] Information must be in sufficient depth consistent with an organization's need to identify, assess, and respond to risk, and remain within its various risk tolerance levels. Information systems process internally and externally generated data into information that is useful for managing risks. Finally, information must be of sufficient quality to support decision-making. COSO notes that information must be:

- Appropriate and at the right level of detail.
- Timely and available when needed.
- Current, reflecting the most recent financial or operational information.
- Accurate and reliable.
- Accessible to those who need it.

COSO goes on to state "Effective communication also occurs, flowing down, across, and up the organization. All personnel receive a clear message from top management that [ERM] responsibilities must be taken seriously. They understand their own role in [ERM], as well as how individual activities relate to the work of others. They must have a means of communicating significant information upstream. There is also effective communication with external parties, such as customers, suppliers, regulators, and shareholders."[18]

There are many different forms of communication, such as policy manuals, memoranda, e-mails, Internet and intranet sites, bulletin board notices, and video messages. When messages are transmitted orally, tone of voice and body language may influence how messages are interpreted.

- **Monitoring.** "Enterprise risk management is monitored — assessing the presence and functioning of its components over time."[19] This type of downstream control can be accomplished through ongoing monitoring activities, separate evaluations, or a combination of the two. Ongoing monitoring will generally occur in the normal course of day-to-day management activities. The nature, scope, and frequency of separate evaluations will depend primarily on management's assessment of the underlying risks and the effectiveness of existing ongoing monitoring procedures. Deficiencies that are noted from these monitoring activities are reported upstream, with the most serious matters reported to senior management and the board.

  In addition to management's ongoing monitoring activities, other individuals may be involved in the monitoring process. For example, individuals responsible for the performance of key activities may perform self-assessments to evaluate the effectiveness of their risk management activities. Internal auditors typically are part of the overall monitoring system, whereby the results of individual audits help assess the effectiveness of the related risk management activities. In certain circumstances, the work performed by the independent outside auditors may also influence management's assessment of ongoing risk management effectiveness.

In essence, the components of ERM provide a context for answering some common, everyday questions that summarize risk management thinking (as linked to the ERM framework):

1. What are we trying to accomplish (what are our objectives)?

2. What could stop us from accomplishing them (what are the risks, how bad could they be, and how likely are they to occur)?
3. What options do we have to make sure those things do not happen (what are the risk management strategies, that is, responses)?
4. Do we have the ability to execute those options (have we designed and executed control activities to carry out the risk management strategies)?
5. How will we know that we have accomplished what we wanted to accomplish (does the information exist to evidence success, and can we monitor performance to verify that success)?

These five questions apply to more than just risk management in the business world. They can apply to almost any objective or decision in life. Answering these questions instills a risk management-based type of thinking and discipline that aligns with COSO ERM and other risk management frameworks.

Roles and Responsibilities in ERM

The board of directors, management, risk officers, financial officers, internal auditors, and indeed, every individual within an organization contribute to effective ERM. The roles and responsibilities of each of these groups align with those discussed in Chapter 3, "Governance."

- **Board of Directors.** The board provides oversight and direction to an organization's management. The board can play a role in strategy setting, formulating high-level objectives, broad-based resource allocation, and shaping the ethical environment. COSO points out that the board provides oversight with regard to ERM by:
    - Knowing the extent to which management has established effective ERM in an organization.
    - Being aware of and concurring with the organization's risk appetite.
    - Reviewing the organization's portfolio view of risk and considering it against the organization's risk appetite.
    - Being apprised of the most significant risks and whether management is responding appropriately.[20]

  The board is also part of the internal environment component of ERM and must have the requisite composition and focus for ERM to be effective. Typically, the board will exercise its responsibilities through its various committees, such as an audit committee and a nominating and governance committee.

- **Management.** Management is responsible for all activities of an organization, including ERM. However, these responsibilities will vary, depending on the level in the organization and the organization's characteristics.

  The CEO is ultimately responsible for the effectiveness and success of ERM. One of the most important aspects of this responsibility is ensuring that a positive internal environment exists. The CEO sets the tone at the top, influences the composition and conduct of the board, provides leadership and direction to senior managers, and monitors the organization's overall risk activities in relation to its risk appetite. When evolving circumstances, emerging risks, strategy implementation, or anticipated actions indicate potential misalignment with risk appetite, the CEO will take the necessary actions to reestablish alignment.

Senior managers in charge of the various organizational units have responsibility for managing risks related to their specific units' objectives. They convert the organization's overall strategy into ongoing operations activities, identify potential risk events, assess the related risks, and implement responses to manage those risks. Managers guide the application of the organization's ERM components relative to and within their spheres of responsibility, ensuring the application of those components is consistent with the related risk tolerances. They assign responsibility for specific ERM procedures to managers of the functional processes. As a result, these managers usually play a more active role in devising and executing particular risk procedures that address the unit's objectives, such as techniques for event identification and risk assessment, and in determining specific risk responses (that is, risk management strategies), for example, developing policies and procedures for purchasing goods or accepting new customers.

Chief Risk Officer

A senior management position established by many companies that acts as the centralized coordinating point to facilitate risk management activities.

Staff functions, such as accounting, human resources, compliance, or legal, also have important supporting roles in designing and executing effective ERM practices. These functions may design and implement programs that help manage certain key risks across the entire organization.

- **Risk Officer.** Some organizations have established a separate senior management position to act as the centralized coordinating point to facilitate ERM. A risk officer — referred to in many organizations as a chief risk officer (CRO) — typically operates in a staff function, working with other managers in establishing ERM in their areas of responsibility. The risk officer has the resources to help effect ERM across subsidiaries, businesses, departments, functions, and activities. This individual may have responsibility for monitoring risk management progress and assisting other managers in reporting relevant risk information up, down, and across the organization.

  COSO outlines the following specific responsibilities of a CRO:

  - Establishing [ERM] policies, including defining roles and responsibilities and participating in setting goals for implementation.
  - Framing authority and accountability for [ERM] in business units.
  - Promoting [ERM] competence throughout the entity, including facilitating development of technical [ERM} expertise and helping managers align risk responses with the entity's risk tolerances and developing appropriate controls.
  - Guiding integration of [ERM] with other business planning and management activities.
  - Establishing a common risk management language that includes measures around likelihood and impact, and common risk categories.

- Facilitating managers' development of reporting protocols, including quantitative and qualitative thresholds, and monitoring the reporting process.
- Reporting to the chief executive on progress and outliers and recommending action as needed.[21]

- **Financial Executives.** Finance and accounting executives and their staffs are responsible for activities that cut across the organization. These executives often are involved in developing organization-wide budgets and plans, and tracking and analyzing performance from an operations, compliance, and reporting perspective. They play an important role in preventing and detecting fraudulent reporting, and influence the design, implementation, and monitoring of the organization's internal control over financial reporting and the supporting systems.
- **Internal Auditors.** The internal audit function plays an important role in evaluating the effectiveness of — and recommending improvements to — ERM. The IIA's *International Standards for the Professional Practice of Internal Auditing (Standards)* specify that the scope of the internal audit function should encompass governance, risk management, and control systems. This includes evaluating the reliability of reporting, effectiveness and efficiency of operations, and compliance with laws and regulations. In carrying out these responsibilities, the internal audit function assists management and the board by examining, evaluating, reporting on, and recommending improvements to the adequacy and effectiveness of the organization's ERM.

- **Other Individuals in the Organization.** In reality, ERM is the responsibility of everyone in an organization and therefore should be an integral part of everyone's job description, both explicitly and implicitly. This is important because:
  - While not every individual may be considered a risk owner per se, virtually all individuals play some role in effecting ERM, ranging from producing information used in identifying or assessing risks, to implementing the strategies and actions needed to manage those risks.
  - All individuals are responsible for supporting the information and communication flows that are an integral part of and inherent in ERM.
- **Independent Outside Auditors.** An organization's independent outside auditors can provide both management and the board of directors an informed, independent, and objective risk management perspective that can contribute to an organization's achievement of its external financial reporting and other objectives. Findings from their audits may relate to risk management deficiencies, analytical information, and other recommendations for improvement that can provide management with valuable information to enhance its risk management program.
- **Legislators and Regulators.** Legislators and regulators can affect the ERM approach of many organizations, either through requirements to establish risk management mechanisms or systems of internal controls (for example, the U.S. Sarbanes-Oxley Act of 2002) or

through examinations of particular entities (for example, by federal and state bank examiners). Legislators and regulators may establish rules that provide the impetus for management to ensure that risk management and control systems meet certain minimum statutory and regulatory requirements. Also, they may conduct regulatory examinations that provide information useful to the organization in applying ERM, and recommendations to management regarding needed improvements.

- **Other External Parties.** Finally, other outside stakeholders may impact an organization's ERM activities:
  - Customers, vendors, business partners, and others who conduct business with an organization are an important source of information used in ERM.
  - Creditors can provide oversight or direction influencing how organizations achieve their objectives. For example, debt covenants may require organizations to monitor and report information differently than they otherwise might.
  - Financial analysts, rating agencies, news media, and other external parties can influence risk management activities. Their investigative and monitoring activities can provide insights on how others perceive the organization's performance, industry and economic risks, innovative operating or financing strategies, and industry trends. Management must consider the insights and observations of these parties and, if necessary, adjust the corresponding risk management activities.
  - Providers of outsourced services are becoming a more prevalent way for organizations to delegate their day-to-day management of certain noncore functions. The external parties discussed above may directly influence an organization's ERM activities; however, using outside service providers may result in a different set of risks and responses than if the organization did not outsource any functions. Although external parties may execute activities on behalf of the organization, management cannot abdicate its responsibility to manage the associated risks and should establish a program to monitor outsourced activities. Refer to Chapter 5, "Business Processes and Risks," where business process outsourcing is discussed in greater detail.

Business Process Outsourcing

The act of transferring some of an organization's business processes to an outside provider to achieve cost reductions, operating effectiveness, or operating efficiency while improving service quality.

Formal ERM is not yet embedded in the business practices of most organizations, but there is a growing trend to either implement ERM or at least practice many of its key principles. COSO identifies the following potential ERM value drivers:

- Aligning risk appetite and strategy.
- Enhancing risk response decisions.
- Reducing operational surprises and losses.
- Identifying and managing cross-enterprise risks.
- Providing integrated responses to multiple risks.
- Seizing opportunities.
- Improving deployment of capital.[22]

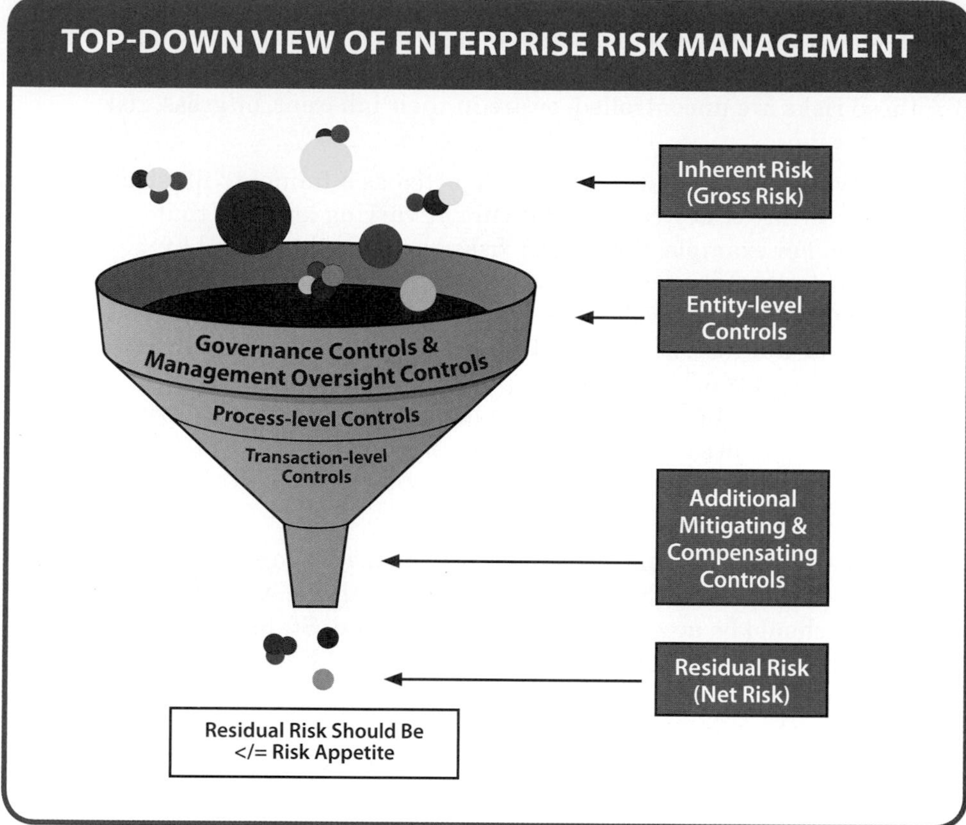

EXHIBIT 4-3

Other Frameworks

While COSO ERM is widely recognized within the United States, other countries have developed their own frameworks. As indicated in Appendix 3-B, "Summary of Governance and Risk Management Codes From Other Countries," which can be found at the end of Chapter 3, "Governance," business conditions and regulatory initiatives have resulted in a variety of codes and regulations to meet the needs of the local capital markets and businesses. While all of these frameworks are fundamentally similar to COSO ERM, each has unique characteristics that readers are encouraged to study. Certain frameworks will prove to be more intuitive to some individuals than to others.

Entity-level Controls

Controls that operate across an entire entity and, as such, are not bound by, or associated with, individual processes.

A Top-down View of Risk

Exhibit 4-3 provides a way of summarizing the role of enterprise risk management. It uses a funnel metaphor to depict the top-down role ERM plays in helping organizations reduce their key risks to acceptable levels. This exhibit is also depicted in Case Study 1, "Auditing Entity-level Controls," which accompanies this textbook. The key points to understand from this illustration are discussed in greater detail in that case study, but are summarized as follows:

- Every organization faces a variety of risks, depending on their business objectives. Some of these business objectives may describe the desired state of operation brought about by an effective system of internal controls.
- Risks that impact an organization's ability to achieve its business objectives are shown in Exhibit 4-3 as colored balls of varying sizes. This reflects the fact that some risks will have greater impact than others. Additionally, some risks are clustered together, representing

Compensating Control

An activity that, if key controls do not fully operate effectively, may help to reduce the related risk. A compensating control will not, by itself, reduce risk to an acceptable level.

the fact that while the risks individually may not be serious, when related risks are aggregated they can become more serious. Initially, these risks are uncontrolled, or are in their inherent, or gross, risk state.

- The system of internal controls is depicted as a funnel to illustrate the "filtering" of key risks that occurs at varying levels of that system. For example, the largest risks should be mitigated by the entity-level controls at the top of the funnel. Those that pass through the entity-level filters are next subjected to the process-level and transaction-level controls. As discussed in Chapter 6, "Internal Control," controls may be considered key or secondary, depending on whether they reduce the risk associated with critical objectives. Additionally, in some cases, management may deploy additional mitigating and compensating controls to further limit the impact of the risks.
- If the system of internal controls is designed adequately and operates effectively, those risks that make it all the way through the funnel should be acceptable to the organization. Stated another way, the overall residual, or net, risk will not exceed the organization's risk appetite.

THE ROLE OF THE INTERNAL AUDIT FUNCTION IN ERM

IIA Standard 2120: Risk Management states "The internal audit activity must evaluate the effectiveness and contribute to the improvement of risk management processes." The skill sets and broad experience levels that internal auditors possess position them to play a valuable role in ERM. In fact, considering the broad purview of most internal audit functions, as well as their role in the overall monitoring process, failure to involve the internal audit function in some manner would likely result in the ERM initiative falling short of expectations. The following discussion focuses on the role that the internal audit function can play in ERM, depending on whether or not the organization is formally implementing ERM.

Organizations with ERM

The IIA's International Professional Practices Framework includes a position paper titled *The Role of Internal Auditing in Enterprise-wide Risk Management*, which outlines several opportunities for internal auditors to get involved. In its summary, the paper states, "Internal auditing's core role with regard to ERM is to provide objective assurance to the board on the effectiveness of an organization's ERM activities to help ensure key business risks are being managed appropriately and that the system of internal control[s] is operating effectively."[23]

The position paper depicts the various roles that the internal audit function should or should not undertake in a fan- or dial-shaped diagram, as shown in Exhibit 4-4. The following types of roles are discussed in the paper.

Core Internal Audit Roles. These roles, which are on the left of the dial in the green section in Exhibit 4-4, represent assurance activities. They are part of the wider objective of providing assurance on risk management activities. These activities include:

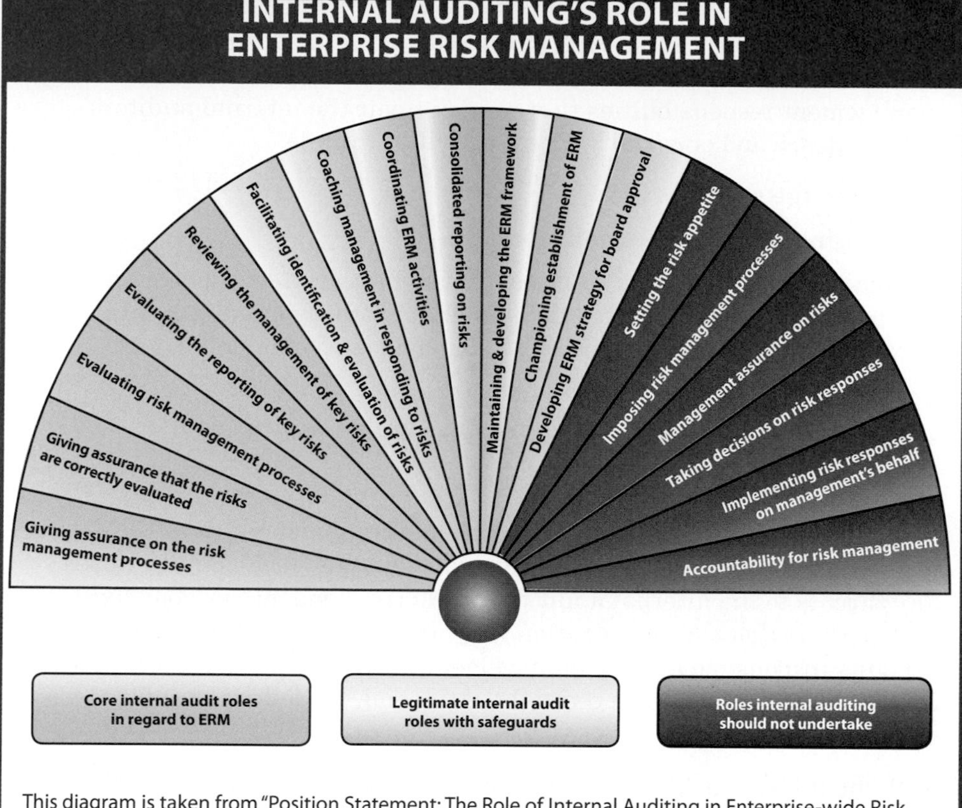

This diagram is taken from "Position Statement: The Role of Internal Auditing in Enterprise-wide Risk Management," reproduced with the permission of The Institute of Internal Auditors – United Kingdom and Ireland. For the full statement, visit www.iia.org.uk. © The Institute of Internal Auditors – UK and Ireland Ltd., July 2004.

EXHIBIT 4-4

- Giving assurance on the risk management processes.
- Giving assurance that risks are correctly evaluated.
- Evaluating risk management processes.
- Evaluating the reporting of key risks.
- Reviewing the management of key risks.[24]

Legitimate Internal Audit Roles with Safeguards. These roles represent consulting services that may improve the organization's governance, risk management, and control processes. The extent of such services will depend on the other resources available to the board and on the risk maturity of the organization. The consulting roles are shown in the middle of the dial in the yellow section in Exhibit 4-4. In general, the further to the right of the dial that the internal audit function ventures, the greater the safeguards that are required to ensure that its independence and objectivity are maintained. These activities include:

- Facilitating identification and evaluation of risks.
- Coaching management in responding to risks.
- Coordinating ERM activities.
- Consolidating the reporting on risks.
- Maintaining and developing the ERM framework.
- Championing establishment of ERM.
- Developing ERM strategy for board approval.[25]

Consulting Services

Advisory and related services, the nature and scope of which are agreed to with the customer, and which are intended to improve an organization's governance, risk management, and control processes without the internal auditor assuming management responsibility.

Roles Internal Auditing Should Not Undertake. These roles, which are depicted on the right of the dial in the red section in Exhibit 4-4, should not be undertaken by the internal audit function as the roles represent management responsibilities that would impair the internal auditors' independence and objectivity. These activities include:

- Setting the risk appetite.
- Imposing risk management processes.
- Management assurance on risks [that is, being the sole source for management's assurance that risks are effectively managed — this would be considered performing a management function].
- Taking [making] decisions on risk responses.
- Implementing risk responses on management's behalf.
- Accountability for risk management.[26]

When determining the role the internal audit function plays in ERM, the chief audit executive (CAE) must evaluate whether each activity raises any threats to the internal audit function's independence or objectivity. It is important that the organization fully understands that management remains responsible for risk management. As the internal audit function extends its roles further to the right of the dial, the following safeguards should be put in place:

- It should be clear that management remains responsible for risk management.
- The nature of the internal audit function's responsibilities should be documented in the internal audit charter and approved by the audit committee.
- The internal audit function cannot manage any of the risks on behalf of management.
- The internal audit function should provide advice, challenge, and support to management's decision-making, as opposed to making risk management decisions itself.
- The internal audit function cannot give objective assurance on any part of the ERM framework for which it is responsible. Such assurance should be provided by other suitably qualified parties, whether internal or external to the organization.
- Any work beyond the assurance activities should be recognized as a consulting engagement, and the implementation standards related to such engagements should be followed.[27]

Organizations with Internal Audit-driven ERM

Practice Advisory 2120-1: Assessing the Adequacy of Risk Management Processes states that "Management and the board are responsible for their organization's risk management and control processes. However, internal auditors acting in a consulting role can assist the organization in identifying, evaluating, and implementing risk management methodologies and controls to address those risks." When an organization has not established a risk management process, the practice advisory offers the following guidance:

> In situations where the organization does not have formal risk management processes, the CAE formally discusses with

management and the audit committee their obligations to understand, manage, and monitor risks within the organization and the need to satisfy themselves that there are processes operating within the organization, even if informal, that provide the appropriate level of visibility into the key risks and how they are being managed and monitored.

The CAE is to obtain an understanding of senior management's and the board's expectations of the internal audit activity in the organization's risk management process. This understanding is then codified in the charters of the internal audit activity and the [audit committee]. Internal auditing's responsibilities are to be coordinated between all groups and individuals within the organization's risk management process.

Ultimately, it is the role of senior management and the board to determine the role of internal auditing in the risk management process. Their view on internal auditing's role is likely to be determined by factors such as the culture of the organization, ability of the internal audit staff, and local conditions and customs of the country. However, taking on management's responsibility regarding the risk management process and the potential threat to the internal audit activity's independence requires a full discussion and board approval.

Impairment to Independence or Objectivity

The introduction of threats that may result in a substantial limitation, or the appearance of a substantial limitation, to the internal auditor's ability to perform an engagement without bias or interference.

This guidance reinforces the importance of bringing the lack of a risk management process to management's attention along with suggestions for establishing such a process. If requested, internal auditors can play a proactive role in assisting with the initial establishment of a risk management process for the organization. A more proactive role supplements traditional assurance activities with a consultative approach to improving fundamental processes. If such assistance exceeds normal assurance and consulting activities conducted by internal auditors, independence could be impaired. In these situations, internal auditors should comply with the disclosure requirements of the *Standards*.

THE IMPACT OF ERM ON INTERNAL AUDIT ASSURANCE

IIA Standard 2010: Planning states, "The chief audit executive must establish risk-based plans to determine the priorities of the internal audit activity, consistent with the organization's goals." Supporting this standard, Practice Advisory 2010-1: Linking the Audit Plan to Risk and Exposures provides guidance to CAEs when developing the annual internal audit plan. This practice advisory offers the following relative to linking the audit plan to risk and exposures:

Audit Universe

A compilation of the subsidiaries, business units, departments, groups, processes, or other established subdivisions of an organization that exist to manage one or more business risks.

1. In developing the internal audit activity's audit plan, many CAEs find it useful to first develop or update the audit universe . . . The CAE may obtain input on the audit universe from senior management and the board.
2. The audit universe can include components from the organization's strategic plan. By incorporating components of the organization's strategic plan, the audit universe will consider and reflect the overall business' objectives. Strategic plans also likely reflect the organization's attitude toward risk and the degree of difficulty to achieving planned objectives. The audit universe will normally be influenced by the results of the

risk management process. The organization's strategic plan considers the environment in which the organization operates. These same environmental factors would likely impact the audit universe and assessment of relative risk.

3. The CAE prepares the internal audit activity's audit plan based on the audit universe, input from senior management and the board, and an assessment of risk and exposures . . . and information to help them accomplish the organization's objectives, including an assessment of the effectiveness of management's risk management activities.
4. The audit universe and related audit plan are updated to reflect changes . . .
5. Audit work schedules are based on, among other factors, an assessment of risk and exposures . . . A variety of risk models exist to assist the CAE. Most risk models use risk factors such as impact, likelihood, materiality, asset liquidity, management competence, quality of and adherence to internal controls, degree of change or stability, timing and results of last audit engagement, complexity, and employee and government relations.

The points above, which apply at the level of establishing an annual internal audit plan, are also relevant at the engagement level. For example, the scope and approach to an individual project will be influenced by:

- How risks at the process level relate to the strategic plans and objectives of the organization. Process-level risks are discussed in greater detail in Chapter 13, "Conducting the Assurance Engagement."
- Changes in the process (for example, objectives, procedures, personnel, and performance measures) that have occurred over the last year or since the last audit of the process.
- Relevant risk model factors (for example, financial impact and asset liquidity).
- The impact and likelihood of the process-level risks.

In summary, management's approach to risk management, regardless of whether or not an organization has implemented ERM, will have a significant influence on both the internal audit charter and annual internal audit plan.

SUMMARY

As COSO defines it, "ERM is a process, effected by the board, management, and other personnel, applied in a strategy setting and across the enterprise, designed to identify potential events that may affect an organization's ability to achieve its objectives and manage risks to be within its risk appetite."[28]

An organization's objectives may be strategic, operational, reporting, or compliance oriented. ERM can be assessed across several components: internal environment, objective setting, event identification, risk assessment, risk response, control activities, information and communication, and monitoring.

The skill sets and broad experience levels that internal auditors possess position them to play a valuable role in ERM. The internal audit function may take on a variety of roles relative to ERM, some of which are consistent with the assurance activities as outlined in its charter, and some of which may be consulting services provided to assist the organization in improving its governance, risk management, and control processes. However, an internal audit function must establish appropriate safeguards to ensure that it does not take on roles that could be equivalent to management's responsibilities, thus impairing independence and objectivity of internal auditors.

An organization's strategic plan and inherent risks will have a direct and profound impact on both the charter of an internal audit function as well as its annual audit plan. Changes in management direction, objectives, emphasis, and focus also may impact the annual internal audit plan. The CAE must consider risks when prioritizing and scheduling the upcoming internal audit engagements.

Review Questions

1. What is the definition of risk used by COSO?
2. What are the four fundamental points embedded in COSO's definition of risk?
3. According to COSO, what are the fundamental concepts in its definition of enterprise risk management (ERM)?
4. What are the four types of objectives in COSO's *Enterprise Risk Management – Integrated Framework* (COSO ERM)? Include a description of each.
5. What are the eight components of COSO ERM?
6. What are the four categories of risk response?
7. What are typical responsibilities of a chief risk officer?
8. In Exhibit 4-3, why are some of the balls representing risks clustered together while some are not?
9. What roles in ERM should the internal audit function not undertake?
10. According to IIA Practice Advisory 2010-1: Linking the Audit Plan to Risk and Exposures, how should the internal audit function's audit plan be determined?

Multiple-choice Questions

Select the best answer for each of the following questions.

1. According to COSO ERM, all of the following are elements of an organization's internal environment except:
   a. Setting organizational objectives.
   b. Establishing risk appetite.
   c. Assigning authority and responsibility.
   d. Having predominantly independent directors on the board.
2. Which of the following external events will most likely impact a defense contractor that relies on large government contracts for its success?
   a. Economic event.
   b. Natural environment event.
   c. Political event.
   d. Social event.
3. Which of the following is not an example of a risk-sharing strategy?
   a. Outsourcing a noncore, high-risk area.
   b. Selling a nonstrategic business unit.
   c. Hedging against interest rate fluctuations.
   d. Buying an insurance policy to protect against adverse weather.

4. An organization tracks a website hosting anonymous blogs about its industry. Recently, anonymous posts have focused on potential legislation that could have a dramatic affect on this industry. Which of the following may create the greatest risk if this organization makes business decisions based on the information contained on this website?
   a. Appropriateness of the information.
   b. Timeliness of the information.
   c. Accessibility of the information.
   d. Accuracy and reliability of the information.

5. Who is responsible for implementing ERM?
   a. The chief financial officer.
   b. The chief audit executive.
   c. The chief compliance officer.
   d. Management throughout the organization.

6. Which of the following is not a potential value driver for implementing ERM?
   a. Financial results will improve in the short run.
   b. There will be fewer surprises from year to year.
   c. There will be better information available to make risk decisions.
   d. An organization's risk appetite can be aligned with strategic planning.

7. Which of the following is the best reason for the CAE to consider the organization's strategic plan in developing the annual internal audit plan?
   a. To emphasize the importance of the internal audit function to the organization.
   b. To ensure that the internal audit plan will be approved by senior management.
   c. To make recommendations to improve the strategic plan.
   d. To ensure that the internal audit plan supports the overall business objectives.

8. When senior management accepts a level of residual risk that the CAE believes is unacceptable to the organization, the CAE should:
   a. Report the unacceptable risk level immediately to the chair of the audit committee and the independent outside audit firm partner.
   b. Resign his or her position in the organization.
   c. Discuss the matter with knowledgeable members of senior management and, if not resolved, take it to the audit committee.
   d. Accept senior management's position because it establishes the risk appetite for the organization.

9. The CAE is asked to lead the enterprise risk assessment as part of an organization's implementation of ERM. Which of the following would not be relevant with respect to protecting the internal audit function's independence and the objectivity of its internal auditors?
   a. A cross-section of management is involved in assessing the impact and likelihood of each risk.
   b. Risk owners are assigned responsibility for each key risk.
   c. A member of senior management presents the results of the risk assessment to the board and communicates that it represents the organization's risk profile.
   d. The internal audit function obtains assistance from an outside consultant in the conduct of the formal risk assessment session.

10. An internal audit engagement was included in the approved internal audit plan. This is considered a moderately high-risk audit based on the internal audit function's risk model. It is currently on a two-year audit cycle. Which of the following will likely have the greatest impact on the scope and approach of the internal audit engagement?
   a. The area being audited involves the processing of a high volume of transactions.
   b. Certain components of the process are outsourced.
   c. A new system was implemented during the year, which changed how the transactions are processed.
   d. The total dollars processed in this area are material.

11. A manufacturing company has identified the following risk: "Failure of employees to conduct required quality control procedures may result in a high level of customer returns." To which type of objective does this risk most directly relate?
   a. Strategic.
   b. Operations.
   c. Reporting.
   d. Compliance.

12. A risk that a new competitor will significantly reduce the market share of an organization's product likely relates to which type of objective?
   a. Strategic.
   b. Operations.
   c. Reporting.
   d. Compliance.

Discussion Questions

1. Describe the difference between risk management philosophy, risk appetite, and risk tolerance. Give examples of each.

2. COSO ERM recognizes four categories of objectives (strategic, operations, reporting, and compliance). If an organization was unable to effectively manage the risks around the objectives in one of those categories, for which category would the impact on the organization be the greatest?

3. Define inherent risk and residual risk. Which of the two types of risk should have a greater impact on the annual internal audit plan?

4. For an organization that has not implemented ERM, describe steps the internal audit function can take to initiate an ERM program without impairing the function's independence and/or objectivity.

5. Risk assessment most commonly focuses on two criteria — impact and likelihood. As an organization's risk assessment process evolves, what other criteria might be valuable to consider and why?

6. One of your classmates, I. M. Motivated, consistently carries a very heavy class load. In addition to his already heavy class load, he is contemplating applying for an internal audit internship at a local company. Discuss the opportunities and risks that are relevant to his decision.

7. Recall the five "everyday questions" outlined earlier in this chapter that can be used to apply risk management thinking:
   a. What are we trying to accomplish (what are our objectives)?
   b. What could stop us from accomplishing them (what are the risks, how bad could they be, and how likely are they to occur)?
   c. What options do we have to make sure those things do not happen (what are the risk management strategies, that is, responses)?
   d. Do we have the ability to execute those options (have we designed and executed control activities to carry out the risk management strategies)?
   e. How will we know that we have accomplished what we wanted to accomplish (does the information exist to evidence success, and can we monitor performance to verify that success)?

   Think about the reasons you decided to take this course and answer each of those questions with a focus on achieving your desired level of success.

CASES

CASE 1 COSO provides a variety of guidance relevant to the internal audit profession. The purpose of this case is to become more familiar with COSO and its guidance. Visit www.coso.org and answer the following questions.

- **A.** Based on the statement on COSO's home page, what is the organization dedicated to?
- **B.** Who are the five sponsoring organizations?
- **C.** What type of internal control guidance does COSO offer? Much of this guidance is discussed in Chapter 6, "Internal Control."
- **D.** Download the COSO ERM executive summary (free of charge). According to the first page of this summary, what does enterprise risk management encompass?
- **E.** Download an article from the Resources page specified by your instructor. What did you find interesting about this article?

CASE 2 Your organization has implemented a robust ERM program similar to the one outlined in this chapter. The audit committee has asked you to assess the design adequacy and operating effectiveness of the program. Because the audit committee members are familiar with COSO ERM, they would like you to assess the veracity of the ERM program relative to the eight components of ERM. Based on this request, develop a list of steps you would follow to test each of the ERM components. Include at least two work steps for each component.

REFERENCES

[1]Bernstein, Peter L., *Against the Gods: The Remarkable Story of Risk* (Indianapolis, IN: John Wiley & Sons, 1996).

[2]Ibid.

[3]Committee of Sponsoring Organizations of the Treadway Commission, *Enterprise Risk Management – Integrated Framework* (Jersey City, NJ: American Institute of Certified Public Accountants, 2004), p. 16.

[4]Ibid.

[5]Ibid, p. 5.

[6]Ibid, p. 22.

[7]Ibid, p. 27.

[8]Ibid, p. 35.

[9]Ibid, p. 41.

[10]Ibid, p. 42.

[11]Ibid.

[12]Ibid, p. 49.

[13]Ibid, p. 55.

[14]Ibid.

[15]Ibid, p. 61.

[16]Ibid, pp. 62-63.

[17]Ibid, p. 67.

[18]Ibid.

[19]Ibid, p. 75.

[20]Ibid, p. 83.

[21]Ibid, p. 87.

[22]Ibid, pp. 14-15.

[23]*The Role of Internal Auditing in Enterprise-wide Risk Management*, International Professional Practices Framework Position Paper (Altamonte Springs, FL: The Institute of Internal Auditors, 2009).

[24]Ibid.

[25]Ibid.

[26]Ibid.

[27]Ibid.

[28]Committee of Sponsoring Organizations of the Treadway Commission, *Enterprise Risk Management – Integrated Framework* (Jersey City, NJ: American Institute of Certified Public Accountants, 2004), p. 16.

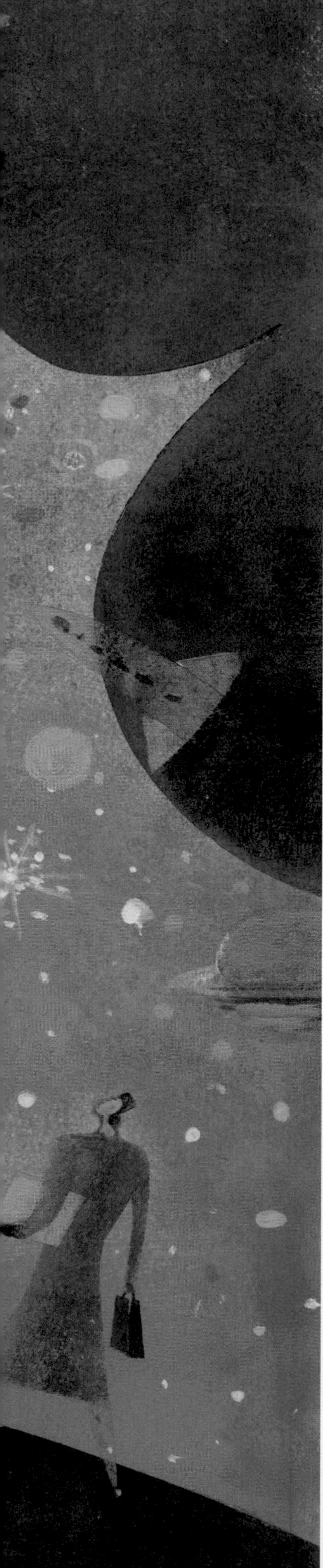

CHAPTER 5
BUSINESS PROCESSES AND RISKS

Learning Objectives

- Understand how organizations structure their activities to achieve their objectives.
- Identify key business processes in an organization.
- Obtain an understanding of a given business process and be able to document it.
- Understand basic types of business risks organizations face.
- Identify and assess the key risks to an organization's objectives and how they are linked to business processes.
- Develop an audit universe for an organization and determine an annual internal audit plan based on key business risks.
- Understand how to use risk assessment techniques within assurance engagements.
- Obtain an awareness of the new risks that arise when an organization outsources some of its key processes.

All of us have objectives in life. You may want to earn your degree by next May. You may want to get a job as an internal auditor when you graduate. You may want to get your master's in business administration degree before you are 30.

Consider a simple objective as an example. You want to get to tomorrow's 8:00 a.m. class on time. What do you need to do?

You might do the following:

- Put the notes, assignments, and books you will need for tomorrow in your backpack along with your cell phone and laptop.
- Set your alarm clock for 6:00 a.m. and then go to sleep.
- Get up when your alarm clock rings.
- Get dressed and eat breakfast.
- At 7:00 a.m., get in your car and drive to campus.
- Find a parking space.

EXHIBIT 5-1

PROFESSIONAL STANDARDS AND PRACTICE ADVISORIES RELEVANT TO CHAPTER 5

2010 – Planning

2120 – Risk Management

2200 – Engagement Planning

Practice Advisory 2010-1: Linking the Audit Plan to Risk and Exposures

Practice Advisory 2120-1: Assessing the Adequacy of Risk Management Processes

Practice Advisory 2200-1: Engagement Planning

Practice Advisory 2210-1: Engagement Objectives

Practice Advisory 2210.A1-1: Risk Assessment in Engagement Planning

Business Process

The set of connected activities linked with each other for the purpose of achieving one or more business objectives.

- Walk to the building.
- Get coffee.
- Walk to the classroom and find a seat.

This is a list of activities you must complete to achieve your objective of getting to class on time. To achieve this objective, you made specific choices from any number of other choices that could have been made. For instance, you could have packed your backpack in the morning instead of doing it the night before, or decided to take the bus to campus instead of driving your car. So, why did you make these choices?

In some cases, it may have been personal preference. For example, if you pack your backpack the night before, you can sleep five minutes longer the next morning. In other cases, your choice may have a direct impact on your ability to achieve your objective. For instance, you decided to drive rather than take the bus because the bus is often late or is frequently full and you might have to wait for the next one. In this case, you are exercising the same type of risk management thinking described in Chapter 4, "Risk Management."

In this chapter, you will learn that organizations go through the same type of thought process to plan steps that will help achieve their objectives, including identifying the potential risks to the objectives and managing those risks to acceptable levels. You also will learn how risk assessment techniques and methodology are used by internal auditors to carry out their responsibilities.

BUSINESS PROCESSES

Chapter 3, "Governance," discussed the importance of the governance process when setting objectives for the organization and the boundaries within which it will operate. This chapter examines how organizations actually structure their activities to implement their strategies and achieve their business (organizational) objectives. Organizations structure activities into business processes or projects. Although there are some common processes across organizations, the exact mix and structure will be unique for each organization. Even within an organization, there may be considerable variability in processes across business areas.

EXHIBIT 5-2

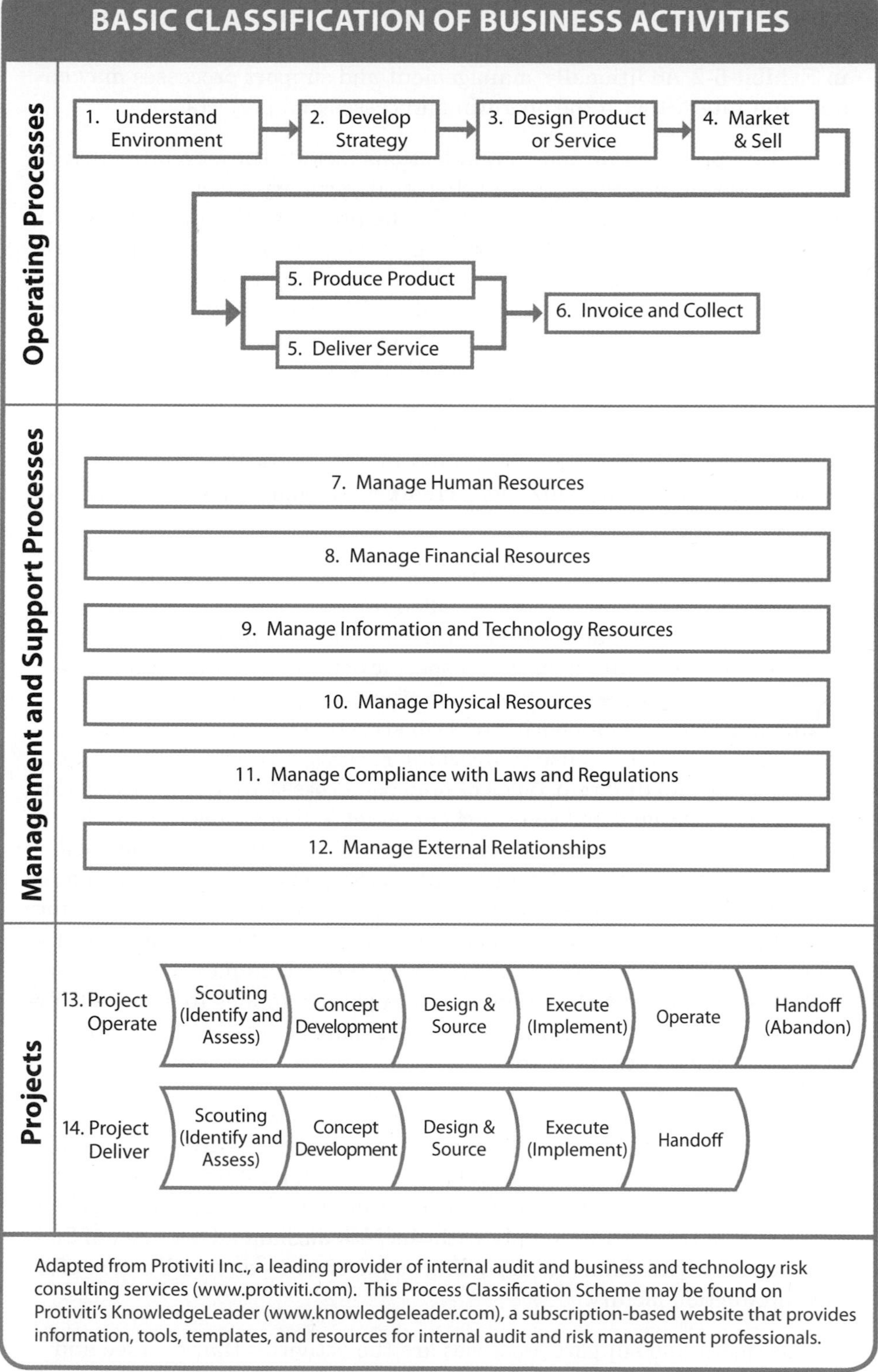

Adapted from Protiviti Inc., a leading provider of internal audit and business and technology risk consulting services (www.protiviti.com). This Process Classification Scheme may be found on Protiviti's KnowledgeLeader (www.knowledgeleader.com), a subscription-based website that provides information, tools, templates, and resources for internal audit and risk management professionals.

What is a business process? It is simply the set of connected activities linked with each other for the purpose of achieving an objective. Exhibit 5-2 outlines a basic classification of business activities. There are three types of business activities: operating processes, management and support processes, and projects. While this exhibit depicts them as separate and distinct processes and activities, the reader should note that they are not independent of one another. For example, the develop strategy activity (process 2) is a more operationally focused element of governance strategic direction that is illustrated in Exhibit 3-3. Strategy development in this operating context may pertain to many of the other activities shown in Exhibit 5-2. Additionally, management and support processes may enable and interact with the operating processes and projects.

Objectives

What an entity desires to achieve. When referring to what an organization wants to achieve, these are called business objectives, and may be classified as strategic, operations, reporting, and compliance.

Operating processes for most organizations include the core processes through which the organization achieves its primary objectives. For a manufacturing company, this would be the processes through which it makes and sells products. For service providers such as a consulting firm or financial institution, it would be the processes by which they market and deliver their services. Government entities such as a city fire department or not-for-profit organizations (for example, the Boy Scouts) also have operating processes through which they deliver services. Once the product or service is designed (processes 1 to 3 in Exhibit 5-2), the remaining operating processes (processes 4 to 6) are viewed as essentially continuous, being repeated many times in a business cycle. It is through these processes that organizations create value and deliver it directly to their customers.

Some organizations may use a different method to organize value-creating activities. This structure, called *projects*, is used when activities happen over an extended period of time, require a complex sequencing, and are relatively unique in that a specific activity is not done continuously. Examples of organizations that often set up their core activities in this manner are engineering and construction firms; mining, oil, and gas companies; and defense contractors. Processes 13 and 14 of Exhibit 5-2 show the two different types of projects. Process 13 applies when the organization designs and constructs an asset and operates it, as well. For example, a petroleum company drills and then operates an oil well. Process 14 applies when the organization designs and constructs an asset and hands it off to another organization to operate (for example, a factory or building is constructed by an engineering firm and then transferred to another company for operation). Note that these examples relate to tangible assets. However, the same project approach applies to firms delivering services. In these instances, the "asset" may be intellectual property or some other intangible asset.

Projects also are frequently used in most organizations to structure nonroutine activities to create assets for the organization's use. For example, a project structure would be used for selection and implementation of a new accounting system, initial implementation of major initiatives, such as what was required to comply with the U.S. Sarbanes-Oxley Act of 2002 or other countries' financial reporting requirements, or construction of a new production facility.

Management and support processes are the activities that oversee and support the organization's core value-creation processes. While these processes will vary between organizations, they generally are necessary across all industries and support, but do not directly create, the value embedded in the organization's objectives. Management and support processes include those used to administer the organization's human, financial, information and technology, and physical resources (processes 7 to 10). Such support processes include recruitment, accounting, cash management, payroll, purchasing, etc. These processes also will encompass the organization's compliance program (process 11). This category also includes processes the organization uses to manage its external relationships (process 12) such as those with suppliers, customers, governmental entities, and regulators, as well as relations with capital markets and venture and alliance partners. Finally, while not specifically depicted in this exhibit, the activities involved in organizational governance that set the strategic direction of the organization and provide oversight of the organization as discussed in Chapter 3, "Governance," also could be considered organizational support processes. Examples of governance processes include strategic planning, the organization's compliance and ethics program, activities of the board and board committees, the enterprise risk management program, and various monitoring and assurance activities.

Exhibit 5-2 illustrates business processes from a high-level perspective. Each of these 14 classification types also can be depicted as more discreet sets of activities. Exhibit 5-3 illustrates this point. For example, a retail organization may depict its general sales process at the highest level for processes 4, 5, and 6. A specific type of sale may be a retail sale, which

EXHIBIT 5-3

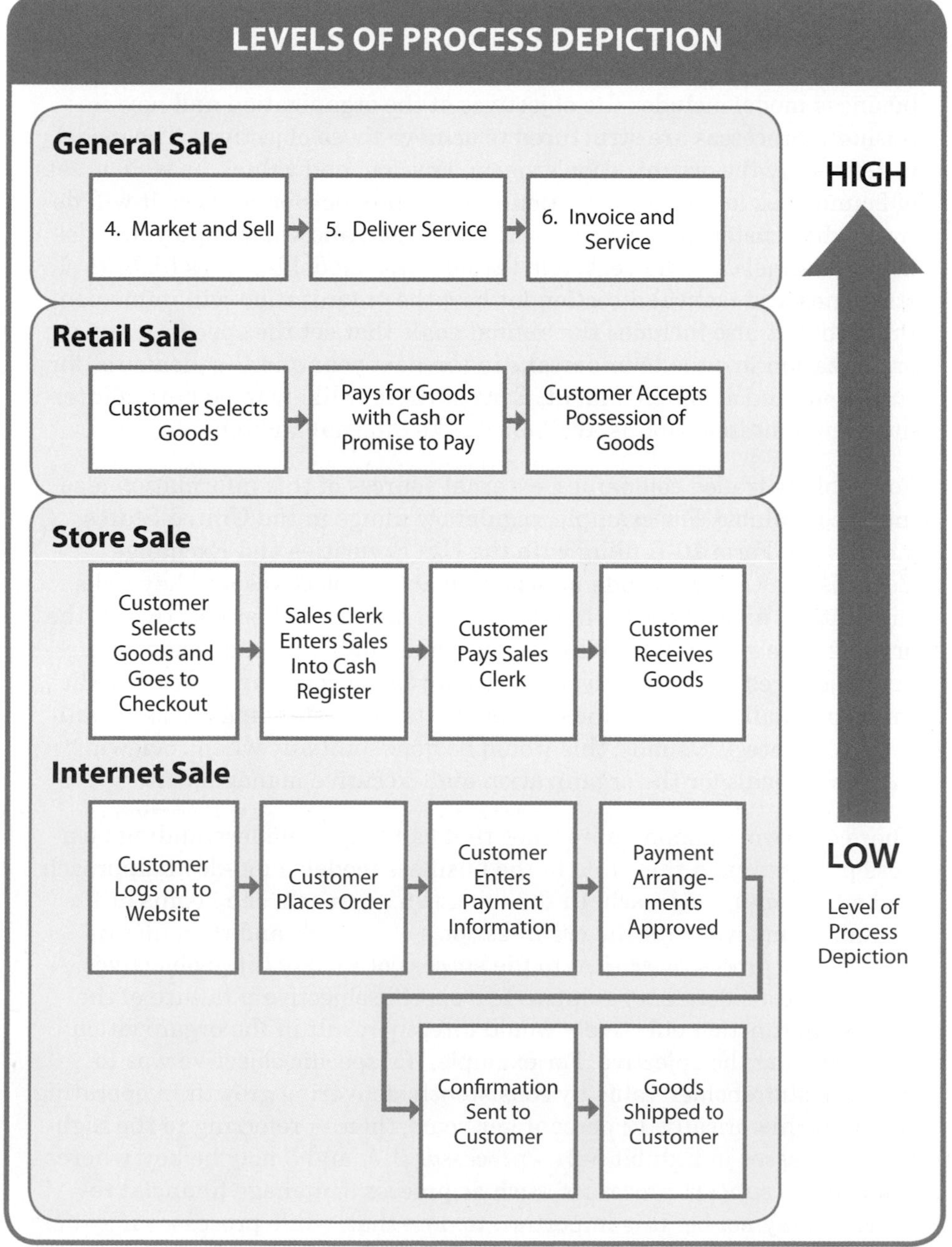

Add Value

Is provided by improving opportunities to achieve organizational objectives, identifying operational improvement, and/or reducing risk exposure.

Strategy

Refers to how management plans to achieve the organization's objectives.

Top-down Approach

Begins at the entity level with the organization's objectives, and then identifies the key processes critical to the success of each of the organization's objectives.

includes processes whereby the customer selects goods, pays for goods with cash or a promise to pay, and accepts possession of goods. Since retail sales may be made in a store setting or over the Internet, more detailed processes can be designed for those unique activities. The level of detail used to depict these processes will vary depending on the desired level of documentation. If an overview is desired, the high-level depiction shown at the top of Exhibit 5-3 is sufficient. If a more detailed level is desired, the middle or lower examples shown in Exhibit 5-3 may be more appropriate. In some instances subprocesses may be shown at even more detailed levels than those shown in Exhibit 5-3. For example, the "store sale" process of entering information into the cash register could involve a number of subprocesses such as updating inventory numbers, recording sales revenue, and opening the cash drawer. Both the high-level and detailed approaches can be valuable to internal auditors, as discussed in the next section.

Understanding Business Processes

For internal auditors to add value and improve an organization's operations, they must first understand the organization's business model. The business model includes the objectives of the organization and how its business processes are structured to achieve these objectives. The model is defined by the organization's vision, mission, and values, as well as sets of boundaries for the organization — what products or services it will deliver, what customers or markets it will target, and what supply and delivery channels it will use. While the business model includes high-level strategies and tactical direction for how the organization will implement the model, it also includes the annual goals that set the specific steps the organization intends to undertake in the next year and the measures for their expected accomplishment. Each of these is likely to be part of internal documentation that is available to the internal auditor.

For publicly traded companies, external sources of this information also may be available. For example, regulatory filings in the United States, such as the Form 10-K filing with the U.S. Securities and Exchange Commission (SEC), include information about objectives and key risks. In addition, analysts' reports may contain an external perspective on the organization's strategies. While an organization's vision, mission, values, and objectives are relatively stable from year to year, the internal audit function should still periodically update its understanding of the organization's strategy. Usually, this would be done annually when reviewing the yearly goals for the organization and executive management.

There are two common approaches that can help in understanding business processes and their role in the business model: a top-down approach and a bottom-up approach. In the top-down approach, one begins at the organization level with the organization's objectives, and then identifies the key processes critical to the success of each of those objectives. A process is considered *key* relative to a specific objective if failure of the process to function effectively would directly result in the organization not achieving the objective. For example, if a specific objective was to increase shareholder value by consistently delivering growth in operating earnings (historically, 12 percent per year), then — referring to the high-level processes in Exhibit 5-2 — processes 3, 4, and 5 may be key, whereas some of the support processes, such as process 8, manage financial resources, may not be. It is important to note that, while processes may not be *key* to one specific objective, they may be key to another. Thus, in the example above, while the monthly accounting closing process might not be a key process to the earnings growth objective, it may be a key process for an organizational objective such as "provide reliable and timely financial information." Once the key processes are identified, they are analyzed in more detail, breaking the process into levels of subprocesses, and eventually reaching the activity level. This approach is effective because it yields a manageable set of critical processes. It is usually undertaken by a team of individuals with a broad perspective of the organization, but not with detailed knowledge of each area. As a result, there is the potential to overlook processes that ultimately prove to be critical but are omitted in the top-down approach.

Bottom-up Approach

Begins by looking at all processes directly at the activity level, and then aggregates the identified processes across the organization.

The bottom-up approach begins by looking at all processes at the activity level. Such an approach requires each area of the organization to identify and document the business processes in which they are involved. This is done by the people in the area who are responsible for the actual activities. The identified processes are then aggregated across the organization. While this approach works well for smaller organizations with a relatively limited number of processes, it is less effective in large and complex organizations as it becomes cumbersome to prioritize the significance of each process relative to the others.

Once a process is identified, the next step in either the top-down or bottom-up approach is to determine the key objectives of the process. Determining the key objectives involves getting answers to questions such as:

- Why does the process exist?
- How does the process support the organization's strategy and contribute to its success?
- How are people expected to act?
- What else does the process do that is important to management?[1]

For an internal auditor, or someone not directly involved in the process, the first source of information is the process owner and the existing policy and procedures documentation for the process. Ideally, the process owner has established formal process objectives that provide the answers to the four questions above. If not, the internal auditor will need to work with key people involved with the process to obtain the necessary information.

Once the process objectives are understood, the next step is to understand the inputs to the process, the specific activities needed to achieve the process objectives, and the process outputs. To understand how inputs and activities combine to generate the outputs, existing documents should be reviewed. Such documents may include, for example:

- Process procedural manuals.
- Policies related to the process.
- Job descriptions of people involved in the process.
- Process maps that describe the process flow.

Although existing documents are an important start, it is usually necessary to discuss aspects of the process with the people performing significant activities in the process. The following questions can be asked of the process owner and other key personnel to help gain an understanding of the business process:

Key Performance Indicator

A metric or other form of measuring whether a process or individual tasks are operating within prescribed tolerances.

Process Map

Pictorial representation of inputs, steps, workflows, and outputs.

1. Why does this process exist?
2. Which of the organization's strategic objectives [does] the process affect and how?
3. What initiatives should the process undertake to help the organization achieve its strategic objectives?
4. What does the process provide the organization, without which the organization would have a difficult time being successful?
5. In the end, what gives employees involved in the process a sense of accomplishment with their jobs?
6. What accomplishments tend to get employees involved in the process recognized by management or internal customers?
7. How are people who are involved with the process expected to act? What happens if they do not meet this expectation?
8. Do key performance indicators (KPIs) exist to help measure and monitor performance?[2]

In addition to identifying the key objectives, understanding the process requires gaining an understanding of how management and the process owner know the process is performing as intended. The process owner should have established KPIs that are used to monitor the performance of the process. These indicators should be observable (they can be measured objectively), be relevant to the objective (not just used because they can be quantified), available on a timely basis, and communicated to people involved in the process. KPIs or other types of performance metrics may indicate management's expectations, or levels of tolerance, related to the process outcomes.

DOCUMENTING BUSINESS PROCESSES

Documentation of the business process is required. Typically, it should be done by the process owner and people involved in the process. However, there are instances when that is not the case because of the daily demands of their jobs or because they do not see the value of formal documentation. While not completing the process documentation may have little immediate consequence, as time passes and those involved in the process move on to other positions or leave the organization, the objectives of the process may be lost or distorted. Process documentation can be very effective in (1) orienting new personnel, (2) defining areas of responsibility, (3) evaluating the efficiency of processes, (4) determining areas of primary concern, and (5) identifying key risks and controls. Internal auditors also must document their understanding to support their overall assessment of risk and control in the organization and in any specific assurance engagements they conduct on the process.

Two commonly used methods for documenting processes are process maps and process narratives. Process maps may be high level or at the detailed activity level and involve pictorial representations of inputs, steps, workflows, and outputs. Process maps also may include some accompanying narrative.

High-level process maps attempt to depict the broad inputs, activities, workflows, and interactions with other processes and outputs. They provide an overall framework to understand the detailed activities and subprocesses. The goal in the high-level process map is to keep it simple

EXHIBIT 5-4

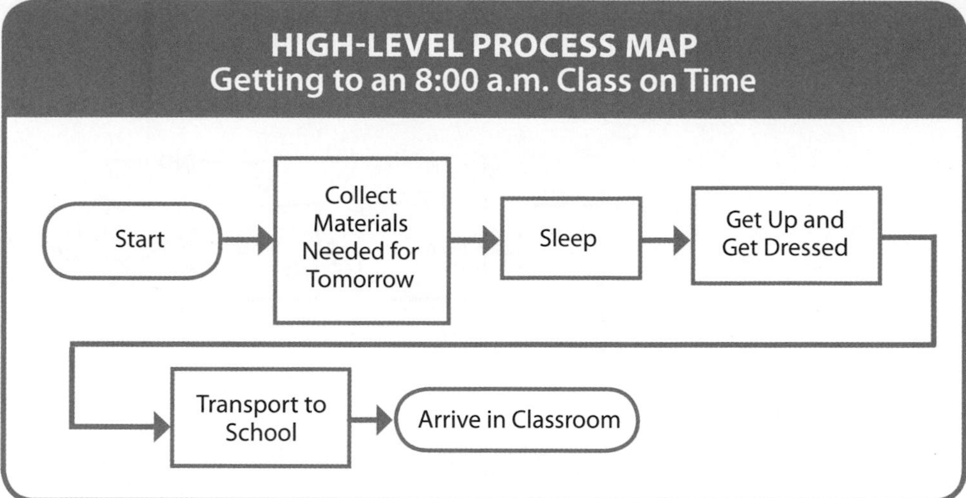

and focus on the forest rather than the trees. Exhibit 5-4 provides an example of a high-level process map of getting to tomorrow's 8:00 a.m. class on time.

There are no absolute standards regarding the format and symbols for process mapping, although internal audit functions and professional service firms typically strive for consistency. Exhibit 5-5 presents the basic symbols with typical meanings. The process maps are usually structured so the sequence of activities runs from left to right, as in Exhibit 5-4, or from top to bottom.

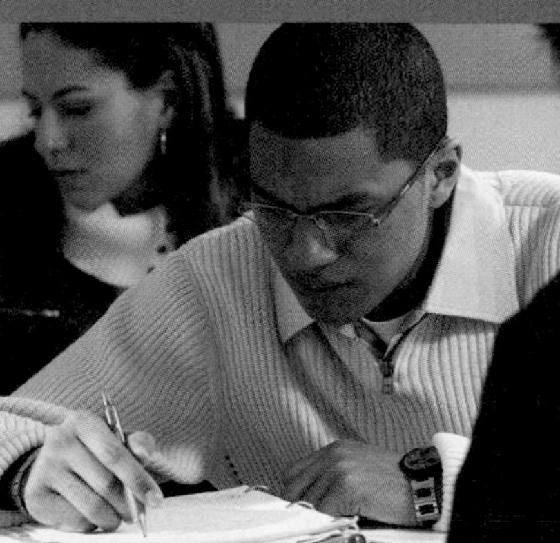

Exhibit 5-6 presents a detailed-level process map for getting to tomorrow's 8:00 a.m. class on time. The high-level process in Exhibit 5-4 is broken down to reflect the specific activities or subprocesses. Narrative is often included along with the process map to explain activities in more detail. Exhibit 5-6 illustrates how narrative supports the process map. In this case, the narrative provides more detail about the activity, but also could include descriptions of controls.

BUSINESS RISKS

Once the internal auditor obtains an understanding of the organization's objectives and the key processes used to achieve those objectives, the next

EXHIBIT 5-5

COMMON PROCESS MAPPING SYMBOLS

(rectangle)	**Process or operation** – A process, subprocess, or activity.
(diamond)	**Decision** – Indicates alternative choices (for example, yes/no or accept/reject), each of which results in different flows of activities.
(arrow)	**Flow line** – The direction of activities, workflow, and handoffs.
(rounded rectangle)	**Terminator** – The start or end of a flow.

EXHIBIT 5-6

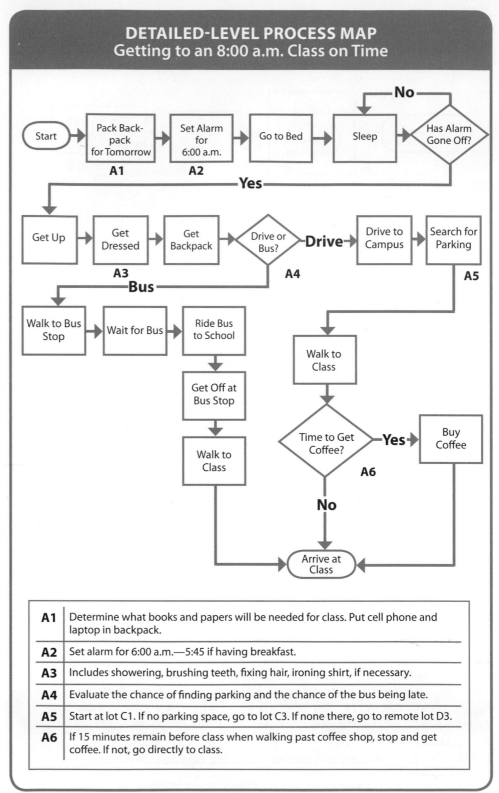

DETAILED-LEVEL PROCESS MAP
Getting to an 8:00 a.m. Class on Time

A1	Determine what books and papers will be needed for class. Put cell phone and laptop in backpack.
A2	Set alarm for 6:00 a.m.—5:45 if having breakfast.
A3	Includes showering, brushing teeth, fixing hair, ironing shirt, if necessary.
A4	Evaluate the chance of finding parking and the chance of the bus being late.
A5	Start at lot C1. If no parking space, go to lot C3. If none there, go to remote lot D3.
A6	If 15 minutes remain before class when walking past coffee shop, stop and get coffee. If not, go directly to class.

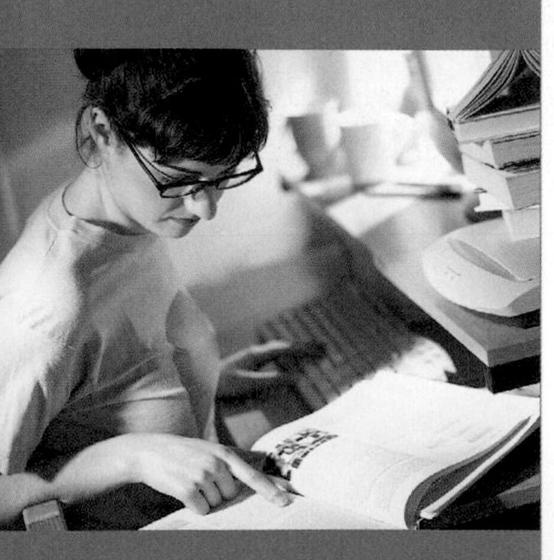

step is to evaluate the business risks that could impede the accomplishment of the objectives. The ability of the chief audit executive (CAE) and internal audit management to get a thorough understanding of the organization's business risks will determine the extent to which the internal audit function will be able to fulfill its mission and add value to the organization. It is helpful to develop an overall risk profile of the organization that identifies the critical risks to achievement of each strategic objective.

EXHIBIT 5-7

BASIC BUSINESS RISK MODEL

Strategic Risks		Compliance Risks		Reporting Risks		
External	*Internal*	*External*	*Internal*	*External*	*Internal*	*Information Resources*
Change in laws and regulations	Reputation	Contractual	Ethics	Accounting and financial reporting	Budgeting	Access
Competition	Strategic focus	Regulatory	Policies	Taxation	Performance measures	Availability
Change in market dynamics	Customer satisfaction	Litigation	Fraud and illegal acts		Internal control and regulatory reporting	Data integrity
Industry	Governance	Permits				Infrastructure
Technology						Privacy

Operations Risks

Process	*People*	*Financial*
Supply chain capacity	Manpower supply	Interest rates
Process execution	Leadership/key employees	Foreign currency exchange
Health and human safety	Performance incentives	Capacity
Business continuity	Empowerment	Default
Cycle time	Change readiness	Concentration
Catastrophic events	Communications	Capital availability
Lack of product innovation		Cash management
		Commodity pricing
		Duration

For the increasing number of organizations that are implementing enterprise risk management (ERM), overall risk profiles may be developed by management. In these cases, each internal audit function can build its risk assessment from the organization's risk profile. However, if such a profile does not exist, the internal audit function will need to create the profile as a starting point for its annual audit planning.

There are a number of different tools and methodologies to assist in developing the risk profile. This chapter looks only at a small set of those. Note also that despite the array of tools available, the assessment of organizational risk remains a very subjective process that requires experience and sound judgment.

A common approach might be to begin by conducting a brainstorming session with senior management or, if they are not available, with members of the internal audit function. The group might start with a generic risk model that depicts the categories and types of risks an organization might encounter. Such a risk model is presented in Exhibit 5-7. In this example, the potential risks are broken down into four categories that align with the Committee of Sponsoring Organizations of the Treadway Commission (COSO) ERM objective categories and 10 subcategories (refer to Chapter 4, "Risk Management," for further discussion of this framework).

The various risks are then assessed in terms of impact and likelihood. Impact, the adverse effect of a risk outcome, is usually assessed in terms of categories. Typically, three (high, medium, low) or five categories are used. A five-category model is presented in Exhibit 5-8. Establishing boundaries for each category is useful for gathering input from multiple

EXHIBIT 5-8

RISK ASSESSMENT MODEL

IMPACT	Remote (0-10%)	Unlikely (10-25%)	Possible (25-50%)	Probable (50-90%)	Certain (90-100%)
Extreme	15	19	22	24	25
High	10	14	18	21	23
Medium	6	9	13	17	20
Low	3	5	8	12	16
Negligible	1	2	4	7	11

LIKELIHOOD

Impact

Extreme: >$100m; threatens ongoing existence
High: $25-$100m; difficult to achieve business objectives
Medium: $5-$25m; makes achieving some business objectives challenging
Low: $1-$5m; some undesirable outcomes
Negligible: <$1m; no noticeable impact on objectives

Critical Risks
High Risks
Moderate Risks
Low Risks

people. In this model, the boundaries for impact are set in terms of dollar values and impact on business objectives. However, some organizations set boundaries for other measures as well. For instance, some organizations establish impact in terms of reputation, health and safety, legal, or damage to assets. For health and safety, the categories might be slight injury, minor injury, major injury, fatality, and multiple fatalities, with the scale going from negligible to extreme (the impact scale shown in Exhibit 5-8), respectively. The reader should note that other terms may be used to signify impact. Significance is sometimes used, although the authors prefer to refer to significance as a combined assessment of impact and likelihood. Less commonly, severity is another term used to signify the adverse effect of a risk outcome.

Likelihood can be evaluated by assessing the odds or probability of the risk impact occurring. However, given the subjective nature of these assessments, most managers and internal auditors are more comfortable expressing likelihood in less precise categories. Again, a three-category scale (high, medium, low) or a five-category scale (as shown in Exhibit 5-8) is often used. As with impact, it does help to specify the category boundaries. This is usually done in terms of specific or ranges of probabilities (as in the scale in Exhibit 5-8).

Using the risk assessment model in Exhibit 5-8, the various risks from the basic business risk model (Exhibit 5-7) can be placed on the matrix. Frequently, this is done in a group session involving senior management or, if they are not available, other levels of management and more experienced individuals from the internal audit function. Using senior management and operations managers is preferable because they have the best understanding of the risks in their areas of responsibility. In this meeting, risks are discussed and consensus is obtained regarding impact, likelihood, and position of the respective risk on the matrix. The combination of impact and likelihood determines the importance of the risks. Exhibit 5-8 shows the matrix broken into 25 boxes. In this model, boxes 20 through 25 represent critical risks, and boxes 16 through 19 represent high risks. These risks present the most serious challenge to meeting the organization's objectives. Boxes 7 through 15 are moderate risks and boxes 1 through 6 are low risks.

Risk

The possibility that an event will occur and adversely affect the achievement of objectives.

Exhibit 5-9 presents a mapping of the risk model to the risk assessment matrix for the online financial services company previously discussed. Four risks identified as critical appear in boxes 21 and 22. The risks in boxes 18 and 19 are considered high and, depending on how many objectives they impact, also may require extensive attention.

The next step is to formally link the identified risks to the specific objectives that each risk may impair. This helps to ensure that all key risks, and the resulting impact, have been identified. Returning to the example of getting to class on time, assume the mission this semester is to gain the necessary knowledge and skills to be successful in an entry-level internal audit position. Several specific strategic objectives could be developed to accomplish this mission:

1. Attend all classes.
2. Be on time for each class.
3. Do assigned reading before the class in which it will be discussed.
4. Complete all assignments on time.
5. Obtain a B+ or better on all exams.

The process depicted in Exhibits 5-5 and 5-7 that outlines getting to an 8:00 a.m. class on time contributes to objective 2 and, to an extent, objective 1. Other processes, such as study processes, would be critical to objectives 3, 4, and 5. Chapter 4, "Risk Management," defines risk as "the possibility that an event will occur and adversely affect the achievement of an objective." Keeping this definition in mind, a number of risks can be identified that could impede the achievement of the five objectives. For instance, becoming sick could impact the achievement of objectives 1, 2, and 4. Exhibit 5-10 presents seven critical risks and their potential to impede these five strategic objectives.

EXHIBIT 5-9

IDENTIFICATION OF CRITICAL RISKS

IMPACT	Remote (0-10%)	Unlikely (10-25%)	Possible (25-50%)	Probable (50-90%)	Certain (90-100%)
Extreme	Catastrophic events Governance	Product stagnation	Availability Economics Business continuity		
High	Changes in laws and regulations Industry Strategic focus	Reputation Technology Competition Customer satisfaction Acct and fin reporting Access Infrastructure Cash management	Litigation Fraud and illegal acts Budgeting Data integrity	Privacy	
Medium	Concentration	Contractual Regulatory IC & reg reporting Duration Capital availability Leadership/key employees Manpower supply			
Low	Health and safety Permits	Taxation Commodity Pricing	Foreign currency Supply chain		
Negligible					

LIKELIHOOD

Risk Assessment

The identification and analysis (typically in terms of impact and likelihood) of relevant risks to the achievement of an organization's objectives, forming a basis for determining how the risks should be managed.

The type of analysis performed to gain the necessary knowledge and skills to be successful in an entry-level internal audit position and the requisite objectives can be applied to organizations as well. As mentioned in our discussion of business processes earlier in the chapter, the objectives can usually be found in regulatory filings, such as the 10-K filing for a publicly traded company in the United States, or in the organization's strategic planning documents.

Mapping Risks to the Business Processes

From the ERM perspective discussed in Chapter 4, "Risk Management," the next step would be to develop appropriate responses to each risk. There are four responses an organization can take:

- **Avoidance.** A decision is made to exit or divest of the activities giving rise to the risk. Risk avoidance may involve, for example, exiting a product line, deciding not to expand to a new geographical market, or selling a division.
- **Reduction.** Action is taken to reduce the risk impact, likelihood, or both. This involves a myriad of everyday business decisions, such as implementing controls.

OBJECTIVES AND CRITICAL RISK MATRIX

EXHIBIT 5-10

Mission: Gain the necessary knowledge and skills to be successful in an entry-level internal audit position.	CRITICAL RISKS						
	CR1 Becomes ill.	CR2 Forgets deadline.	CR3 Oversleeps or is delayed.	CR4 Does not have needed course materials.	CR5 Does not have time to complete all work.	CR6 Unable to understand material.	CR7 Experiences social or other distractions.
OBJECTIVES 1. Attend all classes.	X		X				
2. Be on time for each class.	X		X				X
3. Do assigned reading prior to the class in which it will be discussed.		X		X	X		X
4. Complete all assignments on time.	X	X		X	X	X	X
5. Obtain a B+ or better on all exams.		X			X	X	X

- **Sharing.** The risk impact or likelihood is reduced by transferring or otherwise sharing a portion of the risk. Common techniques include purchasing insurance products, engaging in hedging transactions, or outsourcing an activity.
- **Acceptance.** No action is taken to affect risk impact or likelihood. The organization is willing to accept the risk at the current level rather than spend valuable resources deploying one of the other risk response options.

Risk Response Options:

- **Avoid**
- **Reduce**
- **Share**
- **Accept**

To select appropriate response strategies effectively, an understanding of how risks relate to the organization's business processes is necessary. Internal auditors also must establish the links between risks and business processes to determine whether the risks are being managed to appropriate levels within management's response strategies and to identify where in the organization the critical risks reside. IIA Standard 2010: Planning explicitly requires the CAE to "establish risk-based plans to determine the priorities of the internal audit activity, consistent with the organization's goals."

An effective means of depicting how the processes link to the underlying risks is to create a risk by process matrix (similar to the matrix shown in Exhibit 5-10, which linked objectives with critical risks). Risks are listed along the top of the matrix, and processes are listed down the side. Exhibit 5-11 illustrates this matrix. The risks would be those identified in the business risk model (Exhibit 5-7). Typically, these will be from 30

EXHIBIT 5-11

RISK BY PROCESS MATRIX

K — Key Link S — Secondary Link	Risk 1	Risk 2	Risk 3	Risk 4	Risk 5	Risk 6	Risk 7	...	Risk m
Process 1		S		K					
Process 2				S					
Process 3			S						
Process 4	K						S		
Process 5				S					
Process 6							S		K
Process 7				S	S	S	K		
Process 8		K							S
Process 9	S				K	K			
Process 10		K							S
Process 11	S		K		S				
...									
Process n		S		K			S		

to 70 risks. The risk evaluation process shown in Exhibits 5-8 and 5-9 can be used to shorten the list of risks. For instance, it might be desirable to limit the risks to which processes are linked to only those risks in cells 7 through 25 (see Exhibit 5-8).

Key Link

The process plays a direct and key role in managing the risk.

The next step is to analyze the processes to determine if there are any associations between the processes and the risks. Returning to the initial process example of getting to an 8:00 a.m. class on time, links between that process (Exhibit 5-6) and the seven critical risks listed in Exhibit 5-10 can be assessed. There is clearly a direct association between this process and critical risk 3 (oversleeps or is delayed). There also would be an association with critical risk 4 (does not have needed course materials) because part of getting to the 8:00 a.m. class on time involves gathering needed materials for classes and studying the rest of the day. Critical risk 5 (does not have time to complete all work) and critical risk 6 (unable to understand material) are clearly not related to this process. They would be related to other processes such as time management, scheduling, and study processes.

Secondary Link

The process helps to manage the risk indirectly.

After identifying with which risks a particular process is associated, the associations should be evaluated as to whether the links are key or secondary. Key links are those in which the process plays a direct and key role in managing the risk. Secondary links are ones in which the process helps to manage the risk indirectly. In the example above, critical risk 3 would be judged as a key link, while critical risk 4 may only be considered a secondary link. When the links are viewed across a particular risk, there should be one or two processes (at most three) identified as having key links and any number of additional processes identified as having secondary links.

Once the risk by process matrix is complete, it can be used by the internal audit function to determine which engagements should be included in the function's annual audit plan. A first step could be to count the number of key and secondary links for each process. The number and nature of links between risks and process will influence the type of internal audit that may be conducted. For example, a process with key links to several risks may be a good candidate for a comprehensive audit of the entire process. Alternatively, if a risk has key links to several processes, it may be more appropriate to conduct an audit of all such processes to provide assurance regarding the risk as a whole. Considerable experience is necessary to make these judgments. Also, a cycle for auditing each process could be established based on the impact and likelihood of the related risks. For example, processes with a key link to one or more critical risks or to several high and moderate risks may be audited on a one- or two-year cycle, and those with only secondary links to critical and high risks on a three-, four-, or five-year cycle. Consideration also should be given to past audit results. For instance, even a process on a three- or four-year cycle should be audited before its cycle ends if the prior audit identifies significant issues.

Another, more indirect, approach to linking business processes and risks is through the development of basic risk factors used to evaluate risks across processes (risk factor approach). Typically, risk factor models identify seven to 15 factors that can be used to assess each process. These factors are not identical to risks in the earlier basic business risk model (Exhibit 5-7). They are a higher level of abstraction, one that can be applied to each process. Most models are composed of two basic types of factors, external risk factors and internal risk factors, although other risk factors also may be included. The external risk factors pertain to factors built into the environment and the nature of the process itself. They can be characteristics such as relative level of activity, amount and liquidity of assets involved in the process, complexity of the process in terms of number of steps and inputs, level of legal and regulatory constraints, and so forth. Internal risk factors relate to the extent controls designed into the process assure the process achieves its objectives, performance of the people involved in the activities and in managing the process, and the degree of change in the process and environment in which it operates. Some models include several additional factors, most commonly: time since the last audit, prior audit results, and specific management concerns.

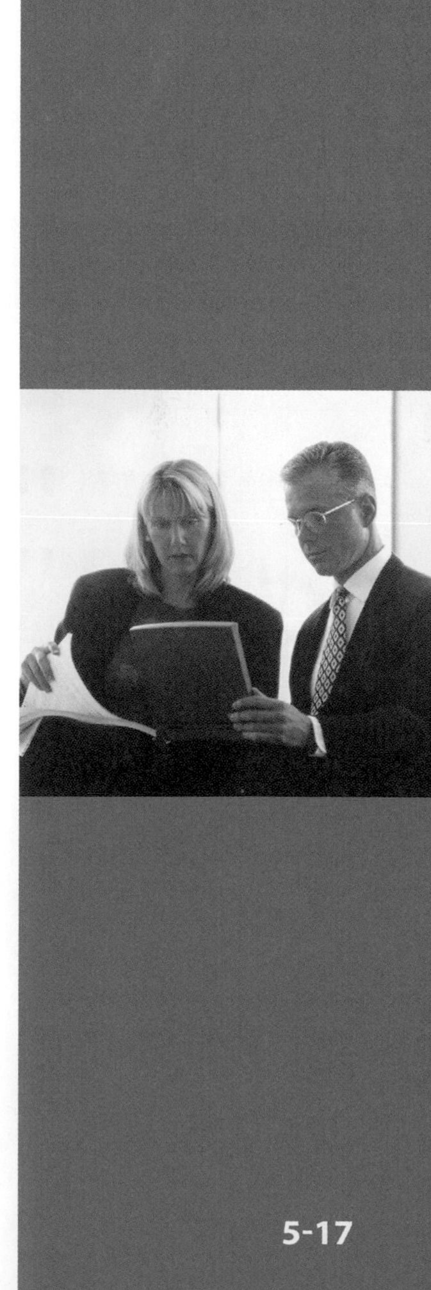

After the factors have been identified, three other decisions must be made before implementing the model. First, the scale used to assess each factor must be set. Typically, a three-, five-, or seven-point scale is used. For example, in a three-point scale, 1 may be low, 2 medium, and 3 high. The boundaries on the three categories also can be set for each factor. For example, if one factor is "amount of assets involved," then low (a score of 1) might be less than US $500,000, medium (a score of 2) from US $500,000 to US $10 million, and high (a score of 3) more than US $10 million. Regardless of which scale is selected (a three-, five-, seven-, or n-point scale), the same scale should be used for the assessment of all factors. Exhibit 5-12 shows an example of a 10-factor model using a three-point scale. The 10 factors are divided among three types of risk factors (external, inter-

EXHIBIT 5-12

RISK FACTOR APPROACH
Factor Descriptions, Weightings, and Scores

Risk Factor	Description	Score (1-3)	X Weight	Weighted Score
External Factors				
1. Assets at risk	1 - Less than $500,000 2 - From $500,000 to $5 million 3 - Greater than $5 million		10	
2. Visibility	1 - Operating unit/direct customer 2 - Divisional/limited set of customers 3 - Organization/national press		10	
3. Complexity	1 - Simple, routine assignments make up process 2 - Requires several steps and interaction of multiple people 3 - Multiple steps, requiring coordination of multiple individuals both within the process and with other processes		10	
4. Size of process/ operation	1 - Process affects less than 3% of the organization's activities 2 - Process affects 3% to 15% of the organization's activities 3 - Process affects more than 15% of the organization's activities		10	
5. Legal/regulatory/external requirements	1 - Few requirements or generally unregulated 2 - Some legal, regulatory, or external requirements 3 - Significant number of and/or complexity of requirements		10	
Internal Factors				
6. Internal control stability	1 - Mature risk and control system 2 - Stable risk and control system with moderate changes 3 - Significant changes to risk and control system		5	
7. Internal control effectiveness	1 - No internal control or compliance issues in past two years 2 - Instances of fraud, internal control weakness, or compliance failures, but none significant in the past two years 3 - Significant fraud, internal control weakness, or compliance failures in past two years		10	
8. Significant changes in operations, processes, personnel, or technology	1 - No significant change in last 12 months 2 - Some changes in process or key personnel in last 12 months 3 - Major change in business and process or new IT system in last 12 months		15	
Other Factors				
9. Management concerns	1 - No concerns expressed 2 - Some concerns expressed by senior management 3 - Notable concerns expressed by senior management or board		10	
10. Prior audit results	1 - No internal control or compliance issues in last audit 2 - Minor internal control or compliance issues in last audit 3 - Significant internal control or compliance weaknesses in last audit		10	
Overall Risk Score				

nal, and other). Exhibit 5-12 shows the name of the risk factor in the first column and explanations of what each of the three scores would mean in the second column.

The next decision pertains to the relative importance (or weight) of one factor to another. If each risk factor is considered to be of equal importance, they may be given the same numeric weighting. Usually, weighting is done by assigning numbers from 0 through 100, so the sum of weights equals 100. Thus, if there are five risk factors and each of the factors is considered to be of the same importance, each factor will be assigned a weight of 20. In the risk factor model shown in Exhibit 5-12, the internal control stability factor is given a weight of 5, which means it is considered only half as important as the assets at risk factor (weight of 10) and only one-third as important as the significant changes factor (weight of 15).

The final decision relates to how the risk factors are combined. Most risk factor approaches use a weighted-additive model — each factor score is multiplied by a factor weight and summed across factors to give an overall risk score (Exhibit 5-12). For example, overall scores can range from 100 through 300 and can be interpreted as low risk (scores below 150), medium risk (scores from 150 through 239), and high risk (scores 240 and greater). The ranges of scores may be adjusted once the distribution of scores over all processes is determined. The categories can then be used to assign each process an audit cycle of one, two, three, or more years. Thus, if a process is assigned to a two-year cycle, it would be scheduled for audit every two years.

As an alternative to assigning each process to a cycle, prioritizing processes can be done by sorting the processes by their risk scores and selecting the ones with the highest scores to include in the internal audit plan until available hours for the planning period have been exhausted. If such an approach is used, it is important to note when the process was last audited. One technique for doing this is to add *time since the last audit* as one of the risk factors. For example, in the model presented in Exhibit 5-12, this factor would be added as a factor under *Other Factors* and could be scored *1 — process audited in the past 12 months, 2 — process audited in the past 12 to 36 months, and 3 — process has not been audited in the past 36 months.*

Some internal audit functions prefer not to make judgments using total scores, but look at the scores by factor (external, internal, other). This can be done by assigning a low, medium, or high rating to each factor. Note that the range of scores varies based on the number of individual factors in each category (5, 3, and 2 in the current example) and differences in weightings. Thus, in the model presented in Exhibit 5-12, the total external risk score can range from 50 through 150, the total internal risk score from 30 through 90, and the total other factors score from 20 through 60. Given these ranges, a low rating for external risks may be scores of less than 90 and a high rating may be scores of 125 or greater. A low rating for internal risks may be scores of less than 50 and a high rating may be scores of 75 or greater. A low rating for other factors may be scores of less than 35 while a high rating may be scores of 50 or greater. Exhibit 5-13 illustrates visually how this might be displayed to help determine the audit cycle. As before, the process can be placed on a cycle of one, two, three, or more years.

EXHIBIT 5-13

RISK FACTOR APPROACH
Risk Analysis by Business Process

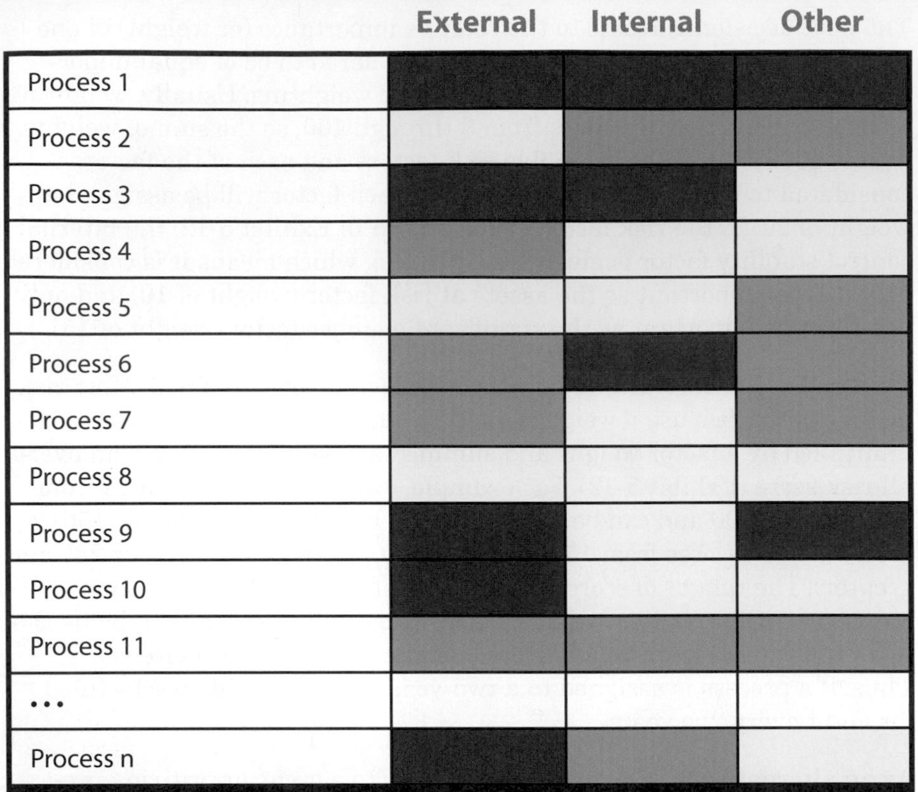

	External	Internal	Other
Process 1			
Process 2			
Process 3			
Process 4			
Process 5			
Process 6			
Process 7			
Process 8			
Process 9			
Process 10			
Process 11			
...			
Process n			

Risk Level	External	Internal	Other
Potential Range of Scores	50 to 150	30 to 90	20 to 60
Low	≤90	≤50	≤35
Medium	90-124	50-74	35-49
High	≥125	≥75	≥50

Business Processes and Risks in the Assurance Engagement

The approach to identifying business processes and risks discussed up to this point also applies at the engagement level. Recall the example presented earlier in this chapter (Exhibit 5-10) — the mission to gain the necessary knowledge and skills to be successful in an entry-level internal audit position and the five objectives established to accomplish this mission. Suppose a student's parents wanted some assurance that the mission and objectives would be accomplished and asked an older sibling, recently graduated and working as an internal auditor, to visit the student and perform an internal audit. This begins with the student and the sibling sitting down and listing a number of activities and processes the student carries out to achieve the mission:

1. Studying for exams.
2. Reading the assigned materials.
3. Completing class assignments and projects.

4. Eating meals.
5. Paying tuition and other bills.
6. Listening and taking notes in class.
7. Selecting and registering for the appropriate classes.
8. Exercising.
9. Cleaning the apartment.
10. Getting to the first class of the day on time.

Process 10, getting to the first class of the day on time, will be the focus of this example. The internal auditor/sibling begins by asking the student a series of questions about how preparations for the next day are conducted and about getting up in the morning and going to class. The student explains that, although classes are held only on Monday, Wednesday, and Friday this semester, the first class begins at 8:00 a.m. After answering all the questions asked, the internal auditor/sibling creates a process map and asks if it represents the information provided. The student suggests a few changes, producing the process map shown in Exhibit 5-6.

Assurance Engagement

An objective examination of evidence for the purpose of providing an independent assessment on governance, risk management, and control processes for the organization.

The next step is to identify and evaluate specific risks in each activity or subprocess within the key process. The internal auditor/sibling does this by placing each activity on a matrix and listing a description of each risk down the side of the page as shown in Exhibit 5-14. Each risk statement describes an event that may adversely affect the activity's or subprocess's ability to achieve its goals. The potential impact of the event is then identified and evaluated by its seriousness. Finally, the likelihood of the event is assessed. The first five columns of Exhibit 5-14 depict this information in a partially completed risk/control matrix for the first nine activities involved in driving to campus.

Risk evaluation also can be displayed using a risk map to prioritize risks within the key process. Those in the upper right quadrant of the risk map would be the most critical, while those in the lower left quadrant would be of relatively low concern. A risk map for the risks identified in Exhibit 5-14 is shown in Exhibit 5-15. On the risk map, impact and likelihood are combined to determine if the risk is of critical, moderate, or low significance.

Once specific risks have been identified, the next step is to determine how these risks are managed and if the response is effective in reducing them to an acceptable level. As mentioned earlier, there are four general responses: avoid, reduce, share, and accept. Within processes, most often the response to a specific risk is either to accept the risk or attempt to reduce it through controls. The topic of controls is addressed in more detail in Chapter 6, "Internal Control," and subsequent chapters. However, to complete the discussion of the risks in our process example, Exhibit 5-14 shows two additional columns in the risk matrix. The sixth column indicates the risk response strategy and the seventh specifies how one might gain assurance that the response strategy (in particular, the control) was effective at managing the risks.

After the response strategies have been determined, and both before and after the strategies have been tested for effectiveness, an overview of the risk response strategies can be obtained by creating a risk control map, which plots risk significance (in this example, impact and likelihood

EXHIBIT 5-14

RISK/CONTROL MATRIX FOR PROCESS 10
Getting to an 8:00 a.m. Class on Time

Activity or Sub-process Within Key Process	Risk Statement	Potential Impact	Impact Rating	Likelihood Rating	Risk Response	Technique for Assessing Effectiveness
Pack Backpack for Tomorrow	1. Forgets to pack homework assignments	• Loss of points for late work	Medium	Medium	Accept	—
	2. Forgets to put in cell phone	• Unable to receive or make calls	Low	High	Always keep cell phone in backpack	Call phone to test location
	3. Forgets to shut down and pack laptop	• Late because of delay with shutdown	Low	Medium	Accept	—
Set Alarm for 6:00 a.m.	4. Forgets to turn on alarm	• Oversleep and miss class	High	High	Turn on alarm in morning when getting up	Inquire and observe to find out if this is being done
	5. Power goes out during the night	• Oversleep and miss class	High	Low	Second battery-powered alarm clock	Observe
Go to Bed	6. Unable to get to sleep	• Tired next day	Medium	Low	Accept	—
	7. Goes to bed too late to get sufficient sleep	• Tired next day	Medium	Medium	Accept	—
Sleep/Get Up	8. Turns off alarm and goes back to sleep	• Miss class	High	Medium	Put alarm across room	Investigate to see if there is an alarm across the room
	9. Pushes snooze repeatedly	• Miss or be late to class	High	Low	Second alarm	Observe

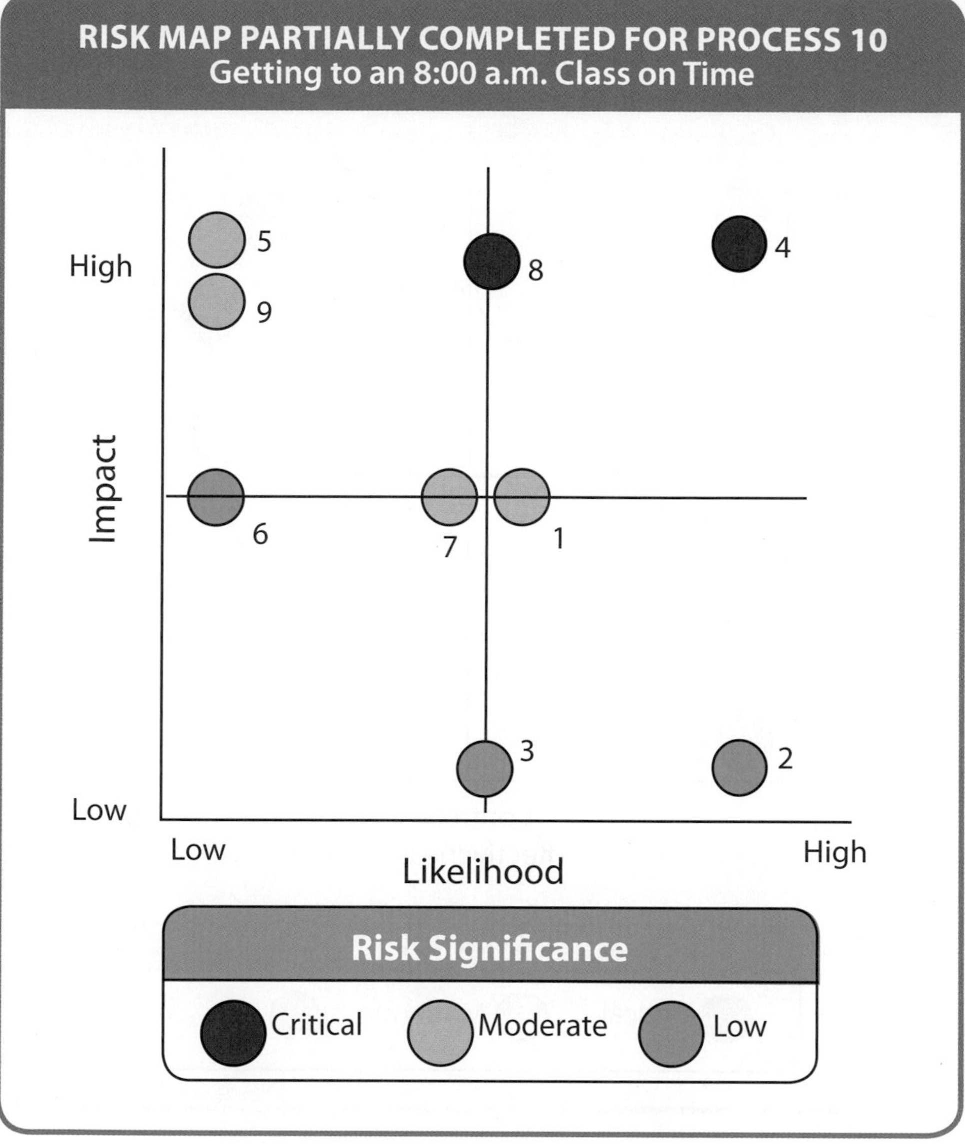

EXHIBIT 5-15

are combined to create low, moderate, and critical significance) against control effectiveness. This is illustrated in Exhibit 5-16 using the specific risks from Exhibit 5-14 for process 10 (getting to the first class of the day on time). The risk control map shows where there is an appropriate balance between risk and the control; that is, more effective controls over critical risks (high-impact and likelihood) than low risks (low-impact and low chance of occurrence). Risks falling between the two dashed parallel lines (risks 4, 8, 1, 3, and 6) are shown to be appropriately balanced. Above and left of the dashed lines on the map (risk 7), the control/risk relationship is not appropriately balanced; the response strategy does not appropriately mitigate the risks. On the other hand, below and right of the dashed lines are a number of risks that may be over-controlled (5, 9, and 2). They represent situations in which efficiencies might be gained by reducing the resources devoted to the related controls.

BUSINESS PROCESS OUTSOURCING

Before concluding the discussion of business processes and risks, it is important to discuss situations in which the process is not executed by employees of the organization. In an effort to streamline operations and

EXHIBIT 5-16

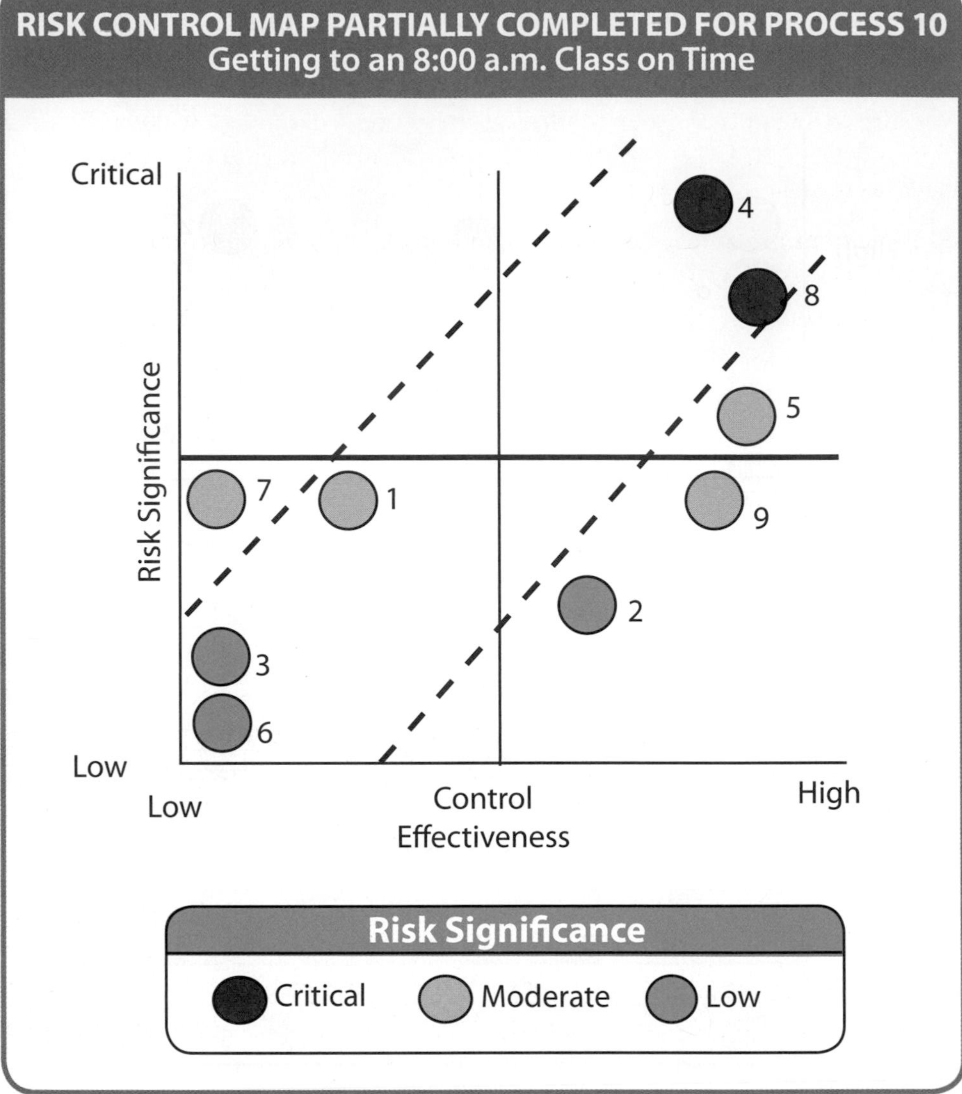

reduce costs, many organizations are increasing the degree to which they are outsourcing specific business processes. Because these processes play an important role in helping organizations achieve their objectives, these outsourced processes should be included in an organization's risk assessment and internal audit universe.

Business Process Outsourcing

The act of transferring some of an organization's business processes to an outside provider to achieve cost reductions, operating effectiveness, or operating efficiency while improving service quality.

Business process outsourcing (BPO) is the act of transferring some of an organization's business processes to an outside provider to achieve cost reductions while improving service quality and efficiency. Because the processes are repeated and a long-term contract is used, outsourcing goes far beyond the use of consultants. Historically, payroll and information technology (IT) functions were the first critical business processes outsourced. However, the trend has grown to include human resources, engineering, customer service, finance and accounting, and logistics as organizations seek to reduce costs through the leverage and economies of scale gained by those in the outsourcing business.

Even though functions may be outsourced, it is critical that management and the internal audit function ensure an adequate system of internal controls exists with the outsource vendor. In many cases, the system of internal controls may be better and more efficient than if the processes were kept internally. However, there are new risks, particularly those encountered in the transition phase of either outsourcing business functions or bringing them back to be managed internally. The following list presents some of the recommended practices that organizations should follow for effective risk management and control of outsourced business processes.

- Document the outsourced process and indicate which key controls have been outsourced.
- Ensure there are means of monitoring the effectiveness of the outsourced process.
- Obtain assurance that the internal controls embedded in the outsourced process are operating effectively, either through internal audits of such controls or an external review of these controls (such as a SAS 70 report in the United States).
- Periodically reevaluate whether the business case for outsourcing the process remains valid.

SUMMARY

The business process and risk concepts discussed in this chapter provide the foundation for understanding how organizations structure their activities to achieve their business objectives. First, it is important to obtain a high-level understanding of these processes and how they support the objectives. Next, the risks that may impact the achievement of the objectives must be identified and assessed. Finally, key processes and subprocesses that are designed to manage the risks consistent with the desired strategies can be identified as potential candidates for internal audits.

However, these concepts are not limited to use by internal auditors. They can be fundamental tools used by other organization personnel, or even individuals in everyday life, to support decision-making. This is illustrated earlier in the chapter through the example of the student with the mission of becoming an internal auditor. Refer to Appendix 5-A for another example of how these principles can be applied.

APPENDIX

Appendix 5-A Student Organization Risk Assessment Example

The following example further illustrates the concepts covered in this chapter by presenting techniques that are applicable to the management of activities and events in student organizations. This particular methodology was developed by the Office of the Dean of Students at The University of Texas at Austin, but draws from similar risk management practices used at several other universities, corporations, and government entities.

The methodology involves a six-step process that the officers or committees of student organizations are encouraged to go through when planning events (for example, a concert or dance) or activities (for example, a field trip to visit organizations or a softball tournament). The steps are:

1. List all aspects of the event on the managing risk worksheet (Exhibit 5-A1).
2. Identify risks associated with each activity, thinking broadly about potential risks.
3. Use the matrix (Exhibit 5-A1) to determine the level of risk associated with each activity before applying any risk management strategies.
4. Brainstorm methods to manage risks. Find strategies that can be applied to reduce the impact and/or likelihood of significant risks.
5. Use the matrix (Exhibit 5-A1) to reassess the activities now that risk management strategies have been applied.
6. Determine whether the application of risk management strategies has resulted in an acceptable level of residual risk. Consider modifying or eliminating activities with intolerable risks. Remember to consider how the activity relates to the mission and purpose of the organization.

Exhibit 5-A2 shows the link between impact and likelihood. It uses slightly different scales and definitions but is conceptually identical with other models discussed in this chapter.

Whether it is a student organization or a multinational corporation, achievement of an organization's mission will involve taking necessary risks. In today's competitive environment, those who best manage risks and focus on improved business processes will outperform the competition. Internal auditors are in a unique position to observe the entire organization and make recommendations that can have an impact across functional boundaries. In addition to providing assurance regarding business processes, the internal audit function can have an even bigger impact when consulting on major changes to business processes (as discussed further in Chapter 15, "The Consulting Engagement"). In today's volatile business environment, it is even more important to look to the future and assess how the business processes can be changed to prepare organizations for the challenges ahead. It is imperative that internal auditors take a leadership role and act as agents of change. The internal audit function can be of great assistance in evaluating the degree of business risk the organization is taking to achieve the goals established by management.

EXHIBIT 5-A1

MANAGING RISK WORKSHEET

Be sure to list all aspects of your event, both risky and less risky ones.	**Think through all the things that could go wrong, including worst-case scenarios.**	**Consider what your organization could do to manage the risk and bring it to a reasonable level.**
Examples: driving, sports/recreation, collecting money, concerts, outdoor events, etc.		

The University of Texas at Austin, Office of the Dean of Students.

APPENDIX

EXHIBIT 5-A2

MANAGING RISK WORKSHEET

Likelihood that Something Will Go Wrong

Impact of Risk

Category	Unlikely Unlikely to occur.	Seldom Not likely to occur but possible.	Occasional May occur at times.	Likely Quite likely to occur in time.	Frequent Likely to occur immediately or in a short period of time.
CATASTROPHIC May result in death.	M	H	H	E	E
CRITICAL May cause severe injury, major property damage, significant financial loss, and/or result in negative publicity for the organization and/or institution.	L	M	H	H	E
MARGINAL May cause minor injury, illness, property damage, financial loss, and/or result in negative publicity for the organization or institution.	L	L	M	M	H
NEGLIGIBLE Hazard presents a minimal threat to safety, health, and well-being of participants.	L	L	L	L	M

E	Extremely High Risk	Activities in this category contain unacceptable levels of risk, including catastrophic and critical injury that are likely to occur. Organizations should consider whether they should eliminate or modify activities that still have an "E" rating after applying all reasonable risk management strategies.
H	High Risk	Activities in this category contain potentially serious risks that are likely to occur. Application of proactive risk management strategies to reduce risk is advised. Organizations should consider ways to modify or eliminate unacceptable risks.
M	Moderate Risk	Activities in this category contain some level of risk that is unlikely to occur. Organizations should consider what can be done to manage the risk to prevent negative outcomes.
L	Low Risk	Activities in this category contain minimal risk that is unlikely to occur. Organizations can proceed with these activities as planned.

Review Questions

1. What is a business process?
2. What are the management and support processes that are common to most organizations?
3. What is a project and how is it different from a business process?
4. What is included in an organization's business model?
5. What is the difference between a top-down and bottom-up approach to understanding business processes?
6. How does an organization determine the key objectives of a business process?
7. What are two commonly used methods for documenting processes? Describe each.
8. What are the two common factors used when assessing risks?
9. After a risk assessment is completed, the next steps involve linking the risks to what two things?
10. What are the four responses an organization can take toward a risk?
11. What is the difference between a key link and a secondary link?
12. How can the risk factor approach be used to identify areas of high risk in an organization?
13. What are the three types of factors typically used when following the risk factor approach?
14. What two axes are typically used in a risk control map?
15. When conducting an assurance engagement, once the objectives are known, what are the three primary steps involved in identifying business risks and processes?
16. What are the four recommended practices that organizations should follow for effective risk management and control of outsourced business processes?

Multiple-choice Questions

Select the best answer for each of the following questions.

1. In assessing organizational risk in a manufacturing organization, which of the following would have the greatest long-range impact on the organization?
   a. Advertising budget.
   b. Production scheduling.
   c. Inventory policy.
   d. Product quality.

2. Internal auditors often prepare process maps and reference portions of these maps to narrative descriptions of certain activities. This is an appropriate procedure to:
   a. Determine the ability of the activities to produce reliable information.
   b. Obtain the understanding necessary to test the process.
   c. Document that the process meets internal audit standards.
   d. Determine whether the process meets established management objectives.

Use the chart to answer questions 3–5

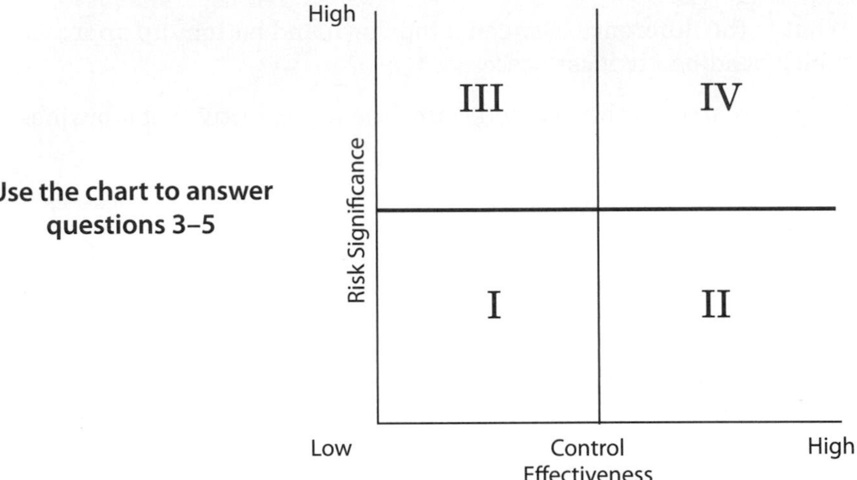

3. If a risk appears in the bottom right of quadrant II in the above risk control map, it means that:
   a. There is an appropriate balance between risk and control.
   b. The controls may be excessive relative to the risk.
   c. The controls may be inadequate relative to the risk.
   d. There is not enough information to make a judgment.
4. If a risk appears in the middle of quadrant IV in the above risk control map, it means that:
   a. There is an appropriate balance between risk and control.
   b. The controls may be excessive relative to the risk.
   c. The controls may be inadequate relative to the risk.
   a. There is not enough information to make a judgment.
5. Which of the following circumstances would concern the internal auditor the most?
   a. A risk in the lower left corner of quadrant I.
   b. A risk in the lower right corner of quadrant II.
   c. A risk in the upper left corner of quadrant III.
   d. A risk in the upper right corner of quadrant IV.

6. Which of the following are business processes?
   I. Strategic planning.
   II. Review and write-off of delinquent loans.
   III. Safeguarding of assets.
   IV. Remittance of payroll taxes to the respective tax authorities.

   a. I and III.
   b. II and IV.
   c. I, II, and IV.
   d. I, II, III, and IV.

7. Which of the following symbols in a process map will most likely contain a question?
   a. Rectangle.
   b. Diamond.
   c. Arrow.
   d. Oval.

8. After business risks have been identified, they should be assessed in terms of their inherent:
   a. Impact and likelihood.
   b. Likelihood and probability.
   c. Significance and severity.
   d. Significance and control effectiveness.

9. In a risk by process matrix, a process that helps to manage a risk indirectly would be shown to have:
   a. A key link.
   b. A secondary link.
   c. An indirect link.
   d. No link at all.

10. A major upgrade to an important information system would most likely represent a high:
    a. External risk factor.
    b. Internal risk factor.
    c. Other risk factor.
    d. Likelihood of future systems problems.

11. Which of the following is true regarding business process outsourcing?
    a. Outsourcing a core, high-risk business process reduces the overall operational risk.
    b. Outsourced processes should not be included in the internal audit universe.
    c. The independent outside auditor is required to review all significant outsourced business processes.
    d. Management's controls to ensure the outsourcing provider meets contractual performance requirements should be tested by the internal audit function.

Discussion Questions

1. How would an oil exploration and production company differ from a global retail company like Wal-Mart in terms of how it organizes business processes?

2. What are five of the most important business processes and business risks for a large automobile manufacturer like Toyota?

3. If internal audit resources are limited to conducting only one audit at a divisional location, should a high-risk process that was audited last year at this location be audited in lieu of a moderately risky process that was last audited four years ago? Explain.

4. The objectives of Sargon Products' purchasing process are to obtain the right goods, at the right price, at the right time. What are the significant risks to achievement of these objectives?

5. Think about the sales and cash receipts process of a men's or women's clothing store where you shop.
   a. What are the key objectives of this process?
   b. What are the key risks that threaten the achievement of those objectives? Key risks are those that have the highest significance (that is, combination of impact and likelihood).
   c. Identify and map the major activities of the process in the order in which they occur.
   d. Based on your review of the major activities, which of the risks identified in b. above likely have the greatest inherent significance?

6. Payswell Company, a small manufacturer, has been in business for 10 years. Senior management is thinking about outsourcing the company's payroll process.
   a. What are three important objectives of a payroll process?
   b. What are the key risks that threaten the achievement of those objectives?
   c. What are the potential benefits of outsourcing the payroll process?
   d. What new risks may arise if the process is outsourced?
   e. How should Payswell's management:
      1. Identify the key controls over the outsourced payroll process?
      2. Determine whether those controls are designed adequately and operating effectively?

CASES

CASE 1

Pizza Inc., a pizza take-out and delivery chain, is experiencing decreasing revenues and is steadily losing market share despite favorable market testing of its products/recipes. The company's strategy has traditionally been defined as gaining increased market share through customer satisfaction. Management has asked your internal audit function to help them understand the reasons for declining sales at the Uptown location and how the decline might be related to internal operations. Your prior internal audit experience and direct observation of work performed at the troubled location identified the following information:

- In 20XX, Pizza Inc.'s corporate office screened this site location prior to construction to ensure that neighborhood demographics supported the ideal business environment. This resulted in locating the chain near a suburb where typical residents were in the mid- to upper-middle class income range and who owned homes with three to four bedrooms. Despite the favorable location, the site you are reviewing continues to have gross and operating margins lower than their local competitors.
- On-the-job training is the primary method used by managers to communicate company policy and procedures. However, documented policies and detailed procedures do exist for each key process and are available by request from the shift manager. Employees are typically male (comprising 65 percent of total staff), 17 to 23 years old, with little or no prior work experience at the time of hire. Unscheduled absenteeism is high and part-time shift assignments are rotated frequently to reward those individuals who regularly work as scheduled. The internal audit team noted in last year's review that management has documented an average annual turnover rate of 18 percent.
- The shift manager is responsible for ensuring that all pizza orders are completed within the advertised time deadlines, a long-held competitive advantage. Drivers are required to record on a delivery ticket the time of their arrival at the delivery location. This time is compared with the time recorded on the order ticket to calculate total elapsed minutes. Review of the last six month's delivery tickets indicates that the company benchmark delivery cycle time of 25 minutes from "placing the order to when we're on the doorbell" has slipped to an average of 43.8 minutes. For months there have been persistent rumors about bets placed on one driver's notorious reputation for beating the delivery deadline every time.

CASE 1 (con't.)

- Delivery promptness is also dependent on the volume of completed pizzas at any given time and the neighborhood traffic pattern. Drivers are initially screened at hire for outstanding traffic violations or other infractions (such as driving while intoxicated). The original site manager posted a large map on the wall so drivers can identify their routes. Mileage is reimbursed as part of the compensation for using their own vehicles so each driver turns in a mileage log at the end of the shift to indicate both starting and ending mileage. The manager randomly checks the recorded starting or ending mileage against the cars' odometers.
- Pizza Inc.'s company policy requires that each location restrict itself to a 5 mile service area; however, if an order comes in, the work is never refused. Phone orders occur in predictable patterns, but walk-in orders are more random and less frequent. Scheduling staff requirements to match the anticipated workload is done one week in advance. The average workload during peak hours is 29 orders taken per hour. Orders are manually written on pre-numbered pads. When mistakes are made, the original order ticket is tossed out and a new order form is created to avoid confusion. Information captured includes: date, time of call (or walk in), name, address, phone number, type of crust, and toppings requested. Hand calculators are available to assist with pricing quotes that are told to the customer and recorded on the delivery ticket. Shift managers check every order to ensure that information is complete prior to processing the order.
- Employees who make the pizza are instructed in the proper quantity of ingredients for various standard topping combinations. Frequently, special request orders are received that add items to the standard recipe. Measuring cups are available, but your internal audit team noted on prior visits that when activity reaches peak load, employees generally "know" how much of key ingredients to use. The manager monitors the supply cabinets and refrigerators at the end of the shift to ensure adequate inventory is on hand. Several months ago, the evening shift manager determined that inventory deliveries should be increased to four per week, up from the usual three. Oven temperatures are monitored closely to ensure that pizzas are properly cooked. Employees who bake the pizza rely on a centrally located wall clock to time the various combinations. There are cooking guidelines posted for each standard topping combination with instructions on what to do if a pizza is overcooked. Generally these are available to employees for snacking.

- All employees are responsible for ensuring the baked pizzas are cut, boxed, hand-labeled for delivery, and assigned to the next available driver. (Drivers work in a first-in first-out method.)

Your internal audit team determined, after reviewing information received from various external sources and reading Pizza Inc.'s internal communications on strategy, mission, and vision, that linking the business risks to business processes will assist Pizza Inc.'s CEO, chief financial officer, and chief operating officer with identifying the critical business processes and key success factors for each process.

As leader of the internal audit team, you have agreed to:

A. Identify and list the key processes used by Pizza Inc. at their individual site locations.

B. Determine 10 business risks for the typical site location and assess the impact and likelihood of these risks.

C. Link the business processes to the business risks. Determine which are key versus secondary links. (Complete a risk by process matrix — Exhibit 5-11.)

D. Select a key process (one you consider critical to the success of an individual site location) and create a detailed-level process map of the activities.

E. Identify the specific risks associated with the activities of the key process (that is, the process you selected for process mapping). (Complete the risk portion of a risk/control matrix — Exhibit 5-14.)

F. Map the identified risks according to their inherent impact and likelihood of occurrence. (Complete a risk map — Exhibit 5-15.)

G. Based on the case facts provided above, identify controls (actions management currently takes) to mitigate the identified risks and put them on the risk/control matrix (in the risk response column — Exhibit 5-14.)

H. Determine techniques for assessing the effectiveness of the existing controls. (Complete the last column in the risk/control matrix — Exhibit 5-14.)

I. Based on your observations and opinion of the potential effectiveness of the current risk response activities to address risks in the critical process you selected, create recommendations to mitigate the existing risks and improve performance.

CASES

CASE 2

Select a company that has undergone an initial public offering within the last five years and obtain the prospectus (these are usually available on the company's website, EDGAR for companies listed on the U.S. stock exchanges, or other information services).

A. What is the business strategy and business model?

B. Identify the strategic objectives.

C. Identify the key risks.

D. Construct a matrix with the strategic objectives on the Y axis and the critical risks on the X axis. For each objective, indicate which key risk applies.

E. Discuss which risk you think the internal audit function should set as the highest priority.

REFERENCES

[1]Sobel, Paul, *Auditor's Risk Management Guide,* 2007 edition (Chicago, IL: CCH, Inc., 2007), pp. 7.04-7.05.

[2]Ibid.

NW
S

CHAPTER 6

INTERNAL CONTROL

Learning Objectives

- Understand what is meant by internal control in a variety of frameworks.
- Identify the components of an effective internal control framework.
- Know the roles and responsibilities each group in an organization has regarding internal control.
- Identify the different types of controls and the appropriate application for each of them.
- Obtain an awareness of the process for evaluating the system of internal controls.

"We can think of few activities within an organization that are more important to its success than maintaining internal control. Internal auditing provides management with genuine assurance that adequate controls are in place, that they are being performed as intended, and that any failures are investigated and remedied on a timely basis."[1]

Every organization has business objectives that it intends to achieve, and every organization has risks that threaten the achievement of those objectives. In this chapter, we discuss the various components of the system of internal controls that organizations develop to mitigate and manage those risks. You will come away from this chapter with an understanding of what is meant by internal control and be able to identify a variety of frameworks that consider internal control. Additionally, you will be able to identify the components that must be present for an adequately designed and effectively operating system of internal controls. Everybody within an organization has responsibility for internal control, and this chapter outlines the specific roles and responsibilities each group of people in the organization has in that respect, including management's process for evaluating the organization's system of internal controls. Most importantly for the purpose of this chapter, we delineate the specific roles the internal audit function has relative to evaluating the system of internal controls. There are several different types of controls employed to mitigate the many varieties of risks facing an organization. By the end of this chapter, you will be able to identify the different types of controls available, as well as the appropriate application of each one. Finally, a high-level overview of the process for evaluating the system of internal controls is covered. This concept is covered in greater detail in the Conducting Internal Audit Engagements chapters (Chapters 12 through 15), as well as the case studies that accompany this textbook.

EXHIBIT 6-1

PROFESSIONAL STANDARDS AND PRACTICE ADVISORIES RELEVANT TO CHAPTER 6

2100 – Nature of Work

2130 – Control

Practice Advisory 2130-1: Assessing the Adequacy of Control Processes

FRAMEWORKS

Framework

A body of guiding principles that form a template against which organizations can evaluate a multitude of business practices.

A framework is a body of guiding principles that form a template against which organizations can evaluate a multitude of business practices. These principles are comprised of various concepts, values, assumptions, and practices intended to provide a benchmark against which an organization can assess or evaluate a particular structure, process, or environment, or a group of practices or procedures. Specific to the practice of internal auditing, various frameworks are used to assess the design adequacy and operating effectiveness of controls.

The IIA provides the following guidance relative to the use of frameworks: "In general, a framework provides a structural blueprint of how a body of knowledge and guidance fit together. As a coherent system, it facilitates consistent development, interpretation, and application of concepts, methodologies, and techniques useful to a discipline or profession."[2]

It is important to begin by making a few distinctions so that there is no confusion regarding the different frameworks discussed in this chapter — specifically, enterprise risk management (ERM) frameworks and frameworks more specifically designed to address internal control. Both deal with risk mitigation and aspects of internal control, however, those frameworks that focus on internal control alone are more narrowly defined and tend to be less strategic in nature. While this chapter deals specifically with the subject of internal control and focuses on internal control frameworks, it would be incomplete without identifying ERM frameworks and other globally recognized frameworks dealing with governance, risk management, and internal control that also have been developed or have evolved over time. Chapter 3, "Governance," addresses the governance, risk management, and internal control hierarchy, while Chapter 4, "Risk Management," specifically discusses the Committee of Sponsoring Organizations of the Treadway Commission (COSO) ERM framework in more detail. Exhibit 6-2 presents these frameworks.

Internal Control Frameworks

Although the frameworks discussed in Exhibit 6-2 contain elements of internal control, there are currently only three internal control frameworks recognized globally by management, independent outside accountants/auditors, and internal audit professionals: *Internal Control – Integrated Framework*, issued by COSO in 1992; *Guidance on Control* (often referred to as the CoCo framework), published in 1995 by the Canadian Institute of Chartered Accountants (CICA), and *Internal Control: Revised Guide for Directors on the Combined Code* (referred to as the Turnbull Report), published by the Financial Reporting Council, which first came out in

GLOBALLY RECOGNIZED FRAMEWORKS

EXHIBIT 6-2

Internal Control Frameworks

Internal Control – Integrated Framework (COSO), Committee of Sponsoring Organizations of the Treadway Commission, United States, 1992

Guidance on Control (CoCo), The Canadian Institute of Chartered Accountants, Canada, 1995

Internal Control: Revised Guide for Directors on the Combined Code (Turnbull), Financial Reporting Council, 2005

COBIT 4.1, IT Governance Institute, United States, 2007

Governance Frameworks

Report of the Committee on the Financial Aspects of Corporate Governance (Cadbury), England, 1992

King Report on Corporate Governance for South Africa (King II), Institute of Directors, South Africa, 2002

Enterprise Risk Management Frameworks

Australian/New Zealand Standard Risk Management (Australian Standard 4360), Joint Technical Committee OB/007 – Risk Management, Australia/New Zealand, Revised 2004

Enterprise Risk Management – Integrated Framework (COSO), Committee of Sponsoring Organizations of the Treadway Commission, United States, 2004

Other Globally Recognized Risk Mitigation Frameworks

International Convergence of Capital Measurement and Capital Standards (Basel Accord), Basel Committee on Banking Supervision, 1988

International Convergence of Capital Measurement and Capital Standards A Revised Framework (Basel II or The New Accord), Basel Committee on Banking Supervision, 2005

1999 and was updated in 2005. COBIT, the information technology (IT) internal control framework referenced in Exhibit 6-2, is specifically designed to provide guidance on the development and assessment of proper information technology governance. As such, it supplements COSO, CoCo, and Turnbull in terms of IT controls, but is not a comprehensive internal control framework itself.

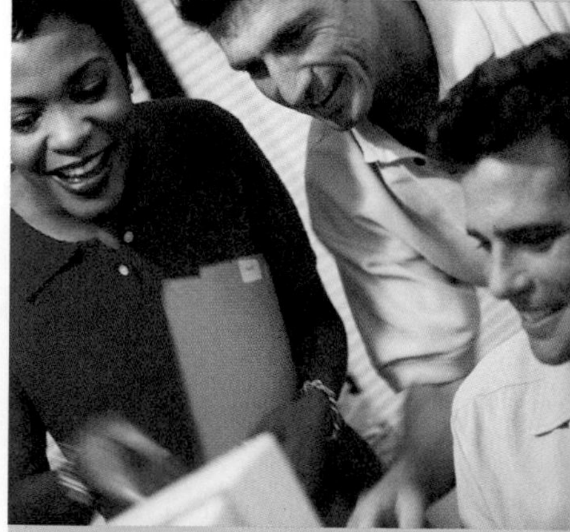

There are no substantive differences among COSO, CoCo, and Turnbull. All of the frameworks include definitions of internal control, describing a process that provides reasonable assurance for achieving the objectives of an organization in three specific categories: effectiveness and efficiency of operations, reliability of reporting, and compliance. The three frameworks also agree regarding responsibility for internal control, specifically putting responsibility not only on the board of directors, senior management, and internal auditors, but also on each individual within the organization. Although called by different titles among the frameworks, the components of each internal control framework are basically the same and can be examined using the COSO titles for each component. They are: Control Environment, Risk Assessment, Control Activities, Information and Communication, and Monitoring. For a comparison of the three internal control frameworks using the language specific to each one, see Exhibit 6-3.

ICFR

Internal Control over Financial Reporting

In the United States, the U.S. Sarbanes-Oxley Act of 2002 legislation put responsibility for the design, maintenance, and effective operation of internal control squarely on the shoulders of senior management, specifically, the CEO and the chief financial officer (CFO). To comply with this legislation, the U.S. Securities and Exchange Commission (SEC) requires the CEO and CFO of publicly traded companies to opine on the design adequacy and operating effectiveness of internal control over financial reporting (ICFR) as part of the annual filing of financial statements with the SEC, as well as report substantial changes in ICFR, if any, on a quarterly basis. Specifically, the SEC requires evidence of compliance, ruling that " . . . management must base its evaluation [or, opinion] of the

EXHIBIT 6-3

COMPARISON OF ACCEPTED INTERNAL CONTROL FRAMEWORKS

	COSO	CoCo	Turnbull
Definition of Internal Control	A process effected by an entity's board of directors, management, and other personnel, designed to provide reasonable assurance regarding the achievement of objectives in the following categories: effectiveness and efficiency of operations, reliability of financial reporting, and compliance with laws and regulations.	Those elements of an organization that support people and offer reasonable assurance in the achievement of the organization's objectives in the following categories: effectiveness and efficiency of operations, reliability of internal and external reporting, compliance with laws and regulations, and internal policies.	Encompasses the policies, processes, tasks, behaviors, and other aspects of a company that offer reasonable assurance in facilitating its effective and efficient operation, enabling it to respond appropriately to significant business, operational, financial, compliance, and other risks to achieving the company's objectives relative to safeguarding assets, identifying and managing liabilities, the quality of reporting, and compliance with laws and regulations.
Components of Internal Control	Control Environment, Risk Assessment, Control Activities, Information and Communication, and Monitoring	Purpose, Commitment, Capability, Monitoring, and Learning	Control Activities, Information and Communication Processes, Monitoring, Embeddedness in Operations of Company, Response to Risk and Changes, and Reporting

U.S. SARBANES-OXLEY ACT OF 2002 COMPLIANCE

The U.S. Securities and Exchange Commission (SEC) in the United States specifically refers to the COSO framework as an example of a framework suitable for organizations to compare their system of internal controls against in order to be compliant with Section 404 of the U.S. Sarbanes-Oxley Act of 2002 which governs all entities, foreign or domestic, wishing to access the United States of America (USA) capital market. The SEC also recognizes the CoCo framework of Canada and the Turnbull Report of England and Wales as suitable frameworks. Outside of England/Wales and Canada, however, COSO represents the primary framework used to assess an organization's system of internal controls.

EXHIBIT 6-4

effectiveness of the company's internal control over financial reporting on a suitable, recognized control framework that is established by a body or group that has followed due-process procedures, including the broad distribution of the framework for public comment."[3] For details regarding the SEC's evaluation of appropriate internal control frameworks, see Exhibit 6-4.

The SEC further ruled, "The COSO framework satisfies our criteria and may be used as an evaluation framework for purposes of management's annual internal control evaluation and disclosure requirements. However, the final rules do not mandate use of a particular framework, such as the COSO framework, in recognition of the fact that other evaluation standards exist outside the United States . . . "[4] The SEC, in footnote 67 of the final ruling, specifically identified the *Guidance on Control* and the Turnbull Report as examples of other suitable frameworks. In addition to the three frameworks specifically referred to, the SEC recognizes " . . . that frameworks other than COSO may be developed within the United States in the future, that satisfy the intent of the statute without diminishing the benefits to investors. The use of standard measures that are publicly available will enhance the quality of the internal control report and will promote comparability of the internal control reports of different companies. The final rules require management's report to identify the evaluation framework used by management to assess the effectiveness of the company's internal control over financial reporting. Specifically, a suitable framework must: be free from bias; permit reasonably consistent qualitative and quantitative measurements of a company's internal control; be sufficiently complete so that those relevant factors that would alter a conclusion [or opinion] about the effectiveness of a company's internal controls are not omitted; and be relevant to an evaluation of internal control over financial reporting [ICFR]" (SEC final ruling 33-8238).[5]

Many organizations were able to successfully apply these frameworks in their efforts to comply with Section 404 of Sarbanes-Oxley, despite encountering significant unanticipated costs. Smaller publicly held companies (as defined in Exhibit 6-5), on the other hand, struggled to comply due to the prohibitive costs as well as several other challenges unique to smaller organizations, including:

- Obtaining sufficient resources to achieve adequate segregation of duties,

COSO

Committee of Sponsoring Organizations of the Treadway Commission, a voluntary private-sector organization dedicated to improving the quality of financial reporting through business ethics, effective internal controls, and corporate governance.

- Management's ability to dominate activities, with significant opportunities for improper management override of processes in order to appear that business performance goals have been met [management override of control],
- Recruiting individuals with requisite financial reporting and other expertise to serve effectively on the board of directors and audit committee,
- Recruiting and retaining personnel with sufficient experience and skill in accounting and financial reporting,
- Taking critical management attention from running the business in order to provide sufficient focus on accounting and financial reporting, [and]
- Controlling information technology and maintaining appropriate general and application controls over computer information systems with limited technical resources.[6]

Supplemental publications to COSO's Internal Control - Integrated Framework*:*

- *Internal Control Over Financial Reporting – Guidance for Smaller Public Companies*
- *Guidance on Monitoring Internal Control Systems*

In response to this, COSO issued *Internal Control Over Financial Reporting – Guidance for Smaller Public Companies (The Guidance for Smaller Public Companies)* in July 2006 as a supplement to the original COSO framework. Primarily designed to provide guidance to smaller public companies to assist them with a cost effective means to comply with Section 404 of Sarbanes-Oxley, *The Guidance for Smaller Public Companies* had the added benefit of supplying direction to all organizations, regardless of size, on the application of the original COSO framework when evaluating the effectiveness of ICFR. It provides "a set of 20 basic principles representing the fundamental concepts associated with, and drawn directly from, the five components of the [COSO] framework."[7] These 20 basic principles are outlined in Exhibit 6-6.

In addition to the difficulties smaller organizations were having with Sarbanes-Oxley Section 404 compliance, some organizations were not using monitoring to its full advantage. As a result, in early 2009, COSO published a supplemental document regarding the use of monitoring to support conclusions on internal control effectiveness called *Guidance on*

EXHIBIT 6-5

CHARACTERISTICS OF "SMALLER" COMPANIES

There is a wide range of businesses that can be classified as "smaller"; many have the following characteristics in common:

- Fewer lines of business and fewer products within lines.
- Concentration of marketing focus, by channel or geography.
- Leadership by management with significant ownership interest or rights.
- Fewer levels of management, with wider spans of control.
- Less complex transaction processing systems and protocols.
- Fewer personnel, many having a wider range of duties.
- Limited ability to maintain deep resources in line as well as support staff positions such as legal, human resources, accounting, and internal auditing.

Copyright 2006 by the Committee of Sponsoring Organizations of the Treadway Commission (COSO). Reproduced with permission from the AICPA acting as authorized administrator for COSO.

20 BASIC PRINCIPLES FOR ACHIEVING EFFECTIVE INTERNAL CONTROL OVER FINANCIAL REPORTING

EXHIBIT 6-6

Control Environment

1. **Integrity and Ethical Values** — Sound integrity and ethical values, particularly of top management, are developed and understood and set the standard of conduct for financial reporting.
2. **Board of Directors** — The board of directors understands and exercises oversight responsibility related to financial reporting and related internal control.
3. **Management's Philosophy and Operating Style** — Management's philosophy and operating style support achieving effective internal control over financial reporting.
4. **Organizational Structure** — The company's organizational structure supports effective internal control over financial reporting.
5. **Financial Reporting Competencies** — The company retains individuals who are competent in financial reporting and oversight roles.
6. **Authority and Responsibility** — Management and employees are assigned appropriate levels of authority and responsibility to facilitate effective internal control over financial reporting.
7. **Human Resources** — Human resource policies and practices are designed and implemented to facilitate effective internal control over financial reporting.

Risk Assessment

8. **Financial Reporting Objectives** — Management specifies financial reporting objectives with sufficient clarity and criteria to enable the identification of risks to reliable financial reporting.
9. **Financial Reporting Risks** — The company identifies and analyzes risks to the achievement of financial reporting objectives as a basis for determining how the risks should be managed.
10. **Fraud Risk** — The potential for material misstatement due to fraud is explicitly considered in assessing risks to the achievement of financial reporting objectives.

Control Activities

11. **Integration with Risk Assessment** — Actions are taken to address risks to the achievement of financial reporting objectives.
12. **Selection and Development of Control Activities** — Control activities are selected and developed considering their cost and their potential effectiveness in mitigating risks to the achievement of financial reporting objectives.
13. **Policies and Procedures** — Policies related to reliable financial reporting are established and communicated throughout the company, with corresponding procedures resulting in management directives being carried out.
14. **Information Technology** — Information technology controls, where applicable, are designed and implemented to support the achievement of financial reporting objectives.

Information and Communication

15. **Financial Reporting Information** — Pertinent information is identified, captured, used at all levels of the company, and distributed in a form and timeframe that supports the achievement of financial reporting objectives.
16. **Internal Control Information** — Information used to execute other control components is identified, captured, and distributed in a form and timeframe that enables personnel to carry out their internal control responsibilities.
17. **Internal Communication** — Communications enable and support understanding and execution of internal control objectives, processes, and individual responsibilities at all levels of the organization.
18. **External Communication** — Matters affecting the achievement of financial reporting objectives are communicated with outside parties.

Monitoring

19. **Ongoing and Separate Evaluations** — Ongoing and/or separate evaluations enable management to determine whether internal control over financial reporting is present and functioning.
20. **Reporting Deficiencies** — Internal control deficiencies are identified and communicated in a timely manner to those parties responsible for taking corrective action, and to management and the board as appropriate.

Copyright 2006 by the Committee of Sponsoring Organizations of the Treadway Commission. Reproduced with permission from the AICPA acting as authorized administrator for COSO.

Monitoring Internal Control Systems (COSO's *Monitoring Guidance*). This guidance does not change the guidance provided by the 1992 COSO framework or *The Guidance for Smaller Public Companies*. Instead, COSO's *Monitoring Guidance* is designed "to help organization's improve the effectiveness and efficiency of their internal control systems" and "provide practical guidance that illustrates how monitoring can be incorporated into an organization's internal control processes."[8] It further elaborates on the two COSO principles relative to monitoring that were included in the 20 basic principles introduced in *The Guidance for Smaller Public Companies*:

- Ongoing monitoring and/or separate evaluations enable management to determine whether the other components of internal control over financial reporting continue to function over time (principle 19).
- Internal control deficiencies are identified and communicated in a timely manner to those parties responsible for taking corrective action, and to management and the board as appropriate (principle 20).[9]

It is also worth noting that COSO's *Monitoring Guidance* is not limited to ICFR, but can, and is intended to, be applied to all internal controls within an organization's system of internal controls. COSO's *Monitoring Guidance* is discussed in more detail later in the chapter.

As a result of the increased public scrutiny over ICFR that ensued from Sarbanes-Oxley, the subject of internal control has been elevated to the prominence formerly reserved for topics such as sales, marketing, profits (EPS), and capital adequacy in many organizations. In addition to using COSO, CoCo, and Turnbull as vehicles to assess ICFR, many organizations also are using these frameworks to more broadly evaluate the entire system of internal controls.

The COSO, CoCo, and Turnbull frameworks

Are used by an increasing number of organizations to evaluate the entire system of internal controls, not just internal controls over financial reporting.

The IIA acknowledged how these frameworks contributed to the shift in thinking about controls in terms of their alignment with the organization's objectives: "Control had long been a component of the 'unique' franchise of internal auditing. The emergence of broad management control frameworks such as *Internal Control – Integrated Framework* from the Committee of Sponsoring Organizations of the Treadway Commission (COSO) and *Criteria of Control* from the Canadian Institute of Chartered Accountants (CoCo) has elevated the internal auditor's focus from financial and compliance-oriented controls to management controls and governance processes that address broad organizational risks. The COSO and CoCo focus widens the spectrum of controls addressed by internal auditors and more closely aligns their control activities with an organization's objectives and core value-creating processes."[10]

As previously indicated, these two frameworks, as well as Turnbull, include similar definitions of internal control describing a process that provides reasonable assurance for achieving the business objectives of an organization in three specific categories: effectiveness and efficiency of operations, reliability of reporting, and compliance. Again, they are called by different titles among the frameworks, but the components of each internal control framework are basically the same. Therefore, throughout the remainder of this chapter, the COSO framework will be used to study the various components of the system of internal controls in more depth, since it reflects the concepts from all three frameworks.

DEFINITION OF INTERNAL CONTROL

COSO broadly defines internal control as:

> . . . a process, effected by an entity's board of directors, management, and other personnel, designed to provide reasonable assurance regarding the achievement of objectives in the following categories:
>
> - Effectiveness and efficiency of operations.
> - Reliability of financial reporting.
> - Compliance with applicable laws and regulations.
>
> This definition reflects certain fundamental concepts:
>
> - Internal control is a process. It is a means to an end, not an end in itself.
> - Internal control is effected by people. It is not merely policy manuals and forms, but people at every level of an organization.
> - Internal control can be expected to provide only reasonable assurance, not absolute assurance, to an entity's management and board.
> - Internal control is geared to the achievement of objectives in one or more separate but overlapping categories.[11]

Although this definition may seem very general, broadly defining internal control accommodates the exploration of its categories individually or taken as a whole. When internal control categories are looked at as a whole, they are collectively referred to as the system of internal controls. COSO indicates, "Those who want to can focus separately, for example, on controls over financial reporting or controls related to compliance with laws and regulations. Similarly, a directed focus on controls in particular units or activities of an entity can be accommodated."[12] Likewise, an organization can choose to focus on its overall system of internal controls. Exhibit 6-7 illustrates the internal control components with emphasis on how they interrelate.

Note that while COSO defines achievement of compliance objectives strictly as "adherence to laws and regulations to which the entity is subject," The IIA's International Professional Practices Framework defines it more broadly as "adherence to policies, plans, procedures, laws, regulations, contracts, or other requirements."[13] COSO considers compliance with those additional governance-related requirements a part of the achievement of operations objectives instead of compliance objectives. The classification is much less important than the actual achievement of the objectives no matter how an organization chooses to classify them. This distinction is, however, an important consideration when the internal audit function is planning and determining the scope of an assurance engagement. For a detailed review of assurance engagement planning, scope setting, and communications, see Chapter 12, "Introduction to the Engagement Process," Chapter 13, "Conducting the Assurance Engagement," and Chapter 14, "Communicating Assurance Engagement Outcomes and Performing Follow-up Procedures."

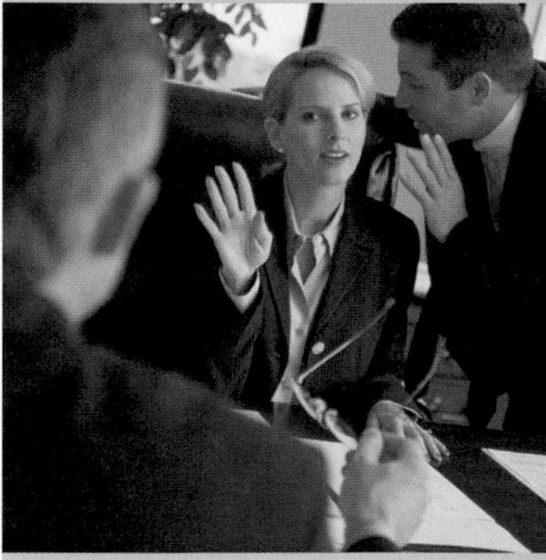

Internal Control (COSO's definition)

A process, effected by an entity's board of directors, management, and other personnel, designed to provide reasonable assurance regarding the achievement of objectives in the following categories:

- **Effectiveness and efficiency of operations.**
- **Reliability of financial reporting.**
- **Compliance with applicable laws and regulations.**

EXHIBIT 6-7

INTERNAL CONTROL COMPONENTS

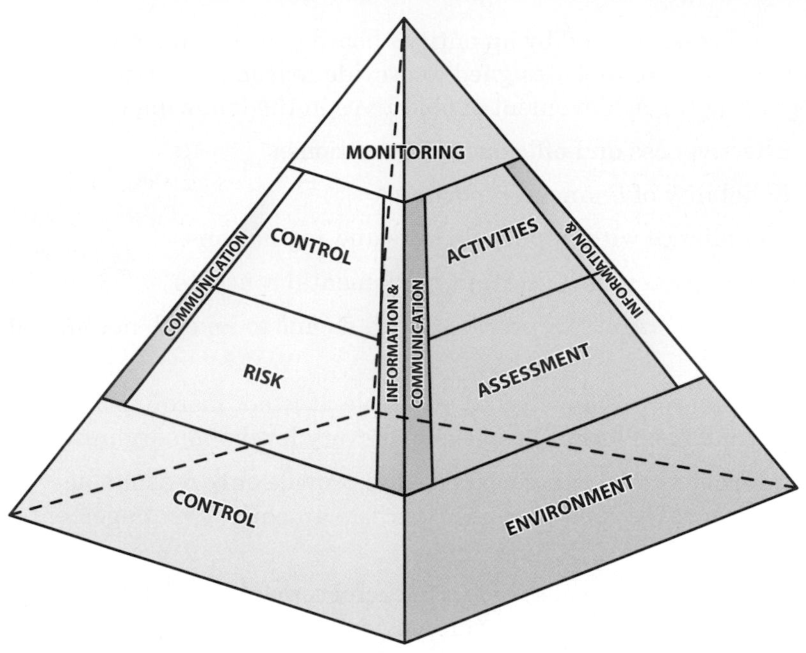

The *control environment* provides an atmosphere in which people conduct their activities and carry out their control responsibilities. It serves as the foundation for the other components. Within this environment, management *assesses risks* to the achievement of specified objectives. *Control activities* are implemented to help ensure that management directives to address the risks are carried out. Meanwhile, relevant *information* is captured and *communicated* throughout the organization. The entire process is *monitored* and modified as conditions warrant.

Copyright 1992. Committee of Sponsoring Organizations of the Treadway Commission (COSO). All rights reserved. Used with permission.

The components of internal control:

- Control Environment
- Risk Assessment
- Control Activities
- Information and Communication
- Monitoring

THE COMPONENTS OF INTERNAL CONTROL

Control Environment

The control environment of an organization permeates all areas of the organization and influences the way individuals approach internal control. This foundational component of internal control creates the context within which the other components of internal control exist. COSO identifies "the integrity, ethical values, and competence of the entity's people; management's philosophy and operating style; the way management assigns authority and responsibility, and organizes and develops its people; and the attention and direction provided by the board of directors" as the factors included in an organization's control environment.[14]

Furthermore, COSO indicates that "the control environment has a pervasive influence on the way business activities are structured, objectives established, and risks assessed. It also influences control activities, information and communication systems, and monitoring activities."[15] The history and culture of the organization directly influence its control environment. The organization's objectives are achieved, in part, through the control environment which, if effectively implemented, results in an organization-wide "attitude of integrity and control consciousness, and set[s] a positive 'tone at the top'" through the establishment of "appropriate policies and procedures, often including a written code of conduct, which foster shared values and team work in pursuit of the entity's objectives."[16]

Risk Assessment

All organizations encounter risks, that is, threats to the achievement of objectives. All risks, both internal and external, need to be assessed. According to COSO, "A precondition to risk assessment is establishment of objectives, linked at different levels and internally consistent. Risk assessment is the identification and analysis of relevant risks to achievement of the objectives, forming a basis for determining how the risks should be managed. Because economic, industry, regulatory, and operating conditions will continue to change, mechanisms are needed to identify and deal with the special risks associated with change."[17] Risk identification and analysis, both of which are important to effective risk assessment, are discussed in more detail later in the chapter.

Setting clear objectives is the precondition to effective identification of, assessment of, and response to risks. There must first be objectives, established in a strategy-setting environment, before management can identify risks that might impede the achievement of the objectives and take necessary actions to manage those risks. As discussed in Chapter 4, "Risk Management," objective setting, event identification, risk assessment, and risk response are key elements of the risk management process. Accordingly, objective setting is a prerequisite to, and enabler of, internal control.

Processes for setting objectives can range from highly structured to very informal. An organization's mission statement often drives entity-level objectives. Together with assessments of the strengths, weaknesses, risks, and opportunities, objectives establish a context for defining an organization's strategy. Typically, the strategic plan that results is general in nature.

From the general strategic plan, objectives are identified that are more specific than the entity-level objectives discussed above. The entity-level objectives are then linked to the specific objectives that have been established for the different activities within the organization. The specific objectives of those activities must align with the entity-level objectives identified by the organization.

Setting objectives at both the entity and process levels is important for the organization to be able to identify *critical success factors* (successes that must be accomplished for objectives to be achieved). Critical success factors are present at all levels of an organization and facilitate the creation of measurable criteria against which performance can be assessed.

Critical Success Factors

Successes that must be accomplished for objectives to be achieved.

Objectives can be divided into the following broad categories established by COSO:

- **Operations Objectives.** These pertain to effectiveness and efficiency of the entity's operations, including performance and profitability goals and safeguarding resources against loss. They vary based on management's choices about structure and performance.

- **Financial Reporting Objectives.** These pertain to the preparation of reliable published financial statements, including prevention of fraudulent public financial reporting. They are driven primarily by external requirements.
- **Compliance Objectives.** These objectives pertain to adherence to laws and regulations to which the entity is subject. They are dependent on external factors, such as environmental regulations, and tend to be similar across all entities in some cases and across an industry in others.[18]

Control Activities

Control activities are the actions taken by management, the board, and other parties to mitigate risk and increase the likelihood that established objectives and goals will be achieved. Management plans, organizes, and directs the performance of sufficient actions to provide reasonable assurance that objectives and goals will be achieved. Like the critical success factors described above, control activities are present at all levels of the organization. And, like the objectives they are designed to help achieve, control activities can be separated into the three categories of operations, financial reporting, and compliance. However, control activities often are designed to mitigate multiple risks which may threaten objectives in more than one category. Remember that it is less important which category a control activity is in than its ability to mitigate the risk(s) to which it corresponds.

Every organization has its own set of business objectives and implementation strategies. Because each organization is managed by different people who use individual judgments in unique operating environments with varying complexity, no two organizations have the same set of control activities, even though they might have very similar business strategies. Control activities, therefore, serve a vital role in the management process of an organization by ensuring that its uniquely identified risks are mitigated, allowing the organization to achieve its business objectives.

Segregation of Duties

Dividing control activities among different people to reduce the risk of error or inappropriate actions taken by any single individual.

One critical concept common to all control activities is the concept that COSO defines as segregation of duties. Segregation of duties is the concept of dividing, or segregating, control activities related to the authorization of transactions from the processing of those transactions from physical access to the assets related to those underlying transactions. The primary purpose of segregating duties (dividing control activities) among different people is to reduce the risk of error or inappropriate actions taken by any single individual.

In addition to segregation of duties, there are many commonly recognized control activities that are present in a well-designed system of internal controls, including:

- Performance reviews and follow-up activities.
- Authorizations (approvals).
- IT access control activities.
- Documentation (rigorous and comprehensive).
- Physical access control activities.
- IT application (input, processing, output) control activities.
- Independent verifications and reconciliations.

Information and Communication

High quality information must be communicated appropriately. This interdependency is why COSO combines information and communication in this component. Relevant, accurate, and timely information must be available to individuals at all levels of an organization who need such information to run the business effectively. Not only must information be provided "to appropriate personnel so they can carry out their operating, financial reporting, and compliance responsibilities," but "communication also must take place in a broader sense, dealing with expectations, responsibilities of individuals and groups, and other important matters."[19] Communications with external parties also are important and can provide critical information on the functioning of controls. These parties include, but are not limited to, customers, suppliers, service providers, regulators, external auditors, and shareholders.

Actions speak louder than words

In addition to hardcopy, electronic, and oral communication formats, management's actions powerfully communicate what is important to the organization.

It is especially important to make sure information remains aligned with current business needs during periods of change. It is equally important to ensure that this information is communicated timely to all interested parties.

There are many ways organizations can choose to communicate. Hardcopy forms of communication include manuals, memoranda, and bulletin boards located in areas where individuals congregate. Communication also can take place in face-to-face meetings or electronically through e-mails, intranet sites, video conferencing, or electronic bulletin boards. The culture of the organization, as well as the content of the information shared, will dictate the best methods of communication. Because individuals accept and process information differently, most organizations will use a combination of media to ensure all individuals can process and understand the information provided to them. COSO argues that management's actions powerfully communicate what is important to the organization as "actions speak louder than words."[20]

Clearly, the culture of an organization plays an important role in communicating its priorities. Typically, organizations that have established a culture of integrity and transparency have an easier time with communication than do other organizations.

Monitoring

To remain reliable, internal control systems must be monitored. Monitoring is "a process that assesses the quality of the system's performance over time. This is accomplished through ongoing monitoring activities, separate [periodic] evaluations, or a combination of the two."[21] While not part of the organization's day-to-day operations per se, monitoring is performed concurrently with those operations on an ongoing basis. The more robust and comprehensive the supervisory and verification procedures, the more confidence management can place in the effectiveness of those procedures to ensure consistent and reliable ongoing operations. With effective ongoing monitoring activities, coupled with accurate and dependable risk assessments, the frequency of separate evaluations may be reduced.

Monitoring is most effective when a layered approach is implemented. The first layer includes the everyday activities performed by management of a given area as described above. The second layer is a separate (nonindependent) evaluation of the area's internal controls performed by management on a regular basis to ensure that any deficiencies that exist are identified and resolved timely. The third layer is an independent assessment by an outside area or function, frequently the internal audit function, performed to validate the results (accuracy and reliability) of management's self-assessment of the effectiveness of controls in their area. This layered approach provides the organization with a higher level of confidence that the system of internal controls remains effective and helps ensure internal control deficiencies are identified and addressed timely.

It is important to note that monitoring activities occur in each of the five components of internal control (Control Environment, Risk Assessment, Control Activities, Information and Communication, and Monitoring), not just as a stand-alone component. Embedding monitoring activities into processes performed during day-to-day business operations allows monitoring to occur regularly, catching problems before they become unmanageable. Separate evaluations lack this advantage due to the timing of their performance, which is later in the process, and because they are performed less frequently. Separate evaluations provide for a supplemental look at the system of internal controls, catch problems that might have been missed during ongoing monitoring, and evaluate the effectiveness of the ongoing monitoring embedded in the day-to-day activities of the area. Despite the various advantages of the two different methods for monitoring, both are needed for a robust monitoring process to exist. Exhibit 6-8 provides examples of different types of monitoring.

As previously indicated, management has primary responsibility for the effectiveness of the organization's system of internal controls, including monitoring. As responsibility for performing certain controls rises in the organization to higher levels of management, traditional supervisory monitoring becomes more challenging. Monitoring activities performed by subordinates in an organization are much less effective than those performed by superiors. In those situations in which senior management performs controls, it might be appropriate for other members of senior management to monitor those controls. In cases that carry the risk of management override, board-level monitoring might be necessary.

Deficiency (COSO's definition)

"A condition within an internal control system worthy of attention" that may represent a perceived, potential, or real shortcoming, or opportunity to strengthen the internal control system to provide a greater likelihood that the entity's objectives will be achieved.

Ultimately, the board of directors is responsible for overseeing whether management has implemented an effective system of internal controls. This responsibility is fulfilled by the board through an understanding of the risks to the organization and by understanding how management mitigates those risks to an acceptable level.

Deficiencies in an organization's system of internal controls might be identified during the performance of either ongoing monitoring or separate evaluations. COSO broadly defines a deficiency as "a condition within an internal control system worthy of attention." COSO elaborates that "a deficiency, therefore, may represent a perceived, potential, or real shortcoming, or opportunity to strengthen the internal control system to provide a greater likelihood that the entity's objectives will be achieved."[22] Deficiencies identified as a result of ongoing monitoring and separate evaluations must be reported in a timely manner to the appropriate parties within the organization. Depending on the impact a specific deficiency has on the potential effectiveness of the system of internal controls, it should be reported to business unit management, senior management,

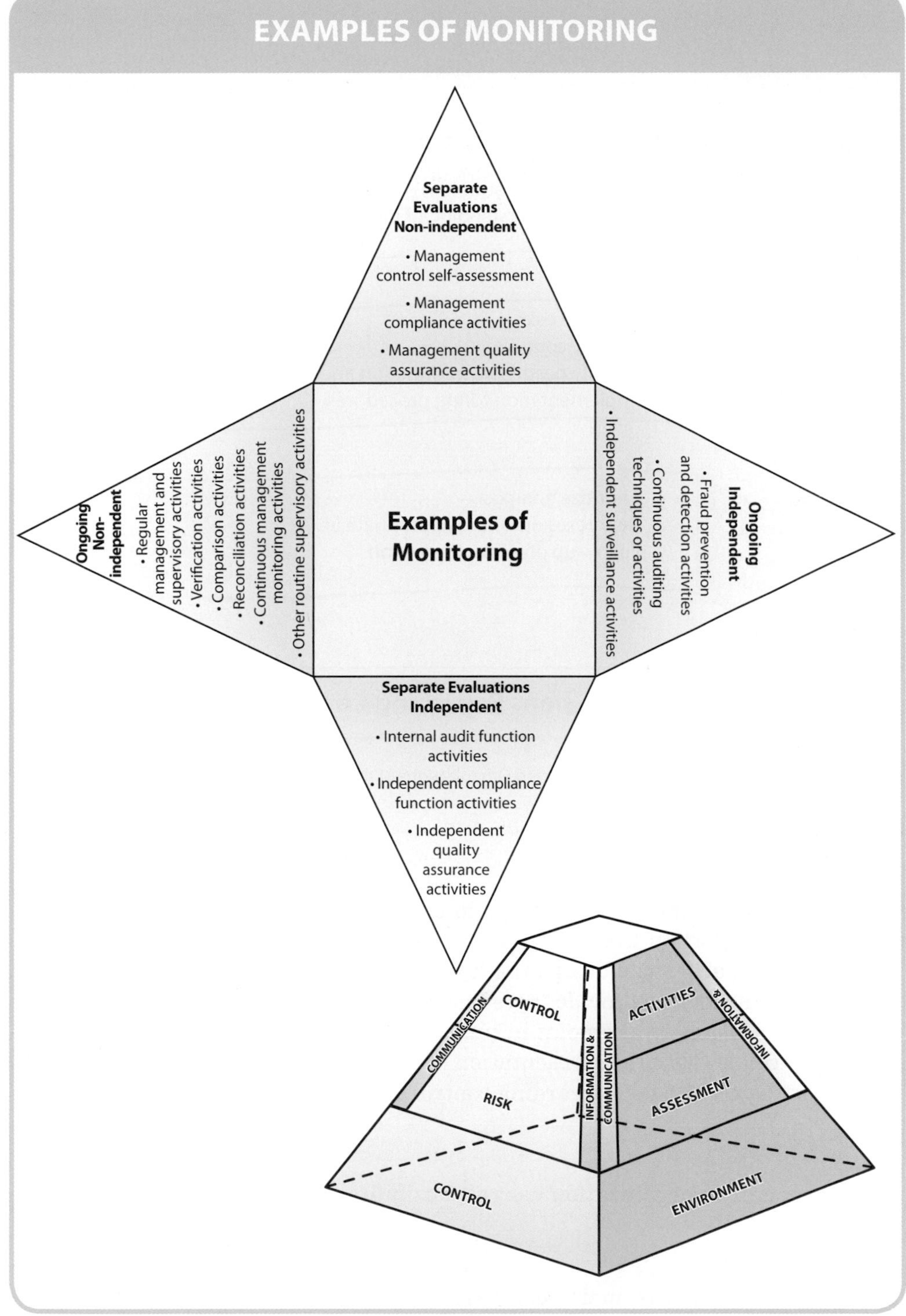

EXHIBIT 6-8

and/or the board of directors. Reported deficiencies are important considerations in the evaluation of the system of internal controls. Evaluating the system of internal controls will be explored in more detail later in this chapter. Formal communications relative to assurance engagements completed by the internal audit function are addressed in detail in Chapter 14, "Communicating Assurance Engagement Outcomes and Performing Follow-up Procedures."

As discussed earlier in the chapter, some organizations underutilize monitoring, particularly with regard to financial reporting requirements. Monitoring can be an effective tool for validating internal control asser-

EXHIBIT 6-9

THE MONITORING PROCESS

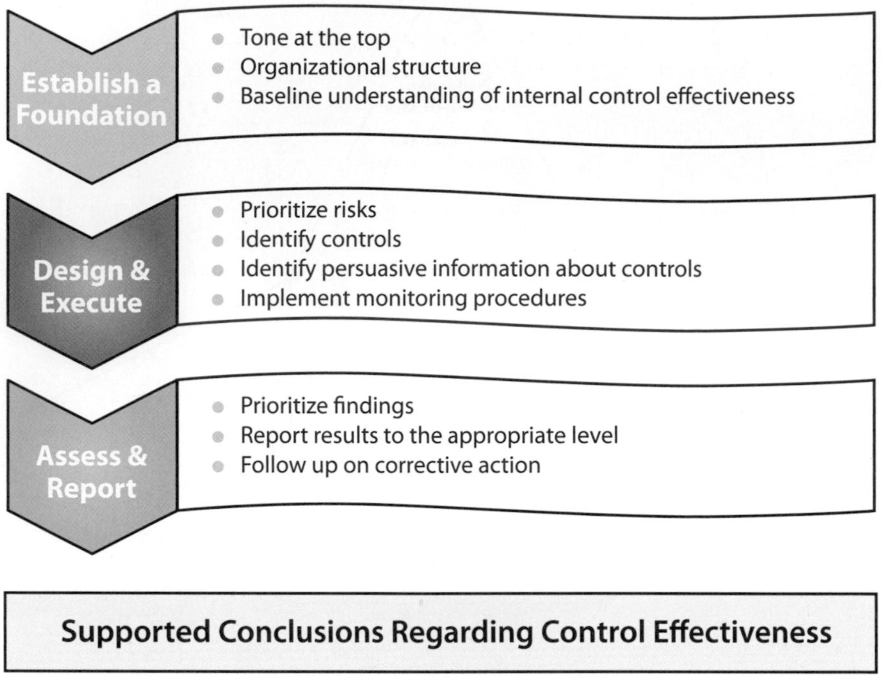

Copyright 2009, Committee of Sponsoring Organizations of the Treadway Commission (COSO). All rights reserved. Used with permission.

tions when designed with that end in mind. Organizations worldwide that must report on the effectiveness of their system of internal controls to external parties can design the "type, timing, and extent of monitoring" that is performed to provide "persuasive information that internal control operated effectively at a point in time or during a particular period."[23] Exhibit 6-9 is COSO's representation of the monitoring process relative to supporting conclusions regarding control effectiveness.

The CEO has primary responsibility for setting the "tone at the top" and establishing a positive control environment.

INTERNAL CONTROL ROLES AND RESPONSIBILITIES

Everyone in an organization has responsibility for internal control:

Management

The CEO assumes primary responsibility for the system of internal controls. The "tone at the top" (how ethical or how much integrity an organization has) is set by the CEO and rolls down from there to senior management, line management, and ultimately to all of the individuals in an organization. The CEO is more or less visible and has more or less of a direct impact depending on the size of the organization. In smaller organizations, the CEO very directly affects the system of internal controls. In larger organizations, the CEO has the greatest impact on senior management who in turn influence their subordinates. In this way, senior and line management act as "CEOs" over the areas for which they are responsible.

Tone at the Top

The entity-wide attitude of integrity and control consciousness, as exhibited by the most senior executives of an organization.

Board of Directors

The board of directors oversees management and provides direction regarding internal control. COSO describes effective board members as "objective, capable, and inquisitive . . . " with "knowledge of the [organization's] activities and environment, and [who] commit the time necessary to fulfill their board responsibilities."[24] Effective board members are essential to an effective system of internal controls because management has the capability to override controls and suppress evidence of unethical behavior or fraud. Such behavior has a greater likelihood of discovery or prevention when the organization has a board that is actively engaged. As previously mentioned, the board of directors has ultimate responsibility for ensuring management has established an effective system of internal controls.

The board of directors' roles and responsibilities as described by COSO form an effective governance "umbrella" for an organization. For a visual depiction of this process, see Exhibit 3-3 in Chapter 3, "Governance." Chapter 3 describes governance as the process conducted by the board of directors to authorize, direct, and oversee management toward the achievement of the organization's business objectives.

Internal Auditors

While management, under the leadership of the CEO, has ultimate responsibility for the adequate design and effective operation of the system of internal controls, internal auditors play a significant role in verifying that management has met its responsibility. Initially, management performs the primary assessment of the system of internal controls, and then the internal audit function independently validates management's assertions. The internal audit function provides reasonable assurance that the system of internal controls is designed adequately and operating effectively, increasing the likelihood that the organization's business objectives and goals will be met. The COSO framework defines the role of the internal auditor similarly, although in more general terms: "Internal auditors play an important role in evaluating the effectiveness of control systems, and contribute to ongoing effectiveness. Because of [its] organizational position and authority in an entity, an internal audit function often plays a significant monitoring role."[25] The relationship between management and the internal audit function relative to evaluating the system of internal controls and reporting on such is further explored later in this chapter and in Chapter 9, "Managing the Internal Audit Function."

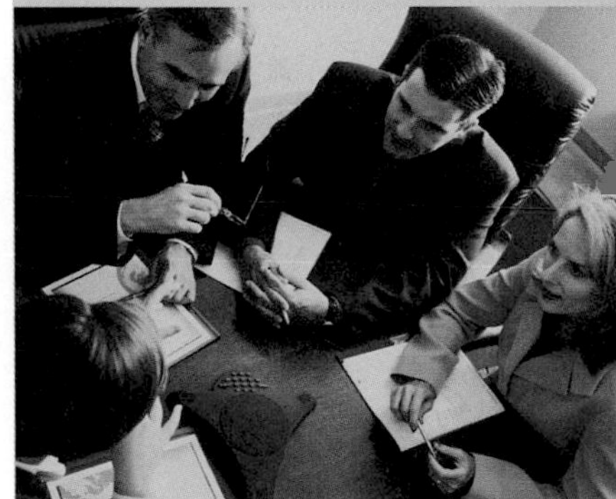

Other Personnel

COSO clearly indicates that everyone in an organization has responsibility for internal control: "Internal control is, to some degree, the responsibility of everyone in an organization and therefore should be an explicit or implicit part of everyone's job description. Virtually all employees produce information used in the internal control system or take other actions needed to effect control." COSO adds that "all personnel should be responsible for communicating upward problems in operations, noncompliance with the code of conduct, or other policy violations or illegal actions."[26]

COSO points out that external parties can be important factors relative to an organization's ability to achieve its objectives. For example, independent outside auditors, while not responsible for the organization's system of internal controls, contribute independence and objectivity through their opinions covering the fairness of the financial statements and the effectiveness of internal control over financial reporting. Other external parties that are not part of an organization's internal control but provide "information to the [organization] useful in effecting internal control are legislators and regulators, customers and others transacting business with the enterprise, financial analysts, bond raters, and the news media."[27]

In many cases, outside vendors are used to perform elements of the internal control system. However, in those cases, ownership and accountability for those outsourced elements remain with internal management, who has the ultimate responsibility for testing and certifying outsourced key controls. Activities commonly outsourced include, for example, data processing, payroll, or even the internal audit function itself. Business process outsourcing is discussed further in Chapter 5, "Business Processes and Risks."

LIMITATIONS OF INTERNAL CONTROL

Internal control is implemented to mitigate risks that threaten the achievement of an organization's objectives or to enable an organization to successfully pursue opportunities. Although management, the board of directors, internal auditors, and other personnel work together to facilitate internal control, no internal control system can ensure that objectives will be achieved. This is due to the inherent limitations of internal control. Specifically, COSO points to the following limitations as inherent to internal control:

Reasonable Assurance

A level of assurance that is supported by generally accepted auditing procedures and judgments.

- Human judgment in decision-making can be faulty.
- Breakdowns can occur because of such human failures as simple error or mistake.
- Controls can be circumvented by the collusion of two or more people.
- Management has the ability to override the internal control system.
- Controls must be considered in terms of their costs compared to their benefits.[28]

While a well designed system of internal controls can provide reasonable assurance to management relative to achievement of the organization's objectives, no system of internal controls can provide absolute assurance for the reasons listed above. This is true regardless of whether objectives fall into the operations, financial reporting, or compliance categories.

As previously indicated, establishing business objectives is a prerequisite to designing an effective system of internal controls. Business objectives provide the measurable targets for which an organization conducts its operations. A key to understanding the concepts of inherent limitations and reasonable assurance lies in also understanding the linkage and interdependency of the business objectives and the risks that directly or indirectly affect an organization's ability to achieve their business objectives. Only then can an organization properly design and implement an effective system of internal controls. As COSO indicates, "The process of identifying and analyzing risk is an ongoing iterative process and is a critical component of an effective internal control system. Management must focus carefully on risks at all levels of the entity and take necessary actions to manage them."[29]

Inherent Risk, Controllable Risk, and Residual Risk

An organization's ability to achieve established business objectives is affected by both internal and external risks. The combination of internal and external risks in their pure, uncontrolled state is referred to as inherent risk. Said another way, inherent risk is the gross risk that exists assuming there are no internal controls in place. Acknowledgement of the existence of inherent risk and that certain events or conditions are simply outside of management's control (external risks) is critical to recognizing the inherent limitations of internal control.

Inherent Limitations of Internal Control

The confines that relate to the limits of human judgment, resource constraints and the need to consider the cost of controls in relation to expected benefits, the reality that breakdowns can occur, and the possibility of collusion or management override.

Identifying external and internal risks at an entity and activity (process and transaction) level is fundamental to effective risk assessment. As discussed in Chapter 5, "Business Processes and Risks," once key risks have been identified, management can link them to business objectives and the related business processes.

Once entity-level and activity-level risks have been identified, they must be assessed in terms of impact and likelihood. Risk analysis processes vary depending on many factors specific to an organization, but typically they include:

- Estimating the [impact (or severity)] of a risk.
- Assessing the likelihood (or frequency) of the risk occurring [probability].
- Considering how the risk should be managed — that is, an assessment of what actions need to be taken.[30]

The results of the risk analysis allow management to consider how best to respond to the risks threatening achievement of the organization's objectives. Risks that are not significant and do not have a high likelihood of occurring will receive little attention. Risks that are significant and/or are likely to occur will receive much greater attention. The risks that fall somewhere in the middle, however, generally require further analysis as care in judgment is necessary to adequately mitigate these risks without using resources inefficiently.

Inherent Risk

The combination of internal and external risk factors in their pure, uncontrolled state, or, the gross risk that exists assuming there are no internal controls in place.

Controls are risk responses management takes to reduce the impact and/or likelihood of threats to objective achievement. Management must consider its overall risk appetite and individual risk tolerances when deciding which actions to take. COSO's *Enterprise Risk Management – Integrated Framework* defines risk appetite as "the broad-based amount of risk a company or other entity is willing to accept in pursuit of its mission (or vision)," and risk tolerance as "the acceptable [levels of size and] variation relative to the achievement of an objective."[31] Risk tolerance must align with the risk appetite.

Additionally, risk tolerance takes into consideration the amount of risk that management consciously accepts after balancing the cost and benefits of implementing controls. It is important to recognize that there is a direct relationship between the amount of risk mitigated and the cost associated with implementing controls designed to achieve that level of mitigation. Consequently, an organization must ensure it has neither

EXHIBIT 6-10

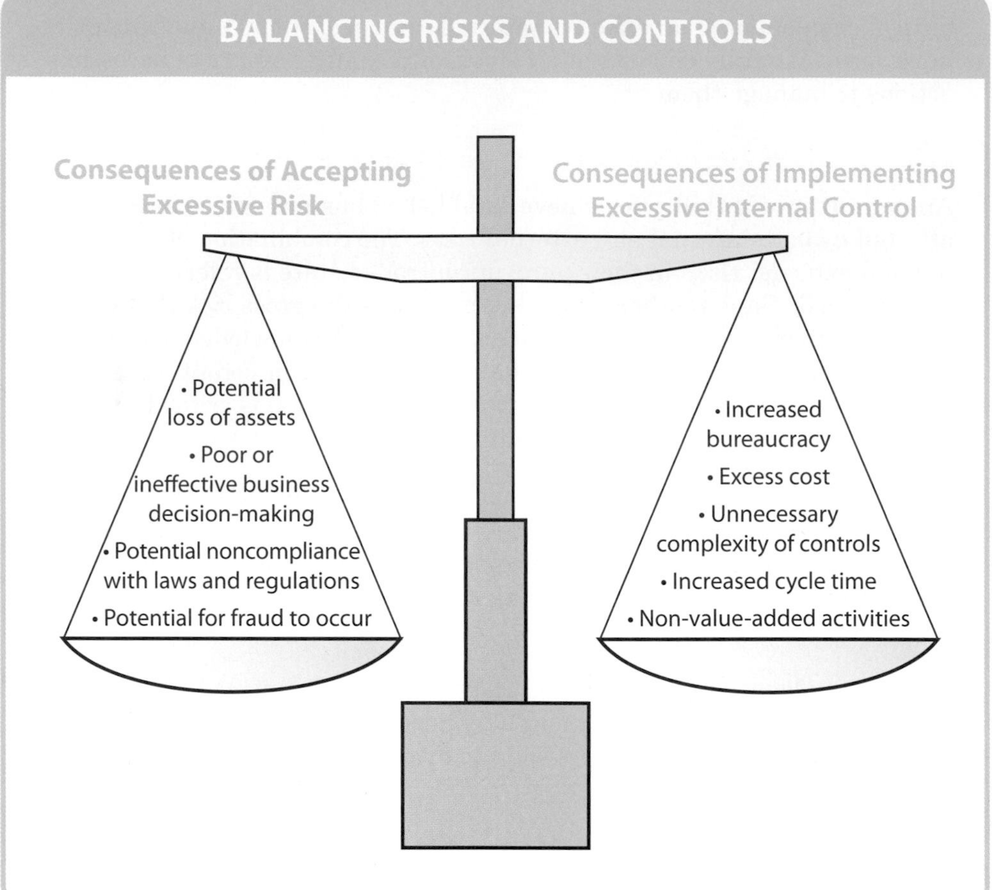
BALANCING RISKS AND CONTROLS
Consequences of Accepting Excessive Risk
• Potential loss of assets
• Poor or ineffective business decision-making
• Potential noncompliance with laws and regulations
• Potential for fraud to occur
Consequences of Implementing Excessive Internal Control
• Increased bureaucracy
• Excess cost
• Unnecessary complexity of controls
• Increased cycle time
• Non-value-added activities

Risk Appetite

The amount of risk, on a broad level, an organization is willing to accept in pursuit of its business objectives. Risk appetite takes into consideration the amount of risk that management consciously accepts after balancing the cost and benefits of implementing controls.

Risk Tolerance

The acceptable levels of risk size and variation relative to the achievement of objectives, which must align with the organization's risk appetite.

excessive risk nor excessive internal control. Exhibit 6-10 lists some of the possible consequences of accepting excessive risk or implementing excessive internal control. The balance that management is able to achieve results in an organization accepting a higher or lower level of risk and depends on the nature of the risk, the regulatory environment in which the organization operates, and management's philosophy.

With that said, there are many factors management must consider when determining the specific actions (controls) management should take to manage inherent risks to an acceptably low level, that is, within their risk tolerances. To begin with, management must consider controllable risk.

Controllable risk is that portion of inherent risk that management can directly influence and reduce through day-to-day business activities. Once management has implemented cost-effective controls to address controllable risks, then and only then can they determine if the organization is operating within the overall risk appetite established by senior management and the board of directors. The portion of inherent risk that remains after mitigating all controllable risks is defined as *residual risk*. If the remaining uncontrolled risk (residual risk) is less than the established risk appetite, then the system of internal controls is operating at an acceptable level and within an organization's defined risk appetite.

If, however, residual risk exceeds the organization's established risk appetite, it is necessary to reevaluate the system of internal controls to determine if additional cost-effective controls can be implemented to further reduce residual risk to a level within management's risk appetite. If not, management must consider other options such as sharing or transferring a portion of the uncontrolled risk to a willing independent third party through insurance or outsourcing. If the uncontrolled risk cannot be effectively transferred or shared, management can either accept the higher level of risk (and adjust their risk appetite accordingly), or the organization must decide if it wants to remain engaged in the activity causing the risk. Refer to Chapter 4, "Risk Management," for an in-depth discussion of risk management and related mitigation techniques.

An adequately designed and effectively operating system of internal controls, by definition, is designed to manage risk within the organization's established risk appetite. It should mitigate inherent risk related to the three COSO categories of objectives (effective and efficient operations, reliable financial reporting, and compliance with applicable laws and regulations) within management's risk appetite.

VIEWING INTERNAL CONTROL FROM DIFFERENT PERSPECTIVES

Because everyone in an organization has some responsibility for internal control, there naturally will be different perspectives from which individuals in the organization approach internal control. "Different perspectives on internal control are not undesirable," according to COSO. "Internal control is concerned with entity objectives, and different groups are interested in different objectives for different reasons."[32]

Management

Because management is responsible for setting the organization's objectives, they naturally view internal control from that perspective. Management must consider internal control in terms of the related costs and benefits and allocate the resources necessary to achieve those objectives.

From management's perspective, internal control includes a number of activities designed to mitigate risks or enable opportunities that affect the achievement of an organization's objectives. Management's involvement with the system of internal controls allows them to react quickly when conditions warrant. It also assists management in terms of complying with national, local, and industry-specific laws and regulations.

Internal Auditors

Like management, internal auditors look at internal control in terms of its role in the achievement of organizational objectives. Whereas management is responsible for the system of internal controls itself, internal auditors are charged with independently verifying that the organization's controls are designed adequately and operating effectively as management intends. This independent validation, which takes into account "all of an entity's systems, processes, operations, functions, and activities," increases the probability of the organization's objectives being achieved.[33]

Independent Outside Auditors

The primary responsibility of an organization's independent outside auditors is to attest to the fairness of the financial statements and, in certain countries, the effectiveness of internal control over financial reporting.

Controllable Risk

The portion of inherent risk that management can reduce through day-to-day operations and management activities.

Residual Risk

The portion of inherent risk that remains after management executes its risk responses (sometimes referred to as net risk).

For this reason, their perspective is focused on internal control relative to how it affects the organization's financial reporting. While independent outside auditors take the organization's objectives and strategy into consideration when fulfilling their role, they do not take the same broad perspective of internal control that is taken by management and internal auditors.

Other External Parties

External parties that have an interest in an organization's internal control include legislators, regulators, investors, and creditors. Because their interests vary, so too will their perspective of internal control. Consequently, "legislators and regulatory agencies have developed various definitions of internal control to conform to their responsibilities. These definitions generally relate to the types of activities monitored, and may encompass achievement of the entity's goals and objectives, reporting requirements, use of resources in compliance with laws and regulations, and safeguarding resources against waste, loss, and misuse." Investors and creditors, on the other hand, primarily need the kind of financial information that the organization's independent outside auditors validate.[34]

TYPES OF CONTROLS

There are many types of controls that are used by an organization to increase the likelihood that objectives will be met. It is important to note that specific controls can be referred to by different organizations (and even different individuals within an organization) by different names. More significant than the name used to describe a particular control is the type of control it is. This can create confusion because many controls fit into more than one category simultaneously. This is addressed in more detail later in the chapter.

Depending on the specific application of these controls, they can be classified any number of ways and may take on multiple classifications simultaneously. The following sections outline the various types of controls and their individual purposes.

Entity-level, Process-level, and Transaction-level Controls

Entity-level Control

A control that operates across an entire entity and, as such, is not bound by, or associated with, individual processes.

All controls are designed to mitigate risk either at the enterprise level or at the operational level within an organization. The 1992 COSO framework uses the terms "entity level" and "activity level" respectively to describe these controls. Although it is not uncommon for organizations within the internal audit profession to use different terminology such as "company-wide" or "entity-wide" to refer to entity-level controls, the more common term "entity level" is used in this chapter. This chapter also describes process-level controls and transaction-level controls, which together comprise activity-level controls. More important than the specific terms used when discussing these types of controls, however, is the purpose of the control and its operating effectiveness. For a visual depiction of these controls, which are discussed below, refer to the funnel in Exhibit 4-3.

Entity-level controls are very broadly focused and often deal with the organizational environment or atmosphere. They are designed to directly mitigate risks that exist at the organization-wide level, including those that arise internally as well as externally, and may indirectly mitigate risks at the process and transaction levels. These controls have a pervasive effect on the achievement of many overall objectives. The U.S. Public Company Accounting Oversight Board (PCAOB) states in its Auditing Standard No. 5 "Entity-level controls include —

- Controls related to the control environment;
- Controls over management override;
- The company's risk assessment process;
- Centralized processing and controls, including shared service environments;
- Controls to monitor results of operations;
- Controls to monitor other controls, including activities of the internal audit function, the audit committee, and self-assessment programs;
- Controls over the period-end financial reporting process; and
- Policies that address significant business control and risk management practices."[35]

Entity-level controls can be divided into two categories: governance controls and management-oversight controls. Governance controls are established by the board and executive management to institute the organization's control culture and provide guidance that supports strategic objectives. Management-oversight controls are established by management at the business unit and line level of the organization to reduce risks to the business unit and increase the probability that business unit objectives are achieved.

Process-level controls are more detailed in their focus than entity-level controls. They are established by process owners to reduce the risk that threatens the achievement of process objectives. While consistent in nature, these controls may vary in their execution between processes. Examples of process-level controls include:

- Reconciliations of key accounts,
- Physical verifications of assets (such as inventory counts),
- Process employee supervision and performance evaluations,
- Process-level risk assessments, and
- Monitoring/oversight of specific transactions.

Process-level Control

An activity that operates within a specific process for the purpose of achieving process-level objectives.

Transaction-level controls are even more detailed in their focus than process-level controls and reduce risk relative to a group or variety of operational-level activities (tasks) or transactions within an organization. They are designed to ensure that individual operational activities, tasks, or transactions, as well as related groups of operational activities (tasks) or transactions, are accurately processed in a timely manner. Examples of transaction-level controls include:

- Authorizations,
- Documentation (such as source documents),
- Segregation of duties, and
- IT application controls (input, processing, output).

Transaction-level Control

An activity that reduces risk relative to a group or variety of operational-level tasks or transactions within an organization.

Adequately designed and effectively operating entity-level, process-level, and transaction-level controls work in unison and serve as an organization's defense against the risks that threaten the achievement of business objectives. Entity-level, process-level, and transaction-level controls are discussed in greater detail in Case Study 1, "Auditing Entity-level Controls," which accompanies this textbook.

Key Control

An activity designed to reduce risk associated with a critical business objective.

Key Controls and Secondary Controls

Controls also can be categorized in terms of their importance. As such, a control can be categorized either as a key control or as a secondary control.

A key control (often referred to as the "primary" control) is designed to reduce key risks associated with business objectives. Failure to implement adequately designed and effectively operating key controls can result in the failure of the organization not only to achieve critical business objectives but to survive.

Secondary Control

An activity designed to either reduce risk associated with business objectives that are not critical to the organization's survival or success or serve as a backup to a key control.

A secondary control is one that is designed to either (1) mitigate risks that are not key to business objectives, or (2) partially reduce the level of risk when a key control does not operate effectively. Secondary controls reduce the level of residual risk when key controls do not operate effectively, but are not adequate, by themselves, to mitigate a particular key risk to an acceptable level. They are typically a subset of compensating or complementary controls.

Compensating Controls

Compensating controls are designed to supplement key controls that are either ineffective or cannot fully mitigate a risk or group of risks by themselves to an acceptable level within the risk appetite established by management and the board. For example, close supervision in instances when adequate segregation of duties cannot be achieved may be a compensating control. Such controls also can back up or duplicate multiple controls.

As previously mentioned, secondary controls and compensating controls are necessary when an effective key control cannot be created or designed to adequately mitigate a risk or group of risks within management's established risk appetite. This may be a result of economic constraints or operational complexity or both. No matter the reason, secondary and compensating controls are required for which no effective key control exists. Often, compensating controls work concurrently with related or overlapping key controls, while serving as a secondary control for a specific key control.

Complementary Controls

A complementary control is a necessary control that is not sufficient by itself to fully mitigate the risk. However, when combined with one or more other controls, a complementary control does help reduce the underlying risk to an acceptable level. For example, segregation of duties is frequently considered a key control. Separating duties relating to custody of cash and recording cash transactions is a specific example. By adding an independent verification (for example, a bank reconciliation), the underlying risks, such as cash misappropriation, are further reduced.

Frequently, complementary controls may operate across multiple processes and risks. In the bank reconciliation example referred to above, this complementary control could help mitigate other risks, including period-end cutoff risk and accuracy risk.

Preventive, Detective, Corrective, and Directive Controls

Often, the many different controls that exist are referred to by labels that describe what they are intended to do in an attempt to differentiate between them. Included here is a short list of these types of controls and their definitions.

A *preventive control* is designed to deter unintended events from occurring in the first place. Because of the dynamic nature and complexity of day-to-day business operations, it is difficult to design a preventive control that is both economical and efficient. As a result, most organizations use a combination of preventive controls and detective controls when designing both an effective and efficient system of internal controls. Examples of preventive controls include physical and logical access controls, such as locked doors and user IDs with unique passwords.

Conversely, a *detective control* is designed to discover undesirable events that have already occurred. A detective control must occur on a timely basis (before the undesirable event has had an unacceptably negative impact on the organization) to be considered effective. Examples of detective controls include security cameras to identify unauthorized physical access and review of computer logs listing unauthorized access attempts.

A *corrective control* is one in which detected omissions and errors are corrected. An example of a corrective control is the resolution of duplicate payments flagged by the cash disbursements system.

A *directive control*, as its name suggests, gives explicit direction regarding what actions need to take place to cause or encourage a desirable event to occur. For example, product assembly instructions provide direction to the individuals involved in the production process.

Information Systems Controls

Due to the prevalent dependence on information systems, controls must be implemented to mitigate the risks associated with automated systems necessary to run the core business of an organization.

There are two types of information systems controls that can be used to mitigate these risks:

1. **General computing controls.** These "apply to many if not all application systems and help ensure their continued, proper operation."
2. **Application controls.** These "include computerized steps within the application software and related manual procedures to control the processing of various types of transactions."[36]

These two types of controls work together "to ensure completeness, accuracy, and validity of the financial and other information in the system."[37]

General computing controls are considered entity-level controls because they apply across the organization and its many computer applica-

Compensating Control

An activity that, if key controls do not fully operate effectively, may help to reduce the related risk. A compensating control will not, by itself, reduce risk to an acceptable level.

Complementary Control

An activity that, when taken together with other controls, contributes to the overall effective mitigation of risk. Frequently, complementary controls operate across multiple processes and risks.

tions. Application controls, on the other hand, are most often considered process-level or transaction-level controls. Additional discussion and examples of general computing and application controls can be found in Chapter 7, "Information Technology Risks and Controls," and Case Study 1, "Auditing Entity-level Controls," which accompanies this textbook.

Simultaneous Categorization of Controls

As alluded to earlier in the chapter, specific controls can fit into several categories at the same time. For example, a control can be an entity-level control at the same time that it is a key control. That same control also can be a directive control. It could not, however, be a secondary control or a transaction-level control at the same time that it is a key control and an entity-level control. While these nuances can be confusing in the beginning, time spent working with controls will lead to a better understanding of how the various categories of controls can exist in a single control.

EVALUATING THE SYSTEM OF INTERNAL CONTROLS – AN OVERVIEW

As previously mentioned, management, under the leadership of the CEO, has ultimate responsibility for the adequate design and effective operation of the system of internal controls. As such, management is responsible for putting in place adequately designed and effectively operating entity-level and activity-level controls to mitigate risks associated with the achievement of business objectives in each of the three COSO-defined categories: effective and efficient operations, reliable financial reporting, and compliance with laws and regulations.

Internal auditors play a significant role in the verification that management has met its responsibility. Initially, management performs the primary assessment of internal controls, using a formalized process developed for that purpose. The internal audit function then independently validates management's results. Additionally, a report is typically submitted to the audit committee by either senior management or the chief audit executive (CAE) outlining the results of management's assessment regarding the design adequacy and operating effectiveness of the organization's system of internal controls.

As indicated in The IIA's *International Standards for the Professional Practice of Internal Auditing* (*Standards*), the internal audit function is responsible for assessing an organization's controls (either elements of, or the entirety of, the system of internal controls) as outlined in Practice Advisory 2130-1: Assessing the Adequacy of Control Processes:

> In evaluating the overall effectiveness of the organization's control processes, the CAE considers whether:
>
> - Significant discrepancies or weaknesses [deficiencies] were discovered,
> - Corrections or improvements were made after the discoveries, and
> - The discoveries and their potential consequences lead to a conclusion that a pervasive condition exists resulting in an unacceptable level of risk [or operating effectiveness].

Sarbanes-Oxley additionally requires management of organizations registered with the SEC to publicly report on the reliability of internal control over financial reporting (ICFR). As previously indicated, in the United States, Sarbanes-Oxley put responsibility for the design, maintenance, and effective operation of ICFR squarely on the shoulders of senior management, specifically, the CEO and CFO. To comply with this legislation, the SEC requires the CEO and CFO of publicly traded companies to opine on the reliability of financial reporting (that is, the adequate design and effective operation of ICFR) as part of the annual filing of financial statements with the SEC, as well as report any substantial changes, if any, in ICFR on a quarterly basis. Many other countries have similar requirements.

Reliable financial reporting, " . . . in the context of published financial statements, . . . is defined [by COSO] as the preparation of financial statements fairly presented in conformity with generally accepted accounting principles and regulatory requirements for external purposes, within the context of materiality. Supporting fair presentation are five basic financial statement assertions:

- Existence or occurrence,
- Completeness,
- Rights and obligations,
- Valuation or allocation, and
- Presentation and disclosure."[38]

Entity-level and activity-level controls specifically designed to provide reasonable assurance that external reporting objectives are achieved and support management's related assertions possess certain common elements. To be designed adequately and operating effectively, these controls should address the concepts of initiation, authorization, recording, processing, and reporting. As mentioned earlier in the chapter, these controls are collectively referred to as internal control over financial reporting.

PCAOB

The U.S. Public Company Accounting Oversight Board

The PCAOB was created to establish guidelines that independent outside auditors and, indirectly, management, must adhere to in order to comply with these reporting requirements. In response, on June 12, 2007, the PCAOB issued Auditing Standard No. 5, An Audit of Internal Control Over Financial Reporting That is Integrated with an Audit of Financial Statements. For additional specific guidelines, refer to Auditing Standard No. 5 itself.

SUMMARY

This chapter discussed the controls that organizations develop to mitigate the risks that could potentially threaten the achievement of business objectives. Beginning with a definition of internal control, the chapter moved on to explain what a framework is and how concepts like internal control and enterprise risk management are more effectively put into practice when they are implemented using well-developed and generally accepted frameworks. Additionally, the variety of frameworks that consider internal control should now be easily identifiable. From there, the components that must be present for an adequately designed and effectively operating system of internal controls were identified and defined. Everybody within an organization has some responsibility for internal control and this chapter outlined the specific roles and responsibilities each group of people in the organization has in that respect, including management's process for evaluating the organization's overall system of internal controls. Additionally, the specific roles and responsibilities the internal audit function has relative to the system of internal controls were discussed. The different types of controls employed to mitigate the many varieties of risks facing an organization were addressed and should now be easily identifiable. The appropriate application of each one also should be well understood. Finally, an overview of the process for evaluating the system of internal controls was presented in this chapter, which will be built on later in the textbook.

Review Questions

1. What does the term internal control mean? Draw from multiple frameworks in your answer.
2. What are the five components of an effective internal control framework?
3. What responsibilities do the following groups of people have regarding internal control?
   - Management.
   - The board of directors.
   - Internal auditors.
   - Others in the organization.
   - The independent outside auditor.
4. Who has ultimate responsibility for internal control within an organization? Why?
5. What does "limits of internal control" mean? Provide examples of limitations that are inherent to internal control.
6. How do entity-level controls differ from process-level and transaction-level controls?
7. What is a key control? What is a secondary control?
8. What is the difference between a compensating control and a complementary control?
9. What is the difference between a corrective and a directive control?
10. What are the two broad types of information systems controls?
11. How is the system of internal controls evaluated?

Multiple-choice Questions

Select the best answer for each of the following questions.

1. Which of the following best describes an internal auditor's purpose in reviewing the organization's existing governance, risk management, and control processes?
   a. To help determine the nature, timing, and extent of tests necessary to achieve engagement objectives.
   b. To ensure that weaknesses in the internal control system are corrected.
   c. To provide reasonable assurance that the processes will enable the organization's objectives and goals to be met efficiently and economically.
   d. To determine whether the processes ensure that the accounting records are correct and that financial statements are fairly stated.

2. What is residual risk?
   a. Impact of risk.
   b. Risk that is under control.
   c. Risk that is not managed.
   d. Underlying risk in the environment.

3. The requirement that purchases be made from suppliers on an approved vendor list is an example of a:
   a. Preventive control.
   b. Detective control.
   c. Corrective control.
   d. Monitoring control.

4. An adequate system of internal controls is most likely to detect a fraud perpetrated by a:
   a. Group of employees in collusion.
   b. Single employee.
   c. Group of managers in collusion.
   d. Single manager.

5. Audit engagement programs should:
   a. Be tailored for the audit of each business area within the organization.
   b. Be generalized to fit all situations without regard to departmental lines.
   c. Be generalized so as to be usable at various international locations of an organization.
   d. Reduce costly duplication of effort by ensuring that every aspect of an operation is examined.

6. The control that would most likely ensure that payroll checks are written only for authorized amounts is to:
   a. Conduct periodic floor verification of employees on the payroll.
   b. Require the return of undelivered checks to the cashier.
   c. Require supervisory approval of employee timecards.
   d. Periodically witness the distribution of payroll checks.

7. An internal auditor plans to conduct an audit of the adequacy of controls over investments in new financial instruments. Which of the following would not be required as part of such an engagement?
   a. Determine whether policies exist that describe the risks the treasurer may take and the types of instruments in which the treasurer may invest.
   b. Determine the extent of management oversight over investments in sophisticated instruments.
   c. Determine whether the treasurer is getting higher or lower rates of return on investments than treasurers in comparable organizations.
   d. Determine the nature of monitoring activities related to the investment portfolio.

8. Appropriate internal control for a multinational corporation's branch office that has a department responsible for the transfer of money requires that:
   a. The individual who initiates wire transfers does not reconcile the bank statement.
   b. The branch manager must receive all wire transfers.
   c. Foreign currency rates must be computed separately by two different employees.
   d. Corporate management approves the hiring of employees in this department.

9. Who has primary responsibility for the monitoring component of internal control?
   a. The organization's independent outside auditor.
   b. The organization's internal audit function.
   c. The organization's management.
   d. The organization's board of directors.

Discussion Questions

1. An audit report contains the following observations:
   a. A service department's location is not well suited to allow adequate service to other units.
   b. Employees hired for sensitive positions are not subjected to background checks.
   c. Managers do not have access to reports that profile overall performance in relation to other benchmarked organizations.
   d. Management has not taken corrective action to resolve past engagement observations related to inventory controls.

   Which two of these observations are most likely to indicate the existence of control weaknesses over safeguarding of assets? Why?

2. To meet waste discharge standards, a factory implements a control system designed to prevent the release of wastewater that does not meet those standards. One of the controls requires chemical analysis of the water, prior to discharge, for components specified in the permit. Is this an appropriate control? Why or why not?

3. An organization has a goal to prevent the ordering of inventory quantities in excess of its needs. One individual in the organization wants to design a control that requires a review of all purchase requisitions by a supervisor in the user department prior to submitting them to the purchasing department. Another individual wants to institute a policy requiring agreement of the receiving report and packing slip before storage of new inventory receipts. Which of these controls is (are) relevant in achieving the stated goal? Explain your answer.

4. COSO is quoted in this chapter as follows: "Internal auditors play an important role in evaluating the effectiveness of control systems, and contribute to ongoing effectiveness. Because of [its] organizational position and authority in an entity, an internal audit function often plays a significant monitoring role." Answer the following questions related to this quote.
   a. Is an organization's internal audit function part of the organization's system of internal controls? If your answer to this question is yes, explain how the internal audit function can evaluate the design adequacy and operating effectiveness of internal controls and at the same time remain independent of the organization's system of internal controls. If your answer to the question is no, explain the internal audit function's role relative to the organization's system of internal controls.
   b. If monitoring is, by definition, a component of internal control for which management is responsible, is it really appropriate for the internal audit function to perform monitoring activities? Explain your answer.

CASE 39

Controls mitigate risks that threaten objectives and thus provide reasonable assurance that objectives will be achieved. Risks encompass both threats of bad things happening and threats of good things not happening. Some controls are visible and therefore can be photographed.

A. Choose one or two classmates you want to work with on this assignment. Each team will need a camera.

B. As a team, photograph five different controls you observe around campus and/or the surrounding community. Use your imagination and ingenuity. Each team must work independently to produce a unique set of pictures. At least two of the controls photographed must be controls designed to mitigate risks of something good not happening (that is, controls designed to help something good happen).

C. For each control photographed:

1. Clearly indicate whether the control is designed to mitigate the threat of bad things happening or the threat of good things not happening.
2. Then briefly and separately describe:
   a. An objective the control is designed to help achieve.
   b. A risk the control is designed to mitigate. (Note: The risk you describe must be something other than merely the inverse of the objective.)
   c. How the control is meant to operate (that is, how the control works).
   d. How you would test the control to determine whether it is operating effectively.

To be submitted:

A. The set of five pictures.

B. The descriptions of the five controls the pictures represent, as called for in requirement C.

REFERENCES

[1]*A Vision for the Future: Professional Practices Framework for Internal Auditing* (Altamonte Springs, FL: The Institute of Internal Auditors, 1999), p. 54.

[2]International Professional Practices Framework (Altamonte Springs, FL: The Institute of Internal Auditors, 2009), p. xv.

[3]U.S. Securities and Exchange Commission. Final Rules 2003 (Rule 33-823). Available at http://www.sec.gov.

[4]Ibid.

[5]Ibid.

[6]*Internal Control Over Financial Reporting – Guidance for Smaller Public Companies,* Volume II: Guidance (Jersey City, NJ: Committee of Sponsoring Organizations of the Treadway Commission, 2006), p. 4.

[7]Ibid, p.15.

[8]*Guidance on Monitoring Internal Control Systems* (Jersey City, NJ: Committee of Sponsoring Organizations of the Treadway Commission, 2009), pp. 7-8. *Guidance on Monitoring Internal Control Systems,* Volume I : Executive Summary.

[9]*Internal Control Over Financial Reporting – Guidance for Smaller Public Companies,* Volume II: Guidance (Jersey City, NJ: Committee of Sponsoring Organizations of the Treadway Commission, 2006), p. 16.

[10]*A Vision for the Future: Professional Practices Framework for Internal Auditing* (Altamonte Springs, FL: The Institute of Internal Auditors, 1999), p. 9.

[11]*Internal Control – Integrated Framework* (Jersey City, NJ: Committee of Sponsoring Organizations of the Treadway Commission, 1992), p. 13.

[12]Ibid, p. 14.

[13]International Professional Practices Framework (Altamonte Springs, FL: The Institute of Internal Auditors, 2009), p. 40.

[14] *Internal Control – Integrated Framework* (Jersey City, NJ: Committee of Sponsoring Organizations of the Treadway Commission, 1992), p. 23.

[15]Ibid.

[16]Ibid.

[17]Ibid, p. 33.

[18]Ibid, p. 34.

[19]Ibid, p. 63.

[20]Ibid, p. 66.

[21]Ibid, p. 69.

REFERENCES

[22]Ibid, p. 74.

[23]*Guidance on Monitoring Internal Control Systems* (Jersey City, NJ: Committee of Sponsoring Organizations of the Treadway Commission, 2009), p. 20.

[24]*Internal Control – Integrated Framework* (Jersey City, NJ: Committee of Sponsoring Organizations of the Treadway Commission, 1992), p. 7.

[25]Ibid, p. 7.

[26]Ibid.

[27]Ibid.

[28]Ibid, p. 79.

[29]Ibid, p. 39.

[30]Ibid, p. 42.

[31]*Enterprise Risk Management – Integrated Framework* (Jersey City, NJ: Committee of Sponsoring Organizations of the Treadway Commission, 2004), p. 124.

[32]Ibid, p. 106.

[33]Ibid.

[34]Ibid, p. 107.

[35]Public Company Accounting Oversight Board. Auditing and Related Professional Practice Standards: Auditing Standard No. 5: An Audit of Internal Control Over Financial Reporting Performed in Conjunction With An Audit of Financial Statements. June 12, 2007, paragraph 24.

[36]*Internal Control – Integrated Framework* (Jersey City, NJ: Committee of Sponsoring Organizations of the Treadway Commission, 1992), p. 52.

[37]Ibid.

[38]Ibid, p. 122.

[39]Adapted from the Snap A Control project created by Dr. Glenn Sumners.

CHAPTER 7
INFORMATION TECHNOLOGY RISKS AND CONTROLS

Learning Objectives

- Understand how information technology (IT) is intertwined with business objectives, strategies, and operations.
- Describe the key components of modern information systems.
- Explain the nature of IT opportunities and risks.
- Understand fundamental IT governance, risk management, and control concepts.
- Understand the implications of IT for internal auditors.
- Identify sources of IT audit guidance.

Organizations invest heavily in IT for several reasons, all of which pertain directly to achieving the organizations' business objectives. For example, IT enables business strategies, enhances the performance of business processes, and facilitates decision-making. In fact, IT has reached the point of being so intertwined with organizations' business objectives, strategies, and operations that IT initiatives must be considered in tandem with business initiatives to ensure alignment between the two.

Consider, for example, that:

- A retail company wants to expand its sales by selling directly to customers via its website. Pursuing a strategy of online sales would not even be an option if e-commerce technology, including the Internet, did not exist.
- A manufacturing company wants to streamline its purchasing process to make it more cost-effective. Electronic data interchange (EDI), which would enable the manufacturer's computer to transact business directly with suppliers' computers, is a technology solution management may consider.
- A large floral company wants to more precisely evaluate the day-to-day operating performance of its geographically dispersed stores. A data warehouse in which pertinent historical information is stored would facilitate calculations of day-by-day, store-by-store performance metrics, analysis of performance trends by product line, and what-if scenario analysis of projected performance.

EXHIBIT 7-1

PROFESSIONAL STANDARDS, PRACTICE ADVISORIES, AND PRACTICE GUIDES RELEVANT TO CHAPTER 7

1210 – Proficiency

1220 – Due Professional Care

2110 – Governance

2120 – Risk Management

2130 – Control

Practice Advisory 1210-1: Proficiency

Practice Advisory 1210.A1-1: Obtaining External Service Providers to Support or Complement the Internal Audit Activity

Practice Advisory 1220-1: Due Professional Care

Practice Advisory 2120-1: Assessing the Adequacy of Risk Management Processes

Practice Advisory 2130-1: Assessing the Adequacy of Control Processes

Practice Advisory 2130.A1-1: Information Reliability and Integrity

Practice Advisory 2130.A1-2: Evaluating an Organization's Privacy Framework

GTAG 1 – Information Technology Controls

GTAG 2 – Change and Patch Management Controls: Critical for Organizational Success

GTAG 3 – Continuous Auditing: Implications for Assurance, Monitoring, and Risk Assessment

GTAG 4 – Management of IT Auditing

GTAG 5 – Managing and Auditing Privacy Risks

GTAT 6 – Managing and Auditing IT Vulnerabilities

GTAG 7 – Information Technology Outsourcing

GTAG 8 – Auditing Application Controls

GTAG 9 – Identity and Access Management

GTAG 10 – Business and Continuity Management

GTAG 11 – Developing the IT Audit Plan

GTAG 12 – Auditing IT Projects

GTAG 13 – Fraud Detection in an Automated World

The GAIT Methodology

GAIT for IT General Control Deficiency Assessment

GAIT for Business and IT Risk (GAIT-R)

Case Studies Using GAIT-R to Scope PCI Compliance

The increasingly pervasive impact of IT on organizations' business strategies and day-to-day operations has significantly affected the internal audit profession. IT has changed the competencies that internal audit functions must possess and how they perform assurance and consulting services. It is virtually impossible in today's business world for any internal audit function to provide value-adding services to their organization unless the function is highly proficient in its knowledge of IT risks and controls and has the capability to effectively apply technology-based audit techniques.

Information Systems (IS) Auditor

An auditor who works extensively in the area of computerized information systems and has deep IT risk, control, and audit expertise.

An internal auditor who works extensively in the area of computerized information systems must possess deep IT risk, control, and audit expertise. Such auditors are commonly referred to as information systems (IS) auditors or IT auditors. Although all internal auditors need not have the expertise of an IT auditor, at minimum, every internal auditor must have a sound understanding of certain fundamental IT concepts. For example, all internal auditors need to understand the basic components of their organizations' information systems, the IT risks that threaten the achievement of their organizations' business objectives, and their organizations' IT governance, risk management, and control processes.

This chapter first provides an overview of selected key components of modern information systems. The opportunities and risks associated with IT are then described. This is followed by coverage of IT governance, risk management, and controls. The chapter then addresses the implications of IT for internal auditors and concludes with sources of IT audit guidance being identified.

KEY COMPONENTS OF MODERN INFORMATION SYSTEMS

Modern information systems vary significantly among organizations and it is beyond the scope of this textbook to cover the wide variety of system configurations that exist in today's business world. There are, however, common key components of information systems that internal auditors need to understand. These components include computer hardware, networks, computer software, databases, information, and people. Exhibit 7-2 illustrates a simple information system configuration that will serve as the context for providing examples of the key components as they are described below.

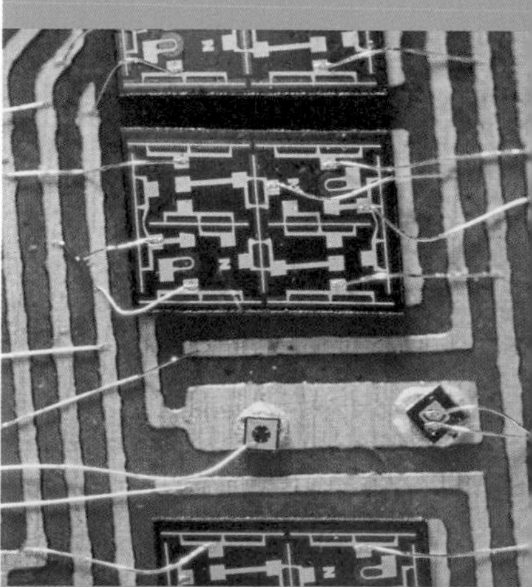

Computer hardware. Computer hardware comprises the physical components of an information system. Hardware includes, for example, central processing units (CPUs), servers, workstations and terminals, computer chips, input/output devices such as scanners and printers, storage devices such as disk drives, and communication devices such as modems and routers.

> **Example:** The computer hardware depicted in Exhibit 7-2 includes two desktop computers, two laptop computers, a printer, a mainframe computer, four servers, and two firewalls.

Networks. A computer network links two or more computers so they can share information and/or workloads. There are many types of networks:

- A client-server network connects one or more client computers with a server and data processing is shared between the client(s) and the server in a manner that optimizes processing efficiency.

EXHIBIT 7-2

ILLUSTRATION OF A SIMPLE INFORMATION SYSTEM CONFIGURATION

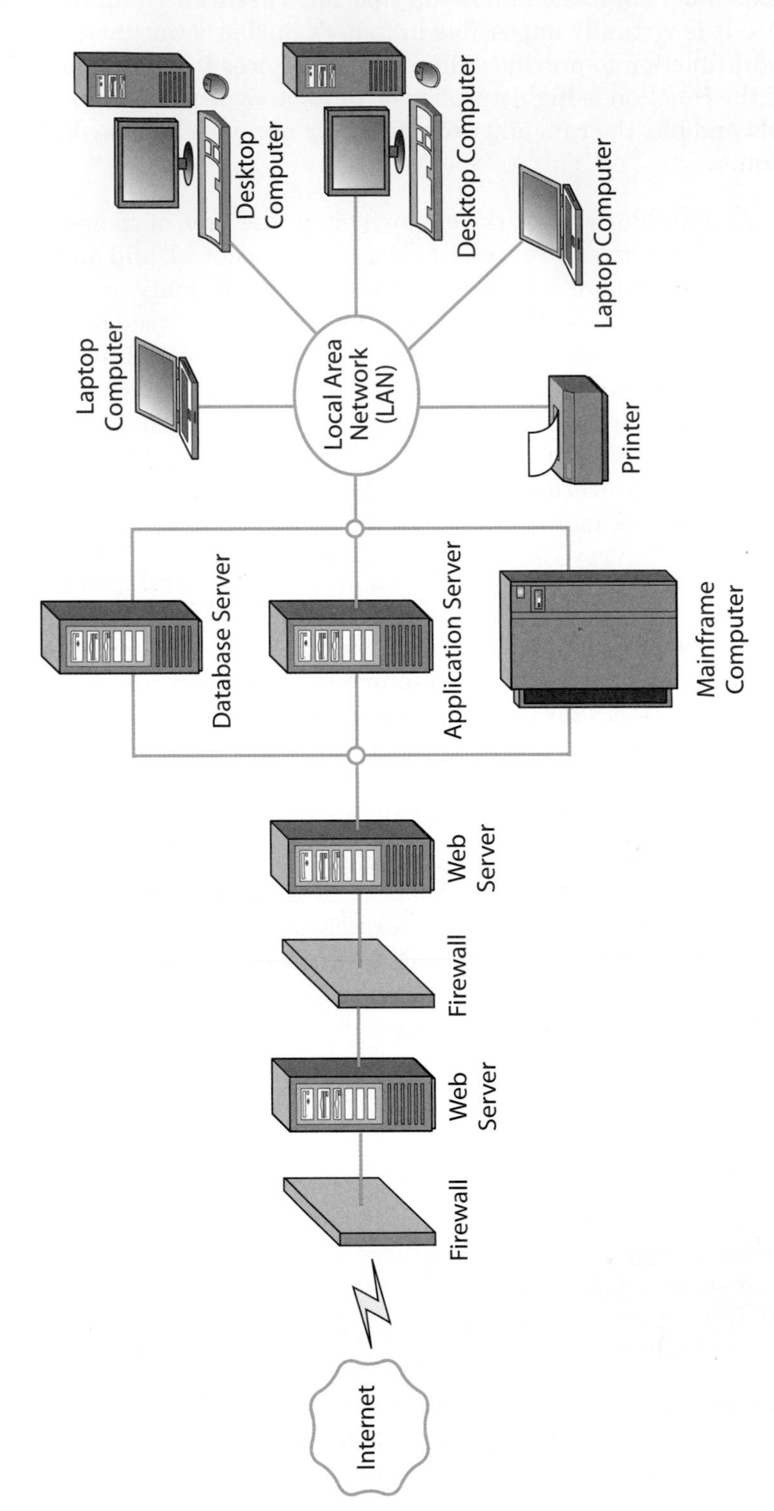

- A local area network (LAN) spans a relatively small area such as a building or group of adjacent buildings.
- A wide area network (WAN) comprises a system of LANs connected together to span a regional, national, or global area.
- An intranet is an organization's private network accessible only to that organization's personnel.
- An extranet is accessible to selected third parties such as authorized suppliers and/or customers.
- A value added network (VAN) is a third-party network that connects an organization with its trading partners.
- The Internet (*inter*connected *net*works) is the very large and complex public system of computer networks that enables users to communicate globally.

  Example: Exhibit 7-2 depicts the interconnection between the LAN, the organization's intranet, and the Internet.

Computer software. Computer software includes operating system software, utility software, database management system (DBMS) software, application software, and firewall software. The operating system controls the basic input, processing, and output of the computer and manages the interconnectivity of the system hardware devices. Utility software augments the operating system with functionality such as encryption, disk space optimization, and protection against viruses. The database management system software manages the data stored in the database, controls access to the database, and automatically backs up the database. Application software includes accounting software that is used to process transactions as well as other types of software, such as word processing and spreadsheet software, that enable end users to perform their assigned tasks. Firewall software enforces access control between two networks by allowing only authorized data transmissions to pass through the firewall in both directions.

> **Example:** Each desktop, laptop, mainframe, and server computer depicted in Exhibit 7-2 contains operating and utility software needed for the computer to function properly and for information to be exchanged among the computers and the printer. Basic application software may reside on each desktop and laptop computer or be stored on the application server to be shared among the users of the desktop and laptop computers. Larger application programs may reside on either the application server or the mainframe and process data as requested by the users. The database server and the mainframe contain database software that manages the stored data and specifies the access and processing privileges of each user. The web servers contain software that directs the flow of information between the Internet and the organization's intranet. The firewalls contain two layers of software that prevent unauthorized transmissions of information into and out of the organization.

Database

A large depository of data, typically contained in many linked files, and stored in a manner that allows the data to be easily accessed, retrieved, and manipulated.

Databases. A database is a large repository of data, typically contained in many linked files and stored in a manner that allows the data to be easily accessed, retrieved, and manipulated. An operating database supports day-to-day transaction processing and is continuously updated as transactions are processed. A data warehouse is a large assemblage of data stored over time to support online data analysis and decision-making.

Example: Each desktop and laptop computer depicted in Exhibit 7-2 may house databases used to store relatively small quantities of data that is useful to the user of that computer. The database server houses bigger databases designed to hold larger volumes of data. Mainframe computers typically house even larger databases that require faster response time due to the volume of inquiries and processing requirements. The DBMS controls which data each user can access and what they can do with the data.

Information. "For many enterprises, information and the technology that supports it represent their most valuable . . . assets."[1] Information systems collect and store data, transform the data into useful information, and provide the information to internal and external decision makers. For information to be useful, it must be relevant, reliable, complete, accurate, and timely.

Example: Each desktop, laptop, server, and mainframe computer depicted in Exhibit 7-2 contains information in various types of files that is useful to the user or users of that computer. Information flows in multiple directions among the various computers, and to and from parties inside and outside the organization.

People. Specific information system roles vary significantly from one organization to another. Typically, these roles include those of a chief information officer (CIO), a database administrator, systems developers, data processing personnel, and end users.

- The CIO is responsible for the day-to-day oversight and direction of IT and for ensuring that IT objectives and strategies are aligned with the organization's business objectives and strategies.
- The database administrator is responsible for supervising the design, development, implementation, and maintenance of the database, controlling access to the database, monitoring database performance, and upgrading the database in response to changes in users' needs.
- Systems developers include analysts and programmers. Analysts survey users' IT needs, perform "what is" versus "what should be" analyses of IT systems, and design new IT systems. Programmers construct and test the software used to execute data processing tasks.
- Data processing personnel manage centralized IT resources and perform centralized day-to-day input, processing, and output activities.
- End users are the managers and employees for whom the information system was built. They use the information produced by the system to carry out their day-to-day roles and responsibilities.

  Example: The people involved in the information system depicted in Exhibit 7-2 include the desktop and laptop users, the database administrators responsible for managing the databases, the individuals responsible for managing and operating the various servers and the firewalls, and the application programmers who constructed and tested the application software. The application software may have been constructed in-house or purchased from a software vendor. The mainframe computer may require individuals with specialized expertise due to its greater level of complexity.

IT OPPORTUNITIES AND RISKS

Opportunity and risk were introduced in Chapter 1, "Introduction to Internal Auditing," and discussed in detail in Chapter 4, "Risk Management." *Opportunity* is the possibility that an event will occur and *positively* affect the achievement of an organization's objectives and *risk* is the possibility that an event will occur and *negatively* affect the achievement of an organization's objectives. Opportunities and risks that arise within an organization because of IT represent a significant portion of the opportunities and risks the organization needs to understand and manage effectively.

ERP System

A modular software system that enables an organization to integrate its business processes using a single operating database.

Opportunities Enabled by IT

Selling goods online is an opportunity enabled by e-commerce technology that many organizations have exploited. Other opportunities that IT advances have enabled include enterprise resource planning (ERP) systems and electronic data interchange (EDI):

- **ERP systems** — An ERP system is a modular software system that enables organizations to integrate their business processes using a single operating database. Benefits organizations expect to gain from implementing ERP systems include online real-time processing of transactions, seamless interaction and sharing of information among functional areas, improved process performance, elimination or reduction of data redundancies and errors, and more timely decision-making. However, implementing an effective and efficient ERP system on time and on budget is a huge undertaking that is fraught with risks. Exploiting the opportunities that an ERP system has to offer depends on effectively mitigating the risks that can cause the initiative to fail.
- **EDI** — EDI involves the computer-to-computer exchange of business documents in electronic form between an organization and its trading partners. Benefits organizations expect to gain from implementing EDI include transaction processing efficiencies and fewer data processing errors. Moreover, recent advances in e-business technology have enabled Internet EDI, which is less expensive than traditional EDI. However, an organization cannot effectively and efficiently implement EDI unless its trading partners also effectively implement EDI. In addition, conducting business over the Internet is not risk free. Fully exploiting the opportunities EDI has to offer depends on mitigating the risks associated with e-business.

EDI

The computer-to-computer exchange of business documents in electronic form between an organization and its trading partners.

IT Risks

Each of the key components of information systems described earlier in the chapter represents a potential source of risk. For example:

- Computer hardware is susceptible to power outages that interrupt the processing of transactions.
- Networks transmit information that may be intercepted and stolen or misused.
- Computer software that is inaccurately programmed may produce invalid, incomplete, and/or inaccurate information.

- Databases may be infiltrated for the purpose of misappropriating or misusing information.
- Information that is invalid, incomplete, and/or inaccurate may result in poor decisions. (The risk that poor information will result in poor decisions is referred to generally as *information risk.*)
- A person may perform incompatible IT duties and thus be in a position to perpetrate and conceal errors or fraud.

The use of IT in information systems opens the door for IT risks. The specific IT risks that a particular organization faces will depend on the nature of the organization's business and operations, the industry within which the organization operates, the configuration of the organization's information systems, and several other internal and external factors. Moreover, risks change as a result of changes in an organization's internal and external environment and nothing in today's business world changes more rapidly than IT. Accordingly, organizations must constantly keep abreast of advances in IT and continuously consider the risk ramifications of these advances.

There are, however, certain types of IT risks that tend to be common across organizations and industries.

- **Selection Risk** — Selection of an IT solution that is misaligned with a strategic objective may preclude the execution of the IT-dependent strategy. Likewise, selection of an IT solution that is insufficiently flexible and/or scalable may result in incompatibilities between the IT solution and the organization's existing systems and/or hinder future organizational changes and growth. Causes of selection risk include, for example, unqualified decision makers and inadequate information supporting the selection decision.
- **Development/Acquisition and Deployment Risk** — Problems encountered as the IT solution is being developed/acquired and deployed may cause unforeseen delays, cost overruns, or even abandonment of the project. Causes of development/acquisition and deployment risk include, for example, insufficient in-house expertise, inadequate vendor support, and resistance to change.
- **Availability Risk** — Unavailability of the system when needed may cause delays in decision-making, business interruptions, lost revenue, and customer dissatisfaction. Causes of availability risk include, for example, hardware/software failures, unscheduled maintenance, and viruses and other malicious acts.
- **Hardware/Software Risk** — Failure of hardware/software to perform properly may cause business interruptions, temporary or permanent damage to or destruction of data, and hardware/software repair or replacement costs. Causes of hardware/software risk include, for example, natural wear and tear, environmental damage caused by such things as excessive humidity, disasters such as fires and floods, and viruses and other malicious acts.
- **Access Risk** — Unauthorized physical or logical access to the system may result in theft or misuse of hardware, malicious software modifications, and theft, misuse, or destruction of data. Causes of access risk include, for example, high-value portable computers (including laptops) dispersed widely throughout the organization, an open floor plan designed to promote and facilitate employee interaction, and wireless networks.

- **System Reliability and Information Integrity Risk** — Systematic errors or inconsistencies in processing may produce irrelevant, incomplete, inaccurate, and/or untimely information. In turn, the bad information produced by the system may adversely affect the decisions that are based on the information. Causes of system reliability and information integrity risk include, for example, software programming errors and unauthorized changes to software.
- **Confidentiality and Privacy Risk** — Unauthorized disclosure of business partners' proprietary information or individuals' personal information may result in loss of business, lawsuits, negative press, and reputation impairment. Causes of confidentiality and privacy risk include, for example, unimpeded access to system networks, software, and databases.
- **Fraud and Malicious Acts Risk** — Theft of IT resources, intentional misuse of IT resources, or intentional distortion or destruction of information may result in financial losses and/or misstated information that decision makers rely upon. Causes of fraud and malicious acts risk include, for example, disgruntled employees and hackers intent on harming the organization for personal gain.

The IT risks described above are intended to be illustrative rather than all-encompassing. Also notice that these risks are not mutually exclusive. For example, an information system may be unavailable (availability risk) due to hardware/software failures (hardware/software risk). Likewise, fraud and other malicious acts may cause any of the other risks.

IT GOVERNANCE

Governance is defined in Chapter 1, "Introduction to Internal Auditing," as the process conducted by the board of directors to authorize, direct, and oversee management toward the achievement of the organization's objectives. As discussed in detail in Chapter 3, "Governance," an organization's governance structure provides assurance that the organization operates within the boundaries and values established by the board and senior management.

IT Governance

The leadership, structure, and oversight processes that ensure the organization's information technology supports the objectives and strategies of the organization.

As indicated in the introduction of this chapter, organizations invest large sums of money in IT because IT enables the execution of business strategies and the achievement of business objectives. In response to the pervasive impact IT has on their business strategies and operations, many organizations have determined that IT governance, by itself, is important enough to warrant special attention. The IT Governance Institute (ITGI), which "was established in 1998 in recognition of the increasing criticality of information technology to enterprise success"[2] states that ". . . the pervasive use of technology has created a critical dependency on IT that calls for a specific focus on IT governance"[3] and defines IT governance as follows:

> "IT governance is the responsibility of the board of directors and executive management. It is an integral part of enterprise governance and consists of the leadership and organizational structures and processes that ensure that the organisation's IT sustains and extends the organisation's strategies and objectives."[4]

The IIA's definition of IT governance is very similar. IT governance:

> "Consists of the leadership, organizational structures, and processes that ensure that the enterprise's information technology sustains and supports the organization's strategies and objectives."[5]

These definitions clearly indicate that the board and senior management "own" IT governance, just as they own all other aspects of governance. Some boards have established governance committees whose spans of responsibility include IT governance. Audit committees often play a key role in IT governance as well. The IT governance roles of the board and its committees are to provide IT governance direction to senior management and oversee senior management's IT governance activities. Senior management is responsible for directing and overseeing the day-to-day execution of IT governance. Some organizations have established IT governance committees, the members of which include the CIO and other senior executives.

The ITGI specifically states that "The purpose of IT governance is to direct IT endeavours, to ensure that IT's performance meets the following objectives:

- Alignment of IT with the enterprise and realisation of the promised benefits
- Use of IT to enable the enterprise by exploiting opportunities and maximising benefits
- Responsible use of IT resources
- Appropriate management of IT-related risks."[6]

The ITGI's IT Governance Framework, which is presented in Exhibit 7-3, depicts the IT governance process as beginning with the definition of IT objectives. These objectives establish the initial direction of IT activities. The IT governance process continues in a loop of measuring IT performance, comparing IT performance with defined IT objectives, revising IT objectives as appropriate, and redirecting IT activities when necessary.[7]

IT RISK MANAGEMENT

IT Risk Management

The process conducted by management to understand and handle the IT risks and opportunities that could affect the organization's ability to achieve its objectives.

Risk management is defined in Chapter 1, "Introduction to Internal Auditing," as the process conducted by management to understand and handle the uncertainties (risks and opportunities) that could affect the organization's ability to achieve its objectives. Chapter 3, "Risk Management," discusses in detail how an organization's risk management process operates within the organization's governance structure to (1) identify and mitigate the risks that threaten the organization's success and (2) identify and exploit the opportunities that enable the organization's success.

As described in the Committee of Sponsoring Organizations of the Treadway Commission's (COSO's) *Enterprise Risk Management – Integrated Framework* and discussed in Chapter 3, enterprise risk management (ERM) comprises eight interrelated components: internal environment, objective setting, event identification, risk assessment, risk response, control activities, information and communication, and monitoring.[8] Each of these components is relevant to IT risk management. For example:

- **Internal environment** — An organization's internal environment includes the "tone at the top" of the organization. As indicated in the

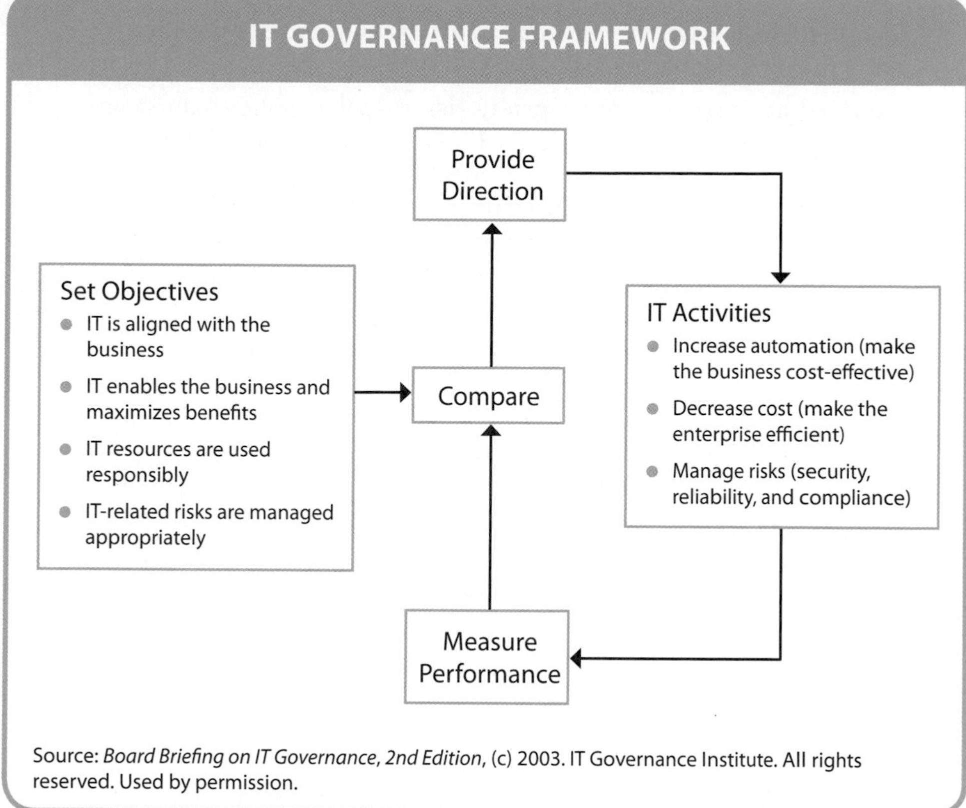
IT GOVERNANCE FRAMEWORK
Provide Direction
Set Objectives
IT is aligned with the business
IT enables the business and maximizes benefits
IT resources are used responsibly
IT-related risks are managed appropriately
Compare
IT Activities
Increase automation (make the business cost-effective)
Decrease cost (make the enterprise efficient)
Manage risks (security, reliability, and compliance)
Measure Performance

Source: *Board Briefing on IT Governance, 2nd Edition*, (c) 2003. IT Governance Institute. All rights reserved. Used by permission.

EXHIBIT 7-3

preceding section of this chapter, the board and senior management are responsible for directing and overseeing the organization's IT governance process. They also are responsible for establishing the organization's IT risk appetite and defining IT risk tolerance thresholds.

- **Objective setting** — As described in the preceding section of this chapter, the IT governance process begins with the definition of IT objectives, which establish the direction of IT activities. Because IT enables the execution of business strategies and the achievement of business objectives, the strategic management of IT operations must be aligned with the overall strategic management of the organization.
- **Event identification** — Potential events arising inside or outside the organization that could affect the execution of the organization's strategies and the achievement of its objectives must be identified. Examples of risk events were described above in the section titled IT Risks.
- **Risk assessment** — Identified IT risk events must be assessed in terms of their inherent impact and likelihood. This assessment involves an analysis of the potential adverse consequences and causes of the risk events. The residual impact and likelihood of the identified IT risk events must also be assessed, taking into consideration existing risk management deficiencies.
- **Risk response** — Appropriate risk responses must be formulated for identified IT risk events. Risk acceptance is an appropriate response for IT risk events with inherent impact and likelihood levels that do not exceed management's risk tolerance. Possible risk responses for IT risk events with inherent impact and likelihood

levels that exceed management's risk tolerance include avoiding, reducing, or sharing the risk.

- **Control activities** — Appropriate risk response policies must be defined and procedures (actions taken to apply the policies) must be designed adequately and operate effectively to provide assurance that residual IT risk levels are within management's risk tolerance. IT controls are discussed in the next section of this chapter.
- **Information and communication** — The purpose of an organization's information systems is to identify, capture, and communicate high quality information to decision makers on a timely basis. For example, information pertinent to identifying, assessing, and responding to IT risk events must be communicated throughout the organization. An important aspect of IT risk management is ensuring that the organization's technology-enabled information systems reliably produce high-quality information.
- **Monitoring** — Management is responsible for monitoring the IT risk management process, including the IT control process, over time to ensure that the process continues to operate effectively and efficiently as internal and external environmental factors affecting the organization change.

IT CONTROLS

Control is defined in Chapter 1, "Introduction to Internal Auditing," as the process imbedded in risk management and conducted by management to mitigate risks to acceptable levels. Chapter 6, "Internal Control," provides in-depth coverage of internal control and introduces the concept of IT controls. IT controls are commonly classified as general or application controls as described in Chapter 6:

- "*General controls* (italics added) . . . apply to all systems components, processes, and data for a given organization or systems environment."[9]
- "*Application controls* (italics added) pertain to the scope of individual business processes or application systems."[10]

Another way to classify controls is "by the group responsible for ensuring they are implemented and maintained properly."[11] For example, as presented in Exhibit 7-4, IT controls may be categorized as a top-down hierarchy of IT governance, management, and technical controls. The top six layers of IT controls illustrated in Exhibit 7-4 represent IT general controls while the bottom layer represents application controls. It is important to understand, however, that "The different elements of the hierarchy are not mutually exclusive; they are all connected and can intermingle."[12] The remainder of this section describes IT controls from "the group responsible" perspective.

IT Governance Controls

As discussed previously in this chapter, IT governance is an integral component of overall governance. Likewise, IT controls at the governance level are an important subset of an organization's overall system of internal controls. IT controls at the governance level fall under the jurisdiction of the board and senior management. The board's responsibility, however, is to oversee the organization's system of internal controls, not to execute controls. It is senior management's job to conduct the control process on a day-to-day basis.

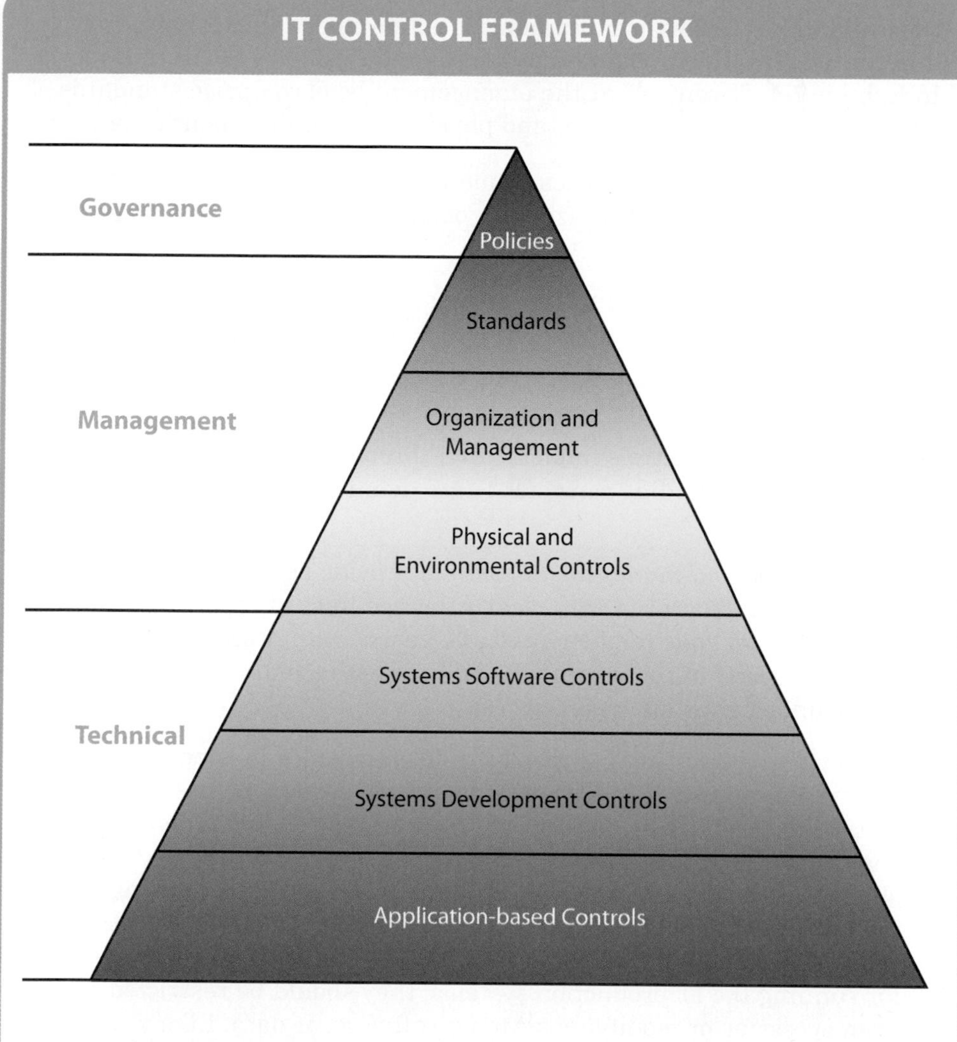

Source: *Global Technology Audit Guide – Information Technology Controls* (Altamonte Springs, FL: The Institute of Internal Auditors, 2006), p. 5.

EXHIBIT 7-4

As illustrated in Exhibit 7-4, IT governance controls comprise IT policies. These policies establish the nature of the controls that should be in place and address, for example:

- IT security and privacy.
- The classification of information and information access rights and usage restrictions.
- Who has responsibility for the organization's systems and data and who has authority to originate, modify, or delete information.
- The extent to which information system end users have authority to develop their own IT applications.
- Personnel policies pertaining to the vetting of new IT personnel and IT employees' control, security, and confidentiality responsibilities.
- Business continuity planning.[13]

IT Management Controls

Management is responsible for ensuring that IT controls are designed adequately and operating effectively, taking into consideration the organization's objectives, risks that threaten the achievement of those objectives, and the organization's business processes and resources. As illustrated in Exhibit 7-4, IT controls at the management level comprise standards, organization and management, and physical and environmental controls.

IT Standards

Support IT policies by more specifically defining what is required to achieve the organization's objectives.

IT standards support IT policies by more specifically defining what is required to achieve the organization's objectives. These standards should cover, for example:

- The processes for designing, developing, testing, implementing, and maintaining information systems and software.
- The configuration of the organization's operating, networking, and database management systems.
- The application controls implemented throughout the organization, including consistent data definitions and appropriate documentation.[14]

IT Organization and Management Controls

Provide assurance that the organization is structured with clearly defined lines of reporting and responsibility and has implemented effective control processes.

IT organization and management controls provide assurance that the organization is structured with clearly defined lines of reporting and responsibility and has implemented effective control processes. Three important aspects of these controls are segregation of duties, financial controls, and change management controls:

- Proper segregation of IT duties provides assurance that no single individual can use IT to both perpetrate and conceal errors or fraud. Initiating, authorizing, inputting, processing, and checking data should be separated to the extent possible. System access privileges should be aligned with individuals' responsibilities for accessing and processing information. Systems development should be separated from operations. Operations personnel should be responsible only for running the IT production systems; they should be restricted from accessing or modifying systems, software, or data. Likewise, IT system developers such as system analysts and software programmers should not be involved in IT operating activities.[15]
- IT financial controls protect against cost overruns in developing and implementing information systems. These controls also provide assurance that investments in IT technology yield expected returns and cost savings.[16]
- Change management controls provide assurance that changes to the IT environment, system, software, and data are properly authorized and appropriate. These controls also provide assurance that any changes made produce the desired results.[17]

IT Physical and Environmental Controls

Protect information system resources from accidental or intentional damage, misuse, or loss.

IT physical and environmental controls protect information system resources (hardware, software, documentation, and information) from accidental or intentional damage, misuse, or loss. Such controls include, for example:

- Placing tangible IT resources in locked rooms with restricted access.
- Installing appropriate fire detection and suppression equipment.
- Locating the IT facilities away from environmental hazards such as flood plains or flammable materials.
- Developing and testing the organization's disaster recovery plan.[18]

IT Technical Controls

"Technical controls form the foundation that ensures the reliability of virtually every other control in the organization . . . These controls are specific to the technologies in use within the organization's IT infrastructure."[19] As illustrated in Exhibit 7-4, IT technical controls include systems software controls, systems development controls, and application-based controls.

Systems software facilitates the use of systems hardware and includes, for example, operating systems, network systems, database management systems, firewalls, and antivirus software. Systems software controls restrict logical access to the organization's systems and applications, monitor systems usage, and generate audit trails. *Systems software controls* include, for example:

- Assigning and controlling systems access rights in accordance with the organization's policy.
- Implementing online configuration controls that enforce appropriate segregation of duties.
- Assessing and testing intrusion vulnerability.
- Preventing and detecting unauthorized intrusions.
- Employing stringent and systematic change management procedures.[20]

Application systems, whether developed in-house or purchased from a vendor, must effectively and efficiently process information in accordance with users' requirements. *Systems development and acquisition controls* include, for example:

- Documenting user requirements and measuring achievement of the requirements.
- Following a formal systems design process to ensure user requirements are met and controls are imbedded as appropriate in the software.
- Testing the system and involving users in the testing process to ensure that specific elements and interfaces of the system work properly and provide the intended functionality.
- Validating changes to applications and testing the changes prior to implementation.[21]

Application-based controls are implemented to ensure that:

- Data input into an application is valid, complete, and accurate.
- Input data is processed as intended.
- Stored data is complete and accurate.
- Output is complete and accurate.
- Movement of data through the system is recorded.[22]

Application-based controls include, for example:

- Input controls designed to check the integrity of data entered into an application.
- Processing controls designed to ensure that processing is valid, complete, and accurate.

EXHIBIT 7-5

EXAMPLES OF IT APPLICATION-BASED CONTROLS

Input Controls: Designed to ensure that data input into the system is valid, complete, and accurate.

- **Source document controls:**
  - Access to documents used to initiate transactions is restricted to authorized individuals.
  - Documents used to initiate transactions are prenumbered when feasible. The source documents are used in numerical sequence and the sequence is verified periodically.
- **Control totals:**
  - **Record count** — A count of the records input for processing. Example: The number of timecards submitted for payroll processing.
  - **Batch total** — A total of an amount included in each record batched for processing. Example: The total number of hours worked in the batch of timecards submitted for payroll processing.
  - **Hash total** — An otherwise meaningless total that is used to ensure the completeness of data input for processing. Example: The sum of the employee numbers in the batch of timecards submitted for processing.
- **Programmed edit checks:**
  - **Completeness check** — Examines the data input to ensure that all critical fields contain values.
  - **Field check** — Examines a field to determine whether it contains the appropriate type of data (alpha or numeric).
  - **Sign check** — Examines a field to determine whether the amount sign is correct (positive or negative).
  - **Limit check** — Examines a field to determine whether the amount is ≤ a prescribed upper limit or ≥ a prescribed lower limit.
  - **Range check** — Examines a field to determine whether the amount falls within a prescribed range.
  - **Reasonableness check** — Compares the data in a field with data in related fields to determine whether the value is reasonable.
  - **Validity check** — Compares the data in a field with a predetermined set of authorized values to ensure the field contains valid data.
- **Input error correction:** Source documents containing errors detected during input are corrected and resubmitted before being processed.

Processing Controls: Designed to prevent, or detect and correct, errors that occur during processing.

- **Run-to-run control totals:** Control totals are calculated and checked at designated points as transactions are processed.
- **Error listings:** Error listings are automatically generated by the computer and errors identified are remediated expeditiously.

Output Controls: Designed to ensure that application system outputs are valid, complete, and accurate and that security over outputs is properly maintained.

- **Output review controls:** Application system outputs are reviewed for validity, completeness, and accuracy before being distributed to users.
- **Distribution controls:** Distribution of application system outputs is restricted to authorized recipients.
- **End-user controls:** End users review the application system outputs they receive for validity, completeness, and accuracy.

Audit Trail Controls: Designed to provide a permanent record of input, processing, and output activity.

- **Transaction logging:** The application system automatically logs the transactions processed.
- **Programmed control logging:** The application system automatically logs the imbedded controls executed during input, processing, and output.
- **Error listing retention:** The error listings generated and remediated during processing are retained.

- Output controls designed to test the validity, completeness, and accuracy of application outputs and to ensure that the outputs go to the intended recipients and only to the intended recipients.
- An audit trail that enables management to trace transactions forward from the beginning of the process to the end and backward from the end of the process to the beginning.[23]

Specific examples of application-based controls are presented in Exhibit 7-5.

Information Security Controls

Information security controls are not explicitly presented in Exhibit 7-4 because "Information security is an integral part of all IT controls."[24] Information security controls protect an information system from unauthorized physical and logical access. Physical access controls provide security over tangible IT resources and include such things as locked doors, surveillance cameras, and security guards. Logical access controls provide security over software and information imbedded in the system and include such things as firewalls, encryption, login IDs, passwords, authorization tables, and computer activity logs. Deficiencies in information security controls compromise the effectiveness of all other IT governance, management, and technical controls.

Physical Access Controls

Provide security over tangible IT resources.

Logical Access Controls

Provide security over software and information imbedded in the system.

IMPLICATIONS OF IT FOR INTERNAL AUDITORS

The previous sections of this chapter describe how IT has affected organizations. IT has changed the manner in which organizations formulate strategies, conduct day-to-day operations, and make decisions. These changes have generated new risks and forced organizations to modify their governance, risk management, and control processes. The pervasive impact of IT on organizations has in turn compelled internal auditors to upgrade their IT knowledge and skills and adjust how they perform their work.

IT Proficiency and Due Professional Care

Two Attribute Implementation Standards specifically address the IT proficiency internal auditors must possess and the consideration they must give to using technology-based audit techniques:

> **1210.A3** – Internal auditors must have sufficient knowledge of key information technology risks and controls and available technology-based audit techniques to perform their assigned work. However, not all internal auditors are expected to have the expertise of an internal auditor whose primary responsibility is information technology auditing.
>
> **1220.A2** – In exercising due professional care internal auditors must consider the use of technology-based audit and other data analysis techniques.

Standards 1210.A3 and 1220.A2 clearly indicate that all internal auditors providing assurance services need at least a baseline level of IT risk, control, and audit expertise. Fundamental IT risk and control concepts that all internal auditors need to understand are discussed in previous sections of this chapter. Technology-based audit techniques (also referred to as computer-assisted audit techniques) are described in Chapter 10, "Audit Evidence and Working Papers." Computer-assisted audit techniques (CAATs) include generalized audit software (GAS) such as ACL and IDEA, both of which are on the CD-ROM accompanying this textbook. GAS is an example of an IT audit tool that internal audit functions are increasingly expecting all staff members to understand and apply effectively. Utility software, test data, application software tracing and mapping, audit expert systems, and continuous auditing are other CAATs described in Chapter 10.

Standard 1220.A3 also indicates that every internal auditor need not have the level of IT audit expertise expected of an IT auditor. However, because the demand for highly skilled IT auditors continues to exceed the supply, readers with an interest in this area are encouraged to investigate further the competencies and credentials needed to succeed as an IT auditor. Such individuals may want to pursue IT-related certifications to complement their Certified Internal Auditor (CIA) credential. Such certifications include, for example, the Certified Information Systems Auditor (CISA) sponsored by ISACA (www.isaca.org) and the Certified Information Systems Security Professional (CISSP) sponsored by the Information Systems Security Association (www.issa.org).

As is the case with all other areas of relevant expertise, the chief audit executive (CAE) is responsible for ensuring that the internal audit function has the IT proficiency needed to fulfill its assurance engagement responsibilities. Some internal audit functions have a sufficient complement of IT audit experts on staff. Those that do not have such experts on staff look to sources outside the internal audit function for such expertise. In some cases, qualified individuals from other areas of the organization may be asked to assist on internal audit engagements requiring IT competencies that the internal audit function does not have. In other cases, the CAE may hire external service providers with the requisite IT knowledge and skills.

Assurance Engagement IT Responsibilities

Three Performance Implementation Standards specifically address internal auditors' assurance engagement responsibilities regarding information systems and technology:

> **2110.A2** – The internal audit activity must assess whether the information technology governance of the organization sustains and supports the organization's strategies and objectives.
>
> **2120.A1** – The internal audit activity must evaluate risk exposures relating to the organization's . . . information systems . . .
>
> **2130.A1** – The internal audit activity must evaluate the adequacy and effectiveness of controls in responding to risks within the organization's . . . information systems . . .

These three standards reflect the fact that an internal audit function cannot effectively evaluate governance, risk management, and control processes without giving due consideration to information systems and technology. To fulfill its IT-related responsibilities, an internal audit function must:

- Include the organization's information systems in its annual audit planning process.
- Identify and assess the organization's IT risks.
- Ensure that it has sufficient IT audit expertise.
- Assess IT governance, management, and technical controls.
- Assign auditors with appropriate levels of IT expertise to each assurance engagement.
- Use technology-based audit techniques as appropriate.

IT Outsourcing

Business process outsourcing was introduced in Chapter 5, "Business Processes and Risks," as the act of transferring some of an organization's business processes to an outside provider to achieve cost reductions while improving service quality and efficiency. It is for these reasons that organizations are increasingly outsourcing IT functions to vendors that specialize in providing IT services.

As is the case with any kind of outsourcing, IT outsourcing brings with it risks that an organization's board and management must understand and manage. Accordingly, they will seek assurance regarding the information upon which their outsourcing decisions are based. The internal audit function can provide such assurance and, in addition, advise the board and management about the risk and control implications of outsourcing IT.

The board and management also retain responsibility for the controls over the outsourced IT functions and will call upon the CAE to provide them with assurance regarding the design adequacy and operating effectiveness of these controls. Depending on the circumstances, the CAE may rely, to some extent, on the reports of the IT service provider's internal and/or independent outside auditors when formulating a conclusion about the controls over outsourced IT functions. If high-risk IT functions have been outsourced, the CAE should allocate an appropriate level of internal audit resources to testing the controls over those functions. Global Technology Audit Guide (GTAG) – *Information Technology Outsourcing* describes in detail some of the key IT outsourcing considerations that warrant the attention of internal auditor functions.

IT Outsourcing

Transferring IT functions to an outside provider to achieve cost reductions while improving service quality and efficiency.

Integrated and Continuous Auditing

Internal audits have historically been conducted retrospectively, for example after transactions have occurred. This after-the-fact audit approach is rapidly becoming outdated as advances in technology give rise to IT-enabled business processes in which online, real-time processing of transactions is common. Paper-based audit trails of transaction processing and controls are increasingly being replaced with paperless audit trails and imbedded automated controls designed to test the propriety of transactions as they occur. In this information systems environment, direct evidence of transaction processing and controls implementation often is temporary in nature. This means that it is becoming less and less feasible for internal auditors to "audit around the computer" and reach a valid conclusion about the overall effectiveness of controls over financial reporting, operations, and compliance. They must instead "audit through the computer," using CAATs, to evaluate IT controls built into the system.

Integrated auditing. The integration of IT controls directly into business processes, together with the availability of user-friendly CAATs, is prompting a growing number of internal audit functions to adopt an approach referred to as integrated auditing. Instead of conducting separate assurance engagements focused strictly on process-level IT risks and controls, these internal audit functions assimilate IT risk and control assessments into assurance engagements conducted to assess process-level financial reporting, operations, and/or compliance risks and controls.

Integrated Auditing

IT risk and control assessments are assimilated into assurance engagements conducted to assess process-level financial reporting, operations, and/or compliance risks and controls.

Internal audit functions that have adopted integrated auditing are finding that this approach benefits their organizations by improving both the effectiveness and efficiency of their internal audit assurance services. Integrated assurance engagements are more effective because the internal auditors are in a much better position to assess the auditee's entire risk portfolio and reach an overall conclusion about the design adequacy and operating effectiveness of controls. The audit process is more efficient because (1) engagements previously conducted separately are combined and (2) the identification and assessment of all key risks and controls are consolidated in integrated audit engagements.

Continuous auditing. Continuous auditing is defined in GTAG 3 – *Continuous Auditing: Implications for Assurance, Monitoring, and Risk Assessment* as "any method used by [internal auditors] to perform audit-related activities on a more continuous or continual basis."[25] As described in GTAG 3, continuous auditing comprises two main activities:

- *Continuous controls assessment*, the purpose of which is "to focus audit attention on control deficiencies as early as possible," and
- *Continuous risk assessment*, the purpose of which is "to highlight processes or systems that are experiencing higher than expected levels of risk."[26]

Assessment of continuous monitoring is a third integral component of continuous auditing. As indicated earlier in the chapter, management is responsible for monitoring the organization's risk management process, including the control process, over time to ensure that it continues to operate effectively and efficiently. The internal audit function's continuous audit responsibility is to assess the effectiveness of management's continuous monitoring activities. In areas of the organization in which management has implemented an effective ongoing monitoring process, internal auditors can conduct less stringent continuous assessments of risk and controls. Conversely, if continuous monitoring is nonexistent or ineffective, the internal audit function must perform more rigorous ongoing risk and control assessments.

GTAG

Provides internal auditors with guidance that will help them better understand the governance, risk management, and control issues surrounding IT.

GAIT

Describes the relationships among financial reporting risks, key process controls, automated controls and other critical IT functionality, and key IT general controls.

SOURCES OF IT AUDIT GUIDANCE

The Institute of Internal Auditors (IIA) has a growing body of IT audit guidance. Two key components of this guidance are the Practice Guides included in The IIA's International Professional Practices Framework:

- **The Global Technology Audit Guide (GTAG) series** — The GTAG series is designed to provide internal auditors worldwide with guidance that will help them better understand the governance, risk management, and control issues surrounding information technology. The 13 GTAG guides available when this textbook was published are listed in Exhibit 7-1. The IIA Advanced Technology Committee (ATC) has identified entity-level IT controls, user development applications, and security management as topics for future GTAG guides.[27]
- **The Guide to the Assessment of IT Risk (GAIT) series** — The GAIT series describes the relationships among financial reporting risks, key process controls, automated controls and other critical IT functionality, and key IT general controls. Each GAIT guide covers a specific facet of IT risk and control assessments. The four GAIT guides available when this textbook was published are listed in Exhibit 7-1.[28]

IIA members can download the GTAG and GAIT guides free of charge at www.theiia.org/guidance/technology/. These practice guides also can be purchased from The IIA Research Foundation Bookstore at www.theiia.org/bookstore/. Other IT audit guidance available through The IIA includes:

- Numerous publications, including IIA Research Foundation handbooks and research monographs, which can be purchased from The IIA Research Foundation Bookstore.
- The *ITAudit* portion of *Internal Auditor Online*, which, before January 2009, was a separate online publication of IT audit articles. Both current and archived *ITAudit* articles can be downloaded by anyone at www.theiia.org/intAuditor/itaudit/.

Many other organizations have published online IT audit information of relevance to internal auditors that is available for downloading. These organizations include, for example:

- The IT Governance Institute (www.itgi.org).
- The IT Compliance Institute (www.itcinstitute.com).
- The IT Process Institute (www.itpi.org).
- ISACA (formally the Information Systems Audit and Control Association) (www.isaca.org).
- The Information Systems Security Association (www.issa.org).
- The American Institute of Certified Public Accountants (www.aicpa.org.
- The Canadian Institute of Chartered Accountants (www.cica.org).

SUMMARY

The pervasive impact of IT on organizations' strategies, information systems, and processes has significantly affected the internal audit profession and this chapter covered fundamental IT concepts that every internal auditor needs to understand:

- Six key components of modern information system — computer hardware, networks, computer software, databases, information, and people — were described and illustrated.
- Opportunities enabled by IT and risk arising as a result of IT were discussed. IT-enabled opportunities include such things as online sales, integration of business processes, and electronic exchange of information between trading partners. Types of risks common across organizations and industries include:
  - Selection risk.
  - Development/acquisition and deployment risk.
  - Availability risk.
  - Hardware/software risk.
  - Access risk.
  - System reliability and information integrity risk.
  - Confidentiality and privacy risk.
  - Fraud and malicious acts risk.

- IT governance was identified as an important subcomponent of overall governance; IT risk management was explained within the context of the COSO ERM components; and IT controls were presented as a top-down hierarchy of IT governance, management, and technical controls.
- The implications of IT for internal auditors were addressed. Internal audit functions need to understand their organizations' information systems and the IT risks that threaten the achievement of their organizations' business objectives. They also must be proficient in assessing their organizations' IT governance, risk management, and control processes and be able to effectively apply technology-based audit techniques.
- Sources of IT audit guidance were identified. Two key components of The IIA's growing body of IT audit guidance are the GTAG series and the GAIT series. Other guidance available through The IIA includes numerous resources that can be purchased through The IIA Research Foundation Bookstore or downloaded from the *ITAudit* portion of *Internal Auditor Online*.

In summary, IT has significantly changed the competencies internal auditors must possess and how they conduct their work. An internal audit function's capacity to provide value-adding assurance and consulting services is highly dependent on its IT expertise.

Review Questions

1. What are the six components of modern IT described in this chapter?
2. How has IT enabled opportunities? Provide two examples.
3. What are the potential effects (adverse consequences) of each of the following types of IT risk?
   a. Development/acquisition and deployment risk.
   b. Hardware/software risk.
   c. System reliability and information integrity risk.
   d. Fraud and malicious acts risk.
4. What are typical causes of each of the following types of IT risk?
   a. Selection.
   b. Availability.
   c. Access.
   d. Confidentiality and privacy.
5. How does the IT Governance Institute define IT governance?
6. How is each of the following COSO ERM components relevant to IT risk management?
   a. Objective setting.
   b. Risk assessment.
   c. Risk response.
   d. Information and communication.
7. What is the difference between general controls and application controls?
8. What should IT governance-level controls (that is, IT policies) address?
9. What are the three types of IT management controls described in the chapter? Provide two examples of each type.
10. What are the three types of IT technical controls described in the chapter? Provide two examples of each type.
11. What is the difference between physical access controls and logical access controls?
12. What must an internal audit function do to fulfill its IT-related responsibilities related to effectively evaluating governance, risk management, and control processes?
13. How does IT outsourcing affect the internal audit function?
14. In what ways might the adoption of integrated auditing improve an internal audit function's assurance engagement process?
15. Continuous auditing involves what three types of assessments?
16. What are the two IT audit guidance series included in The IIA's International Professional Practices Framework as Practice Guides?

Multiple-choice Questions

Select the best answer for each of the following questions.

1. The software that manages the interconnectivity of the system hardware devices is the:
   a. Application software.
   b. Utility software.
   c. Operating system software.
   d. Database management system software.

2. An Internet firewall is designed to provide protection against:
   a. Computer viruses.
   b. Unauthorized access from outsiders.
   c. Lightning strikes and power surges.
   d. Arson.

3. Which of the following best illustrates the use of EDI?
   a. Purchasing merchandise from a company's Internet site.
   b. Computerized placement of a purchase order from a customer to its supplier.
   c. Transfer of data from a desktop computer to a database server.
   d. Withdrawing cash from an ATM.

4. The possibility of someone maliciously shutting down an information system is most directly an element of:
   a. Availability risk.
   b. Access risk.
   c. Confidentiality risk.
   d. Deployment risk.

5. An organization's IT governance committee has several important responsibilities. Which of the following is not normally such a responsibility?
   a. Aligning investments in IT with business strategies.
   b. Overseeing changes to IT systems.
   c. Monitoring IT security procedures.
   d. Designing IT application-based controls.

6. If a sales transaction record was rejected during input because the customer account number entered was not listed in the customer master file, the error was most likely detected by a:
   a. Completeness check.
   b. Limit check.
   c. Validity check.
   d. Reasonableness check.

7. The purpose of logical security controls is to:
   a. Restrict access to data.
   b. Limit access to hardware.
   c. Record processing results.
   d. Ensure complete and accurate processing of data.

8. Which of the following statements regarding an internal audit function's continuous auditing responsibilities is/are true?
   I. The internal audit function is responsible for assessing the effectiveness of management's continuous monitoring activities.
   II. In areas of the organization in which management has implemented effective monitoring activities, the internal audit function can conduct less stringent continuous assessments of risks and controls.
   a. Only statement I is true.
   b. Only statement II is true.
   c. Both statement I and statement II are true.
   d. Neither statement I nor statement II is true.

Discussion Questions

1. a. As stated in the chapter, all internal auditors need at least a baseline level of IT audit-related expertise.
      1. Identify six specific IT-related competencies (that is, knowledge and skills) all entry-level internal auditors should possess.
      2. Discuss how a college student can begin to develop the knowledge and skills identified in 1.a.1. above.
   b. Must all internal auditors have the level of IT audit-related expertise expected of an IT auditor? Explain.

2. Risk, Inherent Risk, and Fraud are defined in the textbook Glossary as follows:

   Risk – The possibility that an event will occur and adversely affect the achievement of objectives.

   Inherent Risk – The combination of internal and external risk factors in their pure, uncontrolled state, or the gross risk that exists, assuming there are no internal controls in place.

   Fraud – Any illegal act characterized by deceit, concealment, or violation of trust. These acts are not dependent upon the threat of violence or physical force. Frauds are perpetrated by parties and organizations to obtain money, property, or services; to avoid payment or loss of services; or to secure personal or business advantage.

   IT Fraud and Malicious Acts Risk is defined in this chapter as follows:

   Fraud and Malicious Acts Risk – Theft of IT resources, intentional misuse of IT resources, or intentional distortion or destruction of information may result in financial losses and/or misstated information that decision makers rely upon. Causes of fraud and malicious acts risk include, for example, disgruntled employees and hackers intent on harming the organization for personal gain.

With the definitions presented above as the backdrop, identify six specific inherent IT fraud and malicious acts risk events that could occur and cause harm to an organization.

3. Download the white paper, "The Risk Intelligent IT Internal Auditor" from the Deloitte U.S. website (www.deloitte.com) (The white paper was available at http://www.deloitte.com/dtt/cda/doc/content/us_risk_RiskIntelligentIT_IA_20080430.pdf when the second edition of the textbook was published). Read the white paper.
   a. What characterizes a "Type 1: Drifting Along" IT internal audit group?
   b. What issues characterize a:
      1. "Type 2: Getting Aloft" IT internal audit group?
      2. "Type 3: Flying High" IT internal audit group?

4. Change management controls are a type of IT organization and management controls, which are a subset of IT management-level (general) controls.
   a. What are change management controls?
   b. Assume that an organization's change management controls pertaining to application software are ineffective. What impact would this have on the reliance that management can place on application-based controls?
   c. Assume instead that the organization's change management controls pertaining to application software are effective. Assume further that the internal audit function determined that the controls imbedded in the purchasing process application software were designed adequately and operating effectively last year. What impact would this have on this year's internal audit testing of the controls imbedded in the purchasing process application software?
   d. Based on the answers to 2.b. and 2.c. above, what general conclusion can be reached about the relationship between IT management-level (general) controls and application-based controls?

5. Download *COBIT® 4.1 Executive Summary and Framework* from the ISACA website (www.isaca.org). (Version 4.1 was available at http://www.isaca.org/AMTemplate.cfm?Section=Downloads&Template=/ContentManagement/ContentDisplay.cfm&ContentID=34172 when the second edition of the textbook was published. A more recent version may be available subsequently.) Read the Executive Overview (pp. 5-8).
   a. What is COBIT® 4.1?
   b. How does COBIT support IT governance?
   c. What are the benefits of implementing COBIT as an IT governance framework?
   d. Why should all internal auditors, at a minimum, be aware of COBIT?

6. Download *Trust Services Principles, Criteria, and Illustrations* from the AICPA website (www.aicpa.org). (The document was available at http://infotech.aicpa.org/NR/rdonlyres/6E7FC695-B160-49F8-91E3-75632E8EA5EE/0/TrustServices_060109.pdf when the second edition of the textbook was published.) Read the following segments of the document:
   - Introduction (paragraphs .01-.18).
   - Paragraph .19, which provides a description of the security principle.
   - Paragraphs .21-.23, which provide a description of the availability principle.
   - Paragraphs .24-.26, which provide a description of the processing integrity principle.
   - Paragraphs .28-.31, which provide a description of the confidentiality principle.
   - Paragraphs .33-.44, which provide a description of the privacy principle.

   a. What are Trust Services?
   b. What are Trust Services principles, criteria, and illustrative controls?
   c. How is "system" defined?
   d. What is the *security* principle?
   e. What is the *availability* principle?
   f. What is the *processing integrity* principle? What is the difference between *processing integrity* and *data integrity*?
   g. What is the *confidentiality* principle? What kinds of information may be subject to confidentiality?
   h. What is the *privacy* principle? What does "privacy" mean? What are some examples of "personal information?" What are some examples of "sensitive personal information?" What is the difference between privacy and confidentiality?

CASE

FPO image.

MVF Company manufactures engine parts for lawn mowers, snow blowers, and other types of yard care equipment. The company employs approximately 300 production employees. Production employees alternate back and forth between two shifts and are sometimes asked to work overtime.

MVF's CAE has asked Alyssa Worcshard, a first-year internal auditor, to gather information about the controls over the company's production payroll process. Worcshard reviewed the process, interviewed selected personnel, and documented the following information about the process.

The personnel department prepares a personnel action form when a production employee is hired or terminated. Action forms also are used to document personnel changes such as changes in pay rates, deductions, employee names, employee addresses, etc. A personnel department employee keys the information from the action forms into the computer each week to update the personnel master file.

Production employees use a time clock to record the hours they work. At the end of each week, production supervisors collect the timecards, verify the number of hours worked for each employee, and document the total number of hours worked on each employee's timecard. Each supervisor also counts the number of timecards collected and e-mails the count to MVF's treasurer.

Every Monday morning, a payroll employee collects the previous week's timecards from the production supervisors, sorts the timecards by employee number, recalculates the total hours on each timecard, keys the data from the timecards into the computer, and processes the production payroll. The system automatically assigns a sequential number to each payroll check produced. Blank checks are stored in a box next to the printer for immediate access. Controls are imbedded in the payroll application software to detect invalid employee numbers, unreasonably high numbers of hours worked, etc. The computer also determines whether overtime has been worked or a shift differential is required. Invalid data is printed on an error listing.

The payroll employee then:

- Prints the payroll register and payroll checks.
- Separates the checks into a valid batch and a batch of those that were included in the error listing.
- Uses the results of the payroll check run to update the employee earnings master file.

- Prepares the weekly payroll journal entry and posts the entry to the general ledger.
- Notifies the payroll manager that the weekly processing of payroll transactions has been completed.

The payroll manager prepares a backup of the employee earnings master file on a CD-ROM for storage in the computer room.

The valid and invalid batches of payroll checks are sent directly to MVF's treasurer. The treasurer agrees the number of valid checks received with the total number of timecards e-mailed by the production supervisors, signs the valid checks, and shreds the invalid checks. The treasurer stores the signed checks in the safe until they are given to the production supervisors for distribution on Friday. If an employee is absent when the checks are distributed, the supervisor returns the unclaimed check to the treasurer who keeps it in the safe until the employee comes to get it.

A. Based on the information presented above, and taking into consideration both manual and automated controls, describe the:

1. Control strengths in MVF Company's payroll process.
2. Control deficiencies in MVF Company's payroll process.

B. MVF Company's senior management, including the CAE, realizes that the company's payroll process needs to be upgraded.

1. Brainstorm ideas as to how the company could more effectively leverage information technology to improve the payroll process.
2. Discuss the risk and control implications of the ideas generated in B.1.

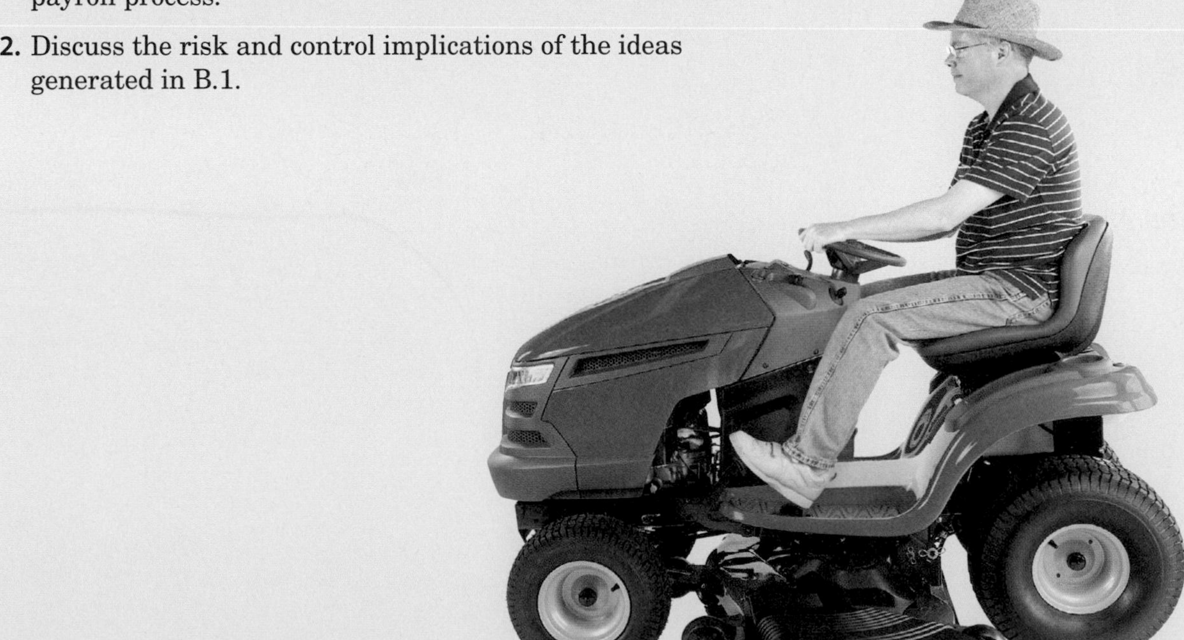

REFERENCES

[1] COBIT 4.1 Executive Summary and Framework (Rolling Meadows, IL: IT Governance Institute, 1996-2007), p. 5. Available for download at www.isaca.org as of May 16, 2009.

[2] IT Governance Institute, www.itgi.org/template_ITGI.cfm?Section=About_ITGI&Template=/ContentManagement/HTMLDisplay.cfm&ContentID=41668 as of May 16, 2009.

[3] *Board Briefing on IT Governance, Second Edition* (Rolling Meadows, IL: IT Governance Institute, 2003), p. 7. Available for download at www.itgi.org as of May 16, 2006.

[4] Ibid, p. 10.

[5] International Professional Practices Framework (Altamonte Springs, FL: The Institute of Internal Auditors, 2009), p. 41.

[6] *Board Briefing on IT Governance, Second Edition* (Rolling Meadows, IL: IT Governance Institute, 2003), p. 10. Available for download at www.itgi.org as of May 16, 2006.

[7] Ibid, p. 11.

[8] *Enterprise Risk Management – Integrated Framework* (Jersey City, NJ: Committee of Sponsoring Organizations of the Treadway Commission, 2004), p. 22.

[9] *Global Technology Audit Guide – Information Technology Controls* (Altamonte Springs, FL: The Institute of Internal Auditors, 2005), p. 3.

[10] Ibid.

[11] Ibid, p. 4.

[12] Ibid, p. 5.

[13] Ibid, pp. 5-6.

[14] Ibid, p. 6.

[15] Ibid.

[16] Ibid, p. 7.

[17] Ibid.

[18] Ibid.

[19] Ibid, pp. 4-5.

[20] Ibid, p. 8.

[21] Ibid.

[22] Ibid.

[23] Ibid.

[24] Ibid, p. 9.

REFERENCES

[25]*Global Technology Audit Guide – Continuous Auditing: Implications for Assurance, Monitoring and Risk Assessment* (Altamonte Springs, FL: The Institute of Internal Auditors, 2005), p. 7.

[26]Ibid, p. 4.

[27]The Institute of Internal Auditors, www.theiia.org/guidance/technology/ as of May16, 2009.

[28]Ibid.

CHAPTER 8
FRAUD RISKS AND CONTROLS

Learning Objectives

- Understand the prevalence of fraud in today's world.
- Compare and contrast various fraud definitions.
- Describe the fraud triangle and why all three elements must exist for fraud to occur.
- Define the types of fraud and fraud risk factors.
- Define governance, risk management, and control in the context of fraud.
- Describe fraud prevention, deterrence, and detection techniques.
- Understand the behavioral aspects of fraudsters.
- Describe internal auditors' fraud-related responsibilities.
- Understand evolving responsibilities of the internal audit function, including the involvement of forensic accountants and fraud examination specialists.

The very mention of the word "fraud" conjures up distinct and negative feelings in most individuals. To many, it immediately suggests a betrayal of trust or the discovery of wrongdoing. Consider your own experience of having heard the term "fraud" used to express moral outrage in general contexts, for example, "She's a fraud!" or "But, wait — isn't that fraud?" Indeed, fraud tends to arouse righteous indignation and emotion because it points to the basic unfairness of scheming, dishonest people knowingly deceiving honest others. In fact, the U.S. public accounting profession, in a civil and professional fashion, continued to refer to fraud as "accounting irregularities" until just before the 21st century. By then, financial statement fraud had increased dramatically in incidence and impact, and it became necessary to dispense with euphemisms and call it what it is.

One of the most significant risks faced by contemporary organizations continues to be the risk of fraud. When fraud surfaces — whether committed by individual employees, collusion among multiple employees, or by outside third parties — the afflicted organization may incur not only significant financial losses but also serious reputational damage. In many cases, the occurrence of fraud at a public company quickly leads to precipitous declines in stock prices and market capitalization, and may be an early indicator of financial distress. Indeed, fraud and financial distress

EXHIBIT 8-1

PROFESSIONAL STANDARDS AND PRACTICE ADVISORIES RELEVANT TO CHAPTER 8

1210 – Proficiency

1220 – Due Professional Care

2060 – Reporting to Senior Management and the Board

2110 – Governance

2120 – Risk Management

2210 – Engagement Objectives

Practice Advisory 1210-1: Proficiency

Practice Advisory 1210.A1-1: Obtaining External Service Providers to Support or Complement the Internal Audit Activity

Practice Advisory 1220-1: Due Professional Care

Practice Advisory 2030-1: Resource Management

Practice Advisory 2060-1: Reporting to Senior Management and the Board

seem to relate to each other in a "chicken-and-egg" sort of way: Fraud can lead to financial distress, but financial distress frequently fuels fraud. Given the serious economic consequences of fraud, senior management and governing boards are increasingly stressing antifraud programs and controls to address key business, regulatory compliance, and marketplace drivers. This renewed global focus on corporate governance comes from a realization that fraudulent financial reporting could easily sound the death knell for any organization.

This chapter starts by comparing and contrasting different definitions of fraud to illustrate the different ways in which fraud can be viewed. Next, the fraud triangle is explored as a means of understanding the key factors that must be present for fraud to occur. This chapter then outlines key principles for a fraud prevention and detection program. Having a good understanding of these principles will lay the foundation for the role an internal audit function can play in such a program. The discussion then moves to the role that a strong fraud prevention and detection program can have in supporting the governance structure. This quite naturally leads to the importance of a fraud risk assessment, and how this assessment enables an organization to develop preventive and detective fraud controls. Finally, the implications fraud has on the role and focus of the internal audit function are explored. The IIA's *International Standards for the Professional Practice of Internal Auditing* (*Standards*) makes several references to the internal audit function's fraud-related responsibilities.

OVERVIEW OF FRAUD IN TODAY'S BUSINESS WORLD

Fraud is not limited to only certain countries or industries. It can arise in virtually any organization at any time. The large accounting scandals in the U.S. (for example, Enron and World Com) were headline news across the globe. These corporate scandals not only cost investors billions of U.S. dollars, they also caused a great reduction in confidence in the U.S. capi-

EXHIBIT 8-2

INTERNATIONAL EXAMPLES OF FRAUD

In January 2009, B. Ramalinga Raju, chairman of Satyam Computer Systems, a leading global technology outsourcing company based in India, made a startling and very public confession. In addition to furnishing details of inflating facts and figures over an extended period of time, he lamented that despite the concerted efforts to cook the books, the gap between actual profits and those reported in the books of accounts remained, ruefully noting that, "It was like riding a tiger, not knowing how to get off without being eaten."[1] After having led the outsourcing company for two decades, possessing over 100 of the Fortune 500 companies as clients, and being a successful business leader representing India at the Davos World Economic Forum Summit, Raju's revelations raised uncomfortable questions about corporate governance in India. The Central Bureau of Investigation (CBI) — similar to the Federal Bureau of Investigation (FBI) in the U.S. — which looks into India's most serious and complex crimes, filed documents in a court in Hyderabad, India, in April 2009 that lay out what it alleges are the outlines of a scandal that has become known as "India's Enron."

The CBI alleges that Raju, two of his brothers, and four other Satyam executives committed the fraud by forging more than 7,000 fake invoices and dozens of bogus bank statements to inflate Satyam's earnings. It all started when, in December 2008, Raju attempted to accomplish unrelated diversification of Satyam's business by combining with related parties — he sought to acquire Maytas Properties and Maytas Infra, companies led by his sons. (Note: Maytas is Satyam spelled backward. "Satyam" means "truth" in several Indian languages.) Institutional investors globally objected to this brazen strategy of browbeating Satyam's Board of Directors into acquiescing with the chairman's wishes — most of the board resigned even before Raju's confession (the global company with some 53,000 employees in 66 countries is listed on the Bombay Stock Exchange, India; the Amsterdam Stock Exchange, the Netherlands; and the New York Stock Exchange, USA).

The two audit partners, S. Gopala Krishnan and Srinivas Talluri, who have been suspended from PriceWaterhouse, the Indian audit arm of PricewaterhouseCoopers (PwC), received certificates of deposit from Satyam's banks that were in "great variance with the figures provided by the company's management" but signed off on the fudged accounts anyway, the CBI claimed.[2] Krishnan and Talluri are in prison in Hyderabad, along with the others that were accused.

The CBI further alleged that the auditors received several times the market rate for the audit work they carried out for Satyam. Since January, furious investors have been demanding to know how the auditors missed a systematic fraud that also severely dented confidence in India's regulatory bodies. Interestingly, news articles in India make no reference to the existence of an internal audit function at Satyam Computer Services.

[1] Source: B. Ramalinga Raju's memo from January 7, 2009, addressed to Satyam Computer Systems' Board of Directors.

[2] The references to the CBI report on Satyam have been culled from the online newsletter available to members of the Institute of Chartered Accountants of India (April 2009).

Other noteworthy examples of massive financial frauds outside the United States include wholesale fraud at the Bank of Credit and Commerce International (BCCI), based in the United Kingdom; the multibillion dollar fraud at Parmalat, the Italian dairy giant; the continuing financial statement re-statements at Nortel Networks, one of Canada's largest companies, that eventually filed for bankruptcy in January 2009; bribery and corruption "on an unprecedented scale and geographic reach" of government officials worldwide by the Siemens Group in Germany; the facilitation of tax evasion by clients of UBS of Switzerland, the largest money manager in the world for the wealthy (note that tax evasion is not illegal in Switzerland); the Dutch food service giant, Royal Ahold NV, engaged in widespread earnings manipulation and securities fraud; and the years of fraudulent financial reporting at Kanebo, a giant cosmetics and textiles company in Japan.

tal markets. This led to passage of the U.S. Sarbanes-Oxley Act of 2002, which was intended to enhance corporate governance and restore investor confidence in the capital markets.

Since 2002, the emphasis on improved corporate governance has become an increasingly global trend, with countries such as the United Kingdom, France, and Germany (and Europe in general), Canada, Indonesia, South Africa, Australia, India, and Japan adopting new rules and regulations. Chapter 3, "Governance," discusses the importance of strong governance, and Appendix 3-B, "Summary of Governance and Risk Management Codes From Other Countries," summarizes many of these codes. Clearly, the driving factor behind such regulatory interest is to preserve market confidence by directly addressing and mitigating the risk of fraudulent financial reporting. Examples of fraud that led to this emphasis on improved corporate governance outside the United States are presented in Exhibit 8-2.

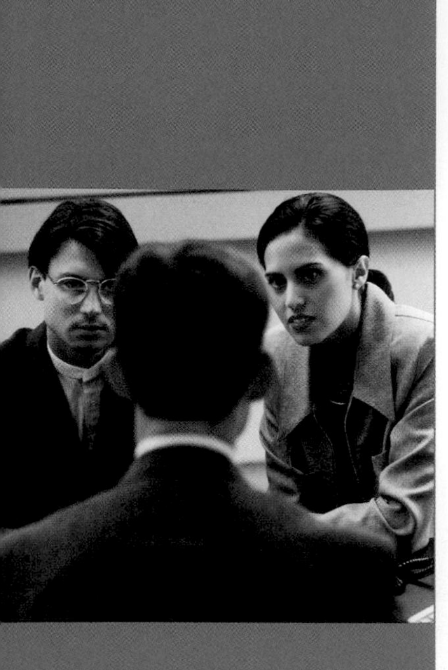

The Association of Certified Fraud Examiners (ACFE) conducts a biannual survey of its members and prepares a *Report to the Nation on Occupational Fraud & Abuse (Report to the Nation).* While this report is largely U.S.-focused, it provides insights into the role of fraud in today's business world. The 2008 *Report to the Nation* is based on data compiled from 959 cases of occupational fraud from a wide range of industries that were investigated between January 2006 and February 2008. Information from these cases was reported by the certified fraud examiners (CFEs) who investigated the cases. The 2008 report summarized the following findings:

- Participants in the survey estimated that U.S. organizations lose 7 percent of their annual revenues to fraud, an increase from the 5 percent estimated in the 2006 *Report to the Nation*. Applied to the projected 2008 United States Gross Domestic Product (GDP), this 7 percent figure translates to approximately US $994 billion in fraud losses.
- Occupational fraud schemes tend to be extremely costly. The median loss caused by the occupational frauds in this study was US $175,000. More than one-quarter of the frauds involved losses of at least US $1 million.
- Occupational fraud schemes frequently continue for years before they are detected. The typical fraud in the study lasted two years from the time it began until the time it was caught by the victim organization.
- The most common fraud schemes were corruption, which occurred in 27 percent of all cases, and fraudulent billing schemes, which occurred in 24 percent (different types of fraud are discussed later in this chapter). Financial statement fraud was the most costly category, with a median loss of US $2 million.
- Occupational frauds are much more likely to be detected by a tip than by audits, controls, or other means. Forty-six percent of the cases were detected by tips from employees, customers, vendors, and other sources.
- The implementation of anti-fraud controls appears to have a measurable impact on an organization's exposure to fraud. For example, organizations that conducted surprise audits suffered a median loss of US $70,000, while those that did not had a median

Corruption

Acts in which individuals wrongfully use their influence in a business transaction in order to procure some benefit for themselves or another person, contrary to their duty to their employer or the rights of another (for example, kickbacks, self-dealing, or conflicts of interest).

loss of US $270,000. Similar reductions were found in fraud losses for organizations that had anonymous fraud hotlines, offered employee support programs, provided fraud training for managers, and had internal audit or fraud examination departments.

- While fraud can occur in any type of organization, the industries most commonly victimized were banking and financial services, government, and health care. The industries with the largest median losses were manufacturing, banking, and insurance.
- Small businesses continue to be especially vulnerable to occupational fraud, with a median loss of US $200,000. Check tampering and fraudulent billing were the most common small business fraud schemes.
- Lack of adequate controls was most commonly cited (35 percent) as the factor that allowed fraud to occur. Next most common were lack of management review (17 percent) and override of existing controls (17 percent).
- Seventy-eight percent of victim organizations modified their anti-fraud controls after discovering that they had been defrauded. This typically involved enhancing controls, conducting surprise audits, and providing fraud training to managers and employees.
- Occupational frauds were most often committed by the accounting department or upper management. Not surprisingly, frauds committed by executives were particularly costly, resulting in a median loss of US $853,000.
- Occupational fraudsters are generally first-time offenders. Only 7 percent had prior convictions and only 12 percent had been previously terminated for fraud-related conduct.
- Fraud perpetrators often display behavioral traits that serve as indicators of possible illegal behavior. The most commonly cited red flags were perpetrators living beyond their apparent means (39 percent) or experiencing financial difficulties (34 percent). In financial statement fraud cases, which tend to be the most costly, excessive organizational pressure to perform was a particularly strong warning sign.[1]

The key point to reinforce here is that no organization is immune to fraud. It can occur in both large and small organizations, and in any country or industry. As long as human beings, with their inherent frailties, are involved in organizations, the risk of fraud is real.

Common Fraud Perpetrator Red Flags:

- **Living beyond their means**
- **Experiencing financial difficulties**
- **Excessive organizational pressure**

DEFINITIONS OF FRAUD

While most individuals have a general understanding of fraud and can probably provide one or more examples, defining it is not so easy. Since most types of fraud are illegal, it is appropriate to start with a legal-focused definition. Exhibit 8-3 provides such a definition from *Black's Law Dictionary*, the most widely used law dictionary in the United States. While some of the terms may differ from those used throughout the rest of this chapter, the focus is similar in that it focuses on acts whereby one individual takes advantage of another.

There are many other definitions of fraud that represent the perspective of both internal and independent outside auditors. Organizations representing auditors as well as fraud examiners have attempted to define

EXHIBIT 8-3

BLACK'S AUTHORITATIVE DEFINITION OF FRAUD

Fraud is a legal term and frequently involves making a legal determination, so the broad definition from *Black's Law Dictionary* may be the most appropriate to consider in this context:

> "[Fraud is] a generic term, embracing all multifarious means which human ingenuity can devise, and which are resorted to by one individual to get advantage over another by false suggestions or by suppression of truth, and includes all surprise, trick, cunning, dissembling, and any unfair way by which another is cheated . . . Elements of a cause of action for "fraud" include false representation of a present or past fact made by defendant, action in reliance thereupon by plaintiff, and damage resulting to plaintiff from such misrepresentation."

Source: *Black's Law Dictionary*, 1979, p. 594.

Fraud

Any illegal act characterized by deceit, concealment, or violation of trust. Frauds are perpetrated by parties and organizations to obtain money, property, or services; to avoid payment or loss of services; or to secure personal or business advantage.

fraud and delineate the roles and responsibilities of their respective member constituency. In 2008, The Institute of Internal Auditors (IIA), The American Institute of Certified Public Accountants (AICPA), and the Association of Certified Fraud Examiners (ACFE) collaborated on a guidance paper titled *Managing the Business Risk of Fraud: A Practical Guide* (the *Fraud Guide*). This guidance outlines five key principles of a fraud risk management process and recommends ways in which boards, senior management, and internal auditors can fight corporate fraud. The report is the result of two years of work from a dedicated task force of more than 20 experts in the field of fraud risk identification, mitigation, and investigation. It contains the following definition:

> Fraud is any intentional act or omission designed to deceive others, resulting in the victim suffering a loss and/or the perpetrator achieving a gain.[2]

The key points from this definition will be discussed in greater detail throughout this chapter. However, each of the sponsoring organizations has their own definitions, reflecting their specific perspectives of fraud. These definitions are shown in Exhibit 8-4.

The IIA's definition is probably the broadest, referring to "Any illegal act characterized by deceit, concealment, or violation of trust." This definition is consistent with the broad role of an internal audit function within an organization. The IIA's definition goes on to cite the types of perpetrators and the potential advantages such individuals may gain. Once again, it is evident how broad The IIA views internal auditors' role within an organization. Many aspects of this definition will be discussed in later sections of this chapter.

The AICPA's definition is, not surprisingly, much narrower. It specifically focuses on "misstatements arising from fraudulent financial reporting and misstatements arising from misappropriation of assets." Given the public accounting profession's primary focus on the financial statement audit, now expanded in the United States and other countries to include an audit of internal control over financial reporting, it is not surprising

EXHIBIT 8-4

DIFFERENT DEFINITIONS OF FRAUD

The Institute of Internal Auditors (IIA)
(From the Glossary to its *Standards* in the International Professional Practices Framework)

> Any illegal act characterized by deceit, concealment, or violation of trust. These acts are not dependent upon the threat of violence or physical force. Frauds are perpetrated by parties and organizations to obtain money, property, or services; to avoid payment or loss of services; or to secure personal or business advantage.

The American Institute of Certified Public Accountants (AICPA)
(From Statement on Auditing Standard No. 99)

> . . . fraud is an intentional act that results in a material misstatement in financial statements that are subject to an audit. [There are] two types of misstatements . . . misstatements arising from fraudulent financial reporting and misstatements arising from misappropriation of assets.

Association of Certified Fraud Examiners (ACFE)
(From the *2008 Report to the Nation on Occupational Fraud*)

> The use of one's occupation for personal enrichment through the deliberate misuse or misapplication of the employing organization's resources or assets.

that the AICPA discusses the concept of fraud by evaluating its relation to, and effect on, the organization's financial statements. Refer to Exhibit 8-5 where the standards relating to independent outside auditors are outlined.

Fraudulent financial reporting involves intentional misstatements or omissions of amounts or disclosures in financial statements designed to deceive financial statement users. The nature of these misstatements or omissions is the failure of the financial statements to be presented, in all material respects, in conformity with Generally Accepted Accounting Principles (GAAP). Fraudulent financial reporting can be accomplished by:

- Manipulating, falsifying, or altering accounting records or supporting documents from which the financial statements are prepared.
- Misrepresenting, or intentionally omitting from, the financial statements events, transactions, or other significant information.
- Intentionally misapplying accounting principles relating to amounts, classification, manner of presentation, or disclosure.

Misappropriation of Assets:

- **Pilferage**
- **Embezzlement**
- **Defalcation**

Misstatements arising from misappropriation of assets (sometimes referred to as pilferage, embezzlement, or defalcation) involve the theft of an organization's assets in which the effect of the theft causes the financial statements not to be presented, in all material respects, in conformity with GAAP. Misappropriation of assets can be perpetrated in various ways, including embezzling receipts, stealing assets, or causing

EXHIBIT 8-5

FRAUD REQUIREMENTS OF INDEPENDENT OUTSIDE AUDITORS

U.S. Public Companies – The Public Company Accounting Oversight Board (PCAOB) promulgates standards that guide the issuance of opinions covering the financial statements of public companies in the U.S. Specific to fraud, the PCAOB standards state in AU Section 110.02 *Responsibilities and Functions of the Independent Auditor,* "The auditor has a responsibility to plan and perform the audit to obtain reasonable assurance about whether the financial statements are free of material misstatement, whether caused by error or fraud." The PCAOB standards address fraud more specifically in AU Section 316, *Consideration of Fraud in a Financial Statement Audit,* the source of which is AICPA Statement of Auditing Standard (SAS) No. 99. Refer to the discussion below for specific guidance provided in SAS No. 99.

U.S. Non-public Companies – Since the PCAOB's authority covers only those audits conducted for U.S. public companies, non-public companies continue to follow the AICPA's standards. SAS No. 99, *Consideration of Fraud in a Financial Statement Audit,* states that

> . . . [independent outside] auditors are responsible for planning and performing an audit to obtain reasonable assurance about whether the financial statements are free of material misstatements whether caused by error or fraud." Specifically, SAS No. 99 contains the following additional guidance for (independent outside) auditors in the U.S.:
>
> - Increased emphasis on fraud awareness and professional skepticism
> - Audit engagement team discussion ("brainstorming session")
> - Gathering information needed to identify the risk of material misstatement due to fraud
> - Summarizing identified fraud and the auditor's planned response
> - Mandatory audit procedures to address the risk of management override of internal controls
> - Evaluating audit results
> - Communications about fraud with management, audit committee, and others

Non-U.S. Companies – The International Auditing and Assurance Standards Board issued International Standard on Auditing (ISA) 240, *The Auditor's Responsibility Relating to Fraud in an Audit of Financial Statements,* which states "In planning and performing the audit to reduce audit risk to an acceptably low level, the auditor should consider the risks of material misstatements in the financial statements due to fraud." ISA 240 provides additional guidance that is similar to SAS No. 99, which is discussed above.

Fraudulent Financial Reporting

Acts that involve falsification of an organization's financial statements (for example, overstating revenues, understating, liabilities and expenses).

an entity to pay for goods or services that have not been received. Misappropriation of assets may be accompanied by false or misleading records or documents, or suppressing evidence, possibly created by circumventing internal controls. Frequently, collusion with other employees or third parties also may be involved.

The ACFE's definition focuses on occupational fraud, that is, fraud in the workplace. Occupational fraud encompasses a wide range of misconduct by employees, managers, and executives. Occupational fraud schemes can be as simple as petty cash theft or as complex as fraudulent financial reporting. Four elements seem to characterize the incidence of occupational fraud. Such an act:

- Is clandestine (that is, secretive and suspicious).
- Violates the perpetrator's fiduciary duties to the victim organization.
- Is committed for the purpose of direct or indirect financial benefit to the perpetrator.
- Costs the employing organization assets, revenues, or reserves.

The ACFE's Occupational Fraud and Abuse Classification System describes three main types of fraud: fraudulent statements, which generally involve falsification of an organization's financial statements (for example, overstating revenues and understating liabilities and expenses); asset misappropriation, which involves the theft or misuse of an organization's assets (for example, skimming revenues, stealing inventory, or payroll fraud); and corruption, in which fraudsters wrongfully use their influence in a business transaction to procure some benefit for themselves or another person, contrary to their duty to their employer or the rights of another (for example, kickbacks, self-dealing, or conflicts of interest). Refer to Exhibit 8-6 for an outline of this classification system.

Internationally, the pertinent standard furnishing guidance for auditors is International Standard on Auditing (ISA) No. 240: The Auditor's Responsibility Relating to Fraud and Error in an Audit of Financial Statements, issued by the International Federation of Accountants (IFAC). Although this standard applies primarily to independent outside auditors, its contents and guidance are relevant to internal auditors as well. Fraud, waste, and abuse are also a big concern in government, and the Governmental Auditing Standards in the United States (also known as the Yellow Book) devotes several sections to government internal auditors' responsibilities in this area.

Each of these fraud definitions supports the focus of the professional organization that created it. However, since these organizations worked together to issue the *Fraud Guide*, the definition used in the guide, specifically that "Fraud is any intentional act or omission designed to deceive others, resulting in the victim suffering a loss and/or the perpetrator achieving a gain," will serve as the basis for discussion throughout the rest of this chapter. It is a simple, yet comprehensive, definition that provides the foundation for the principles and other guidance contained in the *Fraud Guide*.

THE FRAUD TRIANGLE

An important conceptual framework in understanding fraud is Cressey's Fraud Triangle, loosely based on what police officers and detectives

Occupational Fraud

Fraud in the workplace:

- **Falsification of financial statements**
- **Asset misappropriation**
- **Corruption**

EXHIBIT 8-6

OUTLINE OF THE ACFE'S OCCUPATIONAL FRAUD AND ABUSE CLASSIFICATION SYSTEM

1. Intentional manipulation of financial statements, which can lead to:
   a. Inappropriately reported revenues.
   b. Inappropriately reported expenses.
   c. Inappropriately reflected balance sheet amounts, including reserves.
   d. Inappropriately improved and/or masked disclosures.
   e. Concealing misappropriation of assets.
   f. Concealing unauthorized receipts and expenditures.
   g. Concealing unauthorized acquisition, disposition, and use of assets.
2. Misappropriation of:
   a. Tangible assets by:
      i. Employees.
      ii. Customers.
      iii. Vendors.
      iv. Former employees and others outside the organization.
   b. Intangible assets.
   c. Proprietary business opportunities.
3. Corruption including:
   a. Bribery and gratuities to:
      i. Companies.
      ii. Private individuals.
      iii. Public officials.
   b. Receipt of bribes, kickbacks, and gratuities.
   c. Aiding and abetting fraud by other parties (e.g., customers, vendors).

Source: *Managing the Business Risk of Fraud: A Practical Guide*, The Institute of Internal Auditors, The American Institute of Certified Public Accountants, and the Association of Certified Fraud Examiners, p. 24.

Root Causes of Fraud:

- **Perceived need or pressure**
- **Perceived opportunity**
- **Rationalization**

have referred to as "means, motives, and opportunity." First conceived by sociologist Donald Cressey, and widely disseminated by the ACFE, the fraud triangle has three components: perceived need/pressure, perceived opportunity, and rationalization of fraudulent behavior. Exhibit 8-7 is a visual representation of these three components.

The fraud triangle highlights the three elements that may be called the "root causes of fraud." These elements are always present, no matter the type of fraud. Fraud perpetrators want to relieve real or perceived pressure (for example, generating the attitude that when you can't "make" the numbers, you just "make up" the numbers), they need to see ample opportunity so that they can carry out the fraud with ease (for example, nobody's watching the store, the employee is trusted completely), and most importantly, they need to rationalize their action as acceptable (for example, I'm doing it for the good of the company). Rationalization allows fraud perpetrators to believe that they have done nothing wrong and are "normal people." Specifically, fraud perpetrators must be able to justify their actions to themselves as a psychological coping mechanism to deal with the inevitable "cognitive dissonance" (that is, a lack of congruence between their own perception of being honest and the deceptive nature of their action or behavior). Said another way, they need excuses. A typical list includes:

- Everyone's doing it, so I am no different.

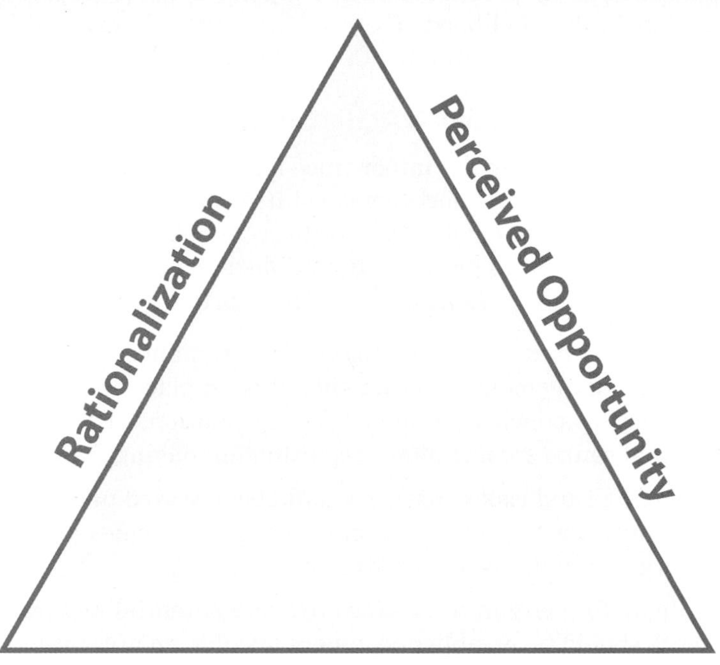

Source: Cressey, D.R., *Other People's Money: A Study in the Social Psychology of Embezzlement* (Glencoe, IL: The Free Press, 1986).

EXHIBIT 8-7

- Taking money from the cash till was just a temporary "borrowing." The money will be returned when the gambling/betting winnings materialize.
- The employer is underpaying me, so I deserve these "perks" as reasonable compensation, and the company can certainly afford it.
- I am not hurting anyone — in fact, it's for a good cause!
- It is not really a serious matter.

Consider a couple of examples: A furniture store employee stealing inventory may be taking advantage of weak internal controls (perceived opportunity), the need to furnish his new apartment with nice furniture instead of the "junk" he can afford (perceived pressure from spouse), and using the rationalization that other store employees are probably stealing too (whether or not this is a fact). In the case of management fraud, the perceived pressure may be to meet earnings targets so that bonuses can be lavish, the opportunity may be weak financial reporting controls or an inactive audit committee, and the rationalization may be that "this is in the organization's best interest and therefore an appropriate use of 'cookie jar reserves' created earlier to get over a temporary hump." Although the fraud triangle is a powerful conceptual tool, there may be other personality factors that do not fit easily into those three categories. Examples of these factors include basic greed and acquisitiveness, a "revenge fraud" orientation to make the organization pay for perceived inequities, or a "catch me if you can" attitude that some fraud perpetrators exhibit. Similarly, the organizational environment and culture may be factors. For

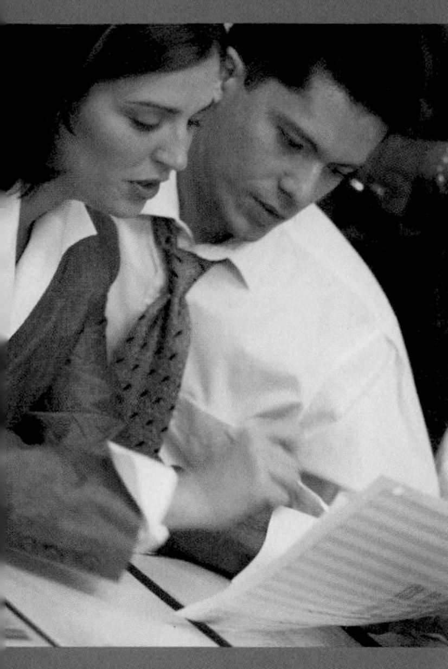

example, a poor tone at the top, as evidenced by organizational inertia and reluctance to take any action, turning a blind eye, being content with a slap on the wrist, or a poor track record in vigorously prosecuting fraud, may contribute to the likelihood of a fraud occurring. Behavioral factors are discussed in greater detail later in the chapter.

KEY PRINCIPLES FOR MANAGING FRAUD RISK

The *Fraud Guide* indicates the importance for organizations to establish a diligent and ongoing effort to protect itself from acts of fraud. To support these efforts, the *Fraud Guide* sets out five key principles that organizations can follow to proactively establish an environment that will help it effectively manage its fraud risk. These principles are:

Principle 1: As part of an organization's governance structure, a fraud risk management program should be in place, including a written policy (or policies) to convey the expectations of the board of directors and senior management regarding managing fraud risk.

Principle 2: Fraud risk exposure should be assessed periodically by the organization to identify specific potential schemes and events that the organization needs to mitigate.

Principle 3: Prevention techniques to avoid potential key fraud risk events should be established, where feasible, to mitigate possible impacts on the organization.

Principle 4: Detection techniques should be established to uncover fraud events when preventive measures fail or unmitigated risks are realized.

Principle 5: A reporting process should be in place to solicit input on potential fraud, and a coordinated approach to investigation and corrective action should be used to help ensure potential fraud is addressed appropriately and timely.[3]

Governance

The combination of processes and structures implemented by the board to inform, direct, manage, and monitor the activities of the organization toward the achievement of its objectives.

The organizations contributing to the *Fraud Guide* believe it "can be used to assess an organization's fraud risk management program as a resource for improvement, or to develop a program where none exists."[4] While key aspects of these principles are discussed in greater detail in subsequent sections of this chapter, the following summarizes these principles.

Fraud Risk Governance (Principle 1)

As discussed in Chapter 3, "Governance," it is important for organizations to develop a strong governance structure to oversee risk management and other activities that are in place to help ensure achievement of business objectives. The same applies to fraud: there must be a structure in place to oversee the identification and management of fraud risks. Effective governance enables the creation and maintenance of an ethical climate within an organization, which can help prevent or deter fraud. The overall tone at the top, in effect, establishes the organization's fraud tolerance.

Similar to the form of governance discussed in Chapter 3, fraud risk governance must start with the governing board. The board helps to set the tone for fraud risk management, and can encourage management to establish specific policies that encourage ethical behavior and promote the prevention and detection of fraud. The board is also responsible for monitoring the effectiveness of the organization's fraud risk management program. It can do this by assigning to a member of management the responsibility for the fraud risk management program and reporting to the board on the effectiveness of this program. The specific elements of a fraud risk management program are discussed later in this chapter.

Fraud Risk Assessment (Principle 2)

A fraud risk management program will not be successful without management first understanding the inherent fraud risks the organization faces. The steps in a fraud risk assessment are similar to those described for an enterprise risk assessment in Chapter 4, "Risk Management." An organization must first identify the potential fraud events or scenarios to which it may be vulnerable. These events or scenarios will vary from one organization to the next, depending on the business model, industry, locations where the organization operates, culture, and other similar factors. When compiling a list of potential fraud scenarios, it may be helpful to gather information from external regulatory bodies, industry sources, guidance-setting groups, and professional organizations. The fraud triangle discussed in the previous section may help guide the brainstorming of fraud risks, particularly the opportunities that could give rise to such scenarios. For example, consideration of current incentives and pressures, together with known systems access shortcomings, may help identify a fraud risk scenario in which management accesses and modifies journal entries to overstate earnings and thereby meet a bonus target.

Risk Assessment

The identification and analysis (typically in terms of impact and likelihood) of relevant risks to the achievement of an organization's objectives, forming a basis for determining how the risks should be managed.

After the potential fraud risks have been identified, the impact and likelihood of each risk must be assessed. It is important to consider all possible effects of fraud scenarios, not just the financial impact. Occurrence of fraud can have a detrimental impact on an organization's reputation or violate laws and statutes, even if the event does not result in a material financial loss. The assessment of fraud risks is an important step because it helps an organization determine the level of resources that should be devoted to preventing or detecting the identified fraud scenarios.

Risk Response

An action, or set of actions, taken by management to achieve a desired risk management strategy. Risk responses can be categorized as risk avoidance, reduction, sharing, or acceptance.

Finally, an organization must decide what to do about the various fraud scenarios, that is, what fraud risk responses are appropriate. Similar to the risk response discussion in Chapter 4, organizations have various options for dealing with each fraud risk: *avoiding* the risk, *sharing* the risk, *reducing* the risk, *accepting* the risk, or some combination of those options. The key is to determine a cost-effective option that will reduce the risk to an acceptable level, giving consideration to all possible risk consequences.

Fraud Prevention and Detection (Principles 3 and 4)

A fraud risk management program must have an appropriate balance between prevention and detection controls. Prevention controls may include policies, procedures, training, and communication, all of which are designed to stop fraud from occurring. Prevention controls may not provide absolute assurance that a fraud will be prevented, but they do serve as an important first line of defense in minimizing fraud risk. Prevention controls, including a strong fraud awareness program, can serve as an important deterrent to fraud (that is, discourage fraud).

While an organization typically prefers to prevent fraud, that is not always possible. Therefore, it is important to design and implement effective detection controls as well. Detection controls may include manual or automated activities that will recognize timely that a fraud has or is occurring. These controls may provide a deterrent to fraud, but they are not designed to prevent the fraud from occurring. Rather, they provide evidence that a fraud has occurred, which can be helpful in an investigation.

Fraud Reporting, Investigation, and Resolution (Principle 5)

As noted earlier in this chapter, the ACFE *Report to the Nation* indicates that frauds are more likely to be detected by a tip than by audits, controls, or other means. Therefore, it is important for an organization to establish a reporting system to facilitate and encourage reporting of potential fraud incidents. For example, a whistleblower hotline provides a means for prompt notification, helps in gathering the necessary information to enable an investigation, if necessary, and provides for confidentiality if desired by the individual reporting the incident. The reporting system can be managed by a member of management, but it may also be appropriate, and even required by regulation, for there to be a reporting mechanism directly to the board in certain circumstances. This provides an avenue of reporting should the individual believe senior management may be involved in the fraud incident.

Fraud Detection

According to the ACFE's *Report to the Nation*, occupational frauds are much more likely to be detected by a tip than by audits, controls, or other means.

Once an allegation has been received, there must be a structured process for evaluating and investigating the incident. In fact, establishing a sound investigation process can improve an organization's chances of recovering losses and may also minimize exposure to litigation. Depending on the circumstances, it may be necessary to involve internal or external legal counsel in the investigation, as well as other functions in the organization, such as human resources, information technology, and internal auditing. Having a formal, structured approach to conducting and reporting on the results of investigations will help an organization complete an investigation timely and develop and maintain the support necessary to facilitate corrective actions.

Regardless of whether an investigation results in prosecution, disciplinary action, or no action at all, it is important for an organization to have a consistent means of resolving investigations. First, timely resolution will help ensure prosecution or disciplinary actions can be taken before "the trail goes cold" (a term often used in investigations to indicate that the collection of evidence will be more difficult and potentially less relevant). Additionally, individuals involved in the fraud have a need, and in many countries a right, to be able to defend themselves timely. Second, organizations must determine what gave rise to the fraud incident so that corrective actions (for example, control enhancements) can be implemented. Finally, management must discipline employees in a consistent manner to avoid the perception of favoritism or that disciplinary actions are arbitrary. This supports the tone at the top, which should send the message: "fraudulent acts will not be tolerated, and will be dealt with swiftly and consistently."

The principles outlined in this section are so important to the establishment and maintenance of an effective fraud risk management program that each will be discussed in greater detail in the following sections. This will help readers gain a greater understanding of how to execute the necessary steps to achieve these principles.

GOVERNANCE OVER THE FRAUD RISK MANAGEMENT PROGRAM

Strong governance provides the foundation for an effective fraud risk management program. The *Fraud Guide* states that organizations' key stakeholders ". . . have raised the awareness and expectation of corporate behavior and corporate governance practices. Some organizations have developed corporate cultures that encompass strong board governance practices, including:

- Board ownership of agendas and information flow.
- Access to multiple layers of management and effective control of a whistleblower hotline.
- Independent nomination processes.
- Effective senior management team . . . evaluations, performance management, compensation, and succession planning.
- A code of conduct specific for senior management, in addition to the organization's code of conduct.
- Strong emphasis on the board's own independent effectiveness and process through board evaluations, executive session, and active participation in oversight of strategic and risk mitigation efforts."[5]

What this emphasizes is the importance of a corporate culture that includes the board obtaining assurances about the ethical conduct of management and employees. The *Fraud Guide* goes on to say, "Effective business ethics programs can serve as the foundation for preventing, detecting, and deterring fraudulent and criminal acts. An organization's ethical treatment of employees, customers, vendors, and other partners will influence those receiving such treatment. These ethics programs create an environment where making the right decision is implicit."[6]

Roles and Responsibilities

The roles and responsibilities in a fraud risk management program must be formal and communicated. Policies and procedures, job descriptions, charters, and delegations of authority are all important in defining the various roles and responsibilities for such a program. Generally, the following roles and responsibilities are embedded in successful fraud risk management programs.

Board of directors — As indicated previously, boards help set the tone at the top. They do so by embracing the governance practices listed above. Many of the specific fraud oversight responsibilities may be carried out by committees of the board, such as the audit committee or the nominating and governance committee. This oversight should generally include:

- A general understanding of fraud-related policies, procedures, incentive plans, etc.
- A comprehensive understanding of the key fraud risks.
- Oversight of the fraud risk management program, including the internal controls that have been implemented to manage fraud risks.
- Receiving and monitoring reports that provide information about fraud incidents, investigation status, and disciplinary actions.

Tone at the Top

The entity-wide attitude of integrity and control consciousness, as exhibited by the most senior executives of an organization. See also Control Environment.

- The ability to retain outside counsel and experts when needed.
- Directing the internal audit function and the independent outside auditor to provide assurance regarding fraud risk concerns.

The board and committee responsibilities should be documented in the respective charters to ensure their roles and responsibilities are clearly delineated and understood. The board should also gain comfort that sufficient resources are being applied to ensure effective operation of the fraud risk management program.

Management — Similar to the board, management plays a very important role in setting the tone for the organization. Beyond what management says, how they act is instrumental in shaping perceptions of the culture and their attitude toward fraud prevention. In addition, management is responsible for implementing the overall fraud risk management program. This includes their direction and oversight over the system of internal controls, which must be designed and operated in a manner to prevent fraud incidents or detect them timely. Management must also establish a system of monitoring and reporting that will enable them to evaluate whether the fraud risk management program is operating effectively. This helps provide them with timely and relevant information that can be reported to the board.

Control Environment

The attitude and actions of the board and management regarding the significance of control within the organization.

It is common in many organizations to assign a member of management the responsibility for overseeing the fraud risk management program. This responsibility may include overseeing fraud and ethics-related policies, conducting the fraud risk assessment, overseeing the controls that are designed to address fraud risks, monitoring the effectiveness of the program, coordinating the investigation and reporting process, and training and educating employees on the program. This individual should be at a sufficiently high level in the organization to reinforce management's commitment to preventing and deterring fraud. Typically there are other functions, most commonly from the legal and human resources areas, that have defined support roles for this individual.

Employees — The day-to-day execution of the fraud risk management program, specifically the controls that are designed to prevent and detect fraud, must involve everyone in the organization. According to the *Fraud Guide*, this means that "all levels of staff, including management, should:

- Have a basic understanding of fraud and be aware of the red flags.
- Understand their roles within the internal control framework. Staff members should understand how their job procedures are designed to manage fraud risks and when noncompliance may create an opportunity for fraud to occur and go undetected.
- Read and understand policies and procedures (e.g., the fraud policy, code of conduct, and whistleblower policy), as well as other operational policies and procedures, such as procurement manuals.
- As required, participate in the process of creating a strong control environment and designing and implementing fraud control activities, as well as participate in monitoring activities.
- Report suspicions of incidences of fraud.
- Cooperate in investigations."[7]

For additional information about fraud risk management activities, and how these activities can be aligned with the Committee of Sponsoring Organizations of the Treadway Commission's (COSO's) *Internal Control – Integrated Framework*, refer to Appendix I in the *Fraud Guide*.

The internal audit function — The internal audit function plays an important role in contributing to the overall governance of a fraud risk management program. This is primarily evident from the independent assurance the internal audit function provides to the board and management that the controls in place to manage fraud risks are designed adequately and operate effectively. The internal audit function's role is discussed in greater detail later in the chapter.

It is recognized that the independent outside auditor has certain responsibilities with regard to the detection of certain types of fraud (primarily financial reporting fraud and misappropriation of certain assets). This role, which is well defined in the standards governing that profession, is not part of an organization's fraud risk management program because such a role would violate the public accounting profession's independence standards.

Components of a Fraud Risk Management Program

While there is no "one size fits all" approach to designing a fraud risk management program, there are certain components that are common among most effective programs. Most organizations have written policies and procedures relating to fraud, and typically have some activities associated with assessing risks, designing effective controls, monitoring compliance, conducting investigations, and educating employees on fraud topics and red flags. However, few organizations have comprehensively tied all of this together into an integrated program. Typically, successful integrated programs have certain key components.

- *Commitment* by the board and senior management. This commitment should be formally documented and communicated throughout the organization.
- *Fraud awareness* activities that help employees understand the purpose, requirements, and responsibilities of the program. These activities may include any or all of the following: written communications to all employees, oral communications during organization-wide meetings, postings on the organization's internal website and external web page, and formal training programs.
- *An affirmation process* that requires employees to affirm periodically, typically annually, that they understand and are complying with policies and procedures.
- *A conflict disclosure* protocol or process that helps employees self-disclose potential or actual conflicts of interest. This would also include a means for timely resolution of matters that have been disclosed.
- *Fraud risk assessment*, which helps to identify all reasonable fraud scenarios. This is discussed further in the next section.
- *Reporting procedures and whistleblower protection* that provide a well-known and easy avenue for individuals, whether inside or outside the organization, to report suspected violations or incidents.

Fraud Awareness

Activities that help employees understand the purpose, requirements, and responsibilities of a fraud risk management program.

- *An investigation process* that ensures all matters undergo a timely and thorough investigation, as appropriate.
- *Disciplinary and/or corrective actions* that address noncompliance with established policies and help deter fraudulent behavior.
- *Process evaluation and improvement* to provide quality assurance that the program will continue to meet its objectives.
- *Continuous monitoring* to ensure the program consistently operates as designed.

Including these components in a fraud risk management program will not eliminate fraud risk. It will, however, provide reasonable assurance that fraud incidents are prevented, or detected timely and dealt with appropriately.

FRAUD RISK ASSESSMENT

As previously stated, the process of conducting a fraud risk assessment is similar to that of conducting an enterprise risk assessment. The three key steps are:

1. Identify inherent fraud risks;
2. Assess impact and likelihood of the identified risks; and
3. Develop responses to those risks that have a sufficiently high impact and likelihood to result in a potential outcome beyond management's tolerance.

Reasonable Assurance

A level of assurance that is supported by generally accepted auditing procedures and judgments

When conducting a fraud risk assessment, it is important to involve individuals with varying knowledge, skills, and perspectives. While the specific individuals will vary from organization to organization, the risk assessment will typically include:

- Accounting and finance personnel to help identify financial reporting and safeguarding of cash fraud scenarios.
- Nonfinancial business personnel to leverage their knowledge of day-to-day operations, customer and vendor interactions, and other industry-related fraud scenarios.
- Legal and compliance personnel to identify scenarios that may include potential criminal, civil, and regulatory liability should fraud or misconduct occur.
- Risk management personnel to help identify market and insurance fraud scenarios, and to ensure the fraud risk assessment is integrated with the overall enterprise risk assessment.
- Internal auditors, who have an understanding of broad fraud risk scenarios and controls.
- Other internal or external parties who can provide additional expertise to the exercise.

The risk assessment process can take many different forms, the most common of which are interviews, surveys, and facilitated meetings. Regardless of the approach, it is important for individuals to remain open and creative to ensure the fraud risk universe is sufficiently comprehensive.

Fraud Risk Identification

An effective means of identifying the most comprehensive list of fraud risk scenarios is through brainstorming. While the actual approach may vary, this exercise should involve all of the individuals who are part of the risk assessment team discussed above. Brainstorming can help the organization identify and discuss the wide array of potential scenarios that may exist. One of the challenges when brainstorming fraud risks is to make sure that the discussion is not limited to scenarios perpetrated by a sole individual. Frequently, fraud includes collusion among multiple individuals, and while it is more difficult to brainstorm these scenarios, it is certainly no less important.

The *Fraud Guide* outlines certain elements that should be considered when brainstorming fraud risk scenarios. All of these elements should be considered to ensure a comprehensive fraud risk universe can be compiled.

- **Incentives, Pressures, and Opportunities —** There are many possible motives for committing fraud. The first challenge when brainstorming fraud risk scenarios is to identify as many of those motives as possible. As described in the section covering the fraud triangle, frauds are committed when there is incentive or pressure to do so, the opportunity exists, and the perpetrator can rationalize the incident. Brainstorming rationalization scenarios is not common, as consideration of the other two sides of the fraud triangle must occur first and rationalization is very individualistic. However, focusing on different incentives, pressures, and opportunities that may exist helps to identify scenarios for which the organization may be vulnerable. Incentives may represent monetary or other rewards that might give people a reason to act differently than they would normally act. Similarly, pressures may cause individuals to act differently because they feel they must relieve whatever is causing such pressures. Opportunities reflect ways through which a fraud can be committed, potentially without detection (for example, when controls are weak). Brainstorming potential incentives, pressures, and opportunities will likely produce the majority of the fraud risk scenarios.
- **Risk of Management's Override of Controls —** Even when a sound system of internal controls exists, controls may still be vulnerable to override. Since management is typically "trusted" to make good decisions, override by management is possible because other employees tend not to question a management decision and assume it is for the benefit of the organization. There have been many chronicled cases of management override to facilitate fraudulent financial reporting or misappropriation of assets. Brainstorming management override scenarios will identify different fraud scenarios than brainstorming about incentives, pressures, and opportunities.
- **Population of Fraud Risks —** There are certain "universal" fraud risks that apply to all organizations and others that are common to those in certain industries or countries. While it is possible to identify most of these risks while brainstorming, such scenarios may already be documented and available through other sources, such as industry organizations, professional societies, consulting firms,

Regulatory and Legal Misconduct

Includes conflicts of interest, insider trading, theft of competitor trade secrets, anti-competitive practices, environmental violations, and trade and customs regulations in areas of import/export.

etc. The ACFE has created a classification structure of occupational fraud risks that can help organizations brainstorm fraud risk scenarios. This structure was previously outlined in Exhibit 8-6.

- **Fraudulent Financial Reporting —** The above elements should help to identify most of an organization's fraud risks. However, it is helpful to also consider specific scenario types to determine whether additional scenarios may exist. Fraudulent financial reporting scenarios have received much notoriety in recent years, culminating in regulations in many countries, such as the Sarbanes-Oxley Act in the United States, which are designed to reduce the likelihood of material financial reporting frauds. This is an area that should be brainstormed with the independent outside auditors since they are likely considering the same scenarios.
- **Misappropriation of Assets —** Another specific scenario type focuses on assets that could be misappropriated. This element begins with identifying what assets belong to the organization that might be valued by employees or outsiders (for example, vendors or customers). Next, scenarios can be identified that would allow such assets to be misappropriated. It is important to remember that physical safeguards may not always be sufficient. While tangible assets, such as cash, inventory, materials, and equipment, certainly need to be considered as part of this element, intangible assets, such as confidential employee or customer data or trade drawings, also may be subject to misappropriation. Therefore, information technology can play an important role in controlling certain misappropriation of assets risks.
- **Corruption —** According to the *Fraud Guide*, corruption "is operationally defined as the misuse of entrusted power for private gain."[8] Examples of corruption include bribery of foreign officials or aiding and abetting other organizations committing fraud. The amount of time spent brainstorming corruption fraud scenarios will depend on the organization's industry and countries of operation, but such scenarios should be given some thought.
- **Other Fraud Risks —** There may be other potential fraud risks that are not inherent in the elements above. The *Fraud Guide* mentions regulatory and legal misconduct, which could include ". . . conflicts of interest, insider trading, theft of competitor trade secrets, anti-competitive practices, environmental violations, and trade and customs regulations in areas of import/export."[9] Another type of fraud risk to consider relates to the organization's reputation. Many of the risks already identified may impact an organization's reputation, but there may be others as well.

Before finalizing the list of fraud risk scenarios, it is important to understand the potential causes and sources of each scenario. If several scenarios have the same root cause, it is possible that the root cause should be assessed, not the other scenarios. Ultimately, an organization should develop responses to the causes of risks, not the symptoms that may be seen on the surface. Similarly, understanding the potential sources of the scenarios, that is where they might occur within the organization, also will help later in the process as responses are determined. Spending extra time at this stage to understand causes and sources will help make the rest of the fraud risk assessment program more successful.

It should be apparent that identifying fraud risk scenarios is not an exact science. It requires contributions from a diverse collection of individuals over a period of time. Moreover, the brainstorming really never ends; the list of potential fraud scenarios continues to evolve over time. But similar to the enterprise risk assessment, identifying potential fraud risks provides the foundation for the next steps in the fraud risk assessment process.

Assessment of Impact and Likelihood of Fraud Risks

Determining the potential impact and likelihood of each fraud scenario is a very subjective process. The risk assessment concepts outlined in Chapter 4 apply to fraud risk assessment as well. Following are key points that should be considered when assessing fraud risks.

- **Impact** — As previously stated, it is important to consider all possible outcomes of a fraud risk scenario, not just the financial statement or monetary impact. The significance of other outcomes may be greater than the financial statement or monetary impact. For example, it is important to consider the legal impact (criminal, civil, and regulatory outcomes), reputational impact (such as damage to a brand), operational impact (such as cost of production and warranty liability), and impact on people (such as health and safety incidents, or inability to attract and retain employees in an organization with low morale). The objective is to identify fraud risk scenarios with outcomes that exceed management's tolerance relative to those outcomes. Given that precise quantification of fraud risk outcomes is difficult, the measurement of impact will typically be in general categories, such as highly significant, somewhat significant, or insignificant.

Impact

The severity of outcomes caused by risk events. Can be measured in financial, reputation, legal, or other types of outcomes.

- **Likelihood** — Judgment regarding the probability or frequency of a fraud scenario is influenced in part by past experience, such as previous incidents of such a scenario within the organization or at organizations in the same industry or geographical location. However, an estimate of likelihood also should be made even if there is no knowledge of past events. As was the case with the impact assessment, precise probability quantifications are typically not possible or even necessary. Therefore general measurement categories, such as probable, possible, or remote, are more commonly used.

Likelihood

The probability that a risk event will occur.

Management's assessment involves considering impact and likelihood together. This assessment provides sufficient context about the fraud risk scenarios to begin making decisions about the resources and priorities that should be devoted to managing the scenarios.

Response to Fraud Risk

As indicated above, management's tolerance to fraud risks influences the fraud risk assessment. Typically, an organization's tolerance to fraud risks is lower than its tolerance to other risks. Specifically, when considering the potential impact on reputation or possible legal liability, an organization may establish a "zero tolerance" to many of the fraud risks. Such a level will influence, and may limit, its options regarding how to respond to the risks. However, there may be some fraud risk outcomes that will be tolerable. There may be more flexible responses that can be applied to these risks.

Risk Tolerance

The acceptable levels of risk size and variation relative to the achievement of objectives, which must align with the organization's risk appetite.

Since risk tolerance will vary from organization to organization, the responses to fraud risks also will vary widely. The concepts from COSO's *Enterprise Risk Management – Integrated Framework* apply when considering responses to fraud risks. This framework outlines four possible responses to risks.

- If a risk is so intolerable that an organization cannot allow for even a single incident to occur, management may need to consider ways to *avoid* the risk. An example would be selling an operation in a country where the risk of bribery is much too great.
- If an organization has little or no tolerance to a risk, but cannot avoid it without adversely affecting its objectives, controls would be designed to *reduce* the likelihood of the incident occurring, or the impact should it occur. This would be accomplished by establishing an appropriate blend of preventive and detective controls, as discussed in the next two sections.
- If an organization desires to reduce the impact or likelihood of a risk, but does not believe it has the skills or experience to do so effectively and efficiently, it may *share* the operation of preventive and detective controls with an organization that is better equipped to execute such controls.
- If the occurrence of a risk is tolerable, management may decide to *accept* the risk at its current level and not make any particular efforts to manage the risk.

Once the risk response decisions are made, management must execute the necessary actions to carry out those responses. Since most fraud risk responses involve reducing the risks, the next two sections focus on fraud prevention and fraud detection.

FRAUD PREVENTION

Preventive Control

An activity that is designed to deter unintended events from occurring.

In a perfect world, an organization would prefer to implement sufficient fraud prevention controls to ensure none of the potential fraud scenarios occurs. However, complete prevention is not possible and in many cases the cost of preventing certain fraud scenarios exceeds the benefits. That is why organizations develop fraud programs that combine an appropriate balance of both preventive and detective controls. Nevertheless, the familiar phrase "an ounce of prevention is worth a pound of cure" provides a good starting point for developing actions to manage fraud risks to an acceptable level.

There are different types of preventive techniques, several of which are discussed below. However, one of the most important forms of prevention relates to organizational awareness. The *Fraud Guide* states "One key to prevention is making personnel throughout the organization aware of the fraud risk management program, including the types of fraud and misconduct that may occur. This awareness should enforce the notion that all of the techniques established in the program are real and will be enforced."[10] In other words, strong organizational awareness serves as a deterrent to fraud.

The "ounce of prevention" part of the familiar phrase represents an organization's proactive way of fighting fraud. By building preventive controls into the system of internal controls, management can establish a foundation that will deter most individuals from even considering fraud.

In addition to implementing a strong fraud governance environment, the *Fraud Guide* outlines common elements that can play an important role in preventing fraud:

- **Performing background investigations —** Some individuals are more susceptible to succumbing to the temptations that may lead to fraud than others. An individual who has committed fraud once is more likely to do so again than one who has not. A comprehensive background investigation can help keep those most likely to commit fraud out of the organization. In addition to performing background investigations on potential employees, some organizations also will perform these investigations on new and existing vendors, customers, and business partners to reduce the risk of fraud from these outside parties.
- **Providing anti-fraud training —** Even if competent and honest employees are hired, they must understand what fraud is, the red flags to watch for, how to report suspected fraud incidents, and the consequences of committing fraud. Such training should be mandatory and also provide periodic updates.
- **Evaluating performance and compensation programs —** Organizations must be careful to not incent the wrong behavior. Compensation programs must be scrutinized carefully to make sure that they not only encourage the right behavior, but even reward it. Conversely, such programs must not inadvertently condone behaviors that might incent, or be perceived to incent, behavior that could be fraudulent.
- **Conducting exit interviews —** Employees leave for a variety of reasons. Frequently, they are willing to share those reasons. Exit interviews are often considered a detection control because individuals may be willing to "tell on" someone who they would not implicate when they were co-employees. However, awareness that exit interviews are conducted also may serve as a deterrent to fraud, which makes such interviews a preventive control as well.
- **Authority limits —** By establishing boundaries of authority, potential fraudulent transactions can be prevented over the established authority limits. A common example is prohibiting wire transfers of funds over a certain amount without the approval of two individuals. This control prevents fraudulent transactions over that amount, assuming there is no collusion among those individuals.
- **Transaction-level procedures —** Many fraud schemes involve third parties, including related parties. By requiring careful scrutiny of those transactions before they are consummated, an organization can prevent inappropriate transactions from occurring.

As part of the organization's system of internal controls, preventive controls must be documented in the same manner as any other control. This will help with the evaluation of whether the preventive controls are designed adequately, and also serve as a deterrent to the extent employees are aware that these controls are in place. Assessing the adequacy of fraud prevention controls takes experience and judgment, but there are tools available that can help with this process. For example, Appendix F, Fraud Prevention Scorecard, of the *Fraud Guide* helps to facilitate the identification and assessment of some of the more common fraud prevention areas.

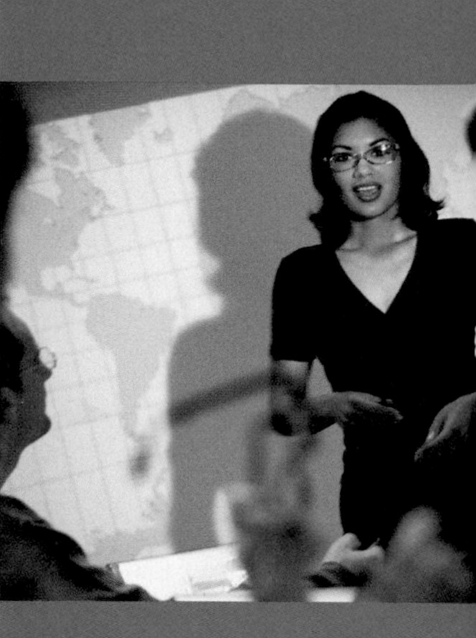

Collusion

Acts involving two or more persons, working together, whereby established controls or procedures may be circumvented for the gain of those individuals.

The *Fraud Guide* reinforces the importance of strong preventive controls, stating "The ongoing success of any fraud prevention program depends on its continuous communication and reinforcement. Stressing the existence of a fraud prevention program through a wide variety of media — posters on bulletin boards, flyers included with invoices and vendor payments, and articles in internal and external communications — gets the message out to both internal and external communities that the organization is committed to preventing and deterring fraud."[11]

FRAUD DETECTION

As previously mentioned, an effective fraud risk management program cannot rely solely on prevention. Not only is the cost of preventing certain fraud scenarios prohibitively high, but it is not possible to prevent all fraud incidents from occurring. Fraud prevention can fail when there is inadequate design or ineffective operation of fraud prevention controls. In addition, collusion among individuals or management override may circumvent established controls that are designed to prevent fraud. As a result, an organization must have a prudent balance of fraud detection controls as well.

By definition, detective controls are those that are designed to identify occurrences of fraud, or symptoms that may be indicative of fraud. Fraud detection techniques may be designed specifically to identify fraud, or they may be built into the system of internal controls and serve other purposes in addition to fraud detection. For example, the preparation and review of a bank reconciliation can serve many purposes, one of which is identifying unusual or suspicious transactions. The *Fraud Guide* outlines several common detection methods.

Detective Control

An activity that is designed to discover undesirable events that have already occurred. A detective control must occur on a timely basis (before the undesirable event has had a negative impact on the organization) to be considered effective.

- **Whistleblower hotlines —** As noted earlier in this chapter, tips are the most common method of fraud detection. Hotlines allow individuals to report their concerns about suspicious activities and remain anonymous. Whistleblower hotlines are frequently operated by third parties to make it easier for people to report matters without fear of reprisal. Broad awareness of a hotline can serve as a deterrent since potential fraud perpetrators realize it is easy for individuals to report their suspicions.

  In connection with maintaining a hotline, organizations must also employ an effective case management process. This process ensures that reported allegations are reported to the right individual, adequately vetted and investigated, if necessary, and receive timely resolution. Case management processes are typically administered by the head of the compliance program, the human resources function, the legal function, or the internal audit function.
- **Process controls —** The most common type of detective controls are built into the day-to-day processes. Examples of process controls that can help to detect fraudulent activity include reconciliations, independent reviews, physical inspections or counts, certain types of analysis, and internal audits or other monitoring activities. The fraud risks with the greatest potential impact may require detective controls that can operate at a lower level of sensitivity to ensure timely detection.
- **Proactive fraud detection procedures —** While detection sounds reactive by nature, it is possible to design more proactive

FRAUD DETECTION MEASUREMENT CRITERIA

EXHIBIT 8-8

- Number of known fraud schemes committed against the organization.
- Number and status of fraud allegations received by the organization that required investigation.
- Number of fraud investigations resolved.
- Number of employees who have/have not signed the corporate ethics statement.
- Number of employees who have/have not completed ethics training sponsored by the organization.
- Number of whistleblower allegations received via the organization's hotline.
- Number of allegations that have been raised by other means.
- Number of messages supporting ethical behavior delivered to employees by executives.
- Number of vendors who have/have not signed the organization's ethical behavior requirements.
- Benchmarks with global fraud surveys, including the type of fraud experienced and average losses.
- Number of customers who have signed the organization's ethical behavior requirements.
- Number of fraud audits performed by internal auditors.
- Results of employee or other stakeholder surveys concerning the integrity or culture of the organization.
- Resources used by the organization.

Source: *The Fraud Guide*, pp. 38-39.

detection procedures. Common proactive procedures include data analysis, continuous auditing, and the use of other technology tools that can flag anomalies, trends, and risk indicators warranting attention. Some of the more creative fraud detection techniques involve analyzing data from multiple sources. For example, a comparison of the database containing employee addresses against the database containing vendor addresses may identify fictitious vendors created by an unethical employee. Also, comparison of employees' Social Security numbers in the U.S. with the national database of active Social Security numbers may detect fictitious employees who are inappropriately being paid, with the funds typically ending up in the account of an existing employee. Another example is software that searches for certain words or phrases in e-mails to identify individuals who may be considering, or already are committing, fraudulent activities.

Continuous monitoring and measurement techniques can help an organization evaluate, enhance, and improve its fraud protection techniques. There are a variety of criteria that can be measured.

Exhibit 8-8 provides a list of criteria that organizations can use to help them monitor, measure, and evaluate the effectiveness of their fraud prevention techniques.

There are countless different controls that can serve to detect fraud. Organizations must focus on those controls that have the greatest likelihood of detecting fraud risk scenarios on a timely basis. Appendix G, Fraud Detection Scorecard, of the *Fraud Guide* helps to facilitate the identification and assessment of some of the more common fraud detection areas.

FRAUD INVESTIGATION AND CORRECTIVE ACTION

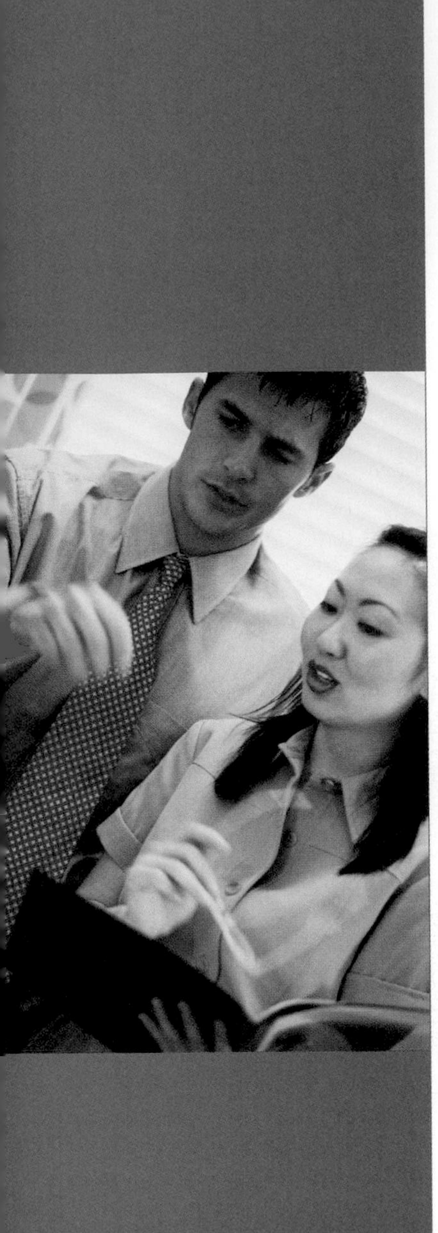

Detecting incidents or symptoms of fraud is obviously quite important. But the battle is not over at that point. Whether an act of fraud is prosecuted through the legal system or handled within an organization, it is critical to understand all of the facts and circumstances surrounding the incident. Thus, the final stage of an effective fraud risk management program focuses on investigating, reporting, and correcting the suspected fraud incidents. There are several discreet steps involved in this stage.

Receiving the Allegation

Allegations may be received from a variety of sources in many different manners. As discussed earlier in the chapter, the ACFE's *Report to the Nation* cites tips, audits, and controls as the most common means of identifying frauds. Regardless of the source, an organization must have a process or protocol for gathering the available information pertaining to an allegation. This will help ensure that the organization ". . . develops a system for prompt, competent, and confidential review, investigation, and resolution of allegations involving potential fraud or misconduct."[12] There is no one-size-fits-all approach to receiving allegations; it will depend on the nature of the allegation, who was purportedly involved, and the potential impact. Regardless of the protocol, the *Fraud Guide* states that "The investigation and response system should include a process for:

- Categorizing issues.
- Confirming the validity of the allegation.
- Defining the severity of the allegation.
- Escalating the issue or investigation when appropriate.
- Referring issues outside the scope of the program.
- Conducting the investigation and fact-finding.
- Resolving or closing the investigation.
- Listing types of information that should be kept confidential.
- Defining how the investigation will be documented.
- Managing and retaining documents and information."[13]

The process must be flexible enough to handle the many different types of allegations, but also structured enough to ensure all key steps are appropriately executed and documented. A formal process will help enable the remaining steps in this stage.

Evaluating the Allegation

Not all allegations of fraud prove to be acts of fraud. It is necessary to evaluate the information received and make many key decisions that can be critical to the effectiveness of the process. The evaluation step involves answering the following questions:

- Does this allegation require a formal investigation or is there enough information now to draw a conclusion?
- Who should lead the investigation?
- Are there special skills or tools needed to conduct the investigation?
- Who needs to be notified and when?

Establishing formal protocols, as discussed below, will help answer these and other questions that are fundamental to evaluating the allegation.

Investigation Protocols

Establishing formal investigation protocols that are approved by management and the board will ensure an investigation achieves its objectives. The *Fraud Guide* states that "Factors to consider in developing the investigation plan include:

- *Time sensitivity* — Investigations may need to be conducted timely due to legal requirements, to mitigate losses or potential harm, or to institute an insurance claim.
- *Notification* — Certain allegations may require notification to regulators, law enforcement, insurers, or external auditors.
- *Confidentiality* — Information gathered needs to be kept confidential and distribution limited to those with an established need.
- *Legal privileges* — Involving legal counsel early in the process or, in some cases, in leading the investigation, will help safeguard work product and attorney-client communications.
- *Compliance* — Investigations should comply with applicable laws and rules regarding gathering information and interviewing witnesses.
- *Securing evidence* — Evidence should be protected so that it is not destroyed and so that it is admissible in legal proceedings.
- *Objectivity* — The investigation team should be removed sufficiently from the issues and individuals under investigation to conduct an objective assessment.
- *Goals* — Specific issues or concerns should appropriately influence the focus, scope, and timing of the investigation."[14]

The investigation should be conducted to address each of these factors. The actual process will depend upon the nature of the allegations, but most investigations include tasks such as interviewing individuals who may have information pertinent to the investigation, gathering hard-copy evidence from both internal and external sources, conducting forensic tests of electronic data, analyzing the data gathered, and documenting the results so that conclusions are supported and others can understand the judgments supporting those conclusions. Finally, an appropriate report will be prepared for those needing to understand the results of the investigation so that they can evaluate the subsequent actions taken.

Legal Privileges

Working with legal counsel to protect the results of investigations, supporting working papers, and communications with counsel.

Corrective Action

The final step is determining the appropriate actions based on the results of the investigation. Possible actions include:

- Legal actions, whether criminal or civil.
- Disciplinary actions, such as warning, demotion, censure, suspension, or termination.
- Insurance claims if losses from the act are covered by insurance policies.
- Redesign or reinforcement of processes and controls that may have been inadequately designed or operated ineffectively, allowing the incident to occur.

Regardless of the choice, actions must be swift and fair. Others in the organization may be watching to see how perpetrators are dealt with. While the ultimate actions may not be made public, employees must sense that the actions were fair under the circumstances and management would treat other perpetrators in the same manner. This is part of what reinforces the tone at the top, a critical element in fraud risk management governance.

UNDERSTANDING FRAUDSTERS

Fraud Perpetrators

Generally fit one of two profiles: greater good oriented or scheming, self-centered types.

It is natural to think of a system of internal controls as being somewhat people neutral. That is, assuming an organization has competent individuals in key control positions, an adequately designed system of internal controls should operate effectively, even when people make mistakes. However, considering that fraud involves intent to act in a manner different than would normally be expected, another element must be considered: how unethical people might act. Internal auditors must have a heightened sense of professional skepticism and not assume that people will "do the right thing." Putting it another way, internal auditors must "think like a crook to catch a crook." They must try to understand why an otherwise honest individual would commit a dishonest act. Gaining this understanding will increase the likelihood that an internal auditor can detect, and in some cases even deter, an individual from committing a fraud.

Behavioral science has thus far been unable to identify a single psychological characteristic or a set of characteristics that can serve as a reliable marker of the propensity of an individual to commit fraud. For example, to say that "greed and dishonesty" — a commonly heard refrain — can account for all that went on during the "irrational exuberance" of the 1990s would be overly simplistic. After all, there are many professionals in the business world who are extremely ambitious, competitive, and wealthy, but nevertheless fully abide by the law. They do not necessarily resort to fraud to achieve their stretch goals. But they are motivated by something, and understanding the different motives that drive fraudsters is an important starting point. For example, one experienced forensic accountant and fraud examiner, Thomas Golden, believes that financial reporting fraud perpetrators fit one of two profiles: "greater good oriented" or "scheming, self-centered" types. Those who fit the greater good oriented profile are "otherwise honest individuals who misrepresent the numbers by rationalizing that what they are doing is best for the company." The scheming, self-centered types are "individuals who exhibit a rampant disregard for the truth, are well aware of what they are doing, and who

CONTROLS VERSUS THE PERCEPTION OF BEING CAUGHT

EXHIBIT 8-9

Joseph Wells provides a penetrating analysis of how fraudsters think. Echoing 18th century economist Jeremy Bentham, he observes that the likelihood of committing a (white-collar) crime is a function of the perpetrator's perception of the risks and rewards, that is, those who assess the probability of getting caught as being high are naturally less inclined to commit fraud. It is well known that, on the effectiveness dimension, fraud risk control activities pale in comparison to the increase in the perception of being apprehended, and the observed follow-up consequences from the organization's track record in the handling of past incidents and allegations. Hence, from a behavioral standpoint, this raises the possibility of creating an "anticipation effect" (that is, the anticipation of being audited), including unannounced surprise checks, as part of the fraud prevention and deterrence controls. Continuing this line of reasoning, both independent outside and internal auditors, through creative and imaginative approaches to their work using technology (for example, continuous control monitoring) or advances in statistics (for example, discovery sampling approaches, Benford's Law) or even "active brainstorming about the ways fraud could be perpetrated" can put up strong deterrents and defenses to fraud, all the while improving fraud detection capabilities. Management must act decisively and swiftly against fraud perpetrators when they are identified as a result of a fraud investigation. Such swift and decisive action can go a long way in cementing fraud deterrence efforts.

Wells, Joseph T., "Let Them Know Someone's Watching," *Journal of Accountancy*, May 2002.

are attempting to attain goals dishonestly."[15] Gaining insights into the potential red flags that may signal individuals who are more vulnerable to committing fraud will help internal auditors understand when fraud risk is heightened. Such red flags include individuals who:

- Exhibit a lifestyle that appears to be well beyond their current means.
- Are experiencing extreme financial problems and/or have overwhelming personal debts.
- Have an unusual propensity to spend money.
- Are suffering from depression or other emotional problems.
- Appear to have a gambling obsession.
- Have a need or craving for status, and believe money can buy that status.

It also may help to view fraud from a criminologist's perspective. They believe fraud, like any other crime, can best be explained by three factors: a supply of motivated offenders, the availability of suitable targets, and the absence of capable guardians — controls systems or someone "to mind the store" so to speak.[16] Notice how similar these three factors are to those in the fraud triangle. Familiarity with these factors may help internal auditors be alert to fraud vulnerabilities. Toward that last point, Joseph Wells, the founder of the ACFE, offers an interesting perspective on how fraudsters view controls versus the perception that they will be caught. This view is summarized in Exhibit 8-9.

Internal auditors are not expected to become behavioral psychologists or criminologists. However, gaining insights into what motivates fraudsters can help internal auditors "keep their antennas up" in the workplace and, potentially, anticipate individuals who may present a greater risk of fraud.

IMPLICATIONS FOR INTERNAL AUDITORS AND OTHERS

It should be evident by now that internal auditors play a key role in a fraud risk management program. The *Standards* provide specific guidance for internal auditors. For example:

Due Professional Care

Applying the care and skill expected of a reasonably prudent and competent internal auditor. Does not imply infallibility.

> **Standard 1210.A2 –** Internal auditors must have sufficient knowledge to evaluate the risk of fraud and the manner in which it is managed by the organization, but are not expected to have the expertise of a person whose primary responsibility is detecting and investigating fraud.
>
> **Standard 1220.A1 –** Internal auditors must exercise due professional care by considering the . . . Probability of significant errors, fraud, or noncompliance . . .
>
> **Standard 2060 –** The chief audit executive must report periodically to senior management and the board on . . . fraud risks . . .
>
> **Standard 2120.A2 –** The internal audit [function] must evaluate the potential for the occurrence of fraud and how the organization manages fraud risk.

These standards make it clear that internal auditors must consider fraud in almost everything they do. But the *Standards* do not provide the only impetus for internal audit functions to focus on fraud. The role of the internal audit function has been emphasized in recent legislation, regulatory mandates, and the proliferation of governance-focused organizations around the world. As a result, the gatekeepers of financial integrity, among them internal auditors, have achieved significant prominence and are increasingly being asked to play a key role in preventing, deterring, and detecting fraud in for-profit, governmental, and nonprofit organizations globally. As the "eyes and ears, and arms and legs of the audit committee," internal auditors need to consider the following questions:

- What fraud risks are being monitored by management on a periodic or regular basis? Are the critical fraud risks subject to frequent, and even continuous, monitoring?
- What specific procedures are being performed by the internal audit function to address management override of internal controls?
- Has anything occurred that would lead the internal audit function to change its assessment of the risk of management override of internal controls?
- What competencies and skills do internal auditors need to address the risk of fraud within organizations? When should they obtain the services of outside specialists to deal with particularly complex issues?
- In addition to establishing direct lines of reporting to the audit committee, how can the independent organizational status of the internal audit function be strengthened? Are they relied upon as competent and objective professionals in addressing fraud risk and control issues?

- How should the internal audit function devote its attention to the preventive, deterrent, detective, and investigative aspects of fraud?

To fulfill this responsibility to the audit committee and other stakeholders, internal auditors must be equipped with skills and experience beyond that which is necessary for most assurance engagements.

Professional Skepticism, Professional Judgment, and Forensic Technology

The exercise of sound professional judgment lies at the heart of the internal audit function's assurance and consulting activities. When assessing fraud risks, the internal auditor must exhibit a high degree of professional skepticism, that is, an ability to critically evaluate the evidence and information available at hand. This is particularly so because fraud perpetrators typically "cover their tracks" and determined persistence may be required to unravel a well-concealed fraud scheme. For example, it required dogged perseverance by 2004 *Time* magazine's Person of the Year, Cynthia Cooper, and her team at WorldCom, to unearth the massive fraud committed by WorldCom management.

Professional Skepticism

The state of mind in which internal auditors take nothing for granted; they continuously question what they hear and see and critically assess audit evidence.

Not all internal auditors exercise the same degree of professional skepticism — some are naturally more skeptical than others, some accept explanations at face value, and others want to probe further and dig deeper. The latter types, who would seem to have natural "sleuthing tendencies," also display higher levels of professional skepticism, in general. While being "paranoid" may frequently result in over-auditing, whenever facts and circumstances suggest a higher likelihood of fraud, exhibiting a heightened degree of professional skepticism may be expected, warranted, and justified.

When leading or participating in a fraud investigation, internal auditors may have to deal with evidence that differs from what they are accustomed to on other engagements. These assignments may be more complex and involve a review of disparate pieces of evidence with diverse characteristics and degrees of reliability. In such contexts, an experienced internal auditor has better ability to "connect the dots" and reconstruct the whole picture from incomplete information and evidence. This is why most fraud investigation groups are staffed with individuals who have significant controls experience. Indeed, research on the applications of artificial intelligence (including neural network technology) has shown that solving the "jigsaw puzzle," that is, aggregating dispersed evidence, is actually a pattern recognition problem. In other words, all the available evidence cannot be considered sequentially; instead, a holistic approach that considers all the available evidence simultaneously may be required. In such circumstances, it may be important for the technology-savvy internal auditor to leverage decision aids, expert systems, and artificial intelligence to increase both effectiveness and efficiency (for example, Benford's Law or digital analysis, advanced computer-assisted audit techniques [CAATs], and predictive analytics, including regression models and neural networks). While movies and television shows may glamorize this process, having a CSI (Crime Scene Investigation) mentality serves internal auditors well when assessing fraud risks and conducting fraud engagements.

With the ubiquitous use of technology-enabled communications, forensic investigations and fraud examinations in the future will depend heavily on computer forensics, computer data imaging, electronic evidence discovery, and the analysis of structured and unstructured data. In other words, the use of technology will not be limited to data analysis (after structured data has been collected); instead, the very extraction and preservation of electronic evidence — usually in the form of textual, unstructured data requiring keyword searches, for instance — will be technology intensive. In such a context, it will be crucial for fraud examiners to have a sound understanding of, and mastery over, "digital forensics" — the latest and emerging forensic technology tools and techniques.

Use of Fraud Specialists

The internal audit function can play a variety of roles to combat fraud in an organization, including conducting fraud awareness training, assessing the design of antifraud programs and controls, testing the operating effectiveness of such controls, investigating improprieties and whistleblower complaints, and conducting a full-fledged investigation at the behest of the audit committee. However, the internal audit function may not have the experience and skills to perform all of these roles. As a result, it is common for the chief audit executive (CAE) to seek the help of fraud specialists to complement the skills of those in the function.

Certified Fraud Examiners

Individuals certified as specialists in conducting forensic accounting investigations and advising on fraud risks and other fraud matters.

The most common specialists engaged are CFEs, who specialize in conducting forensic accounting investigations (usually after the fact, when predication exists) to resolve allegations or suspicions of fraud, reporting to the CAE, an appropriate level of management, or to the audit committee or board of directors, depending upon the nature of the issue and the level of personnel involved. They also may assist the audit committee and the board of directors with aspects of the oversight process, either directly or as part of a team of internal auditors or independent outside auditors, in evaluating the fraud risk assessment and fraud prevention measures implemented by senior management. They can provide more objective input into management's evaluation of the risk of fraud (especially fraud involving senior management, such as financial statement fraud) and the development of appropriate antifraud controls that are less vulnerable to management override. In recent years, several internal audit professionals have obtained the CFE designation and, having acquired this specialized expertise, are better equipped to discharge their responsibilities in this area. Many internal audit functions try to have at least one CFE on the staff. However, individuals with this expertise are not as plentiful as may be necessary. As a result, it is common to source the CFE expertise from outside service organizations.

While the CFE designation is the primary qualification for fraud specialists, other specialties also may be needed. For example, when investigations involve fraudulent financial reporting, possessing the CPA/CA credential can be very helpful. Additionally, technology specialists may be able to conduct advanced investigative techniques using tools that are customized for such purposes.

There are numerous advantages to using outside fraud specialists, in addition to the independence they bring to the job. For example, they have extensive experience with identifying and investigating a variety of different fraud schemes. Therefore, they can help in identifying and assessing the "usual suspects" and recommending the optimal methods of investigation. Additionally, having worked with independent counsel, general counsel, state attorneys, regulators, law enforcement personnel, other accountants and auditors, and prosecutors, they have a good understanding of issues such as:

- The best way to investigate a specific type of fraud scheme.
- Assessing the quality and quantity of evidence needed.
- Evaluating the admissibility of evidence in consultation with outside lawyers.
- Preserving evidence and the chain of custody.
- The need for, as well as potential to act as, a fact witness or as an expert witness.

It is very important for internal auditors to conduct investigations fairly and thoroughly, and develop and maintain the documentation necessary to support any actions that result from the investigation. Using specialists is common practice to ensure these objectives are achieved.

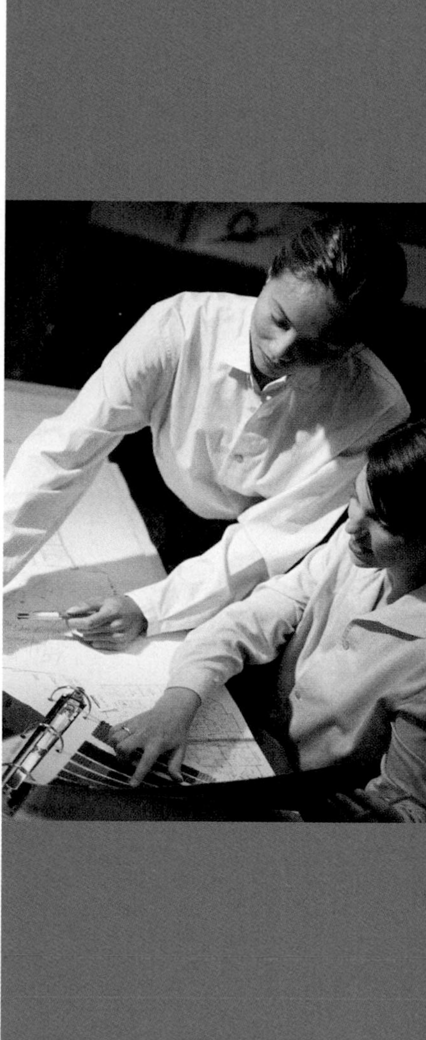

Communicating Fraud Audit Outcomes

When preparing communications concerning the results of fraud audits or investigations, many of the principles discussed in Chapter 14, "Communicating Assurance Engagement Outcomes and Performing Follow-up Procedures," apply. For example, internal auditors should identify the criteria, condition(s), cause, and effect to summarize their findings from a fraud investigation. They should write their communications in a systematic, organized fashion to enhance clarity and comprehension, which typically includes:

- A brief, clear statement of the issue(s).
- A citation of the relevant policies, rules, standards, laws, and regulations that may be applicable to the case at hand.
- The analysis of the evidence gathered to form a professional opinion.
- The conclusions; that is, the findings and recommendations.

This will help make the communication clear and useful, particularly if it is being relied upon by the general counsel or the outside attorney conducting the investigation, who may want to make the communication part of their own communication. At all times, the communications issued by internal auditors should contain facts only, and every effort must be made to eschew personal opinions or any kind of bias or speculation that could potentially enter the analysis. In any case, they should never seek to fix culpability on any particular employee(s), but should merely state that the evidence gathered appears to support the conclusion that fraud may have been perpetrated. Determining culpability and affixing blame are functions of the court (the judge and the jury), and typically outside the scope of the internal auditor's responsibility.

SUMMARY

Fraud is a major concern among all types of organizations. Rising fraud awareness around the world has compelled local regulators to address management's responsibilities for fraud prevention, deterrence, and detection. Audit committees and management are increasingly looking to the internal audit function for help with the design adequacy and operating effectiveness of fraud risk management programs and related controls.

An effective fraud risk management program must have certain key elements. First, there must be sound governance activities in place, both directly related to the program and overall within the organization. Second, a comprehensive fraud risk assessment must be completed. This includes the identification of possible fraud events or scenarios, the assessment of impact and likelihood of those scenarios, and decisions regarding what types of responses should be made to those scenarios. Third, effective controls must be designed and implemented. These controls should be balanced between preventive controls aimed at stopping fraud from occurring and deterring potential fraudsters from considering fraudulent acts, and detective controls, which will help ensure timely identification of fraud incidents. Finally, a process must be established to facilitate reporting of fraud incidents, investigation of those incidents, and implementation of disciplinary and corrective actions.

The internal audit function is key for promoting and supporting an organization's fraud risk management program. The *Standards* require internal auditors to consider fraud in most of their activities. As a result, internal auditors can support all of the elements of an effective fraud risk management program. Understanding the behavioral characteristics of potential fraudsters helps internal auditors stay alert for those situations in which fraud is most likely. This sense of alertness, coupled with a heightened professional skepticism, can help internal auditors prevent or deter potentially fraudulent actions, and detect timely those incidents that have occurred. Finally, while the skills possessed by most internal auditors are valuable, it is important for the CAE to recognize when it is necessary to hire outside fraud specialists, such as CFEs, and use specialized fraud technology to better enable the internal audit function in fulfilling its fraud-related responsibilities.

Review Questions

1. According to the ACFE's *Report to the Nation*, what percentage of their revenues do organizations lose to fraud? Based on the 2008 United States GDP, approximately how much is that in dollars?
2. What is the definition of fraud provided in the *Fraud Guide*?
3. According to the AICPA, by what three ways can fraudulent financial reporting be accomplished?
4. According to the ACFE, what four elements characterize an act of occupational fraud?
5. What are the three elements that may be called the "root causes of fraud" (that is, they are always present, no matter the type of fraud)?
6. The board of directors helps set the tone at the top in an organization. What oversight responsibilities should a board generally have?
7. According to the *Fraud Guide*, what 10 components are typically found in a successful fraud program?
8. What are the three key steps in a fraud risk assessment?
9. In a perfect world, is it better to prevent all fraud incidents or detect all incidents that occur? Explain your answer.
10. What is the most common method of detecting fraud incidents?
11. What does the final stage in an effective fraud risk management program focus on?
12. According to Thomas Golden, what two profiles fit financial reporting fraud perpetrators?
13. What are the different fraud-related roles that an internal audit function can play in an organization?

Multiple-choice Questions

Select the best answer for each of the following questions.

1. Predication is a technical term that refers to:
   - a. The ability of internal auditors to predict fraud successfully.
   - b. The ability of a fraud examiner to commence an investigation if a form of evidence exists that fraud has occurred.
   - c. The activities of fraud perpetrators in concealing their tracks so that fraud is covered up and may not be discovered.
   - d. Management's analysis of fraud risks so they can put in place effective anti-fraud programs and controls.

2. What fraud schemes were found to be most common in 2008 according to the ACFE?
   a. Corruption.
   b. Fraudulent billing.
   c. Misappropriation of assets by employees.
   d. Inappropriately reporting revenues in published financial results.

3. Which of the following is not a typical "rationalization" of a fraud perpetrator?
   a. It's in the organization's best interest.
   b. The company owes me because I'm underpaid.
   c. I want to get back at my boss (revenge).
   d. I'm smarter than the rest of them.

4. Which of the following is not something all levels of employees should do?
   a. Understand their role within the internal control framework.
   b. Have a basic understanding of fraud and be aware of the red flags.
   c. Report suspicions of incidences of fraud.
   d. Investigate suspicious activities that they believe may be fraudulent.

5. An organization that manufactures and sells computers is trying to boost sales between now and the end of the year. It decides to offer its sales representatives a bonus based on the number of units they deliver to customers before the end of the year. The price of all computers is determined by the vice president of sales, and cannot be changed by sales representatives. Which of the following presents the greatest reason a sales representative may commit fraud with this incentive program?
   a. Sales representative may sell units that have a lower margin than other units.
   b. Customers have the right to return a laptop for up to 90 days after purchase.
   c. The units delivered may be defective.
   d. The customers may not pay for the computers timely.

6. How should an organization handle an anonymous accusation from an employee that a supervisor in the organization has manipulated time reports?
   a. Assign a staff internal auditor to review all time reports for the past six months in the supervisor's area.
   b. Make a record of the accusation, but do nothing as anonymous accusations are typically not true.
   c. Assess the facts provided by the anonymous party against pre-established criteria to determine whether a formal investigation is warranted.
   d. Turn the issue over to the human resources department since this type of anonymous accusation is usually just a human resource issue.

7. Which of the following is an example of misappropriation of assets?
   a. A small amount of petty cash is stolen.
   b. A journal entry is modified to improve reported financial results.
   c. A foreign official is bribed by the chief operating officer to facilitate approval of a new product.
   d. A duplicate bill is sent to a customer in hopes that they will pay it twice.

8. Which of the following is not an example of a fraud prevention program element?
   a. Background investigations of new employees.
   b. Exit interviews of departing employees.
   c. Establishing authority limits related to purchasing commitments.
   d. Analyzing cash disbursements to determine whether any duplicate payments have been made.

9. Which of the following types of companies would most likely need the strongest anti-fraud controls?
   a. A manufacturer of popular athletic shoes.
   b. A grocery store.
   c. A bank.
   d. An Internet-based electronics retailer.

10. A payroll clerk increased the hourly pay rate of a friend and shared the resulting overpayment with the friend. Which of the following controls would have best served to prevent this fraud?
   a. Requiring that all changes to pay records be recorded on a standard form.
   b. Limiting the ability to make changes in payroll system personnel information to authorized human resource department supervisors.
   c. Periodically reconciling pay rates per personnel records with those of the payroll system.
   d. Monitoring of payroll costs by department supervisors on a monthly basis.

11. The internal audit function's responsibilities with respect to fraud are limited to:
   a. The organization's operational and compliance activities only, because financial reporting matters are the responsibility of the independent outside auditor.
   b. Monitoring any calls received through the organization's whistleblower hotline, but not necessarily conducting a follow-up investigation.
   c. Being aware of fraud indicators, including those relating to financial reporting fraud, but not necessarily possessing the expertise of a fraud investigation specialist.
   d. Ensuring that all employees have received adequate fraud awareness training.

12. From an organization's standpoint, because internal auditors are seen to be "internal control experts," they also are:
    a. Fraud risk management process owners, and hence, the first and most important line of defense against fraudulent financial reporting or asset misappropriation.
    b. The best resource for audit committees, management, and others to consult in-house when setting up anti-fraud programs and controls, even if they may not have any fraud investigation experience.
    c. The best candidates to lead an investigation of a fraud incident involving the potential violation of laws and regulations.
    d. The primary decision maker in terms of determining punishment or other consequences for fraud perpetrators.

Discussion Questions

1. Discuss why the internal audit function's organizational status, competence, and objectivity are particularly important when considering fraud by senior management. Why might a CAE reporting directly to the CFO, CEO, general counsel, or controller be more problematic than reporting to the audit committee (or equivalent)?

2. The Open Compliance and Ethics Group (OCEG) released a guide for internal auditors to assist them in performing ethics and compliance audits (this guide can be found at www.oceg.org). How will "tone at the top," a control consciousness orientation, and a culture of integrity and ethics within organizations assist, if at all, in preventing, deterring, and detecting fraud? Is it sufficient that organizations effectively deter activities that are "illegal, unethical, or immoral," and if these are observed, ensure that the "whistleblower hotline" will be used to report such wrongful conduct that might well be a precursor to fraud?

3. Fraud appears to come in different colors, stripes, shapes, and sizes. This explains why so many terms exist to describe fraud. Research and provide a brief definition of each of the following terms:

    (1) bribery and kickbacks, (2) conflict of interest, (3) cooking the books, (4) self-dealing and corruption, (5) defalcation/embezzlement, (6) fictitious revenues or expenses, (7) identity theft, (8) industrial espionage, (9) intentionally violating GAAP, (10) kiting, (11) lapping, (12) larceny, (13) breach of fiduciary duty, (14) misrepresentation of material facts, (15) money-laundering, (16) conspiracy, (17) sham entities, (18) round-tripping, (19) forgery, (20) false or manipulated T&E reimbursement claims, (21) theft of trade secrets, (22) topside journal entries, (23) bid-rigging, (24) price fixing, (25) undisclosed side agreements, (26) ghost employees, (27) back-dating stock options, spring loading, and bullet dodging, (28) illegitimate off-balance sheet transactions, (29) false claims, (30) window dressing, (31) channel stuffing, and (32) insider trading.

4. In general, what are the fraud risk indicators that internal auditors should be aware of? How are these "red flags" (fraud risk factors) influenced by industry and geography? Why does it seem that certain areas and assets are more vulnerable to fraud, that is, what "relative risk" considerations need to be factored in? Expand these considerations to materiality (that is, the significance or importance to achieving organizational objectives) and the appropriateness and sufficiency of evidence.

5. How can the internal audit function assist the audit committee by alerting them to instances of management override of internal controls on a timely basis?

6. How should internal auditors help, if at all, with forensic accounting investigations?

7. Internal auditors may be asked to conduct a fraud investigation involving litigation. Is it important to consider conducting the investigation under attorney-client privilege? Explain.

CASES

CASE 1 "Fannie Mae Ex-Officials May Face Legal Action Over Accounting" (*The Wall Street Journal*, May 24, 2006, see pages A1 and A11).

> Mr. James B. Lockhart, acting director of the Office of Federal Housing Enterprise Oversight (OFHEO), Fannie Mae's main regulator, denounced what he called an "arrogant and unethical culture" at the second largest borrower in the U.S. after the federal government. Specifically, the OFHEO's 340-page report blamed both the board and management for a corporate culture that allowed managers to disregard accounting standards when they got in the way of achieving earnings targets. The company then rewarded executives with huge bonuses for hitting those targets, the OFHEO report said.
>
> With reference to internal auditing, the OFHEO report quotes a speech from Mr. Sam Rogers*, a former head of Fannie Mae's auditing office, as telling internal auditors they had a "moral obligation" to strive to meet a goal set by then Fannie Mae CEO, Mr. Frank Raines, in 1999 to double earnings per share to $6.46 by 2003. "By now, every one of you must have $6.46 branded in your brains," the OFHEO report quotes Mr. Rogers as saying. "You must have a raging fire in your belly that burns away all doubts, you must live, breath (sic) and dream $6.46 . . . After all, thanks to Frank [Raines], we all have a lot of money riding on it" in terms of bonuses. Given Mr. Rogers's responsibility for monitoring compliance with accounting rules, those remarks were "inappropriate," OFHEO said.

What's wrong with this picture? Did Mr. Rogers potentially violate The IIA's Code of Ethics and *Standards* by making these remarks? Comment on his organizational status, independence, and objectivity as then Fannie Mae head of internal auditing, and discuss whether there may be a conflict when internal auditors receive stock options and bonuses that are tied to financial performance.

(*Sam Rogers is a fictitious name.)

CASE 2

A number of large cases of fraud have come to trial and the post mortems are completed. You have learned a lot related to identifying fraud risk, mitigating control activities, as well as promoting organizational ethics and compliance. You now should understand that fraud incidence is more common than previously thought, and that there are many techniques, methods, and motivations to fraud. You also should understand that fraud that is uncovered may just be a symptom of other issues and problems (for example, when management lacks integrity, a restatement of the financial statements may mean that the independent outside auditor and/or internal auditor was successful in foiling attempted fraud). We now have a lot more regulation — a classic response to similar periods in history.

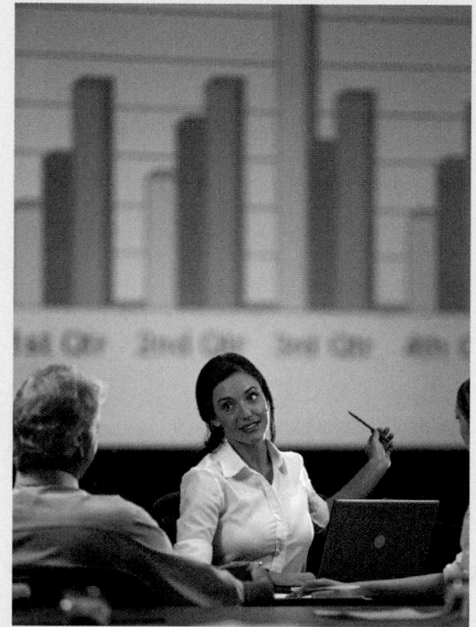

Your group project is strategic in nature and relates to how internal auditors can deal with fraud and the impact of some of the current regulations such as the U.S. Sarbanes-Oxley Act of 2002. The first part of this case study is to select three such cases. Your task is to look at the root cause of each fraud and identify techniques that might have prevented each fraud from occurring, or at least detected it in a timely manner.

As a group, prepare a PowerPoint presentation. The presentation should include two or three slides for each fraud case that summarizes the fraud, approximate loss incurred, the parties involved in the fraud, the root cause of the fraud, and the corrective actions that have been taken since the fraud occurred. Also indicate whether Sarbanes-Oxley (or comparable local legislation and regulation) is robust enough to preclude such a fraud from occurring in the future. Additionally, describe the corrective actions your group would recommend to prevent, or detect on a timely basis, this type of fraud. On a separate slide, compare the root causes of the three fraud cases you study. On a final slide, convey what your group learned as a result of completing this case study.

CASES

CASE 3 The purpose of this case is to familiarize you with the Benford's Law functionality of the ACL and IDEA software. If you have not already done so, install the software on your computer from the CD included with this textbook.

A. Open the ACL software. Locate the description of "Benford command" in ACL Help. Answer the following questions.

1. What does the ACL Benford command do?
2. What caution is provided regarding the use of digital analysis tools such as the Benford command?
3. How is the Benford command activated?

B. Open the IDEA software. Locate the description of "Benford's Law" in IDEA Help. Answer the following questions.

1. Benford's Law analysis is most effective on data with certain characteristics. What are these characteristics?
2. Identify and briefly describe the seven steps used to perform a Benford's Law analysis.
3. What fields are contained in the database created when a Benford's Law analysis is performed?

C. Locate the description of "Fraud Investigations" in IDEA Help. Click on "Payroll frauds." Answer the following questions.

1. What types of payroll fraud are described?
2. How are most payroll frauds found?
3. Describe the payroll fraud tests that can be performed using IDEA.

REFERENCES

[1]Association of Certified Fraud Examiners, *Report to the Nation on Occupational Fraud and Abuse*, pp. 4-5.

[2]*Managing the Business Risk of Fraud: A Practical Guide*, The Institute of Internal Auditors, The American Institute of Certified Public Accountants, and the Association of Certified Fraud Examiners. Available for download at www.theiia.org, p. 5.

[3]Ibid, p. 6.

[4] Ibid.

[5]Ibid, p. 10.

[6]Ibid, p. 11.

[7] Ibid, p. 14.

[8] Ibid, p. 26.

[9]Ibid, p. 28.

[10]Ibid, p. 30.

[11] Ibid, p. 33.

[12]Ibid, p. 39.

[13] Ibid, p. 40.

[14]Ibid, p. 41.

[15]Ballou, B., D.L. Heitger, and C.L. Landes, "The Future of Corporate Sustainability Reporting," *Journal of Accountancy*, (December 2006).

[16]Cohen, I., and M. Felsen, "Social Change and Crime Rate Trends: A Routine Activity Approach," *American Sociological Review*, Vol. 44, (1979), pp. 588-608.

CHAPTER 9
MANAGING THE INTERNAL AUDIT FUNCTION

Learning Objectives

- Understand the importance of proper positioning of the internal audit function within the organization.
- Identify the benefits of various organizational structures for an internal audit function.
- Identify the roles and responsibilities of the key positions in an internal audit function.
- Understand the policies and procedures of internal auditing and how they guide the internal audit function.
- Understand various risk management models and reflect on what role the internal audit function should have in the organization's risk management processes.
- Understand quality assurance, how it operates, and why it is important to the internal audit function.
- Understand how technology is used in the management of the internal audit function.

By now, you should recognize the depth and complexity of an internal audit function and be aware of the critical role it plays in the success of the entire organization. In this chapter, we discuss what is involved in managing the internal audit function. When applicable, the spectrum of methods employed by different internal audit functions is presented and the benefits of each is discussed. We begin with a discussion of the various options regarding organizational structures for an internal audit function, including where it is positioned within an organization. Then, we identify the key positions within the internal audit function, including the chief audit executive (CAE), and outline the roles and responsibilities for each. From there, we move on to the policies and procedures with an overview of how they provide necessary guidance and structure to the internal audit function. Next, we examine various risk management models and look at what role the internal audit function can and should play in the organization's risk management processes. After that, we explain quality assurance and its importance in the internal audit function. Finally, we end the chapter by touching on various technological tools available to an internal audit function and how they are used in managing the function.

EXHIBIT 9-1

PROFESSIONAL STANDARDS, PRACTICE ADVISORIES, AND POSITION PAPERS RELEVANT TO CHAPTER 9

1000 – Purpose, Authority, and Responsibility
1010 – Recognition of the Definition of Internal Auditing, the Code of Ethics, and the *Standards* in the Internal Audit Charter
1100 – Independence and Objectivity
1110 – Organizational Independence
1111 – Direct Interaction With the Board
1120 – Individual Objectivity
1130 – Impairment to Independence or Objectivity
1200 – Proficiency and Due Professional Care
1210 – Proficiency
1220 – Due Professional Care
1230 – Continuing Professional Development
1300 – Quality Assurance and Improvement Program
1310 – Requirements of the Quality Assurance and Improvement Program
1311 – Internal Assessments
1312 – External Assessments
1320 – Reporting on the Quality Assurance and Improvement Program
1321 – Use of "Conforms with the *International Standards for the Professional Practice of Internal Auditing*"
2000 – Managing the Internal Audit Activity
2010 – Planning
2020 – Communication and Approval
2030 – Resource Management
2040 – Policies and Procedures
2050 – Coordination
2060 – Reporting to Senior Management and the Board

Practice Advisory 1000-1: Internal Audit Charter
Practice Advisory 1110-1: Organizational Independence
Practice Advisory 1111-1: Board Interaction
Practice Advisory 1120-1: Individual Objectivity
Practice Advisory 1130-1: Impairment to Independence or Objectivity
Practice Advisory 1130.A1-1: Assessing Operations for Which Internal Auditors were Previously Responsible
Practice Advisory 1130.A2-1: Internal Audit's Responsibility for Other (Non-audit) Functions
Practice Advisory 1200-1: Proficiency and Due Professional Care
Practice Advisory 1210-1: Proficiency
Practice Advisory 1210.A1-1: Obtaining External Service Providers to Support or Complement the Internal Audit Activity
Practice Advisory 1220-1: Due Professional Care
Practice Advisory 1230-1: Continuing Professional Development
Practice Advisory 1300-1: Quality Assurance and Improvement Program
Practice Advisory 1310-1: Requirements of the Quality Assurance and Improvement Program
Practice Advisory 1311-1: Internal Assessments
Practice Advisory 1312-1: External Assessments
Practice Advisory 1312-2: External Assessments: Self-assessment With Independent Validation
Practice Advisory 2010-1: Linking the Audit Plan to Risk and Exposures
Practice Advisory 2020-1: Communication and Approval
Practice Advisory 2030-1: Resource Management
Practice Advisory 2040-1: Policies and Procedures
Practice Advisory 2050-1: Coordination
Practice Advisory 2060-1: Reporting to Senior Management and the Board

Position Paper: The Role of Internal Auditing in Resourcing the Internal Audit Activity

POSITIONING THE INTERNAL AUDIT FUNCTION IN THE ORGANIZATION

There is a broad spectrum of opinions regarding where internal audit functions can and should be positioned in an organization to conform to The IIA's *International Standards for the Professional Practice of Internal Auditing* (*Standards*). On one end of the spectrum, internal audit functions are placed on a senior management level, giving the function the visibility, authority, and responsibility to (1) independently evaluate management's assessment of the organization's system of internal controls, and (2) assess the organization's ability to achieve business objectives and manage, monitor, and mitigate risks associated with the achievement of those objectives. In addition to assurance services, these internal audit functions are commonly asked by management to provide consulting services in the form of initiatives or projects that allow management to use the professional expertise that the internal audit function possesses. (Consulting services are covered more extensively in Chapter 15, "The Consulting Engagement.") On the other end of the spectrum are those organizations that either do not have internal audit functions, or place their internal audit functions much lower in the organizational hierarchy, typically assigning them nonaudit activities to perform on a day-to-day basis, such as quality assurance, compliance, operational, and/or other transaction processing activities.

Chief Audit Executive

A senior position within the organization responsible for internal audit activities. The term also includes titles such as general auditor, head of internal audit, chief internal auditor, internal audit director, and inspector general.

In response to The IIA's definition of internal auditing quoted in Chapter 1, "Introduction to Internal Auditing," as "an independent, objective, assurance and consulting activity designed to add value and improve an organization's operations" that "helps an organization accomplish its objectives by bringing a systematic, disciplined approach to evaluate and improve effectiveness of risk management, control, and governance processes," many organizations have positioned their internal audit function as an activity of the board and senior management. Organizations that continue to position the internal audit function to perform primarily operational and other nonaudit activities, as previously mentioned, essentially render the function unable to provide management with an evaluation of the design and effectiveness of risk management, control, and governance processes because they lack the objectivity to independently evaluate the organization's operations and offer impartial suggestions for improvement.

Organizations that recognize the importance of placing the internal audit function in a position that maximizes its effectiveness and ability to evaluate the efficacy of the risk management, control, and governance processes that are in place often do so through a senior management position described in the *Standards* as a CAE. IIA Standard 2000: Managing the Internal Audit Activity states that "the chief audit executive must effectively manage the internal audit activity to ensure it adds value to the organization." Recognizing that the CAE is pivotal to a successful internal audit function, the interpretation of Standard 2000 goes on to state that "the internal audit [function] is effectively managed when:

- The results of the internal audit [function's] work achieve the purpose and responsibility included in the internal audit charter;
- The internal audit [function] conforms with the Definition of Internal Auditing and the *Standards*; and

- The individuals who are part of the internal audit [function] demonstrate conformance with the Code of Ethics and the *Standards*."

A necessary condition for the CAE to fulfill the responsibilities outlined above is to create a charter that "establishes the internal audit [function's] position within the organization; authorizes access to records, personnel, and physical properties relevant to the performance of engagements; and defines the scope of internal audit activities" (IIA Standard 1000: Purpose, Authority, and Responsibility). In addition to specifying the purpose, authority, and responsibility of the internal audit function, the charter should take into consideration assurance and consulting services. It is important to recognize that the internal audit function and the audit committee have separate charters delineating the specific and separate obligations to the organization of each, while considering and reflecting the inherent interdependencies of the two. The internal audit function's charter is subordinate to the audit committee's charter and must support, not contradict, it. Internal audit functions often supplement the charter with formal vision and/or mission statements, as well as a detailed long-term strategy for the internal audit function. Frequently this supplemental information, along with operating budgets and resource plans, are included in an annual internal audit plan presented, reviewed, and approved by the audit committee. These various separate documents, along with the operating policies and procedures of the internal audit function, are commonly combined into a set of guiding principles (generally referred to as an "audit manual") that, along with other procedural information, drives the internal audit function. Exhibit 9-2 outlines The IIA's recommendations for establishing an internal audit charter.

Internal Audit Charter

A formal written document that defines the internal audit function's purpose, authority, and responsibility. The internal audit charter is subordinate to the audit committee's charter.

In addition to establishing a charter, mission and/or vision, and internal audit plan, the CAE is responsible for establishing and maintaining independence, objectivity, proficiency, and due professional care within the internal audit function. As stated earlier, the positioning of the internal audit function affects the degree to which it can remain objective. Being positioned on a level with senior management with direct access to the

EXHIBIT 9-2

RECOMMENDATIONS FOR ESTABLISHING AN INTERNAL AUDIT CHARTER

Practice Advisory 1000-1: Internal Audit Charter

1. Providing a formal, written internal audit charter is critical in managing the internal audit activity. The internal audit charter provides a recognized statement for review and acceptance by management and for approval, as documented in the minutes, by the board. It also facilitates a periodic assessment of the adequacy of the internal audit activity's purpose, authority, and responsibility, which establishes the role of the internal audit activity. If a question should arise, the internal audit charter provides a formal, written agreement with management and the board about the organization's internal audit activity.
2. The chief audit executive (CAE) is responsible for periodically assessing whether the internal audit activity's purpose, authority, and responsibility, as defined in the internal audit charter, continue to be adequate to enable the activity to accomplish its objectives. The CAE is also responsible for communicating the result of this assessment to senior management and the board.

audit committee gives the internal audit function greater independence and consequently greater objectivity. Audit committee participation in the selection, evaluation, and dismissal of the CAE further enhances the CAE's ability to maintain organizational independence and minimizes the possibility of senior management exerting undue influence that would impact his or her ability to act without bias (individual objectivity). Ideally, the function will be positioned high enough within the organization with direct access to the audit committee to allow conformity with The IIA's requirements and recommendations as detailed below.

Independence and Objectivity

IIA Standard 1110: Organization Independence states, "The chief audit executive must report to a level within the organization that allows the internal audit activity to fulfill its responsibilities." More specifically, Standard 1110.A1 specifies that "the internal audit activity must be free from interference in determining the scope of internal auditing, performing work, and communicating results." Practice Advisory 1110-1: Organizational Independence goes into greater detail, stressing the importance of senior management and board support of the internal audit function to help ensure auditee cooperation and the elimination of interference when the internal audit function is working on an engagement.

IIA Standard 1120: Individual Objectivity states, "Internal auditors must have an impartial, unbiased attitude and avoid any conflict of interest." The IIA further outlines these requirements in Practice Advisory 1120-1: Individual Objectivity:

1. Individual objectivity means the internal auditors perform engagements in such a manner that they have an honest belief in their work product and that no significant quality compromises are made. Internal auditors are not to be placed in situations that could impair their ability to make objective professional judgments.
2. Individual objectivity involves the chief audit executive (CAE) organizing staff assignments that prevent potential and actual conflict of interest and bias, periodically obtaining information from the internal audit staff concerning potential conflict of interest and bias, and, when practicable, rotating internal audit staff assignments periodically.
3. Review of internal audit work results before the related engagement communications are released assists in providing reasonable assurance that the work was performed objectively.
4. The internal auditor's objectivity is not adversely affected when the auditor recommends standards of control for systems or reviews procedures before they are implemented. The auditor's objectivity is considered to be impaired if the auditor designs, installs, drafts procedures for, or operates such systems.
5. The occasional performance of nonaudit work by the internal auditor, with full disclosure in the reporting process, would not necessarily impair objectivity. However, it would require careful consideration by management and the internal auditor to avoid adversely affecting the internal auditor's objectivity.

Individual Objectivity

An unbiased mental attitude that allows internal auditors to perform engagements in such a manner that they have an honest belief in their work product and that no significant quality compromises are made. Objectivity requires internal auditors not to subordinate their judgment on audit matters to that of others.

Organizational Independence

The chief audit executive's line of reporting within the organization that allows the internal audit function to fulfill its responsibilities free from interference.

As discussed in IIA Standard 1130: Impairment to Independence or Objectivity:

> If independence or objectivity is impaired in fact or appearance, the details of the impairment must be disclosed to appropriate parties. The nature of the disclosure will depend upon the impairment.
>
> **Interpretation:**
>
> Impairment to organizational independence and individual objectivity may include, but is not limited to, personal conflict of interest, scope limitations, restrictions on access to records, personnel, and properties, and resource limitations, such as funding.
>
> The determination of appropriate parties to which the details of an impairment to independence or objectivity must be disclosed is dependent upon the expectations of the internal audit activity's and the chief audit executive's responsibilities to senior management and the board as described in the internal audit charter, as well as the nature of the impairment.

Should an impairment to independence or objectivity be identified, the internal auditor must report the impairment or perceived impairment to the CAE who must decide if the internal auditor needs to be reassigned. When the impairment results from a scope limitation, defined in Practice Advisory 1130-1: Impairments to Independence and Objectivity as "a restriction placed on the internal audit activity that precludes the activity from accomplishing its objectives and plans," the CAE must report the limitation to the board. The CAE's communication to the board should be in writing and include the potential effect of the scope limitation. Additionally, to prevent the possibility of an impairment (actual or perceived), internal auditors cannot "accept fees, gifts, or entertainment from an employee, client, customer, supplier, or business associate" (Practice Advisory 1130-1).

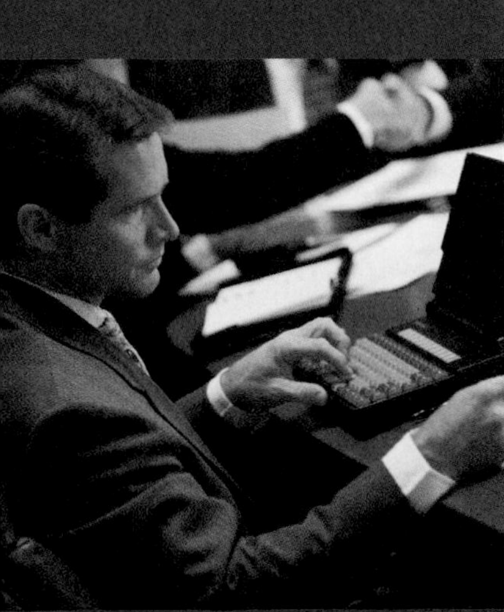

Additional IIA recommendations regarding impairments to independence or objectivity can be found in Exhibit 9-3.

Often the internal audit function will coordinate efforts with other departments in the organization that have similar risk mitigation objectives and responsibilities, such as compliance and risk management. As long as the internal audit function is not asked to perform operating activities or design processes and procedures they will later need to evaluate as part of their duties as an internal audit function, there is no impairment to independence or objectivity. This type of coordination can add significant value to the organization and promote efficient resource utilization in the organization's risk mitigation efforts.

Proficiency and Due Professional Care

IIA Standard 1200: Proficiency and Due Professional Care states simply that "engagements must be performed with proficiency and due professional care." IIA Standard 1210: Proficiency goes into more detail, stating that "internal auditors must possess the knowledge, skills, and other competencies needed to perform their individual responsibilities. The internal audit activity collectively must possess or obtain the knowledge, skills, and other competencies needed to perform its responsibilities." Further-

IIA REQUIREMENTS REGARDING IMPAIRMENTS TO INDEPENDENCE AND OBJECTIVITY

EXHIBIT 9-3

Standard 1130.A1

Internal auditors must refrain from assessing specific operations for which they were previously responsible. Objectivity is presumed to be impaired if an internal auditor provides assurance services for an activity for which the internal auditor had responsibility within the previous year.

Standard 1130.A2

Assurance engagements for functions over which the chief audit executive has responsibility must be overseen by a party outside the internal audit activity.

Standard 1130.C1

Internal auditors may provide consulting services relating to operations for which they had previous responsibilities.

Standard 1130.C2

If internal auditors have potential impairments to independence or objectivity relating to proposed consulting services, disclosure must be made to the engagement client prior to accepting the engagement.

more, IIA Standard 1220: Due Professional Care states that "internal auditors must apply the care and skill expected of a reasonably prudent and competent internal auditor. Due professional care does not imply infallibility."

It is important to note that the interpretation of Standard 1200 defines "knowledge, skills, and other competencies [as] a collective term that refers to the professional proficiency required of internal auditors to effectively carry out their professional responsibilities." This interpretation further encourages internal auditors to "demonstrate their proficiency by obtaining appropriate professional certifications and qualifications, such as the Certified Internal Auditor designation and other designations offered by The Institute of Internal Auditors and other appropriate professional organizations."

Proficiency

The knowledge, skills, and other competencies internal auditors need to perform their individual responsibilities.

PLANNING

As previously mentioned, the CAE is responsible for creating an operating budget and allocating resources in a manner designed to accomplish the annual internal audit plan. The annual plan is developed by the internal audit function through a process that identifies and prioritizes possible audit entities (business units or processes, referred to as the "audit universe") responsible for the mitigating efforts designed to reduce key strategic, operations, reporting, and compliance risks to levels acceptable to the organization's board of directors and senior management. Key risks are those confronting the organization that must be controlled and monitored for an organization to successfully accomplish its defined business objectives. These risks, as identified by senior management, should be independently corroborated by the internal audit function. After the key risks have been identified and agreed upon, the CAE determines which specific business units and processes are responsible for mitigating these risks. The resulting information is then subject to a process that

Due Professional Care

Internal auditors must apply the care and skill expected of a reasonably prudent internal auditor, however, internal auditors are not expected to be infallible.

prioritizes and ranks the risks and associated business units or processes. The CAE takes all of this information and determines the cost in human and financial resources necessary to provide appropriate audit coverage of the prioritized audit universe. The result is a comprehensive internal audit plan that includes both the assurance services and consulting services necessary to assess how effectively the organization is managing the risks that threaten its business objectives. The audit plan can then be implemented by assigning specific personnel to individual engagements in the plan over the following fiscal year. Internal audit functions will implement and assign resources to execute the internal audit plan throughout the fiscal year, and many will update and recast the internal audit plan more frequently than annually (for example, quarterly or monthly).

Audit Universe

A compilation of the subsidiaries, business units, departments, groups, processes, or other established subdivisions of an organization that exist to manage one or more business risks.

There are multiple theories for the structuring of an internal audit plan. Many internal audit functions have moved toward a comprehensive process whereby senior management and the internal audit function collaborate to complete a formal risk assessment on an organization-wide basis to establish a prioritized list of key risk scenarios facing the organization that must be appropriately managed by the organization to achieve key business objectives. It is much more common, however, for the process to be informal and much less collaborative in nature. Whatever process is used, maximum effectiveness is achieved when the risk assessment process is completed annually at the beginning of, or prior to, an organization's fiscal year. This allows the CAE to align audit resources for the upcoming year with the conclusions drawn by management during the risk assessment process. Providing the CAE with a definitive list of audit entities related to the prioritized risks allows for the creation of an internal audit plan using a top-down, risk-based approach. However, many organizations and their internal audit functions still do not use this approach. Instead, they continue to create internal audit plans that cyclically audit each and every area of the organization with highly prioritized business units or processes cycled in for audit coverage more frequently and lower prioritized business units or processes cycled in less frequently.

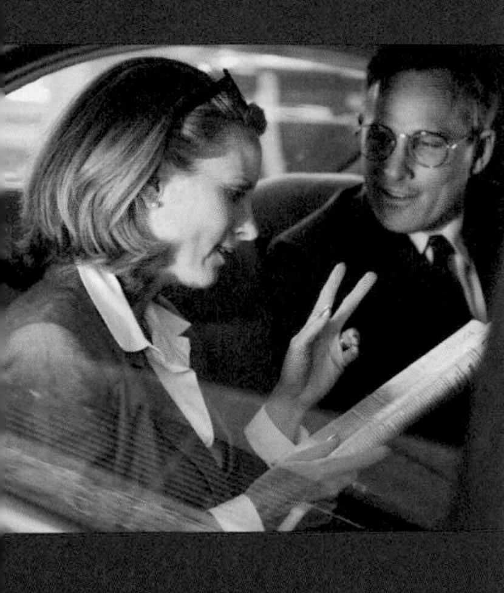

The IIA addresses the differences between assurance services and consulting services relative to IIA Standard 2010: Planning with Standards 2010.A1 and 2010.C1:

> **Assurance Services.** The internal audit activity's plan of engagements must be based on a documented risk assessment, undertaken at least annually. The input of senior management and the board must be considered in this process. (Standard 2010.A1)
>
> **Consulting Services.** The chief audit executive should consider accepting proposed consulting engagements based on the engagement's potential to improve management of risks, add value, and improve the organization's operations. Accepted engagements must be included in the plan. (Standard 2010.C1)

The planning process should include the establishment of goals, engagement schedules, staffing schedules, and financial budgets. Additionally, effective planning should reflect the internal audit charter and be consistent with organizational objectives.

COMMUNICATION AND APPROVAL

After the internal audit plan has been established, it is incumbent upon the CAE to present it to senior management and the board (typically the audit committee) to be approved. Resource requirements, significant interim changes, and the potential implications of resource limitations should all be included in the communication to senior management and the board (IIA Standard 2020: Communication and Approval).

Specific recommendations for meeting this requirement are spelled out in Practice Advisory 2020-1: Communication and Approval:

1. The [CAE] will submit annually to senior management and the board for review and approval a summary of the internal audit plan, work schedule, staffing plan, and financial budget. This summary will inform senior management and the board of the scope of internal audit work and of any limitations placed on that scope. The CAE will also submit all significant interim changes for approval and information.
2. The approved engagement work schedule, staffing plan, and financial budget, along with all significant interim changes, are to contain sufficient information to enable senior management and the board to ascertain whether the internal audit activity's objectives and plans support those of the organization and the board and are consistent with the internal audit charter.

Internal Audit Plan

An outline of the specific assurance and consulting engagements scheduled for a period of time (typically one year) based on an assessment of the organization's risks.

RESOURCE MANAGEMENT

A significant consideration in implementing an internal audit function's plan is how to allocate resources. It is the CAE's responsibility to "ensure that internal audit resources are appropriate, sufficient, and effectively deployed to achieve the approved plan" (IIA Standard 2030: Resource Management). This is achieved by carefully orchestrating a number of factors as discussed below.

Organizational Structure and Staffing Strategy

Internal audit functions should be structured in a way that is consistent with the needs and culture of the organization. The CAE may choose to employ a flat organizational structure in which most of the internal auditors have more or less the same level of skills, experience, and seniority. Typically, this type of organization creates an internal audit function that is stable, highly knowledgeable, and very collaborative. Little supervision is necessary and the work performed is consistent and reliable. However, a flat organizational structure tends to result in a higher cost base due to the higher salaries necessary to retain auditors who all have a high degree of knowledge and experience. Other internal audit functions are much more hierarchical in nature with field auditors reporting to and learning from senior auditors who in turn report to and learn from managers and directors who mentor those in positions subordinate to theirs while supporting the CAE above them.

Internal audit functions that are structured hierarchically tend to be more dynamic due to the fact that positions are often rotating. As the people in the positions near the top of the organizational structure move up and sometimes out of the function, the people in the subordinate positions move up into the recently vacated positions. This allows for growth within the function and leads to the cultivation of diverse skills and fresh perspectives with a lower cost base. Both types of internal audit organization, however, rely on staff members who continue to receive training and broaden their skill base.

The typical hierarchical internal audit function includes associates in a variety of positions that correlate to specific roles within the function, including:

- **Staff auditor or IT staff auditor.** Staff auditors are responsible for performing the fieldwork on financial, operational, compliance, and information system engagements in accordance with the established audit schedule for the purpose of determining the accuracy of financial records, effectiveness of business practices, and compliance with policies, procedures, laws, and regulations.
- **Senior auditor or IT senior auditor (sometimes referred to as an in-charge auditor).** In addition to the responsibilities listed above, senior auditors are responsible for the planning stages of an engagement, guiding staff auditors in their fieldwork, ensuring that engagement timelines are met, reviewing the working papers prepared by the staff auditors, assisting in the preparation of engagement communications, performing the wrap-up steps of the engagement, and evaluating the staff auditors' performance.
- **Audit manager or IT audit manager.** Audit managers supervise and administer engagements in accordance with the established audit schedule. Additionally, audit managers assist in the development and maintenance of the annual internal audit plan and risk model for assigned areas, issue engagement communications, and supervise senior auditors.
- **Audit director or IT audit director.** Audit director positions may exist in larger internal audit functions. In addition to the responsibilities listed above, audit directors assist with the development of the overall internal audit strategy and planning, including the presentation and review of the internal audit strategy, mission, charter, and plan with the audit committee and senior management. Audit directors also supervise audit managers and are responsible for hiring and terminating internal audit associates.
- **Chief audit executive.** The CAE develops, directs, organizes, monitors, plans, and administers the internal audit plan and budget, as approved by the audit committee, for the purpose of determining the accuracy of financial records, effectiveness of business practices, and compliance with applicable policies, procedures, laws, and regulations. The CAE also directly supervises the internal audit management team (audit directors and managers), oversees the entire internal audit function, and approves the hiring and termination of internal auditors.

The Internal Auditor Competency Framework

This resource, published by The IIA, outlines the minimum level of knowledge and skills internal auditors should have at different points in their careers in four areas:

- **Interpersonal skills**
- **Tools and techniques**
- **Internal audit standards**
- **Knowledge areas**

The Internal Auditor Competency Framework, published by The IIA, provides in-depth information regarding the minimum level of knowledge and skills internal auditors should have at different points in their careers in four areas: interpersonal skills, tools and techniques, internal audit standards, and knowledge areas. The Internal Auditor Competency Framework is discussed in Chapter 1, "Introduction to Internal Auditing," and can be found under "Professional Guidance" on The IIA's website.

Right Sizing

Right sizing is an important concept in the staffing and scheduling of an internal audit function. It is important to achieve and maintain a balance of knowledgeable and skilled staff to complete the internal audit plan, without putting undue stress on the staff by creating oppressive workloads, while simultaneously maintaining a reasonable financial budget. This is true whether the internal audit structure is flat or hierarchically organized and is often a factor when determining what type of structure is appropriate for an organization. The CAE relies on various sources to help validate right-sizing decisions, including networking, benchmarking, and other consultative venues.

Staffing Plans/Human Resources

Although some aspects of maintaining appropriate human resources are delegated to other high-level associates in the internal audit function (for example, directors and managers may do much of the recruiting and initial selection of candidates), the CAE is "primarily responsible for the sufficiency and management of internal audit resources in a manner that ensures the fulfillment of internal audit's responsibilities, as detailed in the internal audit charter. This includes effective communication of resource needs and reporting of status to senior management and the board" (Practice Advisory 2030-1: Resource Management). Additionally, the CAE must ensure that the internal auditors in the internal audit function have the skills and knowledge necessary to carry out the internal audit plan and "execute the audit activities in the breadth, depth, and timeliness expected by senior management and the board, as stated in the internal audit charter" (Practice Advisory 2030-1).

The CAE also must assign human resources effectively, meaning that internal auditors are assigned to engagements that they are qualified and capable to perform. In some instances, individuals with specialized knowledge and/or skills from elsewhere in the organization may assist with an internal audit engagement when the necessary competencies are not present within the internal audit function.

From a broader perspective, the CAE takes succession planning into consideration and ensures that there is a robust staff evaluation and development program in place. As with other areas of managing the internal audit function, the CAE must maintain open communication with senior management and the board regarding human resources. Typically this communication takes the form of regular updates during quarterly board meetings, such as audit committee meetings. These updates include "a summary of status and adequacy of resources" along with "metrics, goals, and objectives to monitor the overall adequacy of resources [including] comparisons of resources to the annual audit plan, the impact of temporary shortages or vacancies, educational and training activities, and changes to specific skill needs based on changes in the organization's business, operations, programs, systems, and controls" (Practice Advisory 2030-1).

Hiring Practices

The CAE is responsible for hiring associates to fill the organizational structure of the internal audit function in a way that maximizes efficiency, effectively provides the necessary skill base, and makes good use of

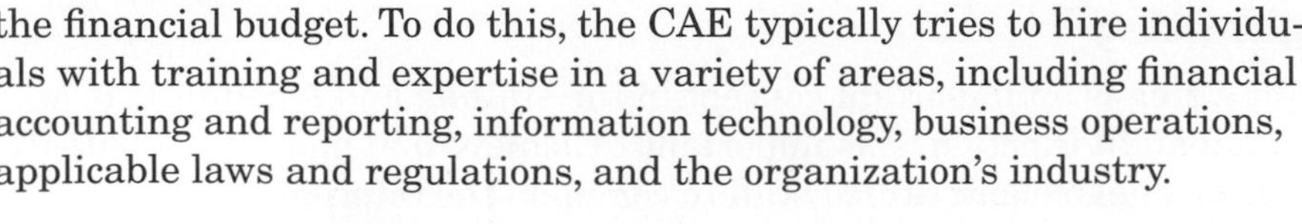

the financial budget. To do this, the CAE typically tries to hire individuals with training and expertise in a variety of areas, including financial accounting and reporting, information technology, business operations, applicable laws and regulations, and the organization's industry.

Strategic Sourcing

Supplements the in-house internal audit function through the use of third-party vendor services for the purposes of gaining subject matter expertise for a specific engagement or filling a gap in needed resources to complete the internal audit plan.

Strategic Sourcing

Strategic sourcing, also referred to as co-sourcing or outsourcing, allows the CAE to optimize both the skill base and the financial considerations related to staffing. The CAE, with the use of strategic sourcing, is able to maintain a cost effective internal audit function by hiring permanent associates who have a broad, more generalized base of skills while maintaining the flexibility of bringing in technical experts that are necessary for specific projects or engagements but who would be cost prohibitive to keep permanently on staff. Strategic sourcing also is used in scheduling when the projected hours necessary to accomplish the internal audit plan exceed the number of hours available from the permanent staff, but when hiring another staff member would be inefficient, cost prohibitive, or impractical under existing market conditions.

Training and Mentoring

Staff development is of particular importance for an internal audit function due to the requirements placed on it regarding proficiency and due professional care as discussed earlier in this chapter. While IIA Standard 1220: Due Professional Care specifically points out that infallibility is not required, it is incumbent on the staff to remain current in their knowledge of the industry and audit skills. This is done primarily through ongoing training and mentoring, as well as continued professional education. Individual internal audit functions establish minimum training and professional development requirements, which typically include professional certifications (for example, Certified Internal Auditor [CIA], Certified Public Accountant [CPA], Certified Information Systems Auditor [CISA], and Certified Fraud Examiner [CFE]) and the related minimum continued professional education required to maintain them.

Career Planning and Professional Development

In addition to the training and mentoring required to meet proficiency and due professional care standards, a good internal audit function will have a process in place for career development. This allows each associate to develop and implement an overall plan to reach long-term career goals while remaining a contributing member of the internal audit function.

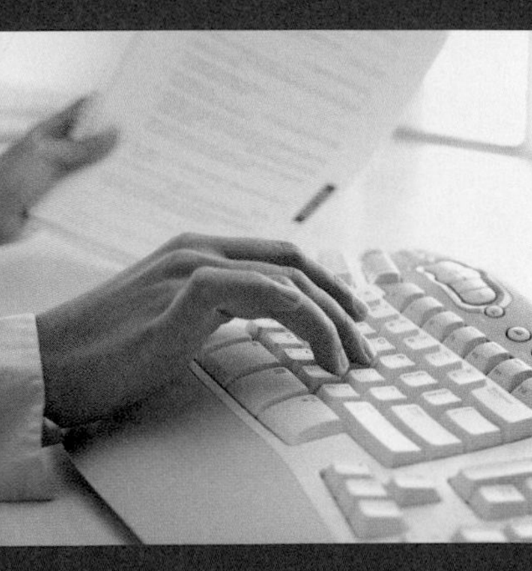

Scheduling

Once the right mix of permanent associates and strategic sourcing is in place and appropriately organized within the internal audit function, the CAE can begin assigning specific engagements and projects to the personnel best suited to perform them. This is where the benefits of good hiring practices and right sizing become apparent. The CAE maximizes the financial budget by creating internal audit teams that, based on their skills and experience, will most effectively and efficiently accomplish the objectives of a specific engagement. At the same time, the CAE takes into consideration the development needs of the staff and works to balance the developmental opportunities a specific engagement can provide to them and the need to complete engagements within the scheduled time frame.

Financial Budget

As mentioned previously in this chapter, the financial budget is driven primarily by the internal audit plan, organizational structure, and staffing strategy. The CAE must carefully evaluate the financial resources necessary to accomplish the objectives set forth. It should be apparent at this point that the financial budget both impacts and is impacted by each of the tasks undertaken by the CAE as described above.

POLICIES AND PROCEDURES

The standard regarding the implementation of policies and procedures simply states that "the chief audit executive must establish policies and procedures to guide the internal audit activity" (IIA Standard 2040: Policies and Procedures). Practice Advisory 2040-1: Policies and Procedures recommends keeping the policies and procedures consistent with the size of the internal audit function: "The [CAE] develops policies and procedures. Formal administrative and technical audit manuals may not be needed by all internal audit activities. A small internal audit activity may be managed informally. Its audit staff may be directed and controlled through daily, close supervision and memoranda that state policies and procedures to be followed. In a large internal audit activity, more formal and comprehensive policies and procedures are essential to guide the internal audit staff in the execution of the annual audit plan."

COORDINATION WITH INDEPENDENT OUTSIDE AUDITORS

According to IIA Standard 2050: Coordination, "The chief audit executive should share information and coordinate activities with other internal and external providers of assurance and consulting services to ensure proper coverage and minimize duplication of efforts." Coordinating the efforts of the internal audit function with those of other internal and external providers of assurance and consulting services is important because of the increase in effectiveness and efficiencies that can be gained. While it is important to leverage the efforts of other internal and external assurance and consulting activities, the most common form of such collaboration is with the independent outside auditors. Therefore, the discussion that follows focuses on these coordination efforts.

Independent Outside Auditor

A registered public accounting firm, hired by the organization's board or executive management, to perform a financial statement audit.

Practice Advisory 2050-1: Coordination outlines the circumstances under which the internal audit function can use work performed by the independent outside auditors. Specifically, Practice Advisory 2050-1 states that the CAE should take "steps necessary to understand the work performed by the [independent outside] auditors (note that the term 'external auditors' has been replaced with the authors' preferred 'independent outside auditors' in the following quoted material), including:

- The nature, extent, and timing of work planned by [independent outside] auditors, to be satisfied that the [independent outside] auditors' planned work, in conjunction with the internal auditors' planned work, satisfies the requirements of Standard 2100 [Nature of Work].
- The [independent outside] auditor's assessment of risk and materiality.
- The [independent outside] auditors' techniques, methods, and terminology to enable the CAE to (1) coordinate internal and [independent outside] auditing work; (2) evaluate, for purposes

of reliance, the [independent outside] auditors' work; and (3) communicate effectively with [independent outside] auditors.

- Access to the [independent outside] auditors' programs and working papers, to be satisfied that the [independent outside] auditors' work can be relied upon for internal audit purposes. Internal auditors are responsible for respecting the confidentiality of those programs and working papers."

To further capitalize on efficiencies between internal auditors and independent outside auditors, the CAE should extend the same opportunities as described above to the independent outside auditors so that they, in turn, can rely on the work performed by the internal audit function. To accomplish this two-way coordination, it is a good idea for the internal auditors and the independent outside auditors to "use similar techniques, methods, and terminology" (Practice Advisory 2050-1). This is attained through regular meetings during which planned audit activities are discussed, including completion timing and the impact, if any, of observations and recommendations on the scope of planned work. Additionally, the internal audit function should make available to the independent outside auditor all final communications, including management's responses to them, and all applicable follow-up reviews. This information allows the independent outside auditors to make any necessary adjustments to the scope and timing of their scheduled work. Conversely, the internal audit function also should have access to the independent outside auditors' materials and communications so that the CAE can ensure "that appropriate follow-up and corrective actions have been taken" (Practice Advisory 2050-1).

Board

An organization's governing body, such as a board of directors, supervisory board, head of an agency or legislative body, board of governors or trustees of a nonprofit organization, or any other designated body of the organization, including the audit committee, to whom the chief audit executive may functionally report.

Although the CAE is responsible for the coordination between the internal audit function and independent outside auditors, the board is responsible for oversight of that coordination as well as the work performed by independent outside auditors. This means that the CAE needs to gain the board's support relative to coordinating the efforts of the internal audit function and the independent outside auditors effectively. The CAE keeps the board apprised of the results of ongoing assessments of these coordination efforts in general and the performance of the independent outside auditors specifically, through regular communication.

REPORTING TO THE BOARD AND SENIOR MANAGEMENT

The CAE has the responsibility to "report periodically to senior management and the board on the internal audit activity's purpose, authority, responsibility, and performance relative to its plan. Reporting must also include significant risk exposures and control issues, including fraud risks, governance issues, and other matters needed or requested by senior management and the board" (IIA Standard 2060: Reporting to the Board and Senior Management). The CAE evidences the completion of these professional responsibilities by periodically reporting the results of ongoing internal audit activities to senior management and the audit committee during routinely scheduled meetings throughout the year. "Significant deviations from approved engagement work schedules, staffing plans, and financial budgets; the reasons for the deviations; and action taken or needed" should be reported, as should significant engagement observations and recommendations (Practice Advisory 2060-1: Reporting to Senior Management and the Board). In instances when senior management and/or the board have assumed the risk of not correcting a significant engagement observation, the CAE makes a decision regarding whether to report it to the board depending on current circumstances, including any recent changes in management or the organization's risk profile.

Additionally, management and the CAE coordinate efforts to routinely report on various risk and control activities performed by either, in accordance with roles and responsibilities set by the board and the audit committee. This typically includes reports covering:

- Business unit monitoring and risk monitoring reports.
- Independent outside auditor activity reports.
- Key financial activity reports.
- Risk management activity reports.
- Legal and compliance monitoring reports.

In addition to this information, a report is typically submitted to the audit committee by either senior management or the CAE outlining the results of management's self-assessment regarding the design adequacy and operating effectiveness of the organization's internal controls. At minimum, the internal audit function should independently assess the process that management underwent to reach their conclusions. However, many CAEs take on the added role of independently opining on the organization's system of internal controls over financial reporting. This opinion is delivered to the audit committee concurrently with management's assertions regarding the system of internal controls. In more limited cases, the CAEs' opinions extend to internal controls over operations and compliance objectives. They see this as a natural extension of completing the annual internal audit plan in which the internal audit function has already independently evaluated the organization's system of internal controls as outlined in the internal audit plan. Other CAEs disagree with this approach and argue that it creates a direct conflict with their responsibility to be independent and objective evaluators of management's self-assessment of the system of internal controls. The approach taken by an organization is largely a result of its culture.

However, because the CAE is responsible for maintaining relationships with organizations that have potentially conflicting expectations, including the audit committee, senior management, line management, and various interested outside third parties (regulators and the independent outside auditors, in particular), this is not always as straightforward as it appears. If an audit report contains no observations and the internal controls are found to be designed adequately and operating effectively, there typically is no misalignment between parties. However, if the internal audit function finds that the internal controls are designed inadequately and/or are operating ineffectively resulting in misalignment between management and one or more of the parties, the situation becomes much more complicated. It is not enough for the CAE to simply report such a misalignment to the board and senior management. In addition to reporting the observation and the misalignment, the CAE is expected to coordinate a resolution to the observation and report to the board and senior management not only what the observation consists of, but how it is being rectified as well. Only in very rare cases when the CAE and management fail to reach agreement regarding the observation and/or its resolution would the CAE report an observation that was not accompanied by its resolution. Communication obligations are covered in detail in Chapter 14, "Communicating Assurance Engagement Outcomes and Performing Follow-up Procedures," and in Chapter 15, "The Consulting Engagement."

GOVERNANCE

Governance

The combination of processes and structures implemented by the board to inform, direct, manage, and monitor the activities of the organization toward the achievement of its objectives.

Governance is defined in Chapter 1, "Introduction to Internal Auditing," and then again in Chapter 3, "Governance," as "a process conducted by the board of directors to authorize, direct, and oversee management toward the achievement of the organization's objectives." Chapter 3 provides detailed information regarding the governance process and the roles and responsibilities of all parties involved. For the purposes of this chapter, however, governance will be discussed only in terms of the CAE's and the internal audit function's specific responsibilities.

IIA Standard 2110: Governance requires the internal audit function to "assess and make appropriate recommendations for improving the governance process in its accomplishment of the following objectives:

- Promoting appropriate ethics and values within the organization;
- Ensuring effective organizational performance management and accountability;
- Communicating risk and control information to appropriate areas of the organization; and
- Coordinating the activities of and communicating information among the board, [independent outside] and internal auditors, and management."

These responsibilities are carried out largely through the assurance services provided by the internal audit function. The internal audit charter defines what role the internal audit function plays in providing assurance relative to the governance process and should reflect the expectations of the board. Chapter 3 provides the following examples of the internal audit function's governance responsibilities:

- Evaluating whether the various risk management activities are designed adequately to manage the risks associated with unacceptable outcomes.
- Testing and evaluating whether the various risk management activities are operating as designed.
- Determining whether the assertions made by the risk owners to senior management regarding the effectiveness of the risk management activities accurately reflect the current state of risk management effectiveness.
- Determining whether the assertions made by senior management to the board regarding the effectiveness of the risk management activities provide the board with the information it desires about the current state of risk management effectiveness.
- Evaluating whether risk tolerance information is communicated timely and effectively from the board to senior management, and from senior management to the risk owners.
- Assessing whether there are any other risk areas that are currently not included in the governance process, but should be (for example, a risk for which risk tolerance and reporting expectations have not been delegated to a specific risk owner).

To carry out these responsibilities, the internal audit function must have a clear understanding of the board's governance direction and expectations, including risk tolerance levels and reporting expectations. The internal audit plan should reflect that understanding by including appropriate governance assurance activities and providing opportunities for regular communication to senior management and the board regarding the effectiveness of risk management activities.

Refer to Chapter 3, "Governance," where governance is covered in greater detail.

RISK MANAGEMENT

Generally defined, risk management is a participatory process designed to identify, document, evaluate, communicate, and monitor the most significant uncertainties facing an organization requiring risk mitigation or exploitation of opportunities to successfully achieve business objectives. In other words, risk management is a process conducted by management to understand and deal with uncertainties (that is, risk and opportunities) that could affect the organization's ability to achieve its business objectives. Risk response is an action or set of actions taken by management to achieve a desired risk management strategy. Effective execution of risk management strategies helps management achieve an organization's business objectives by reducing the potential impact or likelihood (or both) of a potential risk event or, conversely, by taking advantage of (exploiting) a perceived opportunity. Risk mitigation is the act of lessening the severity or potential impact of risks through the use of risk responses. Risk responses are discussed in detail in Chapter 4, "Risk Management."

Risk Management

The process conducted by management to understand and deal with uncertainties (that is, risks and opportunities) that could affect the organization's ability to achieve its objectives.

Risk mitigation is most effectively accomplished when it is decentralized to the areas most affected by the specific risks. In contrast, risk management is typically more effective when it is a centralized function. Risk management is most effective when senior management is actively engaged in the process in a way in which contributors step back from their specific area/department (silo) and consider the risks confronting the organization as a whole. Unfortunately, many organizations make the mistake of letting risk management get dispersed throughout the organization along with risk mitigation. Consequently, the various silos responsible for mitigating risks also become responsible for the risk management activities described above. This results in a situation where different areas of the organization are unaware of what is happening in each others' areas to mitigate similar risk events, culminating in inconsistent risk responses and inefficiencies due to the application of differing risk appetites and mitigation approaches by the individual areas.

Historically, risk management has been designed to focus efforts on avoiding potential danger and preventing harmful actions from negatively impacting an organization. Over time, organizations' risk management models have evolved and are now focusing their risk management efforts on identifying opportunities that can be exploited in addition to risk events that have the potential to negatively affect the organization. In these models, risk management efforts are designed to facilitate the management of both risk and opportunity within a predefined risk appetite set by the board and senior management. Properly executed risk management assists the board and senior management in implementing appropriate risk responses (avoiding, reducing, sharing, and/or accepting risks or exploiting opportunities) by increasing the likelihood of achieving the desired result (mitigating a risk event or taking advantage of an opportunity). Effective risk management also provides reasonable (not absolute) assurance that the business objectives of an organization will be achieved.

As discussed earlier in the chapter, the results of a well-executed risk management process (model) also can be an essential source for identifying an organization's risk drivers and provide invaluable input for the development of the internal audit function's audit universe and audit plan. Consequently, risk management is an area in which the internal audit function can and does have a critical role to play. Just how much involvement the internal audit function should have in the organization's risk management process, however, is the subject of much discussion. Although many organizations now have formal risk management functions that are responsible for monitoring and facilitating risk mitigation efforts throughout an organization, the role of the internal audit function varies widely and is predicated on the division of risk management responsibilities and the culture of the organization. At minimum, the internal audit function should evaluate the design adequacy and operating effectiveness of the organization's risk management processes by providing input and feedback through a periodic review (audit). It is also appropriate for the internal audit function to facilitate the identification and evaluation of risks and opportunities, coach management on appropriate ways to respond to risk events and opportunities, and help an organization coordinate enterprise-wide risk management activities. However, the internal audit function should not set the organization's risk appetite, make decisions on appropriate risk responses, or assume ownership (be accountable for) the risk management processes; only management should take on these roles.

Control

Any action taken by management, the board, and other parties to manage risk and increase the likelihood that established objectives and goals will be achieved. Management plans, organizes, and directs the performance of sufficient actions to provide reasonable assurance that objectives and goals will be achieved.

According to IIA Standard 2120: Risk Management, "the internal audit activity must evaluate the effectiveness and contribute to the improvement of risk management processes." The interpretation for this standard states:

> Determining whether risk management processes are effective is a judgment resulting from the internal auditor's assessment that:
>
> - Organizational objectives support and align with the organization's mission;
> - Significant risks are identified and assessed;
> - Appropriate risk responses are selected that align risks with the organization's risk appetite; and
> - Relevant risk information is captured and communicated in a timely manner across the organization, enabling staff, management, and the board to carry out their responsibilities.
>
> Risk management processes are monitored through ongoing management activities, separate evaluations, or both.

In practical terms, the internal audit function should enhance risk management and mitigation, providing another level of protection. Exhibit 9-4 shows a range of activities that an internal audit function might be asked to perform, detailing which activities are appropriate and which should be avoided. This exhibit was introduced as Exhibit 4-4 in Chapter 4, "Risk Management," where it is discussed in greater depth.

EXHIBIT 9-4

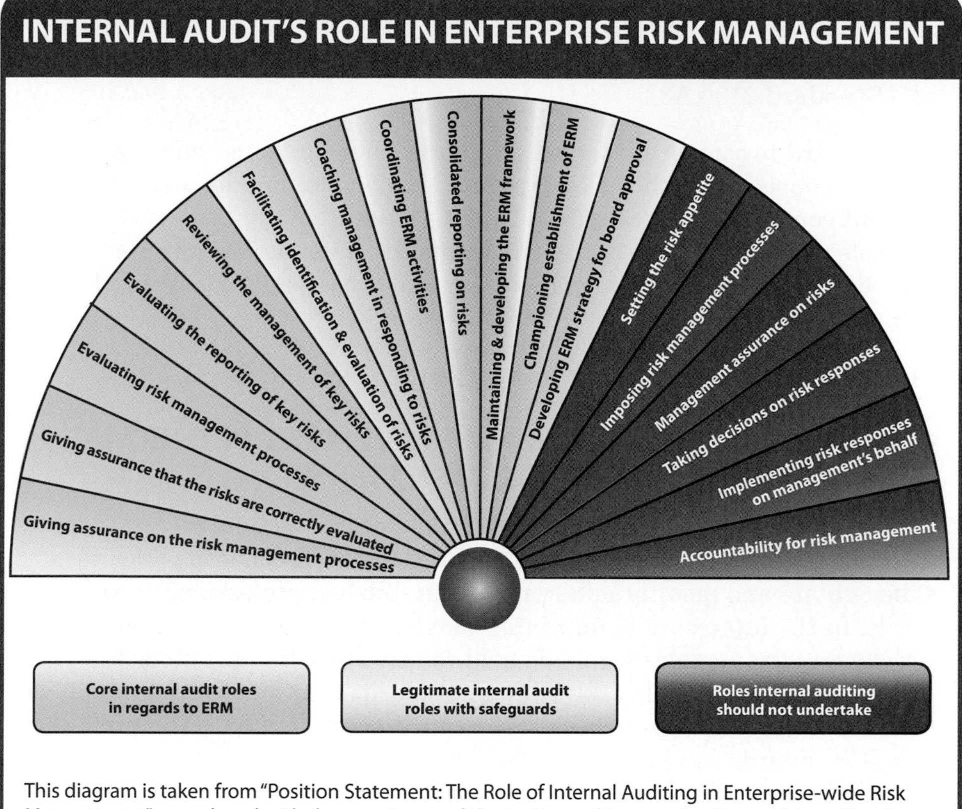

This diagram is taken from "Position Statement: The Role of Internal Auditing in Enterprise-wide Risk Management," reproduced with the permission of The Institute of Internal Auditors – United Kingdom and Ireland. For the full statement, visit www.iia.org.uk. © The Institute of Internal Auditors – UK and Ireland Ltd., July 2004.

Refer to Practice Advisory 2120-1: Assessing the Adequacy of Risk Management Processes for more detail regarding the internal audit function's responsibility regarding risk management.

CONTROL

IIA Standard 2130: Control states that "the internal audit activity must assist the organization in maintaining effective controls by evaluating their effectiveness and efficiency and by promoting continuous improvement."

In terms of providing assurance services, the information that comes out of the risk assessment should drive the internal audit function's direction when evaluating "the adequacy and effectiveness of controls in responding to risks within the organization's governance, operations, and information systems regarding the:

- Reliability and integrity of financial and operational information;
- Effectiveness and efficiency of operations;
- Safeguarding of assets; and
- Compliance with laws, regulations, and contracts." (Standard 2130.A1)

Additionally, the internal audit function "should ascertain the extent to which operating and program goals and objectives have been established and conform to those of the organization" (Standard 2130.A2) and then review "operations and programs to ascertain the extent to which results are consistent with established goals and objectives to determine whether operations and programs are being implemented or performed as intended" (Standard 2130.A3).

With regard to consulting services, "internal auditors must address controls consistent with the engagement's objectives and be alert to significant control issues" (Standard 2130.C1). Additionally, "knowledge of controls gained from consulting engagements" must be incorporated "into [the] evaluation of the organization's control processes" (Standard 2130.C2).

Quality Assurance

The process of assuring that an internal audit function operates according to a set of standards defining the specific elements that must be present to ensure that the findings of the internal audit function are legitimate.

Control is addressed in detail in Chapter 6, "Internal Control."

QUALITY ASSURANCE AND IMPROVEMENT PROGRAM (QUALITY PROGRAM ASSESSMENTS)

In the current corporate governance climate, it has become imperative that internal audit functions have the appropriate tools with which to self-regulate and monitor adherence to established professional standards. In the interest of maintaining consistent standards to which internal audit functions would be held relative to self-regulation, The IIA established formal quality assurance standards that must be followed for internal audit functions to be considered in compliance with the professional standards established by The IIA.

Quality assurance is the process of assuring that an internal audit function operates according to a set of standards defining the specific elements that must be present to ensure that the findings of the internal audit function are legitimate. Specifically, IIA Standard 1300: Quality Assurance and Improvement Program states that "the chief audit executive must develop and maintain a quality assurance and improvement program that covers all aspects of the internal audit activity." The interpretation for this standard goes on to explain that "a quality assurance and improvement program is designed to enable an evaluation of the internal audit activity's conformance with the Definition of Internal Auditing and the *Standards* and an evaluation of whether internal auditors apply the Code of Ethics. The program also assesses the efficiency and effectiveness of the internal audit activity and identifies opportunities for improvement."

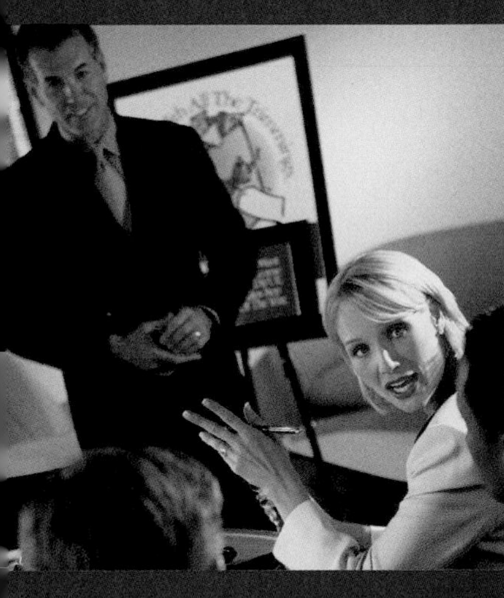

IIA Standard 1310: Requirements of the Quality Assurance and Improvement Program, IIA Standard 1311: Internal Assessments, and IIA Standard 1312: External Assessments detail the specific requirements for IIA Standard 1300 by specifying that internal audit functions must establish both internal assessment and external assessment procedures. In practical terms, internal assessment procedures are the day-to-day quality assurance steps typically outlined in an internal audit function's operating procedures (audit manual) that ensure that the *Standards* are followed, and external assessment procedures are the quality assurance steps that an internal audit function has performed and/or has verified by a qualified, independent party. This process is commonly referred to as an independent peer review. Internal audit functions are required to successfully complete an external assessment periodically (at least once every five years) to confirm that the internal audit function is compliant with the *Standards*. Both internal assessment and external assessment procedures must be established and followed for an internal audit func-

THE INTERNAL AUDIT FUNCTION'S QUALITY ASSURANCE PROCEDURES

EXHIBIT 9-5

Practice Advisory 1311-1: Internal Assessments

1. The processes and tools used in ongoing internal assessments include:
   - Engagement supervision,
   - Checklists and procedures (e.g., in an audit and procedures manual) are being followed,
   - Feedback from audit customers and other stakeholders,
   - Selective peer reviews of workpapers by staff not involved in the respective audits,
   - Project budgets, timekeeping systems, audit plan completion, and cost recoveries, and/or
   - Analyses of other performance metrics (such as cycle time and recommendations accepted).
2. Conclusions are developed as to the quality of ongoing performance and follow-up action taken to ensure appropriate improvements are implemented.
3. The IIA's Quality Assessment Manual, or a comparable set of guidance and tools, should serve as the basis for periodic internal assessments.
4. Periodic internal assessments may:
   - Include more in-depth interviews and surveys of stakeholder groups.
   - Be performed by members of the internal audit activity (self-assessment).
   - Be performed by Certified Internal Auditors (CIAs) or other competent audit professionals, currently assigned elsewhere in the organization.
   - Encompass a combination of self-assessment and preparation of materials subsequently reviewed by CIAs, or other competent audit professionals.
   - Include benchmarking of the internal audit activity's practices and performance metrics against relevant best practices of the internal audit profession.
5. A periodic internal assessment performed within a short time before an external assessment can serve to facilitate and reduce the cost of the external assessment. If the periodic internal assessment is performed by a qualified, independent external reviewer or review team, the assessment results should not communicate any assurances on the outcome of the subsequent external quality assessment. The report may offer suggestions and recommendations to enhance the internal audit activities' practices. If the external assessment takes the form of a self-assessment with independent validation, the periodic internal assessment can serve as the self-assessment portion of this process.
6. Conclusions are developed as to quality of performance and appropriate action initiated to achieve improvements and conformity to the *Standards*, as necessary.
7. The chief audit executive (CAE) establishes a structure for reporting results of internal assessments that maintains appropriate credibility and objectivity. Generally, those assigned responsibility for conducting ongoing and periodic review, report to the CAE while performing the reviews and communicate results directly to the CAE.
8. At least annually, the CAE reports the results of internal assessments, necessary action plans, and their successful implementation to senior management and the board.

tion to be able to state that it "conforms with the *International Standards for the Professional Practice of Internal Auditing*" (IIA Standard 1321: Use of "Conforms with the *International Standards for the Professional Practice of Internal Auditing*"). Exhibit 9-5 presents internal audit function quality assurance procedures suggested in Practice Advisory 1311-1: Internal Assessments.

While Standards 1300, 1310, 1311, and 1312 may seem unambiguous, particularly when clarified by the requisite Practice Advisories, questions as to how these standards should be implemented have sparked debate within the internal audit community. Standard 1312 can be very onerous, especially for "small" internal audit functions. While Practice Advisory 1312-2: External Assessments: Self-assessment With Independent Validation has attempted to address this concern by providing for a self-assessment option with independent validation, and agreement can generally be reached on a philosophical level, problems arise when practitioners try to define what constitutes a "small" internal audit function and the term becomes relative depending on the size of the function defining it. Exhibit 9-6 presents the suggested alternative approach for "small" internal audit functions finding the external assessment quality assurance procedures to be too onerous.

Because neither the *Standards* nor the Practice Advisories make any distinction between functions that are primarily sourced internally to an organization and those that are primarily sourced from outside the organization (strategic sourcing arrangements), much discussion continues about the applicability of, and how best to comply with, the *Standards* when the function is primarily outsourced.

The requirements of a properly designed quality assurance and improvement program are provided in Exhibit 9-7.

Disclosure of Nonconformance

***Nonconformance with the* Standards**

Occurs when the internal audit function is found to be deficient to the point that it impacts the overall scope or operation of the internal audit function. Nonconformance must be disclosed.

In the event that an internal audit function is found to be significantly deficient as to impact "the overall scope or operation of the internal audit activity," IIA Standard 1322: Disclosure of Nonconformance states that "the chief audit executive must disclose the nonconformance and the impact to senior management and the board." At that time, a determination will typically be made regarding whether said noncompliance is intentional or inadvertent, as well as what, if any, corrective action will be taken. Should senior management and the board make the decision not to take corrective action and the internal audit function remains noncompliant, the internal audit function will no longer be able to state that its internal assurance and consulting services conform "with the *International Standards for the Professional Practice of Internal Auditing*" (Standard 1321). The consequences of continuing to offer internal assurance and consulting services that are not conducted in accordance with the *Standards* are far reaching and can significantly inhibit the internal audit function's relationship with interested third parties such as regulators and other interested outside parties (for example, the U.S. Securities and Exchange Commission [SEC] or the organization's independent outside audit firm).

PERFORMANCE MEASUREMENTS FOR THE INTERNAL AUDIT FUNCTION

Performance measurements are integral to the internal assessment requirement outlined in IIA Standard 1311: Internal Assessments discussed earlier. In addition to providing the criteria against which the internal audit function judges its performance in key areas, they gauge how well the internal audit function is accomplishing its mission/goals. The CAE should consider many factors when creating performance

INTERNAL AUDIT FUNCTION SELF-ASSESSMENT QUALITY ASSURANCE PROCEDURES FOR "SMALL" FUNCTIONS

Practice Advisory 1312-2: External Assessments: Self-assessment With Independent Validation

1. An external assessment by a qualified, independent reviewer or review team may be troublesome for smaller internal audit activities or there may be circumstances in other organizations where a full external assessment by an independent team is not deemed appropriate or necessary. For example, the internal audit activity may (a) be in an industry subject to extensive regulation and/or supervision, (b) be otherwise subject to extensive external oversight and direction relating to governance and internal controls, (c) have been recently subjected to external review(s) and/or consulting services in which there was extensive benchmarking with best practices, or (d) in the judgment of the chief audit executive (CAE), the benefits of self-assessment for staff development and the strength of the internal quality assurance and improvement program currently outweigh the benefits of a quality assessment by an external team.
2. A self-assessment with independent [external] validation includes:
   - A comprehensive and fully documented self-assessment process, which emulates the external assessment process, at least with respect to evaluation of conformance with the Definition of Internal Auditing, the Code of Ethics, and the *Standards*.
   - An independent, on-site validation by a qualified, independent reviewer.
   - Economical time and resource requirements — e.g., the primary focus would be on conformance with the *Standards*.
   - Limited attention to other areas — such as benchmarking, review and consultation as to employment of leading practices, and interviews with senior and operating management — may be reduced. However, the information produced by these parts of the assessment is one of the benefits of an external assessment.
3. The same guidance and criteria as set forth in Practice Advisory 1312-1 would apply for self-assessments with independent validation.
4. A team under the direction of the CAE performs and fully documents the self-assessment process. A draft report, similar to that for an external assessment, is prepared including the CAE's judgment on conformance with the *Standards*.
5. A qualified, independent reviewer or review team performs sufficient tests of the self-assessment so as to validate the results and express the indicated level of the activity's conformance with the Definition of Internal Auditing, Code of Ethics, and the *Standards*. The independent validation follows the process outlined in The IIA's *Quality Assessment Manual* or a similar comprehensive process.
6. As part of the independent validation, the independent external reviewer — upon completion of a rigorous review of the self-assessment team's evaluation of conformance with the Definition of Internal Auditing, the Code of Ethics, and the *Standards*:
   - Reviews the draft report and attempts to reconcile unresolved issues (if any).
   - If in agreement with the opinion of conformance with the Definition of Internal Auditing, Code of Ethics, and the *Standards*, adds wording (as needed) to the report, concurring with the self-assessment process and opinion and — to the extent deemed appropriate — in the report's findings, conclusions, and recommendations.
   - If not in agreement with the evaluation, adds dissenting wording to the report, specifying the points of disagreement with it and — to the extent deemed appropriate — with the significant findings, conclusions, recommendations, and opinions in the report.
   - Alternatively, may prepare a separate independent validation report — concurring or expressing disagreement as outlined above — to accompany the report of the self-assessment.
7. The final report(s) of the self-assessment with independent validation is signed by the self-assessment team and the qualified, independent external reviewer(s) and issued by the CAE to senior management and the board.
8. To provide accountability and transparency, the CAE communicates the results of external quality assessments — including specifics of planned remedial actions for significant issues and subsequent information as to accomplishment of those planned actions — with the various stakeholders of the activity, such as senior management, the board, and external auditors.

EXHIBIT 9-7

PRACTICE ADVISORY 1310-1 REQUIREMENTS OF THE QUALITY ASSURANCE AND IMPROVEMENT PROGRAM

1. A quality assurance and improvement program (QAIP) is an ongoing and periodic assessment of the entire spectrum of audit and consulting work performed by the internal audit activity. These ongoing and periodic assessments are composed of rigorous, comprehensive processes; continuous supervision and testing of internal audit and consulting work; and periodic validations of conformance with the Definition of Internal Auditing, the Code of Ethics, and the *Standards*. This also includes ongoing measurements and analyses of performance metrics (e.g., internal audit plan accomplishment, cycle time, recommendations accepted, and customer satisfaction). If the assessments' results indicate areas for improvement by the internal audit activity, the chief audit executive (CAE) will implement the improvements through the QAIP.
2. Assessments evaluate and conclude on the quality of the internal audit activity and lead to recommendations for appropriate improvements. QAIPs include an evaluation of:
    - Conformance with the Definition of Internal Auditing, the Code of Ethics, and the *Standards*, including timely corrective actions to remedy any significant instances of nonconformance.
    - Adequacy of the internal audit activity's charter, goals, objectives, policies, and procedures.
    - Contribution to the organization's governance, risk management, and control processes.
    - Compliance with applicable laws, regulations, and government or industry standards.
    - Effectiveness of continuous improvement activities and adoption of best practices.
    - The extent to which the internal audit activity adds value and improves the organization's operations.
3. The QAIP efforts also include follow-up on recommendations involving appropriate and timely modification of resources, technology, processes, and procedures.
4. To provide accountability and transparency, the CAE communicates the results of external and, as appropriate, internal quality program assessments to the various stakeholders of the activity (such as senior management, the board, and external auditors). At least annually, the CAE reports to senior management and the board on the quality program efforts and results.

Quality Assurance and Improvement Program

An ongoing and periodic assessment of the entire spectrum of audit and consulting work performed by the internal audit function.

measurements, such as the size of the internal audit function, the specific services offered, industry-specific regulations, the operating environment, and the organization's culture. Performance measurements should be aligned with the internal audit function's charter, and all significant services addressed in the charter should be considered when establishing performance measurements. The customized measurement process should outline activities that contribute to the achievement of the goals identified in the charter.

USE OF TECHNOLOGY TO SUPPORT THE INTERNAL AUDIT PROCESS

Technology has an increasingly larger role in the internal audit process. There are more and more technological tools available that enable increased productivity and efficiency, allowing for less time spent on administrative responsibilities and more on assurance and consulting services provided to auditees and customers. In the current environment of technological advancement, it can be difficult not to be distracted by the endless improvements, but it is important to keep in mind that technology should enhance an internal audit function's productivity, not divert attention away from the task of auditing.

In addition to decreasing the amount of time spent on administrative responsibilities, technological tools also should increase productivity of internal audit engagements, allowing for less time spent documenting, retaining, and accessing supporting documentation.

Risk and Control Self-assessment

It should be clear at this point that internal audit functions assist an organization in assessing and mitigating risk in several ways. One way many internal audit functions do this is by establishing self-assessment teams and procedures. Typically, these teams partner with management to perform initial research and interviews to pinpoint potential risk events or scenarios facing an organization. They will assemble senior management representatives to discuss and prioritize these potential risks. The use of voting technology is becoming more widespread and can be a valuable tool in the prioritization of risk events by providing management with the opportunity to communicate their specific views of the impact and likelihood of a given risk while remaining anonymous. Often, this elicits more honest responses since individuals are not influenced by others in the meeting. Once the risk events are identified and prioritized, the internal audit function continues to assist management in identifying, documenting, evaluating, communicating, and mitigating the potential significance (that is, impact and likelihood) of the risks associated with key risk events identified. The use of technology (database repository and tracking tools) can be beneficial to the self-assessment teams, allowing them to assign the various scenarios to those individuals best equipped to manage and mitigate the specific risks causing concern for management. The repository can then be used to document and track action planning and risk mitigation efforts agreed upon with management. Without the use of modern technology, self-assessment efforts are cumbersome, inefficient, and very difficult to manage. Self-assessment can be used on a stand-alone basis to assist in evaluating risk in various areas or processes within an organization or as an effective tool in support of organization-wide risk assessment efforts.

Control Self-assessment

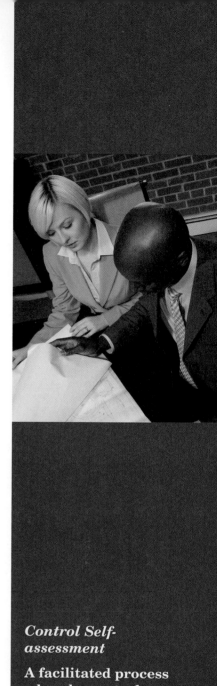

A facilitated process whereby control owners provide a self-assessment of the design adequacy and operating effectiveness of controls for which they are responsible.

On an administrative level, automated risk assessment tools can provide the internal audit function with a repository that allows for the identification, documentation, and prioritization of risks, what areas of the organization own these risks, and key controls designed to manage or mitigate these risks. These tools also document the audit universe, gather information about the different areas in that universe, and are used to evaluate the risks specific to those areas. Additionally, these tools help prioritize the amount of risk that a specific area brings to the organization, which drives how often it is audited. Consequently, the resulting prioritization of the audit universe drives the budget, scheduling, audit plan, and resource requirements as described earlier in the chapter.

Many organizations apply the same techniques described above to self-assess controls. In these situations, control and process owners perform techniques that help them assess the design adequacy and operating effectiveness of the controls within their areas of responsibility. Such techniques may include the use of technology, as described above, and be facilitated by the internal audit function.

Data Interrogation

Often there are large amounts of data that must be reviewed by the internal auditor. This can be very difficult and time consuming without the assistance of technology. Likewise, sampling might not be effective, practical, or preferred. Sampling also can, at times, limit the internal auditor's ability to draw definitive conclusions. In these cases, data interrogation tools can be invaluable because they allow for 100 percent testing, resulting in definitive results and conclusions. In addition, these tools also can be used as a feeder source for continuous monitoring and/or fraud detection and prevention efforts. For a more extensive discussion of computer-assisted audit techniques and sampling, refer to Chapter 10 "Audit Evidence and Working Papers," and Chapter 11, "Audit Sampling."

Automated Monitoring

Continuous Auditing

The use of computerized techniques to perpetually audit the processing of business transactions.

Automated monitoring tools, similar to data interrogation tools, allow the internal audit function to more efficiently perform continuous auditing by allowing internal auditors to monitor and evaluate large amounts of data (information) that otherwise might not be possible or practical. Continuous auditing, in contrast to periodic audit efforts, "is any method used by [the internal audit function] to perform audit-related activities on a more continuous or continual basis."[1] Continuous auditing activities often support or supplement the internal audit function's periodic audit, control assessment, and risk assessment processes. Automated monitoring tools also can enhance the internal audit function's ongoing management communication efforts by providing "near" real-time information about the effectiveness of management's continuous monitoring activities. The availability of timely information about the design adequacy and operating effectiveness of controls can be helpful to an internal audit function in reassessing priorities for planned assurance and consulting services, thus maximizing coverage of the internal audit universe. Automated monitoring tools can better equip an internal audit function to provide value-added services, while managing its human and financial resources in the most efficient manner possible.

Automated Working Papers

The use of automated working papers by an internal audit function enhances productivity by providing a more efficient medium to document, review, store, and access information supporting audit work performed (assurance and consulting services). Productivity enhancements allow more time to be spent doing audit work rather than documenting, storing, and retrieving information. Automated working papers also serve as a repository for evidencing compliance with professional standards and due professional care.

Department Administration and Management

Most of the activities required when managing an internal audit function, including staff evaluations, tracking of time and expenses, and scheduling of audit engagements, can now be done electronically. In fact, many, if not all, of these activities can be done within the same tools that support the automated working papers and risk assessment procedures. This allows for much more efficient management of the internal audit function. Generally, the more activities that can be done with one tool, the more efficient and cost effective it is to implement the tool. When it is not possible to choose a tool that does all of these activities, it is a good idea to choose tools that can easily interact (communicate). Many of the tools available today are cost effective enough to be viable for organizations of all sizes.

The Internet

In addition to the audit-specific tools mentioned above, the Internet can be an effective tool if used properly. It is an efficient way to do research, speeding up access to information that previously had to be retrieved through hard-copy format. An increasing number of internal audit functions use Internet links to enhance the planning and delivery of services and gain access to work programs, working papers, policies, procedures, and other audit tools and resources, which results in increased efficiency and productivity.

SUMMARY

This chapter presented the different philosophies regarding placement of the internal audit function within an organization and the drawbacks and benefits of each. The roles and responsibilities of the key positions within the internal audit function were identified and discussed. The policies and procedures of internal auditing were presented and how those policies and procedures guide the internal audit function was examined. Various risk management models were explored along with what role the internal audit function should take in the organization's risk management processes. Likewise, the internal audit function's responsibility regarding governance was addressed and examples of how those responsibilities can be carried out were provided. The quality assurance requirements, as stated by The IIA, were discussed and the importance of those requirements to the internal audit function was explained. The benefits of using technology, particularly as it relates to the management of the internal audit function, were discussed in detail. It should be clear that managing the internal audit function is a complex undertaking that requires a substantial amount of good judgment from the CAE. For that reason, it is imperative that the CAE use all of the tools available, including guidance from The IIA, and that the internal audit function be staffed with skilled, knowledgeable individuals at every level to assist the CAE in providing the organization with assurance and consulting services that add value and support senior management in the achievement of the organization's objectives.

Review Questions

1. What are the advantages of positioning the CAE on a senior management level within the organization?
2. According to the Interpretation of Standard 2000, the CAE has three specific responsibilities. What are they?
3. What are the differences between organizational independence and individual objectivity?
4. There are multiple approaches a CAE can use to create an annual internal audit plan. What are the advantages of using a top-down, risk-based approach?
5. What key elements are taken into consideration when determining how to manage resources in an internal audit function?
6. What is the difference between a flat organization structure and a hierarchical organization structure in an internal audit function and what are the advantages and disadvantages of each?
7. What are the different positions within a hierarchically structured internal audit function and what are their primary responsibilities?
8. When communicating the annual internal audit plan to senior management and the board, what are the specific items that the CAE should include in the communication?
9. What topics are discussed during coordination efforts between the internal audit function and the independent outside auditors?
10. What are the CAE's responsibilities when reporting to the audit committee?
11. What is the difference between risk mitigation and risk management?
12. According to The IIA, what are the five objectives of a risk management process?
13. The IIA states that the internal audit function can play an important role in improving the "ethical climate" of its organizational culture. What are the ways the internal audit function does this?
14. What are the CAE's and the internal audit function's responsibilities regarding governance?
15. What are the five key elements of a properly designed quality assurance and improvement program?
16. What are the seven areas discussed in this chapter that can be enhanced by the use of technology when managing an internal audit function?

Multiple-choice Questions

Select the best answer for each of the following questions.

1. Which of the following does not represent a key element of The IIA's quality assurance and improvement program?
   a. Implementing quality programs.
   b. Continuous improvement.
   c. Communicating results.
   d. Monitoring risk mitigation.

2. Senior management has requested that the internal audit function perform an operational review of the telephone marketing operations of a major division and recommend procedures and policies for improving management control over the operation. The internal audit function should:
   a. Accept the audit engagement because independence would not be impaired.
   b. Accept the engagement, but indicate to management that recommending controls would impair audit independence so that management knows that future audits of the area would be impaired.
   c. Not accept the engagement because internal audit functions are presumed to have expertise on accounting controls, not marketing controls.
   d. Not accept the engagement because recommending controls would impair future objectivity of the department regarding this client.

3. Who is ultimately responsible for determining that the objectives for an internal audit engagement have been met?
   a. The individual internal audit staff member.
   b. The CAE.
   c. The audit committee.
   d. The internal audit engagement supervisor.

4. Which of the following is the best reason for the CAE to consider the organization's strategic plan in developing the annual internal audit plan?
   a. To emphasize the importance of the internal audit function to the organization.
   b. To make recommendations to improve the strategic plan.
   c. To ensure that the internal audit plan supports the overall business objectives.
   d. To provide assurance that the strategic plan is consistent with the organization's values.

5. The *Standards* requires policies and procedures to guide the internal audit staff. Which of the following statements is false with respect to this requirement?
   a. A small internal audit function may be managed informally through close supervision and written memos.
   b. Formal administrative and technical audit manuals may not be needed by all internal audit functions.
   c. The CAE should establish the function's policies and procedures.
   d. All internal audit functions should have a detailed policies and procedures manual.

6. When conducting a consulting engagement to improve the efficiency and quality of a production process, the audit team is faced with a scope limitation because several months of the production data have been lost or are incomplete. Faced with this scope limitation, the CAE should:
   a. Resign from the consulting engagement and conduct an audit to determine why several months of data are not available.
   b. Discuss the problem with the customer and together evaluate whether the engagement should be continued.
   c. Increase the frequency of auditing the activity in question.
   d. Communicate the potential effects of the scope limitation to the audit committee.

7. Which of the following is not a responsibility of the CAE?
   a. To communicate the internal audit function's plans and resource requirements to senior management and the board for review and approval.
   b. To oversee the establishment, administration, and assessment of the organization's system of internal controls and risk management processes.
   c. To follow up on whether appropriate management actions have been taken on significant issues cited in internal audit reports.
   d. To establish a risk-based plan to accomplish the objectives of the internal audit function consistent with the organization's goals.

8. The *Standards* requires the CAE to share information and coordinate activities with other internal and external providers of assurance services. With regard to the independent outside auditor, which of the following would not be an appropriate way for the CAE to meet this requirement?
   a. Holding a meeting between the CAE and the independent outside audit firm's partner to discuss the upcoming audit of the financial statements.
   b. Providing the independent outside auditor with access to the working papers for an audit of third-party contractors.
   c. Requiring the independent outside auditor to have the CAE's approval of their annual audit plan for conducting the financial statement audit.
   d. Requesting that the internal audit function receive a copy of the independent outside auditor's management letter.

Discussion Questions

1. How do The IIA's quality assurance and improvement program professional standards (Standard 1300) apply to a fully outsourced internal audit function? Specifically discuss the applicability of, and compliance requirements with, the external assessment procedures (Standard 1312).

2. Discuss the various options for properly positioning an internal audit function within an organization and the related advantages and disadvantages for each identified option. What are the primary factors an organization should consider when establishing an effective internal audit function? Where should an effective internal audit function be positioned within an organization?

3. Should the CAE opine on the design adequacy and/or operating effectiveness of the system of internal controls regarding:
   - Reliability of financial reporting? Why or why not?
   - Effectiveness and efficiency of operations? Why or why not?
   - Compliance with applicable laws and regulations? Why or why not?

CASE

Pat Goodly accepted the CAE position at a large, global organization with a well-established internal audit function. The organization is admired as an industry leader and as having very strong corporate governance practices. The organization's board is predominantly made up of outside, independent directors. The audit committee is comprised of outside, independent directors, all of whom are qualified. The chair of the audit committee is designated as the audit committee's "financial expert."

The organization's fiscal year-end is approaching; only a little over a month away. After a brief two months in the new position, Pat is preparing for the upcoming audit committee meeting. This typically is the meeting at which next year's internal audit plan and budget would be presented for approval by the audit committee, as well as any necessary fiscal year-end reporting.

Recently, Pat received a "welcome" call from the audit committee chair, indicating "full" support for Pat and the internal audit function. The audit committee chair expressed an interest in meeting Pat and gaining an understanding of the vision and direction Pat has for the internal audit function going forward. The audit committee chair indicated that periodic communications between them were important and would allow for open and candid dialog in the future.

Pat was hired by, and currently reports to, the chief financial officer (CFO). Historically, the audit committee meeting agenda, and related topic selections for such, have been performed by the CFO. The CFO also has presided over the meetings in the past.

Senior management, including the CEO and the CFO, expressed support for the internal audit function and Pat's vision for the function both during the recruiting process and subsequent to Pat's joining the organization. However, the CFO firmly stated in a recent staff meeting, "I know everyone is very busy and things are going to get even more hectic with year-end upon us. I think it is in everyone's best interest not to make any 'radical' changes in our organizational reporting structure until we get through the fiscal year-end closing and reporting cycle. If we keep our heads down and work hard, we should be able to get through this year-end okay."

In preparation for the upcoming audit committee meeting, Pat contemplated the CFO's comments and reflected on The IIA's professional standards as they relate to the CAE's reporting responsibilities to management and the board. Put yourself in Pat's position as the newly hired CAE and consider the following:

A. How should Pat proceed with the audit committee chair? What obligations does Pat have, if any, to the audit committee chair? As the CAE, what are Pat's role and responsibilities with respect to the audit committee and the audit committee chair?

B. Discuss the key issues that must be understood and addressed (and with whom) to properly discharge any reporting responsibilities noted.

REFERENCES

[1] *Global Technology Audit Guide: Continuous Auditing: Implications for Assurance, Monitoring, and Risk Assessment* (Altamonte Springs, FL: The Institute of Internal Auditors, 2005), p. 7.

E
S
N
W

CHAPTER 10
AUDIT EVIDENCE AND WORKING PAPERS

Learning Objectives

- Understand what it means to gather and appropriately evaluate sufficient appropriate audit evidence.
- Know the manual procedures used by internal auditors to gather audit evidence.
- Be familiar with selected computer-assisted audit techniques, including generalized audit software.
- Understand the importance of well-prepared audit working papers.

In this chapter, we first focus on gathering and documenting audit evidence — a very significant component of all internal audit engagements. The quality of internal auditors' conclusions and advice depends on their ability to gather and appropriately evaluate sufficient appropriate audit evidence. Audit procedures are performed throughout the audit process to gather the evidence needed to achieve the prescribed engagement objectives. Engagement objectives are described and illustrated in Chapters 12 through 15, which we refer to collectively as the Internal Audit Processes chapters.

We then discuss audit working papers, which serve as the principal record of the procedures completed, evidence obtained, conclusions reached, and recommendations formulated by the internal auditors assigned to an engagement (that is, the internal audit team). The working papers also serve as the primary support for the internal audit team's communications to the auditee, senior management, the board of directors, and other stakeholders.

AUDIT EVIDENCE

Recall from Chapter 1, "Introduction to Internal Auditing," that internal auditing is based on logic, which involves reasoning and drawing inferences. Internal auditors rely extensively on seasoned, professional judgment when they formulate conclusions and advice based on evidence they gather and evaluate. The quality of internal auditors' conclusions and advice depends on their ability to gather and evaluate sufficient appropriate evidence upon which their conclusions and advice are based.

Gathering sufficient appropriate evidence requires extensive interaction and communication with auditee personnel throughout the engagement. Such interactions and communications are critical to conducting the engagement effectively and efficiently. It is important, therefore, for internal auditors to be open, communicative, and collaborative. The internal auditor must always be

EXHIBIT 10-1

PROFESSIONAL STANDARDS AND PRACTICE ADVISORIES RELEVANT TO CHAPTER 10

1220 – Due Professional Care
2200 – Engagement Planning
2240 – Engagement Work Program
2300 – Performing the Engagement
2310 – Identifying Information
2320 – Analysis and Evaluation
2330 – Documenting Information

Practice Advisory 2240-1: Engagement Work Program
Practice Advisory 2330-1: Documenting Information
Practice Advisory 2330.A1-1: Control of Engagement Records
Practice Advisory 2330.A2-1: Retention of Records

mindful, however, that the managers and employees from whom evidence is gathered may not adequately understand the purpose, objectives, and scope of the engagement, or the manner in which the engagement is conducted. Moreover, some managers or employees may see the engagement as a threat to them — in other words, think that the internal auditors are specifically looking for things they have done wrong. Unfortunately, the threat of management and/or employee errors and fraud always exists.

Professional Skepticism

The state of mind in which internal auditors take nothing for granted; they continuously question what they hear and see and critically assess audit evidence.

Professional Skepticism and Reasonable Assurance

The internal auditor must always remember to apply a healthy level of professional skepticism when evaluating audit evidence. *Professional skepticism* means that internal auditors take nothing for granted; they continuously question what they hear and see and critically assess audit evidence. They do not assume by default that auditee personnel are either honest or dishonest. Applying professional skepticism throughout the engagement helps internal auditors remain unbiased and maintain an open mind to form judgments based on the preponderance of evidence gained during an engagement, and not just individual pieces of information. Professional skepticism is discussed in the context of fraud in Chapter 8, "Fraud Risks and Controls."

Reasonable Assurance

A level of assurance that is supported by generally accepted auditing procedures and judgments.

Internal auditors are rarely, if ever, in a position to provide absolute assurance regarding the truthfulness of management's assertions regarding the system of internal controls and performance. Even experienced internal auditors are rarely convinced beyond all doubt. This is due to the nature and extent of evidence they gather and the types of decisions they make. Frequently, internal auditors must rely on evidence that is persuasive rather than absolutely convincing, and audit decisions are rarely black and white. Moreover, internal auditors' conclusions and advice must be formed at a reasonable cost within a reasonable length of time to add economic value. Accordingly, internal auditors strive to obtain sufficient appropriate evidence to provide a reasonable basis for formulating their conclusions and advice. This concept is referred to by internal auditors as *reasonable assurance*.

Persuasiveness of Audit Evidence

Audit evidence is persuasive if it enables the internal auditor to formulate well-founded conclusions and advice confidently. To be persuasive, evidence must be:

- **Relevant.** Is the evidence pertinent to the audit objective? Does it logically support the internal auditor's conclusion or advice?
- **Reliable.** Did the evidence come from a credible source? Did the internal auditor directly obtain the evidence?
- **Sufficient.** Has the internal auditor obtained enough evidence? Do different, but related, pieces of evidence corroborate each other?

Persuasive Audit Evidence

Enables the internal auditor to formulate well-founded conclusions and advice confidently.

The American Institute of Certified Public Accountants (AICPA) states that "*Appropriateness* is the measure of the quality of audit evidence, that is, its relevance and reliability . . ." and that "*Sufficiency* is the measure of the quantity of audit evidence."[1] Why audit evidence must be relevant to be persuasive is clear: Relying on evidence that has little or no pertinence to a specific audit objective greatly increases *audit risk*, that is, the risk of reaching invalid conclusions and/or providing faulty advice based on the audit work conducted.

Audit Risk

The risk of reaching invalid audit conclusions and/ or providing faulty advice based on the audit work conducted.

> Example: Assume that an internal auditor wants to determine whether a particular vehicle included in the company's fixed asset ledger exists and is owned by the company. The internal auditor locates the vehicle in the company's parking lot. Can the internal auditor reasonably conclude that the vehicle exists just by seeing it? Yes. Can the internal auditor reasonably conclude that the company owns the vehicle just by seeing it? No. The internal auditor would need to inspect pertinent documentary evidence, such as a title of ownership.

Although there are no hard and fast rules regarding reliability and sufficiency of evidence, there are useful guidelines internal auditors can follow if they remember that guidelines are generally characterized by exceptions. Such guidelines include:

- Evidence obtained from independent third parties is *more reliable* than evidence obtained from auditee personnel.
- Evidence produced by a process or system with effective controls is *more reliable* than evidence produced by a process or system with ineffective controls.
- Evidence obtained directly by the internal auditor is *more reliable* than evidence obtained indirectly.
- Documented evidence is *more reliable* than undocumented evidence.
- Timely evidence is *more reliable* than untimely evidence.
- Corroborated evidence is *more sufficient* than uncorroborated or contradictory evidence.
- Larger sample sizes produce *more sufficient* evidence than smaller samples.

Documentary evidence is a significant portion of the evidence gathered during most internal audit engagements. The reliability of documentary evidence depends, to a large extent, on its origin and the route it follows before being examined by the internal auditor. Exhibit 10-2 illustrates this point.

EXHIBIT 10-2

RELIABILITY OF DOCUMENTARY EVIDENCE

Levels of Reliability	Descriptions	Example Documents
High	Documents prepared by the internal auditor	Inventory test counts Process maps Risk and control matrices
	Documents sent directly from a third party to the internal auditor	Confirmations Cutoff bank statements Letters from outside attorneys
Medium	Documents created by a third party, sent to the organization, and requested from the organization by the internal auditor	Vendor invoices Customer purchase orders Bank statements
	Documents created by the organization, sent to a third party, returned to the organization, and requested from the organization by the internal auditor	Remittance advices Canceled checks Deposit slips
Low	Documents created by the organization and requested from the organization by the internal auditor	Written policy statements Receiving reports Time cards

Audit Procedures

Specific tasks performed by the internal auditor to gather the evidence required to achieve the prescribed audit objectives.

AUDIT PROCEDURES

Audit procedures are specific tasks performed by the internal auditor to gather the evidence required to achieve the prescribed audit objectives. They are applied during the audit process to:

- Obtain a thorough understanding of the auditee, including the auditee's objectives, risks, and controls.
- Test the design adequacy and operating effectiveness of the targeted area's system of internal controls.
- Analyze plausible relationships among different elements of data.
- Directly test recorded financial and nonfinancial information for errors and fraud.

Obtaining sufficient appropriate evidence to achieve the prescribed audit objectives involves determining the nature, extent, and timing of audit procedures to perform.

Nature of audit procedures. The nature of audit procedures relates to the types of tests the internal auditor performs to achieve his or her objectives. One-to-one relationships between audit objectives and audit procedures are rare. Individual audit procedures often provide evidence that is pertinent to more than one audit objective, and more than one audit procedure often is required to meet a particular audit objective. Different types of tests provide varying levels of assurance, take different amounts of time to conduct, and are more or less expensive. The internal auditor must weigh the relative benefits and costs of conducting different types of procedures. Depending on the nature of the engagement, an internal auditor may use manual audit procedures, computer-assisted audit techniques (CAATs), or a combination of the two to gather sufficient appropriate evidence. Manual audit procedures and CAATs are discussed further in subsequent sections of this chapter.

Extent of audit procedures. The extent of audit procedures pertains to how much audit evidence the internal auditor must obtain to achieve his or her objectives. An internal auditor must, for example, determine the appropriate combination of procedures to apply. The degree to which individual tests are to be conducted also must be determined. The internal auditor might decide, for example, that some types of transactions should be tested 100 percent, whereas others may be tested on a sample basis. Audit sampling is discussed in detail in Chapter 11, "Audit Sampling." Ultimately, the internal auditor must gather and evaluate enough evidence to support well-founded conclusions and advice.

Timing of audit procedures. The timing of audit procedures pertains to when the tests are conducted and the period of time covered by the tests. For example:

- An internal auditor testing the operating effectiveness of a manual control over a period of time on a sample basis must take appropriate steps to gain assurance that the sample selected is representative of the entire period.
- An internal auditor testing whether transactions are recorded in the appropriate fiscal year will focus his or her tests on transactions immediately before and after year-end.
- An internal auditor will test the operation of a computerized application control at a given time to determine whether the control is operating effectively at that time. The internal auditor will then rely on different tests, such as tests over access and modification of application programs during a period of time, to gain assurance that the control operated consistently over that period of time.

Manual Audit Procedures

Commonly performed manual audit procedures include inquiry, observation, inspection, vouching, tracing, reperformance, analytical procedures, and confirmation. Each of these procedures is defined and discussed below. Example applications of each procedure are presented in Exhibit 10-3.

Inquiry entails asking questions of auditee personnel or third parties and obtaining their oral or written responses. Inquiry produces indirect evidence, which by itself is rarely persuasive. This is especially true when inquiries are directed to auditee personnel from whom the internal auditor cannot count on receiving unbiased responses. More formal types of inquiry include interviews and circulating surveys and questionnaires. Key components of effective interviewing are outlined in Exhibit 10-4.

Observation entails watching people, procedures, or processes. Observation is generally considered more persuasive than inquiry in the sense that the internal auditor is obtaining direct evidence. For example, the internal auditor's direct personal observation of an employee applying a control generally provides more assurance than simply asking the employee about the application of the control. A significant limitation of observation is that it provides evidence at a certain time. The internal auditor typically cannot conclude that what is observed is representative of what happened throughout the year, especially given the propensity of people to behave differently when they know they are being watched.

EXHIBIT 10-3

ILLUSTRATIVE APPLICATIONS OF MANUAL AUDIT PROCEDURES

Procedures	Illustrative Applications
Inquiry	• Circulate a questionnaire among senior executives asking them to identify the "top 10" risks threatening the organization. • Ask the organization's outside legal counsel to provide information about any litigation, claims, and/or assessments against the organization. • Interview managers and employees involved in the cash disbursements process to identify key process controls.
Observation	• Tour the auditee's facility to gain a general understanding of day-to-day operations. • Observe the care with which employees count the year-end physical inventory. • Watch employees involved in executing and recording cash disbursement transactions to determine whether they are performing their assigned responsibilities and only their assigned responsibilities.
Inspection	• Review the minutes of board of directors' meetings looking for authorization of significant events, for example, the acquisition of another company. • Inspect selected inventory items to determine their condition and salability. • Read the cash disbursements policies and procedures to obtain an understanding of key elements of the process, for example, assigned roles and responsibilities.
Vouching	• Vouch a sample of inventory items from the accounting records to the warehouse to see that the inventory items exist. • Vouch a sample of sales invoices to corresponding shipping documents to verify that the shipments occurred. • Vouch a sample of check copies to supporting voucher packages to test the validity of the checks.
Tracing	• Trace internal auditor test counts of inventory to the auditee's inventory compilation records to verify that the counts are properly included in the compilation. • Trace receiving reports for goods received to the corresponding voucher and then to the voucher register to verify that the receipts of goods are properly recorded as liabilities. • Trace checks dated within a period of several days before and after year-end to the accounting records to ensure the checks were recorded in the proper year.
Reperformance	• Recalculate accumulated depreciation and depreciation expense to verify that they were calculated correctly. • Independently estimate the allowance for doubtful accounts to test the reasonableness of the accounting department's estimate. • Reperform auditee-prepared bank reconciliations to test whether they were completed correctly.
Analytical procedures	• Prepare common-size financial statements for the current year and preceding two years; look specifically for variances or unexpected trends. • Compare the organization's common-size financial statements with published industry common-size information looking for unexpected inconsistencies. • Calculate accounts payable turnover for the current year and preceding two years as evidence of vendor payment periods.
Confirmation	• Confirm a sample of accounts receivable subsidiary ledger balances with customers. • Confirm the principal balance of a notes payable and interest rate with the lender. • Confirm cash account bank balances with banks.

KEY COMPONENTS OF EFFECTIVE INTERVIEWING

EXHIBIT 10-4

Interviewing objectives:

- Gather information (that is, audit evidence) relevant to the engagement.
- Establish a rapport that fosters a positive working relationship throughout the engagement.

The interviewing process:

Prepare for the interview.

- Define the purpose.
- Identify the appropriate interviewee.
- Gather background information about the audit area and interviewee.
- Create the right set of questions (what, why, how, where, when, who).
- Establish expectations with the interviewee and identify information needs.
- Arrange logistics (date, time, location, length).
- Prepare an outline.

Conduct the interview.

- Establish rapport and create an atmosphere that encourages openness.
- Review the purpose of the interview, the topics to be covered, and the estimated time needed.
- Ask straightforward questions and meaningful follow-up questions.
- Avoid technical jargon.
- Use periods of silence effectively.
- Listen.
- Summarize and confirm key points.
- Discuss next steps.
- Arrange follow-up contact.
- Thank the interviewee.

Document the interview outcomes (as soon as possible after the interview).

- Reflect on the interview and review notes.
- Record the results of the interview in good form.

Characteristics common among effective interviewers:

- Professionalism (for example, prepared, respectful, courteous, on time).
- Outstanding interpersonal and oral communication skills, including listening skills.
- The capacity to display confidence and command respect without being arrogant.
- An innate curiosity.
- Objectivity (that is, remain impartial and refrain from interjecting personal opinions).

Common barriers to effective interviews:

- Auditee impediments such as competing demands on time, preconceived notions about internal auditors, and fear of reprisal.
- Flaws in the interview process.
- Lack of requisite competencies on the part of the internal auditor.

Critical success factors:

- Be prepared.
- Know and respect the interviewee.
- Establish credibility and trust.
- Speak the interviewee's language.
- Expect the unexpected.

Inspection entails studying documents and records and physically examining tangible resources. Inspection of documents and records provides direct evidence of their contents. Likewise, physical examination of tangible resources (for example, a building or piece of equipment) provides the internal auditor with direct personal knowledge of the resources' existence and physical condition. Internal auditors must, however, acknowledge and take into account their level of expertise (that is, their capacity to comprehend what they read and see). For example, formulating valid conclusions about the value of precious gems based on inspection may be outside the scope of the internal auditor's expertise. The internal auditor might, in this case, need to rely on the assistance of a precious gems expert to help validate the gems' value.

Vouching

Tracking information *backward* from one document or record to a previously prepared document or record, or to a tangible resource.

Vouching entails tracking information *backward* from one document or record to a previously prepared document or record, or to a tangible resource. Vouching is performed specifically to test the *validity* of documented or recorded information. For example, a sale of goods typically should not be recorded unless the goods have been shipped. Vouching a sales invoice to a shipping document provides evidence that the shipment upon which the invoice is based actually occurred. Likewise, vouching the recording of a vehicle in the fixed asset ledger to the actual vehicle provides evidence that the vehicle really exists. Within the context of financial audits, vouching is used to test for overstatements in recorded amounts.

Tracing

Tracking information *forward* from one document, record, or tangible resource to a subsequently prepared document or record.

Tracing entails tracking information *forward* from one document, record, or tangible resource, to a subsequently prepared document or record. Tracing is performed specifically to test the *completeness* of documented or recorded information. For example, purchases of goods typically should be recorded when the goods are received. Tracing a receiving report for goods received near the end of the year to the accounting records provides evidence that both the asset and liability were recorded in the same year the goods were received. Within the context of financial audits, tracing is used to test for understatements in recorded amounts.

Reperformance entails redoing controls or other procedures. Reperforming a control provides direct audit evidence regarding its operating effectiveness. Reperforming calculations provides direct evidence as to whether the auditee's calculations are correct. Independently formulating an accounting estimate, such as the allowance for bad debts, and comparing it with the auditee's estimate provides direct evidence regarding the reasonableness of the auditee's estimate.

Analytical Procedures

Assessing information obtained during an engagement by comparing the information with expectations identified or developed by the internal auditor.

Analytical procedures entail assessing information obtained during an engagement by comparing the information with expectations identified or developed by the internal auditor. A basic premise underlying the use of analytical procedures in internal auditing is that the internal auditor may reasonably expect certain relationships among different pieces of information to continue in the absence of known conditions to the contrary. It is important for internal auditors to develop expectations independently based on knowledge of the auditee, the organization's industry, and economy before accumulating and analyzing information to ensure that the ensuing comparisons are unbiased.

Internal auditors use analytical procedures while planning and performing an engagement to identify anomalies in information such as unexpected fluctuations, differences, and correlations as well as the absence of expected fluctuations, differences, and correlations. Such anomalies may be indicative of unusual or nonrecurring transactions or events, errors, or fraudulent activities that warrant further attention and the gathering of corroborative audit evidence. Common analytical procedures performed by internal auditors include:

- **Analysis of common-size financial statements.** The internal auditor expresses financial statement line items as percentages of relevant totals (for example, income statement items are expressed as percentages of sales, and balance sheet items are expressed as percentages of total assets).
- **Ratio analysis.** The internal auditor calculates pertinent financial ratios (for example, current ratio, gross profit percentage, inventory turnover, and cost of raw materials purchased divided by cost of finished goods produced) and ratios involving nonfinancial values (for example, sales divided by square footage of sales space, payroll expense divided by average number of employees, and percentage of defective units produced). Illustrative process performance ratios are presented in Exhibit 10-5. It is important, however, to realize that the only true constraints on working with ratios are the availability of the necessary information to calculate the ratios and the internal auditor's creativity.
- **Trend analysis.** The internal auditor compares performance information (for example, individual amounts, common-size percentages, and/or ratios) for the current fiscal period with like information for one or more prior periods.
- **Analysis of future-oriented information.** The internal auditor compares current fiscal period information with budgets or forecasts.
- **External benchmarking.** The internal auditor compares performance information for the organization with like information of other individual organizations or the industry in which the organization operates. Published industry data for specific industries is available for comparison purposes from sources such as Dun & Bradstreet and Standard & Poor's.
- **Internal benchmarking.** The internal auditor compares performance information of one organizational unit with like information for other organizational units.

Confirmation entails obtaining direct written verification of the accuracy of information from independent third parties. Evidence obtained via confirmation generally is considered very reliable because it comes to the internal auditor directly from independent sources. There are two common types of confirmation requests: *positive confirmations* ask recipients to respond regardless of whether or not they believe the information provided to them is correct, and *negative confirmations* ask recipients to respond only when they believe the information provided to them is incorrect. A positive confirmation may ask the recipient to provide the information of interest (referred to as a blank confirmation) or include the information of interest and ask the recipient to indicate agreement or disagreement with the information.

Computer-assisted Audit Techniques

"In exercising due professional care internal auditors must consider the use of technology-based audit and other data analysis techniques." (Standard 1220.A2)

ISACA (formerly known as the Information Systems Audit and Control Association) defines a technology-based audit technique, or computer-

External Benchmarking

Comparing performance information for the organization with like information of other individual organizations or the industry in which the organization operates.

Internal Benchmarking

Comparing performance information of one organizational unit with like information for other organizational units.

EXHIBIT 10-5

ILLUSTRATIVE PROCESS PERFORMANCE RATIOS

Sales, Accounts Receivable, and Cash Receipts:

Net Sales ÷ Average or Year-end Net Accounts Receivable (Accounts Receivable Turnover)

365 ÷ Accounts Receivable Turnover (Average Days to Collect)

Net Sales ÷ Square Footage of Sales Space

On-time Deliveries to Customers ÷ Total Deliveries to Customers

Bad Debt Expense ÷ Net Sales

Year-end Allowance for Bad Debts ÷ Year-end Accounts Receivable

Purchases, Accounts Payable, and Cash Disbursements:

Raw Materials Purchased ÷ Cost of Finished Goods Produced

On-time Deliveries from Suppliers ÷ Total Deliveries from Supplies

Purchase Returns ÷ Total Purchases or Cost of Goods Sold

Cost of Goods Sold or Net Purchases ÷ Average or Year-end Accounts Payable (Accounts Payable Turnover)

Inventory and Cost of Goods Sold:

Cost of Goods Sold ÷ Average or Year-end Inventory (Inventory Turnover)

365 ÷ Inventory Turnover (Average Days to Sell)

Number of Defective Units Produced ÷ Total Units Produced

Cost or Scrap/Waste/Spoilage ÷ Net Sales or Cost of Goods Sold

Gross Profit ÷ Net Sales (Gross Profit Percentage)

Human Resources and Payroll:

Number of Employees Leaving Voluntarily and/or Involuntarily During the Year ÷ Average or Year-end Number of Employees (Employee Turnover)

Man Days Lost to Absenteeism ÷ Total Man Days

Number of Overtime Hours Worked ÷ Total Hours Worked

Payroll Expense ÷ Average or Year-end Number of Employees

Generalized Audit Software (GAS)

Multipurpose software that can be used for audit purposes such as record selection, matching, recalculation, and reporting.

assisted audit technique (CAAT), as "any automated audit technique, such as generalized audit software, test data generators, computerized audit programs and specialized audit systems." Some of the more common CAATs are defined by ISACA as follows:

> *Generalized audit software* (GAS) is "multipurpose software that can be used for [general purposes] such as record selection, matching, recalculation and reporting."
>
> *Utility software* is comprised of "computer programs provided by a computer hardware manufacturer or software vendor and used in running the system . . . This technique can be used to examine processing activities; to test programs, system activities, and operational procedures; to evaluate data file activity; and, to analyze job accounting data."
>
> *Test data* are "simulated transactions that can be used to test processing logic, computations and controls actually programmed in computer applications. Individual programs or an entire system can be tested . . . This technique includes integrated test facilities (ITFs) and base case system evaluations (BCSEs)."

Application software tracing and mapping are "specialized tools that can be used to analyze the flow of data, through the processing logic of the application software, and document the logic, paths, control conditions and processing sequences . . . Both the command language or job control statements and programming language can be analyzed. This technique includes program/system: mapping, tracing, snapshots, parallel simulations and code comparisons."

Audit expert systems are "expert or decision support systems that can be used to assist IS [information systems] auditors in the decision-making process by automating the knowledge of experts in the field . . . This technique includes automated risk analysis, system software and control objectives software packages."

Continuous auditing "allows IS auditors to monitor system reliability on a continuous basis and to gather selective audit evidence through the computer."[2]

Continuous Auditing

Using computerized techniques to perpetually audit the processing of business transactions.

These definitions indicate that internal auditors can use CAATs to directly test (1) controls built into computerized information systems and (2) data contained in computer files. It should be noted that, by directly testing data contained in computer files, internal auditors obtain indirect evidence about the effectiveness of the controls in the application that processed the data.

Example: An internal auditor uses generalized audit software to directly test whether any duplicate payments of invoices exist in the company's cash disbursements transaction file. The internal auditor uncovers several duplicate payments made throughout the year. The internal auditor may correctly infer that controls to prevent and/or detect such payments on a timely basis did not exist, were designed inadequately, or did not operate effectively.

An in-depth discussion of each type of CAAT defined above is beyond the scope of this textbook. However, GAS and the types of data analyses internal auditors can perform with GAS warrant a bit more attention.

Some internal auditors continue to harbor the belief that GAS is a tool to be used only by information technology (IT) audit specialists. This is no longer true because GAS has advanced to the stage where it is relatively easy to use, even by internal auditors with little audit-related IT training. It combines a user-friendly interface with powerful audit functionality and allows internal auditors to extract electronically stored auditee data and perform various operations on the data. Such operations include:

- Examining files and records for validity, completeness, and accuracy.
- Recalculating recorded values and calculating other values of audit interest.
- Selecting and printing samples and calculating sample results.
- Comparing information in separate files.
- Summarizing, resequencing, and reformatting data.
- Creating pivot tables for multidimensional analysis.
- Searching for anomalies in data that may indicate errors or fraud.
- Preparing and printing reports.
- Automatically generating a historical log of data analyses performed.

Benefits of using GAS. There are many benefits of using GAS:

- It allows internal auditors to conduct audit procedures in a wide variety of hardware and software environments with minimal customization.
- It enables internal auditors to perform tests on data independently of the company's IT personnel.
- Using GAS enables the internal auditor to deftly analyze very large quantities of data.
- Some applications of GAS facilitate 100 percent examination of data populations almost instantaneously as opposed to testing a sample of data items manually.
- Using GAS to perform necessary but routine audit tasks frees up time for the internal auditor to think analytically.

Obstacles to implementing GAS successfully. There are also legitimate obstacles that an internal auditor must overcome to implement GAS successfully:

- Obtaining access privileges to relevant and reliable data.
- Gaining physical access to the data.
- Understanding how the data is stored and formatted in the system.
- Extracting the data and downloading it to the internal auditor's personal computer (PC).
- Importing the data in a usable format into the software.

Overcoming these obstacles might, in some cases, require the assistance of an IT audit expert. However, the only "show-stopper" limitations of adding value by using GAS are the availability of relevant data in electronic format and the internal auditor's ingenuity.

ACL and IDEA

The two most widely used, commercially available, audit software programs.

ACL and IDEA software. The two most widely used, commercially available audit software programs, ACL (Audit Command Language) and IDEA (originally an acronym for Interactive Data Extraction and Analysis), accompany this textbook. Both ACL and IDEA are Windows-based and can be operated easily on the internal auditor's PC.

The ACL software is a product of ACL Services Ltd. Interested readers can learn more about ACL Services by visiting the company's website at www.acl.com. The CD-ROM accompanying this textbook contains the following materials relevant to ACL in addition to the software itself:

- Getting Started manual.
- ACL in Practice manual.
- Data Access Guide.
- ACL Help.

The ACL in Practice manual contains an extensive tutorial involving a hypothetical company and real-world data, which provides a good introduction to ACL's analysis and reporting capabilities.

The IDEA software is a product of CaseWare IDEA Inc., a privately held software development and marketing company. Audimation Services Inc., which is referred to on the front of the IDEA CD-ROM, is the U.S. business partner with CaseWare IDEA Inc. Interested readers can learn more about these companies and IDEA by visiting their websites: www.CaseWare-IDEA.com and www.audimation.com. The CD-ROM accompanying this textbook also contains the following materials relevant to IDEA in addition to the software itself:

- Installation Guide.
- IDEA Tutorial.
- Report Reader Tutorial.
- IDEA Help.
- Case Study for IDEA Version Eight.
- IDEA Advanced Statistical Methods Case Study.

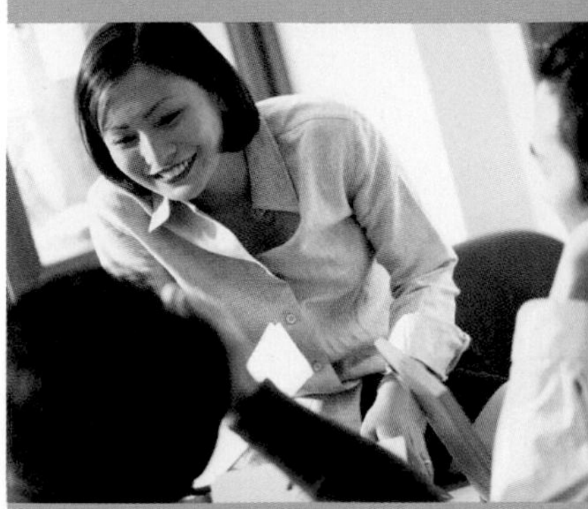

The Getting Started Tutorial in Section Four of the IDEA Tutorial, which can be completed by using the sample data files contained on the CD-ROM, provides a good introduction to IDEA's functionality. The Case Study for IDEA Version Eight and the IDEA Advanced Statistical Methods Case Study can be used for supplemental practice with the software.

WORKING PAPERS

IIA Standard 2330: Documenting Information requires internal auditors to record the evidence they accumulate as support for engagement outcomes. Practice Advisory 2330-1: Documenting Information provides guidance regarding working papers and their preparation.

Purposes and Content of Working Papers

Because of the many purposes working papers serve, it is difficult to overstate their importance. For example, working papers:

- Aid in planning and performing the engagement.
- Facilitate supervision of the engagement and review of the work completed.
- Indicate whether engagement objectives were achieved.
- Provide the principal support for the internal auditors' communications to the auditee, senior management, the board of directors, and appropriate third parties.
- Serve as a basis for evaluating the internal audit function's quality assurance program.
- Contribute to the professional development of the internal audit staff.
- Demonstrate the internal audit function's compliance with The IIA's *International Standards for the Professional Practice of Internal Auditing* (*Standards*).

The content of internal audit engagement working papers will depend on the nature of the engagement. They should always, however, provide complete, accurate, and concise documentation of the engagement process.

Types of Working Papers

A wide variety of working papers are prepared during an internal audit engagement. The following list is intended to be illustrative rather than all-inclusive:

- Work programs used to document the nature, extent, and timing of the specific audit procedures.
- Engagement time budgets and resource allocation worksheets.
- Questionnaires used to obtain information about the auditee, including its objectives, risks, controls, operating activities, etc.
- Process maps or flowcharts used to document process activities, risks, and controls. (Common process mapping symbols and illustrative process maps are presented in Chapter 5, "Business Processes and Risks." Common flowcharting symbols and illustrative flowcharts are presented in Chapter 13, "Conducting the Assurance Engagement.")
- Charts, graphs, and diagrams, such as a risk map used to plot the impact and likelihood of business risks (an illustrative risk map is presented in Chapter 13).
- Agendas for internal audit team meetings and meetings with the auditee.
- Narrative memoranda used to document the results of interviews and other meetings with auditees.
- Pertinent auditee organizational information, such as organization charts, job descriptions, and operating and financial policies and procedures.
- Copies of source documents, such as purchase requisitions, purchase orders, receiving reports, vendor invoices, vouchers, and checks.
- Copies of other important documents, such as minutes of meetings and contracts.
- IT-related documents, such as program listings and exception reports.
- Accounting records, such as trial balances and excerpts from journals and ledgers.
- Evidence obtained from third parties, such as confirmation responses from customers and representations from outside legal counsel.
- Worksheets prepared by the internal auditor, such as a risk and control matrix used to document process-level risks, key control descriptions, the internal auditor's evaluation of control design adequacy, the tests of controls performed, and the test results. (An illustrative risk and control matrix is presented in Chapter 13.)
- Other types of working papers prepared by the internal auditor that reflect work performed (for example, analytical procedures, computerized data analysis, and direct tests of transactions, events, account balances, and performance measurements).
- Evidence compiled by the auditee and tested by the internal auditor.
- Controls performed by the auditee and reperformed by the internal auditor (for example, bank reconciliations).
- Written correspondence and documentation of oral correspondence with the auditee during the engagement.
- The internal audit team's write-ups of observations, recommendations, and conclusions. (Illustrative write-ups are discussed in Chapter 13.)

- Final engagement communications and management's responses. (Illustrative audit communications are presented in Chapter 14, "Communicating Assurance Engagement Outcomes and Performing Follow-up Procedures.")

Guidelines for Working Paper Preparation

The chief audit executive (CAE) is responsible for establishing working paper policies and procedures. Well-written policies and procedures promote effective and efficient work and facilitate consistent adherence to quality assurance standards.

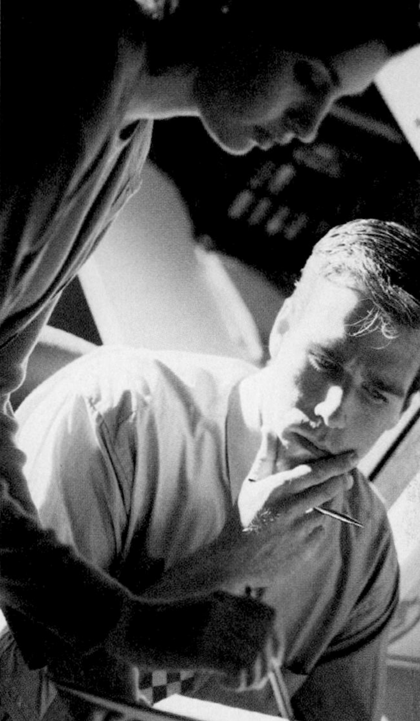

Standardized working paper formats help to streamline the audit process and facilitate consistent, high-quality work across engagements. Care should be taken, however, not to standardize working papers so rigidly that they inhibit internal auditor ingenuity and creativity. Appropriate working paper standardization may include:

- A uniform cross-referencing system for all engagements.
- Consistent working paper layouts.
- Standardized "tick marks" (that is, symbols used on working papers to represent specific audit procedures).
- A prescription for the types of information to store in permanent or carry-forward files (that is, files containing pertinent information of continuing importance for a particular auditee).

Working paper files should be complete and well-organized. At the end of an engagement, the files should be cleared out so they contain only the final versions of the working papers completed during the engagement. Each individual working paper should stand on its own merits. This means, for example, that each working paper should:

- Contain an appropriate index or reference number.
- Identify the engagement and describe the purpose or contents of the working paper.
- Be signed (or initialed) and dated by both the internal auditor who performed the work and the internal auditor(s) who reviewed the work. (Note that such a signature may be electronic.)
- Clearly identify the sources of auditee data included on the working paper.
- Include clear explanations of the specific procedures performed.
- Be clearly written and easy to understand by internal auditors unfamiliar with the work performed (for example, an internal auditor who refers to the working paper at a later date).

The bottom line is that the working paper should contain sufficient information for an internal auditor, other than the one who performed the work, to be able to reperform it. On the other hand, working papers should not contain more information than is necessary; they should be as concise as possible.

Moreover, because time is a precious audit resource, internal auditors must always strive to prepare working papers the right way the first time. There is no time allocated for rewriting them. The vital need for working papers to be prepared correctly, clearly, concisely, and quickly is

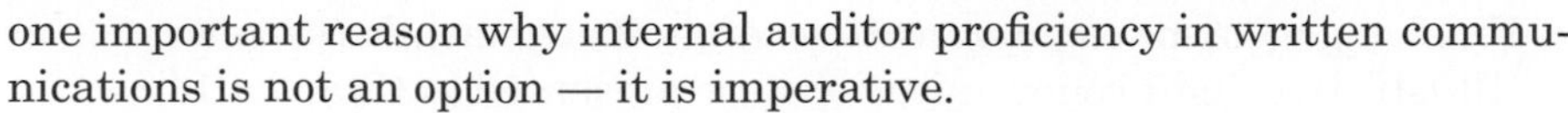

one important reason why internal auditor proficiency in written communications is not an option — it is imperative.

Working papers may be prepared in paper form, electronic form, or both. Automated working paper software, whether purchased from outside vendors or developed in-house, is becoming prevalent. This software increases efficiency and facilitates consistent organization and retention of documentation supporting an internal audit engagement. When fully integrated software is not used, special care must be taken to maintain version control over electronic working papers and to ensure that they are appropriately backed up.

SUMMARY

This chapter focused on gathering and documenting audit evidence. The chapter began with a discussion of audit evidence and the procedures, both manual procedures and computer-assisted audit techniques, that internal auditors use to gather sufficient appropriate evidence. The chapter concluded with a discussion of working papers, which serve as the principal record of the procedures completed, evidence obtained, conclusions reached, and recommendations formulated by the internal audit team during the engagement.

Review Questions

1. What does "professional skepticism" mean?
2. What does "reasonable assurance" mean? Why do internal auditors provide reasonable assurance rather than absolute assurance?
3. What are the defining characteristics of persuasive audit evidence?
4. What is the relationship between audit objectives and audit procedures?
5. What do internal auditors mean when they refer to the nature, extent, and timing of audit procedures?
6. What are some common characteristics of effective interviewers?
7. What is the difference between vouching and tracing?
8. What types of analytical procedures are used by internal auditors?
9. What are some common types of computer-assisted audit techniques?
10. What types of operations can internal auditors perform with generalized audit software?
11. What are the two most widely used, commercially available audit software programs?
12. What are the purposes of internal audit working papers?
13. What are the key characteristics of well-prepared working papers?

Multiple-choice Questions

Select the best answer for each of the following questions.

1. Professional skepticism means that internal auditors beginning an assurance engagement should:
   a. Assume client personnel are dishonest until they gather evidence that clearly indicates otherwise.
   b. Assume client personnel are honest until they gather evidence that clearly indicates otherwise.
   c. Neither assume client personnel are honest nor assume they are dishonest.
   d. Assume that internal controls are designed inadequately and/or operating ineffectively.

2. Which of the following statements regarding audit evidence would be the least appropriate for an internal auditor to make?
   a. "I consider the level of risk involved when deciding the kind of evidence I will gather."
   b. "I do not perform procedures that provide persuasive evidence because I must obtain convincing evidence."
   c. "I evaluate both the usefulness of the evidence I can obtain and the cost to obtain it."
   d. "I am seldom absolutely certain about the conclusions I reach based on the evidence I examine."

3. Audit evidence is generally considered sufficient when:
   a. It is appropriate.
   b. There is enough of it to support well-founded conclusions.
   c. It is relevant, reliable, and free from bias.
   d. It has been obtained via random sampling.

4. Documentary evidence is one of the principal types of corroborating information used by an internal auditor. Which one of the following examples of documentary evidence generally is considered the most reliable?
   a. A vendor's invoice obtained from the accounts payable department.
   b. A credit memorandum prepared by the credit manager.
   c. A receiving report obtained from the receiving department.
   d. A copy of a sales invoice prepared by the sales department.

5. An internal auditor must weigh the cost of an audit procedure against the persuasiveness of the evidence to be gathered. Observation is one audit procedure that involves cost-benefit tradeoffs. Which of the following statements regarding observation as an audit procedure is/are correct?
   I. Observation is limited because individuals may react differently when being watched.
   II. Observation is more effective for testing completeness than it is for testing existence.
   III. Observation provides evidence about whether certain controls are operating as designed.
   a. I only.
   b. II only.
   c. I and III.
   d. I, II, and III.

6. An internal auditor gathered the following accounts receivable trend and ratio analysis information:

	Year		
	3	2	1
Net accounts receivable as a percentage of total assets	30.8%	27.3%	23.4%
Accounts receivable turnover (net sales ÷ average accounts receivable)	5.21	6.05	6.98

   Which of the following is the least reasonable explanation for the changes observed by the auditor?
   a. Fictitious sales may have been recorded in years 2 and 3.
   b. The effectiveness of credit and collection procedures deteriorated over the three-year period.
   c. Sales returned for credit were overstated in years 2 and 3.
   d. The allowance for bad debts was understated in years 2 and 3.

7. Your audit objective is to determine that purchases of office supplies have been properly authorized. If purchases of office supplies are made through the purchasing department, which of the following procedures is most appropriate?
   a. Vouch purchase orders to approved purchase requisitions.
   b. Trace approved purchase requisitions to purchase orders.
   c. Inspect purchase requisitions for proper approval.
   d. Vouch receiving reports to approved purchase orders.

8. A production manager of MSM Company ordered excessive raw materials and had the materials delivered to a side business he operated. The manager falsified receiving reports and approved the invoices for payment. Which of the following procedures would most likely detect this fraud?
   a. Vouch cash disbursements to receiving reports and invoices.
   b. Confirm the amounts of raw materials purchased, purchase prices, and dates of shipment with vendors.
   c. Perform ratio and trend analysis. Compare the cost of raw materials purchased with the cost of goods produced.
   d. Observe the receiving dock and count materials received. Compare the counts with receiving reports completed by receiving personnel.

9. An internal auditor is concerned that fraud, in the form of payments to fictitious vendors, may exist. Company purchasers, responsible for purchases of specific product lines, have been granted the authority to approve expenditures up to $10,000. Which of the following applications of generalized audit software would be most effective in addressing the auditor's concern?
   a. List all purchases over $10,000 to determine whether they were properly approved.
   b. Take a random sample of all expenditures under $10,000 to determine whether they were properly approved.
   c. List all major vendors by product line. Select a sample of major vendors and examine supporting documentation for goods or services received.
   d. List all major vendors by product line. Select a sample of major vendors and send negative confirmations to validate that they actually provided goods or services.

10. Which of the following most completely describes the appropriate content of internal audit assurance engagement working papers?
   a. Objectives, procedures, and conclusions.
   b. Purpose, criteria, techniques, and conclusions.
   c. Objectives, procedures, facts, conclusions, and recommendations.
   d. Subject, purpose, sampling information, and analysis.

Discussion Questions

1. You are studying in the campus library for your next internal audit exam with Mark and Ann, two of your classmates.

   Mark says: "I really don't understand this vouching and tracing stuff. For example, what difference does it make whether I start with sales invoices and match them with shipping documents or start with shipping documents and match them with sales invoices?

   Ann replies: "I don't get it either. I hope there's nothing on the exam about it."

   You respond: "I really don't want to take that chance. Professor Smart seems to enjoy asking us hard questions. I think we better figure it out and be prepared. I'd rather be safe than sorry."

   Consider the following two audit objectives: (1) determine whether sales billed to customers have been shipped and (2) determine whether shipments to customers have been billed. Answer the following questions:

   a. What is the difference between the two audit objectives?
   b. What audit procedure would you perform to achieve each audit objective? Be specific.
   c. Why is it important that for each audit objective, you select the proper document as the starting point for your audit test and match that document with the other document?

2. A division of your company purchased a large quantity of new desktop computers during the current fiscal year. An internal audit manager has asked you to audit the process used to acquire the computers. He also wants you to determine whether the computers have been used properly and accounted for correctly. The manager specified a set of audit objectives to guide your tests. For example, he wants you to determine whether:

   1. The purchases of the computers were properly authorized.
   2. Responsibilities regarding the computers are properly segregated.
   3. The computers, as well as the software and information they contain, are properly safeguarded. Consider both physical and logical access.
   4. Laws and regulations regarding software usage have been complied with.
   5. The computers recorded as being purchased actually exist.
   6. All of the computers that were purchased have been recorded.
   7. The amounts at which the computers are recorded are correct.
   8. The estimated useful lives and salvage values of the computers are reasonable.
   9. Depreciation expense was calculated correctly.

   a. Describe the procedures you might use to gain an understanding of how the computers were acquired, used, and accounted for.
   b. Describe the audit procedure(s) you might to use to achieve each of the audit objectives listed above. Be specific.

3. The following information is available for MVF Company (dollar amounts are in millions):

	2009	2008	2007	2006
Net sales	$23.2	$21.7	$19.6	$17.4
Cost of goods sold	17.1	16.8	15.2	13.5
Beginning finished goods inventory	2.3	2.1	1.9	1.5
Ending finished goods inventory	2.9	2.3	2.1	1.9
Materials purchased	10.6	8.8	7.5	7.1

a. Calculate the following ratios for each year:
   - Gross profit percentage.
   - Inventory turnover.
   - Cost of materials purchased to cost of finished goods produced.

b. Analyze the results obtained in 3.a. above:
   - Describe the change in each ratio you observe in 2009.
   - Discuss at least two possible causes of each change observed.[3]

4. All of Kola Company's sales are credit sales shipped Free on Board (FOB) shipping point. Kola typically records sales transactions (that is, sales and cost of sales) throughout the year on the billing date. The internal auditor gathered the following information and documented it in his working papers.

Invoice Number	Date Shipped	Date Billed
8351	12/28/2008	12/29/2008
8352	12/29/2008	1/2/2009
8353	1/2/2009	12/31/2008
8354	1/2/2009	1/3/2009

a. Describe the specific audit procedures that should be performed to determine whether sales transactions occurring immediately before and after year-end are recorded in the proper period.

b. Record the adjusting journal entries (ignore dollar amounts) the internal auditor should propose based on the cutoff information documented above. Include a clear and concise explanation for each proposed entry.

CASES

If you have not already done so, install the ACL and IDEA software on your computer from the CD included with this textbook.

CASE 1 The purpose of this case is to familiarize you with the ACL software and give you an opportunity to practice its application.

A. Print and read the Getting Started manual.

B. Print the ACL in Practice manual. Work through the tutorial contained in the manual. Beginning in Chapter 2, "Examine Employee Data," print the outcomes of the tasks you are asked to complete.

CASE 2 The purpose of this case is to familiarize you with the IDEA software and give you an opportunity to practice its application.

A. Print the IDEA Tutorial. Read:
- The Forward and Preface.
- Section One, IDEA Overview.
- Section Two, What's On the IDEA Screen.
- Section Three, IDEA Windows and Toolbars.

B. Work through Section Four, Getting Started Tutorial. Print selected task outcomes as you go. The outcomes you print should clearly show that you completed the entire tutorial.

REFERENCES

[1]American Institute of Certified Public Accountants, AU Section 326, Audit Evidence. Available at: http://www.aicpa.org/Professional+Resources/Accounting+and+Auditing/Audit+and+Attest+Standards (as of November 21, 2008.

[2]Available at: http://www.isaca.org/glossary (as of November 21, 2008).

[3]Protivity, *Senior Audit School Participant Guide* (Protivity, Inc., 2006).

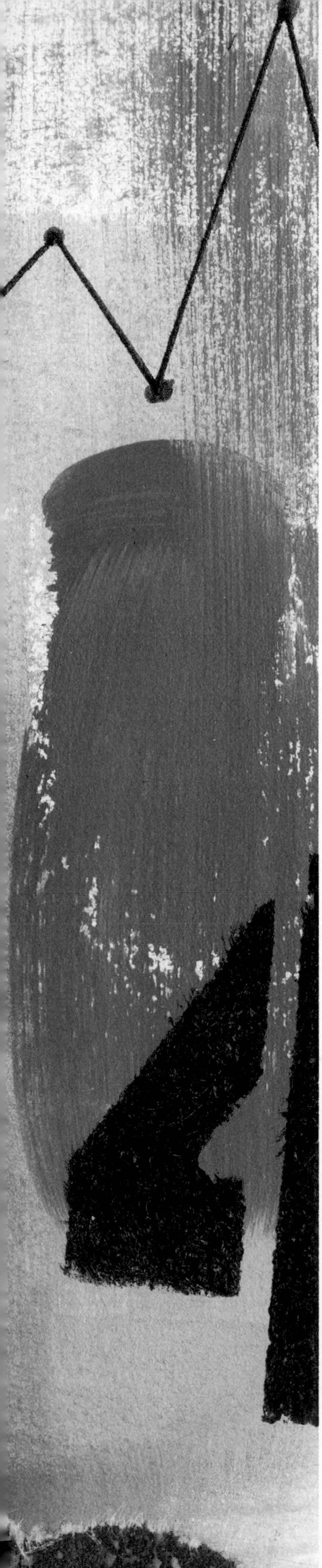

CHAPTER 11 AUDIT SAMPLING

Learning Objectives

- Understand audit sampling and the audit risk concepts associated with sampling.
- Know how to apply statistical and nonstatistical audit sampling in tests of controls.
- Be aware of alternative statistical sampling approaches used in tests of monetary values.

Chapter 10, "Audit Evidence and Working Papers," describes audit procedures as specific tasks performed by internal auditors to achieve the prescribed objectives of an internal audit engagement. It discusses how obtaining sufficient appropriate evidence to achieve the engagement objectives depends on the nature, extent, and timing of the procedures performed.

This chapter primarily focuses on the *extent* of the procedures the internal auditor must perform to obtain the amount of audit evidence required to achieve the engagement objectives. Economic and time constraints generally preclude internal auditors from testing 100% of everything they would like to test. Audit sampling is, by definition, the application of an audit procedure to less than 100 percent of the items in a population of audit interest for the purpose of drawing an inference about the entire population. It is used most commonly by internal auditors to test the operating effectiveness of controls.

Specifically, this chapter introduces the two general approaches to audit sampling, statistical and nonstatistical, and describes sampling and nonsampling risk. It also discusses statistical sampling and nonstatistical sampling as they are applied by internal auditors in tests of controls. It concludes with an overview of two statistical sampling approaches internal auditors use to obtain direct evidence about the correctness of monetary values.

Readers should note that there are currently no IIA *Standards* or Practice Advisories specifically relating to audit sampling. However, there is considerable guidance from other sources, some of which is referred to in this chapter.

INTRODUCTION TO AUDIT SAMPLING

As indicated above, *audit sampling* is the application of an audit procedure to less than 100 percent of the items in a population for the purpose of drawing an inference about the entire population. An audit population might be, for example, all receiving reports prepared during the year or all customer account balances in an accounts receivable subsidiary ledger. Sampling is used most commonly in performing audit procedures such as vouching and tracing, which involve the inspection of some form of manually prepared documentary audit trail. It also may be applicable to the performance of audit procedures such as inquiry and observation. Walking a small set of transactions through a particular process to gain a better understanding of how the process works is not sampling because the purpose is not to reach a conclusion about an entire population of items.

Advances in information technology (IT) have reduced the extent to which internal auditors use statistical sampling. One reason for this is that the operational effectiveness of a control imbedded in an application program needs to be tested only once to determine whether the control is operating effectively at a given time. The internal auditor will then rely on different procedures, such as testing the controls over changes to the application program, to gain assurance that the control operated consistently over a period of time. A second reason is that it is often more expedient to directly test 100 percent of the items stored in a computer file using generalized audit software than it is to select and test a sample of the items.

Two General Approaches to Audit Sampling

There are two general approaches to sampling: statistical and nonstatistical. Both approaches require the use of professional judgment in designing the sampling plan, executing the plan, and evaluating sample results. The internal auditor's choice between the two methods is independent of the specific audit procedures he or she intends to perform, his or her evaluation of the appropriateness of the evidence obtained, and the actions he or she will take based on the outcomes of the sampling application. Both approaches can provide sufficient appropriate evidence if applied correctly. (Some people refer to nonstatistical sampling as "judgmental" sampling. The authors have chosen not to use this term to avoid potential confusion — both statistical sampling and nonstatistical sampling require expert audit judgment.)

The internal auditor's choice between the two methods really boils down to a cost-benefit decision. Statistical sampling is a tool that can help the internal auditor measure the sufficiency of evidence obtained and quantitatively evaluate the sampling results. Most importantly, statistical sampling allows the internal auditor to quantify, measure, and control sampling risk. For these reasons, statistical sampling is normally thought to provide more persuasive evidence than nonstatistical sampling. However, statistical sampling also is generally thought to be more costly. It involves incremental training costs and higher costs associated with designing samples, selecting items to be examined, and evaluating sample results. Statistical sampling and nonstatistical sampling are further differentiated in subsequent sections of this chapter.

Audit Risk

The risk of reaching invalid audit conclusions and/or providing faulty advice based on the audit work conducted.

Audit Risk and Sampling Risk

As defined in Chapter 10, "Audit Evidence and Working Papers," audit risk is the risk of reaching invalid conclusions and/or providing faulty advise based on the audit work conducted. Within the context of sampling, audit risk comprises two types of risk: sampling risk and nonsampling risk.

Sampling risk is the risk that the internal auditor's conclusion based on sample testing may be different than the conclusion reached if the audit procedure was applied to all items in the population. It is a function of testing less than 100 percent of the items in the population because even an appropriately selected sample may not be representative of the population. Sampling risk varies inversely with sample size. If the internal auditor tests 100 percent of a population, and therefore is not sampling, there is no sampling risk.

Sampling Risk

The risk that the internal auditor's conclusion based on sample testing may be different than the conclusion reached if the audit procedure was applied to all items in the population.

In performing tests of controls, the internal auditor is concerned with two aspects of sampling risk:

The risk of assessing control risk too low (type II risk, beta risk). Also known as the risk of over-reliance, this is the risk that the assessed level of control risk based on the sample results is lower than the internal auditor would have found it to be if the population had been tested 100 percent. In other words, it is the risk that the internal auditor will incorrectly conclude that a specified control is more effective than it really is. Stated another way, it is the risk that the internal auditor will overstate the reliance that management can place on the control to reduce residual risk to an acceptably low level.

The risk of assessing control risk too high (type I risk, alpha risk). Also known as the risk of under-reliance, this is the risk that the assessed level of control risk based on the sample results is higher than the internal auditor would have found if the population had been tested 100 percent. In other words, it is the risk that the internal auditor will incorrectly conclude that a specified control is less effective than it really is. Stated another way, it is the risk that the internal auditor will understate the reliance that management can place on the control to reduce residual risk to an acceptably low level.

Control risk, which is referred to for the first time in the preceding two paragraphs, is the risk that controls fail to reduce *controllable risk* to an acceptable level. Remember from Chapter 6, "Internal Control," that controllable risk is that portion of inherent risk that management can reduce through day-to-day operations. Controls are implemented specifically to reduce controllable risk, with the goal of reducing it to management's level of risk tolerance (that is, the level of risk acceptable to management). *Residual risk* is the risk remaining after controls have been implemented. If residual risk exceeds management's risk tolerance, then controls are ineffective, either because they are designed inadequately or operating ineffectively. If the risk is managed to a level below management's risk tolerance, then internal controls are presumed to be designed adequately and operating effectively. However, there also is the possibility that the internal controls are excessive and using more resources than may be required.

Nonsampling risk, unlike sampling risk, is not associated with testing less than 100 percent of the items in a population. Instead, nonsampling risk occurs when an internal auditor fails to perform his or her work correctly. For example, performing inappropriate auditing procedures, misapplying an appropriate procedure (such as failure on the part of the internal auditor to recognize a control deviation or a dollar error), or misinterpreting sampling results may cause a nonsampling error. Nonsampling risk refers to the possibility of making such errors. Nonsampling risk is controlled (reduced to an acceptably low level) through appropriate audit planning, supervision of individual audit engagements, and the overall application of appropriate quality assurance procedures.

STATISTICAL AUDIT SAMPLING IN TESTS OF CONTROLS

Attribute Sampling Approaches

Attribute Sampling

A statistical sampling approach that enables the user to reach a conclusion about a population in terms of a rate of occurrence.

Attribute sampling is a statistical sampling approach, based on binomial distribution theory, that enables the user to reach a conclusion about a population in terms of a rate of occurrence. The binomial distribution is a distribution of all possible samples for which each item in the population has one of two possible states (for example, control deviation or no control deviation). The most common use of attribute sampling in auditing is to evaluate the effectiveness of a particular control. The internal auditor tests the rate of deviation from a prescribed control to determine whether the occurrence rate is "acceptable" and, accordingly, whether reliance on that control is appropriate. Typically, the most basic attribute sampling approach involves the selection of a single sample of a mathematically computed size.

Stratified attribute sampling is a variation of attribute sampling from a population that can be subdivided. For example, a population of purchase transactions may be divided into those of a relatively small amount, which local managers are free to authorize, those of moderately large amounts that regional managers approve, and those of large amounts requiring central management approval. When different controls are applied to different levels of like transactions, the different levels of transactions should be considered separately as different populations. The reason for this is simple: the levels of control effectiveness may vary when different controls are applied.

Stop-or-go sampling is another variation of attribute sampling. Its use is most appropriate when very low deviation rates are expected. Stop-or-go sampling is valuable in these situations, because it minimizes the required sample size for a specified level of sampling risk. An initial, relatively small, sample is drawn and analyzed. The internal auditor then decides, based on the results of this initial sample, whether the sample size should be increased. If a sufficiently low number of deviations are found in the initial sample, the internal auditor stops sampling and formulates his or her conclusion. If more than a sufficiently low number of deviations are found, more sample items are drawn and analyzed before a conclusion is reached.

Discovery sampling is a third variation of attribute sampling. The sample is designed to be large enough to detect at least one deviation if the rate of deviations in the population is at or above a specified rate. A statistical sample is drawn in a manner that enables the internal auditor to test the likelihood of finding at least one deviation. This sampling approach is used most commonly to test for fraud. Its use is appropriate when the expected deviation rate is very low and the internal auditor wants to design a sample based on a specified probability of finding one occurrence. Due to the context in which it is applied and the nature of the potential deviations being investigated, discovery sampling sample sizes are generally much larger than those used in regular attribute sampling applications.

Designing an Attribute Sampling Plan, Executing the Plan, and Evaluating the Sample Results

Attribute sampling involves the following nine steps:

1. Identify a specific internal control objective and the prescribed control(s) aimed at achieving that objective.
2. Define what is meant by a control deviation.
3. Define the population and sampling unit.
4. Determine the appropriate values of the parameters affecting sample size.
5. Determine the appropriate sample size.
6. Randomly select the sample.
7. Audit the sample items selected and count the number of deviations from the prescribed control.
8. Determine the achieved upper deviation limit.
9. Evaluate the sample results.

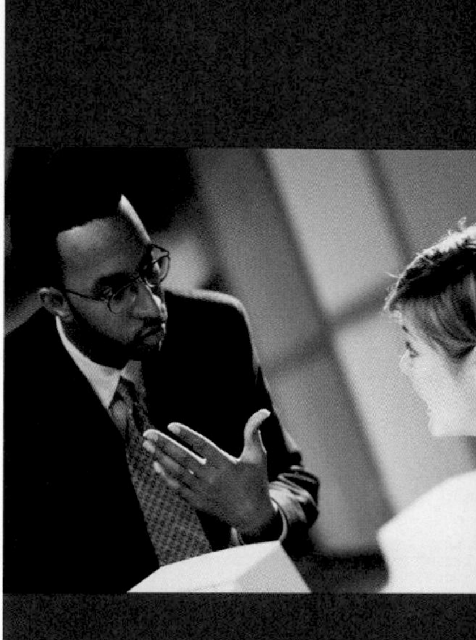

Each of these steps is described here with the following hypothetical situation used as the context for illustrating each step:

> An internal auditor has been instructed to use statistical sampling in her tests of controls over materials acquisitions. The specific audit objective of interest is to determine whether all purchases of materials have been appropriately authorized.

Step 1: Identify a specific internal control objective and the prescribed control(s) aimed at achieving that objective.

The specified audit objective is the key factor in determining what is to be sampled. The audit objective expressed in our illustrative situation above is to determine whether all purchases of materials have been appropriately authorized. This audit objective pertains to the business objective of validity. Management wants to be confident that all purchases are valid — in other words, that no unauthorized purchases have been made. The internal control objective pertaining to this objective is to provide reasonable assurance that management's objective is achieved — specifically, that all purchases are appropriately authorized. Carefully defining the control objective and the control aimed at achieving that objective is very important. If the internal auditor does not do this, there is a risk of performing inappropriate audit procedures and, consequently, drawing inappropriate conclusions. This is an example of nonsampling risk.

For the illustrative example, assume that the company's materials acquisition policies specify that purchases of materials are initiated by authorized warehouse personnel preparing formal written requests (purchase requisitions) for the materials needed. Approved purchase requisitions are forwarded to the purchasing department, where they serve as authorization to order the materials requested. The purchasing department prepares prenumbered purchase orders, which become part of the trail of documentary evidence supporting purchase transactions. The internal auditor decides to test, on a sample basis, whether purchase orders prepared during the past 12 months are supported by appropriately approved purchase requisitions.

Step 2: Define what is meant by a control deviation.

Carefully defining what is meant by a deviation from a prescribed control (that is, the control attribute of interest) is just as important as carefully defining the control objective and control procedure. If the internal auditor fails to do this, there is a risk of not recognizing a deviation, which is another example of nonsampling risk.

In the illustrative example, the internal auditor wants to make sure that purchase orders are supported by appropriately approved purchase requisitions. A deviation from the prescribed control would include any one of the following: a missing purchase requisition, no evidence of a purchase requisition approval, approval by an unauthorized person, or a difference between the item purchased per the purchase order and the item requested per the purchase requisition.

Step 3: Define the population and sampling unit.

As stated in Step 1, the audit objective in this example is to test the validity of purchase orders. Vouching tests the validity of recorded information. It is applied by testing backward to determine whether information in a document is supported by information in previously prepared documents.

The population of interest to the internal auditor in this example is the population of prenumbered purchase orders prepared during the past 12 months. The sampling unit is each purchase order that is tested to determine whether it is supported by an appropriately approved purchase requisition. To test whether each purchase order is supported by an appropriately approved purchase requisition, the internal auditor will vouch each purchase order to the corresponding purchase requisition.

Why would it be inappropriate in this example for the internal auditor to trace purchase orders forward to determine whether a corresponding purchase order was prepared? Remember the audit objective — to determine whether purchase orders are supported by appropriately approved purchase requisitions. If the internal auditor selects a sample of purchase requisitions and traces them forward to subsequently prepared purchase orders, there is absolutely no chance of uncovering a situation in which a purchase requisition was not prepared for an existing purchase order.

Factors Affecting Attribute Sample Sizes:

- **Acceptable risk of assessing control risk too low**
- **Tolerable deviation rate**
- **Expected population deviation rate**

Step 4: Determine the appropriate values of the parameters affecting sample size.

In attribute sampling, the internal auditor must specify, using audit judgment, the appropriate values for three factors affecting sample size:

- The acceptable risk of assessing control risk too low.
- The tolerable deviation rate.
- The expected population deviation rate.

Note that the size of the population has little effect on attribute sample size unless the population is very small. For populations smaller than 200 items, the sample size directly correlates to population size. Sample sizes will increase nominally for populations ranging between 200 and 2,000 items.[1] The statistically derived sample size tables presented below are based on large population sizes, that is, more than 2,000 items. It is, therefore, conservative to use these tables for populations of less than 2,000. It may be appropriate, however, for an internal auditor to consider population size for audit efficiency purposes if a control is applied infrequently (for example, no more than once per week).

Assume for the example above that the population contains 2,500 individual purchase orders.

The acceptable risk of assessing control risk too low. Recall that the risk of assessing control risk too low is the risk that the internal auditor will incorrectly conclude that a specified control is more effective than it really is. The risk of assessing control risk too low is inversely related to sample size; in other words, the lower the acceptable level of risk, the larger the sample size.

Acceptable Risk of Assessing Control Risk Too Low

The risk that the internal auditor will incorrectly conclude that a specified control is more effective than it really is.

The internal auditor's judgment about the acceptable level of assessing control risk too low is based on how confident the internal auditor wants to be in drawing a correct inference about the operating effectiveness of the control procedure being tested. In fact, the risk of assessing control risk too low is the complement of confidence (for example, if the internal auditor chooses to specify a 5% risk of assessing control risk to low, the internal auditor is indicating that 95% confidence in drawing a correct conclusion is desired). The two most commonly used levels of acceptable risk of assessing control risk too low are 5% and 10%. For our case, assume the internal auditor decides to set the acceptable level of control risk at 10%. (Note that the risk of assessing control risk too high is not explicitly controlled in determining the appropriate sample size for an attribute sampling application.)

The tolerable deviation rate. This rate is the maximum rate of deviations the internal auditor is willing to accept and still conclude that the control is acceptably effective (that is, the control can be relied upon to reduce residual risk to an acceptably low level). The tolerable deviation rate is inversely related to sample size.

Tolerable Deviation Rate

The maximum rate of deviations the internal auditor is willing to accept and still conclude that the control is acceptably effective.

The internal auditor's judgment about the tolerable deviation rate is based on the relative importance of the control being tested. If, for example, the internal auditor deems the control to be critical, a low tolerable deviation rate will be set. Assume for the example that the tolerable deviation rate is set at 5%.

The expected population deviation rate. This is the internal auditor's best estimate of the actual deviation rate in the population of items being examined. The expected population deviation rate has a direct effect on sample size. However, this rate will be less than the tolerable rate, or the internal auditor will not conduct the attribute sampling application being considered. Internal auditors refer to the difference between the tolerable deviation rate and the expected population deviation rate as the *planned allowance for sampling risk* or *planned precision.*

Expected Population Deviation Rate

The internal auditor's best estimate of the actual deviation rate in the population of items being examined.

If the internal auditor has previously used attribute sampling to test the effectiveness of a particular control, an appropriate expected population deviation rate would be the one used in the prior audit, adjusted for any known changes in the application of the control. Otherwise, the internal auditor might select and audit a small pre-sample to determine the expected population deviation rate. Assume for the example that the internal auditor estimates the population deviation rate to be 1%.

Step 5: Determine the appropriate sample size.

Once the internal auditor has assigned the values of the factors affecting sample size, the easiest way to determine the appropriate sample size is to refer to readily available sample-size tables such as those presented in Exhibit 11-1.

The internal auditor in the example has set the risk of assessing control risk too low at 10%, the tolerable deviation rate at 5%, and the estimated population deviation rate at 1%. Exhibit 11-1 shows that the appropriate sample size is 77. The internal auditor might round the sample size up to 80 for reasons discussed in step 8 below.

Note that this calculation of sample size illustrates a key benefit of statistical sampling. If the internal auditor wanted to be 100% confident in the conclusion reached about the validity of purchase orders, 100% of them would have to be vouched; however, a conclusion with 90% confidence (the complement of 10% risk of assessing control risk too low) can be reached based on the sample results of vouching 80 purchase orders.

Step 6: Randomly select the sample.

Random Sampling

Each item in the defined population has an equal opportunity of being selected.

When applying sampling in tests of controls, it is important that items from the entire period under audit have a chance of being selected. When applying statistical sampling, it also is very important that the internal auditor use a random-based selection technique (that is, each item in the defined population must have an equal opportunity of being selected). The two most common approaches used to select random attribute samples are simple random sampling and systematic sampling with one or more random starts.

Simple random sampling generally is the easiest approach when sampling prenumbered documents. Using a random number table is one way for the internal auditor to achieve randomness. Another way is to use a computerized random number generator program.

Systematic sampling involves the internal auditor randomly identifying a starting point and then selecting every nth item after that. Systematic sampling is appropriate when there is no reason to believe that the equal intervals will systematically bias the sample. To reduce the likelihood of selecting a biased sample, internal auditors will sometimes select multiple random starting points. Internal auditors most commonly use systematic selection when individual items of the population are not prenumbered.

In the example used in this chapter, the purchase orders are prenumbered, so the internal auditor decides to use a computerized random number generator program to select a random sample of purchase orders prepared during the past 12 months. The 12-month period covers the last three months of the preceding fiscal year and the first nine months of the current fiscal year. Note that it is not always feasible, in terms of timing, for an internal auditor to draw a sample covering one entire fiscal year. The internal auditor needs to take this into consideration when evaluating sample results.

EXHIBIT 11-1

ATTRIBUTE SAMPLING SAMPLE SIZE TABLES

5% Risk of Assessing Control Risk Too Low

Expected Population Deviation Rate (%)	Tolerable Deviation Rate (Number of Expected Errors)								
	2%	3%	4%	5%	6%	7%	8%	9%	10%
0.00	149 (0)	99 (0)	74 (0)	59 (0)	49 (0)	42 (0)	36 (0)	32 (0)	29 (0)
0.50	313 (2)	157 (1)	117 (1)	93 (1)	78 (1)	66 (1)	58 (1)	51 (1)	46 (1)
1.00	590 (6)	257 (3)	156 (2)	93 (1)	78 (1)	66 (1)	58 (1)	51 (1)	46 (1)
1.50	——	392 (6)	192 (3)	124 (2)	103 (2)	66 (1)	58 (1)	51 (1)	46 (1)
2.00	——	846 (17)	294 (6)	181 (4)	127 (3)	88 (2)	77 (2)	68 (2)	46 (1)
2.50	——	——	513 (13)	234 (6)	150 (4)	109 (3)	77 (2)	68 (2)	61 (2)
3.00	——	——	1,098 (33)	361 (11)	195 (6)	129 (4)	95 (3)	84 (3)	61 (2)
4.00	——	——	——	1,348 (54)	421 (17)	221 (9)	146 (6)	100 (4)	89 (4)
5.00	——	——	——	——	1,580 (79)	478 (24)	240 (12)	158 (8)	116 (6)
6.00	——	——	——	——	——	1,832 (110)	532 (32)	266 (16)	179 (11)

10% Risk of Assessing Control Risk Too Low

Expected Population Deviation Rate (%)	Tolerable Deviation Rate (Number of Expected Errors)								
	2%	3%	4%	5%	6%	7%	8%	9%	10%
0.00	114 (0)	76 (0)	57 (0)	45 (0)	38 (0)	32 (0)	28 (0)	25 (0)	22 (0)
0.50	194 (1)	129 (1)	96 (1)	77 (1)	64 (1)	55 (1)	48 (1)	42 (1)	38 (1)
1.00	398 (4)	176 (2)	96 (1)	77 (1)	64 (1)	55 (1)	48 (1)	42 (1)	38 (1)
1.50	1,463 (22)	265 (4)	132 (2)	105 (2)	64 (1)	55 (1)	48 (1)	42 (1)	38 (1)
2.00	——	590 (12)	198 (4)	132 (3)	88 (2)	75 (2)	48 (1)	42 (1)	38(1)
2.50	——	——	353 (9)	158 (4)	110 (3)	75 (2)	65 (2)	58(2)	38 (1)
3.00	——	——	730 (22)	258 (8)	132 (4)	94 (3)	65 (2)	58 (2)	52 (2)
4.00	——	——	——	873 (35)	274 (11)	149 (6)	98 (4)	73 (3)	65 (3)
5.00	——	——	——	——	1,019 (51)	318 (16)	160 (8)	115 (6)	78 (4)
6.00	——	——	——	——	——	1,150 (69)	349 (21)	182 (11)	116 (7)

Note: Sample sizes over 2,000 are not shown. This table assumes a large population.

Copyright 2008. American Institute of Certified Public Accountants, Inc. All rights reserved. Used with permission.

Step 7: Audit the sample items selected and count the number of deviations from the prescribed control.

In the example, the internal auditor vouches each purchase order in the sample to the corresponding purchase requisition. Each purchase requisition is inspected for evidence of approval by an authorized person and correspondence of the item purchased per the purchase order with the item requested per the purchase requisition. Assume two possible outcomes: (1) the internal auditor finds one deviation (that is, one case in which no purchase requisition was found for the purchase order in the sample), and (2) the internal auditor finds two deviations (that is, two cases in which no purchase requisition was found for the purchase order in the sample).

Step 8: Determine the achieved upper deviation limit.

Internal auditors use attribute sampling evaluation tables such as those presented in Exhibit 11-2 to determine the achieved upper deviation limit for an attribute sampling application.

The upper deviation limits for the two possible outcomes indicated would be:

Number of Sample Deviations	Upper Deviation Limit
1	4.8%
2	6.6%

The reason it was indicated in Step 5 that the internal auditor might round the determined sample size of 77 up to 80 is now apparent — the tables presented in Exhibit 11-2 do not contain upper deviation limits for every possible sample size. Rounding the sample size up to the next number in the evaluation table is conservative. An alternative approach would be to audit a sample of 77 items and calculate the achieved upper deviation limit using interpolation.

Step 9: Evaluate the sample results.

Evaluating the results of an attribute sampling application involves:

- Formulating a statistical conclusion.
- Making an audit decision based on the quantitative sample results.
- Considering qualitative aspects of the sample results.

Formulating a statistical conclusion. A key advantage of statistical sampling over nonstatistical sampling is that statistical sampling enables the internal auditor to quantify, measure, and control sampling risk. In attribute sampling, the internal auditor explicitly controls the risk of assessing control risk too low, which is the complement of confidence. In the example, the internal auditor specified a 10% risk of assessing control risk too low, and this value was used to determine the appropriate sample size. When determining the achieved upper deviation limit for the example, refer to the table for a 10% risk of assessing control risk too low.

The internal auditor's best estimate of the deviation rate in the population for the first hypothetical outcome of 1 sample deviation is 1/80 = 1.25%. The internal auditor's best estimate of population deviation rate for the second hypothetical outcome of 2 sample deviations is 2/80 = 2.5%. However, there is uncertainty in these estimates due to the fact that the internal auditor performed the audit procedure on a sample basis as opposed to testing 100%. In other words, the internal auditor cannot conclude with certainty that the population deviation rate is 1.25% or 2.5%.

For hypothetical outcome number 1 (one sample deviation), the internal auditor can express the statistical conclusion:

> I am 90% confident that the true, but unknown, population deviation rate is less than or equal to 4.8%.

EXHIBIT 11-2

ATTRIBUTE SAMPLING EVALUATION TABLES (UPPER DEVIATION LIMITS)

5% Risk of Assessing Control Risk Too Low

Sample Size	Actual Number of Deviations Found								
	0	1	2	3	4	5	6	7	8
20	14.0	21.7	28.3	34.4	40.2	45.6	50.8	55.9	60.7
25	11.3	17.7	23.2	28.2	33.0	37.6	42.0	46.3	50.4
30	9.6	14.9	19.6	23.9	28.0	31.9	35.8	39.4	43.0
35	8.3	12.9	17.0	20.7	24.3	27.8	31.1	34.4	37.5
40	7.3	11.4	15.0	18.3	21.5	24.6	27.5	30.4	33.3
45	6.5	10.2	13.4	16.4	19.2	22.0	24.7	27.3	29.8
50	5.9	9.2	12.1	14.8	17.4	19.9	22.4	24.7	27.1
55	5.4	8.4	11.1	13.5	15.9	18.2	20.5	22.6	24.8
60	4.9	7.7	10.2	12.5	14.7	16.8	18.8	20.8	22.8
65	4.6	7.1	9.4	11.5	13.6	15.5	17.5	19.3	21.2
70	4.2	6.6	8.8	10.8	12.7	14.5	16.3	18.0	19.7
75	4.0	6.2	8.2	10.1	11.8	13.6	15.2	16.9	18.5
80	3.7	5.8	7.7	9.5	11.1	12.7	14.3	15.9	17.4
90	3.3	5.2	6.9	8.4	9.9	11.4	12.8	14.2	15.5
100	3.0	4.7	6.2	7.6	9.0	10.3	11.5	12.8	14.0
125	2.4	3.8	5.0	6.1	7.2	8.3	9.3	10.3	11.3
150	2.0	3.2	4.2	5.1	6.0	6.9	7.8	8.6	9.5
200	1.5	2.4	3.2	3.9	4.6	5.2	5.9	6.5	7.2

10% Risk of Assessing Control Risk Too Low

Sample Size	Actual Number of Deviations Found								
	0	1	2	3	4	5	6	7	8
20	10.9	18.1	24.5	30.5	36.1	41.5	46.8	51.9	56.8
25	8.8	14.7	20.0	24.9	29.5	34.0	38.4	42.6	46.8
30	7.4	12.4	16.8	21.0	24.9	28.8	32.5	36.2	39.7
35	6.4	10.7	14.5	18.2	21.6	24.9	28.2	31.4	34.5
40	5.6	9.4	12.8	16.0	19.0	22.0	24.9	27.7	30.5
45	5.0	8.4	11.4	14.3	17.0	19.7	22.3	24.8	27.3
50	4.6	7.6	10.3	12.9	15.4	17.8	20.2	22.5	24.7
55	4.2	6.9	9.4	11.8	14.1	16.3	18.4	20.5	22.6
60	3.8	6.4	8.7	10.8	12.9	15.0	16.9	18.9	20.8
65	3.5	5.9	8.0	10.0	12.0	13.9	15.7	17.5	19.3
70	3.3	5.5	7.5	9.3	11.1	12.9	14.6	16.3	18.0
75	3.1	5.1	7.0	8.7	10.4	12.1	13.7	15.2	16.8
80	2.9	4.8	6.6	8.2	9.8	11.3	12.8	14.3	15.8
90	2.6	4.3	5.9	7.3	8.7	10.1	11.5	12.8	14.1
100	2.3	3.9	5.3	6.6	7.9	9.1	10.3	11.5	12.7
125	1.9	3.1	4.3	5.3	6.3	7.3	8.3	9.3	10.2
150	1.6	2.6	3.6	4.4	5.3	6.1	7.0	7.8	8.6
200	1.2	2.0	2.7	3.4	4.0	4.6	5.3	5.9	6.5

Note: This table presents upper limits (body of table) as percentages. This table assumes a large population

Copyright 2008. American Institute of Certified Public Accountants, Inc. All rights reserved. Used with permission.

For hypothetical outcome number 2 (two sample deviations) the internal auditor can express the statistical conclusion:

> I am 90% confident that the true, but unknown, population deviation rate is less than or equal to 6.6%.

Achieved Allowance for Sampling Risk

The difference between the sample deviation rate and the achieved upper deviation limit.

Note that the difference between the best estimate of the population deviation rate (the sample deviation rate) and the achieved upper deviation limit is referred to as the *achieved allowance for sampling risk* or *achieved precision*.

Making an audit decision based on the quantitative sample results. The attribute sampling application was designed so that the internal auditor would conclude that the control was effective, based on the sample results, if 90% confidence could be achieved that the true, but unknown, population rate was less than or equal to 5% (the internal auditor's specified tolerable deviation rate). The first hypothetical outcome meets this test because the achieved upper deviation limit (4.8%) is less than 5%. The second hypothetical case does not meet this test because the achieved upper deviation limit (6.6%) is greater than 5%.

If the achieved upper deviation limit is less than or equal to the tolerable deviation rate, the quantitative attribute sampling results indicate that the tested control is effective (that is, it can be relied upon to reduce residual risk to an acceptably low level). Conversely, if the achieved upper deviation limit is greater than the tolerable deviation rate, the quantitative results indicate that the tested control is not effective (that is, it cannot be relied upon to reduce residual risk to an acceptably low level).

At this point, the internal auditor is ready to interpret the quantitative sample results. Recall that the audit objective expressed in our illustrative situation is to determine whether all purchases of materials have been authorized appropriately. The internal auditor predetermined that the goal was to be 90% confident that the true, but unknown, deviation rate is less than 5%. As indicated above, the first hypothetical case meets this test, but the second does not. Accordingly, the internal auditor should conclude for the first case that the level of control effectiveness over the validity of merchandise shipments is acceptable — that is, the sample results indicate that the control can be relied upon to reduce residual risk to an acceptably low level. For the second case, however, the internal auditor should conclude that the level of control effectiveness is not acceptable — that is, the sample results indicate that the control cannot be relied upon to reduce residual risk to an acceptably low level. The second case constitutes an audit observation that the internal auditor should document and include in the engagement communication.

It is important to note that the internal auditor's interpretation of the quantitative sample results pertain to the effectiveness of the control over the past 12 months (the last three months of the preceding fiscal year and the first nine months of the current fiscal year). It would be inappropriate for the internal auditor to draw a conclusion based on the sampling results regarding the effectiveness of the control over the last three months of the current fiscal year because the sample did not include purchase orders from these three months.

Considering qualitative aspects of the sample results. In addition to evaluating the quantitative attribute sampling results, the internal auditor should consider the qualitative aspects of any deviations from prescribed controls uncovered. Of particular importance is the possibility that the deviations might be the result of fraud. Assume, for example, that the quantitative sample results support the conclusion that the control is operating effectively. Evidence that deviations from the control found in the sample were caused by fraud might very well offset the quantitative results and prompt the internal auditor to conclude that the control is not effective (that is, it cannot be relied upon to reduce residual risk to an acceptably low level). The internal auditor also must consider what, if any, impact the discovery of fraud might have on other aspects of the engagement.

Cases of missing or voided documents. What should an internal auditor do if documents pertinent to tests of controls are missing or have been voided? Consider the following cases:

Case 1. As in the illustrative example above, the internal auditor vouches a sample of purchase orders to corresponding purchase requisitions, and two purchase requisitions cannot be found. The two missing purchase requisitions are clearly control deviations; there is no documentary evidence of authorization to prepare the two purchase orders.

Case 2. The internal auditor has randomly selected purchase orders by number to be tested and finds that one of the purchase orders selected was voided. It is determined, after follow-up on the voided purchase order is done, that nothing is amiss. It would be appropriate in this case to select another purchase order for testing purposes. A significant number of voided purchase orders could be indicative of a separate problem warranting further audit attention.

Case 3. The internal auditor has randomly selected purchase orders by number to be tested and finds that one of the purchase orders is missing. The internal auditor follows up on the missing purchase order and is unable to obtain a reasonable explanation for why it is missing. The internal auditor obviously cannot apply audit procedures to a selected item that cannot be found. Should this be considered a deviation from the prescribed control? The American Institute of Certified Public Accountants (AICPA) says yes — "If the auditor is not able to apply the planned audit procedure or appropriate alternative procedures to selected items, he should consider the reasons for this limitation, and he should ordinarily consider these selected items to be deviations from the prescribed policy or procedure for the purpose of evaluating the sample."[2] Some internal auditors disagree with this view because it is impossible to perform the prescribed test of controls to a missing document. They further argue that the missing document represents a different problem that warrants separate consideration. They would select another purchase order for testing purposes. Regardless of whether the missing purchase order is considered a deviation from the prescribed control or a different problem that warrants separate consideration, the internal auditor should document the missing purchase order in the working papers and decide whether it is significant enough to be written up as an audit observation.

NONSTATISTICAL AUDIT SAMPLING IN TESTS OF CONTROLS

Selecting and Evaluating a Nonstatistical Sample

Haphazard Sampling

A nonrandom selection technique that is used by internal auditors to select a sample that is expected to be representative of the population.

Statistical sampling requires two fundamental things: the sample must be selected randomly and the sample results must be evaluated mathematically based on probability theory. Nonstatistical sampling allows the internal auditor more latitude regarding sample selection and evaluation.

However, the internal auditor must still select a sample that is thought to be representative of the population, taking into consideration the factors that affect sample size. *Haphazard sampling* is a nonrandom selection technique that is used by internal auditors to select a sample that is expected to be representative of the population. Haphazard, in this context, does not mean careless or reckless. It means that the internal auditor selects the sample without deliberately deciding to include or exclude certain items.

An internal auditor using nonstatistical sampling also must project the sample results to the population. Moreover, the internal auditor must still gather sufficient appropriate evidence to support a valid conclusion. It is not appropriate, for example, to use nonstatistical sampling to avoid having to justify the size of the sample chosen. In fact, it can be argued that internal auditors applying nonstatistical sampling should err on the side of selecting larger samples to compensate for the less rigorous selection method and the inability to quantitatively control sampling risk.

The inability to quantify sampling risk statistically is the key feature of nonstatistical sampling that differentiates it from statistical sampling. The internal auditor's conclusion about the population from which the sample is drawn is strictly judgmental instead of being based on probability theory. Therefore, it is important for the internal auditors to determine whether they can reach valid conclusions using nonstatistical sampling as opposed to using the potentially more costly and time-consuming statistical sampling approach, which requires random sampling and conclusions based on probability theory.

Commonly Used Nonstatistical Sampling Approaches

One common approach to nonstatistical sampling is to select a relatively small sample haphazardly, such as 25 items for all sampling applications based on a presumption of no control deviations in the population, and to conclude that the control is not acceptably effective if one or more deviations are found. This approach is convenient, but also has a significant shortcoming — it does not take into consideration two of the fundamental factors internal auditors should consider when determining appropriate sample sizes: risk of assessing control risk too low and tolerable deviation rate.

To reinforce this point, take a closer look at Exhibit 11-1. Where in Exhibit 11-1 is there a sample size of 25 items or fewer? The answer is only in the first row of the lower table in the last two columns. What does this mean? It means that if the internal auditor had used statistical sampling to determine the sample size, the following parameters were used: 10% risk of assessing control risk too low, 9-10% tolerable deviation rate, and 0% expected deviation rate. These are very liberal parameters that may not be appropriate across all audit sampling applications used to test the operating effectiveness of controls.

Exhibit 11-3 illustrates a slightly more conservative approach used by some internal auditors to determine nonstatistical sample sizes. This is one firm's view of the sample sizes required to support conclusions that controls are operating effectively if no deviations are found for samples taken from populations of varying sizes. The internal auditor adjusts the sample size within each range, taking into consideration the factors that affect sample size. If, for example, the control being tested is deemed to be critical and the internal auditor wants to assume less sampling risk, sample size at the high end of the relevant range will be used.

A Nonstatistical Sampling Example

Consider the following hypothetical situation:

> An internal auditor has been instructed to test, on a nonstatistical sample basis, whether the bank reconciliations prepared over the past 10 months were completed correctly. The company has 10 bank accounts, all of which were reconciled over the past 10 months by the same person using a prescribed template and method. The internal auditor's expectation is that no incorrectly completed reconciliations will be found. If one or more reconciliations are found that were not completed accurately, the internal auditor will conclude that the operating effectiveness of the bank reconciliation control was not acceptable over the past 10 months.

Using Exhibit 11-3 as a guide, how many bank reconciliations should the internal auditor test? The internal auditor could reasonably decide to test two to five reconciliations for each bank account since the accounts are reconciled monthly. This approach would require the internal auditor to reach a separate conclusion for each account. Another reasonable approach would be to consider the 100 bank reconciliations as one population, because the reconciliations for the 10 accounts are subject to the same controls. In this case, the appropriate sample size range per Exhibit 11-3 falls between the ranges prescribed for controls applied weekly and control applied daily. They might logically decide, in this case, to test 20 to 25 of the 100 bank reconciliations. This approach allows the internal

EXHIBIT 11-3

ILLUSTRATIVE NONSTATISTICAL SAMPLE SIZES

Frequency of Control Application	Appropriate Sample Size
Annually	1
Quarterly	2
Monthly	2 to 5
Weekly	5 to 15
Daily	20 to 40
Multiple times per day	25 to 60

Source: Adapted from *Sarbanes-Oxley Act: Section 404 – Practical Guidance for Management* (PricewaterhouseCoopers, July 2004), p. 61.

auditor to reach one overall conclusion. Care must be taken, however, to select a sample that can be expected to be representative of the population. Consequently, haphazardly selecting sample items across the entire population of 100 bank reconciliations would be appropriate.

Assume the internal auditor haphazardly selects 25 bank reconciliations. After testing the 25 reconciliations, it is determined that each reconciliation was performed correctly. What can the internal auditor conclude? A statistical conclusion about the population of 100 bank reconciliations cannot be expressed, but it would be appropriate to say that the sample result supports the conclusion that bank reconciliations were performed correctly (that is, that the bank reconciliation control was acceptably effective) over the past 10 months.

Assume instead that the internal auditor finds that one of the 25 reconciliations was not performed correctly, which is inconsistent with the expectation that none would be found. Now what should be concluded? Because a control deviation was found, the internal auditor should conclude that the bank reconciliation control was not acceptably effective over the past 10 months. This constitutes an observation that the internal auditor should document and include in the engagement communication.

STATISTICAL SAMPLING IN TESTS OF MONETARY VALUES

In addition to using sampling within the context of testing controls, internal auditors also apply sampling when performing tests designed to obtain direct evidence about the correctness of monetary values — for example, the recorded value of an account balance such as inventory. When performing tests of monetary values, the internal auditor is concerned with two aspects of sampling risk:

The risk of incorrect acceptance (type II risk, beta risk). This is the risk that the sample supports the conclusion that a recorded value (for example, an account balance) is not materially misstated when it is.

The risk of incorrect rejection (type I risk, alpha risk). This is the risk that the sample supports the conclusion that a recorded amount (for example, an account balance) is materially misstated when it is not.

Probability-proportional-to-size Sampling

PPS Sampling

A modified form of attribute sampling that is used to reach a conclusion in monetary amounts rather than rates of occurrence.

Probability-proportional-to-size (PPS) sampling, also called monetary-unit sampling or dollar-unit sampling, is a modified form of attribute sampling that is used to reach a conclusion in monetary amounts rather than rates of occurrence. PPS sampling is primarily applicable for testing recorded monetary amounts for overstatement, especially when the expected number of individual overstatements in the population is small. It is not likely to be a cost-effective sampling approach if these conditions are not met.

Selecting the sample. As with attribute sampling, it is very important in PPS sampling that the sample be randomly selected — that is, each item in the defined population should have an equal opportunity of being selected. The population in a PPS sampling application is the population of individual monetary units contained in the particular account being tested. The sampling unit is the individual monetary unit. The internal auditor uses a systematic sampling approach to select every nth monetary unit in the population after a random start. However, the individual monetary units selected are not the items of audit interest. The items of interest are the "logical units" containing the individual monetary units. A logical unit might be, for example, a specific item of inventory recorded in the inventory records. Larger logical units are more apt to be selected for testing than smaller logical units. In fact, the likelihood of a logical unit being selected is proportional to its size — thus the name probability-proportional-to-size sampling.

The following factors affect PPS sample sizes:

- **Monetary book value of the population.** The book value of the population (for example, the recorded total value of year-end inventory) has a direct effect on sample size.
- **Risk of incorrect acceptance.** The risk of incorrect acceptance was defined above as the risk that the sample supports the conclusion that a recorded value (for example, the recorded inventory balance) is not materially misstated when it is materially misstated. The risk of incorrect acceptance is a component of sampling risk and has an inverse effect on sample size.
- **Tolerable misstatement.** Tolerable misstatement is the maximum misstatement that can exist in the recorded value before the internal auditor considers it materially misstated. It has an inverse effect on sample size.
- **Anticipated misstatement.** Anticipated or expected misstatement is the amount of misstatement the internal auditor expects there to be in the recorded value. It has a direct effect on sample size.

Factors Affecting PPS Sample Sizes:

- **Monetary book value of the population**
- **Risk of incorrect acceptance**
- **Tolerable misstatement**
- **Anticipated misstatement**

Evaluating the sample results. After selecting and auditing the sample, an internal auditor, using PPS sampling, extrapolates the sample results to the population, formulates a statistical conclusion, and determines whether the quantitative and qualitative sample evidence indicates that the recorded monetary value is fairly stated or materially misstated. A description of how an internal auditor performs these steps is beyond the scope of this textbook.

Classical Variables Sampling

Classical variables sampling is based on normal distribution theory. It generally is considered more difficult to apply than PPS sampling, largely because it involves much more complex calculations in determining appropriate sample sizes and evaluating sample results.

Selecting the sample. Again, it is very important in classical variables sampling that the sample be randomly selected. The two approaches used to select random classical variable samples are simple random sampling and systematic sampling with a random start.

The following factors affect classical variable sample sizes:

- **Population size.** The population size is the number of items in the population (for example, the number of different inventory items recorded in the accounting records). It has a direct effect on sample size.

Factors Affecting Classical Variable Sample Sizes:

- **Population size**
- **Estimated population standard deviation**
- **Risk of incorrect acceptance**
- **Risk of incorrect rejection**
- **Tolerable misstatement**

- **Estimated population standard deviation**. The estimated population standard deviation, a measure of population variability, has a direct effect on sample size.
- **Risk of incorrect acceptance.** The risk of incorrect acceptance was defined above as the risk that the sample supports the conclusion that a recorded value (for example, the recorded inventory balance) is not materially misstated when it is materially misstated. The risk of incorrect acceptance is a component of sampling risk and has an inverse effect on sample size.
- **Risk of incorrect rejection.** The risk of incorrect rejection was defined above as the risk that the sample supports the conclusion that a recorded value (for example, the recorded inventory balance) is materially misstated when it is not materially misstated. The risk of incorrect rejection, the second component of sampling risk, has an inverse effect on sample size.
- **Tolerable misstatement.** Tolerable misstatement is the maximum misstatement that can exist in the recorded value before the internal auditor considers it materially misstated. It has an inverse effect on sample size.

Evaluating the sample results. As with PPS sampling, after selecting and auditing the sample, an internal auditor using classical variables sampling extrapolates the sample results to the population, formulates a statistical conclusion, and determines whether the quantitative and qualitative sample evidence indicates that the recorded monetary value is fairly stated or materially misstated. The sample evaluation process is more complex for classical variables sampling than for PPS sampling. A description of how an internal auditor performs the evaluation process is beyond the scope of this textbook.

Probability-proportional-to-size Sampling versus Classical Variables Sampling

Both PPS sampling and classical variables sampling have significant advantages and disadvantages that internal auditors must consider when choosing which approach is best for a particular sampling application. Exhibit 11-4 presents the key advantages and disadvantages of each approach.

SUMMARY

This chapter focused on audit sampling as a tool for applying certain audit procedures to support engagement objectives. It began with an introduction to statistical and nonstatistical sampling and descriptions of sampling and nonsampling risk. This was followed by an in-depth discussion of statistical sampling and nonstatistical sampling as they are applied by internal auditors in tests of controls. The chapter concluded with an overview of two statistical sampling approaches internal auditors use to obtain direct evidence about the correctness of monetary values.

EXHIBIT 11-4

PROBABILITY-PROPORTIONAL-TO-SIZE SAMPLING VERSUS CLASSICAL VARIABLES SAMPLING

Probability-proportional-to-size Sampling

Key advantages:

- Simpler calculations make PPS sampling easier to use.
- The sample size calculation does not involve any measure of estimated population variation.
- PPS sampling automatically results in a stratified sample because sample items are selected in proportion to their size.
- PPS sample selection automatically identifies any individually significant population items, that is, population items exceeding a predetermined cutoff dollar amount.
- PPS sampling generally is more efficient (that is, requires a smaller sample size) when the population contains zero or very few misstatements.

Key disadvantages:

- Special design considerations are required when understatements or audit values less than zero are expected.
- Identification of understatements in the sample requires special evaluation considerations.
- PPS sampling produces overly conservative results when errors are detected. This increases the risk of incorrect rejection.
- The appropriate sample size increases quickly as the number of expected misstatements increases. When more than a few misstatements are expected, PPS sampling may be less efficient.

Classical Variables Sampling

Key advantages:

- Samples are generally easier to expand if the internal auditor should find it necessary.
- Zero balances and negative balances do not require special sample design considerations.
- The internal auditor's objective may be met with a smaller sample size if there is a large number of misstatements, that is, differences between audit values and recorded values.

Key disadvantages:

- Classical variables sampling is more complex. The internal auditor may need to use a computer program to cost-effectively design and evaluate a sample.
- Calculation of the proper sample size requires that the internal auditor first estimate the population standard deviation.

Review Questions

1. How is "audit sampling" defined in this chapter?
2. What are the two general types of audit sampling?
3. How is "sampling risk" defined in this chapter? What are the two aspects of sampling risk that an internal auditor considers when performing tests of controls?
4. How does nonsampling risk differ from sampling risk?
5. What is attribute sampling? What are the three variations of attribute sampling described in this chapter?
6. What are the nine steps involved in attribute sampling?
7. What factors affect the size of an attribute sample?
8. What steps are involved in evaluating the results of an attribute sampling application?
9. What should an internal auditor do if documents pertinent to tests of controls are missing?
10. How is "haphazard sampling" defined in this chapter?
11. What is the key advantage of statistical sampling over nonstatistical sampling?
12. Why do internal auditors sometimes choose to use nonstatistical sampling instead of statistical sampling?
13. How does the purpose of statistical sampling in tests of monetary values differ from the purpose of statistical sampling in tests of controls?
14. What factors affect probability-proportional-to-size (PPS) sample sizes?
15. What are the key advantages of PPS sampling over classical variables sampling? What are the key disadvantages?

Multiple-choice Questions

Select the best answer for each of the following questions.

1. The primary reason for an internal auditor to use statistical sampling rather than nonstatistical sampling is to:
   - **a.** Allow the auditor to quantify, and therefore control, the risk of making an incorrect decision based on sample evidence.
   - **b.** Obtain a smaller sample than would be required if nonstatistical sampling were used.
   - **c.** Reduce the problems associated with the auditor's judgment concerning the competency of the evidence gathered when nonstatistical sampling is used.
   - **d.** Obtain a sample more representative of the population than would be obtained if nonstatistical sampling techniques were used.

2. Which of the following is an element of sampling risk as opposed to an element of nonsampling risk?
   a. Determining a sample size that is too small.
   b. Performing an inappropriate audit procedure.
   c. Failing to detect a control deviation.
   d. Forgetting to perform a specified audit procedure.
3. For which of the following would an internal auditor most likely use attribute sampling?
   a. Determining whether the year-end inventory balance is overstated.
   b. Selecting fixed asset additions to inspect.
   c. Choosing inventory items to test count.
   d. Inspecting employee timecards for proper approval.
4. If all other factors specified in an attribute sampling plan remain constant, changing the expected population deviation rate from 1% to 2% and changing the tolerable deviation rate from 7% to 6% would cause the required sample size to:
   a. Increase.
   b. Decrease.
   c. Remain the same.
   d. Change by 2%.
5. An internal auditor selects a sample of sales invoices and matches them with shipping documents. This procedure most directly addresses which of the following assertions?
   a. All shipments to customers are recorded as receivables.
   b. All billed sales are for goods shipped to customers.
   c. All recorded receivables represent goods shipped to customers.
   d. All shipments to customers are billed.
6. An internal auditor is testing cash disbursement transactions. Internal control policies require every check request to be accompanied by an approved voucher (that is, a package of documents evidencing that a good or service has been received and invoiced by the vendor). The voucher approval is based on a three-way matching of a purchase order, receiving report, and vendor's invoice. To determine whether checks have proper support, the internal auditor should begin her testing procedures by selecting items from the population of:
   a. Check copies.
   b. Purchase orders.
   c. Receiving reports.
   d. Approved vouchers.

7. The achieved upper deviation limit is 7% and the risk of assessing control risk too low is 5%. How should the internal auditor interpret this attribute sampling outcome?
   a. There is a 7% chance that the deviation rate in the population is less than or equal to 5%.
   b. There is a 5% chance that the deviation rate in the population is less than 7%.
   c. There is a 5% chance that the deviation rate in the population exceeds 7%.
   d. There is a 95% chance that the deviation rate in the population equals 7%.

8. An internal auditor should consider the qualitative aspects of deviations found in a sample in addition to evaluating the number of deviations. For which of the following situations should the internal auditor be most concerned?
   a. There were fewer deviations in the sample than expected.
   b. The deviations found are similar in nature to those found during the last audit of the area.
   c. The deviations found appear to have been caused by an employee's misunderstanding of instructions.
   d. The deviations found may have been caused intentionally.

9. An internal auditor wants to test customers' accounts receivable balances for overstatement on a sample basis. Which of the following would be the least valid reason for deciding to use PPS sampling rather than classical variables sampling?
   a. PPS sampling is generally thought to be easier to use than classical variables sampling.
   b. The internal auditor expects to find no misstatements and PPS sampling typically requires a smaller sample size than classical variables sampling in this situation.
   c. PPS sampling automatically stratifies the population.
   d. Using PPS sampling eliminates the need for professional judgment in determining the appropriate sample size and evaluating the sample results.

Discussion Questions

1. The CAE of HVR Company has asked you to explain the fundamental differences between statistical and nonstatistical sampling in a manner that will help him make an informed decision about the nature of the sampling training that his internal audit staff needs. Explain to the CAE how the two sampling approaches differ with respect to:
   a. Sample size determination.
   b. Sample selection.
   c. Evaluating sample results.

2. You and a friend are studying audit sampling together. Your friend is having a hard time understanding the various aspects of risk associated with attribute sampling and has put together the following list of questions she wants to discuss with you. Answer each question.
   a. What is:
      - Audit risk?
      - Inherent risk?
      - Control risk?
      - Controllable risk?
      - Residual risk?
   b. What is sampling risk? How is sampling risk controlled?
   c. What are the two aspects of sampling risk that an internal auditor is concerned with when testing controls? Briefly describe each aspect.
   d. What is nonsampling risk? How is nonsampling risk controlled?

3. AVF Company processes an average of 400 vouchers payable every month. Each voucher package contains a copy of the check disbursed and supporting documents such as vendor invoices, receiving reports, and purchase orders. The internal auditor plans to examine a sample of vouchers listed in the voucher register using attribute sampling to evaluate the effectiveness of several controls. The attributes of interest include:
   - Agreement of voucher amounts with invoice amounts.
   - Voucher canceled after payment.

   Based on past experience, the auditor expects a deviation rate of 2% for the first attribute and 1% for the second. He decides on a tolerable deviation rate of 7% for the first attribute and 6% for the second. He sets the risk of assessing control risk too low at 5%.

   Assume that the auditor's tests uncovered two occurrences of voucher amounts not agreeing with invoice amounts and two occurrences of vouchers not being canceled after payment.

a. Complete the following schedule. (Note: Round sample size per table up to next number ending in zero for sample size used.)

	Attribute 1	Attribute 2
Risk of assessing control risk too low		
Tolerable deviation rate		
Expected population deviation rate		
Sample size per table		
Sample size used		
Number of deviations identified		
Sample deviation rate		
Achieved upper deviation limit		

b. Evaluate the sample results for the two attributes. Your answer should include:

- A statistical conclusion for each attribute.
- The audit decision you would make based on the quantitative sample results for each attribute.[3]

CASES

CASE 1[4]

Ira Icandoit is a staff auditor in the internal audit function of a small manufacturing company located in western Kansas. Ira recently completed a professional development course on statistical sampling and is very excited about the new knowledge he has gained. He decided to apply his newly gained knowledge during the audit to which he had just been assigned. He used attribute sampling when he performed his tests of controls over the company's procurement transactions.

Ira figured that a tolerable deviation rate of 10% and a 5% risk of assessing control risk too low were appropriate for the tests he planned to perform. He had no idea how many deviations actually might exist in the population, so he set the expected deviation rate at 2% to be conservative. Ira selected a sample of 100 items.

Because Ira believed larger items deserved more attention than smaller items, he selected 75 items with values greater than or equal to $2,500 and 25 items with values less than $2,500. He thought it would be most appropriate to select transactions near the end of the fiscal year, so he randomly selected items for testing from the last two months.

Ira was relieved when he found only six deviations from prescribed controls. One deviation was a missing vendor's invoice, so Ira called the vendor to make sure the transaction was valid. The phone conversation convinced him that the transaction was in fact valid. Three deviations were missing signatures by an authorized manager. The manager explained that he had not approved the invoices because he had been out of the office on the date the invoices were prepared. He reviewed the invoices and told Ira there were no problems with them. The other two deviations involved dollar errors. One was an error in the extension of an invoice, and the other was a misclassification error between expenses, which did not affect net income. Ira considered these two dollar errors to be the only two actual control deviations. He determined that the achieved upper deviation limit was 7% at a 5% risk of assessing control risk too low.

Based on these results, Ira concluded that procurement transactions for the year were unlikely to contain more deviations than the allowable rate. Accordingly, he concluded that controls over procurement transactions were effective and could be relied on by management.

Identify and explain any deficiencies you note in Ira's attribute sampling application.

CASES

CASE 2 The purpose of this case is to familiarize you with the attribute sampling functionality of the IDEA software. If you have not already done so, install the software on your computer from the CD included with this textbook.

A. Open the IDEA software. Locate the description of "Attribute Sampling" in IDEA Help. Answer the following questions.

1. How is "attribute sampling" defined in IDEA Help?
2. What are the two attribute sampling planning options? Briefly describe each option.

B. Click on "Planning (Beta Risk Control)" in the Step-by-Step section of the Attribute Sampling description. Answer the following questions.

1. How is "beta risk" defined in IDEA Help? What are some synonyms for beta risk?
2. Identify and briefly describe the five steps used to determine the minimum sample size and critical number of deviations.

C. Click on "Sample Evaluation" in the Step-by-Step section of the Attribute Sampling description. Answer the following questions.

1. What is the relationship between Planning (Beta Risk Control) and Evaluation?
2. Identify and briefly describe the seven steps used to make inferences about the true rate of deviations in a population from which a sample has been selected and tested.

REFERENCES

[1]*Audit and Accounting Guide: Audit Sampling* (New York, NY: American Institute of Certified Public Accountants, 2008), p. 33.

[2]Available at: http://www.aicpa.org/download/members/div/auditstd/AU-00350.PDF. (as of July 28, 2009).

[3]Protiviti, *Senior Audit School Participant Guide* (Protiviti, Inc.: 2006).

[4]Ratliff, Richard L., and Kurt F. Reding, *Introduction to Auditing: Logic, Principles, and Techniques* (Altamonte Springs, FL: The Institute of Internal Auditors, 2002).

CHAPTER 12
INTRODUCTION TO THE ENGAGEMENT PROCESS

Learning Objectives

- Understand the types of engagements internal auditors perform.
- Understand the key activities involved in planning and performing an assurance engagement and reporting the engagement outcomes.
- Describe how the consulting engagement process differs from the assurance engagement process.

The first 11 chapters of this textbook, which we refer to collectively as the Fundamental Internal Audit Concepts section, cover just that — fundamental internal audit concepts that internal auditors need to know and understand. A firm grasp of these concepts is necessary, but not sufficient, for you to understand internal auditing. You also need to understand the internal audit process, that is, how internal audit assurance and consulting engagements are planned and performed and how engagement outcomes are communicated.

This chapter is the first of four chapters we refer to collectively as the Conducting Internal Audit Engagements section of the textbook. We begin the chapter with a brief description of the types of engagements internal auditors perform. We then present an overview of the internal audit assurance engagement process. We conclude the chapter with a discussion of how consulting engagements differ from assurance engagements and the affects of these differences on the consulting engagement process. In Chapter 13, "Conducting the Assurance Engagement," we discuss in detail how to conduct the assurance engagement process, while in Chapter 14, "Communicating Assurance Engagement Outcomes and Performing Follow-up Procedures," we cover the communication of assurance engagement outcomes. We shift our attention to the consulting engagement process in Chapter 15, "The Consulting Engagement."

It is important to point out that throughout this chapter and those that follow, there are multiple references to the "internal audit function," "internal auditor," and the "internal audit team." While there might be subtle differences in the terms depending on the circumstances described or the context in which the terms are used, generally, all of these references are intended to communicate activities performed by the internal audit function under the supervision of the chief audit executive (CAE) and the direction and oversight of the audit committee. As discussed in detail in Chapter 9, "Managing the

EXHIBIT 12-1

PROFESSIONAL STANDARDS AND PRACTICE ADVISORIES RELEVANT TO CHAPTER 12

1220 – Due Professional Care
2000 – Managing the Internal Audit Activity
2200 – Engagement Planning
2201 – Planning Considerations
2210 – Engagement Objectives
2220 – Engagement Scope
2230 – Engagement Resource Allocation
2240 – Engagement Work Program
2300 – Performing the Engagement
2310 – Identifying Information
2320 – Analysis and Evaluation
2330 – Documenting Information
2340 – Engagement Supervision
2400 – Communicating Results
2410 – Criteria for Communicating
2420 – Quality of Communications
2421 – Errors and Omissions
2431 – Engagement Disclosure of Nonconformance
2440 – Disseminating Results
2500 – Monitoring Progress
2600 – Resolution of Senior Management's Acceptance of Risks

Practice Advisory 2200-1: Engagement Planning
Practice Advisory 2210-1: Engagement Objectives
Practice Advisory 2210.A1-1: Risk Assessment in Engagement Planning
Practice Advisory 2230-1: Engagement Resource Allocation
Practice Advisory 2240-1: Engagement Work Program
Practice Advisory 2330-1: Documenting Information
Practice Advisory 2330.A1-1: Control of Engagement Records
Practice Advisory 2330.A2-1: Retention of Records
Practice Advisory 2340-1: Engagement Supervision
Practice Advisory 2410-1: Communication Criteria
Practice Advisory 2420-1: Quality of Communications
Practice Advisory 2440-1: Disseminating Results
Practice Advisory 2500-1: Monitoring Progress
Practice Advisory 2500.A1-1: Follow-up Process

Internal Audit Function," IIA Standard 2000: Managing the Internal Audit Activity states that "the chief audit executive must effectively manage the internal audit activity to ensure it adds value to the organization."

TYPES OF INTERNAL AUDIT ENGAGEMENTS

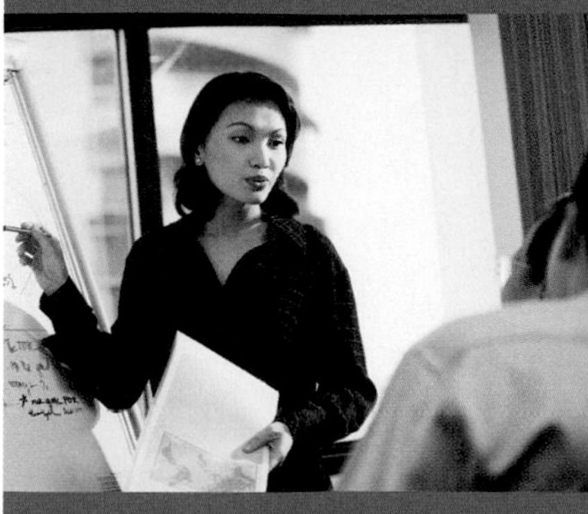

As indicated in Chapter 1, "Introduction to Internal Auditing," internal auditors provide two types of services: assurance services and consulting services. These two types of services are defined in the Glossary to the *International Standards for the Professional Practice of Internal Auditing* (*Standards*) in The International Professional Practices Framework (IPPF) as follows:

> **Assurance Services –** An objective examination of evidence for the purpose of providing an independent assessment on governance, risk management, and control processes for the organization. Examples may include financial, performance, compliance, system security, and due diligence engagements.
>
> **Consulting Services –** Advisory and related . . . service activities, the nature and scope of which are agreed with the [customer], are intended to add value and improve an organization's governance, risk management, and control processes without the internal auditor assuming management responsibility. Examples include counsel, advice, facilitation, and training.

Exhibit 12-2 presents examples of assurance and consulting engagements that internal auditors perform. As reflected in Exhibit 12-2, internal audit assurance and consulting services may be designed to focus directly on operational, reporting, and/or compliance performance or on the controls designed and implemented to provide reasonable assurance that the performance objectives are met. *Controls*-focused engagements performed to assess the design adequacy and operating effectiveness of controls over operations, reporting, and compliance are much more common than *performance*-focused engagements.

Performance-focused Engagements

Focus directly on operational, reporting, and/or compliance performance.

OVERVIEW OF THE ASSURANCE ENGAGEMENT PROCESS

Exhibit 12-3 depicts the controls-focused assurance engagement process, which comprises three fundamental phases — planning, performing, and communicating. Although this exhibit portrays the three phases of the engagement as discrete and sequential steps, actual internal audit engagements do not really work this way. There are no hard lines between planning, performing, and communicating. Where engagement planning ends and performance begins is debatable. In fact, planning typically continues throughout the engagement because adjustments need to be made as new evidence is uncovered. Performing the engagement begins during planning as the internal audit team applies procedures to gather information needed to plan the engagement. Communicating takes place throughout the engagement process as the team communicates important matters to the auditee on an interim basis and not just at the end of the process in the final engagement communication.

Controls-focused Engagements

Focus on the design adequacy and operating effectiveness of controls implemented to provide reasonable assurance that performance objectives are met.

Exhibit 12-3 is useful because it provides a framework for discussing the various activities included in the engagement process. As previously mentioned, it is important to be aware that although various members of the internal audit function will perform the specific activities necessary

EXHIBIT 12-2

EXAMPLES OF INTERNAL AUDIT ASSURANCE AND CONSULTING ENGAGEMENTS

Illustrative Assurance Engagements:

- Assess the design adequacy and operating effectiveness of entity-level controls. Entity-level controls of interest may include, for example:
  - Controls over management override.
  - The organization's entity-level risk assessment process.
  - Controls to monitor the results of operations.
  - Controls over the period-end financial reporting process.
- Assess the design adequacy and operating effectiveness of business process controls. Process controls of interest may include, for example:
  - Controls over the effectiveness and efficiency of operations.
  - Controls over the reliability of financial and/or management reporting.
  - Controls over compliance with applicable laws and regulations.
- Assess the design adequacy and operating effectiveness of information technology (IT) controls. IT controls of interest may include, for example:
  - Entity-level general controls such as system access controls and change management controls.
  - Application controls built into a specific application program.
- Directly assess business process performance. Process performance of interest may include, for example:
  - Operational effectiveness and efficiency reflected in metrics such as customer satisfaction ratings, cycle time, employee turnover, etc.
  - Reporting reliability as reflected in metrics such as the number and monetary magnitude of period-end adjusting entries.
  - Compliance with applicable laws and regulations as reflected in metrics such as the number of reportable accidents or environmental spills.

Illustrative Consulting Engagements:

- Provide advisory services such as:
  - Advice to senior management regarding the risk and control implications of implementing an advanced information technology solution.
  - Advice to process owners about how they can streamline their processes to gain operational efficiencies.
  - Advice to managers at all levels of the organization about how to document and aggregate their risk and control assessments.
- Facilitate self-assessment activities such as:
  - Senior management's assessment of the business risks threatening the organization as a whole.
  - Process owners' assessments of the risks threatening their processes.
- Conduct in-house training such as:
  - Briefing senior management and the audit committee on newly released authoritative guidance pertaining to governance, risk management, and control.
  - Educating process owners and employees about fundamental governance, risk management, and control concepts.

EXHIBIT 12-3

THE ASSURANCE ENGAGEMENT PROCESS

Plan

- Determine engagement objectives and scope.
- Understand the auditee, including auditee objectives and assertions.
- Identify and assess risks.
- Identify key control activities.
- Evaluate adequacy of control design.
- Create a test plan.
- Develop a work program.
- Allocate resources to the engagement.

Perform

- Conduct tests to gather evidence.
- Evaluate evidence gathered and reach conclusions.
- Develop observations and formulate recommendations.

Communicate

- Perform observation evaluation and escalation process.
- Conduct interim and preliminary engagement communications.
- Develop final engagement communications.
- Distribute formal and informal final communications.
- Perform monitoring and follow-up procedures.

to plan, perform, and communicate during an assurance engagement, the CAE retains ultimate responsibility for the work performed. Each of the activities listed in the exhibit under Plan, Perform, and Communicate is briefly described below. The first two phases of the assurance engagement process are covered thoroughly in Chapter 13, "Conducting the Assurance Engagement," and the third phase in Chapter 14, "Communicating Assurance Engagement Outcomes and Performing Follow-up Procedures." Note that a performance-focused assurance engagement will typically include many, but not all, of the activities that are included in Exhibit 12-3. The specific activities and how they are conducted will depend on the objectives of the performance-focused engagement.

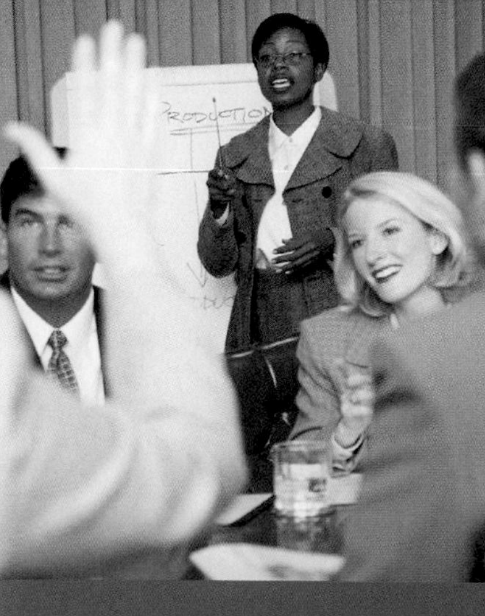

Assurance Engagement Planning Activities

Effective planning is key to the successful completion of any type of project. There is an expression, sometimes referred to as the "six P's," that illustrates this principle: "Proper Prior Planning Prevents Poor Performance." Although it may be tempting to jump right in and start testing, following a structured and disciplined planning approach helps ensure that the engagement is performed effectively and efficiently. Conversely, failure to invest an appropriate amount of time and effort in planning increases the likelihood that the engagement will fail to achieve the desired objectives or that it will achieve the objectives inefficiently. Studying this chapter and the next should deepen readers' appreciation of another expression: "Failing to plan means planning to fail." The following paragraphs discuss planning an engagement.

Determine engagement objectives and scope. An important first step in engagement planning is to determine the engagement objectives (what the engagement is intended to achieve) and scope (what the engagement will and will not cover). One important consideration is the business objective category or categories (strategic, operations, reporting, and/or compliance) of audit interest. For example, will the engagement focus on the operational effectiveness and efficiency of the auditee, the financial reporting aspects of the auditee, or both? Another important consideration is the deliverables the internal audit team is expected to produce. For example, the team might be expected to limit its focus to communicating individual control observations that were identified during the engagement to the appropriate levels of management, or the team might be expected to express an overall conclusion on the controls for the specific area or process in question. A third important consideration is the "boundaries" of the engagement. For example, if the auditee is a business process or subprocess, where does the process or subprocess begin and where does it end? If the auditee is a specified family of geographically separated business units, such as service branches or production facilities, which specific location(s) will the internal audit team visit and what portion(s) of each business unit will the engagement cover?

Auditee Objectives

What the auditee is striving to achieve.

Auditee Assertions

After-the-fact statements of what was achieved.

Understand the auditee, including auditee objectives and assertions. It is virtually impossible to audit effectively something that is not sufficiently understood. The success of any engagement ultimately depends largely on how well the internal audit team understands the auditee. The first thing the internal auditors must understand is the auditee's business objectives and assertions. Business objectives indicate *what the auditee is striving to achieve*. Assertions are after-the-fact statements of *what was achieved*. Although it is preferable for both business objectives and assertions to be expressed explicitly, they are often implicit.

> **Example.** The organization's service department has a written objective of responding to customers' requests for service within 48 hours after the requests are received. Implicit in this objective is the assertion that the service department has implemented the controls necessary to provide reasonable assurance that the objective is achieved. The performance report posted in the service department lobby explicitly asserts that the department met this goal for 92 percent of the customer service requests received over the past three months.

From the auditee's perspective, clear and measurable objectives serve as meaningful targets of performance, and assertions reflect the level of performance achieved. From an internal auditor's perspective, the auditee's objectives and assertions provide a framework for defining the engagement objectives (*what the internal auditor wants to achieve*). Ultimately, the direct link between business objectives and assertions and audit engagement objectives sets the stage for internal auditors to help the auditee achieve its objectives, which in turn helps the organization as a whole achieve its objectives.

Assume, for illustrative purposes, that the auditee is a business process. Other aspects of the process that the internal audit team must understand include:

- How management deploys resources and assigns responsibilities to achieve the objectives of the process.
- The business risks threatening the process.
- The key controls designed and placed in operation to mitigate those risks.
- The relationships between the process and adjoining processes.

- The nature of the outputs (for example, goods and/or services) produced by the process.
- The process activities involved in producing the outputs.
- The process personnel, the responsibilities they are assigned, the authority delegated to them, and the manner in which they are held accountable.
- The tangible and intangible resources used in the process.
- Any recent changes, changes underway, and/or expected changes affecting the process. Note that significant changes affect process risks and, therefore, the design adequacy and operating effectiveness of its controls.

Identify and assess risks. The internal audit team must identify and assess the business risks that threaten the achievement of the auditee's objectives and, ultimately, the organization's objectives. The internal audit team focuses its attention at this stage of the engagement on *inherent risk*, that is, the risk to the auditee in the absence of any actions management might take to reduce or otherwise manage identified risks. Risk assessment involves gauging both the impact of the risk (if it should occur) and the likelihood of the risk occurring. Expressing risks in terms of causes and effects helps the internal auditor assess how big the potential problem is and how likely it is to occur. Take for example the following risk:

> Inefficient processing of vendor invoices for payment (the cause) may result in lost discounts, delays in payment, and vendor dissatisfaction (the effects).

Inherent Risk

The combination of internal and external risk factors in their pure, uncontrolled state.

Analyzing the potential effects (that is, lost discounts, delays in payment, and vendor dissatisfaction) helps the internal auditor judge the size of the potential problem and whether further attention to the risk is warranted. Analyzing the potential cause (that is, inefficiencies), together with the underlying reasons for the potential inefficiencies, helps the internal auditor judge the likelihood of the risk becoming a reality.

The internal audit team also must weigh the assessed risk levels against management's risk tolerance thresholds and decide whether risks are being managed appropriately. Risks assessed at levels within management's risk tolerance thresholds may be *accepted* at their assessed levels. Risks that exceed management's tolerance thresholds must be mitigated to an acceptably low level. Response options to mitigate risks include *avoiding* risks by disbanding the activities that give rise to them, *sharing* risks by transferring a portion of them to third parties (for example, an insurance company), or *reducing* risks by implementing controls designed to lower their impact, likelihood, or both.

Key Control

An activity designed to reduce risk associated with a critical business objective.

Identify key controls. The internal auditor's task at this stage of the engagement planning phase is to identify those controls that are most critical to reducing business risks to acceptably low levels and thus providing assurance that established objectives are achieved. Controls are covered extensively in Chapter 6, "Internal Control." They are discussed again in Chapter 13, "Conducting the Assurance Engagement."

Evaluate the adequacy of control design. The internal audit team must then decide whether the identified key controls are designed adequately to reduce risks, both individually and collectively, to acceptably low levels, assuming that the controls have been placed in operation and are operating as intended. Internal auditors need to recognize at this point that the relationship between risks and controls is not one-to-one — one control may help mitigate several risks, and multiple controls may be needed to mitigate one risk effectively.

Create a test plan. The internal audit team must design the engagement to obtain sufficient appropriate evidence to achieve the engagement objectives. Creating a test plan involves determining the nature, timing, and extent of the procedures needed to gather the required audit evidence. Test plans may include direct tests of controls, tests of performance that provide indirect evidence regarding the operating effectiveness of controls, or both. A plan for testing controls already placed in operation should ensure that sufficient appropriate evidence is gathered and evaluated to determine whether adequately designed controls are operating effectively.

Engagement Work Program

A document that lists the procedures to be followed during an engagement, designed to achieve the engagement plan.

Develop a work program. The work program is an extremely important planning device. It specifically outlines the audit procedures required to accomplish the engagement objectives. Over the course of the engagement, internal auditors sign off on the procedures to indicate that the work has been completed. This, in turn, enables engagement team supervisors to review the work that has been finished and monitor the work that remains to be done. At the end of the engagement, the completed program serves as a record of the work completed and documents who completed the work and when it was completed.

Allocate resources to the engagement. The last step in planning the engagement is to allocate the resources that are needed to successfully (that is, effectively and efficiently) complete the engagement. This involves determining the audit expertise needed, estimating the time it will take to complete the engagement, assigning appropriate internal auditors to the engagement, and scheduling the work so that it is completed timely.

Assurance Engagement Performance Activities

Conduct tests to gather evidence. Performing the engagement involves the application of specific audit procedures to gather evidence. Procedures include, for example, making inquiries, observing operations, inspecting documents, and analyzing the reasonableness of information. A second important aspect of gathering evidence is documenting the procedures performed and the results of performing the procedures. Documenting audit evidence is discussed in Chapter 10, "Audit Evidence and Working Papers." Chapter 13, "Conducting the Assurance Engagement," focuses specifically on conducting and documenting tests to determine whether controls are designed adequately and operating as designed.

Evaluate audit evidence gathered and reach conclusions. Evaluating the audit evidence gathered to determine, for example, whether controls are designed adequately and operating effectively requires a significant degree of professional judgment. The internal audit team must ultimately reach logical conclusions (that is, make informed decisions) based on the evidence gathered. Chapter 13 illustrates how an internal auditor documents conclusions that are reached based on the results of testing. Chapter 14, "Communicating Assurance Engagement Outcomes and Performing Follow-up Procedures," illustrates how an internal auditor formulates and documents conclusions on the engagement as a whole.

Develop observations and formulate recommendations. Observations (also referred to as *findings*) are defined in Practice Advisory 2410-1: Communication Criteria as "pertinent statements of fact" that "emerge by a process of comparing criteria (the correct state) with condition (the current state)." Well-written audit observations contain the following elements (sometimes referred to as the 4 C's):

- The *criteria* are the standards, measures, or expectations used in making an evaluation, that is, the "what should be" (correct) state.
- The *condition* is the factual evidence the internal auditor found, that is, the "what is" (current) state.
- The *consequences* are the real or potential adverse effects of the gap between the existing condition and the criteria. Practice Advisory 2410-1 calls this element the "effect."
- The *causes* are the underlying reasons for the gap between the expected and actual condition, which lead to the adverse consequences.

Note that when the "what is" condition matches the "what should be" criteria, there is no "gap" and, therefore, no consequences or causes to deal with.

"Recommendations are based on the internal auditor's observations and conclusions" (Practice Advisory 2410-1). Audit recommendations (also referred to as *proposed corrective actions*) may be documented as part of the audit observation or separately (some internal auditors refer to corrective actions as the fifth C). Recommendations are aimed at closing the gap between the observation criteria and condition. Meaningful recommendations for corrective actions address the causes of the gap between the criteria and condition, provide long-term solutions rather than short-term fixes, and are economically feasible. Recommendations that address symptoms of problems rather than root causes tend to be of little value.

Observation

A finding, determination, or judgment derived from the internal auditor's test results.

Assurance Engagement Communication Activities

Communicating outcomes is a critical component of all internal audit engagements. Regardless of the content or form of the communication, which may vary, communication of engagement outcomes "must be accurate, objective, clear, concise, constructive, complete, and timely" (IIA Standard 2420: Quality of Communications).

Perform observation evaluation and escalation process. Once one or more observations are identified, the internal audit team must assess each observation using an evaluation and escalation process and determine the implications those observations have on the resulting communications for the area (process) under review. Exhibit 12-4 illustrates one organization's approach to handling observations of varying levels of significance. Chapter 14 includes a detailed description of the observation evaluation and escalation process.

Conduct interim and preliminary engagement communications. As indicated, internal audit communications occur throughout the engagement, not just at the end. Matters often arise during internal audit

EXHIBIT 12-4

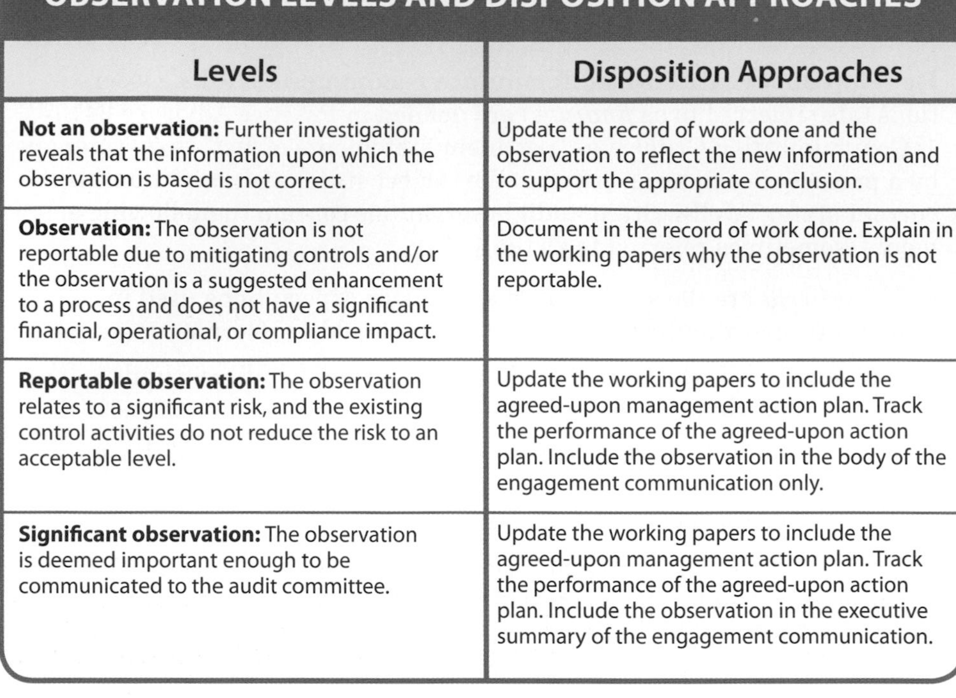

OBSERVATION LEVELS AND DISPOSITION APPROACHES

Levels	Disposition Approaches
Not an observation: Further investigation reveals that the information upon which the observation is based is not correct.	Update the record of work done and the observation to reflect the new information and to support the appropriate conclusion.
Observation: The observation is not reportable due to mitigating controls and/or the observation is a suggested enhancement to a process and does not have a significant financial, operational, or compliance impact.	Document in the record of work done. Explain in the working papers why the observation is not reportable.
Reportable observation: The observation relates to a significant risk, and the existing control activities do not reduce the risk to an acceptable level.	Update the working papers to include the agreed-upon management action plan. Track the performance of the agreed-upon action plan. Include the observation in the body of the engagement communication only.
Significant observation: The observation is deemed important enough to be communicated to the audit committee.	Update the working papers to include the agreed-upon management action plan. Track the performance of the agreed-upon action plan. Include the observation in the executive summary of the engagement communication.

engagements that warrant management's immediate or short-term attention. Timely communication of such matters allows management to address and resolve them sooner, sometimes before the engagement is completed. Other information that may be conveyed to the auditee on an interim basis during the engagement includes, for example, changes in engagement scope and engagement progress.

It is important for the internal audit team to give management a chance to clarify matters and express their thoughts about the team's conclusions and recommendations. Moreover, words stated in writing are sometimes interpreted differently than words spoken, and both are subject to misinterpretation. Reviewing draft versions of the report with management provides assurance that they concur with what the internal auditors have said and what they have written in their report.

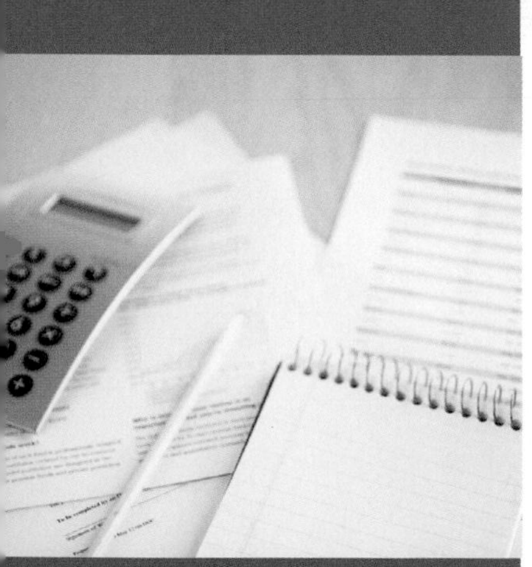

Develop final engagement communications. At this point, the internal audit team is ready to consolidate and synthesize all the evidence gathered during the engagement. There is no single prescribed way for expressing overall engagement results. Options include:

- Listing and prioritizing control observations but stopping short of reaching an overall conclusion or expressing any level of assurance regarding the effectiveness of the auditee's controls.
- Reaching a conclusion known as negative assurance (also referred to as limited assurance). Internal auditors express negative assurance when they conclude that nothing has come to their attention that indicates that the auditee's controls are designed inadequately or operating ineffectively.
- Reaching a conclusion known as positive assurance (also referred to as reasonable assurance). Internal auditors express positive assurance when they conclude that, in their opinion, the auditee's controls are designed adequately and operating effectively.

Distribute formal and informal final communications. Several IIA *Standards* directly pertain to preparing and issuing the final engagement report, including:

> **Standard 2410: Criteria for Communicating.** Communications must include the engagement's objectives and scope as well as applicable conclusions, recommendations, and action plans.
>
> 2410.A1 – Final communication of engagement results must, where appropriate, contain the internal auditors' overall opinion and/or conclusions.
>
> 2410.A2 – Internal auditors are encouraged to acknowledge satisfactory performance in engagement communications.
>
> 2410.A3 – When releasing engagement results to parties outside the organization, the communication must include limitations on distribution and use of the results.
>
> **Standard 2440: Disseminating Results.** The chief audit executive must communicate results to the appropriate parties.
>
> 2440.A1 – The chief audit executive is responsible for communicating the final results to parties who can ensure that the results are given due consideration.
>
> 2440.A2 – If not otherwise mandated by legal, statutory, or regulatory requirements, prior to releasing results to parties outside the organization the chief audit executive must:
>
> - Assess the potential risk to the organization;
> - Consult with senior management and/or legal counsel as appropriate; and
> - Control dissemination by restricting the use of the results.

Also, Practice Advisory 2410-1: Communication Criteria states that all final engagement communications "are to contain, at a minimum, the purpose, scope, and results of the engagement." The purpose represents the engagement objectives, that is, why the engagement was conducted and what it was expected to achieve. The scope defines the activities included in the engagement, the nature and extent of work performed, and the time period covered. The scope also may identify related activities not included in the engagement, if necessary, to delineate the boundaries of the engagement. Results include observations, conclusions, opinions, recommendations, and action plans. The final engagement communications also may contain the auditee's responses to the internal audit team's conclusions, opinions, and recommendations.

The observations that should be included in the formal, final engagement communication are those that must be reported to support, or prevent misunderstanding of, the internal audit team's conclusions and recommendations. Less significant observations may be communicated informally. Conclusions and opinions express the internal audit team's evaluations of the observations. Recommendations, which are based on the observations and conclusions, are proposed actions to correct existing conditions or improve operations. Action plans document what management has agreed to do to address the internal audit team's observations, conclusions, and recommendations.

The CAE, or another high-ranking internal auditor designated by the CAE, should review and approve the final report before it is issued to the auditee's management.

The CAE, or appointed designee, must determine to whom, other than management of the area or process audited, the final engagement report will be distributed. Appropriate recipients are those members of the organization who can ensure that the engagement results will be given due consideration. Such individuals are those who are in a position to take corrective action or ensure that corrective action is taken. Summary reports, which highlight engagement results significant to the organization as a whole, may be more appropriate for senior management, the audit committee, and the board of directors.

Perform monitoring and follow-up procedures. As is apparent in Exhibit 12-3, the assurance engagement process does not end with reporting. IIA Standard 2500: Monitoring Progress states that "the chief audit executive must establish and maintain a system to *monitor* [italics added] the disposition of results communicated to management." Standard 2500.A1 goes on to say that "the chief audit executive must establish a *follow-up* [italics added] process to monitor and ensure that management actions have been effectively implemented or that senior management has accepted the risk of not taking action."

Monitoring Progress

The follow-up process established by the CAE to ensure that management actions have been effectively implemented or that senior management has accepted the risk of not taking action.

It is very important for the internal audit function to determine that corrective actions on engagement observations and recommendations were, in fact, taken by management and that the actions taken remedy the underlying conditions in a timely manner. The internal audit charter should define the internal audit function's responsibility for follow-up, and the CAE should determine the nature, timing, and extent of follow-up procedures appropriate for a particular engagement. The internal audit function's monitoring and follow-up responsibilities are further discussed in Practice Advisories 2500-1: Monitoring Process, and 2500.A1-1: Follow-up Process.

THE CONSULTING ENGAGEMENT PROCESS

Internal audit consulting engagements differ from assurance engagements in certain ways, including:

- Whereas the nature and scope of an assurance engagement are determined by the internal audit function, the nature and scope of a consulting engagement are subject to agreement with the engagement customer.
- Consulting engagements are, accordingly, much more discretionary in nature than assurance engagements. As indicated in the Glossary to the *Standards*, consulting services include "counsel, advice, facilitation, and training."

The consulting engagement process includes the same steps as the assurance engagement process depicted in Exhibit 12-3. However, each step may not be necessary for every consulting engagement, and many of the steps may be conducted differently. As indicated in the relevant standards cited below, the three major phases of the engagement — planning, performing, and communicating — remain the same.

Engagement planning. "Internal auditors must develop and document a plan for each [consulting] engagement, including the engagement's objectives, scope, timing, and resource allocations" (IIA Standard 2200: Engagement Planning). "Internal auditors must establish an understanding with consulting engagement [customers] about objectives, scope, respective responsibilities, and other [customer] expectations" (Standard 2201.C1). The "internal auditors must ensure that the scope of the engagement is sufficient to address the agreed-upon objectives" (Standard 2220.C1). "Work programs for consulting engagements may vary in form and content depending upon the nature of the engagement" (Standard 2240.C1).

Performing the engagement. "Internal auditors must identify, analyze, evaluate, and document sufficient information to achieve the [consulting] engagement's objectives" (IIA Standard 2300: Performing the Engagement). The kind of information identified, analyzed, evaluated, and documented will vary depending on the nature of the engagement, as will the nature, timing, and extent of internal audit procedures performed.

Communicating results. "Internal auditors must communicate the [consulting] engagement results" (IIA Standard 2400: Communicating Results). "Communications must include the engagement's objectives and scope as well as applicable conclusions, recommendations, and action plans" (IIA Standard 2410: Criteria for Communicating). However, "communication of the progress and results of consulting engagements will vary in form and content depending upon the nature of the engagement and the needs of the [customer]" (Standard 2410.C1). For example, the deliverables for a consulting engagement in which the internal audit function has been asked by the customer to provide advice regarding specific matters of interest will differ from the deliverables of facilitation or training engagements.

SUMMARY

Internal auditors provide two types of services: assurance services and consulting services, either of which can be controls focused and/or performance focused. The engagement process for both types of service comprises three major phases — planning, performing, and communicating. The primary steps executed in a controls-focused assurance engagement are outlined in Exhibit 12-3. The nature and scope of assurance engagements are determined unilaterally by the internal audit function, and the process tends to be relatively uniform from engagement to engagement. In contrast, the nature and scope of each consulting engagement are determined jointly by the internal audit function and the customer, and the specific process steps typically vary by engagement.

This chapter is the first of four chapters referred to collectively as the Conducting Internal Audit Engagements section of the textbook. Chapter 13, "Conducting the Assurance Engagement," describes the planning and performing phases in detail, and Chapter 14, "Communicating Assurance Engagement Outcomes and Performing Follow-up Procedures," goes on to cover the communicating phase. Chapter 15, "The Consulting Engagement," provides an in-depth discussion of consulting services and the consulting engagement process.

Review Questions

1. What two types of services do internal auditors provide? Provide three examples of each type of engagement.
2. What are the three phases of the assurance engagement process?
3. What steps are included in the planning phase of an assurance engagement?
4. What is the relationship between business objectives and business assertions?
5. What does "inherent risk" mean?
6. Why is it useful for an internal auditor to express risks in terms of causes and effects?
7. What are management's risk response options?
8. What purposes does a well-written work program serve?
9. What does allocating resources to the engagement involve?
10. What steps are included in the performance phase of an assurance engagement?
11. What elements do well-written observations include?
12. What are the characteristics of meaningful recommendations?
13. What are the key quality characteristics of internal audit engagement communications?
14. What steps are included in the communication phase of an assurance engagement?
15. What is the difference between "negative assurance" and "positive assurance?"
16. What information must final assurance engagement communications include?
17. How do internal audit consulting engagements differ from assurance engagements?

Multiple-choice Questions

Select the best answer for each of the following questions.

1. The tasks performed during an internal audit assurance engagement should address the following questions:

   I. What are the reasons for the results?
   II. How can performance be improved?
   III. What results are being achieved?

   The chronological order in which these questions should be addressed is:

   a. III, I, II.
   b. I, III, II.
   c. III, II, I.
   d. II, III, I.

2. While planning an assurance engagement, the internal auditor obtains knowledge about the auditee's operations to, among other things:

   a. Develop an attitude of professional skepticism concerning management's assertions.
   b. Make constructive suggestions to management regarding internal control improvements.
   c. Evaluate whether misstatements in the auditee's performance reports should be communicated to senior management and the audit committee.
   d. Develop an understanding of the auditee's objectives, risks, and controls.

3. Which of the following statements does not illustrate the concept of inherent business risk?

   a. Cash is more susceptible to theft than an inventory of sheet metal.
   b. A broken lock on a security gate allows employees to access a restricted area that they are not authorized to enter.
   c. Transactions involving complex calculations are more likely to be misstated than transactions involving simple calculations.
   d. Technological developments might make a particular product obsolete.

4. Comprehensive risk assessment involves analysis of both causes and effects. Which of the following statements concerning the analysis of causes and effects is false?

   a. Analyzing the causes and effects of a particular risk should only be performed after the internal auditor has first obtained evidence that a problem has occurred.
   b. Analyzing the causes and effects of a particular risk provides insights about how to best manage the risk.
   c. Analyzing the effects of a particular risk provides insights about the relative size of the risk and the relative importance of the business objective threatened by the risk.
   d. Analyzing the root causes of a particular risk helps the internal auditor formulate recommendations for reducing the risk to an acceptable level.

5. Internal auditors obtain an understanding of controls and perform tests of controls to:
   a. Detect material misstatements in account balances.
   b. Reduce control risk to an acceptably low level.
   c. Evaluate the design adequacy and operating effectiveness of the controls.
   d. Assess the inherent risks associated with transactions.

6. If an internal auditor's evaluation of internal control design indicates that the controls are designed adequately, the appropriate next step would be to:
   a. Test the operating effectiveness of the controls.
   b. Prepare a flowchart depicting the system of internal controls.
   c. Conclude that residual risk is low.
   d. Conclude that control risk is high.

7. Reported internal audit observations emerge by a process of comparing "what should be" with "what is." In determining "what should be" during an audit of a company's treasury function, which of the following would be the least desirable criterion against which to judge current operations?
   a. Best practices of the treasury function in relevant industries.
   b. Company policies and procedures delegating authority and assigning responsibilities.
   c. Performance standards established by senior management.
   d. The operations of the treasury function as documented during the last audit.

8. Internal auditors sometimes express opinions in addition to stating observations in their reports. Due professional care requires that internal audit opinions be:
   a. Based on sufficient appropriate evidence.
   b. Limited to the effectiveness of internal controls.
   c. Expressed only when requested by management or the audit committee.
   d. Based on experience and free from errors in judgment.

9. Which of the following statements best describes an internal audit function's responsibility for assurance engagement follow-up activities?
   a. The internal audit function should determine that corrective action has been taken and is achieving the desired results, or that senior management has assumed the risk associated with not taking corrective action on reported observations.
   b. The internal audit function should determine whether management has initiated corrective action but has no responsibility to determine whether the corrective action is achieving the desired results. That determination is management's responsibility.

c. The CAE is responsible for scheduling audit follow-up activities only if asked to do so by senior management or the audit committee. Otherwise, such activities are discretionary.

d. Audit follow-up activities are not necessary if the auditee has agreed in writing to implement the internal audit function's recommendations.

10. Internal auditors perform both assurance engagements and consulting engagements. Which of the following would be classified as a consulting engagement?

    a. Directly assessing the organization's compliance with laws and regulations.

    b. Assessing the design adequacy of the organization's entity-level monitoring activities.

    c. Facilitating senior management's assessment of risks threatening the organization.

    d. Assisting the independent outside auditor during the financial statement audit engagement.

Discussion Questions

1. Recall the definition of inherent risk. Why is it important for internal auditors to focus on inherent risk during the planning phase of an assurance engagement?

2. COSO defines risk as the possibility that an event will occur and adversely affect the achievement of an objective. An illustrative objective and event are presented below:

Objective	Event
To safeguard the city's citizens and resources	An accident at a four-way intersection

    a. Identify three potential adverse consequences of the event occurring.

    b. Identify three inherent risk factors that make the event more or less probable.

    c. The city's management must decide how to respond to this risk. Two of its choices are to (1) avoid the risk or (2) reduce the risk to an acceptably low level.

        1. Explain how the city can avoid the risk.

        2. Identify *two* ways the city can reduce the risk.

3. Consider the following two statements:

    Evaluating the adequacy of control design is necessary but not sufficient if the objective of an assurance engagement is to reach a conclusion regarding the overall effectiveness of controls.

    If an internal auditor determines that a control is inadequately designed, there is no good reason to test the operating effectiveness of the control.

    Do you agree with each of these statements? Explain.

4. Reflect on the following ways of expressing overall assurance engagement results introduced in this chapter:
   - Listing and prioritizing observations without expressing any level of assurance.
   - Expressing a conclusion known as negative (limited) assurance.
   - Expressing a conclusion known as positive (reasonable) assurance.

   a. Which level of assurance requires the strongest supporting audit evidence? Why?
   b. What other factors, if any, might a CAE consider when deciding which of the three options is the most appropriate for a particular assurance engagement?

5. Internal auditors provide two types of services: assurance services and consulting services.
   a. How do these two types of services differ in terms of purpose?
   b. In what other ways do consulting engagements differ from assurance engagements?

CASE[1]

AFR Manufacturing Company's senior management asked the internal audit function to conduct an operational safety audit of the production facility's metal drill press unit. More specifically, the internal audit function was asked to determine how well the metal drill press equipment and equipment operators comply with company safety policies.

Five downtime injuries of drill press operators occurred in the last six months. The total downtime for the five injuries was 37 hours. Management estimated that the drill press downtime, and the resultant decrease in overall productivity, reduced revenue by approximately $265,000. In addition to the downtime injuries, two drill press operators experienced detectible hearing loss during the six-month period.

The internal auditors learned that the company's safety policies include the following:

- Operators are required to wear safety glasses, ear plugs, and protective gloves.
- The drill presses are required to have a clear, plastic safety shield and a protected channel to safely feed the metal through the press.
- The drill is operated by a knee switch. The operator engages and disengages the drill by shifting his or her right knee.

The internal auditors found the equipment to be in relatively poor condition with little evidence of any regular maintenance. Drill bits were not replaced as they became dull and broken bits often were used because new bits were not kept in supply. Two of the 10 drill press machines were missing safety shields. Five of the 10 machine operators were using the protective ear plugs at the time the auditors visited the plant and six were wearing safety glasses. Four of the knee switches were found to be sticking occasionally in both the off and on positions. The auditors perceived a general sense of negligence — negligence by production management, drill press equipment operators, and maintenance employees.

A. Based on the scenario presented above:

1. Clearly state the internal audit engagement objective.
2. Prepare one or more well-written internal audit observations that include: condition, criteria, consequence(s), and cause(s).

B. Refer to Exhibit 12-4. At what level would you position the observation(s) you prepared in A.2. above? Clearly explain your rationale.

C. Draft a memo to senior management in which you describe a consulting engagement that the internal audit function could perform in response to the operational safety audit results.

REFERENCES

[1]Adapted from: Ratliff, Richard L., and Kurt F. Reding, *Introduction to Auditing: Logic, Principles, and Techniques* (Altamonte Springs, FL: The Institute of Internal Auditors, 2002).

CHAPTER 13
CONDUCTING THE ASSURANCE ENGAGEMENT

Learning Objectives

- Describe how the purpose of an assurance engagement impacts the audit objectives.
- Determine engagement objectives and scope statements.
- Describe different types and sources of information that will help the internal auditor understand the process of conducting an assurance engagement.
- Document simple process flows, showing key process steps, interfaces, and departments involved.
- Perform a process-level risk assessment.
- Distinguish key controls from controls not considered key.
- Describe how to evaluate the design adequacy of process-level controls.
- Design different types of testing approaches, depending on the design of the process and engagement objectives.
- Develop a general work program to guide the engagement process.
- Describe the resource considerations that must be evaluated when determining how to staff and schedule an engagement.
- Conduct and document certain types of tests to gather evidence.
- Evaluate evidence from assurance procedures to reach conclusions based on the results of testing.
- Develop observations and formulate recommendations.

EXHIBIT 13-1

PROFESSIONAL STANDARDS AND PRACTICE ADVISORIES RELEVANT TO CHAPTER 13

2200 – Engagement Planning
2201 – Planning Considerations
2210 – Engagement Objectives
2220 – Engagement Scope
2230 – Engagement Resource Allocation
2240 – Engagement Work Program
2300 – Performing the Engagement
2310 – Identifying Information
2320 – Analysis and Evaluation
2330 – Documenting Information
2340 – Engagement Supervision

Practice Advisory 2200-1: Engagement Planning
Practice Advisory 2210-1: Engagement Objectives
Practice Advisory 2210.A1-1: Risk Assessment in Engagement Planning
Practice Advisory 2230-1: Engagement Resource Allocation
Practice Advisory 2240-1: Engagement Work Program
Practice Advisory 2330-1: Documenting Information
Practice Advisory 2330.A1-1: Control of Engagement Records
Practice Advisory 2330.A2-1: Retention of Records
Practice Advisory 2340-1: Engagement Supervision

Assurance Engagement

An engagement involving an objective examination of evidence for the purpose of providing an independent assessment on governance, risk management, and control processes for the organization.

This chapter describes the various steps necessary to conduct a controls-focused assurance engagement. Specifically, as depicted in Exhibit 13-2, which was introduced as Exhibit 12-2 in the previous chapter, you will learn the key steps necessary to plan and perform the assurance engagement.

The first section of this chapter focuses on the planning steps. This is covered in considerable depth as effective planning is integral to conducting a successful engagement. Executing these steps provides confidence that the engagement will (1) be comprehensive, (2) align with the organization's objectives, and (3) support the internal audit function's charter. After reviewing this section, you should fully appreciate the expression, "failing to plan means you are planning to fail."

The second section of the chapter focuses on executing the test program designed during the planning stage. While performing audit tests typically takes more time than planning an engagement, this section is shorter than the planning section as there are relatively few key steps; these steps are simply performed over and over again to test different control assertions. The assurance engagement performance activities are discussed in Chapter 12, "Introduction to the Engagement Process." Additionally, techniques to evaluate and report on audit observations are covered in Chapter 14, "Communicating Assurance Engagement

THE ASSURANCE ENGAGEMENT PROCESS

EXHIBIT 13-2

Plan	Perform	Communicate
• Determine engagement objectives and scope. • Understand the auditee, including auditee objectives and assertions. • Identify and assess risks. • Identify key control activities. • Evaluate adequacy of control design. • Create a test plan. • Develop a work program. • Allocate resources to the engagement.	• Conduct tests to gather evidence. • Evaluate evidence gathered and reach conclusions. • Develop observations and formulate recommendations.	• Perform observation evaluation and escalation process. • Conduct interim and preliminary engagement communications. • Develop final engagement communications. • Distribute formal and informal final communications. • Perform monitoring and follow-up procedures.

Outcomes and Performing Follow-up Procedures." Therefore, the performance section of this chapter focuses on applying those concepts, rather than restating them. The information contained in this chapter provides a solid understanding of how to plan and perform almost any assurance engagement.

Throughout this chapter, examples are provided for many of the key steps to illustrate how they can be conducted and documented. These examples relate to a fictitious company, Books 2 Buy, and focus on the accounts payable and disbursements process (referred to as the cash disbursements process throughout the chapter). This particular process is being illustrated as it is common to most organizations, regardless of size or industry. Key facts regarding Books 2 Buy can be found in Exhibit 13-3. These facts help make the examples more realistic.

Planning is the first phase of an assurance engagement and involves several steps. Refer to Exhibit 13-4 for a list of these specific steps, each of which will be discussed in more detail in the following sections.

DETERMINE ENGAGEMENT OBJECTIVES AND SCOPE

Reasons for Conducting an Engagement

As discussed in Chapter 12, there are different types of assurance engagements and there may be different reasons for conducting any of them. The type of engagement and reasons for performing it may significantly influence how the engagement is performed. Therefore, it is important to understand the reasons for conducting the engagement before beginning the planning.

There are a number of reasons for performing assurance engagements, including, but not limited to:

- The engagement was identified in the annual internal audit plan because of inherent risks identified during the business

EXHIBIT 13-3

FACTS SUPPORTING BOOKS 2 BUY EXAMPLES IN CHAPTER 13

- Books 2 Buy is a textbook publisher, providing educational tools for the K-8, high school, and post-secondary education markets.
- The company is publicly traded, is based in Dallas, Texas, and has customers in the United States, Canada, England, South Africa, Japan, Australia, and New Zealand.
- Books 2 Buy employs a professional editorial team and contracts with noted academics and other professionals to write the textbooks.
- All printing and binding activities are outsourced, which represents one of the most significant costs to the company.
- The company leases space for its distribution centers, which are located in all of the countries in which it does business.
- Annual revenues for Books 2 Buy total US $550 million, cash expenditures approximate US $480 million, noncash expenditures (for example, depreciation and amortization) approximate US $25 million, and long-term capital expenditures approximate US $40 million.
- On average, the US $480 million in annual cash expenditures are disbursed as follows:

	% of Disbursements	% of US Dollars
Electronic or wire transfers	10%	60%
Computer generated checks	88%	38%
Manual checks	2%	2%

- While disbursements may be made in different currencies, all are processed out of a centralized disbursements function located in Dallas, Texas.

Purpose of Engagements:

- **Part of annual plan**
- **Compliance requirement**
- **Postmortem**
- **Significant changes**

risk assessment process, risks detected the last time the area was audited, and other relevant factors. For these engagements, the internal auditor must understand what underlying business risks caused the engagement to be included in the plan, and then design the engagement plan to provide the appropriate assurance regarding the design adequacy and operating effectiveness of controls implemented to mitigate those risks.

- The engagement is part of an annual requirement to evaluate the organization's system of internal controls for external reporting purposes, such as the U.S. Sarbanes-Oxley Act of 2002 Section 404 requirements in the United States and similar financial reporting laws in other countries. For these engagements, the internal auditor must ensure that the engagement is designed to test the areas covered by the underlying regulations (for example, provide assurance regarding the design adequacy and operating effectiveness of internal control over financial reporting).
- A recent event (for example, natural disaster, fraud, or customer bankruptcy) has tested the process under unusual circumstances and management desires a "post mortem" to determine where the process was effective and where it was not. For these engagements, the internal auditor must tailor the testing and evaluation around the specific event that occurred.
- Changes in the business or industry require immediate modifications to the process and management desires a quick validation that these modifications appear to be designed appropriately to address the changes. For these engagements, the internal auditor may perform a full controls-focused audit or they may scope it to focus only on the controls that changed.

THE ASSURANCE ENGAGEMENT PROCESS

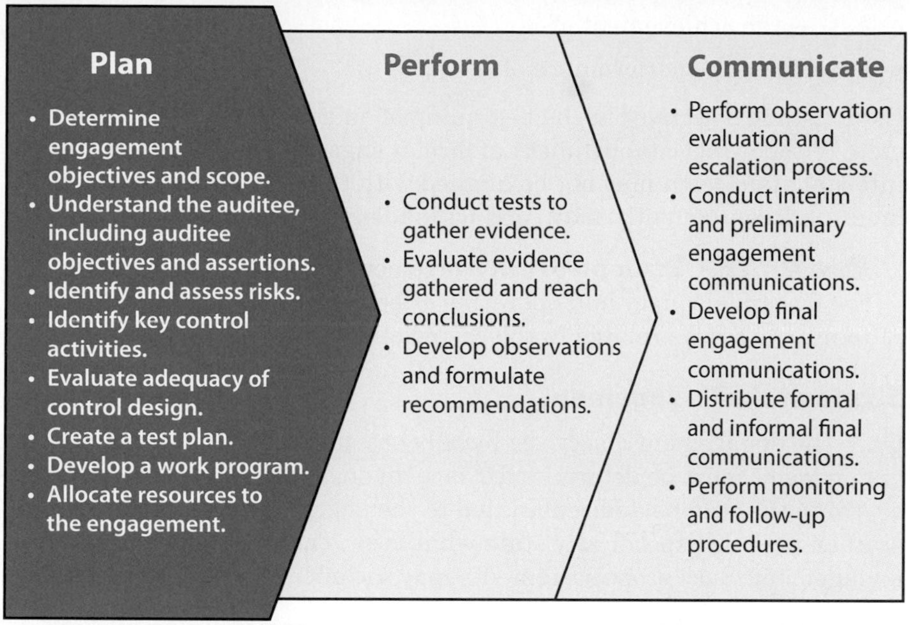

EXHIBIT 13-4

Plan	Perform	Communicate
• Determine engagement objectives and scope. • Understand the auditee, including auditee objectives and assertions. • Identify and assess risks. • Identify key control activities. • Evaluate adequacy of control design. • Create a test plan. • Develop a work program. • Allocate resources to the engagement.	• Conduct tests to gather evidence. • Evaluate evidence gathered and reach conclusions. • Develop observations and formulate recommendations.	• Perform observation evaluation and escalation process. • Conduct interim and preliminary engagement communications. • Develop final engagement communications. • Distribute formal and informal final communications. • Perform monitoring and follow-up procedures.

There may be other factors, in addition to those listed above, that make it important for the internal audit team to be aware of the reasons or drivers that caused the engagement to be performed. For example, instead of looking for assurance regarding the different assertions discussed above, management may desire an engagement be conducted to assess how a process is performing relative to expectations. This type of engagement may necessitate different tests to provide that assessment. Regardless of the reasons for conducting an engagement, understanding such reasons will help ensure that the overall objectives, scope, and focus of the engagement address those drivers and time is not devoted to other, less important drivers.

> *Books2Buy* **Example**: The cash disbursements process engagement was included in the annual internal audit plan because of inherent risks identified during the business risk assessment process (refer to Chapter 5, "Business Processes and Risks," for discussion of the business risk assessment process).

Establishing Engagement Objectives

Once the reasons for the assurance engagement are understood, formal engagement objectives should be established. These objectives, which typically are stated in the final assurance engagement communication, articulate specifically what the engagement is trying to accomplish. While objectives may be stated in a variety of ways, it should be clear what assurance the engagement will provide. For example, objectives could start with the following phrases (different verbs can be substituted for those used in these examples):

Engagement Objectives

What an audit wants to achieve.

- Evaluate the design adequacy of . . .
- Determine the operating effectiveness of . . .
- Assess compliance with . . .

- Determine the effectiveness and efficiency of . . .
- Evaluate the accuracy of . . .
- Assess the achievement of . . .
- Determine the performance of . . .

Establishing objectives at the beginning of an engagement is a critical step. Without the establishment of formal engagement objectives, the internal audit team may not be aligned with the reasons for the engagement and, consequently, may conduct inadequate or unnecessary tasks.

> *Books2Buy* **Example**: The engagement objective is to evaluate the design adequacy and operating effectiveness of controls in place to mitigate risks related to the cash disbursements process.

Scope of the Engagement

Scope

What is or is not included within an engagement.

Once the engagement objectives have been established, the scope of the engagement must be determined. Since an engagement may not cover everything that can be audited related to the engagement objectives, scope statements must specifically state what is or is not included within an engagement. Such scope statements may include:

- **Boundaries of the process.** While some processes are small and self-contained, many are very broad and overlap with other processes. Therefore, it is important to define at what point in the process the engagement will begin (for example, the initial inputs from transactions or other processes) and where it will end (for example, reports, financial statements, or outputs to other processes).
- **In-scope versus out-of-scope locations.** For processes that cover multiple locations, only some of those locations may be included in the engagement.
- **Subprocesses.** Larger processes may be composed of a series of subprocesses (for example, the cash disbursements process may include the invoice matching and validation, disbursements input, and payment processing subprocesses).
- **Components.** Certain portions, or components, of a process may be omitted. For example, if the computer application supporting a process was audited relatively recently, the manual controls related to that process may be included in the scope, while the automated controls are not.
- **Time frame.** An engagement may cover a calendar year, the previous 12 months, or some other time frame.

Subprocess

A discrete and recognizable portion or component of a process.

Decisions regarding scope require a great deal of professional judgment. The internal auditor must ensure that the scope is sufficient to meet the engagement objectives. Articulating the specific scope statements will enable the internal audit team to better focus the specific tests. In addition, recipients of the communication will be better able to interpret the findings within the context of the engagement objectives.

> *Books2Buy* **Example**: The following will be included within the scope of this engagement:
>
> - Cash disbursements procedures, beginning with the receipt of an invoice or a similar document evidencing the creation of a

liability to pay, and ending with the disbursement of funds and recording of such disbursement in the general ledger.

- All three types of disbursements (electronic wires, computer-generated checks, and manual checks).
- Disbursements in U.S. dollars and other currencies.
- Disbursements that were processed during the last 12 months.

Expected Outcomes and Deliverables

Before moving on to the next step in the planning process, one final task should be performed. While the objectives and scope have been determined, it is helpful to apply one of the *Seven Habits of Highly Effective People:* "Begin with the end in mind."[1] There are two important "ends" to consider that will help validate the engagement objectives and scope: (1) potential outcomes of the tests to be performed during the engagement, and (2) auditee expectations regarding engagement communications. Each of these is described more fully as follows:

- **Potential outcomes of the tests to be performed during the engagement**. Being able to anticipate the different types of testing exceptions that may be identified in a given engagement helps the internal auditor plan tests to provide reasonable assurance that such discrepancies are detected. Typical exceptions include:
  - **Financial statement errors or misclassifications** within financial accounts, balances, or disclosures.
  - **Control deficiencies** indicating specific controls that are not achieving the desired effect, that is, mitigating the corresponding risks to the desired level.
  - **Shortfalls in objective achievement**, due to control deficiencies or inadequate performance.
  - **Inefficiencies** due to resources not being deployed in an optimal manner.
  - **Out-of-compliance situations** when laws, regulations, or policies are not complied with consistently.
- **Auditee expectations regarding engagement communications.** Understanding the form and content of the final communication helps the internal auditor ensure that all necessary information is gathered during the engagement. Common types of communication include:
  - Full-scope, internal reports typically have a wide distribution and, thus, require sufficient appropriate evidence to support conclusions and recommendations for improvements.
  - Internal memoranda may be used for more limited distribution, stating the work performed and support for the conclusions and recommendation only to the extent necessary for the intended audience to understand the underlying deficiencies.
  - Reports for third-party use should assume such parties are less familiar with policies and procedures unique to the organization and, therefore, may require greater levels of detail to ensure the readers understand the nature and context of the observations and recommendations.

Auditee

The subsidiary, business unit, department, group, or other established subdivision of an organization that is the subject of an assurance engagement.

- Sometimes, a higher level of confidentiality may be necessary for certain engagements. Such instances should be fully discussed up front with process management to ensure the deliverables support the necessary level of confidentiality.

Books 2 Buy **Example**: All of the potential testing exceptions could occur during this engagement and, as such, the internal audit team will need to design tests accordingly. The deliverable will be a standard, full-scope internal audit communication. (Examples of possible deliverables are discussed in Chapter 14, "Communicating Assurance Engagement Outcomes and Performing Follow-up Procedures.")

UNDERSTAND THE AUDITEE

When planning an engagement, the internal audit team must first understand the auditee (used synonymously with the "process" or "area" within engagement scope in this chapter). Failure to gain a comprehensive understanding of the area under review may result in an incomplete testing plan or a misallocation of internal audit resources deployed in the engagement. Therefore, gaining an understanding of the process is very important.

Determining Auditee Objectives

Auditee Objectives

What the auditee is striving to achieve.

Understanding the process begins with determining the key process objectives. This helps the internal auditor understand why the process exists, which will be important when identifying and assessing process-level risks and controls. It should be noted that this engagement step aligns with the objective setting component of the COSO *Enterprise Risk Management (ERM) – Integrated Framework*, which is discussed in more detail in Chapter 4, "Risk Management," as well as elsewhere in this textbook.

There may be different types of objectives for a given process. These types of objectives can be described to align with the four objective types in the COSO ERM framework. Specifically, process-level objectives may be described as follows (as well as in examples for the Books 2 Buy cash disbursements process):

- Operations objectives are the most common type of objectives at the process level and usually define the reason the process exists. These objectives typically are governance or task-oriented, and, as a result, frequently focus on accuracy, timeliness, completeness, or control attributes. Additionally, operations objectives typically focus on ensuring the effectiveness and efficiency of operations and safeguarding of assets.

  Books 2 Buy **Example**: A cash disbursements process may have objectives that include:

  - Pay bills accurately to avoid adjustments to future bills or penalties due to underpayment of current liabilities.
  - Pay bills timely to take advantage of discounts (if available and appropriate) or avoid late-payment penalties.
  - Record all disbursements accurately in the accounting records and in the appropriate accounting period.
  - Process disbursements within the cost-per-transaction metrics established to ensure cost-effective use of resources.

- Ensure all disbursements represent bona fide obligations to pay.

- Reporting objectives at the process level are those designed to meet the organization's reporting needs, whether internal or external.

  Books2Buy **Example**: Information from the cash disbursements process may be used for:

  - Internal reporting of cash flow information that helps the treasurer prepare weekly cash flow forecasts.
  - Supporting the liquidity disclosures in the organization's regulatory filings.

- Compliance objectives at the process level may relate to compliance with external laws and regulations (COSO's definition), internal policies, or contracts (included in The IIA's definition along with external laws and regulations).

  Books2Buy **Example**: Cash disbursements compliance objectives may include:

  - Ensure disbursements comply with applicable banking regulations.
  - Ensure disbursements are approved in accordance with the organization's delegation of authority policy.

- Strategic objectives at the process level are those created to specifically align with the organization's strategic objectives. While not always evident to individuals performing the specific process tasks, these objectives are important to create a link between the day-to-day activities and the strategies that drive an organization's success. Note that this discussion of strategic objectives differs from the definition of strategic objectives in COSO's *Internal Control – Integrated Framework* discussed in Chapter 6, "Internal Control." Strategic objectives per COSO exist only at the entity level. However, when conducting an assurance engagement, the internal auditor needs to approach the process as a component of the organization as a whole and, thus, certain process-level objectives can be considered strategic in nature.

  Books2Buy **Example**: A cash disbursements function may have the following objective in an organization with a specific cash flow or liquidity strategy:

  - Pay bills in accordance with the cash flow directives provided by the treasury department to support the ongoing liquidity of the organization.

- Other objectives also may be created for a specific process related to individual department initiatives.

  Books2Buy **Example**: If cash disbursements management wanted to develop bench strength among the staff, the following objective may be applicable:

  - Cross-train individuals in all department jobs to ensure at least two people are capable of performing all key departmental tasks.

The process owner or staff involved in the process may be able to provide a list of process objectives. However, in many cases, such objectives may not have been articulated formally. In such situations, the internal auditor may need to facilitate discussions with process individuals to determine the key process objectives. The following questions may prove

COSO Objective Categories:

- **Operations**
- **Reporting**
- **Compliance**
- **Strategic**

helpful during such discussions, or when brainstorming among the internal audit team if process individuals are not available:

- Why does this process exist (that is, what is its primary purpose)?
- Which of the organization's strategic objectives does it affect or influence and how?
- What initiatives does/should the process undertake to help the organization achieve its strategic objectives?
- What does this process provide the organization, without which the organization would have a difficult time being successful?
- At the end of the day/week/month/year, what gives employees a sense of accomplishment with their jobs?
- What accomplishments tend to get employees recognized by management or internal customers?

Once the process objectives are understood, the internal auditor is ready to gather information about how the process operates.

Gathering Information

There are many ways to gather information about a process. The internal auditor should consider different types and sources of readily available relevant information. Additionally, analysis of data and entity-level controls can help provide additional insights into a process.

Types and Sources of Relevant Information

The starting point for understanding a process is reviewing documentation that already exists. For example, the following may be available from process owners or others familiar with the process that may provide useful information regarding how the process works:

- Policies relating to the process.
- Procedures manuals.
- Organizational charts or similar information outlining the number of employees and key reporting relationships.
- Job descriptions for people involved in the process.
- Process maps or flowcharts depicting the overall flow of the process.
- Narrative descriptions of key tasks or portions of the process.
- Copies of key contracts with customers, vendors, outsourcing partners, etc.
- Relevant information regarding laws and regulations affecting the process.
- Other documentation that may have been developed to support required reporting on the effectiveness of the system of internal controls.

This information may provide the internal auditor with much of what is needed to understand the process. However, it still may be necessary to discuss certain aspects of it with key individuals involved in performing the process. If the available documentation is not sufficiently comprehensive, it may be necessary to ask the individuals involved in the process questions such as:

- What key tasks are you responsible for performing?
- What inputs (information, documentation, etc.) do you need to perform these tasks?
- What, specifically, do you do with these inputs?
- What are the outputs that you produce from each task?
- Which other people or areas do you depend on as you perform these tasks?
- Which other people or areas depend on you performing these tasks effectively and timely?
- What information systems do you use when performing these tasks?
- How long does it take to complete each task?
- What types of exceptions or errors do you typically encounter?
- How do you handle these exceptions or errors?
- What other barriers or challenges do you typically encounter when performing these tasks?
- What do you do to remove the barriers or meet the challenges?
- In the end, how do you ensure that you perform the tasks correctly?

Gather Information About:

- **Inputs**
- **Processing**
- **Outputs**

These and other questions can help provide the internal auditor with the information needed to fully understand the process. It can be gained through individual interviews or by performing a walkthrough, which involves following a transaction through each step of a process. Regardless of the approach, it is important to understand the key tasks in sufficient detail to provide the foundation for the subsequent steps in the planning process.

Analytical Procedures

Understanding the tasks in a process, as described above, is an important step in planning an engagement. However, these tasks describe the way a process is designed to perform, but provide little indication regarding how effectively they are carried out. Performing analytical procedures is one way internal auditors conduct high-level assessments that may reveal process activities that warrant closer attention and, accordingly, more detailed testing.

Analytical Procedures

Reviewing and evaluating existing information, which may be financial or nonfinancial, to determine whether it is consistent with predetermined expectations.

Analytical procedures involve reviewing and evaluating existing information, which may be financial or nonfinancial, to determine whether it is consistent with predetermined expectations.

Books2Buy **Example**: For the cash disbursements audit, this analysis may include any or all of the following:

- Comparisons of financial information to prior periods, for example, trends in accounts payable balances from one quarter to the next.
- Ratio analyses, for example, current ratio (current assets divided by current liabilities) and accounts payable turnover (cost of goods sold divided by accounts payable).
- Comparisons of financial or nonfinancial information against budgeted information, for example, actual cash balances versus forecasted cash amounts.

Computer-assisted Audit Techniques

Automated audit techniques, such as generalized audit software, utility software, test data, application software tracing and mapping, and audit expert systems, that help the internal auditor directly test controls built into computerized information systems and data contained in computer files.

Data Analysis Using Computer-assisted Audit Techniques (CAATs)

Data analysis involves compiling and analyzing large amounts of data, typically through the use of technology. This technique is described in greater detail in Chapter 10, "Audit Evidence and Working Papers." While most data analysis is conducted to test the effectiveness of a process, some data analysis tests may provide useful information during the planning process. Data analysis may provide information about the population of transactions that could prove useful when determining the internal audit approach.

Books2Buy **Example**: When conducting an internal audit of the cash disbursements process, the internal audit team may perform the following data analysis tests during the planning phase:

- Number or percent of payments that are made well before or after the due date — this may provide insights into how closely cash flows are managed.
- Number of manual checks — this may indicate process design deficiencies or potential circumvention of established controls.
- Stratification of payment amounts — this may provide information about the level of small payments made, indicating the potential for procurement cards.
- Distribution of the first digits of payment amounts (Benford's Law analysis) — a distribution that does not follow Benford's Law may be an indication of unusual disbursement practices (for example, split invoicing), which may, in turn, influence the internal audit approach. Benford's Law estimates the number of times each of the 10 digits (zero through nine) will typically occur at the beginning of each number in a population with certain characteristics.
- Duplicate payment amounts to the same vendor — this may indicate potential duplicate payments, or provide insights about vendors for which recurring payments are made for like amounts.

Obtaining information about a population during the planning phase can help the internal auditor design tests that most effectively address the inherent risks in the process.

Entity-level Controls

Controls that operate across an entire entity and, as such, are not bound by, or associated with, individual processes.

Entity-level Controls Analysis

While it is important to understand the process-level tasks and controls, it is also important to understand how the entity-level controls may influence the performance of a process. Deficiencies in entity-level controls can circumvent well-designed controls within a process and, in fact, become inherent risks to the effective operation of controls at the process level. For example, if organization-wide policies tend to be informal and inconsistently enforced, then policies specific to the process being audited may not be as important to understanding the process. Similarly, if there is little commitment to attracting, training, and developing competent employees in key areas requiring decision-making abilities and complex judgments, the testing approach may need to be altered as less reliance can be placed on individuals being able to perform complex or highly judgmental tasks.

Entity-level controls are commonly evaluated on an organization-wide basis at periodic intervals (for example, annually). Therefore, it typically will not be necessary to perform an assessment of the effectiveness of entity-level controls on each engagement. However, as described in the previous paragraph, the internal auditor should consider the results of the entity-level control assessment when planning individual engagements to ensure the approach to testing is relevant and efficient.

Documenting the Process Flow

As discussed above, there may be many types of information that can be gathered about a process from a variety of sources. To demonstrate that the internal auditor understands how the process actually operates, the key steps must be documented. This process flow documentation will facilitate a review of the workpapers by the internal auditor's supervisor or others. The most common ways of documenting process flows are flowcharts (high-level or detailed) and narrative memoranda. Before providing a brief description of each, it is important to understand some subtle differences between the documentation of process flows.

Process Map

Depicts the broad inputs, activities, workflows, and interactions with other processes and outputs.

- **Process maps**, as described in Chapter 5, "Business Processes and Risks," attempt to depict the broad inputs, activities, workflows, and interactions with other processes and outputs. They provide a framework to understand the activities and subprocesses.
- **Flowcharts** include additional information, frequently depicting computer systems and applications, document flows, detailed risks and controls, manual versus automated steps, elapsed time for steps in the process, owners of key steps, and any additional information needed to help the reviewer understand the process and its flow.
- **Narrative memoranda** provide information about the process flow using only written words; there is no attempt to use symbols to depict the flow. It is common to combine flowcharts with supplemental narrative information to create a hybrid form of documentation.

Process maps tend to be most useful at the business level, as described in Chapter 5, while flowcharts and hybrid documentation provide the level of information necessary to understand detailed processes. Following is a brief description of those techniques commonly used at the process level.

High-level Flowcharts

The purpose of a high-level flowchart is to depict broad inputs, tasks, workflows, and outputs. A high-level flowchart helps reviewers understand the overall activities, systems, reports, and interfaces with other processes or subprocesses. This understanding will provide a frame of reference for identifying key subprocesses and systems that may be considered for the scope of the engagement. Flowcharts typically are drawn like a process map, with additional information added as necessary to support the understanding of the process flow. The common flowcharting symbols are shown in Exhibit 13-5. These symbols expand on those used for process maps, as discussed in Chapter 5.

Flowchart

Expands on a process map to include computer systems and applications, document flows, detailed risks and controls, manual versus automated steps, elapsed time, and owners of key steps.

Books2Buy **Example**: A high-level flowchart depicting the cash disbursements process is shown in Exhibit 13-6.

A simple, high-level flowchart can be used to confirm the internal auditor's overall understanding of the process with the process owner, help in

EXHIBIT 13-5

COMMON FLOWCHARTING SYMBOLS

(rectangle)	**Process or operation** – A process, subprocess, or activity.
(diamond)	**Decision** – Indicates alternative choices (for example, yes/no or accept/reject), each of which results in different flows of activities and/or documents.
(document shape)	**Document** – A hard copy input source document or output report.
(arrow)	**Flow line** – The direction of activities, workflow, information flow, documents, and handoffs.
(cylinder)	**Computer system or application** – Information technology that is used to store data, run an application, or perform other computer-based functions.
(circle)	**On-page connector** – Used to connect different parts of a flowchart on the same page without the use of flow lines.
(pentagon)	**Off-page connector** – Used to connect parts of a flowchart documented on different pages.
(rounded rectangle)	**Terminator** – The start or end of a flow.
(bracket)	**Annotation** – An explanatory note attached to a specific point in a flowchart.

determining which areas or subprocesses are within scope for the engagement, and serve as a summary view of the detailed flowcharts.

Detailed Flowcharts

While the high-level flowchart is an important starting point, it does not provide the depth and level of detail needed to support the internal auditor's judgments regarding the design of the process. A detailed flowchart documents the more specific inputs, tasks, actions, systems, decisions, and outputs. In addition to providing a more detailed depiction of the process flow, detailed flowcharts provide additional information that enhances the understanding of the process. For example, detailed flowcharts may include some or all of the following:

- Key risks, which may be denoted by a symbol identifying the points in the process where something could go wrong and cause the process to not operate as designed.
- Key controls, which may be denoted by a symbol identifying the tasks, actions, or decisions that are considered critical to the adequate design of the process.
- Individuals or positions performing the key tasks or making decisions.
- The timing of when key tasks, actions, or decisions occur.

EXHIBIT 13-6

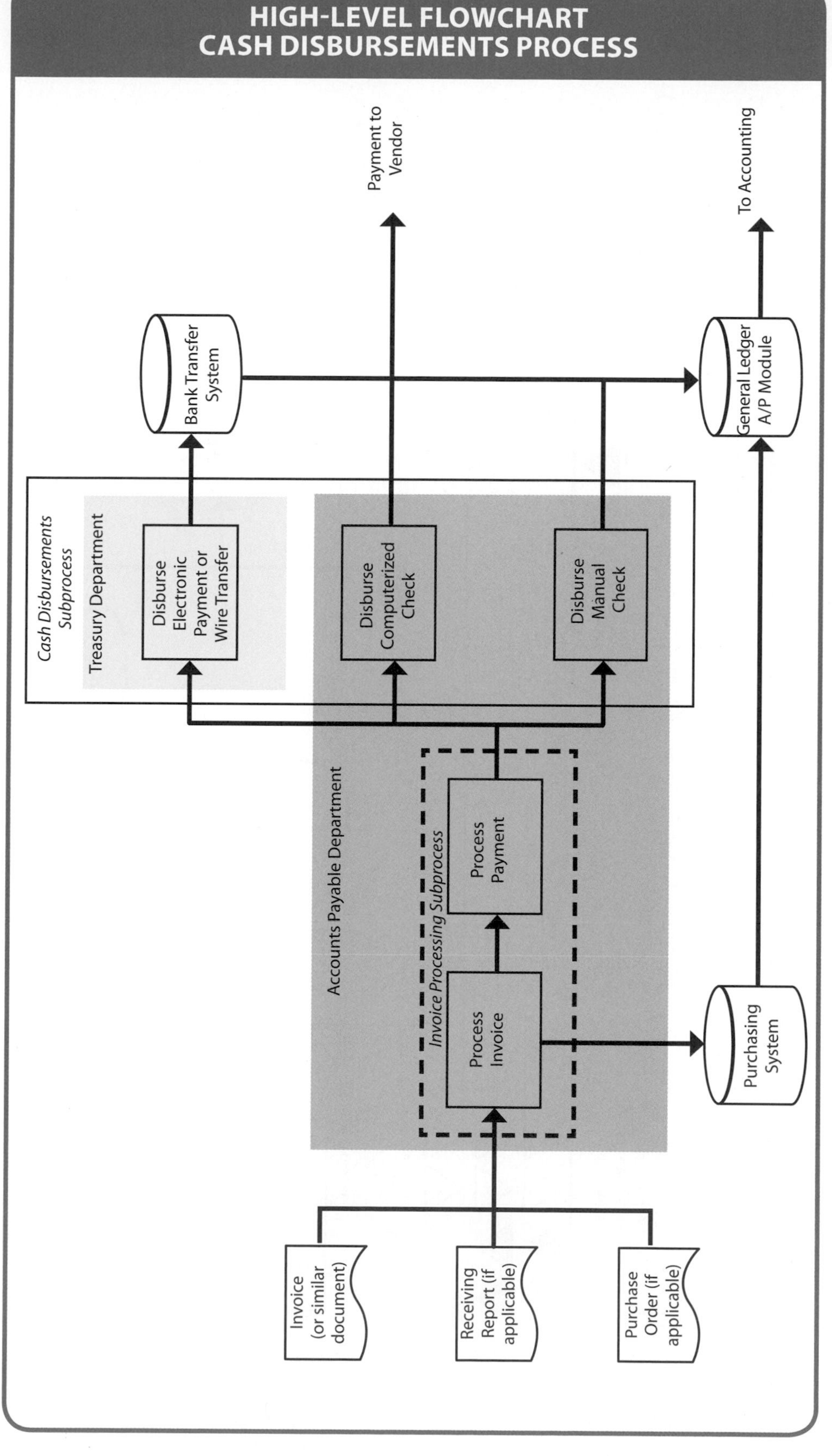
HIGH-LEVEL FLOWCHART
CASH DISBURSEMENTS PROCESS
Invoice (or similar document)
Receiving Report (if applicable)
Purchase Order (if applicable)
Accounts Payable Department
Invoice Processing Subprocess
Process Invoice
Process Payment
Purchasing System
Cash Disbursements Subprocess
Treasury Department
Disburse Electronic Payment or Wire Transfer
Disburse Computerized Check
Disburse Manual Check
Bank Transfer System
General Ledger A/P Module
Payment to Vendor
To Accounting

EXHIBIT 13-7

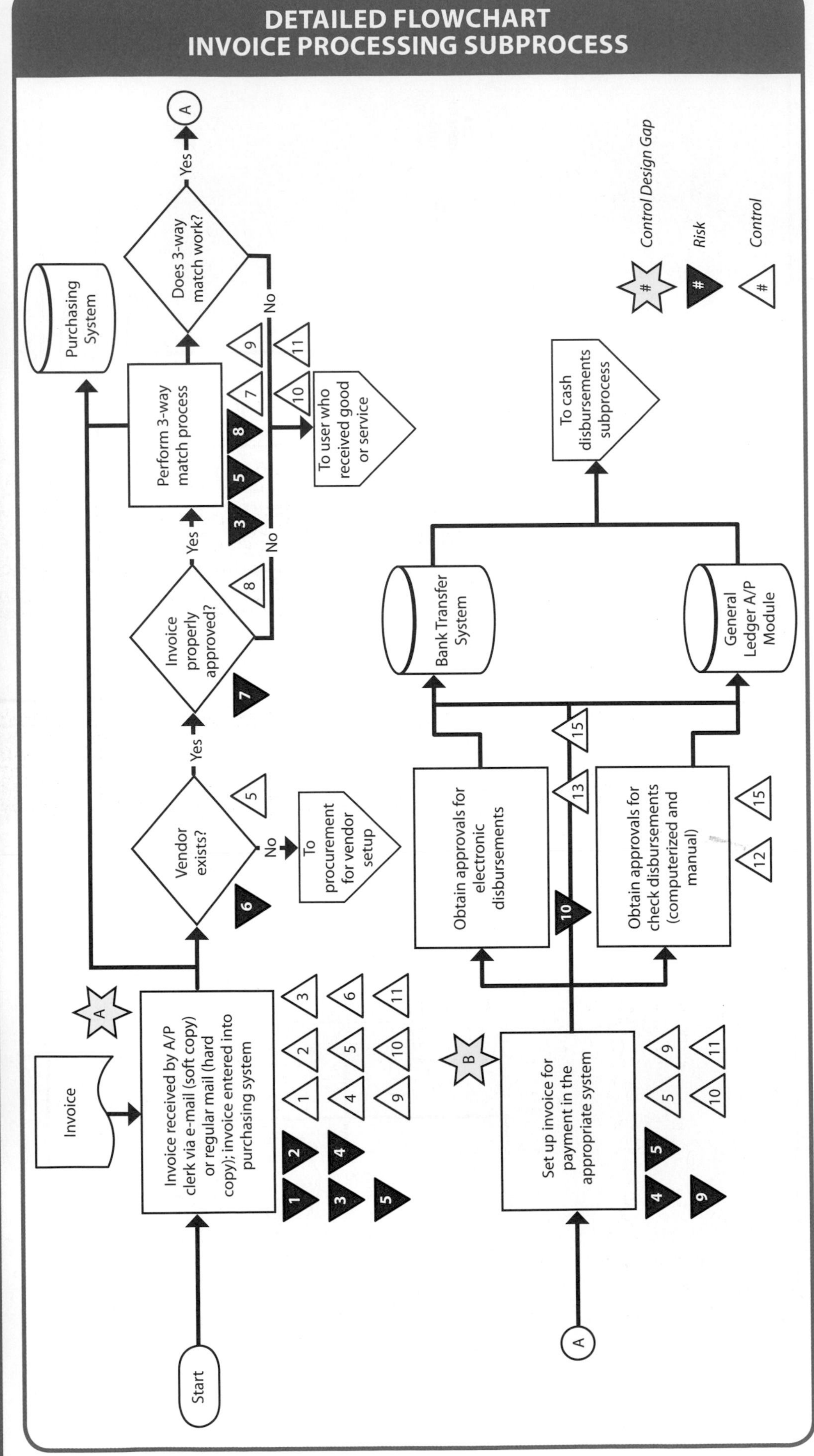

DETAILED FLOWCHART
INVOICE PROCESSING SUBPROCESS
Start
Invoice
Invoice received by A/P clerk via e-mail (soft copy) or regular mail (hard copy); invoice entered into purchasing system
Purchasing System
Vendor exists?
No
To procurement for vendor setup
Yes
Invoice properly approved?
No
Yes
Perform 3-way match process
Does 3-way match work?
No
To user who received good or service
Yes
A
A
Set up invoice for payment in the appropriate system
B
Obtain approvals for electronic disbursements
Obtain approvals for check disbursements (computerized and manual)
Bank Transfer System
General Ledger A/P Module
To cash disbursements subprocess
Control Design Gap
Risk
Control

DETAILED FLOWCHART INVOICE PROCESSING RISKS

Invoice is not received timely by accounts payable, resulting in liability not being properly reflected in the financial statements.

Invoice is not processed timely by accounts payable, resulting in lost opportunities to take discounts or incurring late-payment fees.

Invoice information is entered inaccurately into the purchasing system, resulting in inaccurate or inappropriate payments.

Duplicate invoices are entered and processed for payment, resulting in payment for the same invoice twice.

Accounts payable personnel have inappropriate access to the various systems, allowing them to establish fictitious vendors, create phony purchase orders, and make unauthorized payments.

Payments are processed to the wrong or a nonexistent vendor, resulting in late payments to the correct vendor, the need to collect refunds from the incorrect vendor, or a fraudulent payment.

Payments are processed for invoices that have not been approved yet, resulting in payment before the good or service is received.

Invoices are processed that do not match purchase orders, receiving reports, or other relevant documentation, resulting in establishing a liability and paying an incorrect amount.

Payments are made before the due date, resulting in lost time value of money.

Unauthorized payments are made, resulting in payments being made by a costly or inefficient means, or in a manner inconsistent to meet the cash flow requirements.

EXHIBIT 13-7

continued on pg. 13-18

- The elapsed time it takes to perform a task or make a decision (this may be included if the flowchart is used to evaluate the efficiency of the process).

  Books 2 Buy **Example**: An example of a detailed flowchart is shown in Exhibit 13-7. This example depicts the invoice processing subprocess in the cash disbursements process for Books 2 Buy. The invoice processing subprocess is shown in the high-level flowchart in Exhibit 13-6.

Because many people are visual learners and thinkers, detailed flowcharts are an effective way of presenting a great deal of information in an intuitive and understandable format. The level of information in detailed flowcharts should be sufficient to support the internal auditor's judgments regarding the identification of key controls, the adequacy of the overall process design, and the gaps between the current and desired level of specific controls.

EXHIBIT 13-7

continued from pg. 13-17

DETAILED FLOWCHART — INVOICE PROCESSING CONTROLS AND DESIGN GAPS

As part of the month-end close process, the A/P manager will solicit information on unprocessed invoices and will prepare an accrual accordingly.

Once an approved invoice is entered, the system will automatically book the credit to A/P and debit to the appropriate expense or balance sheet account.

Open purchase orders are reviewed once per month by the purchasing manager to determine their status.

The A/P clerk runs a report at the end of each week showing invoices entered but not approved. For invoices outstanding more than a week, a reminder is sent to the user.

The purchasing system requires that all invoice fields are completed before processing is allowed. An invoice cannot be entered without a match to an approved vendor.

The purchasing system alerts the A/P clerk if the vendor number, invoice number, and invoice amount match an invoice previously entered.

The purchasing system confirms a match between quantities and prices on an invoice, purchase order, and receiving documents. If they do not match, the invoice is placed on hold.

Invoice approval limits are confirmed with department heads annually and updated if necessary.

A user name and password is required to access all of the systems. Passwords are subject to naming parameters, and must be changed every 90 days.

System access rights are reviewed semiannually with department heads to ensure access capabilities align with job responsibilities.

A/P personnel cannot access the vendor masterfile, nor can they make changes to previously entered purchase order and receiving information.

Only the A/P manager can initiate the processing of a computerized check batch.

Only treasury department personnel are entitled to process bank transfers.

The purchasing system interfaces with the general ledger A/P module and the bank transfer system.

Computerized checks over US $50,000 require a manual signature of the treasurer.
Computerized checks over US $100,000 require a manual signature of the CFO.
Manual checks require dual signatures from the treasurer and CFO. The treasurer must authorize individual bank transfers in excess of US $100,000.

There is no check with users to determine whether any goods or services have been received but not invoiced yet (engagement observation written up on working paper Z-1).

While the purchasing system does alert the A/P clerk to potential duplicate invoices, it does not prevent the A/P clerk from continuing to process such an invoice (engagement observation written up on working paper Z-2).

Narrative Memoranda

There may be situations in which the internal auditor believes it is more appropriate to document the understanding of the process using narrative write-ups instead of flowcharts. These situations typically exhibit one or more of the following characteristics:

- The process is simple and, thus, the visual depiction created in flowcharting is not of great value.
- The steps are complicated, making it difficult to describe them effectively in the limited space provided in a flowchart symbol.
- The process owner would like the output to support other process documentation and prefers narrative write-ups over flowcharts.
- Narrative write-ups are a more efficient means of documenting the process.

Narrative memoranda should include the same type of information as is contained in flowcharts. While the specific sections of such a memorandum may vary between processes, a memorandum generally should include the elements from the following outline:

1. Overall description of the process
2. Key inputs
   a. Documents or communications from outside sources (for example, invoices or checks)
   b. Outputs from other processes or subprocesses
   c. Information from outside sources
   d. Data from internal systems
3. Key steps in the process
   a. Tasks that handle, check, change, or monitor the inputs
   b. Analysis that is completed
   c. Decisions or judgments that are made
   d. Computer applications that are updated
   e. New documents or information that are created
   f. Key individuals performing the tasks
   g. Elapsed time for tasks or groups of tasks
4. Key outputs
   a. Documents to be sent to outside parties (for example, bills, checks, or statements)
   b. Reports for internal use
   c. Inputs into other processes or subprocesses
   d. Data to be stored electronically
   e. Hard copy of documentation to be stored internally
5. Risks that threaten the process
6. Key controls (refer to the Identify Key Controls section later in this chapter)

Regardless of whether flowcharts, narrative memoranda, or a combination of the two are used, documenting the process flows helps provide an

Reasons for Narrative Memoranda:

- **Simple process**
- **Complicated steps**
- **Process owner request**
- **More efficient**

understanding that is critical to the next steps in engagement planning. Therefore, care should be taken to invest enough time in understanding the process to enable the internal auditor's assessment of process design adequacy.

It is important to remember that in an assurance engagement, flowcharts and narrative memoranda are used to depict the current or "as is" state, not the desired or "should be" state. A common audit objective is to evaluate the design adequacy and operating effectiveness of a process. The current state is documented to help the internal auditor assess the current design adequacy. The auditee obtains the desired state only after addressing any deficiencies identified by the internal auditor.

Identifying Key Performance Indicators

After gaining an understanding of the process flow, it is helpful for the internal auditor to also understand how process-level management monitors performance. Frequently, there will be key performance indicators (KPIs) which are monitored periodically to provide process owners with information about how well the process is performing. Monitoring these KPIs may be similar to the analytical procedures the internal auditor performed, as described in the previous section, or quite different. There are certain characteristics of good key performance indicators. They should be:

Key Performance Indicator

A metric or other form of measuring whether a process or individual tasks are operating within prescribed tolerances.

- **Relevant**, that is, they measure what is important (for example, disbursement accuracy) as opposed to what is quantifiable (for example, dollar value of disbursements processed).
- **Measurable**, that is, there is quantifiable information to determine successful performance (for example, inaccurate disbursement information is tracked and compiled to monitor accuracy of disbursements).
- **Available**, that is, the information needed is available at the right time and to the right people, allowing for timely measurement of process performance (for example, disbursement statistics are available to the accounts payable manager at the close of each pay cycle).
- **Aligned** with key objectives of the process (for example, duplicate payment information is captured because there is an objective to have none).
- **Articulated** to the people involved in the process so that they understand what is being measured and the importance of achieving those performance levels (for example, accounts payable employees can see the statistics timely and adjust their performance accordingly).

Key performance indicators, whether formal or informal, can define the process owner's tolerance to performance deviations. Management determines what level of errors they are willing to accept when the process does not perform as expected. Knowing these tolerance levels will help the internal auditor evaluate the results of testing. For example, if the internal auditor finds a two percent error rate in a test, knowing whether this frequency of errors is acceptable will help the internal auditor determine whether this error rate is significant.

Books2Buy Example: Examples of key performance indicators for the cash disbursements process are as follows:

- 100 percent of the disbursements are accurate, for example, the monetary amount on the invoice.
- 98 percent of disbursements are paid by the due date. Under no circumstances should the company ever have to pay interest or penalties on late payments.
- There are no duplicate payments.
- 90 percent of payables with early pay discounts exceeding one percent are paid in time to take the discount.

Evaluating Process-level Fraud Risks

Finally, it is important to understand the potential process-level fraud risks. As discussed in the next section in this chapter, most risks are based on the uncertainty of events that may occur due to the inherent nature of the process. The inherent likelihood of certain risks occurring increases if there is intent by an individual to commit fraud and/or collusion among multiple individuals involved in the process. Therefore, before beginning the formal risk assessment process in an engagement, it is important to evaluate potential fraud scenarios in the process. This involves the following three steps:

1. **Identify potential fraud scenarios.** Brainstorming with individuals involved in the process is an effective way to identify the possible means by which individuals, working alone or in collusion with others, could circumvent the process.

   Books2Buy Example: Examples of potential cash disbursements fraud include:

   - An employee creates a fictitious vendor with his or her own address, submits an invoice for processing to that vendor, and deposits the payment into his or her own account.
   - An accounts payable employee processes a duplicate payment and, through collusion with the vendor, agrees to split the proceeds of the additional payment with an individual at that vendor.
   - A treasury employee sets up a bank account in a name similar to a vendor and wire transfers funds to that account.

2. **Understand potential fraud impact.** The potential impact of each fraud scenario should be determined. For example, an organization could:

   - Suffer direct financial loss (through misappropriation of assets).
   - Misrepresent financial results (through fraudulent financial reporting).
   - Suffer reputational damage if the fraud reflects very negatively on the governance of the organization.

3. **Determine whether to test for specific fraud risks.** Based on the first two steps, the internal auditor can assess, based on

Fraud

Any illegal act characterized by deceit, concealment, or violation of trust. These acts are not dependent upon the threat of violence or physical force. Frauds are perpetrated by parties and organizations to obtain money, property, or services; to avoid payment or loss of services; or to secure personal or business advantage.

the inherent risk of fraud within the process, whether specific tests should be designed to determine the vulnerability for fraud.

The intent of this step is not necessarily to identify the occurrence of fraud, but rather to evaluate the possibility of fraud scenarios occurring. If it is reasonably possible that such scenarios will occur, the internal auditor should consider designing specific tests to identify the occurrence of, or potential for, the fraud scenarios. Refer to Chapter 8, "Fraud Risks and Controls," for further discussion about fraud.

IDENTIFY AND ASSESS RISKS

Identifying Process-level Risk Scenarios

An organization establishes processes to execute its business plan and achieve its objectives. These processes may be discrete and focused, or they may be cross-functional. Risks exist in all processes, regardless of their breadth, location, or focus. The first task in assessing process-level risks is to identify the risk scenarios that are inherent in the process. Risk scenarios are potential real-life events that may adversely impact the achievement of objectives.

The risks shown in Exhibit 13-7 may not be identified until the internal auditor has completed this task in the planning process. It is common for these two steps, Understand the Auditee and Identify and Assess Risks, to be conducted iteratively.

Risk

The possibility that an event will occur and adversely affect the achievement of objectives.

The purpose of identifying risk scenarios is to answer the question: What can happen that would prevent the achievement of each of the process-level objectives? To answer this question, internal auditors should brainstorm the possible risk scenarios. The following provides an outline of how this can be done.

1. Choose a single process-level objective. This exercise works best if done one objective at a time.
2. Brainstorm barriers (events, issues, circumstances, etc.) that might threaten the achievement of the objective. Examples include the following:
   a. External events for which the organization is not prepared or does not react to timely or appropriately.
   b. Inadequately designed or poorly documented procedures.
   c. Breakdowns in existing procedures.
   d. Lack of the right people, with the right skills, deployed in the right manner.
   e. Inadequate communication between interfacing areas.
   f. Employees who intentionally violate policies or act unethically.
   g. Inadequately designed or outdated computer applications.
   h. Untimely, inaccurate, or inadequate information for decision-making.
   i. Failure to measure performance.
3. Continue the exercise for the remaining process-level objectives.

4. Since some of the risk scenarios will be similar across process-level objectives, categorize and combine similar risk scenarios. The reason for combining similar risk scenarios will become more evident in the next task, Defining Process-level Risks.

This brainstorming exercise would be optimized if individuals involved in the process participate. They may be able to identify risk scenarios based on first-hand experience. However, experienced internal auditors should be able to conduct this exercise without assistance from process-level individuals.

An effective way for internal auditors to perform such a brainstorming session is to write the different scenarios on self-sticking notes and put them up on a wall or large board. Once the brainstorming is completed, the notes can be (1) arranged by objective to ensure comprehensive coverage of each objective, and (2) categorized by similar scenario type to support risk definition.

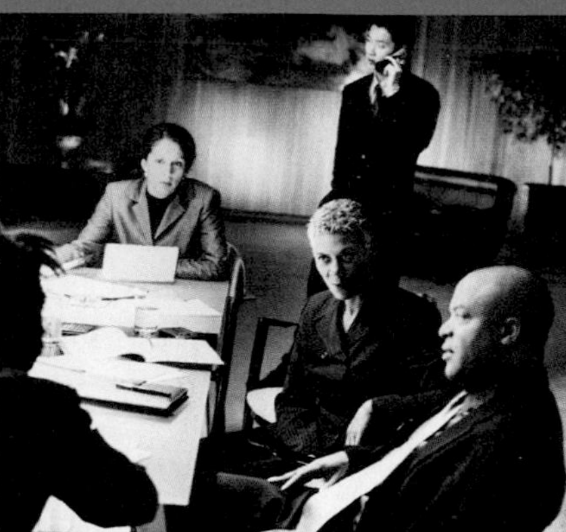

Books2Buy **Example**: The following are a few of the many risk scenario examples for the cash disbursements process:

- Invoices are not processed timely to permit payment by the due date.
- A duplicate payment is made due to an invoice being input twice — once from an approved invoice and a second time off of a statement sent by the vendor.
- An accounts payable clerk accidentally enters the incorrect amount into the system, resulting in payment of that incorrect amount.
- Due to employee turnover in accounts payable, there are input delays resulting in late payments.
- Unauthorized individuals change payment terms within the system resulting in late or incorrect payments.

Defining Process-level Risks

As indicated above, similar risk scenarios provide the foundation for identifying process-level risks. The risk scenarios represent the specific real-life events that could affect the achievement of objectives. Risks are broader descriptions of the causes and effects of such events. The next task in assessing process-level risks is to define the relevant risks.

There are many ways to define risks. The optimal approach depends on the culture and "risk language" of the organization. However, regardless of the unique approaches that may exist from one organization to the next, it is important to be consistent. Lack of consistency may make it more difficult for risks to be broadly understood throughout the organization.

One common and effective approach for defining risks is to use a "cause and effect" protocol. Under this approach, risks begin with a "cause" (for example, failure to . . . , lack of . . . , inability to . . .) and continue with the effect (for example, financial loss, personal injury, data corruption, or reputational damage).

Books2Buy **Example**: A sample of possible cash disbursements risks includes:

- Expectations. Lack of well-developed and well-articulated policies, procedures, and other forms of communication from senior management may result in employees carrying out their responsibilities in a manner that is inconsistent with senior management's expectations and desires.

- Duplicate Payments. Failure to identify multiple inputs of invoices may result in duplicate payments to vendors that could go undetected or prove difficult to collect.
- Timeliness. Inability to process payments on time may result in fines or penalties (for late payments) or missed discounts.
- Systems Access. Lack of effective logical security practices may create opportunities for unauthorized individuals to access, manipulate, or delete key disbursements data.
- Human Resources. Inability to attract, develop, deploy, and retain competent individuals may result in the cash disbursements process performing at a suboptimal level, which could cause inaccurate or untimely payments.

Once the risks are defined, they should be linked to the process-level objectives to ensure there is correlation between each of the risks and objectives. As discussed below, risk assessment involves consideration of the impact on the ability to achieve objectives.

One final task is to validate that the definitions "speak the language" of the process-level employees. Since these employees are responsible for managing the process-level risks, it is important that they have a uniform and consistent understanding of those risks. Therefore, internal auditors should share and discuss the risk definitions with process-level management and employees to validate that the risk list is complete and the definitions make sense. Success with this task will help facilitate success in the Evaluating the Impact and Likelihood of Risks task that follows.

Risk Assessment

The identification and analysis (typically in terms of impact and likelihood) of relevant risks to the achievement of an organization's objectives, forming a basis for determining how the risks should be managed.

Evaluating the Impact and Likelihood of Risks

Now that the risks have been identified and defined, the internal auditor is ready to perform a risk assessment. In this task, the focus is on determining the potential impact and likelihood of each risk. The purpose of this evaluation is to help identify the risks that will have the greatest adverse effect on the achievement of process-level objectives. Such risks deserve most of the attention during an assurance engagement.

The process for conducting a process-level risk assessment generally involves the following three steps:

1. Determine the impact of various outcomes associated with each risk. The following tips may prove helpful when performing this step:
   - Recall that, by definition, risk represents uncertainty; therefore, there may be several possible risk outcomes. The internal auditor must try not to focus only on one possible risk outcome and ignore outcomes that are more likely or carry more impact.
   - Risk is typically measured in terms of the financial impact, which is the most common and easily measured impact. However, there may be other risk outcomes that either cannot be measured in financial terms or may be considered more severe than the financial impact. For example, harm

to an employee's health and safety, or impairment of an organization's reputation due to negative publicity may be considered a more severe outcome than the direct financial impact of such risks.

- Impact should focus on the potential exposure over a specific period of time, typically one year. Because risks may occur more than once during the period, it is important to avoid concentrating on a single-event impact. Estimating the impact over a period of time ensures that the potential worst-case exposure is considered.
- It is not necessary to obtain a high degree of precision when estimating the impact of a risk. Using a generic scale (for example, high/medium/low) will typically suffice. However, it is still important to define the levels of the scale. For example, high impact may be defined as a financial impact greater than US $1 million, medium impact from US $250,000 through US $1 million, and low impact less than US $250,000.

2. The second step is to estimate the likelihood that each risk impact will occur. The following tips may be helpful when performing this step:
   - As discussed above, risks have a range of possible outcomes, each of which will have a different likelihood of occurring. It is important to focus on the risk outcome determined in the previous step.
   - Since there are many risk outcomes, there also may be many root causes for why a risk occurs. Each root cause may have a different likelihood. Therefore, it is important to consider the underlying root cause(s) of the chosen outcome when evaluating the likelihood of a risk occurrence.
   - As is the case when determining risk impact, it is not necessary to obtain a high degree of precision when estimating the likelihood of a risk. Using a generic scale (for example, high/medium/low) will typically suffice. For example, high likelihood may indicate that the risk impact is more likely than not to occur (that is, greater than 50 percent), medium likelihood may indicate that the risk impact is possible (for example, from 10 percent through 50 percent), and low likelihood may indicate that the risk impact is remote (for example, less than 10 percent).
   - When evaluating likelihood, it is important to focus on the inherent likelihood — that is, assessing likelihood without consideration of the controls management may have in place. Since the internal auditor already has some understanding of the process, it may be tempting to estimate likelihood based on the effect of these controls. However, internal auditors should not assume that those controls operate effectively when planning the engagement, otherwise, they may under-assess the related risks and fail to test such controls.
3. The final step is to combine the assessment of impact and likelihood into a single risk assessment. The best way to

Impact

The severity of outcomes caused by risk events. Can be measured in financial, reputation, legal, or other types of outcomes.

Likelihood

The probability that a risk event will occur.

EXHIBIT 13-8

EXAMPLE OF A RISK MATRIX

IMPACT				
	High	7	8	9
	Medium	4	5	6
	Low	1	2	3
		Low	**Medium**	**High**
		LIKELIHOOD		

accomplish this is to create a risk matrix that shows the interrelationship between the impact and likelihood of each risk. For example, the risk matrix shown in Exhibit 13-8 depicts the use of a high/medium/low scale for both the impact and likelihood assessments. When reviewing this risk matrix, note that a number is assigned to each box to signify the overall level of risk. Once each risk is placed in one of the boxes, they can be classified as follows:

- Risks in boxes 8 or 9 (red shading) are considered high risk.
- Risks in boxes 5, 6, or 7 (yellow shading) are considered medium risk.
- Risks in boxes 1, 2, 3, or 4 (no shading) are considered low risk.

Typically, high and medium risks should be included in every internal audit assurance engagement. Low risks may or may not be included, depending on the internal audit function's charter, objectives of the engagement, and resource considerations. Refer to Exhibit 13-9 for an example of a cash disbursements risk matrix that may be a relevant example for Books 2 Buy.

Using a matrix or some other means to visually depict the results of the risk assessment will facilitate an overall review of the judgments made in the risk assessment process by internal audit management and the process owners. Such reviews, particularly by the process owner, will help validate the judgments made by the internal auditor.

Understanding Management's Risk Tolerance

Traditionally, judgments of the internal audit team have been the sole source for evaluating risks. This reflects the internal auditor's governance role in the organization. However, an underlying premise in enterprise risk management is that management must establish tolerances to business risks consistent with the organization's overall risk appetite. This premise applies at the process level as well.

Therefore, it is important for the internal auditor to validate the reasonableness of the high, medium, and low impact thresholds that were employed. It is possible that management may have a different level of risk tolerance for the process. Recall from Chapter 4, "Risk Management," that

EXAMPLE OF A CASH DISBURSEMENTS RISK MATRIX

IMPACT				
	High	7 Expectations Risk	8 Duplicate Payments Risk Systems Access Risk	9
	Medium	4	5 Human Resources Risk	6 Timeliness Risk
	Low	1	2	3
		Low	Medium	High
		LIKELIHOOD		

Expectations Risk is considered *high impact* as lack of sufficient direction and oversight from senior management could result in material disbursements being made in an inappropriate or fraudulent manner. This risk is considered *low likelihood* as there are many examples of good policies and procedures governing disbursement activities, and senior management is not likely to ignore such an important area.

Timeliness Risk is considered *medium impact* as the penalties and interest for being late would not be material, although bad vendor relations would still be of concern. This risk is considered *high likelihood* as there is heavy reliance on others to begin the cash disbursements process and, with generally tight payment terms, there are a variety of delays that could occur in the process, causing a payment to be late.

Human Resources Risk is considered *medium impact* as failure to recruit, develop, and maintain competent people in the accounts payable department could result in a higher-than-desirable number of inaccurate or late payments. This risk is considered *medium likelihood* as the necessary skill sets are not that difficult to find in the market.

Systems Access Risk is considered *high impact* as unauthorized access could result in changes that might conceal material misdirected disbursements. This risk is considered *medium likelihood* as such misdirected disbursements may be detected through other means.

Duplicate Payments Risk is considered *high impact* as a single duplicate disbursement could be material and would represent lost funds if undetected. This risk is considered *medium likelihood* as it is fairly common for duplicate invoices to be presented to a company, however, most vendors are generally honest so it is less likely that a material duplicate payment would go undetected over time.

EXHIBIT 13-9

risk appetite is the amount of risk, on a broad level, an organization is willing to accept, while risk tolerance is the acceptable levels of risk size and variation relative to the achievement of objectives, and must align with the risk appetite. To gain an understanding of management's risk tolerance levels, the following three steps should be conducted:

Risk Appetite

The amount of risk, on a broad level, an organization is willing to accept in pursuit of its business objectives.

Risk Tolerance

The acceptable levels of risk size and variation relative to the achievement of objectives, which must align with the organization's risk appetite.

1. **Identify Possible Risk Outcomes.** As previously discussed, by definition, risks represent a range of possible outcomes. While such outcomes typically are measured in financial terms, there may be other risk outcomes that either do not lend themselves to financial measurement or are more severe than the financial impact. For example, the safety of employees may be more severe than potential fines or penalties due to safety violations. Similarly, the impact of failure to protect the privacy of customer data may be more severe than the cost to recover or protect such data.

2. **Understand Established Tolerance Levels.** Once the different risk outcomes are determined, discussions can be held with process management to identify tolerance levels that they have already established. Such levels may be reflected in documentation of key performance measures, individual performance goals, or in other communications.
3. **Assess Tolerance Levels for Outcomes that Have Not Been Established.** To the extent that established tolerance levels do not comprehensively address all possible risk outcomes, discussions should be held with process management to determine appropriate tolerance levels. Questions to facilitate this discussion include:
   - How much variability can you or senior management tolerate relative to the achievement of process objectives?
   - What types of outcomes would you consider to be unacceptable?
   - What types of risk scenarios would you be uncomfortable dealing with?

Understanding management's tolerance levels is important, but does not necessarily supersede the internal auditor's judgment. Remember, the internal audit function has many stakeholders. Its fiduciary responsibility to other stakeholders should not be subordinated if the internal auditor believes process-level management has a higher level of risk tolerance than other stakeholders. However, having a good understanding of process management's tolerance levels will help the internal auditor finalize the risk assessment judgments, as well as gain an understanding that may prove helpful when evaluating the significance of audit findings later in the engagement.

IDENTIFY KEY CONTROLS

Key Control

An activity designed to reduce risk associated with a critical business objective.

A variety of actions make up a process. All may have a role in achieving the final result, but only a few are truly critical to the outcome, that is, their absence would make it difficult to achieve the desired result. These critical actions are referred to as *key controls*. Chapter 6, "Internal Control," provides a definition of internal control and a detailed discussion of the system of internal controls. Recall also, from earlier in this chapter, that entity-level controls may have an impact on the operation of controls at the process level. Therefore, the internal auditor must consider the impact of entity-level controls on the process under review before proceeding with the identification of key process-level controls.

To execute this task in engagement planning, it is important to understand the different types of controls that may be considered key controls at the process level. Although the following is not an exhaustive list, it represents examples of common control types:

- **Approving** involves obtaining an authorization to execute a transaction by someone empowered to do so (for example, approval of a write-off).
- **Calculating** entails computing or re-computing an amount that results from other data obtained in the process (for example, using historical write-off data to compute a bad debt reserve, or checking a depreciation calculation to ensure the systematically computed amount is reasonable).

- **Documenting** relates to preserving source information or documenting the rationale behind judgments made for future reference (for example, scanning receiving documentation, invoices, and checks to support a payment, or writing a memorandum to the files that outlines the judgments used in determining an accrual).
- **Examining** involves verifying an attribute, that is, a data element, event, or documentary evidence supporting existence or occurrence (for example, evidence that goods paid for were received).
- **Matching** entails making comparisons between two different attributes to verify that they agree (for example, a payment amount agrees with the invoice amount).
- **Monitoring** represents checking to ensure an action is occurring (for example, monitoring that an invoice approver does not exceed his or her limits).
- **Restricting** involves not allowing an unacceptable action (for example, prohibiting speculation on interest rate fluctuations, or not allowing unauthorized individuals to access certain data within key systems).
- **Segregating** focuses on separating incompatible duties that would create the potential for an undesirable action (for example, separating check signing and invoice approval authority).
- **Supervising** involves providing direction and oversight to ensure actions and tasks are carried out as designed (for example, a supervisor approving a batch before computer processing).

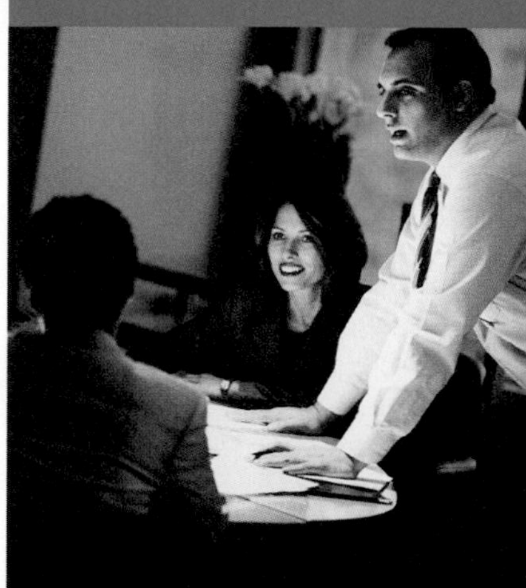

As previously discussed, the identification of process-level controls typically begins in the prior two planning steps: Understand the Auditee and Identify and Assess Risks. The current task involves ensuring that any additional process-level controls have been identified before an assessment is made as to which controls mitigate the key risks.

There are no checklists or formulas that provide the internal auditor with absolute information on which controls are key and which are not. Rather, determining key controls is a judgmental process that can be best accomplished by the internal auditor answering the following question: If not performed as designed, which of these controls would likely result in the inability to achieve the process-level objectives? Those controls that mitigate high or medium risks, as depicted in Exhibit 13-8, are probably key controls. The following are important when determining key controls:

- The internal auditor must have a clear understanding of the process-level objectives.
- The consequences of inadequate control execution must be evaluated to determine whether a control deficiency would significantly impair achievement of the objectives.
- Other compensating controls should be considered as they may indicate that the operation of a given key control is not as critical as first presumed.
- The effect of one control on other controls also must be considered. For example, the execution of a control may not appear to significantly impair the achievement of an objective, but it could impact the execution of other controls, which could impair the achievement of an objective.

EXHIBIT 13-10

EXAMPLE RISK AND CONTROL MATRIX

Process-level Risk	Key Control	Design Adequacy
Risk A – Definition (associated process-level objectives)	• Activity A • Activity B • Activity C	The indicated key controls are designed adequately to manage this risk to an acceptable level.
Risk B – Definition (associated process-level objectives)	• Activity A • Activity D • Activity C	The indicated key controls are **not** designed adequately to manage this risk to an acceptable level (describe design gap).
Rick C – Definition (associated process-level objectives)	• Activity E • Activity F	The indicated key controls are designed adequately to manage this risk to an acceptable level.

- The impact of entity-level controls also should be considered. That is, deficiencies in entity-level controls may diminish the effectiveness of process-level controls. By understanding the effectiveness of entity-level controls, the internal auditor can better assess the impact key controls at the process level will have on the achievement of objectives.
- Redundant controls, or those that are not cost effective, may need to be changed or eliminated. Such controls are probably not key controls.

The final task in this step of engagement planning is to link the process-level controls to the process-level risks. The achievement of objectives is subject to different risk scenarios, and certain controls may only mitigate certain risks. Ultimately, if a control is determined to be ineffective, it may impact a single risk or multiple risks. The documentation of this linkage can be accomplished in a simple matrix, referred to as a Risk and Control Matrix, an example of which is shown in Exhibit 13-10.

Later in this chapter, you will see how this matrix can be used as the beginning for an audit program.

EVALUATE THE ADEQUACY OF CONTROL DESIGN

The next step in the engagement planning process is to evaluate the adequacy of process design. The key to this step is determining whether the key controls are designed adequately to reduce the individual process risks to an acceptable level. The following questions should be considered when evaluating the adequacy of process design:

- Does the internal auditor understand what an "acceptable level" of risk is, based on management's risk tolerance levels for the process?
- Do the key controls, taken individually or in the aggregate, reduce the corresponding process-level risks to acceptable levels?
- Are there additional compensating controls from other processes that further reduce risks to acceptably low levels?
- Does it appear that the key controls, if operating effectively, will support the achievement of process-level objectives?

- To the extent appropriate, does the process design address effectiveness and efficiency of operations, reliability of reporting, compliance with applicable laws and regulations, and achievement of strategic objectives?
- What gaps, if any, exist that impede the process?
    - What specific gaps exist in the design of the process?
    - What are the possible outcomes or effects of those gaps?
    - Why do these gaps exist — that is, what are the root causes (for example, inadequate procedures, unclear policies, noninterfacing systems, or lack of segregation of duties)?

Once the internal auditor has completed the design adequacy evaluation, any gaps that were identified should be discussed with management and documented as preliminary audit observations. Note that the matrix in Exhibit 13-10 contains a column titled "Design Adequacy" where the internal auditor's judgments can be documented. As indicated in that exhibit, the internal auditor's judgment typically is one of the following:

- The indicated key controls are designed adequately to manage this risk to an acceptable level.
- The indicated key controls are not designed adequately to manage this risk to an acceptable level (describe design gap).

Design Adequacy

Assessment of whether management has planned and organized (designed) the controls in a manner that provides reasonable assurance that the related risks can be managed to an acceptable level.

Once the internal auditor has formed judgments on design adequacy for each individual risk, an evaluation can be made regarding the design of the process taken as a whole. Examples of such conclusions include:

- Design is adequate; no significant gaps. Overall, the process and information systems appear to be designed adequately to manage the risks to an acceptable level.
- Design is adequate; however, gaps exist. Overall, the process and information systems appear to be designed adequately to manage the risks to an acceptable level. However, the existence of one or more gaps may result in some exposure that the process owner may find unacceptable.
- Design is inadequate; significant gaps exist. Overall, the process design does not appear to be adequate to manage the risks to an acceptable level. Significant gaps create an intolerable level of exposure that process-level objectives will not be achieved.

These individual observations and the overall evaluation will influence the nature, extent, and timing of tests to be performed.

CREATE A TEST PLAN

Now that the internal auditor fully understands how the process operates and has evaluated the adequacy of process design, the next step is to develop a test plan. A test plan should be designed to gather sufficient appropriate evidence to support an evaluation of how effectively the key controls are operating. This evaluation and the evaluation of the process design adequacy, taken together, provide reasonable assurance that the process-level objectives will be achieved.

Based on the understanding gained from the previous engagement planning steps, the internal auditor is now prepared to: (1) determine which controls are important enough to test, (2) develop an approach for testing those controls, and (3) document judgments supporting the chosen audit tests. Each of these tasks is discussed in more detail in the following sections.

Determining Which Controls to Test

Reasonable Assurance

A level of assurance that is supported by generally accepted auditing procedures and judgments. Reasonable assurance can apply to judgments surrounding the effectiveness of internal controls, the mitigation of risks, the achievement of objectives, or other engagement-related conclusions.

As indicated above, the primary focus of testing is to determine whether the key controls are operating effectively enough to ensure process-level risks are managed sufficiently. While this may be accomplished by simply testing all of the identified key controls, there are other factors the internal auditor must consider when determining which controls to test:

- Are there higher-level controls that might, by themselves, provide reasonable assurance that the relevant risks are managed sufficiently? Higher-level controls may be reconciliation, monitoring, or supervisory controls performed by individuals independent of the detailed control owners, for example, their supervisors or managers. As part of a top-down risk-based controls assessment, the internal auditor should give consideration to these higher-level controls, just as the impact of entity-level controls should be considered (as discussed earlier in this chapter).
- Are there other compensating controls that address multiple risks? If so, it may be more efficient to test these controls rather than focusing on testing of each of the detailed key controls.
- Was the design of controls assessed as being adequate? If not, it may not be necessary to test the controls as, even with effective operation, the risks may not be mitigated due to the inadequate design.
    - However, the internal auditor may decide to perform tests to determine the extent of errors resulting from inadequate control design. The types of tests to quantify the errors (for example, data extraction and analysis) likely will be different than direct tests performed to evaluate the effectiveness of controls.
- When do the key controls operate, and, based on the period within scope for the engagement, is it practical to test certain key controls? For example, certain controls may operate only at year-end. If the engagement is being conducted during the year, it may not be practical to test some of those controls.
- Have there been changes in the process during the period that result in certain key controls operating for only a portion of the period within scope? If so, consideration must be given to how these changes might impact the testing of key controls.

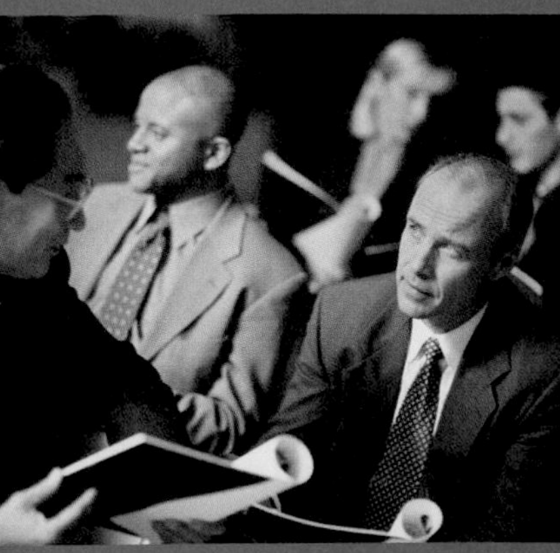

Once these factors have been considered, the internal auditor is ready to develop a specific testing approach. As indicated above, the approach typically focuses on evaluating the effectiveness of controls that are designed adequately, but some testing may be needed to quantify the impact of controls that are not designed adequately.

Developing a Testing Approach

A testing approach involves determining the nature, extent, and timing of tests to perform. The primary objective of testing is to determine whether the controls are operating as designed to reduce the corresponding risks to an acceptable level. The different types of audit tests are described in greater detail in Chapter 10, "Audit Evidence and Working Papers." However, the following outlines the decisions that must be made when developing a testing approach.

- **Nature of Tests.** Different types of tests provide different levels of assurance and will take different amounts of time to conduct.
- **Extent of Tests.** Controls can be tested on a partial or complete basis, that is, a sample of transactions or 100 percent of the transactions. Obviously, testing larger samples provides greater assurance but requires more time. Sampling techniques are discussed in much greater detail in Chapter 11, "Audit Sampling."
- **Timing of Tests.** Tests can be performed at different frequencies or intervals, depending on the period covered in the engagement's scope, the nature of the control, and the type of test being performed.

There may be other factors influencing the nature, extent, and timing of tests. The key is to ensure that the testing approach provides sufficient evidence regarding the management of all key process-level risks.

Documenting the Testing approach

The example Risk and Control Matrix shown in Exhibit 13-10 can be expanded by adding a column to include the Testing Approach for each risk. Exhibit 13-11 provides an example of what this matrix might look like (note that the Design Adequacy column from Exhibit 13-10 has been removed to illustrate the thought link between the Key Control and Testing Approach columns).

Note that some of the individual tests may apply to multiple controls, that is, they are multipurpose tests.

> Books 2 Buy **Example**: Exhibit 13-12 shows a partially completed Risk and Control Matrix for the cash disbursements function.

DEVELOP A WORK PROGRAM

The next step in engagement planning is to document all of the judgments and conclusions made during the planning phase. As can be seen by the breadth of activities covered in this chapter, there are many different but important tasks that were completed, as well as many more yet

EXHIBIT 13-11

EXAMPLE RISK AND CONTROL MATRIX WITH TESTING APPROACH

Process-level Risk	Key Control	Testing Approach
Risk A – Definition (associated process-level objectives)	• Activity A • Activity B • Activity C	• Test A • Test B • Test C
Risk B – Definition (associated process-level objectives)	• Activity A • Activity D • Activity E	• Test A • Test D • Test E

EXHIBIT 13-12

EXAMPLE RISK AND CONTROL MATRIX FOR CASH DISBURSEMENTS

Process-level Risk	Key Control	Testing Approach
Expectations Risk – Lack of well-developed and well-articulated policies, procedures, and other forms of communication from management may result in employees carrying out their responsibilities in a manner that is inconsistent with management's expectations and desires (accuracy, timeliness, recording, compliance, and approval objectives).	• Delegation of authority policy establishes approval levels for procurement and disbursement decisions. • Accounts payable has developed detailed procedures covering all key disbursement tasks.	1. Review delegation of authority policy and evaluate whether it appears to be current and appropriate given the present responsibilities of individuals. 2. Select a sample of 80 disbursements (10% risk, 5% tolerable deviation rate, and 1% expected deviation rate) and test for approvals in accordance with the policy. 3. Review and discuss procedures with accounts payable personnel to determine whether the procedures accurately reflect the required tasks and could be followed by others.
Duplicate Payments Risk – Failure to identify multiple inputs of invoices may result in duplicate payments to vendors that could go undetected or prove difficult to collect (accuracy and recording objectives).	• The purchasing system alerts the A/P clerk if the vendor number, invoice number, and invoice amount match an invoice previously entered. • The cash disbursements run will flag any payments of identical amounts to the same vendor for review prior to disbursement.	1. Test the system's duplicate invoice functionality by attempting to enter duplicate invoice numbers. Also, test what happens if a digit or symbol is added to the end of a duplicate invoice number. 2. Since the system only alerts the user to the possibility of a duplicate payment, extract 100% of the payments for the last year and test for possible duplicate payments. 3. Test to ensure the cash disbursements flag operates as designed.
Timeliness Risk – Inability to process payments on a timely basis may result in fines or penalties (for late payments) or missed discounts (timeliness and cash flow objectives).	• The system requires that a payment date be input during invoice data entry. • An edit report is generated whenever a payment date is more than 30 days after the invoice date. • The invoice input screen has a field that can be checked if the invoice is eligible for an early-pay discount.	1. Test the system functionality for the three key controls. 2. Using data analysis software, compute the difference between the payment date and invoice date for 100% of payments made during the last year. Follow up on any late payments or missed discounts.
Systems Access Risk – Lack of effective logical security practices may create opportunities for unauthorized individuals to access, manipulate, or delete key disbursements data (accuracy, recording, and cash flow objectives).	• Logical security is administered by IT in the same manner as for all applications. • The accounts payable manager must review and confirm access rights to the cash disbursements system twice per year.	1. IT logical security is tested in a separate engagement by the IT audit specialists. Check the results of that audit to ensure there were no design deficiencies relating to the cash disbursements security. 2. Discuss with the accounts payable manager the process for confirming access rights. Examine documentation supporting this procedure.

to be performed (for example, testing and reporting). To ensure all engagement team members understand what has been completed and what remains to be performed, it is common to prepare an engagement work program. This work program may take different forms, such as:

- A standard template or checklist that the lead internal auditor prepares to document the completion of the planning steps. Standard templates are frequently used to ensure each engagement covers all of the necessary tasks.
- A memorandum summarizing the tasks completed. In situations in which the planning is dynamic and not consistent from engagement to engagement, this free-form approach may be more appropriate.
- Additional columns in the Risk and Control Matrix if the internal auditor desires to have everything captured in one document.
- A combination of the three.

Work Program

A document that lists the procedures to be followed during an engagement, designed to achieve the engagement plan.

The format will vary from internal audit function to internal audit function. The key point is that there must be some means of:

- Ensuring all engagement team members understand what has been done and what still needs to be done.
- Communicating who is responsible for performing each engagement task.
- Providing a record of which tasks are completed.
- Facilitating review by an engagement manager or director who provides oversight and direction during the engagement planning process.

Regardless of the format, the following are covered in a typical work program:

- Key administrative tasks, such as preparation of a planning memorandum, scheduling resources, establishing milestone dates, etc.
- Conducting a kickoff meeting with process-level management to discuss the objectives and scope of the engagement, process-level risks, timing of the engagement, information needed from process-level employees, reports or other deliverables, and any expectations management has of the engagement.
- Planning tasks, which list each of the tasks discussed in this chapter (for example, understanding the process, assessing process-level risks, and identifying key controls).
- Fieldwork tasks, which list the specific tests that will be conducted (this may be documented in the Risk and Control Matrix discussed previously).
- Wrap-up steps, such as clearing open review notes, conducting a closing meeting with process-level management, finalizing the working papers, etc.
- Reporting tasks, such as preparing a draft engagement communication, soliciting feedback from process-level management, and issuing a final engagement communication (covered more fully in Chapter 14, "Communicating Assurance Engagement Outcomes and Performing Follow-up Procedures").

Even though the discussion of developing a work program is covered in the latter part of this chapter, its preparation typically is done throughout the engagement planning process. As indicated, the format of the work program is not what is important. The key is to communicate the primary tasks, judgments, and conclusions that were made during this process and help complete the rest of the engagement.

ALLOCATE RESOURCES TO THE ENGAGEMENT

The final step in planning the engagement is to determine the necessary resources needed to carry out the planned tasks. This step involves: (1) estimating, or budgeting, the resources that are needed, (2) allocating the appropriate human resources to the engagement, and (3) scheduling those resources to ensure the engagement is completed on time.

Budgeting

The first task is to estimate the resources that are needed to conduct the engagement. A budget should be prepared that considers the number of hours needed to complete the engagement, as well as other costs that may be required:

- **Hours needed to complete the engagement.** An experienced internal auditor is in a position to develop a reasonable estimate of the number of hours it will take to complete the planning, performing, and communicating phases of an engagement. The estimate should be realistic, but it cannot always be precise as there may be unexpected events that can delay an engagement (for example, unavailability of key process-level employees, delays in obtaining requested information, or illness of internal auditors). It may be appropriate to allow for a variance from the estimate (for example, +/- 10%).
- **Other costs.** In addition to the human resource costs, some engagements may require additional expenditures. Common examples include:
  - Travel and related costs, when the engagement must be performed, all or in part, away from the internal auditors' location.
  - Technology costs, when access to unique or nonroutine technology is needed to complete the engagement (for example, software licenses for data analysis and network security analysis).
  - Supplies, when nonroutine items are needed (for example, steel-toed shoes or hardhats for inventory count observations, or special paper or ink for deliverables that include many pictures or colored charts and graphs).

Engagement Resources:

- **Internal auditors**
- **Other people (internal/external)**
- **Travel**
- **Technology**
- **Other**

Typically, the lead internal auditor on the engagement has the experience to prepare these budgets and will be held accountable for managing the engagement according to budget parameters. The chief audit executive (CAE) relies on the effectiveness of engagement budgeting when determining the overall department budget. Refer to Chapter 9, "Managing the Internal Audit Function," for more details.

Allocating Human Resources

Once the engagement budget has been determined, it is time to identify and allocate the resources needed to complete the engagement. The allocation of human resources is the most important and challenging task. This involves answering the following questions:

- What types of skills are needed on this engagement (for example, financial reporting or IT)?
- What previous experience will be required on the engagement (for example, knowledge about the area or previous experience with similar engagements)?
- Who in the department has the skills and experience to meet these needs?
- Is there a need for any specialty skills that do not exist within the internal audit function (for example, derivatives expertise and environmental expertise)? If so, where can these skills be obtained at a reasonable cost?
- Are there professional development considerations that might impact the allocation of resources to this engagement? For example, do certain internal auditors need a particular type of experience to help them learn and grow professionally?
- Are there any other unique departmental considerations that may impact which internal auditors should be assigned to the engagement?

Strategic Sourcing

Supplements the in-house internal audit function through the use of third-party vendor services for the purposes of gaining subject matter expertise for a specific engagement or filling a gap in needed resources to complete the internal audit plan.

After determining the appropriate human resources, the next task is to formally schedule those resources to the engagement. Resource scheduling can be a very dynamic process, and the following items need to be considered:

- **Availability of Key Process Personnel.** Although it may be convenient for the internal audit function to start an engagement on a certain date, the timing may not work for process personnel. There may be certain times of the month or quarter that are inconvenient (for example, the period when accounting personnel are focused on closing the books). Additionally, the timing of the engagement may need to be changed due to absences of key personnel (travel, vacation, training, etc.), or department initiatives that will divert the attention of key personnel to other matters.
- **Availability of Engagement Resources.** Similar to key process personnel, internal audit employees may have other commitments (for example, vacations, training, department initiatives, etc.) that could impact the scheduling of an engagement.
- **Availability of Outside Resources.** If specialty skills or additional manpower are needed to complete an engagement, the availability of those resources also must be considered. Sometimes, the service firms providing such resources have schedules that differ from the organization's (for example, different holidays, block training weeks, or internal initiatives).
- **Availability of Key Reviewers.** Even if the key engagement resources are available to complete the fieldwork, the internal audit manager or director also must be available to perform the level of

review required on an engagement, otherwise its completion may be delayed.

Once the allocation and scheduling of resources is completed, the engagement is ready to commence. Exhibit 13-13 highlights the next fundamental phase in the assurance engagement process: performing the engagement. The essential steps involved in the performance phase are also listed in this exhibit.

CONDUCT TESTS TO GATHER EVIDENCE

At this point, the assurance engagement transitions from the planning phase to the performing phase. The testing approach developed in the planning phase and outlined in the Risk and Control Matrix (refer to Exhibit 13-11) must now be executed to determine whether the controls are operating as designed. As each test is conducted, evidence will be gathered to support the internal auditor's conclusions regarding how effectively the controls are operating.

The results of testing can be documented in the Risk and Control Matrix. The example Risk and Control Matrix shown in Exhibit 13-11 can be expanded by adding a column to include the Results of Testing. Exhibit 13-14 provides an example of what this matrix might look like. Note that the Key Control column from Exhibit 13-11 has been removed for this illustration. This was done to simplify this example as the Key Control column is not critical to the thought process at this point. However, when conducting an assurance engagement, all of the columns are necessary to evaluate the design adequacy and operating effectiveness of key controls. A complete Risk and Control Matrix can be found in Exhibit 13-21 at the end of this chapter.

Books2Buy **Example**: Exhibit 13-15 shows a partially completed Risk and Control Matrix for the cash disbursements function. At the

EXHIBIT 13-13

THE ASSURANCE ENGAGEMENT PROCESS

Plan

- Determine engagement objectives and scope.
- Understand the auditee, including auditee objectives and assertions.
- Identify and assess risks.
- Identify key control activities.
- Evaluate adequacy of control design.
- Create a test plan.
- Develop a work program.
- Allocate resources to the engagement.

Perform

- Conduct tests to gather evidence.
- Evaluate evidence gathered and reach conclusions.
- Develop observations and formulate recommendations.

Communicate

- Perform observation evaluation and escalation process.
- Conduct interim and preliminary engagement communications.
- Develop final engagement communications.
- Distribute formal and informal final communications.
- Perform monitoring and follow-up procedures.

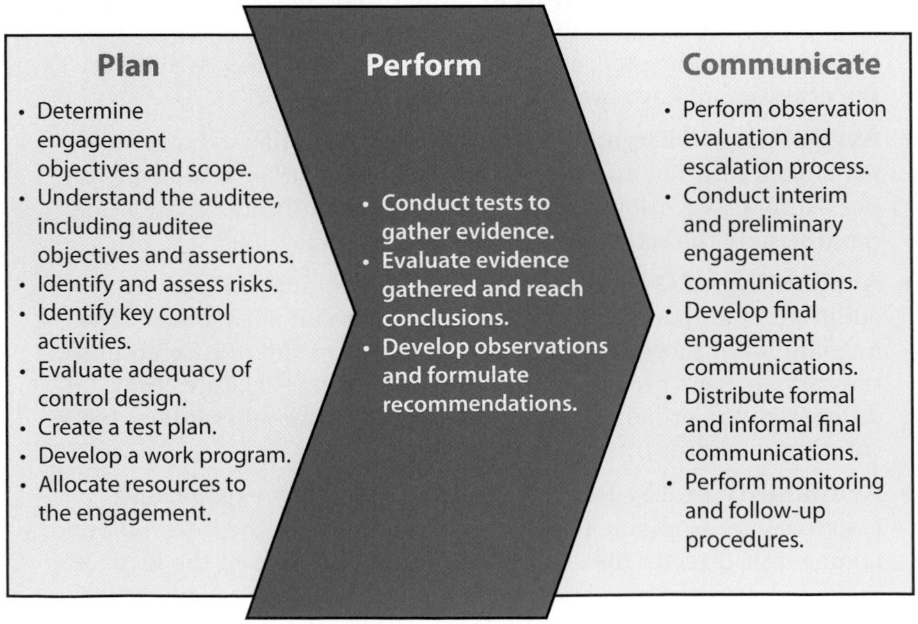

EXHIBIT 13-14

EXAMPLE RISK AND CONTROL MATRIX WITH RESULTS OF TESTING

Process-level Risk	Testing Approach	Results of Testing
Risk A – Definition (associated process-level objectives)	• Test A • Test B • Test C	• Result A • Result B • Result C
Risk B – Definition (associated process-level objectives)	• Test A • Test D • Test E	• Result A • Result D • Result E

end of each Results of Testing entry is a cross-reference to the audit working papers where the test was documented (X-#). Examples of two tests are included in Exhibits 13-16 and 13-17. If an exception or deficiency was found during testing, reference is also made to the working paper documenting the engagement observation (Z-#).

Examples of select working papers supporting this testing are shown in Exhibits 13-16 and 13-17.

EVALUATE EVIDENCE GATHERED AND REACH CONCLUSIONS

Conducting audit tests allows the internal auditor to gather the evidence needed to evaluate the design adequacy and operating effectiveness of key controls and reach conclusions about the effectiveness of the process or area under review. The following are questions that the internal auditor may need to answer, depending on the charter of the internal audit function, the objectives of the engagement, and the expectations of the auditee and other internal audit stakeholders:

- Are the key controls designed adequately?
- Are the key controls operating effectively, that is, as they are designed to operate?
- Are the underlying risks being mitigated to an acceptable level?
- Overall, do the design and operation of the key controls support achievement of the objectives for the process or area under review?

The answers to these questions require the internal auditor to reach conclusions based on the information gathered during the planning phase of the audit and the execution of audit tests. While the conclusions typically require a great deal of judgment, there is a logical thought process that flows from the steps described throughout this chapter. These conclusions can be documented in the Risk and Control Matrix. Similar to past tasks, the example Risk and Control Matrix shown in Exhibit 13-14 can be expanded by adding a column to include the Testing Conclusions. Exhibit 13-18 provides an example of what this matrix might look like. Note that the Testing Approach column from Exhibit 13-14 has been removed for this illustration. This was done to simplify this example as the Testing Approach column is not critical to the thought process in this example. However, as previously stated, all of the columns are necessary to evaluate the design adequacy and operating effectiveness of key controls when

EXHIBIT 13-15

EXAMPLE RISK AND CONTROL MATRIX FOR CASH DISBURSEMENTS

Process-level Risk	Testing Approach	Results of Testing
Expectations Risk – Lack of well-developed and well-articulated policies, procedures, and other forms of communication from management may result in employees carrying out their responsibilities in a manner that is inconsistent with management's expectations and desires (accuracy, timeliness, recording, compliance, and approval objectives).	1. Review delegation of authority policy and evaluate whether it appears to be current and appropriate given the present responsibilities of individuals. 2. Select a sample of 80 disbursements (10% risk, 5% tolerable deviation rate, and 1% expected deviation rate) and test for approvals in accordance with the policy. 3. Review and discuss procedures with accounts payable personnel to determine whether the procedures accurately reflect the required tasks and could be followed by others.	1. The delegation of authority policy lists seven individuals who are no longer with the company. Additionally, nine individuals who are new in their positions or new to the company should be on the list but are not (Z-3). All other responsibilities appear to be appropriate (WP X-1). 2. No observations were identified in this test; all approvals were in accordance with the delegation of authority policy, after taking into consideration necessary changes to the policy as described on working paper X-1 (WP X-2). 3. Based on discussions and observations, it appears that the documented procedures continue to be appropriate, current, and well-understood (WP X-3).
Duplicate Payments Risk – Failure to identify multiple inputs of invoices may result in duplicate payments to vendors that could go undetected or prove difficult to collect (accuracy and recording objectives).	1. Test the system's duplicate invoice functionality by attempting to enter duplicate invoice numbers. Also, test what happens if a digit or symbol is added to the end of a duplicate invoice number. 2. Since the system only alerts the user to the possibility of a duplicate payment, extract 100% of the payments for the last year and test for possible duplicate payments. 3. Test to ensure the cash disbursements flag operates as designed.	1. The system rejected all duplicate invoice entries. However, it accepted invoices in which a digit or symbol was added to the end of the invoice number, creating the opportunity for a duplicate payment (Z-4) (WP X-4). 2. Fourteen (14) potentially duplicate payments were identified, totaling US $357,782. A/P management is following up on all items, which appear to be due to the deficiency noted on working paper X-4 (X-5). 3. The test transactions for this control were all flagged in the cash disbursements run. The 14 transactions identified in the duplicate payments test were from different disbursement batches and, thus, were not flagged by this control (WP X-6).
Timeliness Risk – Inability to process payments on time may result in fines or penalties (for late payments) or missed discounts (timeliness and cash flow objectives).	1. Test the system functionality for the three key controls. 2. Using data analysis software, compute the difference between the payment date and invoice date for 100% of payments made during the last year. Follow up on any late payments or missed discounts.	1. The benchmark testing of all three controls indicated that they operated as designed (WPs X-7, X-8, and X-9). 2. There were 172 payments (1.1% of total disbursements) made late. Late-payment fees were charged on 21 of the payments. Follow-up by A/P management resulted in such fees being waived for nine of the 21 late payments. Fees paid totaled US $24,489 (Z-5). There were no missed discounts identified (WPs X-10 and X-11).
Systems Access Risk – Lack of effective logical security practices may create opportunities for unauthorized individuals to access, manipulate, or delete key disbursements data (accuracy, recording, and cash flow objectives).	1. IT logical security is tested in a separate engagement by the IT audit specialists. Check the results of that audit to ensure there were no design deficiencies relating to the cash disbursements security. 2. Discuss with the accounts payable manager the process for confirming access rights. Examine documentation supporting this procedure.	1. No design deficiencies were noted in the IT logical security testing. 2. Based on the discussion and observations of appropriate documentation, access rights appear to be reviewed appropriately and timely.

EXHIBIT 13-16

EXAMPLE OF EXPECTATIONS RISK TEST #1

X-1
Prepared by: Steve Braveheart
Reviewed by: David Richardson

Purpose of Test: To test whether the delegation of authority policy is complete, appropriate, and current relative to establishing the authority for approving procurement and disbursement transactions.

Testing Approach: Review delegation of authority policy and evaluate whether it appears to be current and appropriate given the present responsibilities of individuals.

Sampling Considerations: There are 147 individuals included in this policy. Given the small population and the nature of the assertion (that all and only appropriate individuals are delegated authority to approve procurement and disbursement transactions), a nonstatistical sample was chosen. Beginning with the first person on the list, every third person was evaluated as to the appropriateness of their inclusion on the delegation of authority policy.

Results of Testing: Following are the results of the test:

- After completing the initial sample, three individuals were identified who were no longer employees of the company.
- Because of this observation, the test was extended to include all 147 individuals, which indicated that seven individuals on the list were no longer employees, one of whom had left the company 15 months ago.
- Recognizing that the list was not being updated timely, the auditor also tested new employees and promotions during the preceding 18 months and found that five of the new employees and four promoted employees should have been on the list based on their assigned responsibilities.

Conclusion: Based on the results of testing, the control relating to reliance on the delegation of authority policy is **not** consistently operating effectively due to failure to update the list timely for changes in employee status (see engagement observation in working paper Z-3).

conducting an assurance engagement. A complete Risk and Control Matrix can be found in Exhibit 13-21 at the end of this chapter.

> Books2Buy **Example**: Exhibit 13-19 shows a partially completed Risk and Control Matrix for the cash disbursements function.

DEVELOP OBSERVATIONS AND FORMULATE RECOMMENDATIONS

After completing the testing, gathering and evaluating the evidence needed, and reaching conclusions, the internal auditor must develop the observations and formulate the recommendations that should be communicated to the auditee and other internal audit stakeholders. The key elements of a well-written observation are discussed briefly in Chapter 12, "Introduction to the Engagement Process." Further elaboration of these elements can be found in Chapter 14, "Communicating Assurance Engagement Outcomes and Performing Follow-up Procedures."

> Books2Buy **Example**: Five potential audit observations were identified. The key elements of audit observations are documented in Exhibit 13-20 for each of these five audit observations.

The examples above reflect the documentation that the internal auditor can complete while conducting the fieldwork. However, there is additional information that may be necessary before including such observations in an engagement communication. Refer to Chapter 14, where the resolution and reporting of observations are discussed in further detail.

EXHIBIT 13-17

EXAMPLE OF DUPLICATE PAYMENTS RISK TEST #2

X-5
Prepared by: Jerry Coxswain
Reviewed by: David Richardson

Purpose of Test: To test whether any duplicate payments were made during the last year.

Testing Approach: Since the system only alerts the user to the possibility of a duplicate payment, extract 100% of the payments for the last year and test for possible duplicate payments.

Sampling Considerations: It is possible to extract all of the disbursements made during the last 12 months. Therefore, all disbursements made during that time frame were extracted from the cash disbursements system. Using the generalized audit software licensed by the department, we selected all payments of equal amounts for a given vendor, regardless of invoice number or payment date. We also reviewed payments of the same amount regardless of vendor to determine if there were payments to a vendor that may have been using different names.

Results of Testing: After analyzing all of the disbursements that met one of our criteria, we determined that the following represent potential duplicate payments:

Vendor	Invoice #	Payment Date	Amount
ABC Office Supplies	8641032	February 21, 20XX	$2,316.50
ABC Office Supplies	8641032A	February 28, 20XX	$2,316.50
Alpha Printing and Binding	48637899	March 15, 20XX	$125,414.22
Alpha Printing and Binding	48637899-1	March 15, 20XX	$125,414.22
Alpha Printing and Binding	48637977	May 15, 20XX	$86,213.47
Alpha Printing and Binding	48637977-1	May 31, 20XX	$86,213.47
Alpha Printing and Binding	48638102	August 15, 20XX	$91,236.17
Alpha Printing and Binding	48638102*	August 31, 20XX	$91,236.17
Daily Shipping Services	12587	April 22, 20XX	$487.95
Daily Shipping Services	12587X	April 22, 20XX	$487.95
Dewey Cheatem Tax Services	489752	April 30, 20XX	$19,495.00
Dewey Cheatem Tax Services	489753	April 30, 20XX	$19,495.00
Dewey Cheatem Tax Services	489960	September 30, 20XX	$21,250.00
Dewey Cheatem Tax Services	489961	September 30, 20XX	$21,250.00
Newtown Catering	NC1568	February 14, 20XX	$685.73
Newtown Catering	NC1568A	February 28, 20XX	$685.73
Newtown Catering	NC1598	March 17, 20XX	$443.65
Newtown Catering	NC1598A	March 31, 20XX	$443.65
Newtown Catering	NC1677	July 4, 20XX	$772.43
Newtown Catering	NC1677A	July 31, 20XX	$772.43
Newtown Catering	NC1751	October 31, 20XX	$875.00
Newtown Catering	NC1751-1	November 30, 20XX	$875.00
Newtown Catering	NC1803	December 12, 20XX	$966.47
Newtown Catering	NC1804	December 31, 20XX	$966.47
Spellmen Training	667305832	June 18, 20XX	$7,500.00
Spellmen Training	667305833	June 18, 20XX	$7,500.00
Thompson Florists	1567	August 22, 20XX	$125.82
Thompson Florists	156X	August 31, 20XX	$125.82
TOTAL DUPLICATE AMOUNTS			**$357,782.41**

Conclusion: It appears that duplicate payments are being made in instances when invoices are presented twice, either with slightly different invoice numbers or with the same invoice number, and the individual entering the invoice has added a digit to the end to prevent the system from rejecting the transaction. Therefore, the controls are **not** operating effectively on a consistent basis (see engagement observation in working paper Z-4).

EXAMPLE RISK AND CONTROL MATRIX WITH TESTING CONCLUSIONS

EXHIBIT 13-18

Process-level Risk	Results of Testing	Testing Conclusions
Risk A – Definition (associated process-level objectives)	• Result A • Result B • Result C	Conclusion covering Risk A
Risk B – Definition (associated process-level objectives)	• Result A • Result D • Result E	Conclusion covering Risk B

SUMMARY

Chapter 12 introduced an expression known as the six P's: Proper Prior Planning Prevents Poor Performance. This expression means that it is critical to effectively plan engagements to ensure success. Time spent in the planning phase of an engagement likely will pay great dividends later, helping to ensure that the overall audit is conducted effectively, efficiently, and comprehensively.

The first phase of an assurance engagement is the planning phase. The key steps in planning an engagement are:

- **Determine Engagement Objectives and Scope.** Each assurance engagement will be a little different, depending on the reason for performing the engagement and the desired end results. The first step is to establish the objectives of the engagement and outline the scope to articulate the time, geographical, and procedural boundaries.
- **Understand the Auditee (including auditee objectives).** To conduct an engagement effectively, the auditor must first understand the auditee's objectives, the tasks undertaken within the area under review to achieve those objectives, and the ways in which performance is monitored and success is measured.
- **Identify and Assess Risks.** The specific events or scenarios that could prevent the achievement of the auditee's objectives must be identified and assessed. This assessment typically involves an evaluation of the impact and likelihood of the risk scenarios.
- **Identify Key Controls.** Key controls are those that, individually or when aggregated with other controls, mitigate the auditee's risk to an acceptable level. While the auditee may have implemented many different controls to achieve a variety of purposes, the key controls are the ones that are truly integral to achievement of objectives.
- **Evaluate the Adequacy of Control Design.** The first key evaluation is the adequacy of control design. This step requires the internal auditor to evaluate whether the controls, if they operate effectively, will mitigate the risks that could prevent the achievement of objectives.
- **Create a Test Plan.** The test plan outlines how each of the key controls will be tested to help the internal auditor evaluate how effectively those controls are operating. The tests also must be

Operating Effectiveness

Assessment of whether management has executed (operated) the controls in a manner that provides reasonable assurance that risks have been managed effectively and that the goals and objectives will be achieved efficiently and economically.

EXHIBIT 13-19

EXAMPLE RISK AND CONTROL MATRIX FOR CASH DISBURSEMENTS

Process-level Risk	Results of Testing	Testing Conclusions
Expectations Risk – Lack of well-developed and well-articulated policies, procedures, and other forms of communication from management may result in employees carrying out their responsibilities in a manner that is inconsistent with management's expectations and desires (accuracy, timeliness, recording, compliance, and approval objectives).	1. The delegation of authority policy lists seven individuals who are no longer with the company. Additionally, nine individuals who are new in their positions or new to the company should be on the list but are not (Z-3). All other responsibilities appear to be appropriate (WP X-1). 2. No observations were identified in this test; all approvals were in accordance with the delegation of authority policy, after taking into consideration necessary changes to the policy as described on working paper X-1 (WP X-2). 3. Based on discussions and observations, it appears that the documented procedures continue to be appropriate, current, and well-understood (WP X-3).	Based on the results of the sample chosen, we can conclude with 90% confidence that the rate of deviations from management's approval policy did not exceed 2.9%, which is less than the tolerable deviation rate of 5%. However, expectations regarding approval authority are not being met due to the fact that the delegation of authority list is not updated consistently to reflect changes in employment status (see working paper Z-3). Therefore, this risk is only partially mitigated.
Duplicate Payments Risk – Failure to identify multiple inputs of invoices may result in duplicate payments to vendors that could go undetected or prove difficult to collect (accuracy and recording objectives).	1. The system rejected all duplicate invoice entries. However, it accepted invoices in which a digit or symbol was added to the end of the invoice number, creating the opportunity for a duplicate payment (Z-4) (WP X-4). 2. Fourteen (14) potentially duplicate payments were identified, totaling US $357,782. A/P management is following up on all items, which appear to be due to the deficiency noted on working paper X-4 (X-5). 3. The test transactions for this control were all flagged in the cash disbursements run. The 14 transactions identified in the duplicate payments test were from different disbursement batches and, thus, were not flagged by this control (WP X-6).	While the systematic controls appear to be operating effectively, it is possible to circumvent these controls through submission and input of a different invoice number or adding a digit at the end of the existing invoice number (see working paper Z-4). This represents a deficiency in the design of controls relating to this risk, which, along with the design deficiency noted in working paper Z-2, indicates that this risk is not adequately mitigated.
Timeliness Risk – Inability to process payments on time may result in fines or penalties (for late payments) or missed discounts (timeliness and cash flow objectives).	1. The benchmark testing of all three controls indicated that they operated as designed (WPs X-7, X-8, and X-9). 2. There were 172 payments (1.1% of total disbursements) made late. Late-payment fees were charged on 21 of the payments. Follow-up by A/P management resulted in such fees being waived for nine of the 21 late payments. Fees paid totaled US $24,489 (Z-5). There were no missed discounts identified (WPs X-10 and X-11).	All of the systematic controls are operating effectively. However, delays earlier in the process (for example, getting invoices approved and processed by initiators of the purchase) result in a relatively small number of payments being delayed. These delays have resulted in an insignificant financial impact (late-payment fees). Therefore, this risk appears to be only partially mitigated.
Systems Access Risk – Lack of effective logical security practices may create opportunities for unauthorized individuals to access, manipulate, or delete key disbursements data (accuracy, recording, and cash flow objectives).	1. No design deficiencies were noted in the IT logical security testing. 2. Based on the discussion and observations of appropriate documentation, access rights appear to be reviewed appropriately and timely.	The controls appear to be designed adequately and are operating effectively to mitigate this risk.

BOOKS 2 BUY AUDIT OBSERVATIONS FOR CASH DISBURSEMENTS

Z-1

Condition: There is no check with users to determine whether any goods or services have been received but not invoiced yet.

Criteria: All goods received for which title has passed to the company, or services that have been rendered, should be recorded in the financial statements.

Cause: Accounts payable management had not previously considered or recognized the value of performing such a check.

Effect: Unrecorded liabilities, along with the corresponding unrecorded assets or expenses, may result when the books are closed at month-end, quarter-end, or year-end.

Z-2

Condition: While the system does alert the A/P clerk to potential duplicate invoices, it does not prevent the A/P clerk from continuing to process such an invoice.

Criteria: The receipt of goods or services should be recorded and processed only once.

Cause: The system was coded to remind the user, but not to prohibit the user from entering an invoice again if circumstances warranted.

Effect: Liabilities, and the corresponding assets or expenses, may be overstated and funds disbursed inappropriately.

Z-3

Condition: The delegation of authority policy lists seven individuals who are no longer with the company. Additionally, nine individuals who are new in their positions or new to the company that should be on the list, are not.

Criteria: Authority over the disbursement of funds should only be delegated to individuals whose responsibilities justify such authority.

Cause: The delegation of authority policy is updated semiannually, rather than each time there is a change in personnel or responsibilities of authorized individuals.

Effect: Disbursements may be made that are not in accordance with management's direction.

Z-4

Condition: The system rejected all duplicate invoice entries. However, it accepted invoices in which a digit or symbol was added to the end of the invoice number, creating the opportunity for a duplicate payment.

Criteria: The receipt of goods or services should be recorded and processed only once.

Cause: In some instances, the A/P clerks appear to be entering certain invoices a second time when sent by the vendor. The clerks are not recognizing that these invoices may have been received before, and, given the control design deficiency as described in Z-2, are adding a digit to the end to facilitate processing. In other instances, the vendor is issuing a duplicate invoice with a different invoice number (typically one higher than the last one) and the A/P clerks did not detect the potential that these were duplicate invoices.

Effect: Liabilities, and the corresponding assets or expenses, were overstated by US $357,782.41 and the same amount of funds were disbursed inappropriately.

Z-5

Condition: There were 172 payments (1.1% of total disbursements) made late resulting in late-payment fees being charged on 21 of the payments. Follow-up by A/P management resulted in such fees being waived for nine of the 21 late payments. Fees paid totaled US $24,489.

Criteria: Payments should be made in a timely manner, consistent with management's expectations regarding avoidance of late-payment fees.

Cause: For a variety of reasons, invoice approvals were not timely in 19 of the 21 instances; thus, the payments missed the company's disbursement processing deadlines. In the remaining two instances, the delays were a result of management's decisions to withhold payment until a disagreement with the vendor could be resolved.

Effect: The company incurred late-payment fees totaling US $24,489.

EXHIBIT 13-20

Observation

A finding, determination, or judgment derived from the internal auditor's test results.

linked to the underlying risks so that any deficiencies identified during testing can be evaluated relative to the impact on risk mitigation.

- **Develop a Work Program.** A formal work program outlines the key tasks in the engagement process and any judgments made regarding the objectives and scope of the engagement.
- **Allocate Resources to the Engagement.** Based on the tasks to be performed during an engagement, personnel with the appropriate level of experience and skills must be identified and assigned to ensure the engagement is completed timely and effectively.

Planning an engagement requires more than just carrying out the steps above. It also requires effective documentation of the information gained and judgments made. While the format of such documentation created during the planning phase may take various forms, typically it includes:

- A planning memorandum or checklist to document the audit approach and judgments made.
- Flowcharts or narrative write-ups describing key process flows.
- A risk map that depicts the judgments made regarding process-level risks.
- A Risk and Control Matrix that documents the linkage between risks, controls, testing approach, results of testing, and testing conclusions.

The second phase of an assurance engagement involves performing the tests that were outlined in the planning phase and evaluating the results. Specifically, the internal auditor conducts the following steps:

- **Conduct Tests to Gather Evidence.** This involves completing each of the tests identified during the planning stage. During this step the internal auditor gathers and documents sufficient appropriate evidence to support the conclusions regarding how effectively the controls are operating.
- **Evaluate Evidence Gathered and Reach Conclusions.** This step requires the internal auditor to consider the initial evaluation of control design as well as the results of testing, and form a conclusion as to whether the underlying risks are being mitigated to an acceptable level.
- **Develop Observations and Formulate Recommendations.** Finally, any control deficiencies identified during the engagement should be documented to facilitate discussion with appropriate management and, ultimately, communication to appropriate stakeholders.

A Risk and Control Matrix is an effective way of documenting the many judgments made and results of testing during the assurance engagement. An example of the full matrix is shown in Exhibit 13-21.

EXHIBIT 13-21

RISK AND CONTROL MATRIX

Process-level Risk	Key Control	Design Adequacy	Testing Approach	Results of Testing	Testing Conclusions
Risk A – Definition (associated process-level objectives)	• Control A • Control B • Control C	The indicated key controls are adequate to manage this risk to an acceptable level.	• Test A • Test B • Test C	• Result A • Result B • Result C	Conclusion covering Risk A
Risk B – Definition (associated process-level objectives)	• Control A • Control D	The indicated key controls are **not** adequate to manage this risk to an acceptable level (describe design gap).	• Test A • Test D • Test E	• Result A • Result D • Result E	Conclusion covering Risk B
Risk C – Definition (associated process-level objectives)	• Control C • Control E • Control F	The indicated key controls are adequate to manage this risk to an acceptable level.	• Test F • Test G • Test H	• Result F • Result G • Result H	Conclusion covering Risk C

Review Questions

1. What are the four reasons for conducting an assurance engagement?
2. What are five types of scope statements?
3. What are the five typical exceptions that may be identified during testing in an engagement?
4. Which type of process objective is the most common and why?
5. What types of information may process owners have available that will help an internal auditor understand the process?
6. Why might an internal auditor perform analytical procedures during the engagement planning process?
7. Why must an internal auditor understand how entity-level controls may influence the performance of a process before auditing that process?
8. What are the three most common ways of documenting a process flow?
9. Why is it important for internal auditors to identify and understand key performance indicators for a process?
10. Why might the inherent likelihood of a risk increase if there is the potential for fraud?
11. What is the difference between a process-level risk scenario and a process-level risk?
12. What three key steps should an internal auditor follow when gaining an understanding of management's risk tolerance levels?
13. Which of the nine examples of common control types typically occur before a transaction is completed?
14. What are the key questions that must be answered when evaluating the design adequacy of controls?
15. When developing a testing approach, what decisions must be made about the tests to be performed?
16. What are the key tasks covered in the typical work program?
17. What four items should be considered when allocating resources and scheduling an engagement?
18. What four questions must be answered to evaluate the evidence gathered from audit testing?

Multiple-choice Questions

Select the best answer for each of the following questions.

1. Which of the following is not likely to be an assurance engagement objective?
   a. Evaluate the design adequacy of the payroll input process.
   b. Guarantee the accuracy of recorded inventory balances.
   c. Assess compliance with health and safety laws and regulations.
   d. Determine the operating effectiveness of fixed asset controls.
2. A process objective stating "All contracts must be approved by an officer of the company before being consummated" is an example of what type of objective?
   a. Strategic.
   b. Operations.
   c. Reporting.
   d. Compliance.
3. Analytical procedures can be applied during which phase(s) of an assurance engagement?
   a. Plan phase.
   b. Perform phase.
   c. Communicate phase.
   d. Plan and perform phases.
4. Which of the following auditee-prepared documents will likely be of greatest assistance to the internal auditor in their assessment of process design adequacy?
   a. Policies and procedures manual.
   b. Organization charts and job descriptions.
   c. Detailed flowcharts depicting the flow of the process.
   d. Narrative memoranda listing key tasks for portions of the process.
5. Which of the following controls is not likely to be an entity-level control?
   a. All employees must receive ongoing training to ensure they maintain their competence.
   b. All cash disbursement transactions must be approved before they are paid.
   c. All employees must comply with the Code of Ethics and Business Conduct.
   d. An organizationwide risk assessment is conducted annually.
6. Which of the following is not typically a key element of flowcharts or narrative memoranda?
   a. Overall process objectives.
   b. Key inputs to the process.
   c. Key outputs from the process.
   d. Key risks and controls.

7. Which of the following external risks is least likely to impact the accuracy of financial reporting?
   a. The standard-setting body in the organization's country issues a new financial accounting standard.
   b. A recent judicial court case increases the likelihood that pending litigation will result in an unfavorable outcome.
   c. Changes in standard industry contracts now allow for netting of payables and receivables.
   d. Competitor pressures cause the organization to pursue new sales channels.

8. Which of the following groups' risk tolerance levels are least relevant when conducting an assurance engagement?
   a. Senior management.
   b. Process-level management.
   c. The internal audit function.
   d. Vendors and customers.

9. Which of the following controls is likely to be least relevant when evaluating the design adequacy of a cash collections process?
   a. Calculating the amount of cash received.
   b. Documenting the rationale for selecting the bank account into which the deposit will be made.
   c. Matching the total deposits to the amounts credited to customers' accounts receivable balances.
   d. Segregating the preparation of deposit slips from the adjustment of customer account balances.

10. An internal auditor determines that the process is not designed adequately to reduce the underlying risks to an acceptable level. Which of the following should the internal auditor do next?
    a. Write the audit report, there's no reason to test the operating effectiveness of controls that are not designed adequately.
    b. Test compensating controls in other (adjacent) processes to see if the impact of the design inadequacy is reduced to an acceptable level.
    c. Test the existing key controls anyway to prove that, despite the design inadequacy, the process is still meeting the process objectives.
    d. Postpone the engagement until the design inadequacy has been rectified.

11. If an internal auditor identifies an exception while testing, which of the following may be appropriate?
    a. Test additional items to determine whether the exception is an isolated occurrence or indicative of a control deficiency.
    b. Gain an understanding of the root cause, that is, the reason the exception occurred.
    c. Draft an observation for the audit report.
    d. All of the above.

12. Which of the following is an appropriate conclusion that can be drawn when the internal auditor identifies an observation from testing controls?
    a. The process objectives cannot be achieved.
    b. The area may be vulnerable to fraud.
    c. Certain risks are not effectively mitigated.
    d. Overall, the process is not operating effectively.

13. Once an observation is identified by the internal auditor, it should be:
    a. Documented in the working papers.
    b. Discussed with the audit committee.
    c. Included in the final audit report.
    d. Scheduled for follow-up.

Discussion Questions

1. Why is it so important to "begin with the end in mind" when planning an assurance engagement?

2. COSO defines an organization's strategic objectives as being "high-level goals, aligned with and supporting its mission" that exist at the entity level. With this definition in mind, how can an administrative, task-oriented process have strategic objectives?

3. Management tends to focus on residual risk instead of inherent risk. Why do you think this is so? Why should internal auditors consider both inherent risk and residual risk when planning an assurance engagement?

4. If the internal auditor fails to identify all key process-level risks, what impact might that have on the overall assurance engagement? If the internal auditor determines that certain process-level risks are key when in fact they are not, what impact might that have on the overall assurance engagement?

5. Besides financial reporting impact, what other types of risk outcomes should be considered when assessing the impact of risks?

6. In anticipation of an upcoming engagement, an internal audit team recently toured the company's receiving, warehousing, and production facilities to obtain a better understanding of day-to-day operations. Listed below are selected items noted by the internal audit team during the tour:
    - A large quantity of materials was sitting in a corner near the unloading docks. The receiving manager informed the audit team that the delivery trucks had already left. The materials had not yet been counted or inspected.
    - One section of the warehouse contained large quantities of items with inventory tags from several physical inventory counts. The warehouse manager told the audit team that this was the company's inventory of spare parts that it was required by law to keep on hand for specified time periods.
    - Hazardous chemicals are used in the inventory finishing process. Waste chemicals are stored in large plastic barrels in a designated area of the factory before being shipped for disposal.

For each item noted by the internal audit team:

a. Describe the potential business risk(s) associated with the item.

b. Discuss how the internal auditors' knowledge of the risks identified might affect a subsequent audit of the materials acquisition and production processes.[2]

7. AVF Inc. manufactures several lines of packaging equipment. The company considers product reliability and outstanding customer service to be critical to its success. The customer service department is responsible for:

- Providing prospective customers with product information.
- Monitoring spare parts availability.
- Providing equipment operating and maintenance information to customers.
- Developing and delivering customer training courses.
- Responding to customer complaints and making service calls.
- Handling customer warranty claims.
- Maintaining good customer relations.

The company recently made a sizeable investment to upgrade its customer service department computer system. The upgrade is expected to improve operational efficiency and customer satisfaction. The outputs of the new system include management reports used to monitor performance in the areas listed above. The audit committee has asked the internal audit function to audit the operational effectiveness and efficiency of the customer service department. This engagement covers the following areas:

- Security of assets, including information.
- Compliance with applicable laws and company policies.
- Reliability of financial records.
- Effectiveness of performing assigned responsibilities.
- Valuation of the spare parts inventory.

a. Discuss why each of the five areas specified by the audit committee may or may not be appropriate for this assurance engagement.

b. Identify three other areas of the customer service department that may warrant the internal auditor's attention.

c. What are the primary audit tasks the internal auditors should perform to evaluate the operational effectiveness and efficiency of the customer service department in meeting the following responsibilities?

  - Developing and delivering customer training courses.
  - Responding to customer complaints and making service calls.
  - Handling customer warranty claims.[3]

8. A staff internal auditor found the following possible deviations from prescribed controls and documented them in her working papers.

Invoice Number	Prescribed Control	Possible Deviation
248	Written authorizations of sales by sales order department.	Verbal authorization by phone by sales order department.
333	Verification of sales order quantities and prices.	No evidence of verification; quantities and prices are incorrect.
377	Verification of sales order quantities and prices.	No evidence of verification, but quantities and prices are correct.
617	Billing department verification of unit prices.	Price verification indicated on invoice; the prices do not agree with the price list in effect at the time of sale.

For each of the items listed above, indicate whether there is or is not a deviation from a prescribed control. Briefly explain your answer.[4]

9. According to COSO ERM, one of the four categories of objectives is strategic objectives. Assuming certain strategic objectives are critical to the success of an organization, what should an internal audit function consider when deciding whether to conduct internal audits that address such objectives? Identify assurance engagement objectives that would and would not be appropriate.

CASE

You are the internal audit senior responsible for conducting an assurance engagement of the XYZ Company payroll process. This process has not been audited for three years and, as such, is due in the normal audit cycle. There have been no significant changes since the previous audit, that is, there were no system changes, no reorganization of personnel, and no substantive procedural changes. However, during the last assurance engagement, the internal audit function identified several observations, some of which were considered significant. The significant observations related to:

- Information pertaining to employees leaving the company was not communicated to the IT department, resulting in extended delays before those employees' systems rights were terminated.
- Hours paid to nonexempt employees were not supported by approved timesheets.
- Amounts withheld for employees were not consistent with elections made by employees.
- The possibility existed that phantom (ghost) employees could be included in the payroll without detection.

Payroll management implemented actions to address all significant observations and the internal audit function conducted limited follow-up procedures to validate that the planned actions were completed. This is the first audit since the follow-up procedures were completed.

The following is pertinent information to the payroll assurance engagement:

- XYZ employs approximately 4,400 employees. Approximately 2,700 of those employees are salaried, the rest are hourly.
- Employees are paid biweekly.
- Hourly employees earn pay at straight time for the first 80 hours in a biweekly pay period, time and a half for the next 20 hours in a pay period, and double time for any hours exceeding 100 hours in a pay period.
- The company utilizes a widely used and market tested payroll package (PayRight) for processing of all payroll transactions.
- The payroll system interfaces with the general ledger system.
- XYZ has established a separate payroll imprest account for the processing of payroll checks. Amounts are deposited in this account from the company's general account to cover any checks presented against the imprest account each day.

- Certain non-payroll items are deducted from the payroll checks, including:
  - Employee loans to cover the cost of extra benefits or computer purchases.
  - Contributions to long-term retirement plans.
  - Contributions to charitable organizations, such as the United Way.
  - Contributions to Political Action Committees (PACs).
- Payroll expenses, and the related payroll accruals, are considered material to the company.

Based on the above information, perform the following steps to conduct a payroll assurance engagement.

A. Determine at least four payroll department objectives that would be relevant to this engagement.

B. Create a list of potential risk scenarios for each objective.

C. Based on the identified risk scenarios, define and assess the key payroll risks.

1. You will need to make assumptions regarding impact and likelihood for this assessment. Document the assumptions made.
2. Also, make assumptions about and document process-level management's risk tolerance levels.

D. Document a potential process flow in a detailed flowchart. Make sure that this flowchart identifies key risks and controls and has at least one potential design inadequacy.

E. Develop potential key performance indicators for the process you documented in step D.

F. Identify which controls are considered key controls. As part of this analysis, document your assumptions regarding the effectiveness of entity-level controls and how such controls affect the payroll process-level controls, if at all.

G. Link the key controls to the identified risks.

H. Prepare a Risk and Control Matrix to cover the appropriate information from steps C through G. Conclude on the overall design adequacy of the payroll process.

I. Create a test plan for gathering evidence regarding the operating effectiveness of all key controls.

J. Develop potential test results of testing for all tests conducted. Make sure to identify at least two observations related to the operating effectiveness of key controls.

K. Add the results of steps I and J above to the Risk and Control Matrix. Document your conclusions on the effectiveness of control operation.

L. Develop observations based on the engagement results that outline the condition, criteria, cause, and effect for each observation.

REFERENCES

[1]Covey, Steven, Seven Habits of Highly Effective People (New York, NY: Free Press, 1989).

[2]Adapted from: Ratliff, Richard L., and Kurt F. Reding, *Introduction to Auditing: Logic, Principles, and Techniques* (Altamonte Springs, FL: The Institute of Internal Auditors, 2002).

[3]Adapted from: Protiviti, *Senior Audit School Participant Guide* (Protiviti, Inc., 2006).

[4]Adapted from: Ratliff, Richard L., and Kurt F. Reding, *Introduction to Auditing: Logic, Principles, and Techniques* (Altamonte Springs, FL: The Institute of Internal Auditors, 2002).

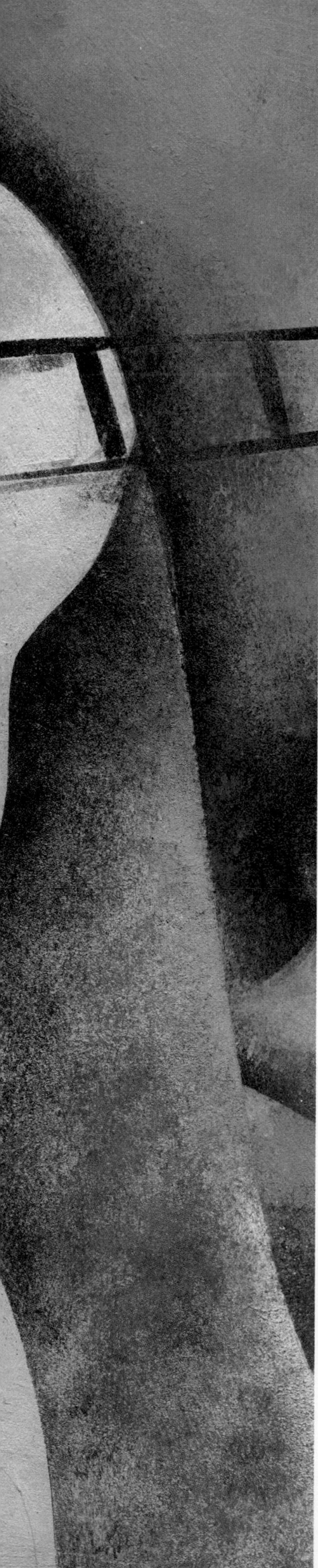

CHAPTER 14
COMMUNICATING ASSURANCE ENGAGEMENT OUTCOMES AND PERFORMING FOLLOW-UP PROCEDURES

Learning Objectives

- Understand why it is appropriate and necessary to communicate assurance engagement outcomes.
- Identify the different forms of assurance engagement communications.
- Identify the steps involved in creating an effective assurance engagement communication.
- Understand the distribution process for effectively communicating assurance engagement outcomes.
- Understand what is involved in effective monitoring of, and follow-up on, assurance engagement outcomes.

Chapter 12, "Introduction to the Engagement Process," provides an overview of the assurance engagement process that depicts three fundamental phases: planning, performing, and communicating. Chapter 13, "Conducting the Assurance Engagement," discusses the first two phases (planning and performing) in detail. Exhibit 14-2 reviews the components of each of these phases. In this chapter, we focus on the communicating phase.

We begin by outlining why it is appropriate and necessary to communicate engagement outcomes. We identify and explain the different forms of communications used to disseminate assurance engagement results and delineate the appropriate use for each one. We also outline the steps involved in creating the appropriate communication for the engagement performed and the distribution process to communicate assurance engagement outcomes effectively. Finally, we identify the necessary steps to monitor and perform follow-up procedures on engagement outcomes that have been communicated.

Because so many engagement communications involve reporting on the design adequacy and operating effectiveness of controls, here, as in Chapter 6, "Internal Control," the Committee of Sponsoring Organizations of the Treadway Commission's (COSO's) *Internal Control – Integrated*

EXHIBIT 14-1

PROFESSIONAL STANDARDS, PRACTICE ADVISORIES, AND PRACTICE GUIDES RELEVANT TO CHAPTER 14

2330 – Documenting Information

2400 – Communicating Results

2410 – Criteria for Communicating

2420 – Quality of Communications

2421 – Errors and Omissions

2430 – Use of "Conducted in Conformance with the *International Standards for the Professional Practice of Internal Auditing*"

2440 – Disseminating Results

2500 – Monitoring Progress

2600 – Resolution of Senior Management's Acceptance of Risks

Practice Advisory 2330-1: Documenting Information

Practice Advisory 2330.A1-1: Control of Engagement Records

Practice Advisory 2410-1: Communication Criteria

Practice Advisory 2420-1: Quality of Communications

Practice Advisory 2440-1: Disseminating Results

Practice Advisory 2500-1: Monitoring Progress

Practice Advisory 2500.A1-1: Follow-up Process

Practice Guide: Formulating and Expressing Internal Audit Opinions

Framework (*Framework*) is used to study the engagement communication process. It is important to note, however, that many assurance engagements are performed with a scope intended to assess or evaluate controls related to matters more narrowly focused than an overall assessment of controls of a business process or area, such as accuracy of account balances, compliance with certain regulations or operating policies and procedures, or the achievement of specific business objectives. In those cases, the corresponding engagement communications will focus on, and provide management with, independent feedback on the internal audit function's results of assessing such matters. The content of such communications will vary somewhat from the control illustrations provided throughout this chapter, but the concepts, methodologies, and approaches described are still applicable.

ENGAGEMENT COMMUNICATION OBLIGATIONS

As discussed in detail in Chapter 9, "Managing the Internal Audit Function," the chief audit executive (CAE) has the responsibility to "report periodically to senior management and the board on the internal audit activity's purpose, authority, responsibility, and performance relative to its plan. Reporting must also include significant risk exposures and control issues, including fraud risks, governance issues, and other matters needed or requested by senior management and the board" (IIA Standard 2060: Reporting to Senior Management and the Board). The CAE evidences the completion of these professional responsibilities by periodical-

EXHIBIT 14-2

THE ASSURANCE ENGAGEMENT PROCESS

Plan
• Determine engagement objectives and scope.
• Understand the auditee, including auditee objectives and assertions.
• Identify and assess risks.
• Identify key control activities.
• Evaluate adequacy of control design.
• Create a test plan.
• Develop a work program.
• Allocate resources to the engagement.
Perform
• Conduct tests to gather evidence.
• Evaluate evidence gathered and reach conclusions.
• Develop observations and formulate recommendations.
Communicate
• Perform observation evaluation and escalation process.
• Conduct interim and preliminary engagement communications.
• Develop final engagement communications.
• Distribute formal and informal final communications.
• Perform monitoring and follow-up procedures.

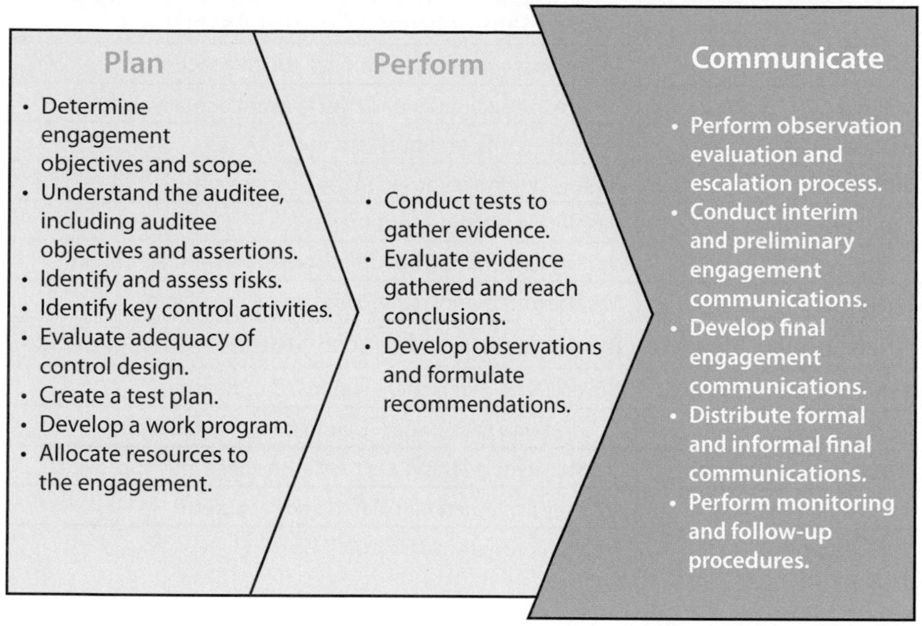

ly reporting, among other things, the results of assurance engagements to senior management and the audit committee during routinely scheduled meetings throughout the year.

Assurance engagements, in part, evidence the internal audit function's independent assessments of how effectively the organization's risks are mitigated. These individual assessments, when taken in the aggregate, help support senior management's assertions regarding the design adequacy and operating effectiveness of the organization's overall system of internal controls.

Communication is an integral part of any assurance engagement and occurs throughout the engagement process. Results are communicated in various ways, including memoranda, outlines, discussions, and draft working papers. In conjunction with concluding an engagement, final results are communicated to affected parties. This final engagement communication is often referred to as an "audit report" and is the formal way an internal audit function communicates the results of an engagement to management and other appropriate parties relying on the engagement outcomes.

As explained in Chapter 13, "Conducting the Assurance Engagement," individual assurance engagements are designed to meet specific audit objectives. These audit objectives are directly tied to the annual risk assessment and internal audit plan. This chapter focuses on reporting on assurance engagements and the follow-up procedures related to observations identified during individual assurance engagements.

Chapter 13 also outlines the steps of conducting an assurance engagement. During the engagement, the internal audit function tests controls to ensure that they are designed adequately and are operating effectively to meet specific control assertions (objectives). Exhibit 14-3 describes

EXHIBIT 14-3

CRITERIA FOR ASSESSING MANAGEMENT'S ASSERTIONS

Criteria for Assessing Management's Control Assertions	
Authorization	Did an approved party authorize the transaction?
Validity	Did the transaction or underlying event actually occur?
Accuracy	Were the terms, amounts, etc. correct?
Timeliness	Was everything recorded in the proper period?
Confidentiality	Was the information kept private?
Integrity	Was the information free from corruption and alteration?
Availability	Was the information stored and readily available?
Criteria for Assessing Management's Financial Statement Assertions	
Existence or occurrence	Is everything that is there supposed to be there?
Completeness	Is everything that is supposed to be there really there?
Rights and obligations	Are the items real, and are they authorized and approved?
Valuation or obligation	Are they accurately calculated and recorded?
Presentation and disclosure	Are they properly classified?

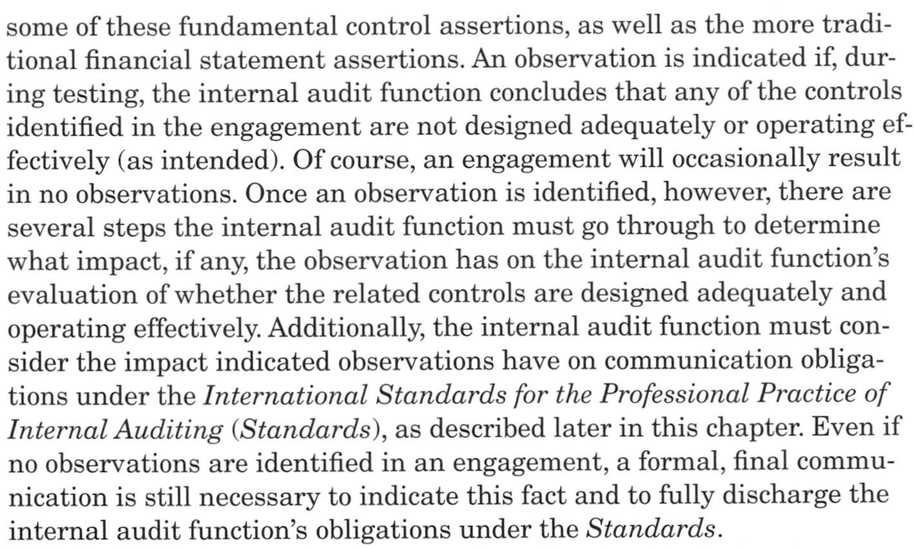

some of these fundamental control assertions, as well as the more traditional financial statement assertions. An observation is indicated if, during testing, the internal audit function concludes that any of the controls identified in the engagement are not designed adequately or operating effectively (as intended). Of course, an engagement will occasionally result in no observations. Once an observation is identified, however, there are several steps the internal audit function must go through to determine what impact, if any, the observation has on the internal audit function's evaluation of whether the related controls are designed adequately and operating effectively. Additionally, the internal audit function must consider the impact indicated observations have on communication obligations under the *International Standards for the Professional Practice of Internal Auditing* (*Standards*), as described later in this chapter. Even if no observations are identified in an engagement, a formal, final communication is still necessary to indicate this fact and to fully discharge the internal audit function's obligations under the *Standards*.

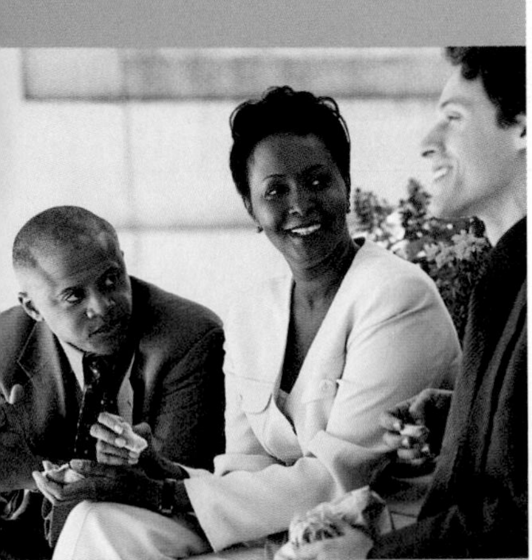

The internal audit function is able to determine the communication obligations indicated by identified observations by progressing through a series of steps that allow them to evaluate factors affecting each individual observation relative to its impact, likelihood, classification, and the way it affects the mitigation of risk. The internal audit function also must determine the cause of the observation, specifically whether the control in question is designed inadequately or operating ineffectively. After those factors have been identified for each observation detected during an engagement, the internal audit function must use judgment in determining the aggregate impact of all observations taken together. For example, an engagement might result in three observations, none of which individually constitutes a "significant" observation. However, the internal audit function might determine that the three observations, when taken together, do constitute a "significant" observation. While the process of evaluating observations applies to all controls whether they are related to operations, compliance, or financial reporting, as discussed in Chapter 6, "Internal Control," the assessment of internal control over financial reporting requires additional consideration of specific communication obligations dictated by the specific financial reporting regulations of the countries in which a given organization operates. Consequently, when communicating an observation regarding a control that pertains to financial reporting, the internal audit function has less discretion when deciding how and to whom that communication should be made.

Exhibit 14-4 illustrates this complex process and shows the various combinations of judgments that the internal audit function will encounter when determining the appropriate escalation and form of assurance engagement communication. This final communication has particular significance because it includes the internal audit function's independent assessment of the design adequacy and operating effectiveness of the controls covered within the scope of the assurance engagement in question, as well as an independent assessment of management's opinion relative to the controls covered by the assurance engagement. Taken collectively, the final communications from all of the engagements included in the annual internal audit plan form the basis on which the internal audit function may provide support for management's assertions on the organization's system of internal controls.

Although determining how and to whom to communicate observations requires the internal audit function to make judgments throughout the process, Exhibit 14-4 illustrates how this process can be broken down into manageable steps. The process begins with determining if any observations were identified during execution of the assurance engagement and concludes with direction on how and to whom to communicate observations identified during the assurance engagement.

PERFORM OBSERVATION EVALUATION AND ESCALATION PROCESS

As indicated earlier, an observation is most commonly identified based on evidence that a control is not operating effectively. However, an observation also can result from improper design when evaluating the control against fundamental control assertions, such as those listed in Exhibit 14-3. Regardless of how an observation is identified, once one or more observations are identified, the internal auditors must assess each observation using an evaluation and escalation process, similar to the one depicted in Exhibit 14-4, and determine the implications those observations have on the resulting communications for the area (process) under review. They are able to make this determination by progressing through a series of steps that allow them to evaluate factors affecting the observation relative to its impact, likelihood, classification, and the way in which it affects the mitigation of risk. The internal auditors also must determine the cause of the observation, specifically, whether the control in question is designed inadequately or operating ineffectively. As indicated in Exhibit 14-4, each time a decision is made in each step of the process, it is carried through to the next step.

Observation

A finding, determination, or judgment derived from the internal auditor's test results from an assurance or consulting engagement.

COSO Category

Once one or more observations have been identified, the next step is to determine which COSO category the compromised control most directly

EXHIBIT 14-4

OBSERVATION EVALUATION AND ESCALATION PROCESS

Observation(s)?

No: If there are no observations made in the course of the evaluation process, by definition impact is insignificant and likelihood is remote.

Formal communication to senior management is necessary to indicate that no observations were identified.

Yes: If there are one or more observations made in the course of the evaluation process, impact and likelihood must be determined.

Determine COSO Objective Category Affected by Each Observation

Operations | Compliance | Financial reporting

Classify Each Observation

Is the control designed inadequately? | Is the control operating ineffectively?

Determine Impact and Likelihood of Each Observation

Insignificant magnitude OR remote likelihood. | More than insignificant magnitude AND more than remote likelihood.

Assessment

Insignificant | Significant | Material

Insignificant: No key control activities involved. | Key controls involved, but adequate compensating controls exist.

After all observations have been classified and assessed, the internal audit function must use judgement to determine if the observations identified, either singularly or in the aggregate, are insignificant, significant, or material.

Form of Communication Required

If observations, either singularly or in the aggregate, are assessed insignificant with no key control activities compromised, communication of any observations relating to secondary control activities will be informal and does not need to include senior management. However, a formal communication to senior management is still necessary to indicate that no observations relating to primary control activities were identified.

If observations, either singularly or in the aggregate, are assessed insignificant with key control activities compromised but adequate compensating controls exist, communication will be formal and must be made to senior management and the organization's independent outside auditor.

If observations, either singularly or in the aggregate, are assessed significant , communication will be formal and needs to include senior management, the organization's independent outside auditor, and the audit committee.

If observations, either singularly or in the aggregate, are assessed material, communication will be formal and needs to include management, the audit committee, the organization's independent outside auditor, and, if the observations relate to internal control over financial reporting, the communication must be provided to other interested parties, as defined by reporting requirements dictated by financial reporting laws in the countries in which the organization operates.

affects, recognizing that an observation may impact more than one category. Controls mitigate risks that threaten the achievement of objectives in three COSO-defined categories:

- Effectiveness and efficiency of operations.
- Reliability of financial reporting.
- Compliance with applicable laws and regulations.[1]

Classification

After the COSO category has been determined for the observation, the next step is to classify the observation in terms of how the control is compromised. The shortcoming will be in one of two areas. Either the control is designed inadequately or operating ineffectively.

Impact and Likelihood of the Observations

The next step in the process involves determining the impact and likelihood of the specific observation in question. This requires that a judgment be made regarding whether the observation represents an insignificant, a significant, or a material breach in the ability of the control to mitigate a specific risk or group of risks. Like all of the other steps, this one will be done for each observation identified during the engagement. After each observation has been taken through this step in the process, however, it will be performed again for all of the observations taken in aggregate. Refer to Exhibit 14-5 for a visual depiction of the relationship and interdependency of impact and likelihood.

There are three different degrees of importance: insignificant, significant, and material. Although the specific terms "significant" and "material"

EXHIBIT 14-5

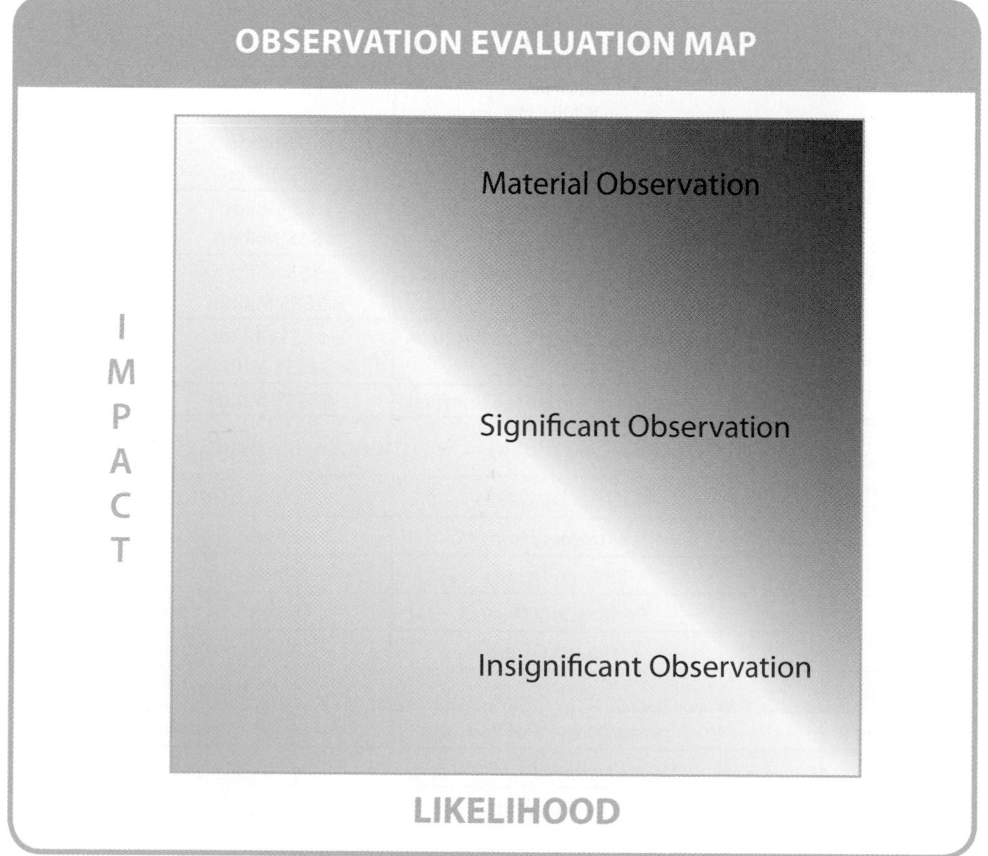

come from the financial reporting regulations that have been instituted in many countries and have particular relevance to internal control over financial reporting, they are used here to apply to controls in the areas of operations and compliance as well as financial reporting. The definitions for each of the three terms will be given shortly, but it is important to keep in mind that they are primarily conceptual. When applying them practically, internal audit functions do well to leverage the organization's existing risk tolerance parameters that are developed and maintained by its risk management function(s). In many organizations, the risk tolerance parameters take into consideration planning materiality of the independent outside auditor, which simplifies the observation assessment process and allows the relevant terms and definitions to be consistently applied to controls related to operations and compliance in addition to internal control over financial reporting. Exhibit 14-6 provides an example of risk prioritization financial metrics, while Exhibit 14-7 illustrates the observation evaluation criteria, including an example of tolerable error and independent outside auditor planning materiality calculation.

Insignificant

Indicates that a control has a remote likelihood of failing or that the impact of its failure is trivial.

Insignificant

An individual observation, or a group of observations, is considered insignificant if the control in question has a remote likelihood (slight chance)[2] of failing or the impact of its failure is insignificant (trivial). If the observation, or a group of observations, is assessed to be insignificant, the

EXHIBIT 14-6

RISK PRIORITIZATION METRICS

Impact (Severity)				
Metric	**Score**	**Description**	**Range** (Pre-tax Income Basis)	**EPS**
Impact	1	Small Loss (De Minimis)	< $ Million	< $.$$$
	2	Medium Loss (Insignificant)	≥ $ Million < $$Million	< $.$$$
	3	Large Loss (Significant)	≥ $$ Million < $$$ Million	≥ $.$$$ < $.$$$
	4	Major Impact on Operations (Material)	≥ $$$ Million < $$$$ Million	≥ $.$$$ < $.$$$
	5	Impact Requiring Board Action	≥ $$$$ Million < $$$$$ Million	≥ $.$$$ < $.$$$
	6	Potential of Imperil to Survival	≥ $$$$$ Million	≥ $.$$$

Likelihood (Probability) = Frequency + Warning			
Metric	**Score**	**Description**	**Range**
Frequency	1	Extremely Rare	Once every 5 years or greater
	2	Seldom Occurs	Once every 1-4 years
	3	Periodically Occurs	Once to 11 times a year
	4	Occurs Often	12 or more times a year
Metric	**Score**	**Description**	**Example**
Warning	1	Months or years of warning	Legislative or regulatory change
	2	Hours or days of warning	Windstorm or flood
	3	No warning	Fire or hacker attack

OBSERVATION EVALUATION CRITERIA IMPACT (SEVERITY)

EXHIBIT 14-7

Examples of Planning Materiality and Tolerable Error	
Description	**Range**
Planning Materiality	5% of Pre-tax Income
Tolerable Error	50% of Planning Materiality
Observation Evaluation Criteria	
Observation Classification	**Range**
Insignificant	<20% of Planning Materiality
Significant	20%-50% of Planning Materiality
Material	>50% of Planning Materiality

internal audit function must further evaluate whether key controls are involved. This is an important consideration when determining how and to whom the observation will ultimately be reported. If the observation(s) is (are) insignificant with no key controls involved, communication will typically be informal and will not need to include management outside of the area(s) subject to the audit. However, a formal communication to senior management is still necessary to indicate that no observations relating to key controls were identified. Remember that Chapter 6, "Internal Control," defined key (primary) controls as those that are designed to mitigate significant risks associated with an organization's critical business objectives. If key controls were involved and adequate compensating controls exist to mitigate the negative impact of the compromised key control, the observation is still considered insignificant. However, communication will be formal, escalated to management external to the area subjected to the audit (that is, those management representatives with oversight responsibility of the area audited), and made available to the organization's independent outside auditor if requested.

Significant

Again, the term significant deficiency is taken from the financial reporting regulations that exist in many countries and refers specifically to observations related to internal control over financial reporting. However, as indicated earlier, some organizations choose, for the sake of conformity, to apply the same definitional criteria to observations related to operations and compliance. The term significant observation is applied in this way here. An individual observation, or a group of observations, is considered significant if the control in question has a more than remote likelihood of failing and the impact of its failure is more than insignificant (that is, significant). If the observation, or a group of observations, is assessed to be significant, communication must be formal and include senior management, the organization's independent outside auditor, and the audit committee.

Significant

Indicates that a control has a more than remote likelihood of failing and that the impact of its failure is more than trivial.

Material

Like significant deficiency, the term material weakness is taken from financial reporting regulations and specifically applies to observations related to internal control over financial reporting. Again, some organiza-

Material

Indicates that a control has a more than remote likelihood of failing and that the impact of its failure exceeds the materiality threshold.

Elements of an Observation:

- **Criteria**
- **Condition**
- **Cause**
- **Effects**

tions apply the same definitional criteria of a material weakness to observations related to compliance and operations. The term material observation is applied in that manner here. An individual observation, or a group of observations, is considered material if the control in question has a more than remote likelihood of failing and the impact of its failure is not only more than insignificant, but also exceeds the financial statement materiality threshold (or other established thresholds for materiality). Refer to Exhibit 14-7 for example observation evaluation criteria. If the observation, or a group of observations, is assessed to be material, communication must be formal and include senior management, the organization's independent outside auditor, and the audit committee. Additionally, if the observation concerns internal control over financial reporting, the U.S. Sarbanes-Oxley Act of 2002 and financial reporting regulations in other countries require management to qualify their opinion on internal control over financial reporting and formulate a remediation plan to correct the weakness identified in the controls in question. Management must continue to qualify its opinion on internal control over financial reporting until the material weakness (observation) is remediated and management has verified such through control retesting that indicates the control in question is designed adequately and operating effectively. If management determines it is necessary to qualify its opinion on internal control over financial reporting, this fact must be reported to its stakeholders according to the laws of the country in which it operates.

Documentation of the conclusions reached as a result of performing the observation evaluation and escalation process is essential to evidencing that the internal audit function has appropriately determined how and to whom to communicate observations indicated by the test results of the assurance engagement. As previously discussed, the process begins with determining if any observations were identified during execution of the assurance engagement and concludes with direction on how and to whom to communicate observations identified during the assurance engagement. Many internal audit functions will use working paper templates or checklists to assist in documenting these results. Exhibit 14-8 is an example of such a template. Additionally, this template helps fulfill the documentation obligations as indicated in the *Standards* and discussed in Chapter 13, "Conducting the Assurance Engagement." Specifically, the *Standards* state, "Internal auditors must document relevant information to support the conclusions and engagement results" (IIA Standard 2330: Documenting Information). Practice Advisory 2330-1: Documenting Information goes on to indicate, "Working papers document the information obtained, the analyses made, and the support for the conclusions and engagement results."

Chapter 13 includes examples of the various steps involved in performing assurance engagements using the fictitious organization Books 2 Buy. Exhibits 14-9 and 14-10 are observation assessment templates that have been completed using the information obtained during the assurance engagement process for Books 2 Buy in Chapter 13. Exhibit 14-9 documents an observation regarding delegation of authority which is determined to be insignificant with no key controls affected. Consequently, it will be communicated informally only to management of the cash disbursements process. Exhibit 14-10 documents an observation regarding the potential for duplicate payments. Although this observation is determined to be

EXHIBIT 14-8

OBSERVATION ASSESSMENT TEMPLATE

Assurance Engagement and Audit Observation Description Engagement Performed: as of DATE	
1. **Observation Summary:**	
2. **Condition (Facts)** — Factual evidence and description of controls as they exist (what is). What was found through testing.	
3. **Criteria** — Standards, measures, expectations, policy, or procedures used in making the evaluation (what should exist).	
4. **Cause** — What allowed or caused the condition to exist (the why).	
5. **Effect** — Risk or exposure encountered because the condition is not consistent with the criteria (what could go wrong, both past and possible future impact). Considers both the impact (financial, reputational, safety, etc.) and the likelihood.	
6. **Compensating Controls** — Other controls in place to mitigate the observation. Includes monitoring.	
7. **Conclusion** — Detailed analysis, assessment, and justification for evaluation classifications and final conclusions.	
8. **Detailed Recommendation** — What the internal audit function recommends. This recommendation must reconcile with management's solution as discussed during the preliminary communication process.	
9. **Management Solution** — What management will do to fix the existing condition or prevent the problem from happening again.	
10. **Observation Evaluation:** • COSO Category • Classification • Assessment **Evaluation performed by:** • Internal Audit Function • Business Unit Management • Outside Independent Auditor	Financial Reporting ___ Material (Weakness) ___ Operations ___ Significant (Deficiency) ___ Compliance ___ Insignificant ___ Inadequate Design ___ Key (Primary) Control ___ Ineffective Operation ___ Secondary Control ___ Name Date
11. **Working Paper Reference**	

insignificant, since key controls are affected, some organizations would still formally communicate this observation to senior management and the audit committee (and the independent outside auditor, if desired) in addition to management of the cash disbursements process.

Engagement Observations and Recommendations

All observations are written to include specific information that must be communicated about them regardless of what form of communication is indicated as a result of performing the observation evaluation and escalation process described above. The criteria, condition, cause, and effect all

EXHIBIT 14-9

OBSERVATION ASSESSMENT TEMPLATE
OUTDATED DELEGATION OF AUTHORITY

Books 2 Buy Holding Corporation Cash Disbursements Process
Engagement Performed: as of February 10, 20XX

1. **Observation Summary:**	Outdated Delegation of Authority Policy
2. **Condition (Facts)** — Factual evidence and description of controls as they exist (what is). What was found through testing.	The delegation of authority policy lists seven individuals who are no longer with the company. Additionally, nine individuals were identified who are new in their positions or new to the company that should have disbursement authority, but are not listed in the policy.
3. **Criteria** — Standards, measures, expectations, policy, or procedures used in making the evaluation (what should exist).	Authority over the disbursement of funds should only be delegated to individuals whose responsibilities justify such authority.
4. **Cause** — What allowed or caused the condition to exist (the why).	The delegation of authority policy is updated semiannually and not as changes in personnel or responsibilities of authorized individuals occur.
5. **Effect** — Risk or exposure encountered because the condition is not consistent with the criteria (what could go wrong, both past and possible future impact). Considers both the impact (financial, reputational, safety, etc.) and the likelihood.	Disbursements may be made that are not in accordance with management's or the board's direction.
6. **Compensating Controls** — Other controls in place to mitigate the observation. Includes monitoring.	• Once an employee leaves the company, all access rights to the system are eliminated. Therefore, even though seven individuals who have left the company remain in the policy as authorized signers, they could not get online to approve transactions. • A budget-to-actual analysis is performed monthly by all department heads and cost center owners.
7. **Conclusion** — Detailed analysis, assessment, and justification for evaluation classifications and final conclusions.	Based on the compensating controls, the risk of an inappropriately authorized disbursement is minimal. While management may make efforts to update the policy more frequently, they are relying on other key controls to mitigate the risk and are willing to accept the current level of risk. Therefore, this audit observation will *not* be included in the final report.
8. **Detailed Recommendation** — What the internal audit function recommends. This recommendation must reconcile with management's solution as discussed during the preliminary communication process.	Management should implement procedures to update named individuals and corresponding disbursement limits listed in the delegation policy.
9. **Management Solution** — What management will do to fix the existing condition or prevent the problem from happening again.	Management believes the risk is minimal relative to this observation and, therefore, is willing to live with the weakness as identified between policy updates. **Responsibility:** N/A **Target Date:** N/A
10. **Observation Evaluation:** • COSO Category • Classification • Assessment **Evaluation performed by:** • Internal Audit Function • Business Unit Management • Outside Independent Auditor	Financial Reporting _X_ Material (Weakness) ___ Operations _X_ Significant (Deficiency) ___ Compliance ___ Insignificant _X_ Inadequate Design _X_ Key (Primary) Control ___ Ineffective Operations ___ Secondary Control _X_ Name Date Robert Cratchert mm/dd/yy
11. **Working Paper Reference**	Z-3, X-1

OBSERVATION ASSESSMENT TEMPLATE
POTENTIAL DUPLICATE PAYMENTS

EXHIBIT 14-10

Books 2 Buy Holding Corporation Cash Disbursements Process
Engagement Performed: as of February 10, 20XX

1. **Observation Summary:**	Potential Duplicate Payments
2. **Condition (Facts)** — Factual evidence and description of controls as they exist (what is). What was found through testing.	The system rejected all duplicate invoice entries. However, it accepted invoices when a digit or symbol was added to the end of the invoice number, creating the opportunity for a duplicate payment.
3. **Criteria** — Standards, measures, expectations, policy, or procedures used in making the evaluation (what should exist).	The receipt of goods or services should be recorded and processed only once.
4. **Cause** — What allowed or caused the condition to exist (the why).	In some instances, the A/P clerks are entering certain invoices a second time when a duplicate invoice is submitted by the vendor. The clerks are not recognizing that these invoices may have been received before and, given the control design weakness as described in Z-2, are adding a digit to the end to facilitate processing. In other instances, the vendor is issuing a duplicate invoice with a different invoice number (typically one higher than the last one) and the A/P clerks did not detect the potential that these were duplicate invoices.
5. **Effect** — Risk or exposure encountered because the condition is not consistent with the criteria (what could go wrong, both past and possible future impact). Considers both the impact (financial, reputational, safety, etc.) and the likelihood.	Liabilities and the corresponding assets or expenses were overstated by $357,782.41 and the same amount of funds were disbursed inappropriately.
6. **Compensating Controls** — Other controls in place to mitigate the observation. Includes monitoring.	A budget-to-actual analysis is performed monthly by all department heads and cost center owners.
7. **Conclusion** — Detailed analysis, assessment, and justification for evaluation classifications and final conclusions.	While the compensating control activities may detect very large duplicate payments, there is still the challenge of collecting the duplicate payment from the vendor. Also, smaller, insignificant payments may not be detected (as proven in the audit test). Management agrees with the observation and has proposed a plan to address the weakness. Therefore, *this audit observation will be included in the final report.*
8. **Detailed Recommendation**— What the internal audit function recommends. This recommendation must reconcile with management's solution as discussed during the preliminary communication process.	It is recommended that A/P create a query routine that mirrors the tests run by the internal audit function and perform it before processing each batch. The results of this query then need to be reviewed by the A/P supervisor and, if any payments are identified as potentially duplicative, those transactions should be removed from the batch and researched before payment.
9. **Management Solution** — What management will do to fix the existing condition or prevent the problem from happening again.	A query routine will be written that operates similarly to the test performed by the internal audit function. This routine will be run before a batch is processed and reviewed by the A/P supervisor. If there are any potentially duplicate payments identified, these transactions will be removed from the batch and researched before payment. **Responsibility:** A/P Supervisor **Target Date:** mm/dd/yy
10. **Observation Evaluation:** • COSO Category • Classification • Assessment **Evaluation performed by:** • Internal Audit Function • Business Unit Management • Outside Independent Auditor	Financial Reporting _X_ Material (Weakness) ___ Operations ___ Significant (Deficiency) ___ Compliance ___ Insignificant _X_ Inadequate Design _X_ Key (Primary) Control _X_ Ineffective Operations ___ Secondary Control ___ Name Date Robert Cratchert mm/dd/yy
11. **Working Paper Reference**	Z-4, X-5

must be included for each observation being communicated. As indicated earlier, engagement observations are items that have come to the attention of the internal audit function that can influence management's assertions on the design adequacy and/or operating effectiveness of the controls. As such, they must be handled in a way consistent with, and as indicated by, the evaluation and escalation process. In those cases when formal communication is indicated, in addition to the items listed above (criteria, condition, cause, and effect), the internal audit function makes recommendations to provide the auditee with guidance on appropriate ways to resolve the observation and enhance either the design or operation of the controls.

Practice Advisory 2410-1: Communication Criteria provides more details relative to the elements that must be contained in each engagement observation when communicated: "Engagement observations and recommendations emerge by a process of comparing criteria (the correct state) with condition (the current state). Whether or not there is a difference, the internal auditor has a foundation on which to build the report [communication] . . . Observations and recommendations are based on the following attributes:

Criteria

What should exist.

Condition

What does exist.

Cause

Why there is a difference between what should exist and what does exist.

- Criteria — The standards, measures, or expectations used in making an evaluation and/or verification (the correct state).
- Condition — The factual evidence that the internal auditor found in the course of the examination (the current state).
- Cause — The reason for the difference between expected and actual conditions.
- Effect — The risk or exposure the organization and/or others encounter because the condition is not consistent with the criteria (the impact of the difference). In determining the degree of risk or exposure, internal auditors consider the effect their engagement observations and recommendations may have on the organization's operations and financial statements.
- Observations and recommendations can include [auditee] accomplishments, related issues, and supportive information."

Criteria, condition, cause, effect, and recommendation are discussed in greater detail below.

Criteria

The criteria states what should be. This component of an observation identifies the standard of performance that should be accomplished. The criteria may already be outlined in a policy, procedure, law, regulation, etc., or it may need to be determined by the internal auditor based on reasonable standards for achievement of the organization's objectives.

Condition (Facts)

The condition describes controls as they exist and are functioning at the time of the audit or evaluation. It states what was found through testing. This is the heart of the engagement observation and must be supported by sufficient appropriate (relevant and reliable) evidence and information.

Cause

The cause explains what allowed the condition to exist. The cause describes the elements of management's processes that either did not exist or that failed, thus allowing the condition to occur. This is an essential component because unless it is known, recommendations or corrective action may not be possible, thus allowing recurrence of the condition.

Effect

The effect outlines the consequence (both past and possible future) of the observation. It describes what did or could happen as a result of conditions not meeting the criteria (in other words, adverse consequences). This component is necessary to convince management that corrective action is necessary. Whenever possible, this component should be quantified by indicating the dollar amount of exposure, number of occurrences, etc.

Effect

The consequence of the difference between what should exist and what does exist.

Detailed Recommendation

The recommendation offers suggestions regarding how to correct the condition. It describes the course of action management should consider to correct the condition and eliminate its adverse effect. The recommended action should address the condition's cause and should include measures to prevent its recurrence.

Recommendation

Suggested corrective actions to correct the condition.

Practice Advisory 2410-1: Communication Criteria states "The internal auditor may communicate recommendations for improvements, acknowledgements of satisfactory performance, and corrective actions. Recommendations are based on the internal auditor's observations and conclusions. They call for action to correct existing conditions or improve operations and may suggest approaches to correcting or enhancing performance as a guide for management in achieving desired results. Recommendations can be general or specific."

CONDUCT INTERIM AND PRELIMINARY ENGAGEMENT COMMUNICATIONS

As previously discussed, communication is an integral part of any assurance engagement and occurs throughout the engagement process. During the course of performing an assurance engagement, the internal audit function communicates routinely and regularly with the key individuals in the area subject to audit. Much of this communication is done via e-mail and in face-to-face meetings or on conference calls. The purpose of these communications is to discuss observations as they are identified during the engagement. This allows the internal audit function to make sure the facts are accurate and also initiates dialogue regarding the best method of remediation for identified observations. When an observation calls for immediate attention, interim communication allows it to be brought to the attention of the appropriate individuals in a timely manner and increases the likelihood of prompt resolution. The internal audit function will use the information gathered during these interim communications to finalize the observations that will ultimately go into the final communication and to formalize management's action plan for inclusion in the final communication.

Although the observation evaluation and escalation process took the engagement observations through a step-by-step process to determine what is required for final communication, the internal audit function must confirm these preliminary facts and conclusions with appropriate management representatives of the area that was covered by the engagement before it is distributed in its final form. This can be accomplished in many ways, but most commonly is done through a formal meeting with management, typically referred to as an exit interview or closing conference, followed by a draft of the final communication in whatever form it will take. As part of this process, the internal audit function meets with appropriate management representatives from the area covered by the engagement and confirms agreement with preliminary observations and conclusions discussed throughout the engagement. This allows all parties to review what is anticipated to be contained in the formal engagement communication and provides a final opportunity for any misunderstandings to be resolved. Additionally, it provides the management of the area that was the target of the assurance engagement with a way to present their thoughts and planned actions regarding the items to be covered in the final engagement communication and give feedback regarding how well the engagement team executed the assurance engagement. Management's action plan to address and resolve control deficiencies identified during the assurance engagement is commonly referred to as management's response. These corrective actions are formulated with input from the internal audit function, but are ultimately the responsibility of management to implement. Many internal audit functions include management's response in the final engagement communication.

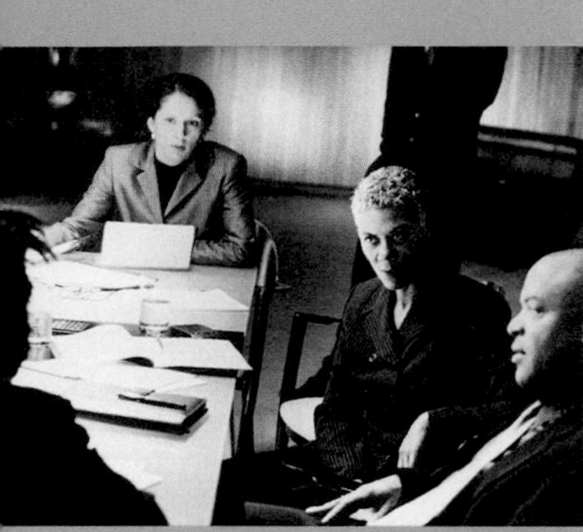

Practice Advisory 2410-1: Communication Criteria gives guidance regarding the inclusion of management's response in engagement communications: "As part of the internal auditor's discussions with the [auditee], the internal auditor obtains agreement on the results of the engagement and on any necessary plan of action to improve operations. If the internal auditor and [auditee] disagree about the engagement results, the engagement communications state both positions and the reasons for the disagreement. The [auditee's] written comments may be included as an appendix to the engagement report, in the body of the report, or in a cover letter."

Furthermore, Practice Advisory 2410 goes on to state that "Use [of] interim reports to communicate information that requires immediate attention, to communicate a change in engagement scope for the activity under review, or to keep management informed of engagement progress when engagements extend over a long period . . . does not diminish or eliminate the need for a final [communication]."

Final Communication

The vehicle through which the internal audit function informs interested parties of engagement outcomes.

In conjunction with concluding an engagement, final results must be communicated to the appropriate and affected parties. This final engagement communication can take on different forms, as discussed in detail later in the chapter, and is the formal way an internal audit function discharges its professional communication obligation under the *Standards*, also discussed in detail later in the chapter.

DEVELOP FINAL ENGAGEMENT COMMUNICATIONS

The final assurance engagement communication is important for a number of reasons. As discussed in both Chapter 1, "Introduction to Internal Auditing," and Chapter 2, "The International Professional Practices Framework: Authoritative Guidance for the Internal Audit Profession," a primary difference between an assurance engagement and a consulting engagement is that in an assurance engagement there are three parties involved: (1) the person or group directly involved with the process, system, or other subject matter — the auditee, (2) the person or group making the independent assessment — the internal audit function, and (3) the person or group relying on the independent assessment — the user. A consulting engagement, on the other hand, typically involves only two parties: (1) the person or group seeking and receiving the advice — the customer, and (2) the person or group offering the advice — the internal audit function. Because the results contained in the final assurance engagement communication will be used by someone other than the auditee (for example, the audit committee), it is imperative that the communication be concise, comprehensive, and accurate. In addition, the final communication evidences the internal audit function's independent assessment of the area's controls and serves as the permanent record of the work performed on the assurance engagement and its results.

Final assurance engagement communications ensure the internal audit function fulfills the following obligations:

- Communicate timely, pertinent information to management concerning deficiencies in controls (lack of design adequacy or operating effectiveness), strengths in controls, opportunities to maximize resource utilization or reduce costs, and areas for increased productivity or efficiency.
- Document the scope, conclusion, observations, recommendations, and resulting management action plans of an engagement.
- Become a part of the permanent record of the work performed during an engagement and the results of that engagement.

Like all engagement communications, the final communication should be professional, accurate, comprehensive, and distributed in a timely manner. Accomplishing all of these objectives is often a balancing act since a quality engagement communication must offer the assurance that an appropriate amount of time has been allocated to complete the work correctly and thoroughly and still be disseminated timely to meet management's need for current information. The time required to prepare an engagement communication will vary depending on the amount of time spent on the engagement and the number and complexity of any observations contained in the communication. However, a leading practice is to provide final engagement communications to management within 10 business days after completing the preliminary engagement communication (exit conference or closing conference).

A well-designed final communication should include:

- **Purpose and scope of engagement** — The objectives (that is, what the engagement was intended to achieve) and scope of the engagement. Practice Advisory 2410-1: Communication Criteria specifies that "scope statements identify the audited activities and may include supportive information such as time period reviewed and related activities not reviewed to delineate the boundaries of the engagement. They may describe the nature and extent of engagement work performed."
- **Time frame covered by the engagement** — The period of operations covered by the engagement scope typically either as of a certain time or for a period of time.

Scope

What is or is not included within an engagement.

- **Observations as required by the evaluation and escalation process (see Exhibit 14-4) and recommendations** — Details regarding the communication of observations and recommendations are discussed later in the chapter.
- **Engagement conclusions and rating (if applicable)** — The internal audit function's assessment of the design adequacy and operating effectiveness of the area's controls subject to audit, in addition to the internal audit function's rating of the area if a rating system is used. Ratings are discussed in more detail below. Practice Advisory 2410-1: Communication Criteria provides the following information regarding conclusions: "Conclusions and opinions are the internal auditor's evaluations of the effects of the observations and recommendations on the activities reviewed. They usually put the observations and recommendations in perspective based upon their overall implications. Conclusions may encompass the entire scope of an engagement or specific aspects. They may cover, but are not limited to, whether operating or program objectives and goals conform with those of the organization, whether the organization's objectives and goals are being met, and whether the activity under review is functioning as intended. An opinion may include an overall assessment of controls or may be limited to specific controls or aspects of the engagement."
- **Management's action plan to appropriately address reported observations (if applicable)** — Summarized response of management to the audit observations contained in the final communication, including the agreed-upon action plan for remediation with a projected timeline for completion that will be used as a basis for the internal audit function's follow-up work. The action plan should include the name(s) of the specific individual(s) responsible for carrying it out.

Conclusion

The internal audit function's assessment of the design adequacy and operating effectiveness of the controls subject to audit.

In addition, Practice Advisory 2410-1: Communication Criteria states that "final engagement communications may include background information and summaries. Background information may identify the organizational units and activities reviewed and provide explanatory information. It also may include the status of observations, conclusions, and recommendations from prior reports and an indication of whether the report covers a scheduled engagement or is responding to a request." This practice advisory also indicates that "the internal auditor may communicate [auditee] accomplishments in terms of improvements since the last engagement or the establishment of a well-controlled operation. This information may be necessary to fairly present the existing conditions and to provide perspective and balance to the engagement final communications."

Rating System

The assignation of a numeric or descriptive appraisal of engagement results for the purpose of comparing or trending them with other engagement results.

Rating Systems

There is no single prescribed way for expressing engagement outcomes (observations, recommendations, and effects these observations and recommendations have on management's assessment of the activities reviewed). Options range from listing observations indicated from the assurance engagement to expressing an overall conclusion on the effectiveness and efficiency of controls reviewed. As indicated in Chapter 12, "Introduction to the Engagement Process," the internal audit function's assessment of controls that is included in the final engagement communication can be stated either positively or negatively. If the internal auditors choose to state that the controls are designed adequately and operating effectively, they have given positive assurance. If, on the other hand, they choose to communicate that nothing has come to their attention that leads them to believe that the controls are not designed adequately and operating effectively, they have given negative assurance. Either expression of assurance is acceptable and constitutes compliance with the *Standards*. However, many CAEs consider positive assurance to be a best practice. The IIA supports this position, stating that "Positive assurance (reasonable assurance) provides the highest level of assurance and one of the strongest types of audit opinions."[3] When the internal audit function provides negative assurance (limited assurance), they take " . . . no responsibility for the sufficiency of the audit scope and procedures to find all significant concerns or issues."[4]

Positive Assurance

A rating or conclusion by the internal auditor that provides specific assurances about an engagement.

Many internal audit functions and audit committees have chosen to use a formal rating system in conjunction with their conclusions. Such a system provides a way for management and the audit committee to compare the results of assurance engagements across functional areas within an organization, as well as a means to trend audit results for a specific area over time. There are many types of rating systems, ranging from numerical (for example, one through five) to those that are more descriptive in nature (for example, a descriptive rating system may include ratings such as satisfactory versus unsatisfactory). If an internal audit function chooses to employ a rating system, there must be congruence between the rating assigned and the internal audit function's conclusion regarding management's assertion that the controls subject to the assurance engagement are designed adequately and operating effectively. When the internal audit function's conclusion and/or rating is inconsistent with management's initial assertion, management would be compelled to reevaluate that assertion to reconcile it with the internal audit function's conclusion (rating). For example, an unsatisfactory rating typically indicates that the internal audit function has identified one or more risks that have not been mitigated to a tolerable level. In this instance, management needs to reassess their evaluation of the design adequacy and operating effectiveness of existing controls. In addition, they should seek to understand why their own self-assessment did not identify the deficiency(ies). No matter how the internal audit function chooses to provide engagement conclusions, ultimately the intent is to provide the auditee and other users of the communication with sufficient information to understand the effects of the internal audit function's observations and how the recommendations will address the root causes of those observations.

Negative Assurance

A rating or conclusion indicating that nothing negative has come to the internal auditor's attention.

Some internal audit functions make a conscious choice not to include ratings in engagement reports because of the perception that if they distribute communications that rate areas or processes as less than satisfactory, it will result in antagonistic relationships between the internal audit function and the rest of the organization. Moody's Investor Services disagrees with this perspective, however, and argues that providing ratings is a best practice. " . . . audit professionals [should] adopt a simple, yet sensible, grading or rating [in] their reports, to help users distinguish problematic reports from other audit reports. The audit committee should be able to distinguish the various kinds of reports generated from the audit team:

- Highly critical reports where significant remedial actions are recommended.
- Reports that cite deficiencies that need to be corrected, but where the lapses are not significant.
- Reports that are, effectively, a clean bill of health, even though some improvement opportunities are identified."[5]

DISTRIBUTE FORMAL AND INFORMAL FINAL COMMUNICATIONS

Once all observations have been identified and assessed using the observation evaluation and escalation process individually and in the aggregate, they must be communicated according to the results of that process. Practice Advisory 2410-1: Communication Criteria reiterates the importance of such communication, stating that "observations are pertinent statements of fact. The internal auditor communicates those observations necessary to support or prevent misunderstanding of the internal auditor's conclusions and recommendations. The internal auditor may communicate less significant observations or recommendations informally."

Before communications can be distributed, they must be reviewed and approved by the CAE or designee. Then, " . . . the CAE distributes the final engagement communication to the management of the audited activity and to those members of the organization who can ensure engagement results are given due consideration and take corrective action or ensure that corrective action is taken. When appropriate, the CAE may send a summary communication to higher-level members in the organization. When required by the internal audit charter or organizational policy, the CAE also communicates to other interested or affected parties such as external auditors and the board" (Practice Advisory 2440-1: Disseminating Results).

Additionally, Practice Advisory 2410-1: Communication Criteria states that "certain information is not appropriate for disclosure to all report recipients because it is privileged, proprietary, or related to improper or illegal acts. [The CAE should] disclose such information in a separate report [and] distribute the report to the board if the conditions being reported involve senior management."

Assurance engagement communications are formal or informal depending on the outcome as determined by the observation evaluation and escalation process. For every assurance engagement, however, there will always be a final, formal communication, even if there are no observations to report to management.

Formal

Typically, the recipients of formal assurance engagement communications are senior management, the audit committee, the organization's independent outside auditor, and/or auditee management. Formal communications are indicated when the controls evaluated during an assurance engagement are assessed to be:

- Insignificantly compromised, although key controls are affected.
- Significantly compromised.
- Materially compromised.

Historically, formal audit communications have been in hardcopy (written reports) or, if distributed electronically, in a Word document. As technology has become more pervasive, however, internal audit functions are beginning to migrate to other formats such as PowerPoint presentations. The format used to communicate is less important (as long as it is appropriate to the information presented and the audience receiving it) than covering all of the elements of a formal communication.

As indicated earlier in the chapter, formal communications are the final, permanent record of the results of an assurance engagement. As such, they need to contain the information necessary to reflect accurately the work performed and conclusions drawn. Remember, as stated earlier, all formal communications should include:

- The purpose and scope of the audit.
- The time frame of the audit.
- The observations and recommendations (results) of the audit, if any.
- The conclusion (opinion and/or rating) of the internal audit function.
- Management's response (action plan) to the recommendations.

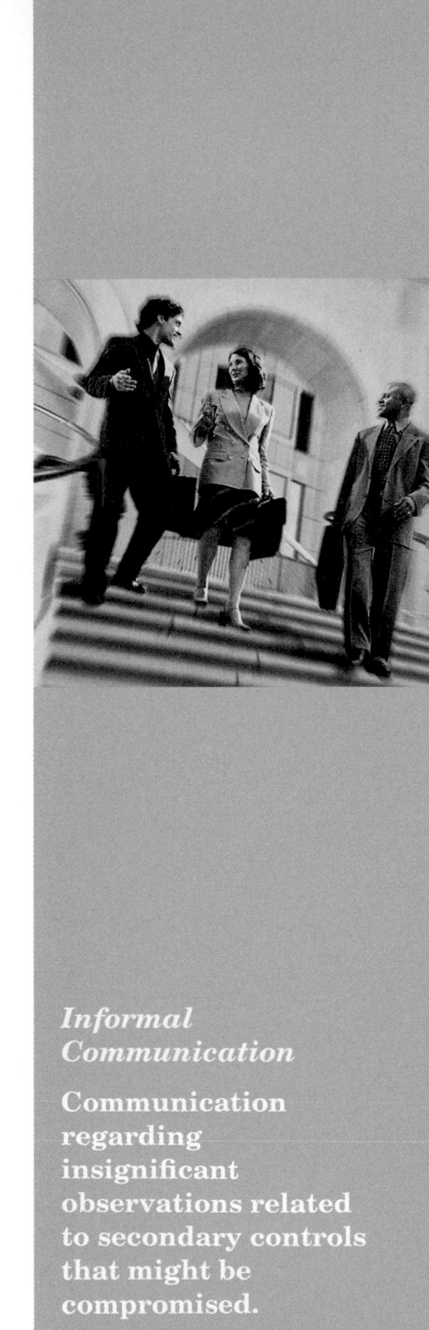

The information listed above should be organized clearly and incorporated into the communication using concise, specific language that leaves no room for ambiguity. An example of a final, formal communication is included as Exhibit 14-11.

Informal

When observations are determined to be insignificant through application of the evaluation and escalation process, the internal audit function may opt to communicate these observations to management of the area subject to the audit informally via memoranda, e-mail, in face-to-face meetings, or on conference calls. No matter the form or medium chosen, informal assurance engagement communications of insignificant observations are still considered final communications and serve to fulfill the internal audit function's reporting obligations under the *Standards*. The audience for informal, final communications is limited to management of the area that was the target of the audit. Informal communication is considered appropriate only when, during the observation evaluation and escalation process, all observations were assessed to be insignificant with no key controls compromised. The informal communication will cover insignificant observations related to secondary controls that might be compromised and, again, will only be distributed to management of the area that was the target of the engagement. An example of a final, informal communication is included as Exhibit 14-12. Even when an informal communication is indicated, to fully discharge the obligations outlined in the *Standards* relative to communicating assurance engagement outcomes, it is still necessary to communicate to senior management, the audit committee, and the independent outside auditor that no observations were identified related to key controls.

Informal Communication

Communication regarding insignificant observations related to secondary controls that might be compromised.

Additional Assurance Engagement Communication Standards

The *Standards* offer guidance regarding the quality of assurance engagement communications as well as what is required in the event of an error or omission. The relevant standards and practice advisories are included here.

EXHIBIT 14-11

FINAL, FORMAL COMMUNICATION EXAMPLE (Audit Report)

TO:	Chief Accounting Officer, Books 2 Buy Holding Corp.
FROM:	Audit Director/Manager, Books 2 Buy Holding Corp.
SUBJECT:	Books 2 Buy Holding Corp. Cash Disbursements Audit Report SATISFACTORY RATING
DATE:	April 27, 20XX

The Books 2 Buy internal audit function completed an internal control review of the cash disbursements function on March 24, 20XX. The scope of the review, performed as of Feb. 10, 20XX, was to evaluate the design adequacy and operating effectiveness of the system of internal controls within the cash disbursements process. The review included verification procedures to ensure proper authorization, validity, accuracy, timeliness, completeness, existence, classification, confidentiality, integrity, and availability of books, records, and other relevant documentation supporting cash disbursements processed during the fiscal year ended Dec. 31, 20XX.

The scope of the review included, but was not limited to, documenting, evaluating, and testing:

- Procedures for receiving and validating requests for disbursements.
- Procedures for approving and processing disbursements (wires or checks).
- Procedures for validating disbursements for distribution.
- Procedures for recording and balancing cash disbursements.
- Procedures for reconciling detailed records to general ledger cash disbursements control accounts.

CONCLUSION

In our opinion, the cash disbursements process is reasonable and the system of internal controls is acceptable, resulting in a SATISFACTORY audit rating. This rating indicates that overall internal controls are acceptable to safeguard assets and minimize exposure to loss. This rating also indicates that there are relatively few deficiencies and that an appropriate level of management attention exists. The internal control environment rating definitions are included as Attachment A.

MANAGEMENT'S ACTION PLAN

Management has established a satisfactory action plan to resolve the observation presented in this report. A detailed explanation of our findings and recommendations, together with management's response, is provided in the attached report.

Copies to:

Chairman of the Board	Audit Committee	General Counsel
CEO	Independent Outside Auditor	Chief Administrative Officer
CFO	Controller	Chief Compliance Officer

FINAL, FORMAL COMMUNICATION EXAMPLE Attachment A

Books 2 Buy audit reports include an overall rating of controls based on the objectives, scope, and conclusions of detailed work performed. The control ratings are defined as follows:

SATISFACTORY
Overall, controls are designed adequately and operating effectively to mitigate the underlying risk to an acceptable level. This rating indicates that there are relatively few minor deficiencies and that an appropriate level of management attention exists.

NEEDS IMPROVEMENT
Overall, controls need improvement to consistently mitigate the underlying risk to an acceptable level. This rating indicates that the number and nature of deficiencies require prompt management attention to reduce exposure to a more acceptable level.

UNSATISFACTORY
Overall, controls are not designed adequately and/or operating effectively to mitigate the underlying risk to an acceptable level. This rating indicates that the number and nature of deficiencies are of critical importance and require substantial management attention. Immediate corrective action is essential to prevent further deterioration.

FINAL, FORMAL COMMUNICATION EXAMPLE
Page 2

1. Enhance cash disbursement review and approval procedures.

Our testing of the cash disbursements system confirmed that the system appropriately rejects all duplicate invoice entries based on invoice number. However, the system edit is not comparing other invoice information for potential duplicates. Our testing indicated the system accepts invoices when a digit or symbol is added to the end of the invoice number, creating the opportunity for a duplicate payment. The receipt of goods or services should be recorded and processed only once.

As a result, we expanded our testing to include all invoices processed for payment from Jan. 1, 20XX through Dec. 31, 20XX for possible duplicate payments. Using generalized audit software, we selected all cash disbursement payments of equal amounts for a given vendor, regardless of the invoice number or payment date. Our query revealed several instances (14 invoices totaling $357,782) in which the A/P clerks possibly entered certain invoices a second time when a duplicate invoice was submitted by the vendor. Follow up with the clerks indicated they are not recognizing that these invoices may have been received before and were adding a digit to the end to facilitate processing. In other instances, the vendor issued a duplicate invoice with a different invoice number (typically one higher than the last one) and the A/P clerks did not detect that these were potentially duplicate invoices. As a result, liabilities, and the corresponding assets or expenses, were overstated by $357,782 and the same amount of funds were disbursed inappropriately. A budget-to-actual analysis is performed monthly by all department heads and cost center owners, but is not designed to detect insignificant errors such as these.

We recommend that a query routine be developed that matches the vendor name, invoice amount, invoice date, and any other key invoice characteristics considered appropriate by A/P and compares these characteristics to previously processed invoices before processing each cash disbursements batch. The results of this query should be reviewed by the A/P supervisor for potentially duplicative invoices. Any suspect transactions should be removed from the batch and investigated before processed for payment.

Management Response:

A query routine will be written that compares "key" invoice characteristics (invoice dollar amount, vendor description, invoice number, and invoice date) to previously processed invoices flagging the invoice as a potential duplicate if any characteristics are a match. This routine will be run before a batch is processed and reviewed by the A/P supervisor. If there are any potentially duplicate invoices identified, these transactions will be removed from the batch and researched before processed for payment.

Accountability: Chief Accounting Officer
Responsibility: Accounts Payable Supervisor
Implementation Date: June 30, 20XX

EXHIBIT 14-11
continued

Quality of Communications

Standard 2420: Quality of Communications states that "communications must be accurate, objective, clear, concise, constructive, complete, and timely." The interpretation to Standard 2420 defines these terms.

- **Accurate** communications are free from errors and distortions and are faithful to the underlying facts.
- **Objective** communications are fair, impartial, and unbiased and are the result of a fair-minded and balanced assessment of all relevant facts and circumstances.
- **Clear** communications are easily understood and logical, avoiding unnecessary technical language and providing all significant and relevant information.
- **Concise** communications are to the point and avoid unnecessary elaboration, superfluous detail, redundancy, and wordiness.
- **Constructive** communications are helpful to the engagement client and the organization and lead to improvements where needed.

Rating Definitions

It is important to ensure readers of an audit communication understand what the ratings used by the internal audit function mean.

EXHIBIT 14-12

FINAL, INFORMAL COMMUNICATION EXAMPLE (MANAGEMENT DISCUSSION MEMORANDUM)

TO: Chief Accounting Officer, Books 2 Buy Holding Corporation

FROM: Audit Director/Manager, Books 2 Buy Holding Corporation

SUBJECT: Management Discussion Findings – Cash Disbursements Process

DATE: April 27, 20XX

The internal audit function performed a review of the cash disbursements process to evaluate the design adequacy and operating effectiveness of the system of internal controls within the cash disbursements process. During the course of the review, the following observation came to our attention that affects the operational efficiency of your area. In our opinion, this observation does not constitute a reportable control deficiency and, as a result, is not included in the formal audit report.

We recommend management evaluate the impact the observation has on operational efficiency and the cost/benefit of implementing corrective action, if any.

Enhance the process for updating and maintaining the delegation of authority policy.

Our review of the delegation of authority policy indicated there were seven individuals listed with disbursement authority in the policy who are no longer employed by the company and nine individuals acting with disbursement authority that are not identified in the policy as having such authority. Authority over the disbursing of funds should be limited to individuals currently employed by the company, individuals authorized to perform cash disbursements under the policy, and individuals whose job responsibilities justify such authority. The absence of such limits creates the risk disbursements might be made by individuals not authorized by the policy.

Upon further investigation, we determined the delegation of authority policy is only updated semiannually. Currently, no updates are made when there is a change in personnel or a change in responsibilities affected by the policy. For individuals acting with disbursement authority, but not listed in the policy, all were appropriately approved to perform disbursements and required such to perform assigned job responsibilities. Additionally, our testing revealed that access rights to the cash disbursements system are eliminated upon an individual leaving the company. Therefore, even though individuals who have left the company remain in the policy as authorized signers, they could not access the system to approve disbursement transactions. In all seven cases noted during our review, system access had been disabled at termination of the individuals. Finally, we noted that a budget-to-actual analysis is performed monthly by all department heads and cost center owners. Any unauthorized disbursements of consequence would be identified and investigated immediately.

We recommend management consider enhancing procedures for updating the delegation of authority policy. Individuals named with disbursement authority should be incorporated into the policy via an exhibit that would list individuals with disbursement authority. The exhibit could be updated and maintained as part of the new employee on-boarding and terminated employee exit processes in a similar manner as system access rights are added or deleted allowing for the policy to be updated as changes occur.

Management's Response:

Management believes the risk of an inappropriately authorized disbursement is minimal and, therefore, is willing to live with the current level of risk as identified between policy updates. However, management does see value in separating the list of individuals with disbursement authority from the policy itself, as well as incorporating the maintenance of this list as part of the processing of new and terminated employees. Management will evaluate the cost/benefit of making these changes to the process for updating and maintaining the delegation of authority policy.

Accountability: Chief Financial Officer
Responsibility: Chief Accounting Officer
Implementation Date: Not Applicable

- **Complete** communications lack nothing that is essential to the target audience and include all significant and relevant information and observations to support recommendations and conclusions.
- **Timely** communications are opportune and expedient, depending on the significance of the issue, allowing management to take appropriate corrective action.

Quality Communications must be:

- Accurate
- Objective
- Clear
- Concise
- Constructive
- Complete
- Timely

Practice Advisory 2420-1: Quality of Communications provides additional guidance regarding the steps internal auditors should take to ensure communications meet the criteria of Standard 2420. Specifically, internal auditors should:

1. Gather, evaluate, and summarize data and evidence with care and precision.
2. Derive and express observations, conclusions, and recommendations without prejudice, partisanship, personal interests, and the undue influence of others.
3. Improve clarity by avoiding unnecessary technical language and providing all significant and relevant information in context.
4. Develop communications with the objective of making each element meaningful but succinct.
5. Adopt a useful, positive, and well-meaning content and tone that focuses on the organization's objectives.
6. Ensure communication is consistent with the organization's style and culture.
7. Plan the timing of the presentation of engagement results to avoid undue delay.

Errors and Omissions

Error

An unintentional misstatement or omission by the internal audit function of significant information in the final engagement communication.

Although a lot of attention is spent on accuracy and completeness in an engagement communication, there will be times when an error or omission will occur. The *Standards* have accounted for that with Standard 2421: Errors and Omissions: "If a final communication contains a significant error or omission, the chief audit executive must communicate corrected information to all parties who received the original communication." An error is defined as an unintentional misstatement or omission of significant information in the final engagement communication.

PERFORM MONITORING AND FOLLOW-UP

The internal audit function's responsibilities do not end when engagement results are distributed. Remember that during the course of the engagement, as observations were identified, management of the area that was the target of the assurance engagement either committed to take corrective action to remediate the observations or they chose not to take action. The collaborative process that took place during the engagement ensured the internal audit function was in agreement with the proposed action plan as documented in the final engagement communication. As a result, monitoring and follow-up procedures are designed to ensure observations have been addressed and resolved in a manner consistent with management's response included in the final engagement communication. The CAE is instructed by the *Standards* to "establish a follow-up process to monitor and ensure that management actions have been effectively implemented or that senior management has accepted the risk of not taking action" (Standard 2500.A1). In other words, management must make one of two choices: either implement changes to remediate the observation or accept the risk associated with making no changes to the control. If changes are implemented, the internal audit function must have a process in place to monitor and follow up on agreed-upon actions to ensure management has done what they intended.

If management chooses to accept the risk, the *Standards* indicate that the CAE must make a judgment regarding the prudence of that decision. Furthermore, "when the chief audit executive believes that senior management has accepted a level of residual risk that may be unacceptable to the organization, the chief audit executive must discuss the matter with senior management. If the decision regarding residual risk is not resolved, the chief audit executive must report the matter to the board for resolution" (Standard 2600: Resolution of Senior Management's Acceptance of Risks).

If, on the other hand, management accepts responsibility for implementing changes to remediate the observations, the internal audit function must monitor the progress management makes relative to the remediation of the observations. Regular follow-up procedures should ensure that enhancements are made on schedule with the time frame outlined in the final engagement communication. Ultimately, it is the CAE's responsibility to "establish and maintain a system to monitor the disposition of results communicated to management" (Standard 2500: Monitoring Progress). This system should be delineated in the internal audit function's audit manual. At minimum, follow-up actions should be documented and retained in the internal audit function's working papers of the next assurance engagement relating to the area that was subject to audit originally. Additionally, in the case in which engagement observations were evaluated as significant or material, a follow-up engagement is typically scheduled with a targeted scope to evaluate and test whether the controls of the area have been improved and the risks have been reduced to an acceptable level. This engagement should be planned, executed, and reported on in a manner consistent with any other assurance engagement.

In 2009, the Committee of Sponsoring Organizations of the Treadway Committee (COSO) issued *Guidance on Monitoring Internal Control Systems*, which is covered in more detail in Chapter 6, "Internal Control." While this guidance is focused on management activities within an organization, aspects of the guidance are relevant to internal audit functions as well.

For example, when conducting a targeted review of control enhancements, COSO indicates that the internal audit function has the responsibility to communicate the outcome of that review to the same audience that received the communication from the original assurance engagement. Additionally, when the controls that were assessed to be significantly or materially compromised in the original assurance engagement communication pertain to financial reporting, the financial reporting regulations relative to the countries in which the organization operates must be followed in terms of communication requirements. Furthermore, the remediation of the significant deficiency or material weakness, as well as the outcome of the targeted review, should be reported to senior management, the audit committee, and the independent outside auditor. In the case of a material weakness, the remediation and corresponding control enhancements also must be disclosed to the organization's stakeholders according to the laws of the country in which it operates.

OTHER TYPES OF ENGAGEMENTS

This chapter addresses reporting on assurance engagement outcomes only. Consulting engagements, including investigations, projects, due diligence efforts, etc., have different communication requirements. Refer to Chapter 12, "Introduction to the Engagement Process," and Chapter 15, "The Consulting Engagement," for examples of consulting engagements and details on the requirements pertinent to consulting engagement communication.

SUMMARY

Communication is an integral part of any assurance engagement and occurs throughout both interim and final communications. Because of their immediacy, interim communications tend to happen through face-to-face meetings, conference calls, and e-mail messages, while final engagement communications tend to be documented more formally with reports and memoranda.

Final communications disseminate the results of an assurance engagement and should include:

- Scope and purpose of the engagement,
- Time frame covered by the engagement,
- Any observations as required after performing the evaluation and escalation process, as well as the related recommendations,
- Engagement conclusions and the overall rating (if applicable), and
- Management's action plan to appropriately address reported observations.

Each observation that is reported should include the following: criteria, condition, cause, and effect. Additionally, there should be a recommendation for remediating each observation included in the report. The significance of the observations, both individually and in the aggregate, as well as whether key controls are compromised, will dictate whether communication should be formal or informal, or if both types of communication are appropriate for an engagement. Formal communications typically are distributed to senior management, the audit committee, the organization's independent outside auditor, and/or auditee management and are appropriate when controls are assessed to be:

- Insignificantly compromised, although key controls are affected,
- Significantly compromised, or
- Materially compromised.

Informal communications are typically distributed only to management of the area that was subject to the engagement and are only appropriate when the observations being reported are assessed as insignificant with no key controls compromised.

All communication, whether formal or informal, interim or final, must be "accurate, objective, clear, concise, constructive, complete, and timely" according to Standard 2420: Quality of Communications. Additionally, any errors or omissions that are identified in a final communication, if significant, must be corrected and communicated "to all parties who received the original communication" (Standard 2421: Errors and Omissions).

Distribution of final communications for an engagement does not complete the internal audit function's role in the engagement. It is still necessary to follow up and monitor to ensure that management has implemented the action plan that was agreed upon to remediate any observations in the final communication. This includes following up with management to determine whether progress is consistent with agreed-upon time frames and can be expanded to include a follow-up engagement to assess whether controls have been enhanced to a sufficient degree to reduce risks to an acceptable level.

In the event that auditee management chooses not to take action to remediate communicated observations, the CAE must assess the prudence of that decision. If the CAE decides that auditee management has accepted an amount of risk that exceeds senior management's risk tolerance, this must be communicated to senior management and, if necessary, the board.

Review Questions

1. Why is communication an important part of assurance engagements?
2. How is engagement communication to auditees related to the CAE's communication to senior management and the board?
3. What are the steps an internal auditor takes to assess the observations identified during an assurance engagement?
4. Why is interim and preliminary communication important in an assurance engagement?
5. What is the purpose of a closing conference?
6. What attributes need to be present for each observation when communicated in the final assurance engagement communication?
7. What is the internal audit function's responsibility after the assurance engagement communication is disseminated?
8. What is the difference between final formal communications and final informal communications and when is each appropriate?
9. What information should be included in a well-designed final assurance engagement communication?
10. What is the difference between providing positive assurance versus negative assurance in an audit report?

Multiple-choice Questions

Select the best answer for each of the following questions.

1. Recommendations should be included in final audit communications to:
   a. Provide management with options for addressing audit observations.
   b. Ensure that problems are resolved in the manner suggested by the auditor.
   c. Minimize the amount of time required to correct audit observations.
   d. Guarantee that audit observations are addressed, regardless of cost.
2. Once an observation is identified by the internal auditor, it should be:
   a. Documented in the working papers.
   b. Reported to the independent outside auditors.
   c. Scheduled for follow-up.
   d. Included in the final audit report.

3. According to the IPPF, which of the following are part of the minimum requirements for an engagement final communication?

   I. Background information.
   II. Purpose of the engagement.
   III. Engagement scope.
   IV. Results of the engagement.
   V. Summaries.

   a. I, II, and III.
   b. I, III, and V.
   c. II, III, and IV.
   d. II, IV, and V.

4. Which of the following would not be considered a primary objective of a closing or exit conference?

   a. To resolve conflicts.
   b. To identify concerns for future audit engagements.
   c. To discuss the engagement observations and recommendations.
   d. To identify management's actions and responses to the engagement observations and recommendations.

5. During a review of purchasing operations, an internal auditor found that procedures in use did not agree with stated company procedures. However, audit tests revealed that the procedures used represented an increase in efficiency and a decrease in processing time, without a discernible decrease in control. The internal auditor should:

   a. Report the lack of adherence to documented procedures as an operational deficiency.
   b. Develop a flowchart of the new procedures and include it in the report to management.
   c. Report the change and suggest that the change in procedures be documented.
   d. Suspend the completion of the engagement until the engagement client documents the new procedures.

6. A formal engagement communication must:

   a. Provide an opportunity for the auditee to respond.
   b. Document the corrective actions required of senior management.
   c. Provide a formal means by which the independent outside auditor assesses potential reliance on the internal audit function.
   d. Report significant observations.

7. Which of the following does the CAE need to consider when determining the extent of follow-up required?

   I. Significance of the reported observation.
   II. Past experience with the manager charged with the corrective action.
   III. Degree of effort and cost needed for the corrective action.
   IV. The experience of the internal audit staff.

   a. I and III.
   b. I, II, and III.
   c. II, III, and IV.
   d. I, II, III, and IV.

8. An excerpt from an internal audit observation indicates that travel advances exceeded prescribed maximum amounts. Company policy provides travel funds to authorized employees for travel. Advances are not to exceed 45 days of anticipated expenses. Company procedures do not require justification for large travel advances. Employees can, and do, accumulate large unneeded advances. In this audit observation, the element of an audit finding known as "effect" is:

   a. Advances are not to exceed estimated expenses for 45 days.
   b. Travel advances exceed prescribed maximum amounts.
   c. Employees accumulate large, unneeded advances.
   d. Unauthorized employees are given travel advances.

9. Internal audit reports can be structured to motivate management to correct deficiencies. Which of the following report-writing techniques is most likely to be effective?

   a. State the procedural inadequacies and resulting improprieties in specific terms.
   b. Recommend changes and state the punitive measures that will follow if the recommendations are not implemented.
   c. List the deficiencies found so as to provide an easy-to-follow checklist.
   d. Suggest practical improvements to address the identified observations.

10. The primary purpose of issuing an interim report during an internal audit is to:

   a. Provide auditee management the opportunity to act on certain observations immediately.
   b. Set the stage for the final report.
   c. Promptly inform auditee management and their supervisors of audit procedures performed to date.
   d. Describe the scope of the audit.

Discussion Questions

1. The process of evaluating and escalating observations during an assurance engagement can be relatively complex. It involves several steps and requires a number of professional judgments.
   a. What judgments must an internal audit team make during the observation evaluation and escalation process?
   b. What are the three levels of observation importance described in this chapter? Briefly describe each level.
   c. Why is it important to carefully document the conclusions reached as a result of performing the observation and escalation process?

2. Must all observations identified by an internal audit team during an assurance engagement be acted upon by management? Explain. What are the implications for the internal audit function if management fails to respond appropriately to an observation warranting corrective action?

3. Consider the facts presented below. Using the Observation Evaluation and Escalation Process (see Exhibit 14-4), assess the facts presented and determine the following:
   a. What observation(s) is (are) indicated?
   b. What COSO objective categories are affected?
   c. Classify the observation(s) as inadequately designed, ineffectively operating, or both.
   d. Determine the impact and likelihood of the observation(s).
   e. Assess whether the observation(s) is (are) insignificant, significant, or material.
   f. Based on your answers, how and to whom would you communicate the observation(s)?

   Facts:

   ABC Company is a major wholesaler of electrical lighting fixtures and ceiling fans.

   The company opened a large store in a growing metropolitan area near the beginning of the company's fiscal year.

   The following facts surfaced during post-year-end audit procedures performed by the company's financial statement auditor (independent outside auditor):

   - The manager of the new store had booked a large year-end adjustment — a debit to sales and a credit to accounts receivable. The journal entry explanation indicated that the entry was made to adjust the general ledger accounts receivable account to the accounts receivable subsidiary ledger.
   - The year-end gross margin percentage at the new store was significantly lower than the average gross margin percentage of the company's other stores.

- The manager of the new store was stealing payments customers made on account. That is why the general ledger was out of balance with the subsidiary ledger. The store manager made the large year-end adjusting entry to cover up the theft, which is why the store's gross margin was lower than the average of other stores.
- The year-end adjustment was material to the store but not to the company as a whole.

4. Some internal auditors take the view that the internal audit profession should require that internal audit functions adopt a simple, yet sensible, grading or ranking of their engagement reports to better communicate their overall conclusions expressed in these reports. They propose that an overall rating be included in the audit report for each business unit or function audited. The purpose of the rating is to indicate the design adequacy and operating effectiveness of internal controls. For example one proposed rating system is:

A	Controls are designed adequately and operating effectively to provide reasonable assurance that risks are being managed to an acceptable level.
B	Some opportunities for improvement were identified; generally, however, controls are designed adequately and operate effectively to provide reasonable assurance that risks are being managed to an acceptable level.
C	Significant opportunities for improvement were identified. Numerous specific control weaknesses were noted resulting in areas where controls are unlikely to provide reasonable assurance that risks are being managed to an acceptable level.
F	Unsatisfactory. Controls are designed inadequately and/or operating ineffectively; therefore there is no reasonable assurance that risks are being managed to an acceptable level.

Present arguments for and against the use of internal audit ratings. Do you believe the use of ratings is appropriate or not? Explain your reasons.

5. The audit committee chair has asked your boss, the CAE, to explore the possibility of giving an overall annual opinion each year on the organization's state of internal controls. The CAE has done some preliminary research and designed the following potential form for such an opinion:

> To: Chair, Audit Committee
>
> From: Executive VP - Internal Audit
>
> Subject: Internal Audit Opinion of the System of Internal Controls for the Period Ended December 31, 20XX.
>
> We have completed the annual internal audit plan for the company. This plan was designed in such a manner that allows us to assess the adequacy of the company's system of internal controls relating to operational risks, financial reporting risks, and compliance risks.
>
> The plan was prepared considering the results of the risk assessment completed as a part of the company's enterprise risk management process and the risk assessments completed by internal audit and the organization's external auditors. Our work was conducted in accordance with the *International Standards for the Professional Practice of Internal Auditing*.
>
> The criteria used to assess the company's system of internal controls are reflected in the company's internal control framework, which is based on the COSO internal control framework. The criteria were discussed and agreed upon with management of each area before the individual engagements included in the annual internal audit plan were conducted.
>
> Our overall opinion is that on December 31, 20XX, internal controls over operations, financial reporting, and compliance are designed adequately and operating effectively. We have conducted sufficient appropriate audit procedures and gathered the necessary evidence to support this conclusion. The evidence gathered meets professional internal audit standards and is sufficient to provide reasonable assurance.

The CAE has asked you to do additional research regarding the appropriateness of internal audit functions giving such opinions and to develop a preliminary list of issues that the department would need to consider if it were to give such an opinion. He suggests that you might begin by reviewing The IIA's *Practice Guide: Formulating and Expressing Internal Audit Opinions*.

a. Is the type of opinion the CAE is considering to the audit committee positive or negative assurance? Explain.

b. What does this opinion imply about the scope of internal audit work performed?

c. In your report to the CAE, what factors would you recommend the internal audit function consider before committing to issuing an overall opinion on the organization's system of internal controls?

CASES

CASE 1

Review the engagement observation that follows and record the specific information that represents the recommendation and each of the following observation attributes: criteria, condition, cause, and effect.

Audit Observation and Recommendation:

Corporation X associates are required to abide by the organization's formal Code of Business Conduct & Ethics (the Code). To ensure all employees are aware of the Code and their obligations under it, Corporation X requires all associates to acknowledge receipt of the Code. A global e-mail was sent to all associates on July 1st informing them of their obligation to read and acknowledge the Code. Associates were instructed to complete and return acknowledgments by December 1st. Our audit testing indicated the following relative to the acknowledgment process:

- As of March 1st, fewer than 50 percent of associates had completed and returned acknowledgments.
- Follow-up procedures have not been performed by human resources (HR) or department management to date.
- There is not a formal policy indicating actions to be taken if and when associates do not return acknowledgments.
- No disciplinary actions have been taken regarding associates who have not completed acknowledgments of the Code to date.

Improving the acknowledgment process will help Corporation X demonstrate compliance with external regulations requiring a Code of Ethics. It will also help to ensure all associates are aware of their responsibilities and obligations to the organization under the Code.

We recommend management enhance the acknowledgement tracking process to ensure all associates acknowledge receipt of, compliance with, and understanding of the Code. Policy and procedures need to be developed and implemented to take appropriate action when associates do not respond. Disciplinary action should be taken if associates refuse to complete and return acknowledgments, as required by policy.

Management Response:

Associates who have not acknowledged the Code as of March 24th will be sent a reminder notification the week of April 3rd inform-

CASE 1 con't.

ing them of the requirement to acknowledge the Code. A report of all associates who continue to be delinquent in acknowledging the Code will be provided to the applicable HR liaison for review and follow-up the week of April 17th. The HR function will partner with the department business heads of delinquent associates to obtain the necessary acknowledgments. A final report will be generated the week of April 24th to determine the remaining associates who have not acknowledged the Code. A verbal warning will be issued to all associates who have not acknowledged the Code by April 24th and a written warning will be provided to associates who have not acknowledged the Code by April 30th.

Accountability: Jane Doe
Responsibility: John Smith
Implementation Date: March 24

Does the observation, as presented, adequately address all of the suggested observation attributes? If not, explain why.

CASE 2 Consider the following facts.

During its assessment of the accounts payable department, the internal audit function identified the following observations:

- Inadequate segregation of duties over certain information system access controls. Potential loss exposure of $45 million.
- Several instances of transactions that were not properly recorded in subsidiary ledgers. Transactions were not material, either individually or in the aggregate. Potential loss exposure of $60 million.
- A lack of timely reconciliations of the account balances affected by the improperly recorded transactions. Potential loss exposure of $25 million.

Based on the context in which the observations occur, management and the internal audit function agree on the potential loss exposure represented by these observations individually.

The organization has a risk management function that, together with the independent outside auditor, has determined that an amount less than $20 million is insignificant in impact and that an amount greater than $80 million is material in impact.

Based only on these facts, determine the COSO objective category affected by each observation, classify each observation in terms of its design adequacy and operating effectiveness, determine the impact and likelihood for each observation, and assess whether each observation is insignificant, significant, or material. After that has been done, outline the next steps an internal audit function should take and the ramifications of the overall conclusion, including how and to whom communication should be made.

REFERENCES

[1]*Internal Control – Integrated Framework* (Jersey City, NJ: Committee of Sponsoring Organizations of the Treadway Commission, 1994), p. 13.

[2]*Statement of Financial Accounting Standards No. 5: Accounting for Contingencies* (Norwalk, CT: Financial Accounting Standards Board of the Financial Accounting Foundation, 1975), p. 4.

[3]*Practice Guide – Formulating and Expressing Internal Audit Opinions* (Altamonte Springs, FL: The Institute of Internal Auditors).

[4]*Practical Considerations Regarding Internal Auditing Expressing an Opinion on Internal Control* (Altamonte Springs, FL: The Institute of Internal Auditors), p. 8.

[5]Watson, Mark, *Moody's Special Comment Report Number 99909* (New York, NY: Moody's Investor Services, Inc.), p. 3.

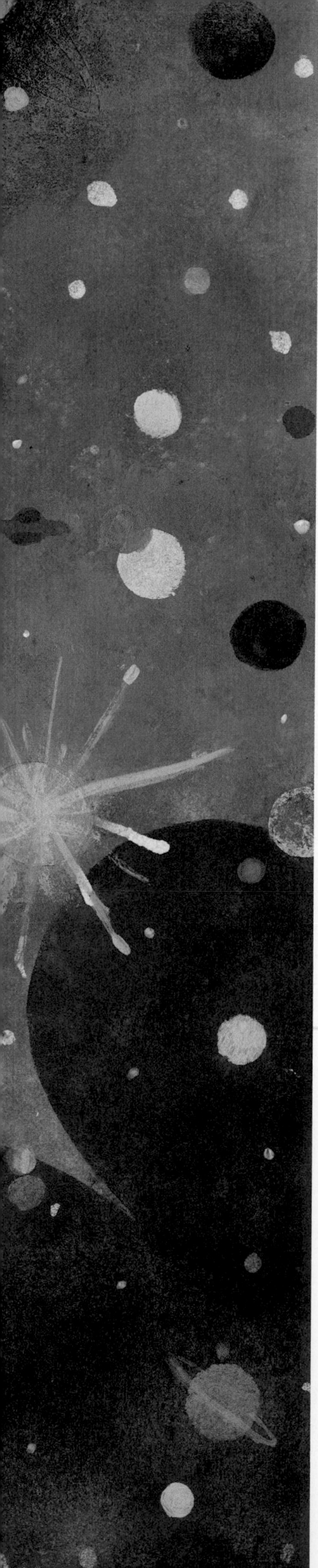

CHAPTER 15
THE CONSULTING ENGAGEMENT

Learning Objectives

- Articulate the difference between assurance and consulting engagements.
- Discuss the various types of consulting services provided by internal auditors.
- Understand how internal audit functions select which requested consulting engagements to perform.
- Understand the process for conducting an advisory consulting engagement.
- Describe the benefits to an organization when the internal audit function provides consulting services.
- Understand the importance of determining customer expectations for consulting activities.
- Discuss the *Standards* as they pertain to consulting engagements.
- Understand the need for the internal audit function to set boundaries for consulting activities.

Many internal auditors acting in a consulting capacity love the excitement of receiving an unexpected call from senior management asking them to help solve a problem. For example, the CEO may need someone to go to India as soon as possible to help resolve an issue with the customer service call center. Perhaps the call center has had a significant increase in complaints and the CEO wants the internal audit function to report back by the end of the week with recommendations for both short-term and long-term corrective actions. In this example, a team of internal auditors will fly out over the weekend to interview key personnel and report back on the state of call center operations in India.

Another call may come from the manager who oversees an outsourced payroll operation that has been having difficulty getting employee paychecks out correctly and on time. For this scenario, imagine that complaints have come from the president's office that his paycheck, among others, was posted at least a day late and that some employee paychecks bounced. The manager would like someone from the internal audit function to review these issues and provide advice regarding the implementation of appropriate corrective actions immediately. An audit team needs to be on site with the vendor the next morning in Dallas, Texas, to help management resolve the issue.

EXHIBIT 15-1

PROFESSIONAL STANDARDS AND PRACTICE ADVISORIES RELEVANT TO CHAPTER 15

1000.C1 – Purpose, Authority, and Responsibility
1130.C1 – Impairment to Independence or Objectivity
1130.C2 – Impairment to Independence or Objectivity
1210.C1 – Proficiency
1220.C1 – Due Professional Care
2010.C1 – Planning
2110.C1 – Governance
2120.C1 – Risk Management
2120.C2 – Risk Management
2120.C3 – Risk Management
2130.C1 – Control
2130.C2 – Control
2201.C1 – Planning Considerations
2210.C1 – Engagement Objectives
2220.C1 – Engagement Scope
2240.C1 – Engagement Work Program
2330.C1 – Documenting Information
2410.C1 – Criteria for Communicating
2440.C1 – Disseminating Results
2440.C2 – Disseminating Results
2500.C1 – Monitoring Progress

Practice Advisory 1000-1: Internal Audit Charter
Practice Advisory 1110-1: Organizational Independence
Practice Advisory 1120-1: Individual Objectivity
Practice Advisory 1130-1: Impairment to Independence or Objectivity
Practice Advisory 1200-1: Proficiency and Due Professional Care
Practice Advisory 1210-1: Proficiency
Practice Advisory 1220-1: Due Professional Care
Practice Advisory 2020-1: Communication and Approval
Practice Advisory 2030-1: Resource Management
Practice Advisory 2040-1: Policies and Procedures
Practice Advisory 2060-1: Reporting to Senior Management and the Board
Practice Advisory 2120-1: Assessing the Adequacy of Risk Management Processes
Practice Advisory 2130-1: Assessing the Adequacy of Control Processes
Practice Advisory 2200-1: Engagement Planning
Practice Advisory 2210-1: Engagement Objectives
Practice Advisory 2230-1: Engagement Resource Allocation
Practice Advisory 2240-1: Engagement Work Program
Practice Advisory 2330-1: Documenting Information
Practice Advisory 2340-1: Engagement Supervision
Practice Advisory 2410-1: Communication Criteria
Practice Advisory 2440-1: Disseminating Results
Practice Advisory 2500-1: Monitoring Progress

In another example, a team is assembled to review the controls of a company that is a potential acquisition target in China. This due diligence assignment involves looking at what it will take to implement the same level of controls at the newly acquired company as the controls of the existing organization. The chief operations officer (COO) wants a report back by the end of the month.

These are just a few examples of the challenging and rewarding consulting engagements an internal auditor may be called upon to perform.

For internal auditors who regularly perform consulting engagements, a very exciting part of their job is coming to work on Monday and not knowing exactly what they may be working on that week. Consulting services, such as fraud investigations, special task force assignments, merger and acquisition studies, due diligence reviews, third-party vendor or service provider reviews, executive management special requests, and analyses to identify root causes of operational performance problems can hit the internal auditor's desk on any given day. These projects can cause an unexpected diversion from day-to-day internal audit assurance activities and tax available resources. Many of these projects require a very timely response to management and may have stricter deadlines than already scheduled assurance projects.

David Richards, immediate past president of The IIA, has long been an advocate of internal audit consulting services. In his former role as chief audit executive (CAE) at First Energy, he noted:

> For some internal auditors, the concepts of consulting and auditing are at odds with one another because they see consulting as putting the auditor too close to the customer and potentially compromising the auditor's independence. Actually, consulting has been part of internal auditing for years . . . The current definition of internal auditing recognizes that the focus of internal auditing should include both assurance and consulting services. It is clear that internal auditors can add value to consulting assignments by providing the methodologies, facilitation, focus, knowledge, technology, best practices, and independence that help solve customers' problems.[1]

The internal audit function is uniquely positioned to add value and make an impact on the organization when performing consulting engagements. Because internal auditors are often viewed as risk and control experts within an organization, this expertise can be leveraged to assist the organization in keeping abreast of emerging risks. For example, the internal audit function can act in a consulting capacity by initiating discussions that explore the increased risk in areas that are particularly affected by an economic downturn. Additionally, because internal auditors are very familiar with most, if not all, areas of the organization due to the assurance services they perform, they are acutely aware of the changes occurring in these areas. They are in a unique position to advise management about how to deal effectively with these changes. Today's business environment, more than ever, presents many opportunities for internal auditors to provide consulting services that add value at a critical point in the organization's evolution.

For these reasons and more (which are discussed in greater depth throughout the chapter), the addition of, or increase in, consulting services provided by the internal audit function can be very valuable to the organization. Additionally, consulting services provide internal auditors with opportunities to diversify their skills and work in a dynamic, interesting work environment. Increasing the focus on consulting services, especially in an uncertain environment, is clearly a win-win situation.

EXHIBIT 15-2

DEFINITIONS OF CONSULTING AND ASSURANCE SERVICES FROM THE *STANDARDS* GLOSSARY

Consulting Services – Advisory and related client service activities, the nature and scope of which are agreed with the client, are intended to add value and improve an organization's governance, risk management, and control processes without the internal auditor assuming management responsibility. Examples include counsel, advice, facilitation, and training.

Assurance Services – An objective examination of evidence for the purpose of providing an independent assessment on governance, risk management, and control processes for the organization. Examples may include financial, performance, compliance, system security, and due diligence engagements.

Source: International Professional Practices Framework (Altamonte Springs, FL: The Institute of Internal Auditors, 2009), p. 40.

THE DIFFERENCE BETWEEN ASSURANCE AND CONSULTING SERVICES

There are several fundamental differences between assurance services and consulting services: the number of parties involved in the engagement, the application of the *International Standards for the Professional Practice of Internal Auditing* (*Standards*) to both types of services, the purpose of the engagement, and communication of engagement results. As noted in Exhibit 15-2, consulting services are advisory in nature and many times are conducted at the request of management. Consequently, the nature and scope of the consulting engagement are subject to agreement with the engagement customer.

Engagement Parties

Customer

The subsidiary, business unit, department, group, individual, or other established subdivision of an organization that is the subject of a consulting engagement.

Consulting services generally involve two parties:

1. The person or group seeking and receiving the advice — the engagement customer.
2. The person or group offering the advice — the internal audit function.

In contrast, assurance services typically involve three parties:

1. The person or group directly involved with the process, system, or other subject matter — the auditee.
2. The person or group making the independent assessment — the internal audit function.
3. The person or group relying on the independent assessment — the user.

Application of Standards

While the Attribute and Performance Standards apply equally to both assurance and consulting services, there is a set of Implementation Standards for each type of service. The differences in the two sets of Implementation Standards reflect the differences between assurance and consulting services, most notably the difference in the parties involved.

Because consulting services involve only the two parties previously discussed (the engagement customer and the internal audit function), their structure is less complex than assurance services, which involve three parties (the auditee, the internal audit function, and the third-party user). Based on this structural difference, the Implementation Standards for assurance services are more stringent and numerous than the Implementation Standards for consulting services. As stated in Chapter 2, "The International Professional Practices Framework: Authoritative Guidance for the Internal Audit Profession," Implementation Standards specific to assurance engagements are identified with an "A" after the standard number (for example, Standard 1130.A1), and with a "C" for consulting engagements (for example, Standard 1130.C1).

Engagement Purpose

Whereas assurance engagements are conducted for the purpose of providing independent assessments, consulting engagements are conducted for the purpose of providing advisory, training, or facilitation services. Like the scope of a consulting engagement, the type of engagement that is most conducive to providing the specific service requested is agreed upon between the internal audit function and the consulting customer based on the customer's needs.

Engagement Communication

In many internal audit functions, there is a prescribed audience who receives communication regarding assurance engagement outcomes. Because the purpose of assurance engagements is to provide an independent assessment, and a third party exists that will use the information, communications must include not only the auditee, but the members of the third party as well. Additionally, because the type of information communicated is similar for all assurance engagements, the format of the communications does not vary much. This makes it easier for the audience to immediately find the information they are looking for within the communication. Communication of engagement outcomes for consulting services, on the other hand, varies based on the scope and purpose of the engagement. It may be formal or informal and can be distributed in any number of different formats so that the system of delivery is chosen based on what will be most effective and efficient given the specific content of the communication and the audience receiving it.

TYPES OF CONSULTING SERVICES

Consulting services comprise a wide range of activities based on management's needs. These services can be tailored to resolve specific issues that senior management has identified as requiring attention and can be advisory, educational, and/or facilitative in nature. The specific consulting engagements that an internal audit function can perform are limited only by the needs of the organization and the resources of the function so long as they do not impair the independence of the internal audit function or the objectivity of the internal auditors.

Types of Consulting Engagements:

- **Advisory**
- **Training**
- **Facilitative**

Advisory Consulting Engagements

Many consulting engagements are designed to offer advice. As organizations go through changes, such as staff reductions or redesign of business processes, the internal audit function can be called on to provide insight.

For example, management may ask the internal audit function to help review and recommend improvements in the effectiveness and efficiency of a particular business process or participate in specific quality assurance initiatives.

Consulting engagements that are advisory in nature include, for example:

- Advising on control design.
- Advising during development of policies and procedures.
- Participating in an advisory role for high-risk projects such as information systems development.
- Advising on certain enterprise risk management activities.

Training Consulting Engagements

As previously mentioned, the internal audit function has specialized knowledge in many different areas that are important to the organization. Because of the assurance services they provide, internal auditors understand specific industry regulations, risk assessment, risk mitigation, control design, best practices, etc. Often, management asks the internal audit function to serve as educators on this and other topics to appropriate areas of the organization. The internal audit function serves in this capacity by holding special training sessions, presenting on a requested topic to specific groups or individuals, or working one-on-one with high-level individuals as they are hired into the organization.

Consulting engagements that are educational in nature include:

- Training on risk management and internal control.
- Benchmarking internal areas with comparable areas of other, similar organizations to identify best practices.
- Post mortem analysis (that is, determining lessons learned from a project after it has been completed).

Facilitative Consulting Engagements

Control Self-assessment (CSA)

A methodology encompassing facilitated meetings and surveys that enables internal auditors and managers to collaborate in assessing business risks and evaluating internal controls.

Sometimes management asks the internal audit function to go a step further than just providing education on a subject. In these cases, the internal audit function takes a facilitative role. Facilitation requires the internal audit function to be more involved with the activity in question rather than just offering the necessary knowledge needed for an individual outside the internal audit function to carry it out. For example, control self-assessment (CSA), which is discussed further in Chapter 9, "Managing the Internal Audit Function," is one activity the internal audit function may facilitate. The knowledge internal auditors have in this area can be used to facilitate discussions regarding business processes and controls. Internal auditors facilitating a CSA discussion go beyond educating management on the process, they actually focus management's attention on the goals of the organization and the business processes needed to support those goals. Internal auditors then guide management through an analysis of the gaps between the existing and desired states of a process, and steps to close those gaps. As stressed throughout this chapter, care must be taken not to go too far and assume management responsibility, which would be a violation of IIA Standard 2120.C3 which states that "When assisting management in establishing or improving risk management processes, internal auditors must refrain from assuming any management responsibility by actually managing risks."

Consulting engagements that are facilitative in nature include, for example:

- Facilitating the organization's risk assessment process.
- Facilitating management's control self assessment.
- Facilitating a task force charged with redesigning controls and procedures for a new or significantly changed area.
- Acting as a liaison between management and the independent outside auditors, government agencies, vendors, and contractors on control issues.

While there is often clear delineation between the types of consulting engagements described above, they are not mutually exclusive. For example, when performing a facilitative consulting engagement, internal auditors also will be serving as educators to some degree even as they facilitate the process or activity. Similarly, there will be crossover between advisory and training consulting engagements and so on with any combination of types of engagements. Typically, however, there will be an overriding intent to the engagement that will be one of the three types mentioned.

Overall, the process for conducting consulting engagements is essentially the same as for assurance engagements. There is a planning stage, a performance stage, and a communication stage. However, depending on the type of consulting engagement, the individual steps within each of these stages may or may not be performed. The consulting engagement process is discussed in greater depth later in this chapter.

Blended Engagements

It is important to point out that consulting and assurance services are not always an either/or proposition. Internal auditors should recognize that assurance and consulting services are sometimes combined in a single engagement, often referred to as a blended engagement. Blended engagements incorporate elements of both consulting and assurance services into one consolidated approach. Any engagement in which there is a component of assurance, such as the independent assessment of a process or controls, as well as a component of consulting, such as advising or facilitation, is a blended engagement. As is true of any consulting or assurance engagement, care must be taken to ensure that neither independence nor objectivity is compromised. Although these engagements have both an assurance and a consulting element, it is often necessary to communicate the outcomes separately since the purpose and scope will differ between the assurance and the consulting component of the engagement.

Blended Engagements

Internal audit engagements that incorporate elements of both consulting and assurance services.

Not all internal audit functions believe that assurance and consulting engagements can or should be combined. Whether or not an internal audit function structures engagements this way is dependent on the organization's philosophy toward internal auditing, as documented in the internal audit function's charter.

SELECTING CONSULTING ENGAGEMENTS TO PERFORM

Because internal audit functions have finite resources, not all potential consulting engagements can be conducted. Consulting engagements are selected based on the magnitude of the associated risk or opportunity. There are several different ways that potential consulting engagements are identified: (1) engagements are proposed during the annual risk assessment process and, if identified as high-priority, included in the annual internal audit plan, (2) specific engagements are requested by management, or (3) new or changing conditions warrant the internal audit function's attention. Regardless of how potential consulting engagements are identified, they are typically put through the internal audit function's risk assessment process to determine whether the risk or opportunity warrants the expenditure of scarce internal audit resources.

Annual Internal Audit Plan

Typically, the internal audit plan is created annually and includes those areas within the organizations that have gone through the risk assessment process and were selected as priorities for the internal audit function. For many internal audit functions, these priorities represent both assurance and consulting engagements. Although, assurance engagements typically make up the bulk of the internal audit plan, some consulting engagements, such as systems development projects, due diligence, and large change initiatives, may be known when the internal audit plan is being created and could be included. Additionally, hours may be reserved in the internal audit plan for consulting engagements that may arise during the year. Although consulting engagements are often identified after the internal audit plan has been created, they usually are still subjected to the internal audit function's risk assessment process before being added to the internal audit plan.

Sources of Consulting Engagements:

- **Annual internal audit plan**
- **Requests from management**
- **New or changing conditions**

Requests from Management

In many cases, events arise that are unforeseen at the time the internal audit plan is created, resulting in a request for a consulting engagement by management. Examples of unforeseen events include fraud investigations, special projects, ad hoc committees, and reviews of new procedures. These management requests vie for resources out of the planned internal audit budget. Many of these projects are time sensitive and may preempt assurance engagements in the annual internal audit plan. Alternatively, some consulting engagements may not require a full-time effort during the engagement and can be performed simultaneously with assurance engagements without too much disruption. Clearly, the selection of consulting engagements that the internal audit function will perform requires thoughtful consideration. This frequently translates into the performance of the internal audit function's risk assessment process to determine which consulting engagements requested by management are truly critical enough to warrant the expenditure of scarce resources.

New or Changing Conditions

Consulting engagements are often the result of new or changing conditions. While management may request consulting engagements as a result of such conditions, frequently the internal audit function itself is in the position to identify potential consulting engagements this way. Because the internal audit function has a presence in every area of the organization, it very often receives advance notification of management reorganization, department restructuring, new product offerings, etc. which may warrant internal audit involvement. Additionally, assurance engagement results may indicate a need for the internal audit function to provide consulting services. For example, after conducting an assurance engagement related to business continuity planning, the internal audit function may be asked to conduct a consulting engagement to help the organization develop a plan to address emerging pandemic risks. As with other methods of identification, potential consulting engagements identified this way are often subjected to the risk assessment process to determine the true level of risk or opportunity represented by the engagement.

Risk Assessing Potential Consulting Engagements

The internal audit function's risk assessment process is similar to management's assessment and prioritization process (as discussed in both Chapter 4, "Risk Management," and Chapter 9, "Managing the Internal Audit Function"), and more often than not evaluates risks based on many more factors than just impact and likelihood. Those factors are frequently individually weighted as well, and each factor is specifically defined according to a scale. In addition to assigning an overall risk score to each potential consulting engagement, some internal audit functions add a subjective priority rating that is applied to each potential consulting engagement according to the importance the internal audit function places on it. The internal audit function will consider management's assessment and prioritization process results when determining their subjective priority rating. Additionally, the internal audit function will consider the amount of resources required and the skills necessary to perform the consulting engagement, as well as the customer's needs and expectations. For more detailed information regarding this risk assessment process, including exhibits that illustrate its application, see Case Study 3, "Performing the Consulting Engagement," which accompanies this textbook.

Based on the prioritization process described above, the internal audit function determines the consulting engagements that will be performed. Through these consulting engagements, the internal audit function will attempt to maximize the value provided to management relative to resources committed, perceived risk mitigated or opportunities exploited, and timeliness of services provided. The internal audit function's ultimate goal is to provide management with the information they need to mitigate the risks and maximize the opportunities inherent in the business activities and initiatives intended to carry out the organization's strategic objectives. Once those consulting engagements have been determined, the internal audit function must schedule them and assign resources.

THE CONSULTING ENGAGEMENT PROCESS

Because consulting engagements can differ so greatly in nature and scope, the process for conducting them also varies from engagement to engagement. Among the three types of consulting engagements discussed previously, advisory engagements most closely resemble assurance engagements. In general, the three phases of the advisory consulting engagement process are the same as they are for the assurance engagement process as shown in Exhibit 15-3. There are, however, differences in how the steps within each phase of the advisory consulting engagement process are executed. In fact, some steps may not be required at all.

Remember that a primary difference between consulting and assurance engagements is that consulting engagements do not require an independent assessment for use by a third party. Instead, they involve only two parties: the internal audit team performing the engagement and the indi-

vidual or group requesting the independent advisory, training, or facilitation services (the customer). Because training and facilitation consulting engagements are very diverse in nature and scope from one engagement to another, these types of engagements do not conform to one general process. The processes for these types of consulting engagements are often customized to the specific engagement. However, advisory consulting engagements generally follow the approach depicted in Exhibit 15-3 and, as such, are the focus of the discussion throughout this section.

Planning the Advisory Consulting Engagement

Planning an advisory consulting engagement is very similar to assurance engagement planning with certain exceptions. First, if the advisory consulting engagement is selected after the internal audit plan is finalized, planning is typically more time sensitive and may need to be completed on a stringent timeline. Often the time frame for this type of engagement is inflexible due to circumstances beyond the internal audit function's control or because feedback is time sensitive. Second, as indicated in Exhibit 15-3, not all assurance engagement planning steps may be appropriate. The circumstances in which these steps may not be appropriate are discussed in the respective steps below.

Determine engagement objectives and scope. Once the advisory consulting engagement is identified and scheduled, planning begins. Initial scope discussions with the customer to determine the appropriate level of services, along with consulting engagement objectives, should be performed by a member of the internal audit management team. Internal auditors assigned to the engagement must then meet with the customer to gain a detailed understanding of their expectations. IIA Standard 2300: Performing the Engagement states that "internal auditors must identify, analyze, evaluate, and document sufficient information to achieve the engagement's objectives." The success of the advisory consult-

EXHIBIT 15-3

THE ADVISORY CONSULTING ENGAGEMENT PROCESS

Plan	Perform	Communicate
• Determine engagement objectives and scope. • Obtain final approval of objectives and scope from engagement customer. • Understand the engagement environment and relevant business processes. • Understand relevant risks, if appropriate. • Understand relevant controls, if appropriate. • Evaluate control design, if appropriate. • Determine engagement approach. • Allocate resources to the engagement.	• Gather and evaluate evidence. • Formulate advice.	• Determine nature and form of communications with engagement customer. • Vet advice with engagement customer. • Conduct interim and preliminary engagement communications. • Develop final engagement communications. • Distribute final engagement communications. • Perform monitoring and follow-up, if appropriate.

ing engagement is highly dependent on the internal audit function's ability to understand the customer's expectations for the engagement.

As with an assurance engagement, formalizing objectives at the beginning of an advisory consulting engagement is important. However, in a consulting engagement, the objectives may not be well defined initially and may change during the engagement as more information becomes known. Examples of advisory consulting engagement objectives include:

- Reviewing the design of controls and providing suggestions for improvement.
- Providing input on the design of a new process.
- Reviewing a new computer system prior to implementation.
- Providing advice during a due diligence review for a potential merger or acquisition.

Advisory consulting engagements are most often conducted at the request of management and, because the internal audit function is focused on being responsive to the customer, it is imperative that the scope and time frame be established. During the engagement, the scope may change based on the information that is gathered along with additional input from the customer. However, since internal audit resources are limited, it is important that boundaries are established related to scope and time frame.

Obtain final approval of objectives and scope from consulting engagement customer. The objectives and scope of an advisory consulting engagement should be approved by the engagement customer before the engagement commences. As stated in IIA Standard 2201.C1, "Internal auditors must establish an understanding with consulting engagement clients about objectives, scope, respective responsibilities, and other client expectations. For significant engagements, this understanding must be documented." In most consulting engagements, internal auditors should document the engagement scope and responsibilities and review them with the engagement customer before performing the work. This helps avoid misunderstandings as the consulting engagement progresses.

Also important to the advisory consulting engagement is discussion with the customer regarding the engagement deliverables. The expectation of what will be delivered at the end of the engagement must be established. This could vary based on the nature and scope of the advisory consulting engagement and may be handled formally or informally.

Understand the engagement environment and relevant business processes. As is the case when beginning an assurance engagement, it is important for the internal auditors assigned to the advisory consulting engagement to gather information about the area of the organization in which consulting services are being performed. The internal audit function brings value to each consulting engagement it undertakes by leveraging the broad perspective it has of the organization as a whole. However, real value can be added only if internal auditors fully understand the area covered by the engagement.

Understand relevant risks, if appropriate. If appropriate, the internal auditors conducting the engagement should understand the nature of risks relevant to the area covered by the engagement. Internal auditors

providing advice regarding risks and risk management should have a good understanding of both the organization's and customer's risk tolerance.

Understand relevant controls, if appropriate. In some, but not all, advisory consulting engagements, it may be necessary to understand certain controls. This step requires internal auditors to use their judgment when deciding which controls are relevant to the objectives of the engagement. Once the relevant controls are understood, they should be linked to the corresponding risks identified in the preceding step.

Evaluate control design, if appropriate. If relevant to the advisory consulting engagement, the design of controls identified in the previous step may need to be assessed. For example, when evaluating how to make a process more efficient, it may be necessary to evaluate whether the existing controls efficiently reduce the corresponding risks to an acceptable level. If the internal auditor advises the customer that controls should be eliminated, modified, or added, it will be important to ensure that the new, more efficient process continues to mitigate the corresponding risks to an acceptable level.

Determine engagement approach. An engagement approach must be designed to achieve the advisory consulting engagement objectives. This involves the internal auditors determining the nature, timing, and extent of evidence needed and the procedures required to obtain that evidence. If an understanding of risks and controls is appropriate, the approach may be similar to that of an assurance engagement as described in Chapter 13, "Conducting the Assurance Engagement." Such engagements may be blended engagements, that is, designed to achieve both consulting and assurance objectives.

Allocate resources to the engagement. As previously stated, advisory consulting engagements often are time sensitive. Therefore, if the requested engagement is accepted, it is important to ensure that the internal auditors with the right experience and expertise are assigned promptly and the engagement is started timely. Typically, more experienced internal auditors are assigned to lead consulting engagements. These individuals usually have the most functional business experience relative to the area that has requested the consulting services.

Resource Considerations:

- **Experience**
- **Expertise**
- **External resources**
- **Staff development**

Resources for consulting engagements are allocated in much the same way they are for assurance engagements. IIA Standard 2230: Engagement Resource Allocation advises that "Internal auditors must determine appropriate and sufficient resources to achieve engagement objectives based on an evaluation of the nature and complexity of each engagement, time constraints, and available resources." Additionally, Practice Advisory 2230-1: Engagement Resource Allocation continues, "Internal auditors [should] consider the following when determining the appropriateness and sufficiency of resources:

- The number and experience level of the internal audit staff.
- Knowledge, skills, and other competencies of the internal audit staff when selecting internal auditors for the engagement.
- Availability of external resources where additional knowledge and competencies are required.

- Training needs of internal auditors as each engagement assignment serves as a basis for meeting the internal audit [function's] developmental needs."

Performing the Advisory Consulting Engagement

The execution of advisory consulting engagements is typically more involved than either facilitative or training engagements. Execution of an advisory consulting engagement can take on many forms. As indicated earlier in this chapter, the steps involved in performing an advisory consulting engagement are similar to those performed during an assurance engagement. However, much of the work done to create documentation and perform testing of controls may not be performed in an advisory consulting engagement and there may be greater reliance on department documentation provided by the customer of the engagement. Although each advisory consulting engagement may involve different steps, some procedures that may be conducted in such engagements include:

- Understanding management issues related to the area under review.
- Gathering information.
- Performing analytical procedures.
- Reviewing various department documentation, including organization charts, process flows, and departmental procedures.
- Using computer-assisted audit techniques.
- Understanding key risks.
- Understanding controls and determining which controls need to be improved.
- Evaluating the efficiency of existing controls.

Depending on the nature of the advisory consulting engagement, some of these procedures may or may not be applicable. However, both steps depicted in Exhibit 15-3 in the Perform phase are relevant, in some form, to all advisory consulting engagements.

Gather and evaluate evidence. Internal auditors performing advisory consulting engagements must gather sufficient appropriate evidence to support the engagement objectives. Internal auditors then evaluate the evidence gathered and determine the nature of advice to be given. It is important to document the procedures performed, the evidence gathered, and the evaluation of that evidence. Documentation should be done in working papers created for that purpose. These working papers may be similar to the assurance engagement working papers described in Chapter 13, "Conducting the Assurance Engagement."

Formulate advice. After gathering and evaluating evidence, internal auditors formulate the advice that will be provided to the engagement customer. It is important to ensure that this advice is pertinent to the objectives, understandable to the customer, and actionable. The advice should clearly indicate to the customer that the improvements they seek are achievable. While the format for delivering the advice will be described in the next section, the advice itself is the ultimate deliverable desired by the engagement customer.

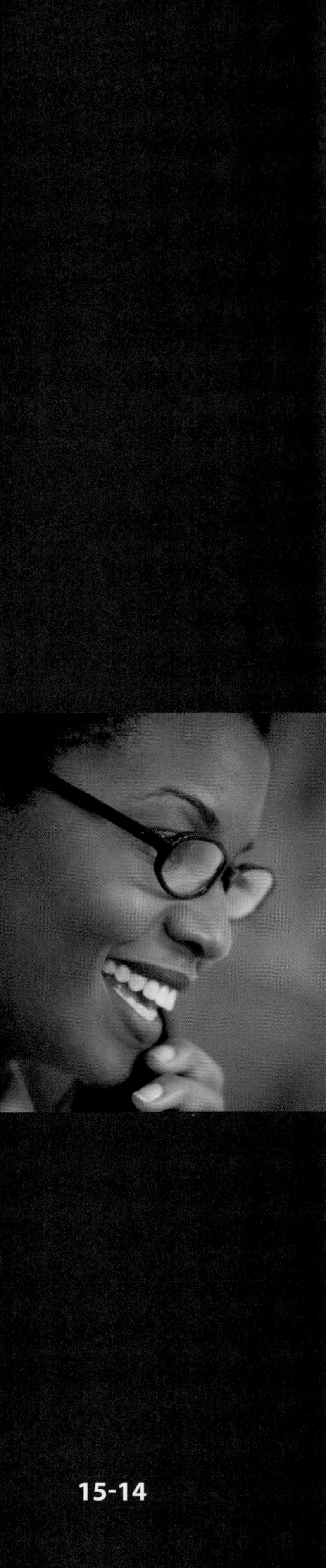

Communication and Follow-up

Communication is just as important in consulting engagements as it is in assurance engagements. There are many similarities between communicating assurance engagement outcomes and communicating consulting engagement outcomes, but there are some differences as well. The steps for communicating consulting engagement outcomes are outlined below.

Determine nature and form of communications with engagement customer. Communication for a consulting engagement can take many forms. Depending on the nature of the engagement and expectations of the customer, a consulting communication format may be less formal than in an assurance engagement, for example, a presentation, memorandum, or e-mail. In other situations, management may ask the internal audit function to provide impromptu advice, for example, about the pros and cons of insourcing versus outsourcing a business function. Conversely, there may be times when a formal report is desired. For example, the internal audit function may be part of a committee or project team that is evaluating a process or product and the advice may be integral to the success of that project. In these instances, a formal deliverable may be desired to ensure the advice is appropriate and addressed timely.

Vet advice with engagement customer. While the advice may seem appropriate to the internal auditors conducting the consulting engagement, there may be other information or factors that the internal auditors are not aware of that could influence the appropriateness of the advice. The advice must be vetted with the customer to ensure that it (1) is understood by the customer, (2) meets the objectives of the consulting engagement, and (3) is practical and cost effective to implement.

Conduct interim and preliminary engagement communications. Because of the time urgency associated with many advisory consulting engagements, communication to the engagement customer should be frequent during the execution of the engagement. This communication can take many forms, but in the interim stages of the engagement, it is often done orally or through conference calls and e-mail chains. Often, consulting engagement communication is tied to specific dates of importance throughout the engagement (milestones) and key decision points. Additionally, as more details of the project are known, or as factors change, the consulting requirements may change and consequently must be communicated.

Develop final engagement communications. As with interim communications, the final communications will vary in format and formality. As previously stated, the communication of final consulting engagement results may be less formal, such as a presentation, memorandum, or e-mail. However, the format and formality of the final communication also will be driven by what was agreed upon with the engagement customer. For example, the engagement customer may require an oral sign-off before a system conversion or major initiative. The internal audit function might be one of many parties that support this type of go/no-go decision before the organization moves forward. If monitoring or follow-up is required or agreed upon with the engagement customer, the final communication may indicate that such actions will occur. Exhibits 15-4 and 15-5 are examples of interim and final communications for an advisory consulting engagement.

EXHIBIT 15-4

INTERIM CONSULTING ENGAGEMENT E-MAIL COMMUNICATION

From: Moritz, Lenny F.
Sent: Thursday, March 13, 20XX, 2:44 p.m.
To: Fish, Kerry S.
CC: Sellers, Julie M.

Subject: Client Data Conversion Project – Advisory Consulting Review Status and Next Steps

Corporate audit has completed the first phase of our pre-conversion advisory consulting review of the Bank of China Client Data Conversion Project. We received and reviewed all requested documentation and believe that the project is consistent with the BUS System Development and Conversion methodology. Adequate resources have been allocated and a detailed timeline of key milestones has been established. Based on our review to date, our only concern is that the process for resolving data format inconsistencies has not been defined. We encourage the Conversion Steering Committee to address this potential issue immediately to ensure these inconsistencies do not cause a conversion delay.

Corporate audit plans to perform the following steps prior to conversion, which is currently scheduled for June 12, 20XX:

- Monitoring project progress by participating in the weekly Conversion Steering Committee meetings.
- Evaluating the remediation efforts related to identified functional gaps.
- Reviewing the system and process capabilities.
- Monitoring the status of required regulatory approvals.
- Monitoring project risk management.

We plan to complete our pre-conversion review procedures by May 11, 20XX, and will issue a final report by May 30, 20XX. Please let me know if you have any questions or comments on the current status and planned next steps of our advisory consulting review. Thanks.

Lenny Moritz
Audit Consulting Manager
BUS Financial Services
lmoritz@BUS.com

Distribute final engagement communications. Unlike assurance engagements in which the recipients of final communications include a number of individuals that may or may not be directly related to the assessed area, in consulting engagements final communications are distributed to the customer for whom the internal audit function provided the service. Unless a final communication covers a blended engagement that includes assurance services, typically it is at the discretion of the customer to expand the distribution of the communication to other parties.

Perform monitoring and follow-up, if appropriate. Monitoring and follow-up procedures related to consulting engagements may not be necessary due to the fact that management may be asking for any number of things during a consulting engagement that do not require any kind of follow-up. As part of the completion of the consulting engagement, the internal audit function should communicate with management and come to agreement regarding any ongoing monitoring or follow-up that will be performed related to the engagement area. When applicable, "the internal audit [function] must monitor the disposition of results of consulting engagements to the extent agreed upon with the [customer]" (IIA Standard 2500.C1).

CONSULTING ENGAGEMENT WORKING PAPERS

As in assurance engagements, the work performed in an advisory consulting engagement, regardless of the type, must be documented in work-

EXHIBIT 15-5

FINAL CONSULTING ENGAGEMENT COMMUNICATION

To: Conversion Steering Committee
Kerry Fish and Julie Sellers, Co-chairs

From: Lenny Moritz, Audit Consulting Manager
Bus Financial Services

Subject: Bank of China Client Data Conversion Project
Pre-conversion Advisory Consulting Review

Date: May 30, 20XX

Corporate Audit completed a pre-conversion advisory consulting review of the Bank of China Client Data Conversion Project. The scope of the review, performed as of May 11, 20XX, was to advise the Conversion Steering Committee on the bank's readiness to complete the conversion of client data on June 12, 20XX.

The scope of the engagement included, but was not limited to, a review of the following pre-conversion activities:

- Identification and remediation of all functional gaps between legacy BUS and Bank of China systems.
- Evaluation of system and process capabilities to support an accurate and timely conversion of client data (including accounts, assets, and web experience).
- Receipt of required regulatory approvals to proceed with the Client Data Conversion Project.
- Identification and management of project, technology, and operational risks.

OUTCOMES

Overall, pre-conversion activities have been effectively managed and monitored by the Conversion Steering Committee. During the course of our review, several items came to our attention that we believe must be completed or resolved prior to commencement of the data conversion. Without appropriate resolution, the success of the conversion will be subject to increased risk. If timely resolution is not possible, consideration should be given to postponing the data conversion. The Conversion Steering Committee should work to resolve these concerns expeditiously.

SIGNIFICANT CONCERNS

Functional Gap Completion – Several functional gaps remain open which have been deemed "showstoppers" for the Client Data Conversion Project. The Conversion Steering Committee is actively tracking these items and has high confidence they will be resolved prior to conversion weekend.

BUS Client Support Information System Testing – Complete validation testing for the Client Support application software has not been completed and there are outstanding data format inconsistencies that impair the system's ability to fully accept all Bank of China data. The Conversion Steering Committee has high confidence that testing will be completed and all inconsistencies will be resolved prior to the conversion of client data.

Regulatory Approval – Regulatory approval to proceed with the Client Data Conversion Project has not been received from FINRA. Approval is anticipated the week of June 7th and the Conversion Steering Committee is confident approval will be granted prior to conversion weekend.

ing papers. IIA Standard 2330.C1 requires the CAE to "develop policies governing the custody and retention of consulting engagement records, as well as their release to internal and external parties. These policies must be consistent with the organization's guidelines and any pertinent regulatory or other requirements." The level of documentation required for consulting engagements will vary by internal audit function and the nature of the specific engagement. However, in most cases, the amount of documentation and time spent documenting will be significantly less than for an assurance engagement. The focus typically will be on the final product and providing observations and recommendations to management. Sufficient documentation should be maintained to support those overall internal audit recommendations.

As consulting work is performed, it is important to document the results as they become known. There should be a record of the work performed to support advice provided to the customer. Specifically, this documentation should corroborate the assumptions and hypotheses underlying the advice. Additionally, the internal audit function may find that this documentation will enhance the effectiveness and efficiency of similar internal audit engagements in the future.

THE CHANGING LANDSCAPE OF CONSULTING SERVICES

Traditionally, internal audit functions have focused primarily on assurance services because this aspect of internal auditing is relied upon by organizations to be confident that the risks threatening the achievement of objectives are sufficiently mitigated. The current regulatory environment across the globe certainly contributes to this reliance on assurance services. Many organizations, however, are increasingly recognizing the value an internal audit function can add through the performance of consulting services. Because internal auditors' knowledge and skills relating to governance, risk management, and control have advanced in recent years, there are ample opportunities for them to leverage this expertise and add value through consulting services.

Add Value

Value is added by providing opportunities to achieve organizational objectives, identifying operational improvement, and/or reducing risk exposure through both assurance and consulting services.

While a greater proportion of internal audit resources are being allocated to consulting services, there are still many lost opportunities for internal audit functions to increase the value they add to the organization through the wide range of activities that fall into the consulting category. The accelerating pace of global change presents superb opportunities for expanding consulting services as organizations continuously focus on enhancing revenues and controlling costs. Given the internal audit function's knowledge and expertise, it is a prime source from which management can draw to serve as advisors, facilitators, and trainers. Forward-thinking leaders in a growing number of organizations recognize this and are partnering with the internal audit function in new and creative ways.

When management of an organization does not recognize the opportunity to tap the internal audit function in this way, the CAE should educate them on the value the internal audit function can add when partnered with other areas of the organization to work toward achieving non-assurance-related objectives. As CAEs increasingly become agents of change within their organizations, they must ensure that their internal audit functions are prepared to deliver value-adding consulting services. CAEs can lay the foundation for partnering with other areas by:

- Building relationships with other departments in the organization.
- Increasing internal auditors' subject matter expertise through:
    - Training.
    - Rotating internal auditors into other business units.
- Hiring associates from other business units into the internal audit function.
- Obtaining buy-in from the audit committee and senior management by communicating the benefits of increasing consulting services.

CAPABILITIES NEEDED

The increased opportunities that result from this changing landscape have provided the impetus for progressive CAEs to ensure that their internal audit functions have the requisite skills to provide value-adding consulting services. These CAEs know that, to effectively provide these services, internal auditors need to be very versatile and able to learn new things quickly. Additionally, depending on the consulting engagement, internal auditors may need significant experience and expertise in process design and engineering, facilitation skills, strategic thinking, consensus building, and/or creative problem solving. Due to the dynamic nature of internal auditing in general, many internal auditors already have the skills necessary to serve as consultants. Those auditors who operate with a "checklist" mentality and are more comfortable using common standardized audit techniques, however, tend to be significantly challenged when asked to provide consulting services due to the unstructured and dynamic nature of the work that is required.

Skills and Experience Required

Impairment to Independence or Objectivity

The introduction of threats that may result in a substantial limitation, or the appearance of a substantial limitation, to the internal auditor's ability to perform an engagement without bias or interference.

Internal auditors who are interested in performing consulting services within their internal audit functions can acquire the specific skills to perform consulting services effectively. While many of the skills necessary for conducting consulting engagements are the same as the skills necessary for assurance engagements, internal auditors performing consulting engagements must be even more proficient with these skills. Specifically, internal auditors performing consulting engagements are expected to have the ability to:

- Exhibit facilitation and collaboration skills.
- Demonstrate both broad business experience and specific subject matter expertise (such as accounting, technology, and regulatory).
- Build relationships quickly and demonstrate strong interpersonal skills.
- Think analytically and solve unstructured problems.
- Learn and adapt quickly in a dynamic environment.
- Process information and respond quickly to requests.
- Articulate and communicate results quickly, whether through presentations, written communications, or oral communications.

Sourcing

There will be times when the internal audit function may not have the specialized skill sets required to perform certain consulting engagements. When the internal audit function lacks the specialized technical skills required for a consulting engagement, those skills may need to be obtained from internal sources or external subject matter experts as stated in IIA Standard 1210.C1: "The chief audit executive must decline the consulting engagement or obtain competent advice and assistance if the internal auditors lack the knowledge, skills, or other competencies needed to perform all or part of the engagement." Areas in which outside specialists may need to be engaged can include:

- Financial reporting.
- Technology.

- Treasury/cash management.
- Fraud examination, including forensic accounting.
- Engineering and environmental compliance.
- Regulatory compliance.

The type of outside specialist needed depends on the specialized knowledge that is required for a particular engagement. Specialists from whom supplementary advice and assistance may be acquired include:

- Internal audit service providers.
- Independent outside accountants or tax specialists.
- Information technology and security specialists.
- Fraud investigators.
- Actuaries, statisticians, and appraisers.
- Engineers, geologists, and environmental specialists.
- Lawyers.

The CAE may determine that the needed resources are available from within the organization. However, when this is not the case, it is prudent to bring in outside specialists to serve a specific need in a consulting engagement. In either case, the *Standards* are clear that providing quality services and adding value to the organization are more important than who provides those services. Even when outside specialists are used on an engagement, however, the internal audit function must maintain overall control of, and supervisory responsibility for, the consulting engagement. Refer to Chapter 9, "Managing the Internal Audit Function," for more on co-sourcing internal audit services.

SUMMARY

With increased economic pressure on organizations to optimize the use of the resources they have on hand, internal audit functions are in a prime position to step up and increase the value they add to the organization by expanding the amount of consulting services they provide. As enumerated in this chapter, there are many benefits to both the organization and the internal audit function when the number of consulting engagements conducted increases.

By committing to the training of internal auditors and adhering to the guidance provided in the *Standards*, the internal audit function can maintain its independence and internal auditors can maintain their objectivity while delivering high-quality consulting services to their organizations. Using a robust risk assessment process, internal auditors can select the consulting engagements that provide the greatest value to the organization. Following the advisory consulting engagement process outlined in the chapter helps ensure such engagements meet customers' specific expectations.

Consulting services provide many opportunities for internal auditors to increase their knowledge and skills in areas that may not be part of the assurance engagement environment. As internal audit functions allocate more resources to consulting engagements, organizations will recognize the full value of internal auditing.

Review Questions

1. What are the differences between an assurance engagement and a consulting engagement?
2. What are three types of consulting engagements the internal audit function can perform? Give an example of each.
3. What is a blended engagement and when is it appropriate?
4. What are the three ways potential consulting engagements are identified?
5. How does the internal audit function choose which consulting engagements to perform?
6. How are consulting services addressed in the annual internal audit plan?
7. What are the three phases of an advisory consulting engagement?
8. Why is it important to create and maintain robust working papers for a consulting engagement?
9. How can the CAE educate management regarding the value of consulting services to the organization?
10. What skills are required of an internal auditor performing consulting engagements?
11. What types of outside specialists may be asked to assist in consulting engagements?

Multiple-choice Questions

Select the best answer for each of the following questions.

1. Which of the following would be a typical consulting engagement activity performed by the internal audit function?
   - a. Testing compliance with accounts payable policies and procedures.
   - b. Determining the scope of an engagement to test IT application controls.
   - c. Reviewing and commenting on a draft of a new ethics policy created by the company.
   - d. Testing the design adequacy of controls over the termination of employees.
2. Which of the following is not a required consideration regarding proficiency and due professional care when choosing to perform a consulting engagement?
   - a. Availability of adequate skills and resources to conduct the engagement.
   - b. Needs and expectations of the engagement customer.
   - c. Cost of the engagement relative to the potential benefits.
   - d. Potential impact on the independent outside auditor's financial statement audit.

3. Senior management of an organization has requested that the internal audit function help educate employees about internal control concepts. This work is an example of which type of engagement:
   a. An assurance engagement.
   b. A training consulting engagement.
   c. A facilitative consulting engagement.
   d. An advisory consulting engagement.

4. It would be appropriate for the internal audit function to perform which of the following:
   a. Design controls for a process.
   b. Develop a new whistleblower policy.
   c. Review a new IT application before implementation.
   d. Lead a process reengineering project.

5. Which of the following is not likely to be a step during a consulting engagement?
   a. Understanding the objectives of a process.
   b. Assessing the risks in a process.
   c. Flowcharting the key steps in a process.
   d. Expressing a conclusion on the design adequacy and operating effectiveness of a process.

6. The chief operating officer (COO) has requested that the internal audit function advise her regarding a new incentive plan being developed for sales representatives. Which of the following tasks should the CAE decline with respect to providing advice to the COO?
   a. Researching and benchmarking incentive plans provided by other companies in the industry.
   b. Determining the appropriate bonus formula for inclusion in the plan.
   c. Recommending monitoring procedures so that appropriate amounts are paid under the plan.
   d. Determining how to best document the support for amounts paid to provide a sufficient audit trail.

7. When conducting a consulting engagement to improve the efficiency of a production process, the internal audit team is faced with a scope limitation because several months of the production data has been lost or is incomplete. Faced with this scope limitation, the CAE should:
   a. Halt the consulting engagement and conduct a separate assurance engagement to determine why the data was not available.
   b. Discuss the problem with the customer and together evaluate whether the engagement should be continued.
   c. Complete the analysis without the data but include a scope limitation in the engagement report.
   d. Report the scope limitation to the independent outside auditors.

8. The audit committee has requested that the internal audit function assist with the annual risk assessment process. What type of consulting engagement does this assistance represent?
   a. An assurance engagement.
   b. A training consulting engagement.
   c. A facilitative consulting engagement.
   d. An advisory consulting engagement.

Discussion Questions

1. Explain how the internal audit function can maintain its independence while working with management to deploy improved risk management practices and improve the system of internal controls throughout the organization.

2. An internal audit function has agreed to conduct an advisory consulting engagement related to evaluating the efficiency of a process. During this engagement, an internal auditor identifies a control weakness that could be material to the company. Since a consulting engagement is between two parties, the customer and the auditor, is there any obligation to disclose this weakness to senior management and the audit committee? What are the benefits and drawbacks of an internal auditor communicating such a weakness?

3. Describe a situation in which the internal auditor could be accused of having impaired objectivity while providing consulting services.

4. Typically, an internal audit charter will determine the nature of services provided by an internal audit function. What are the benefits and drawbacks of developing a charter that does not expressly authorize the performance of consulting services?

5. Why is it important for an internal audit function to assess the relevant risks before agreeing to conduct a consulting engagement? Consider risks to both the organization and the internal audit function in your answer.

6. Can consulting engagements be structured to also provide assurance? Why or why not?

7. For an organization going through an acquisition, would involvement by the internal audit function be considered an assurance or consulting activity? Explain your answer.

8. Describe the key steps an internal audit function should follow if asked to facilitate an enterprise risk assessment.

CASES

CASE 1 You are working for a new company that is primarily an Internet-based seller of goods whose business model is similar to eBay's. The company was founded on principles similar to eBay's and is an online auction business, but has the added benefit of having one common site that deals with customers worldwide. The CEO knows that privacy is very important in the online business and has requested that the internal audit function draft a best practices privacy policy for customers since the motto for the new company is "Your Privacy is Our Policy." The company neither has, nor plans to hire, a privacy or compliance officer. The CEO expects the CAE to lead this effort and ensure the campaign delivers on the company's motto. With the advertising campaign slated to launch in one month, the CEO wants the privacy documentation finalized as soon as possible.

A. Identify key sources on privacy that are available for you to reference as you define best practices.

B. Determine the consulting engagement steps you would take and the areas of the company from which you would ask representatives to participate in the project.

C. Identify the consulting engagement documentation you would prepare and the information you would present to the CEO.

CASE 2 A large, international bank is considering outsourcing all facets of the human resources function, including recruiting, benefits, payroll, employee training and development, compensation, and information systems. Three potentially viable vendors have been identified. The internal audit function has been asked to review the vendor selection process and evaluate each vendor's system of internal controls. Senior management has decided they want a 10 percent equity stake in the company that performs the outsourcing function.

The original terms of the agreement call for 1,000 employees to be moved from the bank's human resources function to the company who ultimately receives the contract. The vendor will then be responsible for evaluating the employees' performance and determining which employees will be terminated after a six-month period.

The vendor has the option to determine which computer systems are used. The length of the contract will be either five or 10 years, depending on its pricing structure.

CASE 2 con't.

The bank expects to achieve significant financial gains from this outsourcing arrangement, including significant cost reductions associated with the conversion to standard applications provided by the vendor. The vendor will be expected to leverage existing systems, processes, and personnel and be able to make a profit based on the economies of scale, particularly in the systems areas.

A. What role should the internal audit function play in the bank's decision to outsource this function?

B. What specific areas should the internal audit function review during the transition phase?

C. What areas of risk should the bank consider during the transition phase? After the transition is complete?

D. What types of internal audit consulting activities related to the outsourced human resources function might be appropriate once the transition is complete?

REFERENCES

[1]Richards, David, "Consulting Auditing – Charting a Course," *Internal Auditor*, December 2001, pp. 30-35.

GLOSSARY

NOTE: Many of the definitions in this glossary are taken from the glossary in The IIA's International Professional Practices Framework, or have been modified as appropriate to conform to the discussions in this textbook.

Add Value
Value is provided by improving opportunities to achieve organizational objectives, identifying operational improvement, and/or reducing risk exposure through both assurance and consulting services.

Adequately Designed — See Controls are Adequately Designed.

Application Systems
Sets of programs that are designed for end users such as payroll, accounts payable, and in some cases, large applications such as enterprise resource planning (ERP) systems that provide many business functions.

Appropriate Evidence
Any piece or collection of evidence gained during an engagement that provides relevant and reliable support for the judgments and conclusions reached during the engagement.

Asset Misappropriation
Acts involving the theft or misuse of an organization's assets (for example, skimming revenues, stealing inventory, or payroll fraud).

Assurance Services
An objective examination of evidence for the purpose of providing an independent assessment on governance, risk management, and control processes for the organization. Examples may include financial, performance, compliance, system security, and due diligence engagements.

Audit Engagement — See Assurance Services.

Audit Observation
Any identified and validated gap between the current and desired state arising from an assurance engagement.

Audit Risk
The risk of reaching invalid audit conclusions and/or providing faulty advice based on the audit work conducted.

Audit Sampling
The application of an audit procedure to less than 100 percent of the items in a population for the purpose of drawing an inference about the entire population.

Audit Universe
A compilation of the subsidiaries, business units, departments, groups, processes, or other established subdivisions of an organization that exist to manage one or more business risks.

Auditee
The subsidiary, business unit, department, group, or other established subdivision of an organization that is the subject of an assurance engagement.

Board
An organization's governing body, such as a board of directors, supervisory board, head of an agency or legislative body, board of governors or trustees of a nonprofit organization, or any other designated body of the organization.

Bottom-up Approach
To begin by looking at all processes directly at the activity level, and then aggregating the identified processes across the organization.

Business Process
The set of connected activities linked with each other for the purpose of achieving one or more business objectives.

Business Process Outsourcing (BPO)
The act of transferring some of an organization's business processes to an outside provider to achieve cost reductions, operating effectiveness, or operating efficiency while improving service quality.

Cause
The reason for the difference between the expected and actual conditions (why the difference exists).

Chief Audit Executive
A senior position within the organization responsible for internal audit activities. When internal audit activities are obtained from external service providers, the chief audit executive is the person responsible for overseeing the service contract and the overall quality assurance of these activities, and follow-up of engagement results. The term also includes titles such as general auditor, head of internal audit, chief internal auditor, internal audit director, and inspector general.

Code of Ethics
The Code of Ethics of The Institute of Internal Auditors contains principles relevant to the profession and practice of internal auditing and Rules of Conduct that describe behavior expected of internal auditors. The Code of Ethics applies to both parties and entities that provide internal audit services. The purpose of the Code of Ethics is to promote an ethical culture in the global profession of internal auditing.

Compensating Control
An activity that, if key controls do not fully operate effectively, may help to reduce the related risk. A compensating control will not, by itself, reduce risk to an acceptable level.

GLOSSARY

Complementary Control
An activity that, when taken together with other controls, contributes to the overall effective mitigation of risk. Frequently, complementary controls operate across multiple processes and risks.

Compliance
Conformity and adherence to applicable laws and regulations (COSO definition). May also include conformity and adherence to policies, plans, procedures, contracts, or other requirements.

Computer-assisted Audit Techniques (CAATs)
Automated audit techniques, such as generalized audit software, utility software, test data, application software tracing and mapping, and audit expert systems, that help the internal auditor directly test controls built into computerized information systems and data contained in computer files.

Condition
The factual evidence that the internal auditor found in the course of the examination (what does exist).

Conflict of Interest
Any relationship that is, or appears to be, not in the best interest of the organization. A conflict of interest would prejudice an individual's ability to perform his or her duties and responsibilities objectively.

Consulting Services
Advisory and related services, the nature and scope of which are agreed to with the customer, and which are intended to improve an organization's governance, risk management, and control processes without the internal auditor assuming management responsibility. Examples include advice, facilitation, and training.

Continuous Auditing
Using computerized techniques to perpetually audit the processing of business transactions.

Control
Any action taken by management, the board, and other parties to manage risk and increase the likelihood that established objectives and goals will be achieved. Management plans, organizes, and directs the performance of sufficient actions to provide reasonable assurance that objectives and goals will be achieved (also see Internal Control and System of Internal Controls).

Control Environment
The attitude and actions of the board and management regarding the significance of control within the organization. The control environment provides the discipline and structure for the achievement of the primary

objectives of the system of internal controls. The control environment includes the following elements:

- Integrity and ethical values.
- Management's philosophy and operating style.
- Organizational structure.
- Assignment of authority and responsibility.
- Human resource policies and practices.
- Competence of personnel.

Control Risk
The potential that controls will fail to reduce controllable risk to an acceptable level.

Controllable Risk
The portion of inherent risk that management can reduce through day-to-day operations and management activities.

Controls are Adequately Designed
Present if management has planned and organized (designed) the controls or the system of internal controls in a manner that provides reasonable assurance that the organization's entity-level and process-level risks can be managed to an acceptable level.

Controls are Operating Effectively
Present if management has executed (operated) the controls or the system of internal controls in a manner that provides reasonable assurance that the organization's entity-level and process-level risks have been managed effectively and that the organization's goals and objectives will be achieved efficiently and economically.

Corrective Control
An activity in which detected omissions and errors are corrected.

Corruption
Acts in which individuals wrongfully use their influence in a business transaction in order to procure some benefit for themselves or another person, contrary to their duty to their employer or the rights of another (for example, kickbacks, self-dealing, or conflicts of interest).

Criteria
The standards, measures, or expectations used in making an evaluation and/or verification of an observation (what should exist).

Customer
The subsidiary, business unit, department, group, individual, or other established subdivision of an organization that is the subject of a consulting engagement.

GLOSSARY

Database
A large repository of data, typically contained in many linked files, and stored in a manner that allows the data to be easily accessed, retrieved, and manipulated.

Detective Control
An activity that is designed to discover undesirable events that have already occurred. A detective control must occur on a timely basis (before the undesirable event has had a negative impact on the organization) to be considered effective.

Directive Control
An activity that gives explicit direction regarding what actions need to take place to cause or encourage a desirable event to occur.

Effect
The risk or exposure the organization and/or others encounter because the condition is not consistent with the criteria (the consequence of the difference).

Engagement
A specific internal audit assignment or project that includes multiple tasks or activities designed to accomplish a specific set of objectives. See also Assurance Services and Consulting Services.

Engagement Work Program
A document that lists the procedures to be followed during an engagement, designed to achieve the engagement plan.

Enterprise Risk Management — See Risk Management.

Entity-level Control
A control that operates across an entire entity and, as such, is not bound by, or associated with, individual processes.

External Auditor — See Independent Outside Auditor.

Framework
A body of guiding principles that form a template against which organizations can evaluate a multitude of business practices. These principles are comprised of various concepts, values, assumptions, and practices intended to provide a yardstick against which an organization can assess or evaluate a particular structure, process, or environment or a group of practices or procedures.

Fraud
Any illegal act characterized by deceit, concealment, or violation of trust. These acts are not dependent upon the threat of violence or physical force. Frauds are perpetrated by parties and organizations to obtain money,

property, or services; to avoid payment or loss of services; or to secure personal or business advantage.

Fraudulent Financial Reporting
Acts that involve falsification of an organization's financial statements (for example, overstating revenues, or understating liabilities and expenses).

General Information Technology Controls
Controls that operate across all information technology systems and are in place to ensure the integrity, reliability, and accuracy of the application systems. Also represents a specific example of an "entity-level control."

Governance
The combination of processes and structures implemented by the board to inform, direct, manage, and monitor the activities of the organization toward the achievement of its objectives.

Impairment to Independence or Objectivity
The introduction of threats that may result in a substantial limitation, or the appearance of a substantial limitation, to the internal auditor's ability to perform an engagement without bias or interference.

Independence
The freedom from conditions that threaten objectivity or the appearance of objectivity. Such threats to objectivity must be managed at the individual auditor, engagement, functional, and organizational levels (also see Organizational Independence).

Independent Outside Auditor
A registered public accounting firm, hired by the organization's board or executive management, to perform a financial statement audit providing assurance for which the firm issues a written attestation report that expresses an opinion about whether the financial statements are fairly presented in accordance with applicable Generally Accepted Accounting Principles.

Individual Objectivity
An unbiased mental attitude that allows internal auditors to perform engagements in such a manner that they have an honest belief in their work product and that no significant quality compromises are made. Objectivity requires internal auditors not to subordinate their judgment on audit matters to that of others.

Information Technology Governance
The leadership, structure, and oversight processes that ensure the organization's information technology supports the objectives and strategies of the organization.

GLOSSARY

Information Technology Operations
The department or area in an organization (people, processes, and equipment) that performs the function of running the computer systems and various devices that support the business objectives and activities.

Inherent Limitations of Internal Control
The confines that relate to the limits of human judgment, resource constraints and the need to consider the cost of controls in relation to expected benefits, the reality that breakdowns can occur, and the possibility of collusion or management override.

Inherent Risk
The combination of internal and external risk factors in their pure, uncontrolled state, or, the gross risk that exists, assuming there are no internal controls in place.

Internal Audit Charter
A formal, written document that defines the internal audit function's purpose, authority, and responsibility. The charter should (a) establish the internal audit function's position within the organization, (b) authorize access to records, personnel, and physical properties relevant to the performance of engagements, and (c) define the scope of the internal audit function.

Internal Audit Function
A department, division, team of consultants, or other practitioner(s) that provides independent, objective assurance and consulting services designed to add value and improve an organization's operations.

Internal Control
A process, effected by an entity's board of directors, management, and other personnel, designed to provide reasonable assurance regarding the achievement of objectives in the following categories:

- Effectiveness and efficiency of operations.
- Reliability of financial reporting.
- Compliance with applicable laws and regulations.

Key Control
An activity designed to reduce risk associated with a critical business objective.

Key Performance Indicator
A metric or other form of measuring whether a process or individual tasks are operating within prescribed tolerances.

Material Observation
An individual observation, or a group of observations, is considered "material" if the control in question has a reasonable possibility of failing and the impact of its failure is not only significant, but also exceeds management's materiality threshold.

Monitoring
A process that assesses the presence and functioning of governance, risk management, and control over time.

Network
A configuration that enables computers and devices to communicate and be linked together to efficiently process data and share information.

Objectives
What an entity desires to achieve. When referring to what an organization wants to achieve, these are called business objectives, and may be classified as strategic, operations, reporting, and compliance. When referring to what an audit wants to achieve, these are called audit objectives or engagement objectives.

Objectivity — See Individual Objectivity.

Observation
A finding, determination, or judgment derived from the internal auditor's test results from an assurance or consulting engagement.

Operating Effectively — See Controls are Operating Effectively.

Operating System
Software programs that run the computer and perform basic tasks, such as recognizing input from the keyboard, sending output to the printer, keeping track of files and directories on the hard drive, and controlling various computer peripheral devices.

Opportunity
The possibility that an event will occur and positively affect the achievement of objectives.

Organizational Independence
The chief audit executive's line of reporting within the organization that allows the internal audit function to fulfill its responsibilities free from interference (also see Independence).

Preventive Control
An activity that is designed to deter unintended events from occurring.

GLOSSARY

Process-level Control
An activity that operates within a specific process for the purpose of achieving process-level objectives.

Professional Skepticism
The state of mind in which internal auditors take nothing for granted; they continuously question what they hear and see and critically assess audit evidence.

Reasonable Assurance
A level of assurance that is supported by generally accepted auditing procedures and judgments. Reasonable assurance can apply to judgments surrounding the effectiveness of internal controls, the mitigation of risks, the achievement of objectives, or other engagement-related conclusions.

Residual Risk
The portion of inherent risk that remains after management executes its risk responses (sometimes referred to as net risk).

Risk
The possibility that an event will occur and adversely affect the achievement of objectives.

Risk Appetite
The amount of risk, on a broad level, an organization is willing to accept in pursuit of its business objectives. Risk appetite takes into consideration the amount of risk that management consciously accepts after balancing the cost and benefits of implementing controls.

Risk Assessment
The identification and analysis (typically in terms of impact and likelihood) of relevant risks to the achievement of an organization's objectives, forming a basis for determining how the risks should be managed.

Risk Management
The process conducted by management to understand and deal with uncertainties (that is, risks and opportunities) that could affect the organization's ability to achieve its objectives.

Risk Mitigation
An action, or set of actions, taken by management to reduce the impact and/or likelihood of a risk to a lower, more acceptable level.

Risk Response
An action, or set of actions, taken by management to achieve a desired risk management strategy. Risk responses can be categorized as risk avoidance, reduction, sharing, or acceptance. Exploiting opportunities that, in turn, enable the achievement of objectives, is also a risk response.

Risk Tolerance
The acceptable levels of risk size and variation relative to the achievement of objectives, which must align with the organization's risk appetite.

Secondary Control
An activity designed to either reduce risk associated with business objectives that are not critical to the organization's survival or success or serve as a backup to a key control.

Significant Observation
An individual observation, or a group of observations, is considered "significant" if the control activity in question has a reasonable possibility of failing and the impact of its failure is significant.

Standard
A professional pronouncement promulgated by the Internal Audit Standards Board that delineates the requirements for performing a broad range of internal audit activities, and for evaluating internal audit performance.

Strategic Objectives
What an entity desires to achieve through the value creation choices management makes on behalf of the organization's stakeholders.

Strategy
Refers to how management plans to achieve the organization's objectives.

Sufficient Evidence
A collection of evidence gained during an engagement that, in its totality, is enough to support the judgments and conclusions made in the engagement.

System of Internal Controls
Comprises the five components of internal control: the control environment, risk assessment, control activities, information and communication, and monitoring that are in place to manage risks related to the financial reporting, compliance, and operational objectives of an organization. See also Internal Control.

Third-party Service Provider
A person or firm, outside of the organization, who provides assurance and/or consulting services to an organization.

Tone at the Top
The entity-wide attitude of integrity and control consciousness, as exhibited by the most senior executives of an organization. See also Control Environment.

Top-down Approach
To begin at the entity level, with the organization's objectives, and then identify the key processes critical to the success of each of the organization's objectives.

Transparency
Communicating in a manner that a prudent individual would consider to be fair and sufficiently clear and comprehensive to meet the needs of the recipient(s) of such communication.

Work Program — See Engagement Work Program.

APPENDICES

Appendix A

The Institute of Internal Auditors' Code of Ethics

The purpose of The Institute's Code of Ethics is to promote an ethical culture in the profession of internal auditing.

> *Internal auditing is an independent, objective assurance and consulting activity designed to add value and improve an organization's operations. It helps an organization accomplish its objectives by bringing a systematic, disciplined approach to evaluate and improve the effectiveness of risk management, control, and governance processes.*

A code of ethics is necessary and appropriate for the profession of internal auditing, founded as it is on the trust placed in its objective assurance about governance, risk management, and control.

The Institute's Code of Ethics extends beyond the Definition of Internal Auditing to include two essential components:

1. Principles that are relevant to the profession and practice of internal auditing;
2. Rules of Conduct that describe behavior norms expected of internal auditors. These rules are an aid to interpreting the Principles into practical applications and are intended to guide the ethical conduct of internal auditors.

"Internal auditors" refers to Institute members, recipients of or candidates for IIA professional certifications, and those who perform internal audit services within the Definition of Internal Auditing.

Applicability and Enforcement of the Code of Ethics

This Code of Ethics applies to both entities and individuals that perform internal audit services.

For IIA members and recipients of or candidates for IIA professional certifications, breaches of the Code of Ethics will be evaluated and administered according to The Institute's Bylaws and Administrative Directives. The fact that a particular conduct is not mentioned in the Rules of Conduct does not prevent it from being unacceptable or discreditable, and therefore, the member, certification holder, or candidate can be liable for disciplinary action.

APPENDICES

Principles

Internal auditors are expected to apply and uphold the following principles:

1. Integrity

The integrity of internal auditors establishes trust and thus provides the basis for reliance on their judgment.

2. Objectivity

Internal auditors exhibit the highest level of professional objectivity in gathering, evaluating, and communicating information about the activity or process being examined. Internal auditors make a balanced assessment of all the relevant circumstances and are not unduly influenced by their own interests or by others in forming judgments.

3. Confidentiality

Internal auditors respect the value and ownership of information they receive and do not disclose information without appropriate authority unless there is a legal or professional obligation to do so.

4. Competency

Internal auditors apply the knowledge, skills, and experience needed in the performance of internal audit services.

Rules of Conduct

1. Integrity

Internal auditors:

1.1. Shall perform their work with honesty, diligence, and responsibility.

1.2. Shall observe the law and make disclosures expected by the law and the profession.

1.3. Shall not knowingly be a party to any illegal activity, or engage in acts that are discreditable to the profession of internal auditing or to the organization.

1.4. Shall respect and contribute to the legitimate and ethical objectives of the organization.

2. Objectivity

Internal auditors:

2.1. Shall not participate in any activity or relationship that may impair or be presumed to impair their unbiased assessment. This participation includes those activities or relationships that may be in conflict with the interests of the organization.

2.2 Shall not accept anything that may impair or be presumed to impair their professional judgment.

2.3 Shall disclose all material facts known to them that, if not disclosed, may distort the reporting of activities under review.

3. Confidentiality

Internal auditors:

3.1 Shall be prudent in the use and protection of information acquired in the course of their duties.

3.2 Shall not use information for any personal gain or in any manner that would be contrary to the law or detrimental to the legitimate and ethical objectives of the organization.

4. Competency

Internal auditors:

4.1. Shall engage only in those services for which they have the necessary knowledge, skills, and experience.

4.2 Shall perform internal audit services in accordance with the *International Standards for the Professional Practice of Internal Auditing.*

4.3 Shall continually improve their proficiency and the effectiveness and quality of their services.

APPENDICES

Appendix B

International Standards for the Professional Practice of Internal Auditing

Attribute Standards

1000 – Purpose, Authority, and Responsibility

The purpose, authority, and responsibility of the internal audit activity must be formally defined in an internal audit charter, consistent with the Definition of Internal Auditing, the Code of Ethics, and the *Standards*. The chief audit executive must periodically review the internal audit charter and present it to senior management and the board for approval.

Interpretation:

The internal audit charter is a formal document that defines the internal audit activity's purpose, authority, and responsibility. The internal audit charter establishes the internal audit activity's position within the organization; authorizes access to records, personnel, and physical properties relevant to the performance of engagements; and defines the scope of internal audit activities. Final approval of the internal audit charter resides with the board.

> **1000.A1** – The nature of assurance services provided to the organization must be defined in the internal audit charter. If assurances are to be provided to parties outside the organization, the nature of these assurances must also be defined in the internal audit charter.
>
> **1000.C1** – The nature of consulting services must be defined in the internal audit charter.

1010 – Recognition of the Definition of Internal Auditing, the Code of Ethics, and the *Standards* in the Internal Audit Charter.

The mandatory nature of the Definition of Internal Auditing, the Code of Ethics, and the *Standards* must be recognized in the internal audit charter. The chief audit executive should discuss the Definition of Internal Auditing, the Code of Ethics, and the *Standards* with senior management and the board.

1100 – Independence and Objectivity

The internal audit activity must be independent, and internal auditors must be objective in performing their work.

Interpretation:

Independence is the freedom from conditions that threaten the ability of the internal audit activity or the chief audit executive to carry out internal audit responsibilities in an unbiased manner. To achieve the degree of independence necessary to effectively carry out the responsibilities of the internal audit activity, the chief audit executive has direct and unrestricted access to senior management and the board. This can be achieved through a dual-reporting relationship. Threats to independence must be managed at the individual auditor, engagement, functional, and organizational levels.

Objectivity is an unbiased mental attitude that allows internal auditors to perform engagements in such a manner that they believe in their work product and that no quality compromises are made. Objectivity requires that internal auditors do not subordinate their judgment on audit matters to others. Threats to objectivity must be managed at the individual auditor, engagement, functional, and organizational levels.

1110 – Organizational Independence

The chief audit executive must report to a level within the organization that allows the internal audit activity to fulfill its responsibilities. The chief audit executive must confirm to the board, at least annually, the organizational independence of the internal audit activity.

1110.A1 – The internal audit activity must be free from interference in determining the scope of internal auditing, performing work, and communicating results.

1111 – Direct Interaction With the Board

The chief audit executive must communicate and interact directly with the board.

1120 – Individual Objectivity

Internal auditors must have an impartial, unbiased attitude and avoid any conflict of interest.

Interpretation:

Conflict of interest is a situation in which an internal auditor, who is in a position of trust, has a competing professional or personal interest. Such competing interests can make it difficult to fulfill his or her duties impartially. A conflict of interest exists even if no unethical or improper act results. A conflict of interest can create an appearance of impropriety that can undermine con-

fidence in the internal auditor, the internal audit activity, and the profession. A conflict of interest could impair an individual's ability to perform his or her duties and responsibilities objectively.

1130 – Impairment to Independence or Objectivity

If independence or objectivity is impaired in fact or appearance, the details of the impairment must be disclosed to appropriate parties. The nature of the disclosure will depend upon the impairment.

Interpretation:

Impairment to organizational independence and individual objectivity may include, but is not limited to, personal conflict of interest, scope limitations, restrictions on access to records, personnel, and properties, and resource limitations, such as funding.

The determination of appropriate parties to which the details of an impairment to independence or objectivity must be disclosed is dependent upon the expectations of the internal audit activity's and the chief audit executive's responsibilities to senior management and the board as described in the internal audit charter, as well as the nature of the impairment.

1130.A1 – Internal auditors must refrain from assessing specific operations for which they were previously responsible. Objectivity is presumed to be impaired if an internal auditor provides assurance services for an activity for which the internal auditor had responsibility within the previous year.

1130.A2 – Assurance engagements for functions over which the chief audit executive has responsibility must be overseen by a party outside the internal audit activity.

1130.C1 – Internal auditors may provide consulting services relating to operations for which they had previous responsibilities.

1130.C2 – If internal auditors have potential impairments to independence or objectivity relating to proposed consulting services, disclosure must be made to the engagement client prior to accepting the engagement.

1200 – Proficiency and Due Professional Care

Engagements must be performed with proficiency and due professional care.

1210 – Proficiency

Internal auditors must possess the knowledge, skills, and other competencies needed to perform their individual responsibilities. The internal audit activity collectively must possess or obtain the knowledge, skills, and other competencies needed to perform its responsibilities.

Interpretation:

Knowledge, skills, and other competencies is a collective term that refers to the professional proficiency required of internal auditors to effectively carry out their professional responsibilities. Internal auditors are encouraged to demonstrate their proficiency by obtaining appropriate professional certifications and qualifications, such as the Certified Internal Auditor designation and other designations offered by The Institute of Internal Auditors and other appropriate professional organizations.

1210.A1 – The chief audit executive must obtain competent advice and assistance if the internal auditors lack the knowledge, skills, or other competencies needed to perform all or part of the engagement.

1210.A2 – Internal auditors must have sufficient knowledge to evaluate the risk of fraud and the manner in which it is managed by the organization, but are not expected to have the expertise of a person whose primary responsibility is detecting and investigating fraud.

1210.A3 – Internal auditors must have sufficient knowledge of key information technology risks and controls and available technology-based audit techniques to perform their assigned work. However, not all internal auditors are expected to have the expertise of an internal auditor whose primary responsibility is information technology auditing.

1210.C1 – The chief audit executive must decline the consulting engagement or obtain competent advice and assistance if the internal auditors lack the knowledge, skills, or other competencies needed to perform all or part of the engagement.

1220 – Due Professional Care

Internal auditors must apply the care and skill expected of a reasonably prudent and competent internal auditor. Due professional care does not imply infallibility.

1220.A1 – Internal auditors must exercise due professional care by considering the:

- Extent of work needed to achieve the engagement's objectives;
- Relative complexity, materiality, or significance of matters to which assurance procedures are applied;
- Adequacy and effectiveness of governance, risk management, and control processes;
- Probability of significant errors, fraud, or noncompliance; and
- Cost of assurance in relation to potential benefits.

1220.A2 – In exercising due professional care internal auditors must consider the use of technology-based audit and other data analysis techniques.

1220.A3 – Internal auditors must be alert to the significant risks that might affect objectives, operations, or resources. However, assurance procedures alone, even when performed with due professional care, do not guarantee that all significant risks will be identified.

1220.C1 – Internal auditors must exercise due professional care during a consulting engagement by considering the:

- Needs and expectations of clients, including the nature, timing, and communication of engagement results;
- Relative complexity and extent of work needed to achieve the engagement's objectives; and
- Cost of the consulting engagement in relation to potential benefits.

1230 – Continuing Professional Development

Internal auditors must enhance their knowledge, skills, and other competencies through continuing professional development.

1300 – Quality Assurance and Improvement Program

The chief audit executive must develop and maintain a quality assurance and improvement program that covers all aspects of the internal audit activity.

Interpretation:

A quality assurance and improvement program is designed to enable an evaluation of the internal audit activity's conformance with the Definition of Internal Auditing and the Standards *and an evaluation of whether internal auditors apply the Code of Ethics. The program also assesses the efficiency and effectiveness of the internal audit activity and identifies opportunities for improvement.*

1310 – Requirements of the Quality Assurance and Improvement Program

The quality assurance and improvement program must include both internal and external assessments.

1311 – Internal Assessments

Internal assessments must include:

- Ongoing monitoring of the performance of the internal audit activity; and
- Periodic reviews performed through self-assessment or by other persons within the organization with sufficient knowledge of internal audit practices.

Interpretation:

Ongoing monitoring is an integral part of the day-to-day supervision, review, and measurement of the internal audit activity. Ongoing monitoring is incorporated into the routine policies and practices used to manage the internal audit activity and uses processes, tools, and information considered necessary to evaluate conformance with the Definition of Internal Auditing, the Code of Ethics, and the Standards.

Periodic reviews are assessments conducted to evaluate conformance with the Definition of Internal Auditing, the Code of Ethics, and the Standards.

Sufficient knowledge of internal audit practices requires at least an understanding of all elements of the International Professional Practices Framework.

1312 – External Assessments

External assessments must be conducted at least once every five years by a qualified, independent reviewer or review team from outside the organization. The chief audit executive must discuss with the board:

- The need for more frequent external assessments; and
- The qualifications and independence of the external reviewer or review team, including any potential conflict of interest.

Interpretation:

A qualified reviewer or review team consists of individuals who are competent in the professional practice of internal auditing and the external assessment process. The evaluation of the competency of the reviewer and review team is a judgment that considers the professional internal audit experience and professional credentials of the individuals selected to perform the review. The evaluation of qualifications also considers the size and complexity of the organizations that the reviewers have been associated with in relation to the organization for which the internal audit activity is being assessed, as well as the need for particular sector, industry, or technical knowledge.

An independent reviewer or review team means not having either a real or an apparent conflict of interest and not being a part of, or under the control of, the organization to which the internal audit activity belongs.

1320 – Reporting on the Quality Assurance and Improvement Program

The chief audit executive must communicate the results of the quality assurance and improvement program to senior management and the board.

Interpretation:

The form, content, and frequency of communicating the results of the quality assurance and improvement program is established through discussions with senior management and the board and considers the responsibilities of the internal audit activity and chief audit executive as contained in the internal audit charter. To demonstrate conformance with the Definition of Internal Auditing, the Code of Ethics, and the Standards, *the results of external and periodic internal assessments are communicated upon completion of such assessments and the results of ongoing monitoring are communicated at least annually. The results include the reviewer's or review team's assessment with respect to the degree of conformance.*

1321 – Use of *"Conforms with the International Standards for the Professional Practice of Internal Auditing"*

The chief audit executive may state that the internal audit activity conforms with the *International Standards for the Professional Practice of Internal Auditing* only if the results of the quality assurance and improvement program support this statement.

1322 – Disclosure of Nonconformance

When nonconformance with the Definition of Internal Auditing, the Code of Ethics, or the *Standards* impacts the overall scope or operation of the internal audit activity, the chief audit executive must disclose the nonconformance and the impact to senior management and the board.

Performance Standards

2000 – Managing the Internal Audit Activity

The chief audit executive must effectively manage the internal audit activity to ensure it adds value to the organization.

Interpretation:

The internal audit activity is effectively managed when:

- *The results of the internal audit activity's work achieve the purpose and responsibility included in the internal audit charter;*
- *The internal audit activity conforms with the Definition of Internal Auditing and the* Standards*; and*
- *The individuals who are part of the internal audit activity demonstrate conformance with the Code of Ethics and the* Standards.

2010 – Planning

The chief audit executive must establish risk-based plans to determine the priorities of the internal audit activity, consistent with the organization's goals.

Interpretation:

The chief audit executive is responsible for developing a risk-based plan. The chief audit executive takes into account the organization's risk management framework, including using risk appetite levels set by management for the different activities or parts of the organization. If a framework does not exist, the chief audit executive uses his/her own judgment of risks after consultation with senior management and the board.

2010.A1 – The internal audit activity's plan of engagements must be based on a documented risk assessment, undertaken at least annually. The input of senior management and the board must be considered in this process.

2010.C1 – The chief audit executive should consider accepting proposed consulting engagements based on the engagement's potential to improve management of risks, add value, and improve the organization's operations. Accepted engagements must be included in the plan.

2020 – Communication and Approval

The chief audit executive must communicate the internal audit activity's plans and resource requirements, including significant interim changes, to senior management and the board for review and approval. The chief audit executive must also communicate the impact of resource limitations.

2030 – Resource Management

The chief audit executive must ensure that internal audit resources are appropriate, sufficient, and effectively deployed to achieve the approved plan.

Interpretation:

Appropriate refers to the mix of knowledge, skills, and other competencies needed to perform the plan. Sufficient refers to the quantity of resources needed to accomplish the plan. Resources are effectively deployed when they are used in a way that optimizes the achievement of the approved plan.

2040 – Policies and Procedures

The chief audit executive must establish policies and procedures to guide the internal audit activity.

Interpretation:

The form and content of policies and procedures are dependent upon the size and structure of the internal audit activity and the complexity of its work.

2050 – Coordination

The chief audit executive should share information and coordinate activities with other internal and external providers of assurance and consulting services to ensure proper coverage and minimize duplication of efforts.

2060 – Reporting to Senior Management and the Board

The chief audit executive must report periodically to senior management and the board on the internal audit activity's purpose, authority, responsibility, and performance relative to its plan. Reporting must also include significant risk exposures and control issues, including fraud risks, governance issues, and other matters needed or requested by senior management and the board.

Interpretation:

The frequency and content of reporting are determined in discussion with senior management and the board and depend on the importance of the information to be communicated and the urgency of the related actions to be taken by senior management or the board.

2100 – Nature of Work

The internal audit activity must evaluate and contribute to the improvement of governance, risk management, and control processes using a systematic and disciplined approach.

2110 – Governance

The internal audit activity must assess and make appropriate recommendations for improving the governance process in its accomplishment of the following objectives:

- Promoting appropriate ethics and values within the organization;
- Ensuring effective organizational performance management and accountability;
- Communicating risk and control information to appropriate areas of the organization; and
- Coordinating the activities of and communicating information among the board, external and internal auditors, and management.

2110.A1 – The internal audit activity must evaluate the design, implementation, and effectiveness of the organization's ethics-related objectives, programs, and activities.

2110.A2 – The internal audit activity must assess whether the information technology governance of the organization sustains and supports the organization's strategies and objectives.

2110.C1 – Consulting engagement objectives must be consistent with the overall values and goals of the organization.

2120 – Risk Management

The internal audit activity must evaluate the effectiveness and contribute to the improvement of risk management processes.

Interpretation:

Determining whether risk management processes are effective is a judgment resulting from the internal auditor's assessment that:

- *Organizational objectives support and align with the organization's mission;*
- *Significant risks are identified and assessed;*
- *Appropriate risk responses are selected that align risks with the organization's risk appetite; and*
- *Relevant risk information is captured and communicated in a timely manner across the organization, enabling staff, management, and the board to carry out their responsibilities.*

Risk management processes are monitored through ongoing management activities, separate evaluations, or both.

2120.A1 – The internal audit activity must evaluate risk exposures relating to the organization's governance, operations, and information systems regarding the:

- Reliability and integrity of financial and operational information;
- Effectiveness and efficiency of operations;
- Safeguarding of assets; and
- Compliance with laws, regulations, and contracts.

2120.A2 – The internal audit activity must evaluate the potential for the occurrence of fraud and how the organization manages fraud risk.

2120.C1 – During consulting engagements, internal auditors must address risk consistent with the engagement's objectives and be alert to the existence of other significant risks.

2120.C2 – Internal auditors must incorporate knowledge of risks gained from consulting engagements into their evaluation of the organization's risk management processes.

2120.C3 – When assisting management in establishing or improving risk management processes, internal auditors must refrain from assuming any management responsibility by actually managing risks.

2130 – Control

The internal audit activity must assist the organization in maintaining effective controls by evaluating their effectiveness and efficiency and by promoting continuous improvement.

2130.A1 – The internal audit activity must evaluate the adequacy and effectiveness of controls in responding to risks within the organization's governance, operations, and information systems regarding the:

- Reliability and integrity of financial and operational information;
- Effectiveness and efficiency of operations;
- Safeguarding of assets; and
- Compliance with laws, regulations, and contracts.

2130.A2 – Internal auditors should ascertain the extent to which operating and program goals and objectives have been established and conform to those of the organization.

2130.A3 – Internal auditors should review operations and programs to ascertain the extent to which results are consistent with established goals and objectives to determine whether operations and programs are being implemented or performed as intended.

2130.C1 – During consulting engagements, internal auditors must address controls consistent with the engagement's objectives and be alert to significant control issues.

2130.C2 – Internal auditors must incorporate knowledge of controls gained from consulting engagements into evaluation of the organization's control processes.

2200 – Engagement Planning

Internal auditors must develop and document a plan for each engagement, including the engagement's objectives, scope, timing, and resource allocations.

2201 – Planning Considerations

In planning the engagement, internal auditors must consider:

- The objectives of the activity being reviewed and the means by which the activity controls its performance;
- The significant risks to the activity, its objectives, resources, and operations and the means by which the potential impact of risk is kept to an acceptable level;
- The adequacy and effectiveness of the activity's risk management and control processes compared to a relevant control framework or model; and
- The opportunities for making significant improvements to the activity's risk management and control processes.

2201.A1 – When planning an engagement for parties outside the organization, internal auditors must establish a written understanding with them about objectives, scope, respective responsibilities, and other expectations, including restrictions on distribution of the results of the engagement and access to engagement records.

2201.C1 – Internal auditors must establish an understanding with consulting engagement clients about objectives, scope, respective responsibilities, and other client expectations. For significant engagements, this understanding must be documented.

2210 – Engagement Objectives

Objectives must be established for each engagement.

2210.A1 – Internal auditors must conduct a preliminary assessment of the risks relevant to the activity under review. Engagement objectives must reflect the results of this assessment.

2210.A2 – Internal auditors must consider the probability of significant errors, fraud, noncompliance, and other exposures when developing the engagement objectives.

2210.A3 – Adequate criteria are needed to evaluate controls. Internal auditors must ascertain the extent to which management has established adequate criteria to determine whether objectives and goals have been accomplished. If adequate, internal auditors must use such criteria in their evaluation. If inadequate, internal auditors must work with management to develop appropriate evaluation criteria.

2210.C1 – Consulting engagement objectives must address governance, risk management, and control processes to the extent agreed upon with the client.

2220 – Engagement Scope

The established scope must be sufficient to satisfy the objectives of the engagement.

2220.A1 – The scope of the engagement must include consideration of relevant systems, records, personnel, and physical properties, including those under the control of third parties.

2220.A2 – If significant consulting opportunities arise during an assurance engagement, a specific written understanding as to the objectives, scope, respective responsibilities, and other expectations should be reached and the results of the consulting engagement communicated in accordance with consulting standards.

2220.C1 – In performing consulting engagements, internal auditors must ensure that the scope of the engagement is sufficient to address the agreed-upon objectives. If internal auditors develop reservations about the scope during the engagement, these reservations must be discussed with the client to determine whether to continue with the engagement.

2230 – Engagement Resource Allocation

Internal auditors must determine appropriate and sufficient resources to achieve engagement objectives based on an evaluation of the nature and complexity of each engagement, time constraints, and available resources.

2240 – Engagement Work Program

Internal auditors must develop and document work programs that achieve the engagement objectives.

2240.A1 – Work programs must include the procedures for identifying, analyzing, evaluating, and documenting information during the engagement. The work program must be approved prior to its implementation, and any adjustments approved promptly.

2240.C1 – Work programs for consulting engagements may vary in form and content depending upon the nature of the engagement.

2300 – Performing the Engagement

Internal auditors must identify, analyze, evaluate, and document sufficient information to achieve the engagement's objectives.

2310 – Identifying Information

Internal auditors must identify sufficient, reliable, relevant, and useful information to achieve the engagement's objectives.

Interpretation:

Sufficient information is factual, adequate, and convincing so that a prudent, informed person would reach the same conclusions as the auditor. Reliable information is the best attainable information through the use of appropriate engagement techniques. Relevant information supports engagement observations and recommendations and is consistent with the objectives for the engagement. Useful information helps the organization meet its goals.

2320 – Analysis and Evaluation

Internal auditors must base conclusions and engagement results on appropriate analyses and evaluations.

2330 – Documenting Information

Internal auditors must document relevant information to support the conclusions and engagement results.

2330.A1 – The chief audit executive must control access to engagement records. The chief audit executive must obtain the approval of senior management and/or legal counsel prior to releasing such records to external parties, as appropriate.

2330.A2 – The chief audit executive must develop retention requirements for engagement records, regardless of the medium in which each record is stored. These retention requirements must be consistent with the organization's guidelines and any pertinent regulatory or other requirements.

2330.C1 – The chief audit executive must develop policies governing the custody and retention of consulting engagement records, as well as their release to internal and external parties. These policies must be consistent with the organization's guidelines and any pertinent regulatory or other requirements.

2340 – Engagement Supervision

Engagements must be properly supervised to ensure objectives are achieved, quality is assured, and staff is developed.

Interpretation:

The extent of supervision required will depend on the proficiency and experience of internal auditors and the complexity of the engagement. The chief audit executive has overall responsibility for supervising the engagement, whether performed by or for the internal audit activity, but may designate appropriately experienced members of the internal audit activity to perform the review. Appropriate evidence of supervision is documented and retained.

2400 – Communicating Results

Internal auditors must communicate the engagement results.

2410 – Criteria for Communicating

Communications must include the engagement's objectives and scope as well as applicable conclusions, recommendations, and action plans.

2410.A1 – Final communication of engagement results must, where appropriate, contain internal auditors' overall opinion and/or conclusions.

2410.A2 – Internal auditors are encouraged to acknowledge satisfactory performance in engagement communications.

2410.A3 – When releasing engagement results to parties outside the organization, the communication must include limitations on distribution and use of the results.

2410.C1 – Communication of the progress and results of consulting engagements will vary in form and content depending upon the nature of the engagement and the needs of the client.

2420 – Quality of Communications

Communications must be accurate, objective, clear, concise, constructive, complete, and timely.

Interpretation:

Accurate communications are free from errors and distortions and are faithful to the underlying facts. Objective communications are fair, impartial, and unbiased and are the result of a fair-minded and balanced assessment of all relevant facts and circumstances. Clear communications are easily understood and logical, avoiding unnecessary technical language and providing all significant and relevant information. Concise communications are to the point and avoid unnecessary elaboration, superfluous detail, redundancy, and wordiness. Constructive communications are helpful to the engagement client and the organization and lead to improvements where needed. Complete communications lack nothing that is essential to the target audience and include all significant and relevant information and observations to support recommendations and conclusions. Timely communications are opportune and expedient, depending on the significance of the issue, allowing management to take appropriate corrective action.

2421 – Errors and Omissions

If a final communication contains a significant error or omission, the chief audit executive must communicate corrected information to all parties who received the original communication.

2430 – Use of *"Conducted in Conformance with the International Standards for the Professional Practice of Internal Auditing"*

Internal auditors may report that their engagements are "conducted in conformance with the *International Standards for the Professional Practice of Internal Auditing*," only if the results of the quality assurance and improvement program support the statement.

2431 – Engagement Disclosure of Nonconformance

When nonconformance with the Definition of Internal Auditing, the Code of Ethics, or the *Standards* impacts a specific engagement, communication of the results must disclose the:

- Principle or rule of conduct of the Code of Ethics or Standard(s) with which full conformance was not achieved;
- Reason(s) for nonconformance; and
- Impact of nonconformance on the engagement and the communicated engagement results.

2440 – Disseminating Results

The chief audit executive must communicate results to the appropriate parties.

Interpretation:

The chief audit executive or designee reviews and approves the final engagement communication before issuance and decides to whom and how it will be disseminated.

2440.A1 – The chief audit executive is responsible for communicating the final results to parties who can ensure that the results are given due consideration.

2440.A2 – If not otherwise mandated by legal, statutory, or regulatory requirements, prior to releasing results to parties outside the organization the chief audit executive must:

- Assess the potential risk to the organization;
- Consult with senior management and/or legal counsel as appropriate; and
- Control dissemination by restricting the use of the results.

2440.C1 – The chief audit executive is responsible for communicating the final results of consulting engagements to clients.

2440.C2 – During consulting engagements, governance, risk management, and control issues may be identified. Whenever these issues are significant to the organization, they must be communicated to senior management and the board.

2500 – Monitoring Progress

The chief audit executive must establish and maintain a system to monitor the disposition of results communicated to management.

2500.A1 – The chief audit executive must establish a follow-up process to monitor and ensure that management actions have been effectively implemented or that senior management has accepted the risk of not taking action.

2500.C1 – The internal audit activity must monitor the disposition of results of consulting engagements to the extent agreed upon with the client.

2600 – Resolution of Senior Management's Acceptance of Risks

When the chief audit executive believes that senior management has accepted a level of residual risk that may be unacceptable to the organization, the chief audit executive must discuss the matter with senior management. If the decision regarding residual risk is not resolved, the chief audit executive must report the matter to the board for resolution.

Glossary

Add Value
Value is provided by improving opportunities to achieve organizational objectives, identifying operational improvement, and/or reducing risk exposure through both assurance and consulting services.

Adequate Control
Present if management has planned and organized (designed) in a manner that provides reasonable assurance that the organization's risks have been managed effectively and that the organization's goals and objectives will be achieved efficiently and economically.

Assurance Services
An objective examination of evidence for the purpose of providing an independent assessment on governance, risk management, and control processes for the organization. Examples may include financial, performance, compliance, system security, and due diligence engagements.

Board
A board is an organization's governing body, such as a board of directors, supervisory board, head of an agency or legislative body, board of governors or trustees of a nonprofit organization, or any other designated body of the organization, including the audit committee to whom the chief audit executive may functionally report.

Charter
The internal audit charter is a formal document that defines the internal audit activity's purpose, authority, and responsibility. The internal audit charter establishes the internal audit activity's position within the organization; authorizes access to records, personnel, and physical properties relevant to the performance of engagements; and defines the scope of internal audit activities.

Chief Audit Executive
Chief audit executive is a senior position within the organization responsible for internal audit activities. Normally, this would be the internal audit

director. In the case where internal audit activities are obtained from external service providers, the chief audit executive is the person responsible for overseeing the service contract and the overall quality assurance of these activities, reporting to senior management and the board regarding internal audit activities, and follow-up of engagement results. The term also includes titles such as general auditor, head of internal audit, chief internal auditor, and inspector general.

Code of Ethics
The Code of Ethics of The Institute of Internal Auditors (IIA) are Principles relevant to the profession and practice of internal auditing, and Rules of Conduct that describe behavior expected of internal auditors. The Code of Ethics applies to both parties and entities that provide internal audit services. The purpose of the Code of Ethics is to promote an ethical culture in the global profession of internal auditing.

Compliance
Adherence to policies, plans, procedures, laws, regulations, contracts, or other requirements.

Conflict of Interest
Any relationship that is, or appears to be, not in the best interest of the organization. A conflict of interest would prejudice an individual's ability to perform his or her duties and responsibilities objectively.

Consulting Services
Advisory and related client service activities, the nature and scope of which are agreed with the client, are intended to add value and improve an organization's governance, risk management, and control processes without the internal auditor assuming management responsibility. Examples include counsel, advice, facilitation, and training.

Control
Any action taken by management, the board, and other parties to manage risk and increase the likelihood that established objectives and goals will be achieved. Management plans, organizes, and directs the performance of sufficient actions to provide reasonable assurance that objectives and goals will be achieved.

Control Environment
The attitude and actions of the board and management regarding the significance of control within the organization. The control environment provides the discipline and structure for the achievement of the primary objectives of the system of internal control. The control environment includes the following elements:

- Integrity and ethical values.
- Management's philosophy and operating style.
- Organizational structure.
- Assignment of authority and responsibility.
- Human resource policies and practices.
- Competence of personnel.

Control Processes
The policies, procedures, and activities that are part of a control framework, designed to ensure that risks are contained within the risk tolerances established by the risk management process.

Engagement
A specific internal audit assignment, task, or review activity, such as an internal audit, control self-assessment review, fraud examination, or consultancy. An engagement may include multiple tasks or activities designed to accomplish a specific set of related objectives.

Engagement Objectives
Broad statements developed by internal auditors that define intended engagement accomplishments.

Engagement Work Program
A document that lists the procedures to be followed during an engagement, designed to achieve the engagement plan.

External Service Provider
A person or firm outside of the organization that has special knowledge, skill, and experience in a particular discipline.

Fraud
Any illegal act characterized by deceit, concealment, or violation of trust. These acts are not dependent upon the threat of violence or physical force. Frauds are perpetrated by parties and organizations to obtain money, property, or services; to avoid payment or loss of services; or to secure personal or business advantage.

Governance
The combination of processes and structures implemented by the board to inform, direct, manage, and monitor the activities of the organization toward the achievement of its objectives.

Impairment
Impairment to organizational independence and individual objectivity may include personal conflict of interest, scope limitations, restrictions on access to records, personnel, and properties, and resource limitations (funding).

Independence
The freedom from conditions that threaten objectivity or the appearance of objectivity. Such threats to objectivity must be managed at the individual auditor, engagement, functional, and organizational levels.

Information Technology Controls
Controls that support business management and governance as well as provide general and technical controls over information technology infrastructures such as applications, information, infrastructure, and people.

Information Technology Governance
Consists of the leadership, organizational structures, and processes that ensure that the enterprise's information technology sustains and supports the organization's strategies and objectives.

Internal Audit Activity
A department, division, team of consultants, or other practitioner(s) that provides independent, objective assurance and consulting services designed to add value and improve an organization's operations. The internal audit activity helps an organization accomplish its objectives by bringing a systematic, disciplined approach to evaluate and improve the effectiveness of governance, risk management and control processes.

International Professional Practices Framework
The conceptual framework that organizes the authoritative guidance promulgated by The IIA. Authoritative Guidance is comprised of two categories – (1) mandatory and (2) strongly recommended.

Must
The *Standards* use the word "must" to specify an unconditional requirement.

Objectivity
An unbiased mental attitude that allows internal auditors to perform engagements in such a manner that they have an honest belief in their work product and that no significant quality compromises are made. Objectivity requires internal auditors not to subordinate their judgment on audit matters to others.

Residual Risk
The risk remaining after management takes action to reduce the impact and likelihood of an adverse event, including control activities in responding to a risk.

Risk
The possibility of an event occurring that will have an impact on the achievement of objectives. Risk is measured in terms of impact and likelihood.

Risk Appetite
The level of risk that an organization is willing to accept.

Risk Management
A process to identify, assess, manage, and control potential events or situations to provide reasonable assurance regarding the achievement of the organization's objectives.

Should
The *Standards* use the word "should" where conformance is expected unless, when applying professional judgment, circumstances justify deviation.

Significance
The relative importance of a matter within the context in which it is being considered, including quantitative and qualitative factors, such as magnitude, nature, effect, relevance, and impact. Professional judgment assists internal auditors when evaluating the significance of matters within the context of the relevant objectives.

Standard
A professional pronouncement promulgated by the Internal Audit Standards Board that delineates the requirements for performing a broad range of internal audit activities, and for evaluating internal audit performance.

Technology-based Audit Techniques
Any automated audit tool, such as generalized audit software, test data generators, computerized audit programs, specialized audit utilities, and computer-assisted audit techniques (CAATs).

INDEX

A

B

INDEX

C

INDEX

G

H

I

INDEX

J

K

INDEX

Q

R

S

INDEX

W

Y